DISCOVERING MASS COMMUNICATION

THIRD EDITION

Samuel L. Becker
University of Iowa

Churchill L. Roberts
University of West Florida

HarperCollins*Publishers*

Sponsoring Editor: Melissa A. Rosati
Project Editor: Cindy Funkhouser
Design Supervisor: Dorothy Bungert/Molly Heron
Text Design Adaptation: North 7 Atelier Ltd.
Cover Design: Heather Ziegler
Photo Research: Carol Parden
Production Manager/Assistant: Willie Lane/Sunaina Sehwani
Compositor: BookMasters, Inc.
Printer and Binder: R. R. Donnelley & Sons Company
Cover Printer: The Lehigh Press, Inc.

Discovering Mass Communication/Third Edition

Library of Congress Cataloging-in-Publication Data

Becker, Samuel L.
Discovering mass communication / Samuel L. Becker, Churchill Roberts. — 3rd ed.
p. cm.
Includes index.
ISBN 0-673-46119-X
1. Mass media. I. Roberts, Churchill Lee, 1940– . II. Title.
P90.B343 1992
302.23—dc20 91-29619
CIP

95 94 9 8 7 6 5 4 3

Overview

CONTENTS

Preface

Do you believe that advertising for cigarettes and beer causes young people to smoke and drink more than they would if there were no advertising?

Do you believe that cigarette and beer advertising has that effect on you?

If you are like most of us, you are convinced the mass media have tremendous impact on people: making children more aggressive, instilling the wrong values in adults, shaping the outcomes of elections, and so forth. On the other hand, like most of us, you probably think the media do not have much effect on you. You believe that you eat what you do, drink what you do, see the movies that you do, vote the way you do, and otherwise live the way you do because you make free, rational choices on the basis of the facts and what is best for your life.

We must admit we are usually motivated to believe that about ourselves also. On the other hand, when we think about it, and when we examine the research on the causes of people's behaviors and attitudes, we are convinced that all of us are probably wrong in our estimates of how the media affect other people, and even more wrong in our estimates of how the media affect us personally. In other words, we know far less about the role media play in our lives and the lives of others than we think we do.

This is interesting because, in some ways, we know a great deal about the media, as well as about ourselves. You, for example, know who your favorite authors are, your favorite recording artists, your favorite movie stars, and when your favorite television shows are on the air. You may know how newspapers or movies or television programs are put together. You may be experienced and skilled in journalism or film and television production. You could even be one of those rare individuals who has thought seriously about what the media are doing to *other* people. In spite of that, you—like most of the rest of us—are probably relatively naive about the ways in which the media affect *you* and your life.

In a sense, most of us are like the fish who are unaware of the role water plays in their lives because they have always been totally immersed in it and so do not think about it. In the same way, most of us do not think about our media environment because we have been so immersed in it for all of our lives. It seems natural because it has always been there; the media have always been around. We have no trouble using them to get the information or entertainment we want, so we assume that we understand them quite adequately. We know where the local movie theaters are and how to find out what is playing. We know how to turn on the television set or videotape recorder and how to find the programs we want.

Despite all of this, most of us know far less about the media than we think we do, and we are especially naive about their role in our lives. If we want to have greater control of our lives, we must overcome that naiveté; we must gain greater understanding of how the media operate and how and why we use them as we do. That understanding will be even more important for you if you enter one of the media professions. It will be critical that you as a professional, know not only the mechanics of your job and how your communications industry operates, but also how other people use the product of your labors.

Discovering Mass Communication is designed to help you gain these understandings. If this book works as we hope it will, it should help you develop a better understanding not only of the communication media but also of yourself and other people as well. Whatever effects the media have on you, whatever functions they serve for you, depends more on you and the way you use them than they do on the media or their content. So a major result of understanding the lessons of this book should be a rethinking and revision of the way you use media.

A second and related goal of *Discovering Mass Communication* is to stimulate you to see and think about the media in some ways you have never done before. We want you to see how all of the media are part of the total system of communication in our society. We want you to better understand the similarities and differences among the media. And we want you to recognize the ways the media affect each other, as well as the ways they affect you and the society in which you live.

Discovering Mass Communication is divided into four major parts. Part One, "Your Role in Mass Communication," provides a framework for the receiver-oriented approach that informs the remainder of the book. It explains the ways you and others who read newspapers, go to the movies, watch television, and so on are "active" in the process of mass communication. It argues that you are at least as much a "creator" of the messages you take in as are the writers, editors, directors, actors, and producers. It suggests that all of the media of communication available to you at any moment, along with the various people with whom you can communicate, form a type of communication environment—what we call a "mosaic" of communication. From this environment or mosaic, you grasp different combinations of information and use that information, along with all of the other information you gathered over the years, to construct your reality—what you believe the world is like.

Part Two, "Individual Media in the System," devotes a chapter to each of the major media we frequently find in our mosaic environments. These chapters discuss the historical development of each medium, the ways we receive and process messages from it, and its functions in and effects on our lives. This section of the book concludes with a chapter on new technologies and other recent developments that have implications for the future of mass communication.

In order to control the impact of the media on us, we must understand the factors that influence them and their content. Such an understanding can help you become one of those influences, rather than just a target of the media's influence. Part Three, "Media Controls" discusses the major sorts of influences on media that exist: economic influences, such as advertising, government regulation and pressure groups, and even the working practices of people working in the media.

Finally, we come full circle in Part Four, "The Influence of the Media on Your Life," and discuss the ways you and others use the media, the functions those uses may serve for you, the functions the media serve for our society, and the impact they have on you and the society.

You will not find answers in this book to all the important questions about mass communication. For many of the questions, there are no answers. For others, the answers are different for different individuals. We provide answers to some questions, but more often we try to stimulate you to develop your own. There are a number of features in the book that should aid in that stimulation: the list of *Objectives* at the beginning of each chapter, the *Bylines* scattered through the chapters, and the discussion questions at the end of each chapter. As you read, try to answer the questions posed by the *Bylines* and at the ends of chapters. After completing each chapter, test your knowledge and understanding against the *Objectives* outlined at the front of the chapter.

One of the new features in this edition, besides the chapter objectives, are the reviews of key points found throughout each chapter. We hope these features will help you to more fully master all of this material.

For most of modern civilization, three institutions—government, the church, and business—have been the dominant forces in people's lives. Today, in the United States and most other developed countries of the world, there is a fourth major force: the mass media—primarily television, newspapers, books, radio, motion pictures, magazines, and recordings. Some scholars believe these media to be collectively more powerful and influential today than either the government or the church, especially when allied with all of the other businesses with which they are closely associated.

If *Discovering Mass Communication* helps you to better understand this tremendous force, if it encourages and helps you to think about yourself and the role of the media in your life, and especially what you might do to make the media serve you and your society better than they do now, our goal in writing this book will have been fulfilled.

We are indebted to many people for their help in this latest revision. We would like to thank the following reviewers: James A. Anderson, University of Utah; Eldean Bennett, Arizona State University; Don E. Black, Western Illinois University; Beverle R. Bloch, Bowling Green State University; John Cambus, California State University, Hayward; Rod Carveth, University of Hartford; Mary B. Cassata, State University of New York at Buffalo; Robert K. Daly, Kansas State University; Phyllis M. Endreny, University of Illinois, Chicago; Edward Funkhouser, North Carolina State University; Bruce Garrison, University of Miami; Mazharul Haque, University of Southern Mississippi; Jay B. Korinek, Henry Ford Community College; Sue Lafky, Temple University; Val E. Limburg, Washington State University; Jeanne Meadowcroft, Indiana University; Michael Murray, University of Missouri, St. Louis; Doug Newsom, Texas Christian University; Robert M. Ours, West Virginia University; Robert T. Ramsey, Stephen F. Austin State University; Michael Ryan, University of Houston; John P. Smead, Central Missouri State University. They offered a plethora of ideas for making the chapters more lively and meaningful. Larry Day, Sandra Dickson, and Amir Karimi of the University of West Florida read portions of the manuscript and made many thoughtful suggestions. The staff at HarperCollins assisted in myriad ways. Cynthia Funkhouser, Melissa Rosati, Joan Petrokofsky, Maureen O'Neill, and Jim Donohue provided important professional help in designing, editing, and producing the third edition. Much of the clerical work was facilitated by the able assistance of Florence Lee of the University of West Florida.

We are especially indebted to our students, past and present, from whom we learned much about the role of mass communication in the lives of young men and women today. We also learned from them about what works in the classroom, what does not; what interests students, what does not; what students need and want, what they do not.

Finally, and most important, to Gay and Ruth we dedicate this work with love and thanks.

Samuel L. Becker
Churchill L. Roberts

PART ONE

YOUR ROLE IN MASS COMMUNICATION

The most important element in the mass communication system is not the printing press, the camera, or the communication satellite; it is you. Whether you recognize it or not, you have far more control over the information you get from the media and the meanings you construct from that information than all of the journalists, producers, and advertisers in the world. The chapters in this first section of the book explain how you exercise that control, the many sources from which you get information, and the way you use that information to construct your vision of reality.

Although the mass media often operate relatively independently of each other, they form a tightly integrated system in your use of them. As you will learn in this section, your exposure to one medium tends to be influenced by others. Equally important, your *perception* of the information you get from a medium is affected by information you received earlier from other media. Virtually no one forms a picture of the world based on one medium alone. Each of us gets bits and pieces from a great variety of media and from talking with other people. Sometimes, consciously or unconsciously, we check the same bit of information in various media. At other times, from the different media we learn different kinds of things about an event, idea, or person.

Understanding mass communication as a system, and from the vantage point of a receiver, should help you understand individual media in different and more useful ways than you did before. It will also help you better understand yourself and how you came to believe the things you do about your world. Even beyond that, it should help you in the future to develop fuller and more valid beliefs about the world.

CHAPTER 1

YOUR FOUR WORLDS

OBJECTIVES

After studying this chapter, you should be able to

- **Differentiate between the idea of a "communication receiver" and a "communication participant."**
- **Describe the four "worlds" in which each of us lives.**
- **Explain the communication mosaic.**
- **Explain why people have such different beliefs about reality.**
- **Explain communication models and their value.**

An interesting experiment was once carried out in Ridgewood, New Jersey. At the urging of their teachers, all of the fourth-, fifth-, and sixth-grade pupils in one elementary school agreed to swear off television for a week. It was not easy for these children, but apparently most of them stuck with it. One fifth-grader said she cried a lot and sang to keep her mind off television. What surprised teachers, however, were the many complaints they received from *parents* because their children were pressuring them not to watch television either. Most of the parents absolutely refused. For example, when one ten-year-old girl told her parents she could not eat with them if they watched television during dinner, they told her to eat elsewhere. A mother complained to the school that it was the worst idea they ever had. Her nine-year-old son was pestering her with questions, and it was interfering with her lifestyle. Some parents even tried to sabotage the experiment. One boy reported that his father turned the volume of the television set up extremely high so the youngster could not avoid hearing it.

THE IMPORTANCE OF COMMUNICATION IN OUR LIVES

That experiment demonstrates clearly the important role of television in the lives of the vast majority of Americans. The adults in Ridgewood are not unintelligent or uncaring. They are well-educated, upper-middle-class suburbanites—people who probably do not perceive, or would not admit to friends, that they are addicted to television. Whether or not they admit it, though, and despite all of their criticisms of the medium, most adults in our society spend a tremendous portion of their lives staring at the "tube," and they will not easily give it up.

Although television is clearly the dominant medium of mass communication today, it is not the only one that is tightly woven into the fabric of our lives. Many people find newspapers, stereos, books, radio, motion pictures, or other media equally difficult to stay away from. One study of people's behavior during a newspaper strike some years ago found that many persons were so addicted to newspaper reading that they simply began rereading old newspapers when new ones were not available.

Estimates of the time most people spend with the mass media depend in part on how you define "spending time with." However defined, though, it adds up to a great deal of time. Individuals who make little use of the media are extremely rare. One large national study showed that the average American adult has almost 34 hours a week of free time—time not

Great quantities of information are available in the home communication center.

spent sleeping, going to school, working for pay, taking care of the family, or looking after oneself (eating, washing, and so on). Of those 34 hours, at least 50 percent—or slightly over 17 hours a week—are devoted to mass media use.

In addition to those 17 hours of leisure time a week spent exclusively with the media, people often attend to one of the media while involved in other activities—driving to and from school, eating, cooking, doing housework, or engaging in some other type of work. You have probably listened to records while studying or working around the house, or to the radio while traveling to school or work, during meals, at your place of employment, or even while jogging. Television accompanies many of our meals; some of us also watch it on and off while working around the house or taking care of children. And a number of people read newspapers, magazines, or even novels while they are supposed to be working. If you wander through almost any office first thing in the morning, you will find many people with their faces buried in the morning paper. If these hours of media use during nonleisure time are added to the hours of our leisure devoted to the media, the sum represents a vast portion of our day-to-day lives.

REVIEW

Americans are heavy media consumers. On average, 50 percent of their leisure time is spent with media, and media use accompanies much of their work and other activities.

We are not suggesting that all people use all of the media in the same way or to the same degree. Obviously they do not; the statistics we have cited are averages. The amount of time different people spend with media varies greatly. Some adults spend much time reading newspapers or magazines, while others spend none at all. The same is true for television, radio, and movies. Virtually all adults, however, spend a great deal of their lives with at least *some* media. When we think of all of that media use, along with all of the direct communication we have with other people, it becomes clear that each of us lives in what is truly a communication environment.

YOUR COMMUNICATION ENVIRONMENT

Have you thought about your particular communication environment, the time you spend with the media, the kinds of face-to-face communication you regularly have, the ways these various forms of communication are interrelated and woven into the fabric of your life and the patterns of that weaving? Is it possible that you would be like the parents in Ridgewood, New Jersey, if your children tried to get you to avoid all television for a week? Do you know how many of your waking hours are accompanied by some sort of talk and exposure to the media? Do you recognize why your read, hear, or see the things you do? Are you aware of how much of your involvement in communication is the result of conscious selection for some particular purpose, how much of it is habitual, and how much occurs simply because of circumstance: where you are at the moment, who you are with, how available a medium is when you simply want something to occupy your time, or—most important—how your behaviors and perceptions of your world are influenced by your media exposure and other communication? This chapter and those that follow will help you answer these questions.

BYLINE

Estimate the amount of time you spend with each medium of communication on the average day. Then, keep a diary for a few days, trying to follow your normal routine otherwise. In your diary, keep an accurate record of the frequency and amount of time you are exposed to radio, newspapers, television, books, and other media. With this diary record, determine the accuracy of your original estimates.

The Worlds Outside and the World in Your Head

To understand communication, it is useful to keep in mind that you live in **four worlds**. There is one world out there, your **first world**, that you *can never know directly, the world that is beyond your line of vision or range of hearing*. For most of us, that world includes what is going on in other countries, in other parts of this country, and even other parts of our homes. It also includes the thoughts and feelings of other people.

The **second world** in which you live is made up of *everything around that you could see, hear, or otherwise experience if you chose to do so*. It includes the sights outside that you could see if you looked out your window, the stories and advertisements in your newspaper that you could read if you liked, the radio and television material available for you to tune to, the books in your local stores or library that you could obtain without too much difficulty, the conversations going on in your vicinity that you could hear if you wanted to, and a great variety of sights around to which you could direct your eyes.

The **third world** consists of *those available sights, sounds, and other experiences that you attend to or that, somehow, strike your senses*. These are the newspaper stories or parts of stories that you decide to read, the movies and television programs you choose to watch or happen to see, the things people around you say that you listen to, and all of the other bits and pieces of information to which you attend at some level of consciousness. To put this another way, the third world in which you live is made up of those parts of your second world that touch you.

REVIEW

Your reality, the world in which you believe, the world to which you respond when you vote or buy, cheer or cry, is the world you constructed in your head. You do not, you cannot, respond directly to the worlds outside your head—your first, second, or third worlds.

The **fourth world** is *the world in your head*. It is the world you constructed from all of the bits and pieces of information and experience that you encountered since you left the womb, if not before. It is a world you are constantly *re*constructing as you encounter new bits of information and have other new experiences. Most important, this fourth world is your reality. As a journalist, Walter Lippmann, noted many years ago, in a very real sense, each of us lives in a world that does not exist anywhere except in our heads. It is this world to which we are responding when we vote, express an opinion, or make other decisions. We cannot respond to the world outside, what some would call the "real world"; we can respond only to the world in our heads, for that is the only world, or "reality," that we know.

War in Your Four Worlds

You might better grasp this idea of the world you construct in your head and the three worlds outside if you think about war, a plague our world has suffered from the dawn of history to the present moment. Although many of us think of wars in relatively simple-minded ways—gun fights between the good guys and the bad guys—wars are extremely complex phenomena. They involve economic, political, social, ethical, and even religious issues. They involve the lives and actions, hopes and despair of a great many individuals, no two of whose stories are exactly the same. These are important aspects of wars, both past and present, that you cannot possibly get all of the information about, even while the wars are going on.

As an illustration, no matter how hard you try, you cannot get all of the facts about the causes of a war. For example, there is no way you can know all of the circumstances surrounding Saddam Hussein's decision to invade Kuwait in 1990. It is impossible for you or anyone else to know precisely what was going on inside his head, or all of the forces pushing him to act as he did. Nor can you truly know the feelings of all of the Iraqi people about that occurrence. Even closer to home, no one except the closest advisers to President Bush knows most of the considerations that went into the decision to respond to the invasion of Kuwait by sending American troops to the Middle East. This information simply is not available to you, just as many other kinds of relevant information about this or any war are not available. This is part of the world you can never come close to knowing.

On the other hand, there is a great deal of information about this most recent war, or about wars in general, that you could readily encounter by chance or by searching it out, generally from one of the mass media. There is information about wars in various parts of the world reported on television, in newspapers, and in magazines; claims about the right or wrong of American involvement in the Persian Gulf War that commentators in the media or perhaps even your friends or other students argue about; news stories in all of the media about the fighting that took place in Kuwait and Iraq; facts and opinions about past wars presented in history and political science classes; countless war novels and poems that have been published; the stories of wars from Greek times through at least the Vietnam War that have been dramatized and are available in print form and, frequently, in the theatre. There are reruns of "M*A*S*H" that are available frequently on local television stations, as well as documentaries about many of the wars in which America has been involved. The "Beetle Bailey" comic strip provides a perspective on some of the kinds of people who fight America's wars. Religious positions on war can be heard on Sunday mornings in

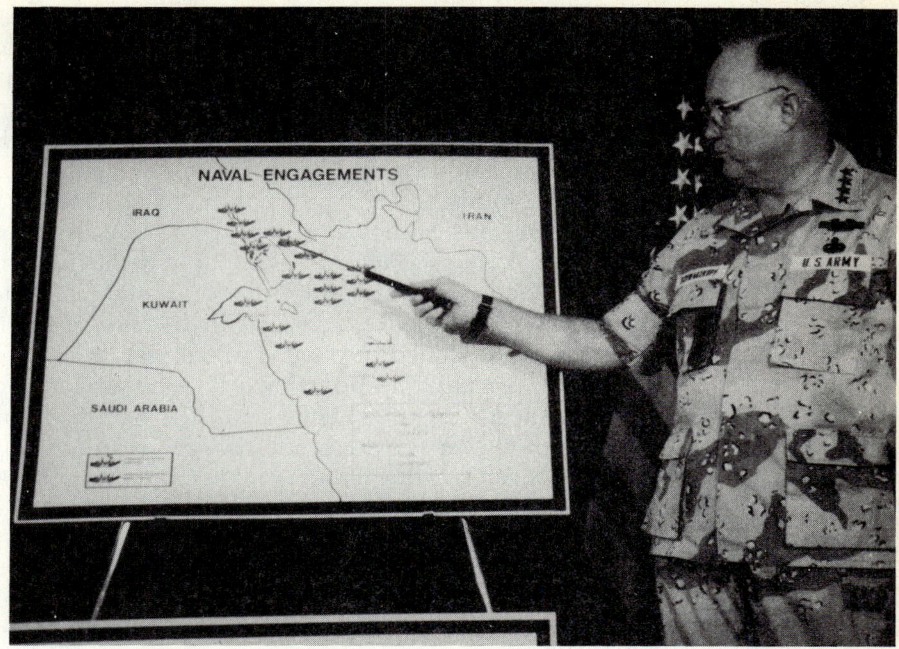

Some of the kinds of information you encountered about the Persian Gulf War: a press conference with General Schwarzkopf.

many churches and pacifist arguments are available at periodic rallies and peace vigils on almost any college campus. And war songs, from "Yankee Doodle" to the latest country-and-western tune about the Persian Gulf War, are almost impossible to avoid.

It is the rare individual who does not have at least one family member, relative, or friend who served in one of the armed services from whom information could easily be obtained. Among that group may even be someone who, during the days of compulsory military service, faced the decision about whether to accept the military draft or be a conscientious objector.

In short, even though there are some kinds of information about wars or about some particular war that you can never know, a tremendous amount of information is available in what we have called your second world. Authors, publishers, broadcasters, directors, and others who control or work in the media have ensured a more than ample supply of information on almost every conceivable topic. No matter how hard you might try, though, it is impossible to be exposed to all of it. There simply is not enough time or, for most of us, enough energy to grasp as much as we might like. None of us can possibly read, listen to, or view more than a minute fraction of what is available.

When you consider that war is only one of an infinite number of issues or stories about which you have a large amount or information in your environment, the impossibility of encountering much of it becomes even clearer. So, by a combination of circumstance and choice, you are exposed to a highly selective sample of the bits of information about war. Over time, this sample has probably become extremely large. Never, though, can you encounter all the information that is available to you on this or any other issue. Never can you come even close to encountering everything there is to know about the subject. To put this in terms of our analogy of four worlds, never can your third world—the world to which you become exposed—be any more than a small fraction of the first world, the total universe of possible information about war.

In many ways, your fourth world—the world inside your head—is the most interesting of all. That part of the world in your head that is your understanding of war does not have a one-to-one relationship with all of the bits of information about war that you encountered through your lifetime. Although you constructed it from those bits, you interpreted all of them as you took them in, organized them to meet your particular needs and interests, and categorized the result in some particular way. You may have categorized those bits as political issues, ethical or religious issues, issues of patriotism, economic issues, or some combination of these. In Chapter 2 we will discuss some of the major factors that caused you to interpret, organize, and categorize that information as you did, that led you to construct that particular world in your head.

BYLINE

Describe each of your "four worlds" in your own words. It may be helpful, in doing this, to use some real example other than war: perhaps college athletics, the Soviet Union, or America's space program.

The Uniqueness of Your Worlds

We mentioned before that not all people are involved in communication in the same way. The fact is, no two people in the world have precisely the same communication environment or expose themselves to the same bits of their environment. The first world is the same for all of us—that "reality" that consists of everything going on in the world—but our other three worlds differ widely from those of other people. No two people have the opportunity to read precisely the same combination of materials, to talk to the same combination of people, or to hear and see the same combination of movies or radio and television programs. The pattern of selection from that environment is even more heterogeneous. And because we bring such different backgrounds, needs, and interests to the task, the worlds we ultimately create in our heads are different; even those

REVIEW

No two people in the world have exactly the same communication environment, or the same world in their heads.

No matter where we are these days, the media bring us information.

we create from fairly similar experiences are different. As a result, each of us lives in a unique set of worlds.

Think again about the way your understanding of war developed, the way you constructed and reconstructed that part of the world in your head. When did you first encounter information that made you aware of wars? What were all of the sources of information from which you got additional bits of information? Were some of the messages redundant; that is, did you encounter some bits of information a number of times? Did you see something on television, then read about it in the newspaper, and then hear some of your friends talking about it? For example, just think about all of the situations and sources from which you got information about the Persian Gulf War and about other events related to it.

BYLINE

If your memory is good, you should be able to recall a tremendously large number of encounters with bits of information about this war. Can you recall ever changing or refining your understanding of what was happening in Iraq? If so, what were the circumstances? What media messages were involved? What conversations with other people were involved?

Not only have you almost certainly been exposed to many bits of information about this situation in the Middle East; you have probably been involved in conversations about it with friends or family members. During those conversations, you had to respond to questions about some of the issues involved, thus creating additional information for yourself as well as for others about how you perceive those issues. In this way, you developed even firmer views about what was going on. The more you talked about it, the more complete, clear, and unchangeable became this world in your head.

In short, two kinds of things happened as you constructed your understanding of the war in the Middle East. (1) You were exposed to an ever-increasing number and variety of pieces and sources of information about it. (2) At the same time, you were exposed to a certain amount of repetitiveness, to the same or similar kinds of information again and again. And this process of constructing your understanding of these occurrences is not over; you are likely to continue to receive both new and redundant information for many years to come. Even if all of the problems in the Middle East get settled, novels, television series, film documentaries, poems, exposes, memoirs, and histories will continue to be produced based on these events. Men and women who served in the war will tell and retell stories about it for years to come. As a result, you will continue to reconstruct that part of the world in your head.

REVIEW

On almost any important issue, as time goes on you are exposed to a steadily increasing number and variety of bits of information. In addition, over time, you are exposed to some of the same bits of information many times.

Your Control of Exposure

You may have sought much of the information you have about war, or at least paid attention when it was available. *You* decided whether to read the newspaper story about national guard or military reserve units from your region called into active duty. *You* decided whether to watch the television documentary on women at the front or to read Ernest Hemingway's *For Whom the Bell Tolls*. And you decided if you should discuss with your friends whether to vote for the candidate for Congress who voted against giving President Bush authority to go to war against Iraq. You may even have initiated a discussion in a journalism class about military censorship of news from the front or about the appropriateness of newspapers or television stations showing vivid photographs of the maimed and bloody bodies after a land mine explosion or a bombing. At the minimum, you must have wondered about what factors a responsible editor takes into account in deciding how much space and prominence to give to war coverage and how much to devote to all of the other events in the world. To a great extent, you controlled your exposure to this information and the amount of time you spent thinking and talking about these issues.

Of course, you could not control all of your exposure to information about the Persian Gulf War. Sometimes you encountered news about it when you just happened to turn on the television set, although even then you controlled—consciously or unconsciously—the amount of attention you gave it and the parts of the story on which you focused. Nor were you totally in control of the nature of this information; it varied depending on whatever local, state, national, and world events made the war situation more or less newsworthy on any given day.

In any case, you have much greater control of the kinds and amounts of war-related information you are exposed to than most critics of "mass society" give you credit for. If you did not have that control, we would not find such great variation in people's knowledge and beliefs about war. The image of war that you developed over the years is truly your personal construction.

Not only have your beliefs about war been developed in this way, but also your beliefs about almost everything else—the President, minority groups, nuclear power, the economy, the Soviet Union, our educational system, appropriate sex roles, and so forth. All of these parts of your reality—these parts of the world in your head—have been shaped and reshaped by the bits of information and other experiences to which you have been exposed throughout your life.

BYLINE

Think back about your exposure to information the past few days. Other than information related to the courses you are taking this term, what are some of the bits of information to which you were exposed without any effort or intention on your part? What are some of the bits of information you exposed yourself to intentionally? From these examples, can you generalize about the kinds of information exposure over which you have more control and the kinds over which you have less control?

THE FUNCTIONS OF COMMUNICATION MODELS

In the remainder of this chapter, and in other parts of this book, we will be discussing communication **models**. Because the idea of models may be new to you, it is probably helpful to explain what they are and what they are good for.

Models are abstract descriptions of a phenomenon. Models, or abstract descriptions of communication, for example, help us think about communication more analytically, whether we are (1) trying to solve a specific, immediate problem—such as assessing the effectiveness of a particular advertisement so we can decide whether to use it, or (2) developing and testing a theory that can help us solve a wider range of problems. For either of these purposes, we always need to have some image, picture, blueprint, or "model" of how the phenomenon works. For the study of communication or the solving of a communication problem, we need a communication model.

Models can help us perceive things we would not otherwise have perceived or thought of. They can also help us organize our ideas about the phenomenon. They facilitate our thinking beyond the specific instances of communication that are before us so that we can consider more general problems. Conversely, they can help us understand a particular problem by stripping away the immediate context so we can get down to fundamentals. The fact that a model is an *abstract* description helps us do that. It strips away the elements that are tied to specific instances.

It is this abstract quality of models that bothers some people. They say that no model describes communication in all its richness, that the model is different from the instances they know about. And they are perfectly right. No model describes everything about communication. In this sense, models are like any other kind of description, including verbal descriptions. When we use words to describe your college or class, when we describe you, or when we describe communication with words, our description is an abstraction. It is not the thing itself.

All of the sciences use models and all encounter some of the same criticisms of them. You may have encountered models of molecules in a chemistry class or a model of the solar system in an astronomy class. The explanation of models by a philosopher of science named Hesse (1966) may clarify our point about the differences between a model and the phenomenon it helps us to understand:

> *When we take a collection of billiard balls in random motion as a model for a gas, we are not asserting that billiard balls are in all respects like gas particles, for billiard balls are red and white, and hard and shiny, and we are not intending to suggest that gas molecules have these properties. We are in fact saying that gas molecules are analogous to billiard balls, and the relation of analogy means that there are some properties of billiard balls which are not found in molecules* [**negative analogies**] *and there are some which are* [**positive analogies**] . . . . *Now the important thing about this kind of model-thinking in the sciences [and social sciences] is that there will generally be some properties of the model about which we do not yet know whether they are positive or negative analogies; these are the interesting properties, because . . . they allow us to make new predictions.* [These are the **uncertain analogies**.][1]

Review

A model is an abstract description of a phenomenon that helps us (a) think about the phenomenon in new ways, (b) perceive some aspects of the phenomenon we would not otherwise have thought of, (c) organize our ideas about the phenomenon, and (d) make new predictions about the phenomenon that we can then test.

Let us give you another example, the example of the floor plan of a house. In a sense, a model has the same relationship to the phenomenon it is describing as a floor plan does to the structure on which it is based. A floor plan is clearly different from the house, and yet it often helps us to see the house in fresh and useful ways.

Just as a floor plan is but one way of conceiving of a particular house, or perhaps of the general concept "house," so a model is just one way of conceiving of a particular phenomenon or concept. The criterion for judging a floor plan is whether it is useful or whether it stimulates you to think of fresh ideas about how to decorate the house or how to use the rooms. That is also true of the scientific model. Like the floor plan, in assessing scientific models we are primarily concerned with utility. Is the model useful? Does it help us perceive some aspects of communication that we would not have perceived without it? Does it help guide our study of communication in useful ways? Are there some properties or aspects of the model whose relationship to the phenomenon we are unsure about—we do not know whether they are analogous to our phenomenon or not? Models with such properties are especially useful for scholars because, as Hesse pointed out, we can get new hypotheses from them—new ideas for testing.

So far, our discussion of models has been rather abstract and perhaps confusing. Any confusion should be cleared up, though, as we look at some models of communication and discuss their utility.

> **BYLINE**
>
> Before turning to the communication models, review what you have learned about models in general. How would you define a model in your own words? What is a "negative analogy"? A "positive analogy"? An "uncertain analogy"? Which of these three types of analogies is most useful to scholars? Why?

FIGURE 1.1 *Communication is far more complex than simply pouring information or meanings from one person's head into another's.*

SOME TRADITIONAL MODELS OF COMMUNICATION

If you are like most people, you usually think about communication as *receiving* information or messages from the mass media or other people or *sending* information or messages to others. It is like pouring lemon-

FIGURE 1.2
Source control model.

ade from one person's pitcher into another person's glass, the pouring of meaning from one head into another.

Communication scholars have depicted this view of communication in a **source-message-receiver** model, or if they were concerned with mass communication, in a **source-message-channel-receiver** model.

This model suggests that a source sends a message through some channel to a receiver who absorbs it in just the way in which it was sent, unless the receiver is inattentive. In general, the source or sender is in control of what the receiver learns.

In much the same way, you may have envisioned mass communication as simply the pouring or transmission of the same meanings into the heads of a large number of anonymous, isolated, and passive individuals—"the masses"—as in Figure 1.3. But this model grossly distorts the great differences among individuals in patterns of exposure and ways of processing the information they receive. The vast majority of people may be anonymous, as far as mass communicators are concerned, but they are neither isolated nor passive.

Bruce Westley and Malcolm MacLean (1957), two communication scholars disturbed by the oversimplification of existing models of mass communication, developed a more elaborate model. It stresses that much of what we get from the mass media, before it ever reaches us, has been shaped by a variety of individuals, institutions, and technologies. An adaptation of their model can be seen in Figure 1.4.

The Westley-MacLean model points up the fact that, in any form of mass communication, information goes through a series of gatekeepers, labeled in our adaptation of the model, observers / interpreters / translators. A reporter, for example, is an observer / interpreter / translator. A military censor is a different type of observer / interpreter / translator. The editor who decides whether the reporter's translation of an event will be used observes and interprets not only the reporter's copy, but also other related information. The editor may even have been exposed first-hand to the event being reported. If the decision is positive, the editor translates the information again through editing. If such a situation involves a large newspaper, someone else on the staff observes and interprets the information to decide on which page it will go and how prominently it will be displayed, a process that is also a type of translation. The headline writer also observes and interprets this version of the story and translates it further by deciding on the kind and size of headline. If such a scenario in-

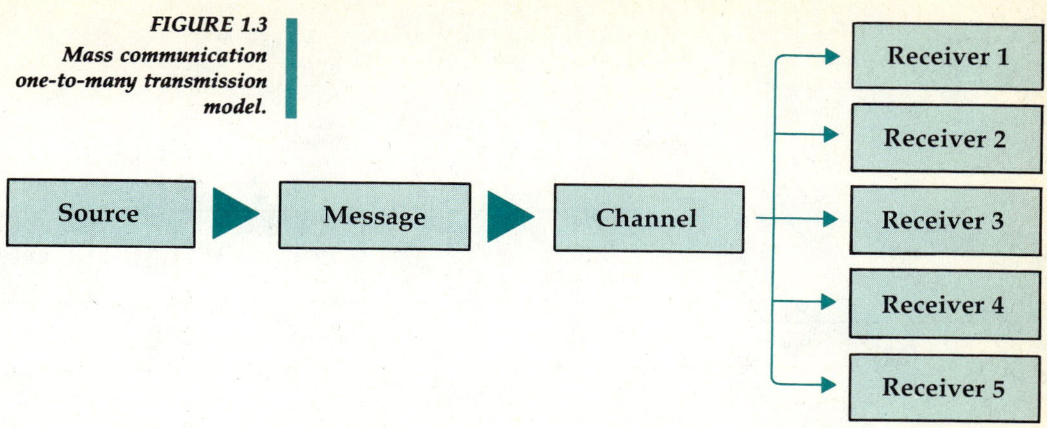

FIGURE 1.3 ***Mass communication one-to-many transmission model.***

volves a radio or television newscast, the on-air reporter or anchor provides yet another translation by deciding on the placement of the story within the newscast, by choosing the visuals to accompany it, by deciding whether to use the original reporter's voice-on-tape or to substitute the anchor's voice, and, if the latter, by choosing the tone of voice with which to present the copy on the air.

Still another type of observer / interpreter / translator is the technology used. That technology is as much a gatekeeper as an editor is; a story reported with a video camera can never be precisely the same as a story reported with just a lap-top word processor.

Even the readers, viewers, or listeners are not only observers and interpreters but, quite often, translators as well, because they put the information into yet another form as they talk about it with friends and family members, or when they write or call a station or newspaper to compliment or complain about it.

The Westley-MacLean model takes into account that response of audience members as it points up the fact that communication goes in more than one direction: receivers often provide **feedback** to the original sources, *responses or reactions to the sources' messages, which can cause the sources, consciously or unconsciously, to alter their communicative behavior*. Journalists not only send stories to their editors, they get reactions back, just as editors get reactions from readers or viewers. There are few, if any, people involved in mass communication who do not get feedback in one form or another.

In addition, just as readers or viewers are influenced by what they read and see, media people are influenced by this feedback. What they select to transmit, the way they shape that material, and even the way they perceive it are influenced by this feedback. One of the important contributions of the Westley-MacLean model is to remind us that communication is a continuing, multidirectional process.[2]

FIGURE 1.4
Adaptation of Westley–MacLean feedback model.

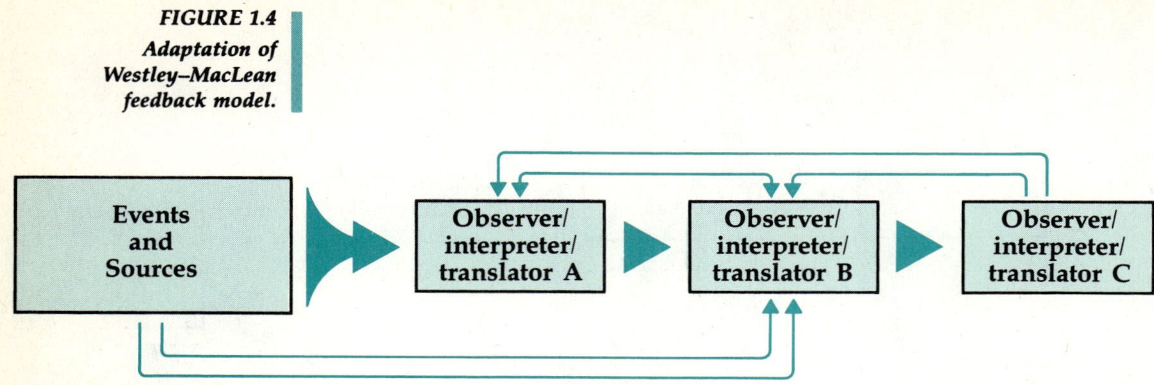

> **BYLINE**
>
> For what kind of communication is the model in Figure 1.2 probably the best representation? For what kind is Figure 1.3 the best? Figure 1.4? Why?

A NEW MODEL OF MASS COMMUNICATION

Although each of these models of mass communication provides insight into some aspect of communication processes, none gives us an adequate picture of the contemporary world of communication that you and others experience. Nor do these provide any insight into our role—the role of audience members—in the communication process. The **mosaic model** overcomes those deficiencies.[3]

We call this a mosaic model because *the communication environment in which all of us live—what we labeled our "second world" earlier in this chapter—* is like a vast mosaic of information bits. Readily available to all of us at virtually any time are newspapers, books, magazines, television, radio, motion pictures, recordings, pamphlets, and other people. Each of these is a source of countless bits of information on almost an infinite variety of topics. From this vast mosaic of information bits in our environment, we select or are exposed to a limited number. These comprise what we earlier called our "third world." And it is from this limited number of bits of information that we construct our "fourth world"—that world in our heads.

Representing the Communication Mosaic Visually

In visualizing the communication mosaic model, think first about just one topic, perhaps the topic of war we discussed earlier. Consider all of the possible *sources* of information on this topic to which you might turn and the vast number of possible *bits of information* available in those sources. We can picture those sources and information bits as a matrix of

REVIEW

The mosaic model is an abstract description of your environment. This environment is like a vast mosaic composed of all the bits of information available to you from a great variety of sources. You are exposed to, or attend to, only a tiny fraction of what is available. From this relatively small sample, you construct—and constantly reconstruct—the world in your head.

squares, like the matrix shown in Figure 1.5. This figure suggests what your communication environment is like at one moment in time. Each row stands for one of the almost infinite number of sources you have available, if you choose to use them. Some of these are newspapers, others are television channels, books, persons, and so forth. Each column stands for one of the available bits of information about war that might be found through those sources. Some of those bits of information are available from many sources; others are available from only one or two. At times, there are probably some bits not available from any source.

You will notice that some of the squares are colored in, while most are not. The filled-in squares represent those few bits of information you attend to or happen to notice and the sources in which you encounter them. As you can see, only a small number of the squares are filled in. This indicates that you, or any of us, encounter only a small fraction of the great number of the bits of information about war that are available in our environment. Some of these bits are those you looked for; others are those you encountered by accident, perhaps hearing them when some friend or family member turned on the radio. Thus, there is a certain amount of chance or randomness in the information about war that you encounter. It is not totally a matter of chance, of course. If you are a member of the National Guard or of the reserves, you are almost certain to encounter more bits of information about war than if you are not. If you have friends or family members who are in the service or who are active in either the ROTC or some pacifist group, you are almost certain to hear more about the issue than if your friends and family are indifferent to it. If you

FIGURE 1.5
At almost any time, there are many bits of information about war available in your communication mosaic.

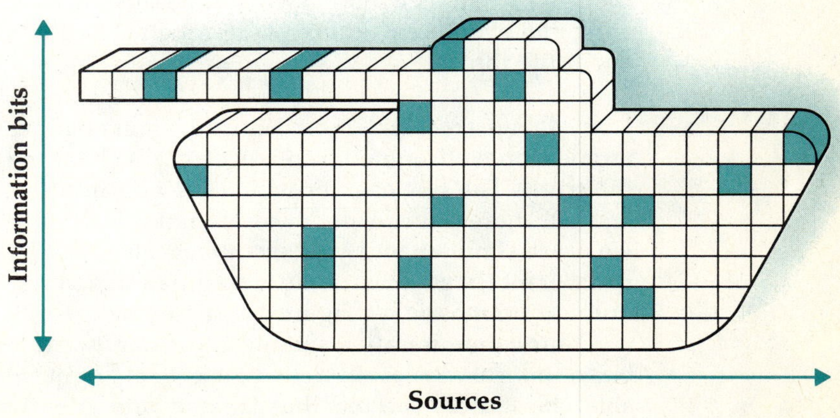

live in an area where there is a large military base you are almost certain to run into more information on the topic than people who live in other areas.

> **BYLINE**
>
> Try to list all of the sources from which you have ever gotten any bits of information about the Persian Gulf War, both media and interpersonal sources. Rank them in terms of the relative amounts of information you have received from each. Is that rank order the same as or different than what it would be for other types of issues, such as the issue of tuition increases? How do you explain the similarity or difference?

The interaction of sources. Some media, such as television and the motion picture, are each multiple sources. We simultaneously get both aural and visual information from each. These aural and visual "tracks" interact, just as the various images or bits of information that we get from completely different sources interact as we use them to create our meanings. By **interaction** we mean *they affect each other; the meaning you construct from a visual image will be different when it is accompanied by different sounds, just as your interpretation of different sounds will be different when accompanied by different visual images*. For example, assume that you are watching a story on television about yet another possible war in the Middle East. While the anchor person is reading the story, the producer could insert many different kinds of visual images: starving refugee children, soldiers in the desert, burning tanks, bombed-out buildings, Saddam Hussein, American General Colin Powell, or diplomats arguing about the issue at the United Nations. The same words accompanied by each of these different kinds of pictures would tend to lead viewers to construct completely different meanings for the story of the new military threat because the viewers would be associating quite different kinds of information with the bits of information about the threat.

Your changing mosaic. From Figure 1.5 you might conclude that your communication environment is relatively static. Nothing could be further from the truth. The bits of information we get from the media, other people, and our more direct experiences do not interact solely with other bits that we sense simultaneously. They interact also with bits that we have sensed at different times. Thus, time is an important third dimension in our communication mosaic, as Figure 1.6 suggests.

Your communication mosaic is constantly changing. The sources and bits of information available to you keep changing and, from what is available, the sources and bits that come to your attention also keep changing.

FIGURE 1.6
Over time, an almost infinite number and variety of bits of information about war are available to you.

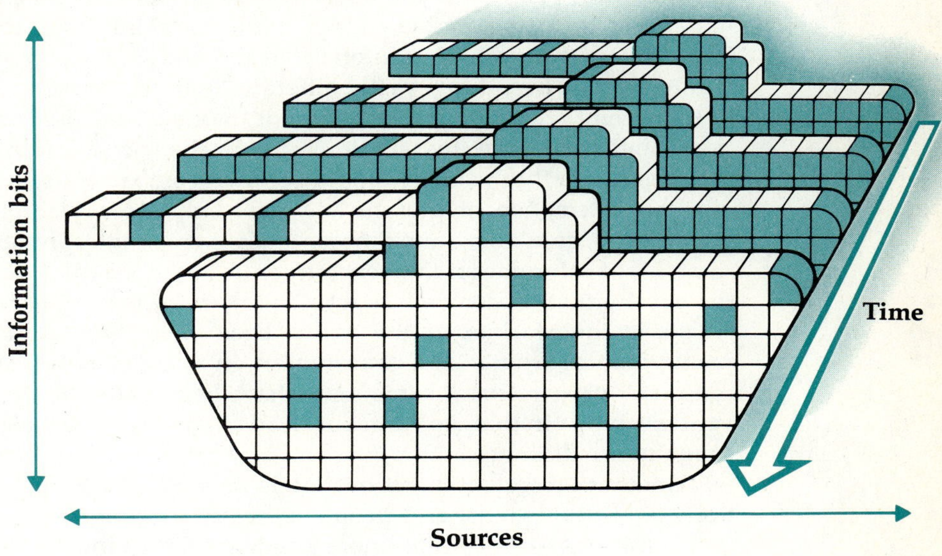

For example, the information available on radio, television, or from other people changes steadily. If you do not hear what newscasters are saying as they say it, you cannot ordinarily have it repeated, although you may hear it again on a later newscast. The newscasters, like your friends, move on from one topic to another. Other media, such as newspapers, do not change as steadily, but each day a new newspaper appears, and the old one is used to wrap the garbage or is recycled, thus disappearing from your environment.

REVIEW

Your communication mosaic is constantly changing. And the bits of information to which you were exposed in the past interact with those to which you are exposed now, just as the sights and sounds you sense simultaneously interact.

Another source of change in your communication environment over time is your movement from place to place. Clearly, when you leave your home and go to class, or when you go from class to work, or even when you move from one friend or group of friends to another, the sources and kinds of information available to you change quite substantially, as do the sources and kinds of information to which you attend.

All of these kinds of changes are indicated by the time dimension in Figure 1.6. Thus, over time, you are exposed to a great variety of different sources and bits of information.

Time and memory. Insofar as the time dimension affects the construction and reconstruction of that world in your head, it is analogous to your memory. New information that you encounter can often stir that memory and make vivid in your mind some information or event that you experienced long ago and have not thought of for a long time. There can even be an interaction between the present and past experience that leads you to see that past in a totally new way. For example, you may once have had a negative view of a friend you knew in high school who enlisted in the military when he or she graduated. All of the recent information about American soldiers defending our interests in the Middle East, however, has led you to see this friend in a vastly different light. Conversely, your memory of this friend affects your perception of the new information you are getting about soldiers in the Middle East or, if the friend is female, for example, about whether women should serve in combat units.

This interaction of present and past helps to explain why different people often construct quite different meanings or interpretations from the same bit of information they encounter. A large group of us might watch the same situation comedy about a family in which the son or daughter enlists in the Marines or the Army. Each of us will "understand" that young man or woman and the program in a somewhat different way because our prior relevant experiences have been different, and so the relevant meanings in that world in our heads that we use to make sense of the program are different.

Another important effect of time is its tendency to make our perceptions of issues, events, and people increasingly complex and yet increasingly clear. As we encounter more and more bits of information about war in general, or about the Persian Gulf situation in particular, our picture of it tends to become clearer. At the same time, however, it becomes more complex; we see many aspects of war that we never thought about before.

Still another way to think of time or memory is as one additional source to which you turn for information. Just as you search a newspaper for some bit of information you want, you sometimes search your memory also. In addition, just as you sometimes happen to encounter some relevant bit of information on television just by chance, so you can suddenly recall some relevant bit of information from memory just by chance—probably stimulated by something in the present.

In a way, your memory—all of the nooks and crannies of that world in your head—is like a library packed with your history. An even better analogy might be the old-time general store that you have probably seen depicted in some television show, encountered in old movies, or read about in histories of America. The general store had everything in it that the owner-manager had ever come across: brooms, books and baseball bats, meats and matches, tables and tobacco, nails and netting, spices and suspenders, apples and aspirin, gasoline, garden hoses and galoshes, pickles, and powder puffs.

REVIEW

Your memory may be one of the most fully packed sources of information to which you turn for information to supplement or help you understand material from other sources.

Sometimes you forget what is stocked in that old-time general store that is your memory until something happens that reminds you, or you stumble across it while searching for something else. On the other hand, you are almost always aware of the items in your storehouse that many customers are interested in, and you can pull them out of their bin with hardly a thought. So it is with items in memory that you need to recall often.

The fourth dimension of the mosaic. To this point, we talked about the interaction among sources of information relevant to your image of war: bits of information about war that you sense in the present, and the picture of war that you constructed in the past and now have stored in memory. To better understand why you have constructed your particular meaning or understanding of war, you must take into account at least one other factor. Every time you encounter or remember anything about war, your interpretation of it will be affected by the other issues or topics about which you are getting information.

For example, your interpretation of new information regarding the issue of war might be shaped by information you are getting at roughly the same time on world hunger, the dependence of our country on oil, progress on achieving equal rights for women, the poor treatment of political dissidents in many countries, the inefficiency of government agencies, the corruption among government officials in many countries that are our allies, or any number of other topics. These other messages form a context for your construction of the meaning of war.

In fact, these other messages can increase or decrease the level of attention you give to news about war. If a major story grabs your attention, such as a story about the threat of a major economic recession, you are more likely to ignore completely any story about war or the threat of war. On the other hand, if the major story of the day is focused on all of the political abuses being practiced in a country we oppose, or on ways in which that country is getting a stranglehold on our economy through its control of oil prices, you will probably give more attention to the story about the war than you would otherwise.

REVIEW

Your interpretation of information on one topic is often affected by information on other topics that you are aware of at the same time.

These different topics for which sources and bits of information are available in our environment form the fourth dimension of our communication mosaic. Because four dimensions are difficult to visualize, however, and because these sources and bits of information on other topics act as a context around the other dimensions of the mosaic, we can think of it that way—a sort of information atmosphere or context through which and within which we experience the information on any one topic. This idea is portrayed in Figure 1.7 as the area or atmosphere surrounding and impinging on the mosaic.

BYLINE

Define the communication mosaic in your own words. What are the four dimensions of this model? How does the mosaic model relate to the four worlds that we discussed in the early part of this chapter?

FIGURE 1.7
Your interpretation of all of the bits of information about war to which you are exposed is influenced by the information you encounter about all sorts of other topics.

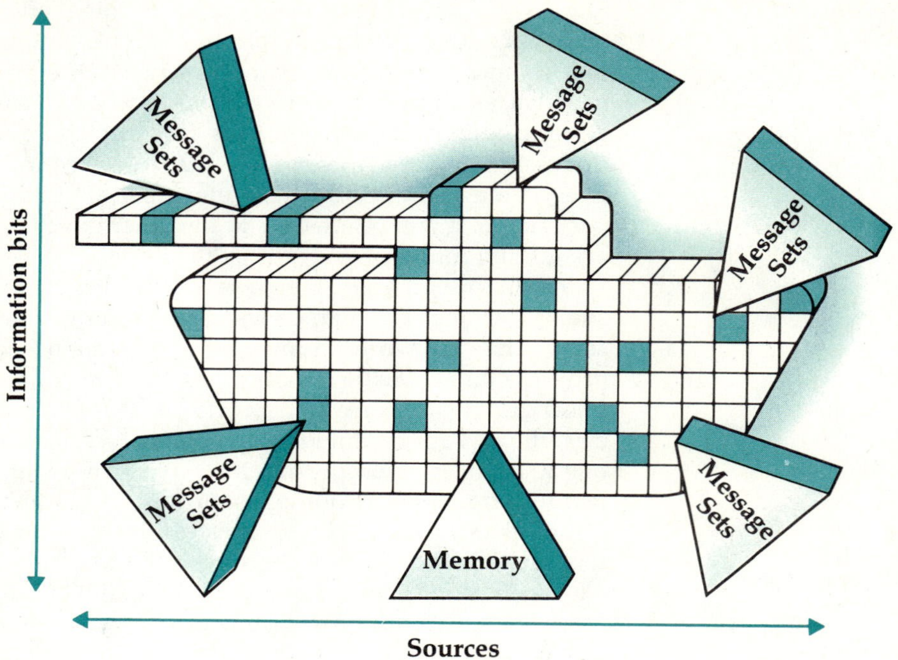

The Value of the Mosaic Model

Receivers versus participants. Although each of the models of communication presented in the early part of this chapter provides insight into some aspect of communication processes, none gives us insight into the role of people such as ourselves, who depend on the mass media and on other people for most of our information. Most of these models seem to picture us as passive sponges, soaking up whatever messages the media send our way and soaking them up in exactly the way in which they are sent. In fact, as we indicated with the example of the war, we are far from passive. Neither the simple source-message-channel-receiver model, the transfer-of-meaning model, the source-message-channel-many-receivers model, or even the feedback model of Westley and MacLean adequately describes our role in communication processes or the way in which any of us experience mass communication. The mosaic model better fits our real-life communication. It takes into account the various kinds of communication in which we engage, the close relationship of mass communication and interpersonal communication, and the active role you play in this process.

First of all, the mosaic model is based on a very different conception of communication than that underlying all of the other models. Each of those earlier models we talked about suggests that the important people in communication are the *sources*. They are in the driver's seat; they control the communication process. The mosaic model, on the other hand, suggests that the important people in communication—the people in the driver's seat—are the *audience members*, those to whom communication is being directed. Given this mosaic conception of communication, it is a mistake to think of anyone as a mere "receiver" of information. It is far more valid to think of yourself and others as *participants*.

REVIEW

You are never simply a *receiver* of communication; you are always a *participant* in the communication process because you *select* much of the information to which you are exposed and you *construct* meanings from it.

To put this another way, those other models define communication in terms of someone *sending* messages to someone else. The mosaic model defines communication in terms of you, or ourselves, or anyone else *constructing* our own messages from the words, pictures, objects, odors, or actions that we encounter in our environment.

The Construction of Meaning

There are two key concepts to consider when you think about communication in this way. One is *construction*. We do not *receive* messages; we *construct* messages. No one can *pour* messages into our heads; we *create* the messages in our own heads.

The second key term is *meaning*. An important implication of the mosaic model is that meanings are not in words or news stories, television programs or photographs; *meanings are in people*. You *interpret* the words or stories, programs, or photographs; this is simply a different way of saying that you construct meanings from them.

BYLINE

What do we mean when we say that meanings are not in words or pictures, newspapers or television programs, but that meanings are in people?

REVIEW

No one media message or interpersonal message has much impact on your beliefs. You construct your beliefs with bits of information gathered from various sources over a long period of time.

Not only do you *construct* meanings from the bits of information or stimuli you encounter in the mass media and elsewhere; you constantly *reconstruct* those meanings as you encounter new bits of information or as your needs or experiences change. Few if any of your meanings were constructed on the basis of information from a single message in isolation. Any one news story, conversation, motion picture, radio program, or television program was but a small part of the information that you have received about the Persian Gulf War. As a result, any one of these stories, by itself, had only a small impact on that world in your head.

Reconstructions of meaning. On the other hand, over time, as you continue to get information from these various sources, you regularly reassess and refine your meanings. Once in a while, you even revise some of them quite drastically, especially when you get a flood of information from a variety of sources about some new development. Thus, for example, what "war" means to you, that part of the world in your head that is your understanding of what war is like, is constantly evolving. When the Persian Gulf War broke out and there was a heavy flow of news about it in most of the media you use, and people around you talked a great deal about it, you must have reconstructed your understanding, or meaning, of war quite substantially, as well as your meanings for Iraq, Kuwait, Saudi Arabia, and other countries in that part of the world.

There is a term used by some contemporary artists that describes this continual construction and reconstruction of our meanings quite well. It is **cumulative meanings**. By this we mean that *your beliefs about the world are based on bits of information and experiences that you accumulated over time*. Thus, your meanings for most of the important events, people, and ideas in the world are not static, *they evolve as you experience or accumulate bits of relevant information*.

One of this country's important communication scholars, Wilbur Schramm, likened this process to the gradual building up of a stalagmite in a cave. As you know, a stalagmite is formed by the constant drip of calcareous water upon it, each drop leaving a residue so small as to be invisible until the dripping has continued for hundreds of years. In the same way, except in extremely unusual cases, any one bit of information about war—or anything else—has only an imperceptible effect on that world in your head. Although it does not take hundreds of years for recognizable change to occur in that world in your head, it generally takes a fair amount of time and many bits of information.

The particular bits of information that are relevant to the construction and constant reconstruction of your meanings are not always obvious. Your meaning of war and peace, and whether any particular war was justifiable, may be shaped by what you know about the people of other countries and cultures, about politics and economics, psychology and nuclear science, and about the many wars that have affected this world. Your religious beliefs may also strongly influence your views of war, as will your friends' and family members' beliefs about war.

BYLINE

Why is the idea of "cumulative meanings" particularly apt for describing your beliefs about the world, for describing the world in your head? Does it fit your recollection of how you constructed your message of the Persian Gulf War?

A broadened conception of information. Some of those bits of information that you use in constructing your fourth world, that world in your head, may not even be "information" in the usual sense of that term. They may come from comic strips, novels, situation comedies, or other experiences we think of as entertainment. For example, when a television soap opera character is considering enlisting in the army in order to help defend his or her country and discusses the matter with family and friends, some of whom favor the idea and some of whom oppose it, how do those bits of information differ in your use of them from the bits of information you encounter in the news? Research evidence indicates that they differ little, if at all.

You are probably constructing your meanings for law officers and the kinds of crime that go on in large cities at least as much from police and private eye shows on television as you are from news stories and personal observation.

The point of all this is that the differences between entertainment content in the media and news or information content is not nearly as important as most people believe, at least not when we are trying to explain how and why people construct the worlds in their heads that they do. It is an error to assume that a television series about crime and police work is merely entertainment, while only newspaper stories about crime and police work are "news." Programs such as "60 Minutes" or a situation comedy, cartoons, novels and motion pictures, and the lyrics of popular music all provide bits of information that we use to construct the world in our heads.

BYLINE

Describe a fictional movie or situation comedy you saw that illustrates the idea that what appears to be simply diversion is sometimes informative. Describe a news item from the newspaper or television news that illustrates the idea that what appears to be informative is sometimes simply diversion or entertainment.

Paths through the mosaic. As you look at the representation of the mosaic, you must visualize a person moving through it, just as you move through your communication environment, encountering some bits of information in some sources on some topics and missing others that are there. Obviously, no two people go through their environments in precisely the same way; no two people encounter or attend to all of the same bits of information.

In addition, you, like others, go through your mosaic in different ways at different times. Sometimes you rush madly through, with your mind on other things, and so avoid or hardly notice any of the new information available to you. At other times, you move more slowly, studying the bits of information carefully, turning from one source of information to another in order to build as complete and valid a picture as possible of some event, person, or issue. At still other times you are relatively passive, neither seeking nor avoiding information, just noticing the information that happens to cross your path.

The particular path you take through the mosaic affects not only which bits of information you encounter, but also the context for each bit—what comes before and after it. As we indicated earlier, that context can affect your interpretation of the information almost as much as the information itself does. We will talk more about the influence of context on meaning construction, as well as other influences on that construction, in Chapter 2.

BYLINE

Think about the way you use the media. Are there particular patterns in your use? For example, do you usually read a daily newspaper before or after hearing a radio or television newscast (assuming that you do both)? When you read a newspaper, what "path" through the paper do you usually follow? Do you start at page 1 and read straight through the paper, or do you read it in a different order? Does the way you read the paper increase or decrease the probability of your noticing certain kinds of items in the paper?

Gaps in the mosaic. From our discussion so far, it should be clear that all of us have **gaps** in the information to which we have been exposed, *important information about a topic that was not in any of the messages we received, or information that we did not notice*. No individual is probably ever exposed to all possible information about a topic. At the same time, all of us have within ourselves a need for order, for wholeness, for seeing the complete picture. Therefore, we fill those gaps, usually without even being aware that we are doing so.

Imagine, for example, that you see four photographs in succession. The first shows a child glaring at another child. The second shows a small child's fist. The third has that fist against the nose of the second child. And the fourth shows that second child lying on the floor with tears streaming from both eyes. Before going on, think about those photographs and the message you constructed from them. If you are like other people, you filled in the gaps between those photographs. You "saw" the fist being formed, then being swung through the air, and the child falling. You might even have "heard" the second child falling. Again, stop for a moment here and, before reading on, picture that scene. Can you get an image of it in your mind? Can you see those children? Quickly: Are they boys or girls?

Given the worlds in the heads of most of us, constructed from images encountered in children's books, television, and elsewhere, you probably "saw" that both of those children were boys. Nothing in the description of the photographs mentioned their sex. That was a gap in the set of information given to you. In creating your world, in constructing the "reality" of that fight in your head, you filled that gap, along with all of the others that were there. In the same way and for the same reasons, you fill the gaps in the messages you encounter about war, crack and cocaine, the abortion issue, your friends and enemies, China, the dangers of tobacco and alcohol, the President of the United States, intercollegiate athletics, and all of the other ideas or topics that are important to you and about which you get bits of information from the mosaic that is your environment.

Unintended bits of information. Because most of us do not read, hear, or see every bit of information in the messages contained in the media or in the conversations of our friends, we are not aware of all of the meanings intended by the message creators. On the other hand, we often get some **unintended bits of information** from their messages. That is, we notice some *bits of information in a message that the source did not consider or plan to have there*. Almost any motion picture, television or radio program, magazine article, or newspaper story that is intended to communicate information about some particular subject also communicates information about a host of other topics to some receivers.

Those unintended bits of information may be present because of the content of the message (the "thing" a creator is telling us about), the background or setting, or perhaps even the medium itself. For example, a magazine photograph of Michael Chang making the winning tennis shot for the deciding match in a Davis Cup competition carries innumerable elements that are irrelevant to the intended message—that his victory ensured a victory for the American team against Austria—but that are necessary to include. Chang's tennis outfit has no necessary relationship to the intended message but, in visual media at least, must be included, and some viewers will use it in their construction, or reconstruction, of the message of tennis fashions in their heads. Michael Chang himself might also fit into various messages in people's heads, in addition to the one intended by the publication of the photograph. He might fit into a message about athletes, tennis, America's standing in world tennis, sportsmanship, and the integration of Asian-Americans into our society. Information bits in that photograph could affect our meanings for any or all of those

Into which of your messages does Michael Chang fit?

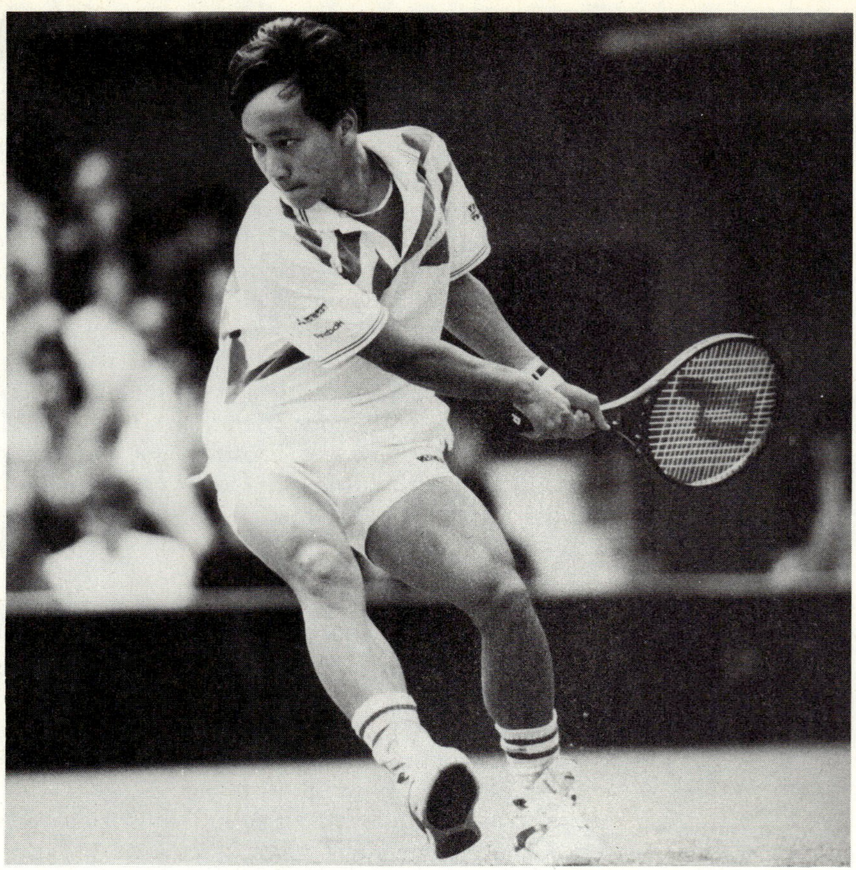

messages. Some who see the photograph may not even notice that it has anything to do with the Davis Cup, nor will they catch the player's name; the message for them will be one about the photographer's skill and perhaps even about the art of photography itself. In later chapters we will talk about some of the factors that cause different people to "read" photographs, motion pictures, television programs, news stories, or books in such different ways.

YOUR COMMUNICATION MOSAIC: SUMMARY AND IMPLICATIONS

The mosaic model gives us not simply a different way of thinking about communication, but a different *definition* of communication. Since meaning is not in words or pictures, objects or actions, but rather in people, communication is something that takes place when a person constructs meanings from words, pictures, objects, or actions that have symbolic value for him or her.

Thus, it is not the sender who is in control of whether communication takes place; it is the audience members whom that message hits who are in control. So it makes good sense to think of those audience members—those meaning constructors—as *participants* in the communication process, not simply as *receivers*.

Another implication of the mosaic model is that you are mistaken if you believe you take in or consume media content in rather large and well-organized segments—for example, that you watch and take into your memory system *programs, newspaper stories, movies,* or *books*. In fact, you never take into your memory bank an entire program, news story, movie, or book. You take in *bits of information* and you *construct* those larger entities in your head. And because no two persons exposed to the same movie, for example, ever take in *precisely* the same bits of information, the world you construct in your head of the movies you see, or of anything else, is bound to be at least somewhat different than the worlds constructed by everyone else. And each of the movies, television programs, newspaper stories, books, and other such images you have constructed in your head becomes a building block for larger messages—messages about the television industry, the field of journalism, politics, intercollegiate athletics, the military, the abortion issue, war, and so forth.

If you think about the image of politics that you have in your head, or your image of intercollegiate athletics, and about how you came to have that image, you should begin to understand better the mosaic concept. You must have constructed that image over a long period of time from many different bits of information that you encountered in a variety of media, interpersonal communication, and perhaps even first-hand experiences.

Here are some of the major points that may help you to understand and remember the concept of the communication mosaic:

1. Each of us lives in four worlds: the vast universe or world that is largely beyond our view; that world or mosaic of information that is available to us if we search for or attend to it; that world to which we are exposed; and that world in our heads we construct.
2. It is useful to think of the second, third, and fourth of those worlds as *mosaics* of information bits.
3. Each of these mosaics is an interpretation and representation of that first world.
4. From the large mosaic that is your environment (your second world), you *select* or are *exposed to* many bits of information (your third world).
5. You *interpret* those bits to which you are exposed and use them to *construct* your reality, the world in your head (your fourth world).

DISCUSSION QUESTIONS

1. What are the "four worlds" in which you live? Using the President of the United States as the example, how do your four worlds of President Bush probably differ?
2. Why do Becker and Roberts claim that your worlds are unique, unlike those of anyone else?

3. What difference does it make whether we think of ourselves as "receivers" of communication or as "participants" in the communication process?
4. What are the possible functions or values of a good communication model?
5. What do the authors mean by "positive," "negative," and "uncertain analogies" of models? Which kind of analogy is most important to communication scholars? Why?
6. Does "feedback" increase or decrease the chances that the people involved in a communication situation will ultimately construct similar meanings for the event being covered?
7. How does the mosaic model differ from Westley and MacLean's feedback model?
8. What are the four dimensions of the mosaic model?
9. In what ways does memory work as if it were one of the many other sources of information?
10. What helps you fill the gaps in your meanings or images of events about which you have encountered scattered and incomplete bits of information?
11. How is the idea of "cumulative meanings" related to the mosaic model?

NOTES

1. M. B. Hesse, *Models and Analogies in Science* (Notre Dame: University of Notre Dame Press, 1966), p. 8.
2. For a more complete description and discussion of the Westley-MacLean model, see Bruce H. Westley and Malcolm S. MacLean, Jr. "A Conceptual Model for Communication Research." *Journalism Quarterly* 34 (1957): 31–38.
3. The mosaic model was first described and explained in Samuel L. Becker, "Toward an Appropriate Theory for Contemporary Speech-Communication," in *What Rhetoric (Communication Theory) Is Appropriate for Contemporary Speech Communication*? David H. Smith, ed. (Minneapolis: University of Minnesota, 1969), pp. 9–25.

SUGGESTED READINGS

Classic Works in the Field

Boulding, Kenneth E. *The Image*. Ann Arbor: University of Michigan Press, 1956.

Lasswell, Harold D. "The Structure and Function of Communication in Society." In *The Communication of Ideas*, ed. Lyman Bryson. New York: Institute for Religious and Social Studies, 1948.

Lippmann, Walter. *Public Opinion*. New York: Macmillan (Free Press), 1965. See especially Chapter 1, "The World Outside and the Pictures in Our Heads."

McLuhan, Marshall. *Understanding Media: The Extensions of Man*. 2nd ed. New York: New American Library, 1964.

Schramm, Wilbur. "The Nature of Communication Between Humans." In *The Process and Effects of Mass Communication*, ed. Wilbur Schramm and Donald F. Roberts, pp. 1–53. Rev. ed. Urbana: University of Illinois Press, 1971.

Relevant Contemporary Works

Anderson, James A., and Timothy P. Meyer. *Mediated Communication: A Social Action Perspective*. Newbury Park, CA: Sage, 1988.

Ball-Rokeach, Sandra, and Melvin DeFleur. "A Dependency Model of Mass Media Effects." *Communication Research 3* (1976): 3–21.

McQuail, Denis. *Mass Communication Theory: An Introduction*. 2nd ed. Newbury Park, CA: Sage, 1987.

McQuail, Denis, and Sven Windahl. *Communication Models For the Study of Mass Communications*. New York: Longman, 1981.

Severin, Werner J., with James W. Tankard. *Communication Theories*. 2nd ed. New York: Longman, 1988.
See especially Chapter 3, pp. 30–41, on communication models.

CHAPTER 2

YOUR FOURTH WORLD: ITS CONSTRUCTION AND RECONSTRUCTION

OBJECTIVES

After studying this chapter you should be able to

- Explain what perception is.
- Describe some of the major reasons people process information as they do.
- Explain some of the major theories regarding why people expose themselves to the information they do.
- Explain why the world in your head is a "fiction."
- Describe how "scripts" or "schemata" help you to understand movies, television programs, and newspaper stories.
- Give examples of how our personal characteristics can affect processing of information.
- Explain why different students perceive your college in such different ways.

An artist once was walking through a museum when she saw a well-dressed young man examining one of her paintings. It was a highly abstract work titled simply *Man*. The museum patron first stood far back and stared at the painting. Then he got up close, studying it from side to side and top to bottom, very much in the style of a true connoisseur of art. Then he moved back to study it in its entirety again. Finally he shrugged his shoulders and growled, "Humph, that's not a man!" At this, the artist could contain herself no longer. She tapped him on the shoulder and said, "You are right, my dear fellow, that is *not* a man. *You* are a man. *That* is a painting."

Much the same can be said about the images in your head. They are *not* the things in the world outside. Like works of art, they are your *representations* of those things. In a sense, that world in your head—everything you know—is a construction, a fiction.

Reality: fact or fiction? That may seem too far-fetched a statement to you, but let us examine it for a moment. If you are like most people, you are pretty certain you know what a fact is. You have no hesitation in calling some things "fact" and other things "fiction." Stories that an author makes up and descriptions that are inconsistent with your observations you label "fiction," while your account of what you observe, the accounts of others that are consistent with your observations, and the accounts of others whom you trust you label "fact." Fortunately or unfortunately, the world is not that simple. If it were, all of us—you and your parents, your teachers and the local garbage collectors, people in this country, in Iran, and the Soviet Union—would see the world in much more similar ways than we do. The fact is that every observation, even yours, is a **perception**, *an interpretation of an experience—an interpretation based only in part on that experience and in part on the context of that experience and memory of other experiences.* In other words, it is a fiction.

REVIEW

Perception is the meaning you construct of something. It is an *interpretation* of present experiences based, in part, on what you sense through your eyes, ears, nose, and skin, in part on the context of those experiences, and in part on your memory of related experiences in the past. Your perception is what you *believe* you have seen, heard, or felt.

If this claim is hard for you to believe, think again about our story of the man and the painting. No painting of a man is a man. Not even a photograph truly captures the "real" man. It is merely a representation of a man, or of men in general. It is something constructed by the photographer, the camera, and the developer. Obviously, a photograph is affected by the appearance of the object at the moment the shutter is clicked, but that appearance is just one of the factors affecting the final picture.

General semanticists, scholars who study the way people use language in everyday life, have a favorite saying: "The word is not the thing." In the same way, photographs of objects, accounts of events, descriptions of people, or explanations of ideas are not the objects, events, people, or ideas. They are constructions. Thus, the images, accounts, descriptions, and explanations in your head of everything you believe you know are constructions. They are fictions you created that *represent* some parts of the world around you.

What reality do you construct from the televangelists frequently seen on television or cable? Is it fact or fiction?

All of us, to varying degrees, construct different meanings for what seem to be the same phenomena, even when we have been exposed to those phenomena in roughly the same way. Whether or not you accept that generalization, why do you suppose it might be so? Why do people construct different worlds in their heads about chemical warfare, the Middle East, student government, professional football, our president, and the many other people, events, and places about which they observe bits of information directly or through the media? This chapter provides some answers to these questions. These answers, in turn, should help you understand and, to some extent at least, control the way you see your world—the way you construct that world in your head.

BYLINE

Why do people who see the same event remember it differently? In what sense is it valid to say that what you know is a "construction"?

NEGOTIATING OUR MEDIA MOSAICS PERCEPTUALLY

In the last chapter we talked about the ways in which individuals physically negotiate their communication environments, exposing themselves more to those media, people, and content that best fit their needs, wants, and styles of life. In this chapter we will discuss the ways in which people negotiate their communication environments *perceptually*, in ways that fit their personal limitations and needs.

To understand communication, you must recognize that there are differences between your perception—what you believe you have seen, heard, or felt—and what is truly there. Perception is a creative process. It is not simply observing, hearing, or sensing what is out there in your environment. It also involves assigning meaning to those stimuli. In fact, what you experience is more a product of your interpretations of information than of the information itself. For example, there is strong evidence that the physiological states associated with being frightened, angered, or pleasantly excited are almost, if not completely, identical. Whether you *experience* fear, anger, or excitement depends on your *interpretation* of those physical states. For example, if you are watching a movie and feel your heart beating faster, you decide whether you are frightened, pleasantly excited, or angry on the basis of whether you are seeing a chase scene or a love scene, or hearing the people behind you loudly talking and munching on strong-smelling popcorn. In all three cases, your physiological response (increased heart rate, blood pressure, and so on) is the same. But the way you *interpret* that response depends on the context or external cues you use to label the emotional state associated with it.

In the same way, as the media or other sources stimulate our senses, we interpret those sensations, in part, by associating them with bits of information in memory. Using patterns we have developed over time, we invent a reality and then constantly reinvent it or reshape it as we encounter additional fragments of information. This sort of invention, or the construction and reconstruction of our realities, is something each of us does all of the time in his or her role as receiver. These "pictures in our heads" are important because they represent our perceptions of reality. And, as Walter Lippmann pointed out, even if these pictures are inaccurate, we behave as if they were true. We react not to what is true but to what we *perceive* to be true.

Lippmann's example, described in his famous book on public opinion, is the group of Germans, French, and British who were living on an isolated island when World War I broke out among their countries. It was over six weeks before the islanders discovered they were at war with each other. As Lippmann put it:

> *For over six weeks now those of them who were English and those of them who were French had been fighting . . . those of them who were Germans. For six strange weeks they had acted as if they were friends, when in fact they were enemies.*[1]

SCRIPTS/SCHEMATA: AIDS TO PERCEPTION

Communication scholars refer to those patterns we have developed over time as **scripts** or **schemata**. More specifically, scripts, or schemata, are *stereotyped sequences of events in memory that are activated by observations or experiences in the present*. They are important because they help us organize incoming information so that we can understand it. Put another way, a script gives you a framework for constructing or assigning meaning to new information. Scripts also affect your expectations

Where is reality?

about the order of events or parts of an event and lead you to fill in missing parts in a particular way. For example, when you read in a novel or newspaper about a character entering a restaurant, your "restaurant-going script" is activated, and you automatically fill in missing information: being seated at a table or counter, studying the menu, ordering, being served by the waiter, calculating the tip, paying your bill, and so on.

Scripts provide interpretive frameworks for media material that might otherwise be difficult to understand. The following paragraph beautifully illustrates this phenomenon:

> *With hocked gems financing him, our hero bravely defied all scornful laughter that tried to prevent his scheme. Your eyes deceive, he had said. An egg, not a table, correctly typifies this unexplored planet. Now three sturdy sisters sought proof. Forging along sometimes through calm vastness, yet more often over turbulent peaks and valleys, days became weeks. As many doubters spread fearful rumors about the edge, at last, from nowhere, welcome winged creatures appeared signifying momentous success.*[2]

Can you make sense of this paragraph? Do the sentences seem to have any relationship to each other? What does it all mean? After thinking about that for a while, read it again, this time with the knowledge that the paragraph comes from a story titled "Christopher Columbus Discovering America." Unless your mind works in very different ways from most people's, that title will activate your "Christopher Columbus script," and you will find it easy to interpret the paragraph within that framework. Not only will you now be more certain that you understand it, you will find that it takes less effort to read.

REVIEW

Scripts or schemata are patterns or frameworks that we develop on the basis of past experiences. We use them to help us interpret similar experiences in the present.

It may help you understand the way you use the scripts in your head to cope with and interpret experiences if you think of a reporter covering a three-alarm fire or a meeting of the local city council. Exposure to one of those events activates the reporter's "fire script" or "city council script," and the story that results is heavily influenced by the set of expectations that script generates, as well as by the events that occur at the fire or meeting. (We will return to this point in Chapter 14 as we talk about the norms of journalists.)

Maintaining and Adjusting Our Realities

The scripts or pictures of the world in our heads, our realities, have been shaped by our particular experiences, knowledge, needs, values, and beliefs. And they are constantly tested against new fragments of information we sense from our environment. Sometimes these new fragments simply reinforce an existing script. At other times they make the script clearer, add a new element to it, or force a restructuring of it. In these ways, the bits of information we are continually sensing from our communication mosaics cause us to maintain, strengthen, or revise those scripts or pictures in our heads.

For example, you have some sort of image or script about Hollywood in your head. Each time you encounter some mention of Hollywood in one of the media, that script is likely to be activated and to aid your interpretation of what you are reading, seeing, or hearing. As you encounter new fragments of information about Hollywood from your communication environment, those fragments have meaning for you only insofar as they fit with the pattern or script in your head that is your prior image of that West Coast wonderland. You may not comprehend a discussion of Hollywood's history unless you have already acquired meanings for such concepts as the Trust, vertical integration, or four-walling (all terms that are defined in Chapter 7).

This explains why many communicators claim you cannot tell people anything they do not already know. On the face of it, that seems a rather extreme and pessimistic statement, especially for those of us concerned with helping the public become better informed or better educated. But it is more true than false. Neither you nor any member of the mass media audience can perceive or understand anything you cannot relate in some way to your prior experience—that you cannot fit in some way into one of the scripts or realities in your head. In addition, once you process these new fragments of information that fit your script or prior image of the object or idea, these new fragments in turn reshape that image or script.

You probably have difficulty accepting that generalization, especially when you think of your visual experiences. Surely, what you see is what is there—at least most of the time. Most likely, you are confident that you can perceive objects you have not seen before, or that you have no meaning for. Surprisingly, though, this is not the case. Testimony in support of that conclusion comes from biologist John Young:

> *The visual receiving system in its untrained state has only very limited powers. We are perhaps deceived by the fact that the eye is a sort of camera. Contrary to what we might suppose, the eyes and brain do not simply record in a sort of photographic manner the pictures that pass in front of us. The brain is not by any means a simple recording system like a film. . . . Many of our affairs are conducted on the assumption that our sense organs provide us with an accurate record, independent of ourselves. What we are now beginning to realize is that much of this is an illusion, that we have to learn to see the world as we do. . . . In some sense we literally create the world we speak about.*[3]

To put this more plainly, what you see is not the world "out there"; it is the world you created in your mind.

This quality of perception—this demand that a perception be meaningful—helps prevent our being overwhelmed by the infinite number of information fragments in our environments; it helps us select and organize the relatively small number of fragments from our mosaic that we can handle. We do the selecting and organizing in terms of the meaning those fragments have for us.

> **BYLINE**
>
> Can you think of any experience you have had that supports Young's claims? Have you ever perceived something one way, only to discover later that your perception was totally wrong? What about some of the visual illusions? (Later in this chapter, we will provide some examples of those, in case you have not seen any.)

Set or Expectation and the Processing of Information

Our scripts are shaped not only by our ancient past (going back virtually to birth or even, some would say, into the womb), but also by our very recent past. One important effect of both recent and ancient past is to create expectations or sets, assumptions about the world in which we live. Because of your prior experience, for example, if you hear someone mumbling what sounds like "A, B, C, D," and then something else, your expectation or set leads you to perceive that the person said "E."

That is the reality you create. Whatever was said, that part of the world in your head is an "E." A rather simple experiment suggests one of the ways expectations are created and demonstrates their effect.

One communication scholar has studied the way a headline can affect readers' perceptions of what a newspaper story said. He constructed two news stories for this experiment: one about a murder suspect being interrogated by the police, the other about an accelerated program of instruction being developed for a college. For each story he had three headlines, two biased in opposite ways and one neutral. For example, one headline for the murder investigation story suggested the suspect was guilty; the other suggested he was innocent. Subjects who read the story with the "guilty" headline were significantly more likely to conclude that the person was guilty than those who read the same story with the "innocent" headline. Biased headlines did not have the same effect on perceptions of the story about the accelerated college program. This was an issue in which these readers had more of a personal stake, and so they tended to read it more carefully. And, as you might expect, the study found that the more carefully a subject read a story, the less effect the headline had. Careful reading resulted in a more relevant script being evoked, rather than the irrelevant script evoked by the headline.

BYLINE

Do you think your perceptions are affected by newspaper headlines? Why do you believe this is so? In the headline study, the researcher found that expectations created by headlines had less effect when people read the stories more carefully. Do most people read, listen, or view the media carefully enough to counteract the effect of expectation? Do you?

Our knowledge of and attitudes toward a newspaper or columnist, newscaster or station, or perhaps even toward the mass media in general probably act in the same way as a headline. They affect our set or expectations; hence, they affect the way we perceive the information received from those media.

The Absence of Set or Expectation: Passive Perception

The research described thus far involves the effect of expectation or set on perception. But what about your perception of material that you happen to see or hear or read for which you have no prior expectation? This may be the case when you listen to a radio or television station you have not heard before, or read a newspaper story without noticing the headline and without prior information about the event. Normally, unless you are almost totally passive during that exposure, you will quickly develop expectations based on the first bits of information you notice—the opening scene of a drama, the introductory lines of a news story, or the first bars of music. From then on, all of the effects of expectation apply.

If you remain passive during such exposure to the media, developing no expectations of what is to come, the effects are less certain. In fact, total passivity may not even be possible unless you are asleep or hypnotized or are paying no attention to the medium. Assuming such passivity is possible, it seems likely you will not understand as much of the information as you would otherwise. You will not have the aid of a relevant script that may be stored in your memory, and therefore you will not have the aid of appropriate expectations. Expectations make media content easier to grasp, as long as that content is reasonably consistent with them—as it usually is. Returning to an earlier example, when someone is reciting the alphabet in the normal order, your expectations help you "hear" and perceive accurately what is being said. If the letters are being recited in random order, you will have more trouble grasping them because you have no expectations to help. On the other hand, when a mistake is made in the normal recitation of the alphabet, you are more likely to pick it up if you have no expectations but are listening carefully.

Review

In general, expectations help us understand what we read, hear, see, or feel. These expectations can be caused by scripts based on similar experiences, by cues—such as newspaper headlines, or by the early part of the experience itself. The introduction of a book or television program affects your expectations of what is to follow.

Just as expectations that are reasonably consistent with the material you are hearing, reading, or seeing make that material easier to understand, expectations also make them easier to remember. Scripts serve not only as aids in interpreting information, but also as useful frameworks for recalling that information.

Whether you realize it or not, you are generally fairly good at predicting much of what you are exposed to—the next word, the next sound, the next turn of the plot. On the whole, these expectations help you process, comprehend, and remember the bits of information you sense from your communication mosaic. We will return to this concept of expectation when we discuss the way you use those bits of information to fill the gaps in the meanings you construct.

PERSONAL CHARACTERISTICS: IMPACT ON PERCEPTION

The process of perceiving—the construction of meanings from the stimuli we sense in our communication mosaics—is affected by many of our personal characteristics. To some extent, the particular stimuli we sense and the stimuli we ignore are also affected by those characteristics.

The Impact of Attitudes, Personality, and Expectations on Exposure: Variety and Consistency Theories

There are a number of explanations of why different individuals become exposed to the particular news stories, television programs, books, conversations, and other forms of communication that they do. None of these explanations is completely satisfactory, but communication scholars are hard at work attempting to improve them. In the meantime, these existing theories provide some useful insights. **Variety theory** and **consistency theory**, for example, explain why people differ in the degree to which they seek or are receptive to information and why each of us is sometimes receptive and sometimes unreceptive.

Variety theory assumes that people need a certain amount of variety or new sensations. They find such variety pleasurable. Studies show, however, that people vary considerably in the degree to which they seek such sensations. Some people almost always need them more than others do. But in addition, most of us seem to need them more at some times than at other times. This explains why all of us at times, and some of us almost constantly, seek new kinds of information and other media experiences, even when the information or experiences may conflict with what we believe.

REVIEW

Variety theory argues that people have a tendency to seek the pleasant stimulation that comes from new experiences. Consistency theory argues that people avoid information or experiences that might make their beliefs, attitudes, and behaviors inconsistent and seek those that make them consistent. These latter tendencies result in what some scholars have labeled "selective exposure."

Consistency theory, on the other hand, *assumes that people need consistency among their beliefs, their attitudes, and their behaviors. If these are not consistent, a person tends to be uncomfortable.* This theory is used to explain why some of us actively avoid some kinds of information. You can probably recall times when information that contradicted your attitudes or beliefs made you uncomfortable. For example, if you are very close with all members of your family, knowledge that one of them has done something dishonest can make you quite uneasy. Similarly, if you are a strong supporter of the president, negative information about him is somewhat disturbing. Or if you are a fan of your college athletic teams, any information that they have violated conference regulations can make you uncomfortable. All of us seem to feel internal pressure to avoid such discomfort. This pressure is so strong within some of us all of the time, and within most of us at least some of the time, that we tend to avoid information that might conflict with our beliefs. At the same time, and for the same reason, we are more likely to seek or pay attention to information that is consistent with our beliefs. This *tendency to avoid information that is inconsistent with our beliefs, attitudes, or behaviors and to attend more to information that is consistent with them* is called **selective exposure**.

The combination of pressure to avoid conflict and pressure to seek sensations suggests another way to think about our media exposure. The relationship between variety-seeking and conflict-avoidance behavior is shown in Figure 2.1.

As the figure indicates, those two distinct types of motivation, if taken together, predict four different types of exposure behavior:

1. You can seek or be receptive to information on all sides of an issue, or
2. You can seek or be receptive only to information on the particular side that will support your existing point of view, so as to avoid or reduce discomfort, or
3. You can avoid discomfort by actively avoiding any kind of information, or
4. You can be a passive participant, neither actively seeking information nor actively avoiding that which you encounter.

FIGURE 2.1
Relationship between variety-seeking and conflict-avoiding behavior.

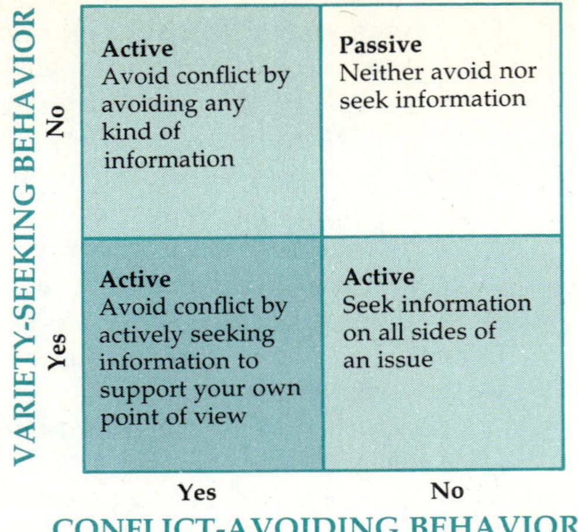

BYLINE

Where do you fit in Figure 2.1? On such issues as the Persian Gulf War, abortion, the honesty of college sports, or the latest political campaign, do you seek information on all sides or do you attend largely to information that just supports your point of view? Do you sometimes do one and sometimes the other? Can you identify the kinds of issues or circumstances that cause you to seek information and the kinds that cause you to avoid information?

Impact on perceptions. Just as attitudes, personality, and expectations tend to affect exposure to information, they also affect perceptions. A large number of studies and many of our personal experiences have demonstrated that most of us tend to perceive messages from the mass media or elsewhere in a way that is consistent with our beliefs and attitudes. This means that we tend to misperceive messages that are not consistent with them.

You have probably seen some of the many reruns of the television series "M*A*S*H" that have flooded the airways for a number of years. A pacifist with very strong attitudes against war is likely to perceive this series as a depiction of the senselessness and futility of war. Someone without strong feelings on the subject probably sees it simply as a comedy, with no special "message." On the other hand, someone who believes firmly that America is always right, that it enters wars only to make the world a freer and safer place, probably sees "M*A*S*H" as a demonstration of the courage of America's "citizen soldiers" under fire. *The tendency to interpret or perceive information in a way that makes it consistent with one's prior knowledge, attitudes, and behavior* is called **selective perception.**

REVIEW

Selective perception can be explained either by consistency theory or the principle of least effort. Consistency theory argues that all of us feel pressure to avoid discomfort by keeping our knowledge, our behaviors, and our attitudes consistent. The principle of least effort argues that we tend to perceive things in the easiest way possible, and that it is easiest to perceive things as consistent with our beliefs, attitudes, and expectations.

A study of partisan viewing of the film of a football game has provided additional evidence of the way people's attitudes create a set or expectation that in turn affects perception. Students from the teams' schools who watched the film reported "seeing" twice as many rule violations committed by players from the other school as by players from their own school. Regardless of which school the viewers were from, the same phenomenon occurred; they always perceived more violations by the other side.

Two explanations for these phenomena have been suggested. The explanation accepted by most scholars is a version of the consistency theory described earlier. One way in which we avoid the discomfort caused by inconsistency is to misperceive any new information that is not consistent with our attitudes or behaviors. For example, if you are prejudiced against political conservatives, and your local newspaper publishes a story that is favorable to Vice-President Dan Quayle, you can avoid inconsistency by perceiving the story as somehow damaging to Quayle, or you can discredit the newspaper, accusing it of distorting the news.

The other explanation of this effect of attitudes and expectations on perceptions is the **principle of least effort.** This is *the theory that people perceive things in the simplest or easiest way they can, and it is easiest to perceive them in ways consistent with their prior expectations, attitudes, or beliefs.* It takes more effort to perceive a message that is contrary to the way you see the world or that is different than what you expect.

> **BYLINE**
>
> Think about one of the television comedies you particularly like, especially one involving some minority group. Is it possible that you misperceived this show at times because your attitudes differ from those of the program's producers? Compare your perceptions of the program's treatment of minority groups with the perceptions of others whose attitudes differ from yours.

The Influence of Needs The need to maintain consistency among our attitudes, beliefs, and actions is only one class of needs. Other kinds of needs also influence our exposure and perception: the needs or drives for power, security, social esteem, and self-esteem. Individuals vary greatly in their drive to satisfy each of these needs. In addition, for each of us, some of these needs are felt more strongly at some times than at others. As a result, at times you probably actively seek information to satisfy some particular need; at other times, you attend to such information only when you happen to encounter it and perceive that it can serve your needs. In addition, you probably encounter and notice a certain amount of information that serves no apparent need.

REVIEW

Many kinds of needs affect the way we process information: more-or-less permanent needs, such as our needs for self-esteem, social esteem, security, and power, as well as momentary needs such as hunger.

Needs and information processing. Your needs are also important factors in the way you process information. The probability is high that you usually process or perceive the information you encounter in a way that is relevant to the needs you feel most strongly at that moment. When you are hungry you are more likely to notice the food present in a dramatic scene in a movie than when you are not hungry. Similarly, if you dislike a character in a movie, you are more likely to interpret what that person does as showing negative attributes than if you like or admire him or her. If the character you dislike is very polite to elderly people, you are likely to see it as a sign of phoniness or showing off, whereas you will see it as a sign of thoughtfulness or good breeding in someone you like.

Reference groups and information processing. Just as our needs affect what we select from the communication environment, how we process or interpret that material, and what we remember of it, so too do our **reference groups**, *the groups of individuals with whom we identify and to whom we look for guidance or reinforcement*. Thus, our information processing is affected by our family, friends, and others with whom we associate or with whom we would like to associate. We interact with these groups and test our interpretations of what we read, hear, and see. As a result, our scripts are shaped by those interactions with other people, just as they are shaped to some extent by our interactions with the media.

As you know, the interpretations of our family, friends, and others who are important to us are not always consistent with each other. In these instances, we see an interesting phenomenon. When we are exposed to material in the company of our family, we process it in a way more consistent with their pattern. On the other hand, when we are exposed to the same material in the company of friends, we process it in a different way—in a way more consistent with the pattern of these friends. In a sense, we use a different script for interpreting this material, depending on our social context.

BYLINE

Try this mental experiment to test our claim about the effect of social context. Imagine watching an NC-17-rated movie with some of your college friends. Now imagine watching the same movie with your parents or a much younger sibling. Do you believe you would see the movie in the same way? Would you perceive the extremely violent or pornographic scenes the same way in the two situations? How would they probably differ?

We would predict that you would "see" quite a different movie when watching that NC-17-rated film in the company of your parents or a younger sibling than watching it in the company of friends.

Even the expectation of being with one of these groups in the near future can affect your processing of media content. For example, knowing you are soon going to be with your family, with different friends, or with one of your professors may cause you to read and process the morning newspaper in very different ways. You might be influenced by quite a different script in each of those instances.

In these ways, reference groups shape our sets or expectations for certain kinds of information. Some evidence even suggests that any audience with whom you are listening to or observing one of the mass media tends to be a type of reference group for you at the moment. That group, that audience of which you are a part, affects how you organize the information being communicated and what you remember of it.

Reference groups and opinions/behaviors. As you probably know, those of us who study mass communication audiences rely heavily on surveys in our research. We are constantly interviewing people or sending them questionnaires. Many of these surveys include opinion or attitude questions such as "What do you think about the president's proposal to reduce federal aid to education?" Or "What is your reaction to the proposal to raise tuition 6 percent in this college?" We ask these kinds of questions again and again and publish the results in newspapers or scholarly journals. However, some scholars have criticized such questions. They claim, with some justification, that when we ask questions of these sorts we are not simply *measuring* opinions; we are *creating* opinions. Many people we ask about the president's proposal or the tuition proposal would not have thought about it before we asked their opinion. Therefore, they had no opinion *until we asked the question*. Once they are asked, though, most of them think about it and come up with an opinion. The question is, are the public opinion pollsters or the scholars who measure opinions in this way misleading themselves and the rest of us by claiming their results are meaningful?

At first glance, it might appear they are misleading, that such research is invalid. But that initial reaction is wrong. When pollsters create opinions that did not exist in some people before they were asked questions about them, these researchers are duplicating the conditions under which most, if not all, of us form our opinions. Let us explain.

We do not form opinions simply because we are exposed to some information. Just because we read or hear about a proposal from the president does not mean we form an opinion about it. In most cases, our development of an opinion depends on whether someone confronts us with a question about it, or on our anticipating that we will be talking with someone else about it. The opinion or point of view we then develop is in part a function of who the other individual is and of our relationship to him or her. Thinking about this other person in connection with the information we encountered affects the way we organize and use that information.

Thus, the opinions we developed about the federal aid proposal or the tuition increase are not solely the result of our individual analyses and beliefs. They are heavily influenced by our reference groups, especially those with whom we are interacting or expect to be interacting on the subject. Most of your opinions, whether you realize it or not, are strongly influenced by the people around you. And, thus, the opinions you develop and state when confronted with a public opinion pollster are probably reasonable approximations of the opinions you would develop when interacting with other strangers about those topics.

Another way to think about this matter is to consider each of your reference groups as a type of "audience" for you. That "audience" can affect your perceptions and your other behaviors, even when it is not present. In fact, an audience that is not present can sometimes affect you more than one that is. For example, consider a physician speaking to a lay audience about some particular health problem. She is probably constantly conscious of how her medical colleagues will view what she is saying. Thus, her remarks—and, hence, her points of view—are shaped by that absent audience.

Let us consider an example closer to home. Think about the behavior of college professors talking to an undergraduate class—perhaps the authors of this book talking to your class. The way we behave, the way we perceive information and talk about it to you, is influenced not only by that information and by you who are in this class, but also by our perceptions of our colleagues and how they would react to what we are saying. In fact, our comments on this page are influenced by at least two reference groups who will probably never see what we have written. One is that set of professional colleagues. The other is the set of friends who are strong feminists. It is the existence of this latter reference group that led us to refer to the physician in this example as "she." This reference group has increased the probability that when we read the word "physicians" or "police officers," we will construct in our minds an image of women as well as of men.

REVIEW

The world in our heads is a product of the information we heard, read, and saw, that we processed, and that we then tested and refined through our interactions with other individuals, especially our reference groups. Thus, our realities are socially constructed; they are intersubjective realities.

So be aware of the way your language, your behavior, and the way you process or perceive mass media messages are affected by the people with whom you interact. Even when absent, they affect what you think you are "seeing" and "hearing" in the mass media. When you hear people talking about the **social construction of reality**, it is this phenomenon to which they are referring, at least in part. *Our beliefs and interpretations of information, even our definitions of words and other symbols, are influenced by the people with whom we interact*. Thus, the realities we create in our minds are, to some extent, *social* constructions because they are influenced by our reference groups.

Some scholars believe the influence of other people on our processing of information is even more basic than we have suggested. They take the position that the reality each of us constructs from our communication mosaics is an **intersubjective reality**. According to this theory, *people's beliefs* *about the world are shaped in part by comparing them to the beliefs* of *other people*. We constantly test our perceptions of reality as we interact with others.

Personality traits. Another influence on your information processing is your personality. At least one personality trait, **dogmatism**, has even been defined by some social scientists in terms of the way we process information.[4] Dogmatism is *the degree to which people are unable to perceive or evaluate information independent of their prior attitudes, beliefs, and needs, the source of the information, and its context*.

The more you receive, evaluate, and act on information from your environment on its own merits, uninfluenced by irrelevant information or by your attitudes, beliefs, or needs, the more open-minded you are. On the other hand, the more your reception, evaluation, and actions concerning that information are influenced by your attitudes, beliefs, and needs or by irrelevant information, the more dogmatic or closed-minded you are. For example, the more your evaluation of a disarmament plan is affected by whether the idea came from the president, Mikhail Gorbachev, or your roommate, the more closed-minded you are, according to this definition. The more your judgment of the quality of a motion picture is affected by knowing who the director was or by the judgments of your friends, the more closed-minded you are. Or the more easily you can be fooled by a visual illusion, the more closed-minded you are. Research has shown that a closed-minded person usually has extreme difficulty isolating an object or idea and evaluating or perceiving it independently of its context. Similarly, when a closed-minded individual is evaluating a newspaper column or broadcast commentary, he or she is more affected by the knowledge of its author's identity than is the person with an open-minded belief system. The closed-minded or dogmatic individual is especially influenced by authority figures.

Dogmatic persons also have difficulty tolerating ambiguity. They have a strong tendency to categorize everything immediately. Such persons, when trying to solve problems, have difficulty thinking about them in more than one way. When they first encounter a problem, they assume it must be solved in a particular way. Even when that doesn't work, they can't seem to shake themselves loose from that frame of reference—that way of thinking. Consider, for example, the problem of connecting these nine dots with four straight lines:

•   •   •

•   •   •

•   •   •

REVIEW

Our personalities affect the way we process information. Dogmatism, for example, affects how our perception of information is influenced by its context and source as well as by our prior attitudes, beliefs, and needs.

The four straight lines must be formed without lifting pen or pencil from the paper and without retracing all or part of any line.

What do you perceive when exposed to those nine dots? You probably perceive a square, and that square becomes a frame of reference. In weighing the problem, it is difficult to even consider solutions that go outside the frame of reference—that go outside the square. Yet, you must go outside that frame of reference to solve the problem. Presumably, the individual with the closed-minded belief system will fail to do so, whereas the individual with an open-minded belief system is more likely to solve the problem by going outside the frame of reference and drawing the lines more or less as shown on page 54.

Your Language and Information Processing

Still another influence on the way we process or construct meanings from the material we read, see, and hear in the mass media is our language. Even when you are exposed to nonverbal material, such as a photograph, your language plays a large role in the way you process that information. Your everyday language, the language with which you are most familiar, gives you a set of categories or frames in which to "see" things.

Earlier we talked about patterns or scripts we acquire from past experiences and then use to organize and interpret new experiences. In a sense, our language serves that same function. The fact that we have the word "tree" and the word "bush" increases the probability that we will see the distinction between these different kinds of vegetation growing in our back yards. Having different words for each helps you see greater differences than you would if you had only one word to use for both.

The most famous example of this phenomenon is that described by linguist Benjamin Whorf, a pioneer in the study of the influence of language on thought.[5] Whorf observed that Eskimos have many words for describing snow, in contrast to the single word available in English. He attributes this variety of labels to Eskimos' greater ability to perceive small differences among various kinds of snow. English-speaking people, on the other hand, can do little more than distinguish snow from rain or sleet.

Words helps us objectify—to give meaning to the mass media material we encounter as well as to our other experiences in the world. If you had no word for homosexual, if you had never heard that word or the word "gay" or any other word that signified that particular concept, it is unlikely you would perceive that distinction among people in a motion picture or television drama. That is, you would not make the distinction between gays and heterosexuals. Without knowledge of that word or concept, you probably would interpret signs of affection between two men or between two women on the screen in quite a different way than you do now.

As Peter Berger and Thomas Luckman put it in their book, *The Social Construction of Reality,* symbols—primarily language—are the key elements in the creation of our realities. For each of us,

> *. . . the reality of everyday life appears already objectified, that is, constituted by an order of objects that have been designated as objects before my appearance on the scene. The language used in everyday life continuously provides me with the necessary objectifications and posits the order with which these make sense and within which everyday life has meaning for me. . . . Language marks the co-ordinates of my life in society and fills that life with meaningful objects.*[6]

REVIEW

Our language helps us make sense of our experiences: to make distinctions among elements, to organize them, and to make them meaningful.

"And fills that life with meaningful objects." That is the critical phrase. Language helps you give meaning to your experiences. If you can give something a label—if you have a word for it—it becomes meaningful. If you have no word—no label—it is less likely to have meaning, and you may have difficulty perceiving its existence.

Styles of Media Use A scholar named Roland Barthes once talked about different styles of reading. See whether you recognize your usual style of reading among these:

1. *The spearing method of reading:* simply spearing bits from what you are reading—a bit here, a bit there—without plan or system. Many people read the newspaper this way.
2. *The aromatic or gourmet method:* savoring each idea or story as a gourmet savors a choice wine. If this is your style, you linger over a good story as though it were an especially tasty morsel, rolling it around in your mind so the experience will stay with you for a long time.

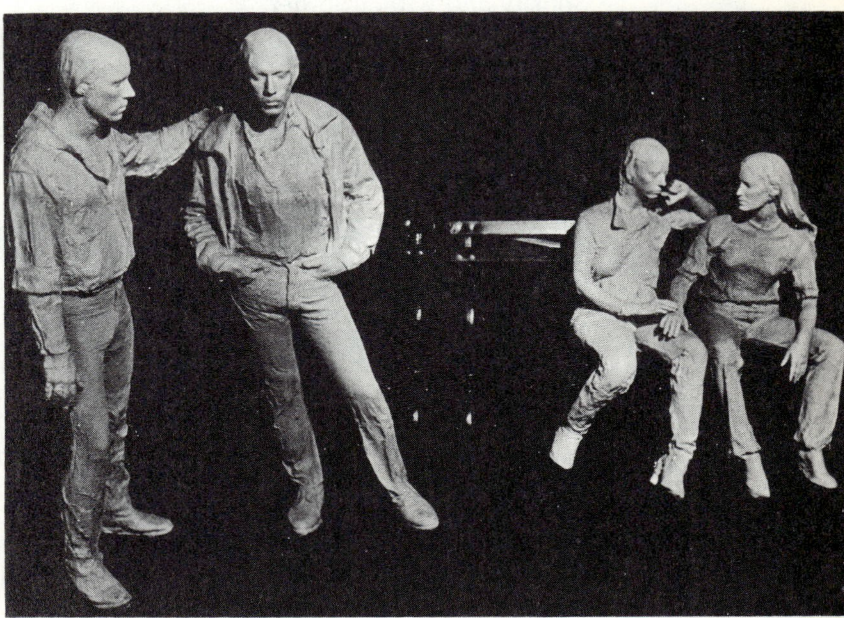

Labels often shape the meaning of some image or experience. In a general sense, this sculpture depicts friendship and affection. But knowing that it is titled "Gay Liberation," you probably construct different and more specific meanings for it.

3. *The nose-to-the-ground method:* reading one word at a time, digging slowly, diligently through a story, never stepping back to consider the whole, or the way that story fits into a larger context.
4. *The rolldown method:* reading down each page as though it were on a steadily rolling teleprompter, giving everything the same amount of time and attention—the important and the unimportant, the interesting and the dull.

Barthes's categories describe not only the various ways we read, but also the various ways we expose ourselves to all of the media. Think about your exposure to different media, including even conversations with friends. That is, think about your exposure to your communication mosaic. Are there certain times when you are a *spearer*—grabbing bits at random here and there? Are there other times when you are a *gourmet*—savoring the best of what you encounter, perhaps even looking down your nose at the "junk food" of the media world? We suspect you are sometimes a *rooter*, with your nose to the ground, concentrating on each blade of grass, and missing the forest or the contour of the lawn. Perhaps you study for examinations in this way, concentrating on little facts that might show up in multiple-choice questions and missing the overall idea. If you do not think about why you are studying and precisely what you are trying to get out of it, or if you do not think about the purposes for which you are using the media at any given time, yet feel pressured to learn all that you can, you probably have become a *rolldown* expert, taking in everything, without priority and without order.

A fifth style of media use needs to be added to those suggested by Barthes, one that could be labeled the *suntan* style. As you might expect, *suntanners* are the individuals who enjoy relaxing and letting the waves of sound from the stereo or radio, or the visual images of the television set or movie, wash over them like the rays of the sun.

BYLINE

Which of these five styles best describes your usual use of the media? Do you use different styles for different purposes?

The truly skilled users of the mass media are those persons who adapt their style of media use to their needs of the moment and to the nature of the media content with which they are dealing. Conversely, the skilled and sensitive media professionals find ways to *cue* us to the style they believe most appropriate for each particular media product they present. This is done in the print media, for example, with headlines, subheadings, print size, the way material is laid out on the page, and the page on which it is placed.

Do you often use more than one of the media at a time like this student studying in the park?

Effects of "chunking style" on memory. Our styles of media use, as some of Roland Barthes's categories suggest, are very much like our styles of eating. One of the important differences in eating style is the size of the bite. Some people eat their food quickly, in large bites; others go slowly, taking one small bite at a time. Just as our bites of food can vary in size, so our bites of information can vary in size—we can "chunk" our information in large, medium-sized, or small bites. You can see this clearly if you examine the ways different people read. Some individuals fixate on one word at a time. Others fixate on a phrase or a line at a time, chunking in larger units. Similarly, in watching a television program you can fixate upon the larger story line and not "see" some of the details of costume, set, light, and other elements, or you can fixate on these details and perhaps fail to grasp some of the program's plot or theme. Thus, when we talk about **chunking** in communication, we are referring to *the size of the information bits* or *the number of information bits you are attending to at one time.*

With reading, at least, you can cover more ground—read faster—by chunking in larger units. Some experts say you also have a better chance of grasping major ideas when you chunk in larger units. However, you probably miss some of the detail—the nuances of language, particular differences in sentence construction, and so on. Which type of reading is better depends on your purpose in reading. When you are proofreading newspaper copy, for instance, you probably ought to chunk by words or, at times, even by letters. When you are reading something to see if it has information about Iraq, you probably ought to chunk by phrases or lines of type.

REVIEW

Your style of media use affects the information you sense and, therefore, the world you construct in your head. Among the important styles of use are the size "chunks" of information you tend to grasp and whether you are using a spearing, aromatic (gourmet), nose-to-the-ground, rolldown, or suntan style.

These differences in chunking style probably account for many students' observation after they have taken a television or film production class that they no longer enjoy television programs or movies as much. They tend to notice the editing and the other techniques of production, and this distracts them and prevents them from enjoying the show. They have not yet learned to control their chunking behavior so it will be appropriate for their viewing purposes.

One theory of memory suggests that chunking—grouping items together to reduce the number of individual units to retain—helps us remember more material. We retain the group as a unit, rather than remembering each individual item. It seems that an editor of a newspaper or a newscast can help audience members do this by precoding for them, grouping similar or related items. The result should be better recall of the items by readers, listeners, or viewers.

VARIABLES IN THE COMMUNICATION MOSAIC

Up to this point we have been considering the way differences between you and other people, or even the differences within you over time, can affect your processing of information. We turn now to some other kinds of differences that affect your processing: variables in your communication mosaic.

Prior Exposure and the Processing of Information

When considering the role of prior exposure in information processing, a good starting place is the saying attributed to Greek philosopher Heraclitus who lived in the fifth or sixth century B.C.: "You can't step into the same river twice." Not only is there constant change in the river—in our case, the communication mosaic—there is also constant change in you. Each prior experience, however slight, changes you in some respect. Each bit of information that you sense affects your response to later information, especially to related, similar, or "identical" information. It appears, in other words, that repetition affects you even when you do not recall your prior exposure to the information. Support for this generalization is found in studies that show you will learn things more quickly if you have learned them before and forgotten them than if you never knew them. It is likely, then, that the second or third time you get a particular bit of information (about a kidnapping or about the president, for example)—even if you do not recall getting that information before—it has a different effect than it had the first time.

Repetition and Persuasion

One body of evidence suggests that repetition of persuasive messages—that is, hearing a persuasive message such as a political commercial more than once—causes people to agree more rapidly with the statement of opinion. Repetition has also been shown to affect choice of a product. However, we do not know whether a commercial can be played too often, whether there is a point of diminishing returns—or even a reversal—after a certain amount of repetition. Nor do we know much about the effect of short or long time periods between repetitions of the message, although some evidence suggests that a broadcast commercial is more effective if it comes in bursts rather than being evenly distributed over a long period of time. Thus, if you are going to run for political office and can afford an average of only one commercial a day throughout the campaign period, you are probably wiser to schedule seven commercials on one day each week, instead of running just one commercial every day.

Repetition can also occur across as well as within media. Thus you can boost your political candidacy by transmitting your name or campaign slogan through a variety of media so voters will likely encounter it repeatedly, not only when they listen to the radio but also when they turn from radio to the newspaper, when they pass some billboards, when they see people sporting political buttons, and so on.

REVIEW

Repeated exposure to information tends to aid learning and positive attitude change, at least up to a point. We do not know when repetition might boomerang, or what is the ideal time period between repetitions.

With enough repetition, even mere exposure, with no apparent attempt at persuasion, seems to affect attitude. For example, one study showed that the more frequently subjects were exposed to some Chinese symbols whose meanings they did not know, the more likely they were to believe that the symbols represented something "good." This suggests that just showing minority group members in advertisements so that the audience is exposed to them frequently may have a positive effect on attitudes toward these groups, at least among children who have no preconceived notions about these groups.

Gaps and the Processing of Information

In 1890, William James, an American psychologist and philosopher, discussed the fact that many gaps exist in the information we receive and that the degree to which we can fill those gaps varies widely among individuals:

> *When we listen to a person speaking or read a page of print, much of what we think we see or hear is supplied from memory. We overlook misprints, imagining the right letters, though we see the wrong ones; and how little we actually hear, when we listen to speech, we realize when we go to a foreign theatre; for there what troubles us is not so much that we cannot understand what the actors say as that we cannot hear their words. The fact is that we hear quite as little under similar conditions at home, only our mind, being fuller of English verbal associations, supplies the requisite material for comprehension upon a much slighter auditory hint.*[7]

Ample evidence suggests that James' generalization is valid, and that the extent and ways we fill the gaps depend in good part on the kinds of scripts or schemata we have stored in memory, as discussed in the first part of this chapter.

Solution to the nine-dot problem. The problem of connecting the nine dots, described on page 47, is not only an example of the way one's personality and frame of reference can affect perception, it is also a good analogy for the many gaps we find in the body of information we get from the media and the ways we tend to fill them. The shape of those nine dots was familiar to anyone raised in a western culture; it immediately brought to mind a square, a concept for which you have a well-established script in your memory. Therefore, you probably tried to close the gaps among those dots by completing the square. However, if you did, you found it impossible to do so without lifting your pen or pencil from the paper and without retracing any lines. As you see in the solution below, you needed to go outside the frame of reference of the square and form a totally different shape in order to close the gaps without violating the conditions. In this case, your "square" script or schema interfered with effective processing of that problem.

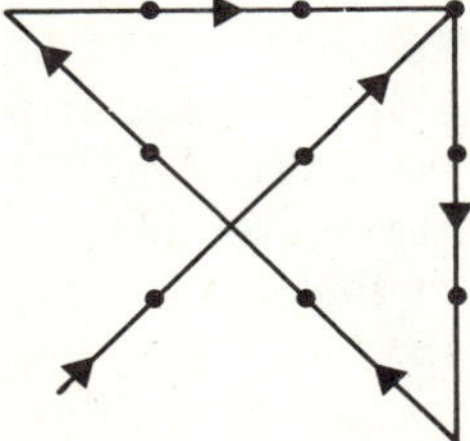

Gaps in the information we sense from the media. As suggested in Chapter 1, there are many gaps or missing pieces in the array of information we get from the media. We read about one political candidate answering the charges of an opponent, but we miss the opponent's original charges. We do not get enough information about political candidates, or persons charged with crimes, or characters in soap operas or other dramas, to know for certain what their motivations are. We hear charges about some large industries ruining the air and streams and, at the same time, charges that pollution is far less serious than the damage that overregulation is doing to the American economy, but we do not get enough facts to know for certain where "truth" lies. When it comes to foreign affairs, the bits of information we get are even more scattered and, hence, the gaps far greater.

REVIEW

We have a natural tendency to fill all gaps in messages. We tend to create "whole pictures" from the bits of information to which we are exposed.

In spite of these gaps, in spite of the incomplete information we sense from our communication mosaics, the worlds we create in our heads are whole. When we must think about or act on any of these matters, we think about or act on a complete picture. In judging the political candidate's response to charges, we infer what those charges are on the basis of a "political" script we have in our heads. Often without realizing it, we create motivations for the candidates and characters. We "know" whether industry leaders or the environmentalists are right in their debate because we fill in the scenario from another script we have stored away.

The Effect of Iconicity on the Processing of Information

Iconicity is the *degree to which a symbol is similar to that which it represents.* The family photograph you managed to shoot with reasonably sharp focus is a good example of a highly iconic image. At the opposite end of the dimension of iconicity is the arbitrary symbol, such as the word *family*, or a group of stones an artist might arrange to represent a family or—even less iconic—to represent humanity. Theorists label this end of the continuum "non-iconic," "symbolic," or "abstract."

The importance of iconicity for our present purposes is that the more iconic or realistic a stimulus, according to theorists, the more specific the referent with which receivers will associate it; the less realistic a stimulus—the more abstract it is—the more general the referent with which it will be associated. For example, according to the theory, you are more likely to perceive an abstract drawing of an athlete than a realistic photograph of an athlete as a symbol for all athletes, for athletics in general, or for health and physical fitness. On the other hand, you are more likely to associate the realistic photograph with a particular athlete rather than generalizing it.

What gaps must you fill to make sense of this photograph of homeless shelters in New York City?

An understanding of this theory is important for you both as a receiver and processor of information and as a potential creator of films or other media messages. It can help explain why you sometimes perceive that a drama or a photograph is not just about the particular individuals or things being portrayed but that it has far wider implications. Knowing about this theory can also help you recognize how photographers or directors want you to interpret their work.

REVIEW

The more iconic an image, the more specific the referent or meaning receivers tend to construct for it. The less iconic the image—that is, the more abstract—the more general the meaning or referent constructed.

When you are on the other side of the camera or computer, creating rather than receiving messages, this theory should help you do the things that will increase the probability your audience will interpret your creations as you want them to. The more realistic you make a description or representation of a person or object, the more the audience is likely to interpret it as a specific person or thing. The more abstract you make it, the more they are likely to generalize it to some more general class of persons or objects, or even to some abstract idea such as "evil" or "love."

Order of exposure to the communication mosaic. An ample body of evidence suggests that the order in which you get bits of information affects what you recall and what you think about what you recall. In the short run, there appears to be both a **primacy effect** and a **recency effect**. In general, *the bits of information you remember best and that have most influence on your attitudes and meaning constructions are those you receive first* (the primacy effect) *and those you receive last* (the recency effect). For example, if you hear a series of stories or read a large number of facts within a relatively brief period, you will tend to remember best the earliest and latest ones.

This generalization has been tested in a variety of ways. For example, in one study researchers had subjects listen to radio newscasts and rotated the order of news items for different test audiences (in order to counterbalance any effects due to variations in interest value of stories). A relationship, shown in Figure 2.2 was found between recall and the order of presentation.

For many issues about which we get information from the mass media and elsewhere, we encounter arguments on different sides. We encounter some arguments to vote for a bond issue for a community center and some arguments to vote against it. Or we receive bits of information that give us different impressions of a person, object, or idea—for example, contradictory information about the personality of a political figure or about the dangers of a nuclear power plant. Whether we are more affected relatively by the arguments we encounter first or by those we encounter last depends on a number of factors:

1. When we are not particularly interested in the issue and have no opinion about it, we tend to be more influenced by the information we receive first. In one study that demonstrated this phenomenon,

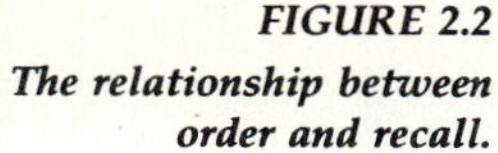

FIGURE 2.2
The relationship between order and recall.

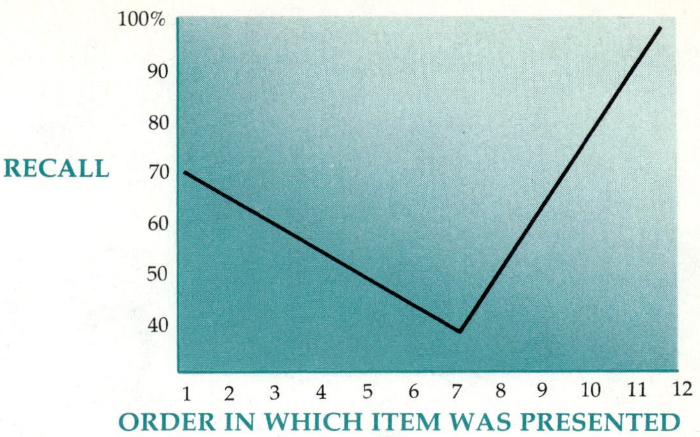

subjects were exposed to two descriptions of the behavior of someone called "Jim." One description showed Jim as an extrovert and one as an introvert. The impressions of Jim that subjects had afterward were influenced primarily by the description to which they were exposed first.

2. When we are highly interested in an issue, *when we have a strong need to know or understand* (what some scholars term a high **need for cognition**), the order in which information is received makes little difference.
3. When we expect someone is trying to influence us, the impact of the initial bits of information to which we are exposed is reduced. The same occurs when we expect to get information on various sides of the issue and, therefore, are aware we should avoid early judgment.
4. If we become involved in a conversation about the issue and take a position based on the information received up to that time, the ultimate effect of that early information is increased. Our taking a position, even in casual conversation, seems to commit us to that view. In addition, the more "public" that commitment, the greater its influence.
5. Time and the distraction caused by other activities in the intervals between bits of information increase the probability that the most recent information to which we have been exposed will have the greatest influence on our perceptions of the message.

REVIEW

Primacy and recency effects are strongest when we have no interest in or opinion on a topic. Primacy and recency effects are weakest when we have a high need for cognition or are suspicious that someone is trying to influence us. The greater the time or distraction between the early and late information, the greater will be the influence of the latter.

The Effect of Context on the Processing of Information

The final stimulus variable to consider is context. All sorts of contextual variables affect the meaning or reality we perceive. The kind of drama in which a particular scene is embedded can affect the interpretation of the scene. The other stories on the front page of the newspaper can affect the way each individual story is perceived. This phenomenon is seen most easily in visual illusions such as Figure 2.3.

FIGURE 2.3
The effect of context on perception.

You can see how context alters our perception of the relative sizes of the cylinders. The combination of context and placement of the figures on the right side of the illustration causes us to perceive all three cylinders as roughly the same size. The combination of context and placement on the left causes us to perceive far greater differences in size among the cylinders than actually exist. Similarly, a label or word can sometimes so structure a message for some people that parts of it are effectively blocked out. For instance, if we label a message as a "commercial" or as "persuasive," that context reduces its persuasibility. Precisely the same story about a political candidate will be perceived differently when it is run during the break in an entertainment program and labeled a political commercial than when it is embedded in a television newscast as one of the regular news stories.

BYLINE

Consider the relationship between commercials and programs you have seen on television. Do you see ways exposure to some commercials can affect people's perceptions of the program—for example, of some news stories or of a movie in which commercials are inserted? Do you see ways exposure to a program can alter perception of a commercial?

Composition as context. The composition of a photograph or of words or letters on a page provides a different type of context. But it is a context that can also have a strong impact on our constructions of meaning. You are probably quite familiar with the way photographic composition can alter meaning: camera angle, type of lens, closeness of camera to subject, and so forth. We suspect, though, that you probably never thought about the fact that the composition of printed matter can also affect meaning.

One of America's most imaginative poets, e. e. cummings, clearly thought about it and used it in his work. In "a leaf falls," which is probably his most delicate and beautiful poem, he uses both composition and the juxtaposition of words to stimulate readers to construct a variety of fresh meanings. This poem consists simply of the phrase "a leaf falls" and the word "loneliness" intertwined and arranged on the page in an unusual, falling order. This is the poem:

l(a
le
af
fa
ll
s)
one
l
iness

We mentioned earlier the fact that audience members are far more than simply receivers; they are full participants in the process of communication. Nowhere is that fact clearer than in the case of this poem. The context that each of the ideas in this poem provides for the other and the context of the composition interact with the ideas readers bring to the work—including ideas about loneliness, about falling leaves, about poetry, and about novelty. From this interaction, each reader constructs a meaning.

Impact of contextual cues on attributions. Contextual cues can also affect whether we perceive something in the media as "natural" or "symbolic" and, therefore, in need of interpretation. And if we think it is symbolic, contextual cues can influence the meaning or intent we attribute to the symbol's creator.

For example, a piece of torn window screen shown in a television drama will be perceived as "natural" if it appears in a brief shot of an old, abandoned house. On the other hand, if we see it during the titles of the show, isolated from the window, with a strong spotlight shining on it, we will almost certainly perceive it as "symbolic," and we will try to figure out what the director was trying to communicate by that symbol.

We perceive a set of random words as a "natural" error by a typist or editor if we see them on the pages of a newspaper or coming over the wire service, but we will probably perceive them as "symbolic" if we encounter the same set of random words in a book of poetry or the arts section of the newspaper. If those random words are arranged in "stanzas," the perception of them as poetry will be almost certain, and we will work hard to figure out what that odd poem means.

Creators of most kinds of media content, from movies to news stories and from television programs to novels, use contextual cues to help you perceive what to interpret as symbolic and what to interpret as natural. To understand the creator's intent, you need to become sensitive to these cues.

BYLINE

Think about the movies or television programs you have seen recently or the novels you have read. Do you think any of them, or characters in them, were symbols for something else or for some class of individuals? What in the film, the program, or the novel led you to perceive it in this way?

REVIEW

The context in which we hear, read, or see something affects the meaning we create for that message and its influence on us. The context of a stimulus can influence whether we perceive it as a symbol or as some natural phenomenon. The context may even be part of the world in our heads, a theme we treat as the frame of reference for something we are reading, seeing, or hearing.

Context as a figure-ground phenomenon. One way to think of context is in terms of the **figure-ground phenomenon**. This contextual phenomenon is similar to what occurs with any type of perception: *when you focus on one pattern, the rest becomes background*. A familiar optical illusion, shown in Figure 2.4, demonstrates this phenomenon.

This illusion is called the Peter-Paul goblet. When first looking at the figure, some people will see a goblet; others will see two faces. You can see both of them if you try, but not at one time. At any moment you can perceive either the goblet or the faces, and the other part of the drawing becomes background. When you see the faces, the goblet is background; when you see the goblet, the faces are background. You can focus on only one at a time. Thus, in your communication mosaic, you might focus on all of the fragments that have a conceivable relationship to the economy, and everything else becomes ground—foreign policy, politics, and so on. Once you find a particular theme of this sort—just as you find a pattern in visual perception—you tend to keep on perceiving that theme. The theme could be that young people are going to hell, that the capitalists dominate everything, or that God controls our actions and our fate. Given any one of these themes as the figure, you would perceive quite a different world in the messages in your environment than if any other theme was the figure.

THE PROCESSING OF NEWS VERSUS ENTERTAINMENT

If you have a special interest in literature, you may be aware of the debate going on today in literary circles concerning what is and is not fiction, or what is and is not literature. For example, consider Truman Capotes' book *In Cold Blood*, based on the actual murder of a family and the

FIGURE 2.4
The Peter-Paul goblet illusion.

men who did it. In gathering the material for his book, Capote studied all of the news accounts of the brutal and senseless affair and interviewed the murderers, friends and relatives of the murdered family, and others who were involved in the trial. But in addition to descriptions of actual events and people, he added conversations that may or may not have taken place and additional events to aid the flow of the story. Which parts of the book are journalistic or historical description and which are fiction is unclear—and probably was unclear even to Capote.

Critics have argued whether this and similar books comprise a new literary genre, or whether they are simply part of a continuum on which every piece of literature lies. In a sense, every work of fiction contains some germ of fact. No writer can make a story out of nothing; he or she must build on experience with people and events. Thus, every story is some blend of fact and fiction.

Some literary theorists have gone even further. Just as any novel can be read, in some sense, as a description of reality, any piece of writing that purports to be a description of reality, for example, a work of history, can be read as fiction. It is impossible to truly recreate the past. All a historian can do is tell a story that is an analogy or model of the past. In the same way, news stories are, to some extent, fiction—selective interpretations of events as filtered through the eyes and camera angles and words of observers, journalists, and editors and molded into coherent stories.

Just as many contemporary literary critics and theorists are trying to break down the boundaries between literature and nonliterature, so are critics and theorists of mass communication beginning to break down the boundary between news and entertainment. When one considers that most news or information is almost immediately used in entertainment, this breakdown seems essential. The latest news event becomes, almost overnight, part of the plot of soap operas, made-for-television movies, and situation comedies.

This incorporation of nonentertainment into entertainment has been going on since the beginnings of literature and drama. The Greek dramas and the early religious dramas were attempts to communicate moral lessons and the events of the day in more interesting and effective ways. The songs of wandering minstrels centuries ago were essentially news stories set to music. The extreme of this confounding of literature and nonliterature can be seen in the work of a poet some years ago who found a unique source for his creations. His "poems" consisted of classified advertisements, unchanged except for the arrangement of the lines.

So when we see a motion picture about the latest million-dollar robbery or the latest war, is it any less "real" than the newspaper or television news account of the event? Both are selective. Both are translations of the event into words and pictures. The only difference is that one claims to be news and the other claims to be fiction or entertainment or, sometimes, **docudrama**—*a blend of documentary and dramatization*. In fact, the news story, like the dramatization, is *both* news and fiction; neither can possibly be anything else.

BYLINE

Instances have been documented of a television network having people restage news occurrences so they could be videotaped for broadcast on news programs. Is this practice consistent with responsible journalism? What about docudramas? Why might one consider the creation of docudramas ethical but the recreation of news events for broadcast on news programs unethical?

Looking at the reverse side of this coin, we can see that the news and informational or educational materials presented through the media also incorporate elements of fiction or entertainment. When we report in the newspaper or newscast about a city council meeting, a women's basketball game, or the latest doings of the student senate, how do we shape that material? We shape it into a "story"—a story with a beginning, a middle, and an end—a story with a plot and, if we are clever enough, a story with a villain and a hero or heroine.

It is interesting, by the way, that as our news stories and documentaries take on more and more the form of traditional fiction, much of fiction is taking on more and more the form—or formlessness—of events out in the world, without beginning, middle, or end; without heroes, heroines, or villains; without logical order. At its most extreme, this form of literature gives us an almost random set of bits of information from which each reader creates his or her own story.

The point of all this—the effect of all of these phenomena—is that just as the boundaries between news and entertainment have broken down in good part for the creators of those forms of mass communication, so have they broken down for the consumers of those forms: for you and us as the audience. In fact, for us consumers, they may have broken down even more. We probably can make no meaningful distinction between them in their impact on the creation of our realities. Entertainment can shape that world in our heads—our images of reality—as much as news can; at times it can shape it even more.

As evidence, consider the Korean War. It is an important part of our history. You probably have some conception of Korea and of that war; it is part of the world in your head, even if you were not alive when it occurred. You almost certainly were exposed to historical accounts in some of your high school and, perhaps, college classes. You may have read about it or talked to a parent, relative, or friend who took part in that war. So you have been exposed to so-called "factual" accounts. If we could examine that part of the world in your head that is the Korean War, though, it would be a safe bet that more of that world was constructed from bits of information you got from reruns of "M*A*S*H" than from all of those factual accounts.

REVIEW

There is far less difference between news reports and many forms of entertainment than most people realize. Both contain elements of fact and fiction and both can be "read" as either fact or fiction.

Not only is this true for those who were not alive in that day; it is true for those who were and who followed the war day by day in the newspapers and newscasts. We would not be surprised if it were true even for some of the people who actually participated in that war. As time has passed, the fiction has become more real than the actual, on-the-scene experiences. So, as you think about your impressions of reality—that world in your head—and as you attempt to gain greater control over its future construction and reconstruction, try to be sensitive to the fact that some of the building blocks come from that part of your mosaic environment that is fiction or entertainment.

WHY ALL OF THESE FACTORS AFFECT OUR INFORMATION PROCESSING

Why do all of the effects discussed in this chapter occur? At least part of the reason is that each of us is faced with far more information than we can take in and process in a rational way. We can cope with only a small part of that information and must make inferences about much of the rest; we must fill the gaps left by what we skimmed over or simply missed. We do this in part by anticipating what the information will be. We anticipate the future in the only way we can: through inference based on prior experience. Then, when the future becomes the present—or the past—we have some check on our inference; either it worked or it didn't work. The results of this test affect the kind of inference we make in the future—our expectation.

These unconscious processes of perception are much like the processes a scientist goes through consciously. Each time we perceive something in our communication environment, it is as though we are experimentally testing a hypothesis about what that thing is. Our hypothesis—or expectation—is then confirmed and reinforced or disconfirmed and modified according to the results of the test. For example, from the fragments of sports news that we accept from the media, we make an inference about whether it will be worthwhile to buy a season ticket for the football games. Our experiences in the stadium serve to confirm or deny the inference.

That confirmation or lack of confirmation, in turn, affects the way we perceive or make inferences from future sports news we encounter.

Many scholars today talk about **information overload**, by which they mean *the constant exposure to more information than individuals can process.* These scholars assume that, because of all of the new communications technologies, the amount of information overload is far greater than it has ever been in the past. We believe that assumption is wrong. Information overload is not the result of the increasing amounts of processed information coming at us from the mass media. Those who claim it is fail to consider the fact that not all of our information comes from the media and, even more important, that we have always had communication overload—more stimuli or fragments of information available to each of us than we can handle. Just look out of the window and try to notice every single thing. Obviously, that is an impossible task, for there are almost an infinite number of minute fragments in that scene. An examination of one of your hands may provide a clearer example. Under normal circumstances, we perceive little more than its grossest characteristics. A careful examination, however, shows that we could study one of our hands for a long time and still not see all that is there. Look at the myriad lines, various colors, hairs, and interesting shapes. And each finger is unique. The hand contains far more information than we can absorb. But normally we do not even try to absorb all of it; there is no need to do so. We abstract what we need and ignore the rest. This is precisely what we do when we process information we receive from the mass media.

REVIEW

Many of the unconscious processes of perception—such as chunking or filling gaps in the array of information to which we are exposed—occur because most of us are confronted with more information than we can handle easily. These processes help us cope with this information overload.

HOW AND WHY WE PROCESS INFORMATION AS WE DO: A SUMMARY

The major point of this chapter is that the perception or understanding of your communication environment is a creative process in which you are engaged throughout all of the waking hours of your lifetime. We looked at the major factors that affect that creative process—that affect the way you construct and constantly reconstruct all of the meanings that fill the world in your head.

We talked about two major sets of factors that affect the way you process information. One set is composed of all of your personal qualities and habits that influence the way you see your environment. Central to these personal characteristics are the patterns we called "scripts" or "schemata" that you built up over the years. These scripts were shaped by your particular experiences, knowledge, needs, values, and beliefs. You match incoming stimuli against these scripts and use what seems to be the most relevant script to organize, fill in, and make sense of each set of stimuli. These scripts are not static; they are constantly evolving as you encounter new information and as you test their validity. It does not take much interaction with other people for you to learn which of your interpretations of information from your communication mosaic are sharply inconsistent with the interpretations of others. A friend might have said to you, "You thought that movie was a *comedy?* You certainly didn't see the same movie I did." Such reactions can bring a sharp change in the script you use to assess that sort of movie in the future.

Another major function of a script is to shape your expectation or set, making it easier to process and to remember information. Your needs, attitudes, and beliefs also affect your expectations in such a way that you are more likely to perceive and remember messages that are consistent with them; you are less likely to perceive or remember messages that are inconsistent with them.

People who are close to you—family members, friends, others with whom you identify—also affect the set with which you approach the media, how you process information you encounter, and what you remember of that information. These people are your reference groups. Just being in the company of one of these reference groups when you are being exposed to a television program, movie, or some other media content, or just being aware that you soon will be in their company, can affect what you see in that content and what you bring away from that experience. Reference groups affect you in this way because each one's presence or expected presence tends to activate a different script. In addition, each of your reference groups is a type of audience for you. And the kinds of ideas you are likely to extract or construct from your media experiences for one of these audiences (such as your friends) is often quite different from the kinds you are likely to construct for another of these audiences (such as your parents).

Another major factor in the way you process information from your communication mosaic is your language. That language influences the kinds of things you see and the kinds of distinctions you make. Words are necessary tools for making sense of your environment.

Your construction of the world in your head is influenced not only by your personal characteristics or internal environment, but also by the characteristics of the information you encounter in your external environment. Among the many characteristics of that information is its redundancy or repetitiveness. The more often you encounter information, the greater influence it tends to have on you. Similarly, the order in which you receive bits of information affects both which ones you are likely to recall and which ones you are more likely to believe. However, as we saw in this chapter, the effect of order varies with circumstances.

Although it may seem odd to you to call the absence of information a characteristic of messages, that is precisely what a gap is. As we noted, no message is complete; every message has gaps that its recipient must fill in. Here again, the scripts we have stored in memory play an important role in determining how those gaps are filled.

Another interesting characteristic of the messages we encounter in our communication mosaics is their relative iconicity or, at the opposite extreme, their symbolic value. We noted that the less iconic a message or stimulus, the more likely most receivers are to perceive a general rather than a specific referent. For example, we are more likely to think of all mankind or humanity when we see a highly abstract drawing of a man than when we see a realistic photograph of a particular male.

The last major characteristic of messages that we discussed was their context. Context affects the interpretation of information in a great variety of ways. For example, it can increase the probability that you will perceive a stimulus as a symbol, rather than as something standing only for itself.

In characterizing mass media messages, the distinction between "entertainment" and "information" or "news" is often considered highly important. If we think of the effects of these two forms, and the way they appear to blend into each other in our contemporary media environment, the distinction between them may not be nearly as important as many of us believed. People get a great deal of useful information from what we generally label entertainment and find much entertainment in what we label news.

In explaining the various effects of both our internal characteristics and the characteristics of our external communication environment, we suggested that we perceive or process information much the way scientists explore the world. Our scripts provide hypotheses about how to interpret information, and we test those hypotheses as we interact with other people and as we respond in other ways. In the process, we discover that some of our hypotheses work and some do not. As a result, we either reinforce those scripts in our head or revise them, and continue our eternal journey of exploration through our communication mosaics.

DISCUSSION QUESTIONS

1. What are the major factors that influence the way you process information? How does each one work?
2. What are your personal characteristics that might lead you to perceive what you read, see, and hear in a different way than someone else might perceive it?
3. What factors in the exposure situation—the context of your exposure—might influence your perceptions?
4. Why do Becker and Roberts claim that the difference between news and entertainment is not as great as most people think? Do you agree or disagree with them? Why?
5. How might thinking of news stories as "fictions" rather than "truths," as "one possible way" to construct reality rather than "the way," affect the way journalists do their work? How might it affect the way, as a reader, listener, or viewer, you process news stories?
6. Do you have a "war script" or "war schemata" that you use to interpret news coming from the Middle East? How similar is it to the war scripts of your classmates? Why do you believe this is so?

NOTES

1. Walter Lippmann, *Public Opinion* (New York: Macmillan, 1922), p. 3.
2. Roy Lachman, Janet L. Lachman, and Earl C. Butterfield, *Cognitive Psychology and Information Processing: An Introduction* (Hillsdale, New Jersey: Lawrence Erlbaum Associates, 1979), p. 454.
3. John Z. Young, *Doubt and Certainty in Science: A Biologist's Reflections on the Brain* (Oxford: Clarendon Press, 1951).
4. Milton Rokeach, *The Open and Closed Mind* (New York: Basic Books, 1960).
5. John B. Carroll, *Selected Writings of Benjamin Whorf* (New York: John Wiley & Sons, 1956).
6. Peter Berger and Thomas Luckman, *The Social Construction of Reality* (Garden City, N.Y.: Doubleday, 1966), pp. 21–22.
7. William James, *Principles of Psychology* (New York: Holt, 1890).

SUGGESTED READINGS

Classic Works in the Field

Bauer, Raymond A. "The Obstinate Audience: The Influence Process from the Point of View of Social Communication." *American Psychologist*, 19 (1964): 319–328.

Berger, Peter L., and Luckmann, Thomas. *The Social Construction of Reality*. Garden City, NY: Doubleday, 1966.

Lang, Kurt, and Lang, Gladys Engel. "The Unique Perspective of Television and Its Effects: A Pilot Study." In *The Process and Effects of Mass Communication*, ed. Wilbur Schramm and Donald F. Roberts. Rev. ed. Urbana: University of Illinois Press, 1971.

Schwartz, Tony. *The Responsive Chord*. New York: Doubleday, 1973.
An imaginative book on the way sound works on people. It was written by an experienced creator of radio and television commercials.

Relevant Contemporary Works

Bordwell, David. *Making Meaning: Inference and Rhetoric in the Interpretation of Cinema*. Cambridge, MA: Harvard University Press, 1989.

Donohew, Lewis, Sypher, Howard E., and Higgins, E. Tory, eds. *Communication, Social Cognition, and Affect*. Hillsdale, NJ: Lawrence Erlbaum Associates, 1988.

Graber, Doris A. *Processing the News: How People Tame the Information Tide*. 2nd ed. New York: Longman, 1988.

Pettey, Gary R. "The Interaction of the Individual's Social Environment, Attention and Interest, and Public Affairs Media Use on Political Knowledge Holding." *Communication Research* 15 (June 1988): 265–281.

Rounder, Donna, and Perloff, Richard M. "Selective Perception of Outcome of First 1984 Presidential Debate." *Journalism Quarterly* 65 (Spring 1988): 141–147.

Severin, Werner J., with Tankard, James W. *Communication Theories*. 2nd ed. New York: Longman, 1988.
See especially Chapter 9, pp. 120–133, on perception and communication.

Zillmann, Dolf, and Bryant, Jennings. *Selective Exposure to Communication*. Hillsdale, NJ: Erlbaum, 1985.

PART TWO

INDIVIDUAL MEDIA IN THE SYSTEM

In Part One we examined how you operate within a mass communication system or environment, exposing yourself and being exposed to many and varied bits of information. We also discussed the ways you create the world in your head from those bits of information. In that discussion, we treated the mass media as an integrated system—a type of environment that you live in, use, and react to.

Understanding the mass media in this systematic way is important. But it is equally important to understand each of the elements that make up that system—how each medium works and how it fits into the total media environment.

To discover that working and that "fit," in this section we will examine the history of each medium, the way it operates, and the direction in which it seems to be moving. A knowledge of media history will give you a context for understanding why the media are the way they are. And by seeing where the media have been, along with where they are now, you will have a better basis for predicting the future. In addition, these understandings will help you see how you might help change and improve the media and your use of them.

As we examine each medium, we will vary our coverage to emphasize the most important factors. For some media we will stress their news functions; for others, we will focus more on their entertainment content. We will focus on the processing of information from some media, while placing greater emphasis, for other media, on how they operate, how information gets into them, or perhaps on how they developed. By learning about its key elements, you should more fully appreciate each medium and be able to use it more effectively and efficiently.

In considering the history of mass communication, note the rapid and continuously accelerating rate of new developments. We can illustrate this accelerating rate with an analogy that gives us a better feel for relative time spans. Imagine that the past thirty-five thousand years—from the beginnings of human speech to the present—were just one year.[1] The development of writing, which occurred about 5000 B.C., falls well into the autumn of our year, on about October 20. Movable type came sixty-five hundred years later, or December 27 on our calendar. The telegraph, developed near the start of the nineteenth century, would make its appearance at about 4 A.M. on December 30. Radio and the motion picture grew to popularity in the first half of the twentieth century, placing them at about 10 A.M. on December 31 of our year. Television, which emerged in the late 1940s, would arrive about 5:15 P.M. of that same day. The satellite communication of the 1960s would appear at 9 P.M., and home video recordings and video discs would arrive shortly before midnight on the last day of our year.

From the perspective of thirty-five thousand years, mass communication is an infant. More important, it is growing and developing at an ever faster rate.

1. I am indebted for this analogy to Frederick Williams, "President's Column," *ICA News*, Fall, 1978, p.2.

CHAPTER 3

BOOKS: THE BIRTH OF MASS COMMUNICATION

OBJECTIVES

After studying this chapter, you should be able to

- Trace the major developments in the history of the book.
- Describe the book-publishing industry.
- Discuss the factors that affect the probability that a book manuscript or idea will be published.
- Explain the legal ramifications of copyright and the First Amendment as they apply to authors and publishers.
- Identify the factors that must be considered in determining whether using a portion of a copyrighted work can be considered "fair use."
- Explain how books are marketed and the reasons book marketing is so difficult.

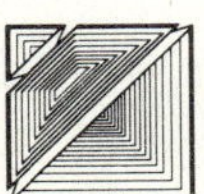

All that mankind has done, thought, gained or been: it is lying as in magic preservation in the pages of books.

from Thomas Carlyle's *Heroes and Hero Worship*

Books are not absolutely dead things, but do contain a potency of life in them to be as active as that soul whose progeny they are; nay they do preserve as in a vial the purest efficacy and extraction of that living intellect that bred them.

from John Milton's *Areopagitica*

Books are the carriers of civilization. Without books, history is silent, literature dumb, science crippled, thought and speculation at a standstill.

Barbara Tuchman in address at the Library of Congress

Books, like television, are so much a part of our social fabric that we cannot imagine life without them. Nor can we imagine the threat they posed—and in some cases continue to pose—to existing values and ideas. Elizabeth Eisenstein argues that the availability of printed material led to the societal, cultural, familial, and industrial changes that brought about the Renaissance, the Reformation, and the scientific revolution.[1] The resistance to such monumental upheavals can be seen in the sentencing of a seventeenth-century English printer who published a book that argued that the king should be accountable to the people and should be removed or even put to death if he did not carry out the people's will. Having been charged with treason, John Twyn was informed:

you [will] be led back to the place from whence you came and from thence to be drawn upon an hurdle to the place of execution; and there you shall be hanged by the neck, and being alive, shall be cut down, and your privy-members shall be cut off, your entrails shall be taken out of your body, and you living, the same to be burnt before your eyes; your head to be cut off, your body to be divided into four quarters and your head and quarters to be disposed of at the pleasure of the king's majesty. And the Lord have mercy upon your soul.[2]

Chilling as that punishment was, the "potency of life" that John Milton wrote about was out of the bottle. Printing presses, and the books that flowed from them, would usher in new ideas and new knowledge on a scale heretofore unimaginable.

You may never have thought of books as part of our mass communication system, but they are. And they are an important segment of your communication mosaic. For this reason, and because the book has influenced other mass communication media, it is important for you to understand how this medium came to be and how it works. In this chapter, we will consider not only the birth and development of the book, but something of its parentage as well. We will also look at how books come into being, factors that affect the probability that a book will be published, factors that affect the probability of your being exposed to books, and some of the major functions and effects of books.

EARLY DEVELOPMENTS

The ancestors of books are the early attempts of people to speak, to draw, and to write. It is impossible to estimate when human beings began to make sounds we could call speech. We do have evidence that pictures were used as symbols twenty-five thousand years ago and that some sort of writing has existed for five to six thousand years.

As far as we can determine, the need for nonoral communication first became strong when people began to settle down, turning from a nomadic

Cave and wall art, such as that created by American Indians at Nine Mile Canyon in Utah, was one of the earliest forms of "written" communication.

to a relatively stable, agrarian life. They began to feel the need for some sort of record keeping and so developed a system of writing. Using the only means of visual communication they knew at the time—drawings of objects—they developed a type of picture writing or sign-writing, a form of writing that still exists to some extent in China. The system of sound-writing, writing with symbols that stand for sounds rather than objects, evolved much later, about 1500 B.C. This is the sort of writing we have in most languages today, including English.

Initially, not many people needed this new-fangled trick of writing. They had always gotten along with just talk, punctuated once in a while, perhaps, by a kick or a shove. Why would anyone want to waste time learning to write? Besides, those with whom they wanted to communicate could not read anyway. Then, as now, it was the interest of commerce that gave the new form of communication a boost—and probably kept it alive. The first people who saw a use for writing were those who needed it as an aid in business.

Although business stimulated the development and establishment of writing, drama stimulated its rapid spread. Business and the arts have played interacting roles in the development of every communication innovation since that time. Drama was flourishing in Greece, even before the days of Aeschulus, Euripides, and Aristophanes. Those involved in this

c4000 BC
Sign-writing—using symbols based on pictures—develops

c1500 BC
Sound-writing—using symbols standing for sounds—evolves

c105 AD
Paper developed in China

c1100
Chinese use movable type

c1400
Gutenberg develops integrated system for printing with movable type

4000 BC–c1400

1518
England enacts copyright statute protecting work of royal printers

1638
First printing press arrives in American colonies

1640
The Whole Book of Psalmes printed at Harvard College

1662
Massachusetts requires approval of copy by licensing board before publication

1674
First privately owned press begins operating in Boston

1744
First novel published in American colonies

1499–1749

1783
Noah Webster's spelling book published

1790
Congress enacts federal copyright statute

1791
Bill of Rights ratified—First Amendment becomes constitutional

1798
Sedition law prohibits printing of libel against Congress or President

1840
Rotary press developed

1842
Tariff Act prohibits obscene books and pictures into U.S.

1750–1849

1852
First free public library in U.S. opens

1873
Post Office gains power to exclude obscene books and pictures from U.S. mails

1884
Linotype machine perfected

1850–1899

1918
Last of states adopts compulsory school attendance law

1933
U.S. district court rules *Ulysses* not obscene; can be imported legally

1939
Inexpensive paperback books, $4\frac{1}{4}'' \times 6\frac{1}{2}''$, introduced

1900–1950

1978
Copyright revision protects works from creation until 50 years after creator's death

1982
Supreme Court says removal of books from school library involves First Amendment and rights of students

1987–1989
Mergers and acquisitions realign the book industry

1950–1989

art quickly saw the usefulness of being able to put all or parts of their plays in some relatively permanent form so that different groups could produce them. The alternative, dominant prior to the use of writing, was to have the play passed on by word of mouth from one group to the next, and from one generation to another. We can well imagine why playwrights welcomed a more reliable means of passing their works along, so that their words and ideas would not be mutilated by word-of-mouth transmission.

Appearance of the Book The date of the first book ever written is difficult to determine. It depends in part upon what you want to call a book. In some sense, the first "books" were those cumbersome objects made of clay, shaped into flat rectangles or circles or into bricks or columns, with symbols etched into the clay. These books date from many centuries before the Christian era.

Throughout the history of communication, technological developments have been important. This early history was no exception. One technological development important for the book was the invention of papyrus about 4000 B.C. Clearly, the spread of writing was limited when it depended on a heavy and cumbersome clay tablet as the medium. Even the wax tablet used in Rome by some of Cicero's contemporaries did not solve the problem. The Egyptians' invention of papyrus, the first paperlike substance on which people could write, was a major step in its solution.

Papyrus was made by slicing the inner pith from the papyrus plant, spreading it on some sort of flat surface, moistening it with a sticky substance, pressing, and drying it. Papyrus was not bulky and, unlike clay or wax, its smooth surface facilitated an easy, cursive style of writing. In addition, sheets of papyrus could be glued together to form scrolls. Some scrolls were as long as 120 feet; normally they measured about 15 feet. Scholars estimate that in the third century B.C. the royal libraries in Alexandria held as many as four hundred ninety thousand scrolls.

An improvement on papyrus was parchment, made from specially prepared animal skins. It appears to have been the major medium for writing during the period just before and after the birth of Christ.

Evidence shows that libraries were established by the time of Aristotle, in the fourth century B.C. As you know, many libraries today have storage problems—the problem of storing books so they will be preserved and the problem of finding space for the rapidly expanding number of books. The libraries in the early days of Greece had a similar problem: how to store the large scrolls so that they would not be damaged. The problem was solved by standing each rolled scroll in a large vase.

Sometime during the first century A.D., the Chinese developed an even better material on which to write. They took vegetable fibers of various sorts, softened them in vats of water, pressed the resulting mushlike material, and let it dry. The product was a primitive form of paper. Another technological development important for mass communication was the water mill, invented in about the twelfth century. Water mills produced power that accelerated the processing of the pulp, thus making possible the production of large amounts of paper.

Up to the middle of the fifteenth century, all books had to be written and copied by hand, a slow, laborious, and expensive process. The library of even a wealthy person, therefore, was small—probably less than two dozen volumes. The poor could afford none at all. One historian estimates that if an average court official of that day had wanted to buy one book—one bound manuscript—it would have cost a month's salary. In the early fifteenth century, a major university—Cambridge—had only 22 volumes, compared to the 1 million to 5.5 million volumes in a major university research library today.

Review

Writing of some kind has existed for five to six thousand years. The first paperlike substance on which people could write was called papyrus. It was invented by Egyptians around 4000 B.C. Until the middle of the fifteenth century, books had to be prepared by hand.

By the middle of the fifteenth century, all of the components needed for the mass production of books were available. Woodblock printing of textiles was fairly common, and some of this printing was being done with a screw press. Oil-based pigments had been used for about a hundred years. Methods were being developed to make molds from engraved wood or metal letters. And, as previously noted, the art of papermaking had been developed fourteen hundred years earlier.

Initially, printed pages were made from engraved wooden blocks. Some of these pages were put together to form books—primarily collections of religious pictures, although some included textual material.

The Printing Press

The last major technological development needed for the production of printed material was movable type. Credit for this development is generally given to a German, Johann Gutenberg; however, evidence shows that movable type was used in Asia as far back as the eleventh century. Both the Chinese and Koreans were casting symbols from lead long before the birth of Gutenberg. Movable type was probably invented by a Chinese named Pi Ching. Gutenberg developed the technique into an integrated system around 1400 and improved many details. The earliest known material produced by Gutenberg's press is a poem. The Gutenberg Bible came a short time later.

Of all the inventions and developments in history up to that time, probably none spread faster than the process of printing from movable type. Within twenty years from the time Johann Gutenberg set that first poem in type, his method of printing was being used throughout Europe. It took almost two hundred years for a printing press to find its way across the Atlantic to the American colonies. A press arrived at Harvard College in 1638, the year that institution opened its doors.

Government Control of Printing

Most of the materials printed on the Harvard press had nothing to do with the college. They were either government or religious publications, the same sort of materials that dominated printing throughout the American colonies for most of the seventeenth century. For example, the

Johann Gutenberg displays a page from his printed Bible. No other technological development has matched the impact of Gutenberg's press on the mass media.

"Freeman's Oath," an oath to which one had to agree to become a citizen of the Massachusetts Colony, was printed at Harvard. The Harvard press also printed the *Whole Book of Psalmes*, sometimes called the *Bay Psalm Book*. This was apparently the first book printed in the colonies. The reason most of the material printed in those days was either religious or government-related is that the king's governors in the colonies permitted little else. As a matter of fact, they permitted very few presses to operate. None other than the one at Harvard was allowed in Massachusetts until 1674, and none whatever in either Pennsylvania or Virginia. An explanation for this control is evident in the words of Sir William Berkeley, governor of Virginia, in 1671:

> *But, I thank God, there are no free schools nor printing . . . for learning has brought disobedience, and heresy, and sects into the world, and printing has divulged them, and libels against the best government. God keep us from both.*[3]

No press in the colonies was free of either church or government ownership until one was set up in Boston in 1674. Although free of government ownership, this press was not free of government control. The owner needed government permission to operate it.

A few years later, King James II of England made clear that actions by the Royal Governors in America limiting and controlling printing were done at his command. He issued these orders:

> *And for as much a great inconvenience may arise by the liberty of printing within our province of New York, you are to provide by all necessary orders that noe person keep any press for printing, nor that any book, pamphlet, or other matters whatsoever bee printed without your special leave & license first obtained.*[4]

Early Printers By the beginning of the eighteenth century, printing was spreading rapidly throughout the colonies. In 1717, James Franklin obtained a license for a press in Boston. His apprentice was his younger brother, Benjamin Franklin. Being rather independent of mind, Benjamin soon quarreled with his brother, moved to Philadelphia, and set up his own press with a partner. There he introduced one of the most famous of America's early books, *Poor Richard's Almanac,* full of useful information and wise sayings. Almanacs, by the way, were a staple of the American publishing industry almost from its beginning. For the colonists, they served many of the functions that today are served by newspapers, magazines, and even radio and television. They contained poetry and short stories for entertainment, a wealth of information for education—from mean temperatures in different parts of the country to lists of public officials—and articles on public affairs for readers' general enlightenment. One reason that almanacs were so popular during the first century of printing in America was that the only alternative for reading in most homes was the Bible.

BYLINE

Have you ever examined a modern almanac? If not, you should do so. They still provide a load of information. Do you think people use them for different purposes today than they did in Benjamin Franklin's time? For what purposes do people buy almanacs today?

Benjamin Franklin soon became one of the major publishing figures in the colonies. In 1744 his press printed the first novel in America: *Pamela*, by Samuel Richardson. Franklin was evidently also involved in politics from the earliest days of his career, for he soon became the official printer for the colonies of Pennsylvania, New Jersey, and Delaware.

REVIEW

The printing press was invented by a German, Johann Gutenberg. As presses spread, so did attempts to control them. In colonial America, one of the major publishers was Benjamin Franklin.

Another Franklin—Ann Smith Franklin, widow of Benjamin's older brother—was also an important printer in the colonies. Calling herself the Widow Franklin, she took over her husband's printing and newspaper publishing business on his death in 1735. The Widow Franklin was not the earliest female printer in America, however. That honor apparently belongs to Dinah Nuthead, who also took over the operation of a family press when her husband died in 1695. Being a female in the printing business was unusual in the seventeenth century. Even more unusual, at least from our perspective, is the fact that Mrs. Nuthead could neither read nor write; she could not even sign her name. She set type visually, simply by matching the letters of the alphabet, which she could recognize.

THE BOOK AS A MASS MEDIUM

Bookstores played an extremely important role in the life of the colonies. They were gathering places for intellectuals, where important ideas of the day were discussed and local literary talent nurtured. However, during the early history of this country the frequenting of bookstores and the reading of books were largely confined to the elite; few of the masses had those opportunities. It was almost the end of the nineteenth century before the book became truly a mass medium, in terms of both its production processes and its audience.

Until that time, those involved in publishing were largely generalists. The printer, the publisher, and the seller of books were often one person. Some authors even published their own books. One could hardly talk of a publishing "industry." By the end of the century, however, that situation had largely changed; specialization was the norm, as it was in other mass production industries. As the industry became more complex, it was increasingly difficult for one person to handle more that one major function.

Authors began getting out of the publishing business when the royalty system became established in the latter half of the nineteenth century. Under this system—still the dominant contractual arrangement between authors and publishers—the publisher pays an author a percentage of the net price of each book that is sold.

Even more important in the development of the book as a mass medium were the successful attempts of publishers to appeal to a broad segment of the public, rather than to a small elite. Publishing was and is a business, and the owners wanted to sell as many books as possible. Therefore, they were most interested in books with wide, popular appeal. The result was a scramble among publishers to sign up well-known authors or would-be authors. For example, in 1872, more than twenty American and British publishers vied for the right to publish the story of David Livingstone, the lost African explorer whom journalist Henry Stanley had found. (You may be familiar with the story from the old motion picture, featuring Spencer Tracy, about Stanley and Livingstone.)

The drive to appeal to large numbers of readers was not without its price, of course. The publishing industry was charged with pandering to the masses, appealing to the lowest common denominator, and forsaking quality for quantity—charges familiar to later mass communicators in the motion picture, radio, and television industries. Although not without some basis in fact, the charges were overblown. As in other mass communication industries, many people working in the book industry were—and are—concerned with publishing works of merit. Except for subsidized university presses, however, each publisher must produce enough popular books to keep the company profitable, or it will cease to exist.

There is still strong competition to sign "hot" authors to publishing contracts. Australian author Colleen McCullough, who wrote *The Thorn Birds,* was recently lured from Harper and Row—now HarperCollins—to Morrow and Avon for a reported $7.5 million. The new contract calls for five books making up a historical series. Bill Cosby is another writer who recently changed publishers. He switched from Doubleday, which had just sold 2.6 million hardcover copies of his book, *Fatherhood,* to Putnam, which offered some $4 million for his next book. Philip Roth, the author of *Goodbye, Columbus,* has changed publishers a number of times. In 1989 he moved to Simon and Schuster to write three novels for a reported $1.2 to $1.7 million. Mary Higgins Clark, often referred to as the "Agatha Christie of the '80s," received $11.4 million from Simon and Schuster to produce four novels and a short-story collection. While this may seem like an extraordinary commitment, the publisher is confident that Clark's track record—six previous novels, all of which were best-sellers and four of which were adapted for motion picture or television—justifies the amount. Prior to the publication of her first book, *Where Are the Children?*, Clark received an advance of only $3000. In a bidding contest among six major publishers, Dell Publishing Company paid a whopping $12.3 million for the rights to English author Ken Follett's next two books—subjects for which have not even been determined! Dell believes, however, that sales of Follett's previous books—an average of two hundred fifty thousand copies in hardcover and approximately 4 million in paperback—warrant the high cost.

REVIEW

Books became a mass medium when they began appealing to large numbers of people. Today there is much competition for popular authors. Some, such as Mary Higgins Clark, are offered multimillion dollar contracts by publishers.

HOW BOOKS GET INTO OUR MOSAICS

A large portion of the adults in the United States never read a book once school is behind them. However, this medium contributes a rich array of information and entertainment to the communication mosaics of those of us who wish to take advantage of it. In local and school libraries, on racks in a variety of stores, and available through the mails are books on almost every conceivable subject, for any level of literacy, and in every major language.

Amount of Book Production

Close to ten thousand publishers operate in the United States, individuals or companies that will publish one or more books this year. Most of these are quite small. Slightly more than one-tenth of them will publish at least five new titles during the year. Fewer than twenty-five firms—between 2 and 3 percent of the total number of publishers—account for roughly half the book sales in the country.

This year that total group of publishers will turn out between forty thousand and fifty thousand new books and between seven thousand and eight thousand new editions of old books. These are in addition to all of the books that are being published in other countries and imported to the United States and all that have been published here and abroad in years past, many of which are still available. The number of new books and of new editions published in this country has risen steadily since 1638, when the first printing press arrived on these shores. That number now seems to have leveled off, at least for the present. Future growth or decline will depend on population trends, lifestyle, education, and developments in communication technologies.

The growth in the number of new books published was slow at first. By the 1830s, the number had risen to only about a hundred a year, but then the pace picked up. By 1853 almost nine hundred titles a year were published, by 1855 almost eleven hundred, by 1884 over four thousand, by 1900 over six thousand, and by 1910 over thirteen thousand. Growth stopped and the output declined somewhat from this period just before World War I until after World War II, but then the industry came back stronger than ever, its production rising steadily and rapidly almost to the present day.

Book Sales and Types of Books Published

Book sales in the latter part of the 1980s continued to rise, owing mainly to three factors: higher levels of library and educational funding, more disposable personal income, and gains in the reading population and school enrollments. Sales rose from $10.5 billion in 1986 to $12.9 billion in 1987, $13.2 billion in 1988, and $14.7 billion in 1989. Predictions are that sales will continue to rise at about 4 percent a year into the 1990s, although profits may lag behind somewhat because of increases in the price of paper.

The spoken-word audio publishing business—books on audio cassette—is now a $100-million-a-year industry. Although there has yet to be a real bestselling audio book, there is growing interest in this form of publication. Random House, for instance, issued a first-run printing of fifty thousand copies of the audio version of Nancy Reagan's book, *My Turn* (recorded incidentally, by the former First Lady herself). One factor that may further stimulate sales is the attention given to packaging audio books. Simon and Schuster's audio release of former President Ronald Reagan's book, *Speaking My Mind,* featured a two-cassette, three-hour edition and a multicassette deluxe edition in a leatherette portfolio. A forty-page color photo-booklet accompanied the cassettes.

REVIEW

Between forty thousand and fifty thousand new books are published each year in the United States. Yearly book sales approach $14 billion. When we think of the book as a mass medium, we often think of the trade book or mass market paperback. Yet this kind of book accounts for less than half of the total book sales.

When most people think of the book business, and especially of the book as a mass medium, they think of the novel and popular biography—what are called trade books and mass market paperbacks by those in the industry. These are the books most often sold at bookstores and bookstands or through book clubs. However, **trade books**—*a category that includes cookbooks, children's books, atlases and almanacs, and other popular nonfiction as well as novels and biographies*—and **mass market paperbacks**—*pocket-size books that generally sell for less than $7*—account for less than half of the book sales in this country. Textbooks account for 26 percent of all book sales, and professional books such as medical, technical, legal, or scientific books account for 21 percent (Table 3.1). The remaining income of publishers comes from religious books, mail-order publications, and subscription reference books such as encyclopedias sold through the mail or door to door.

BYLINE

What difference do you believe the increase in the proportion of our population that is fifty years old and older will make in the kinds of books being published? What other factors do you imagine will affect the number or kinds of books published in the next twenty-five years?

How Books Come to Be

Ideas for books are born in a variety of ways. Some spring from the imagination of authors, stimulated by events in their lives or by their observations of the world, either directly or through the mass media. This is the usual genesis of novels and, of course, autobiographies. Other books are the inspiration of publishers or editors who find authors to translate their visions into book manuscripts. The ideas for textbooks often originate with teachers dissatisfied with the material available to teach their subjects, or they originate with a publisher's marketing or editorial personnel, who identify a market for a particular sort of book and then contract with a teacher or teachers to write it. Some books and series are the products of publisher's research and development departments. And, as in the other mass communication industries, major successes—best-sellers, whether novels, biographies, or textbooks—spawn innumerable imitators. For example, consider the stacks of books—biographical, fictional, or some combination of the two—based on the events surrounding former President Nixon's tumultuous final years in office.

TABLE 3.1 Breakdown of Publishing Industry Sales

	Percentage of Sales
Professional	18
Adult Trade	17
Elementary and High School Text	13
College Text	13
Mass Market Paperback	8
Juvenile Trade	6
Religious	5
Book Club	5
Mail Order	5
Subscription Reference	4
University Presses	1
Other	5

Source: Association of American Publishers press release, August 31, 1989. Reprinted courtesy of Association of American Publishers, Inc.

Despite myths to the contrary, most professional authors do not create solely on the basis of inspiration or at the behest of demons; rather, they consider the kinds of works that have audiences, that some publisher is likely to be willing to support, and for which their writing talent is suitable. Only the amateur author can afford to do otherwise.

A major criterion in the decision of a publisher to contract with an author is the potential size of the market—the number of persons who might buy the book. This potential is affected by, among other things, the reputation of the author, the number of people in the population for whom the book is relevant, the number and quality of similar books on the market, current fads or trends, and the possibility for secondary sales to paperback publishers or to the television or motion picture industry. In addition, of course, there are those intangible qualities in some books and in the time at which they are published that help them to become big sellers. The fact that these qualities are intangible and difficult to predict is one of the many factors that make publishing such an interesting business.

Reputation of the author. The reputation of an author (and not necessarily his or her reputation *as an author*) generally has a major impact on a book's sales. For this reason, publishers often contract with well-known personalities whose names will be on the title pages while the books will be written by more experienced writers. The latter are sometimes acknowledged and sometimes not. You are familiar with examples of the "autobiography" of X "as told to" Y. Books bearing the names of well-known political, sports, or show business personalities that were actually written by these personalities are probably the exception rather than the rule. Writers who create books for which others get the credit have come to be called, with justification, "ghost writers."

Generally, of course, the reputation of an author as an author affects the probability of publication. Understandably, publishers are more willing to sign contracts with authors who have proven their ability to write well and in ways that are appealing to readers and who have shown reliability in completing books for which they have signed contracts. A publisher who signs a contract with an unknown author for a book that is not yet completed is taking a double risk: that the author will not complete the book, and that the product will not be of the quality that will sell. Sometimes, of course, an unknown author will bring a completed manuscript with great potential to a publisher—as Margaret Mitchell did with the complete manuscript of *Gone with the Wind*—but that situation is increasingly unusual.

Market potential. The potential market for a book also affects the probability of its publication. Thus, all else being equal, a textbook for a popular beginning college course is more likely to be published than a textbook for an advanced course, because beginning courses usually have far larger enrollments and, hence, the potential sales are greater. Similar assessments are made of the potential number of purchasers for novels, hobby books, and every other sort of book to determine whether enough sales are likely to justify publication. For this reason, a book of poetry is less likely to be published than a detective story, and a book on furniture upholstery is less likely to get into print than a cookbook. An exception would be if the market were so flooded with cookbooks, for example, that a new cookbook would be unlikely to win a very large share, whereas a book on amateur upholstering, even though its potential market is small, would have that market virtually to itself and so could produce greater sales.

Fads and trends are among the more interesting and unpredictable aspects of the publishing business. Thirty years ago, no one would have predicted a large audience for books on jogging. If someone had written such a book then, it is unlikely any publisher would even have considered it. In the 1970s and 1980s, though, along with the fitness boom, jogging books became highly popular.

Potential for secondary sales. Secondary sales of books have become increasingly important to the financial health of many publishers. Hence, a book that is likely to be purchased for reprinting in paperback form or a book that has the potential for adaptation to a motion picture or television program is more likely to be published than a book without such potential.

Undoubtedly, the publisher of the book titled *Rambo* decided to take it on after reading the manuscript, at least in part, because it was the type of book a movie producer would be interested in adapting to film. And as you know, that was a sound judgment, for a highly successful film was produced based on the book. In fact, the film, *First Blood*, was so successful the producer decided to create a sequel, *Rambo: First Blood II*. The symbiotic relationship between books and movies can be seen in the fact that when this sequel proved as successful as the first one, the producer hired the author of the original *Rambo* book, David Morrell, to write a new book based on *Rambo: First Blood II*. Thus we have a case of a film being adapted from a book, and then a book being adapted from the first film's sequel. Rather an incestuous business.

Judgments of publishers. In light of all these factors, it is difficult to understand how some books get published—books that seem to have none of the attributes generally important for success yet that some editors and publishers have supported. The fact is that such books come into being because an editor or publisher sees something special in them and has sufficient faith to gamble. It is people with such insights and with the willingness to gamble on those insights who insure that books continue to contribute a great deal of richness to our media environments.

Unlike the directors of many industries, publishers are not influenced strongly by market research, except in their textbook divisions. In addition, because publishers recognize that only a relatively small number of the books they produce will be highly profitable, idiosyncratic judgments play a large role in publishing decisions. Thus, noncommercial considerations are probably more important in publishing companies than they are in most other kinds of commercial companies. This is especially true of large, successful publishing firms that can afford to experiment with unknown authors and different kinds of books.

Author-editor relationship. For an author, an important figure is the editor in the publishing house who usually works closely with him or her throughout the process of revision and of turning a manuscript into a finished book. Some editors have become famous for their ability to bring out the best in authors. Several now-famous authors would certainly not have achieved the success they did without the help of particularly able and sensitive editors. Scribners editor Maxwell Perkins, for example, was responsible for creating two best-selling novels out of a mass of material written by undisciplined Thomas Wolfe.

The literary agent. Another important figure for the professional writer, especially the novelist, is the **literary agent,** *the person who sells the work of an author to publishers or, at times, to television or motion picture companies.* The most able agents do far more than that. They help guide their authors' careers, encouraging them to do the kind of writing for which they are most talented and that is most likely to sell. They act as business managers, negotiators, record keepers, and often as shields between authors and a distracting world. Publishers have also come to depend on literary agents to such an extent that most of them will not even read the manuscript of a novel unless it comes from an established literary agent. Literary agents have become gatekeepers who determine which manuscripts for novels get through to publishers for consideration and in what form they arrive. (Gatekeepers are discussed in greater detail in Chapter 14.) Publishers depend on agents to screen out manuscripts that are inappropriate for their company, to find new writers, to help authors polish their manuscripts, and even to think up ideas for books and recruit authors to turn the ideas into realities.

Review

Many factors affect the likelihood that a book will reach publication. The author's reputation, the likely market for the book, and the potential for adaptation to another medium are all taken into consideration. A key figure in the publication procedure is the literary agent, who represents the author.

This increase in the importance of the literary agent as gatekeeper has created a problem for many untested novelists. They cannot get their work considered for publication unless it goes through a literary agent, but many of the literary agents will not accept authors as clients until they have published. A similar problem exists for authors who are attempting to sell scripts for television or motion pictures.

For many kinds of books other than novels, and especially for textbooks, publishers will contract directly with authors rather than working through agents. This is also generally the case when a publisher has the idea for a book and commissions an author to write it.

The Business of Books

Of all the mass media, perhaps the greatest tension between aesthetics and economics is found in the book industry. Although there is often great concern for the artistic quality of works published, book publishing in this country is primarily a business. Publishers, essentially, are investors. They invest money in books in the hope of making a profit. They buy paper and ink and printing presses. They pay money to authors, editors, illustrators, printers, publicists, and others. They get money back from libraries and stores that sell books and from others who want the right to use the content of the book in some way. If they take in more money than they spend, they are successful. If they spend more than they take in, they go out of business. Recognizing these simple economic facts will help you understand why you are more likely to be exposed to some kinds of books than others. These are not the only relevant facts, of course, but they are fundamental ones.

Two trends, one minor and one major, are visible today in the publishing business. The minor trend is the move toward printing fewer copies of a book at any one time, but producing them faster. As one publisher put it, we are moving toward "books on demand." This trend has come about because of the rapidly rising costs of storing books. Publishers can no longer afford to carry a large stock, especially since the Internal Revenue Service ruled in 1981 that the value of publishers' inventories could not be reduced for tax purposes, as was allowed previously.

The other trend in publishing, as in all mass communication industries, is toward the merging of small firms into large firms, and these large firms into still larger ones. This is occurring both through the merger of companies and the acquisition of one company by another. With increased size a publisher is able to reduce overhead, warehouse, salary, and distribution costs per book produced by distributing these set costs over a large number of books. Almost all of the current major publishers are parts of larger media corporations. Bantam Doubleday Dell, for example, is a subsidiary of the German communication giant, Bertelsmann AG, while Harper and Row—renamed HarperCollins in 1990—is a part of Rupert Murdoch's News Corporation Ltd. In 1988 the Macmillan Company was acquired by British tycoon Robert Maxwell, who also owns a U.S. textbook publishing house, Science Research Associates. Crown, one of the largest independent publishers, was recently acquired by Random House. The 1989 merger of Time and Warner made that organization one of the ten largest trade book publishers in America (Table 3.2). One industry observer, noting the constant change of ownership among publishers, said that hardly a single publishing firm of any size was in the same hands in 1989 as it was at the start of the decade, and that many were part of corporations with headquarters in other countries.

REVIEW

Book publishing is primarily a business, and like other mass media, publishing houses tend to be parts of larger media corporations. In the 1980s there were many changes of ownership among publishers. Today ten publishing companies dominate the market.

TABLE 3.2 The Ten Largest Trade Book Publishers in America

Bantam Doubleday (Bertelsmann)
HarperCollins (News America Corp.)
Hearst Trade Book Group
Houghton Mifflin
Macmillan (Maxwell Communication Corp.)
Penguin USA (Pearson)
Putnam Berkley Group (MCA)
Random House, Inc. (Newhouse)
Simon & Schuster (Gulf + Western)
Time Warner

BYLINE

There is much debate about whether consolidation of publishing firms is beneficial or harmful to the interests of the reader. Do you think such consolidation increases or decreases the chances that aesthetics and the variety of readers will be considerations in publishing decisions?

Controls: Legal Constraints and Aids

Two major legal controls affect the presence and shape of books in our communication mosaics: copyright laws and censorship laws. These controls serve to constrain certain publishing practices. Overall, however, in this country they have probably aided publishers more than constrained them. This is especially true of copyright laws.

Copyright laws. The motive for the original copyright legislation in the United States was not simply the protection of the interests of authors or publishers, but the promotion of the public good. This was made clear in the report of a congressional committee in 1909 that recommended some revisions in the **Copyright Act,** *the law that protects an author's published works:*

> *The enactment of copyright legislation . . . is not based upon any natural right that the author has in his writings, for the Supreme Court has held that such rights as he has are purely statutory rights; but upon the ground that the welfare of the public will be served and progress of science and useful arts will be promoted by securing to authors for limited periods the exclusive rights to their writings.*[5]

In other words, copyright laws originally were not based primarily on the belief that individuals have rights to their intellectual and artistic property, in the same way that they have rights to their own tangible property such as real estate. The laws were based rather on the assumption that it is in the best interest of society to encourage the intellectual and creative activity of authors by protecting their rights to the materials they create. In fact, the preambles or title clauses of the copyright laws in 10 of the original 13 American states, enacted before there was federal legislation, state specifically that the purpose of these laws was to improve learning and to encourage the arts and sciences and other aspects of civilization.

The idea of copyright protection apparently originated in ancient Rome, back in the time of Cicero. Our own copyright legislation is based on the English law of the sixteenth century. Interestingly, that English statute, which dates from 1518, did not protect authors; it protected only the royal printer. The early copyright protection in the American colonies also ignored authors. Publishers and booksellers were protected from plagiarism, but not authors. Noah Webster, the famous compiler of dictionaries, and other authors both before and during the Revolutionary War fought unsuccessfully to get copyright protection for authors.

Not until 1781 did an American author win copyright protection. This was an author not of a book, but rather of a collection of songs. He got the Assembly of the State of Connecticut to pass a special act giving him exclusive rights to the printing and sale of his song for five years. A general statute protecting authors, titled an "Act for the encouragement of Literature and Genius," was enacted by the Connecticut Assembly in 1783. The first federal statute in the United States, passed in 1790, was based on the Connecticut law.

The federal copyright law, which restricted reprinting or importing copies of a work without an author's permission, stated that the courts could withdraw a copyright if an author did not make enough copies of a book available to the public or did not set a reasonable price on a book. The major intent of the legislation continued to be the spread of learning. A copyright protected an author's work for up to 28 years (14 years, plus an additional 14 if the copyright was renewed).

In 1831 the initial coverage period was extended to 28 years, with the renewal period kept at 14. The copyright act of 1909 extended the renewal period to 28 years, so that total coverage could be 56 years. The latest copyright statute, effective January 1, 1978, provides protection from the day of a work's creation until 50 years after the creator's death.

The present copyright law covers not only literary works, but also musical works (including lyrics); dramatic works; pantomimes and choreographic works; pictorial, graphic, and sculptural works; motion pictures and other audiovisual works; and sound recordings. Copyright protection does not extend "to any idea, procedure, process, system, method of operation, concept, principle, or discovery, regardless of the form in which it is described, explained, illustrated, or embodied."[6]

Because of the continuing congressional concern that copyright law facilitate rather than hinder the spread of learning, the statue provides for **fair use** of copyrighted material *without the prior permission of the copyright holder. A limited portion can be reproduced for purposes such as criticism, comment, news reporting, teaching, scholarship, or research.* Determining the amount of work that can be reproduced for these purposes is difficult. The copyright law states that:

> *In determining whether the use made of a work in any particular case is a fair use the factors to be considered shall include—*
>
> *(1)–the purpose and character of the use, including whether such use is of a commercial nature or is for nonprofit educational purposes;*
> *(2)–the nature of the copyrighted work;*
> *(3)–the amount and substantiality of the portion used in relation to the copyrighted work as a whole; and*
> *(4)–the effect of the use upon the potential market for or value of the copyrighted work.*[7]

In other words, a teacher has somewhat greater freedom to copy a small portion of a copyrighted work for classroom use than does an author who wants to use the material in a book that will be sold—even a textbook. You have greater freedom to use a newspaper story without the written consent of the copyrighted holder than you do a piece of music or a portion of a dramatic work. And the quotation of a sentence or two is more likely to be considered fair use than the quotation of an entire chapter.

Censorship. Censorship by government is not a problem for book publishers in the United States today. However, this has not always been the case.

Freedom of the press was not a characteristic of the American colonies. Printers were afraid of displeasing the king or his royal governors. As the Revolutionary War approached, they were also afraid of displeasing their increasingly militant fellow colonists. In spite of those fears, and in spite of the threats of the governors, political tracts began appearing with increasing frequency. One of the most important of these was Thomas Paine's *The American Crisis*, published in 1776. It did much to crystallize American public opinion in favor of independence:

> *These are the times that try men's souls. The summer soldier and the sunshine patriot will, in this crisis, shrink from the service of his country; but he that stands it now, deserves the love and thanks of man and woman. Tyranny, like Hell, is not easily conquered; yet we have this consolation with us, that the harder the conflict, the more glorious the triumph. What we obtain too cheap, we esteem too lightly; it is dearness only that gives everything its value. Heaven knows how to put a proper price upon its goods; and it would be strange indeed, if so celestial an article as FREEDOM should not be highly rated.*[8]

This "article"—freedom—was advanced later that year when the Continental Congress adopted the Declaration of Independence. It was advanced further, especially for the fledgling mass media, when the First United States Congress, at its initial session in New York City, submitted to the states a set of amendments to the Constitution. Freedom of the press, presumably, was ensured by the first of these amendments:

> *Congress shall make no law respecting an establishment of religion, or prohibiting the free exercise thereof; or abridging the freedom of speech, or of the press, or the right of the people peaceably to assemble, and to petition the Government for a redress of grievances.*[9]

This amendment and the rest of the **Bill of Rights**—*the first ten amendments to the Constitution*—were adopted by Congress at its first session on September 25, 1789, and submitted to the states for ratification. It went into effect on December 15, 1791, when the last of the required number of states had ratified it.

Threats to the principle of the First Amendment arose almost from the day it was ratified, and they continue to the present day. The first major threat came just seven years after ratification in the form of the **Sedition Law** of 1798, which, among other things, *prohibited the printing of libel against Congress or the president*. This act was used to prosecute some unfriendly editors, but it was soon drowned in the growing flood of belief in the importance of press freedom.

As indicated earlier, religious books dominated the American market in the 1700s, but then, as now, erotica was not unknown. The first and most famous book of erotica was titled *Memoirs of a Woman of Pleasure*. (You may know it under its more popular title, *Fanny Hill*.) It was published in England about 1749 and created a sensation. Copies could soon be found throughout much of the western world. Other books of erotica were published in America during this period, but *Fanny Hill* received most of the publicity and was the one most involved in censorship battles for almost one hundred fifty years.

This type of material—material related to sex—has been censored more consistently and successfully in this country than any other type. During the eighteenth century even dictionaries were expurgated to remove words that might offend adults or harm children. Noah Webster not only expurgated his dictionaries of all potentially offensive words; he even tried to cleanse the Bible of offensive language.[10]

REVIEW

Copyright laws protect authors from having their works reproduced without their consent or without compensation. Ever since colonial days government officials have attempted to censor books they considered offensive or obscene. In recent years the U.S. Supreme Court has severely limited this practice.

There is little censorship of books today by any level of government in the United States. Almost all the existing censorship is being done by a few isolated school boards worried about the content of some textbooks and school library books available to young students. But in 1982 the U.S. Supreme Court said that students were not without First Amendment rights when school board officials tried to remove library books they considered objectionable. The case involved the Island Trees School District in Long Island, New York. Board members declared that several junior and senior high school library books—such as Eldrige Cleaver's *Soul on Ice*, Kurt Vonnegut's *Slaughterhouse-Five*, and Bernard Malamud's *The Fixer*—were anti-American, anti-Christian, anti-Semitic, and just plain filthy. Although the court was divided in its opinion, the message to school boards across the country was that decisions to remove books based on objections to ideas in those books would be unconstitutional.

BYLINE

Where do you stand on the censorship issue? Should school board members, who are elected by the citizens of a community, have the power to censor the textbooks or library books used in a school, or should the selection of textbooks and library books be controlled totally by trained teachers and librarians? Should a book ever be censored in school because of the way it discusses or depicts sexual relationships? Because of the way it stereotypes women? Because it stereotypes or is derogatory to a particular ethnic group? Do you think you would respond to these questions in the same way if you had a ten-year-old child in the involved school?

OUR EXPOSURE TO BOOKS

Some social critics look at the statistics showing the large number of adult Americans who read no books and conclude either that television has caused a decline in the popularity of books or that the schools are not teaching people to read as well as they once did. There is only one problem with these explanations: The popularity of books has not declined. In fact, books have been steadily gaining in popularity during most of the period of television's growth—that same period during which the schools have been so heavily criticized.

Though censorship is rare in this country, there are those who deem certain books as inappropriate for children. The ad for People for the American Way, an anticensorship group, displays a few of the titles that have been removed from schools and library shelves.

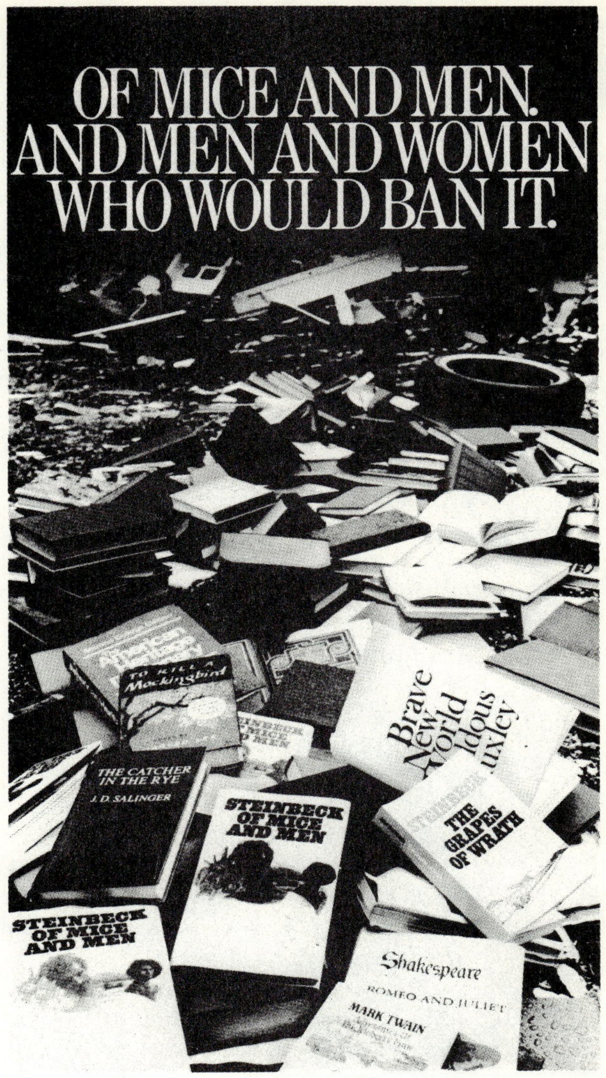

Despite the large number of nonreaders, an average of well over 3 million books are sold in the United States every day. In addition, millions of books are checked out from libraries and borrowed from friends. One sign of the increase in reading is the fact that a best-seller in the mid-1950s, such as *Marjorie Morningstar,* was bought by about 2 million people. Today, a best-seller such as *Windmills of the Gods* or *Fine Things* will be bought by more than twice that number in a single year.

Because books can be obtained in such a variety of ways, because more than one person can read each one, and because some books that are bought or borrowed go unread, it is difficult to discover precisely how many people in this country read books or how frequently they read. We do know there is great variability in the amount of book reading done by adult Americans. A surprising number read none at all. During any given year, less than half of adult Americans buy at least one book. One study estimated that a quarter of the population of the United States read ten books or more during the past six months, and another 30 percent read between one and nine books. About 39 percent read newspapers and magazines but no books. The remaining 6 percent read nothing.

Most book readers (58 percent) are women. They tend to be above average in education and income and under age fifty. Survey data show that most book reading is done in the evening, often in bed just before going to sleep. It also appears that most women read primarily for pleasure, most men for information.

Marketing Books Marketing is one of the most difficult problems the industry has. It is a far greater problem for books than for any other medium of mass communication. And because it is so difficult, it is expensive; marketing accounts for a large portion of each book's retail price.

Just consider the problems. Between forty thousand and fifty thousand completely new books are published each year—an average of about one hundred every single day—and many times that number continue to be available from previous years. Undoubtedly, many of these books would be interesting to you, and some would be interesting and useful to almost any other person. Probably no book is published that would not be of interest to some people somewhere, if those people were only aware of it. But there is the rub. How can publishers get information about each of these hundreds of thousands of books to the right individuals among the over two hundred million in our population, to say nothing of the hundreds of millions more potential readers in other countries? The answer is that they can't. The job of the marketing personnel in the publishing firms, however, is to try.

Publicists use every conceivable medium of communication to alert potential readers to the virtues of their particular books. They are constantly thinking of ways to get the books mentioned on television or radio programs, reviewed in newspapers, magazines, and journals, and displayed prominently in the windows and on the counters of bookstores and book departments in other stores. Sample copies of textbooks are distributed to teachers in the hope that they will find them interesting and adopt them for their classes. Authors are encouraged to travel about the country, appearing at autographing parties or in bookstores or, better yet, being interviewed on radio or television. An appearance by an author on a major television talk show ensures a sharp rise in sales for virtually any book.

Television appearances have become so important for the sales of some kinds of books that placing authors on major television programs has developed into a specialized business. In addition, publishers coach authors so that they will be better at selling themselves—and their books—on television. The national tour, with appearances on local radio and television stations, is often seen as an out-of-town tryout before an author is offered to one of the big-time programs such as the "Today" show, "Donahue," or "The Tonight Show." According to some publishers, an appearance on such programs is one of the most valuable sales boosters a book can have, second only to being a Book-of-the-Month Club selection.

Television can be a boon for publishers in another way. The dramatization of a book on television or in a theatrical film is profitable for an author and publisher both in the direct income from the sale of rights and in the increased book sales that result. In fact, there is a type of reciprocal relationship here. Large book sales increase the probability of a television or film adaptation, and the television or film presentation further increases the sales of the book. That happened to Alex Haley's *Roots*, for example, and to innumerable other books.

Computers may help publishers reduce, at least to some extent, the problem of getting information about the right books to the right potential readers. Publishers can pinpoint the most likely readers for almost any type of book by purchasing computerized mailing lists from a variety of sources. For example, if you were publishing a political novel, you might purchase the mailing list of *Time* or *Newsweek*, since their subscribers are more likely to want such a novel than people who do not read news magazines.

Publishers constantly seek the most cost-effective method of marketing books—the optimum balance of advertising, author tours, promotion to booksellers, and so on. The best combination, of course, varies with the kind of book, its potential market, and the fame and personality of its author.

Although it may seem like a high proportion, the rough guideline for money spent on promoting hardcover books is "a buck a book"—a dollar on promotion for every copy expected to be sold. Spending less than that will usually mean too many potential readers are not reached; spending more will probably reduce profits too much.

Spending a dollar a book for promotion is not out of line with the marketing budgets of other products in this country. In fact, it is a good bit less, proportional to the cost of the product, than what is spent for marketing consumer goods such as cereal or toothpaste.

Once potential readers know about a book, there is still the problem of getting it into their hands. A publisher has four primary means for distributing books: directly to individual consumers (through direct-mail promotion and sale or the publisher's own bookstores or subscription-selling system); to institutions, such as school systems or libraries; to retailers, such as retail bookstores or book clubs or sale-by-mail retailers; or through **jobbers,** *wholesalers who sell to retailers and institutions.*

The traditional, individually owned bookstore, once the heart of the book distribution system, is in serious difficulty today. It can no longer afford to keep large numbers of hardcover trade books in stock and is even having difficulty handling special orders for customers because high postage rates are eroding the profit margin. The result is disappointed customers who cannot find or obtain the books they want. These bookstores have lost customers to the paperback counters in department stores, drugstores, supermarkets, and a variety of other outlets. They have been hurt by the mail-order houses, which can afford postage because they have little overhead, and probably most especially by the book clubs.

Book clubs, which distribute books to their subscribers through the mail, are a twentieth-century phenomenon. More than one hundred fifty clubs, most of which cater to special interests, operate in the United States today. There are book clubs that distribute only books on science fiction, mystery, cooking, dieting, history, or even nostalgia. The two major and oldest book clubs, created in 1926 and 1927, are the Book-of-the-Month Club and the Literary Guild. Both handle general works of fact and fiction. Each has well over a million subscribers, as does the Reader's Digest Book Club, which distributes condensed books. Selection for distribution by one of the two main book clubs can guarantee the success of a book.

REVIEW

While there is a great deal of variability in book reading, less than half the adult population buys one book a year. Most book readers are women. One of the main problems facing publishers is how to reach potential readers. Publicists use every means possible to promote a new book. To market their books, publishers sell to individual consumers, institutions, retailers, and jobbers.

Some promising signs indicate that the bookstore may again become a familiar American phenomenon. It will not be the individually owned store, however, but part of a chain. Bookstore chains are expanding rapidly, with most of their stores located in shopping centers and malls. The two largest of these chains today, B. Dalton/Barnes & Noble and Waldenbooks, account for between one-third and one-half of all hardcover trade book and mass-market paperback sales. In contrast to the independent bookstore, chain stores are able to keep prices down and profits up through efficient management. Their large–scale purchasing keeps their costs down. They also keep their markup on books low, but make up for the lower profit on each individual book through the high volume of their sales. By using computerized inventory control they are able to ensure having in stock most of the books that customers want, rapid turnover, and little storage problem because they do not keep books in stock that fail to sell. Discount chains such as Crown are able to sell books at even lower prices by purchasing very cheaply stocks of former best sellers and other works that publishers have overstocked and either cannot sell or cannot afford to store.

Three major factors in the widespread distribution of books in America today are the free public library, the increasing availability of relatively cheap paperbacks, and the popularity of higher education—coupled, of course, with compulsory education at lower levels.

The Growth of Libraries

As indicated earlier, libraries have existed since at least the fourth century B.C. However, until after the American Civil War, they tended to be either individually owned, part of an educational institution, or a commercial enterprise that rented books. We have had free public libraries in this country only since 1852. Free public libraries spread rapidly in the latter part of the nineteenth century, spurred by endowments from some wealthy industrialists, especially Andrew Carnegie, and by state legislatures that made the establishment of community libraries compulsory. New Hampshire passed the pioneer statute of that sort in 1895.

The public library today is an important element in almost every American community; some believe it is second in importance for a community only to the local school system.

The Mass Market Paperback

The inexpensive, pocket-size paperback has also contributed to making the book more of a mass medium, both because of its price and because of its availability. Paperback stands are found today almost everywhere—in drugstores, newsstands, department stores, supermarkets, toy stores, bus and train stations, and airports.

Although paperback books were being produced even before the Civil War, they were not a tremendously important part of the industry until relatively recent times. Because of their price and clever marketing, they make up a healthy portion of books sold today. The classic book on child care by Dr. Benjamin Spock has sold more than 39 million copies since Pocket Books introduced it in 1946. It's a fairly safe bet that this book, and several of the other best-selling paperbacks shown in Table 3.3, have been

TABLE 3.3 Pocket-size Paperbacks: The Twenty All-time Best Sellers

	Number of Copies Sold
Baby and Child Care by Dr. Benjamin Spock (1946)	39,200,000
Merriam Webster Dictionary (1974)	19,700,000
New American Roget's College Thesaurus (1957)	17,620,000
How To Win Friends and Influence People by Dale Carnegie (1940)	17,400,000
The Hobbit by J. R. R. Tolkien (1972)	14,500,000
The American Heritage Dictionary (1970)	12,983,480
1984 by George Orwell (1950)	12,800,000
The New American Webster's Handy College Dictionary (1956)	12,600,000
The Exorcist by William Peter Blatty (1972)	12,400,000
French/English, English/French Dictionary, Larousse (1955)	11,300,000
The Thorn Birds by Colleen McCullough (1978)	10,880,000
Spanish/English, English/Spanish Dictionary edited by Carlos Castillo and Otto F. Bond (1950)	10,800,000
Animal Farm by George Orwell (1956)	10,470,000
Mythology by Edith Hamilton (1953)	10,000,000
Catcher in the Rye by J. D. Salinger (1964)	9,650,000
Love Story by Erich Segal (1970)	9,500,000
Peyton Place by Grace Metalious (1957)	9,468,566
Valley of the Dolls by Jacqueline Susann (1967)	9,451,000
The Pearl by John Steinbeck (1948)	9,430,000
The Sensuous Woman by "J" (1971)	9,377,592

Source: Compiled by Daisy Maryles for a forthcoming PW/Bowker Book, *Bestsellers, 1895–1990*. Reprinted from the October 27, 1989 issue of PUBLISHERS WEEKLY, published by Cahners Publishing Company, a division of Reed Publishing USA. Copyright © 1989 by Publishing USA.

a part of your mosaic environment. And years from now you will probably have in your home some dog-eared, pocket-size paperbacks—including such best-sellers as the dictionary and *Roget's Thesaurus*—that you purchased in college.

The parent, or perhaps the grandparent, of the paperback was the dime novel—short, easy-to-read western, love, or adventure stories, popular in the latter half of the nineteenth century, that sold, of course, for ten cents. The modern counterparts of the dime novel are among the top-selling books in the country. They even follow the same format, although many rely a good bit more on sex. Three of the most popular authors of these modern dime novels (which sell for considerably more than ten cents these days) are Harold Robbins, who builds his novels around sex and celebrities, Barbara Cartland and her historical romances, and the late Louis L'Amour, whose western novels were very much in the traditional mold. L'Amour wrote some 103 westerns, 90 of which sold more than a million copies.

REVIEW

Public libraries and inexpensive paperbacks—especially pocket-sized paperbacks—have contributed to the popularity of books.

FUNCTIONS AND EFFECTS OF BOOKS

Books serve a variety of functions for most of us. If we want to learn something other than current events, whether in school or out, we are more likely to turn to books than any other medium of communication. Many of us also use books for inspiration—religious material, history, the biographies of great people—and entertainment—mysteries, love stories, adventures, and poetry.

Some books have had surprising impact. Harriet Beecher Stowe's *Uncle Tom's Cabin* is credited with helping to precipitate the Civil War. Noah Webster's spelling book, first published in 1783 because he was unhappy about the use of British textbooks in a country that had won its independence, helped break England's hold over our language and, in effect, taught America how to spell.

Books provide, in large part, the cultural standards for our country. And the mark of the cultivated citizen is more often knowledge of books, especially the novel, than any other quality.

The book has also been the model for much of contemporary film, television, and radio drama, since these follow the narrative forms first developed in novels and short stories. And most news stories today, though less obviously, follow the narrative form.

Some observers attribute even further-reaching impact to the development of printing and books. It has been claimed that because the ready availability of printed material reduced the importance and the practice of memorizing in the schools, most people are unable to commit to memory the large amount of matter that their forebears did. It has also been claimed, most notably by the late Canadian media guru Marshall McLuhan, that the linear, one-at-a-time structure of printing has shaped the way

The Jesse James stories and other dime novels were the predecessors of today's mass-market paperbacks.

REVIEW

Books function for us or affect us in many ways. They provide information, inspiration, cultural standards, and a model for other media. One media scholar believes books shape the way we think.

we think. According to McLuhan's theory, people brought up primarily on print, as opposed to radio, television, and the motion picture, are more likely to analyze problems in a linear fashion, taking one thing at a time and tracing the straight logic. Although neither of these claims—that print affected our ability to memorize and the structure of our thinking—has been proven, each may have some validity. They are interesting ideas to contemplate with all of the other wonders of books.

BYLINE

How do you use books? Are there particular times that you are more likely to read books that are unrelated to your academic work? Do you read books for relaxation or stimulation? Or do you read them for some totally different reasons?

BOOKS, THE FIRST OF OUR MASS MEDIA: A SUMMARY

The clearest way to summarize most of the major points in this chapter is with Figure 3.1. This chart suggests the variety of relationships that must exist and functions that must be carried out in order to get ideas into book form and the book into the hands of readers.

Books are the most varied of our mass media of communication, both in content and in the ways in which we become exposed to them. The first exposure for most of us was to those picture and number books our relatives bought to stimulate and entertain us in our preschool years. Our teachers introduced us to the range of knowledge to be found between book covers. If we were lucky, we discovered the local public library at an early age and found we could travel alone in the world of Oz and the Wild West, through a wonderland with Alice or the dens of London with Sherlock Holmes and Oliver Twist. We learned of the unexpected pleasures to be gained from books we had never heard of, and we also learned that we could find a book about almost anything if we searched hard enough. Almost half of American adults apparently never learned of these wonders, for they seldom if ever read a book. Even when you graduate from college, the chances are greater than one in five that you will not be a regular book reader.

Costs of books have been held down to some extent and availability expanded by the phenomenal spread of paperback books. In a sense, the paperback has democratized the purchase and reading of books.

Books come into being in a variety of ways. For the novel and many general interest books, the literary agent has become a type of midwife, helping the author through the difficult birth period. Even more, the literary agent introduces the fertile idea at times and, when the infant book is born, carries it lovingly to a publisher for discipline and refinement and proper introduction to society.

Publishing is a business in this country, as other mass communication industries are. For publishers, however, there are greater difficulties in getting the right product into the right hands; from the point of view of the audience member—you and us—there are greater difficulties learning about all of the books available and then locating copies of those that interest us.

Periodically we hear that the book is dead, a victim of creeping illiteracy or the latest communications technology. Mark Twain, after seeing his obituary in a newspaper, cabled the Associated Press, "The reports of my death are greatly exaggerated." So it is with the book.

FIGURE 3.1
The book cycle.

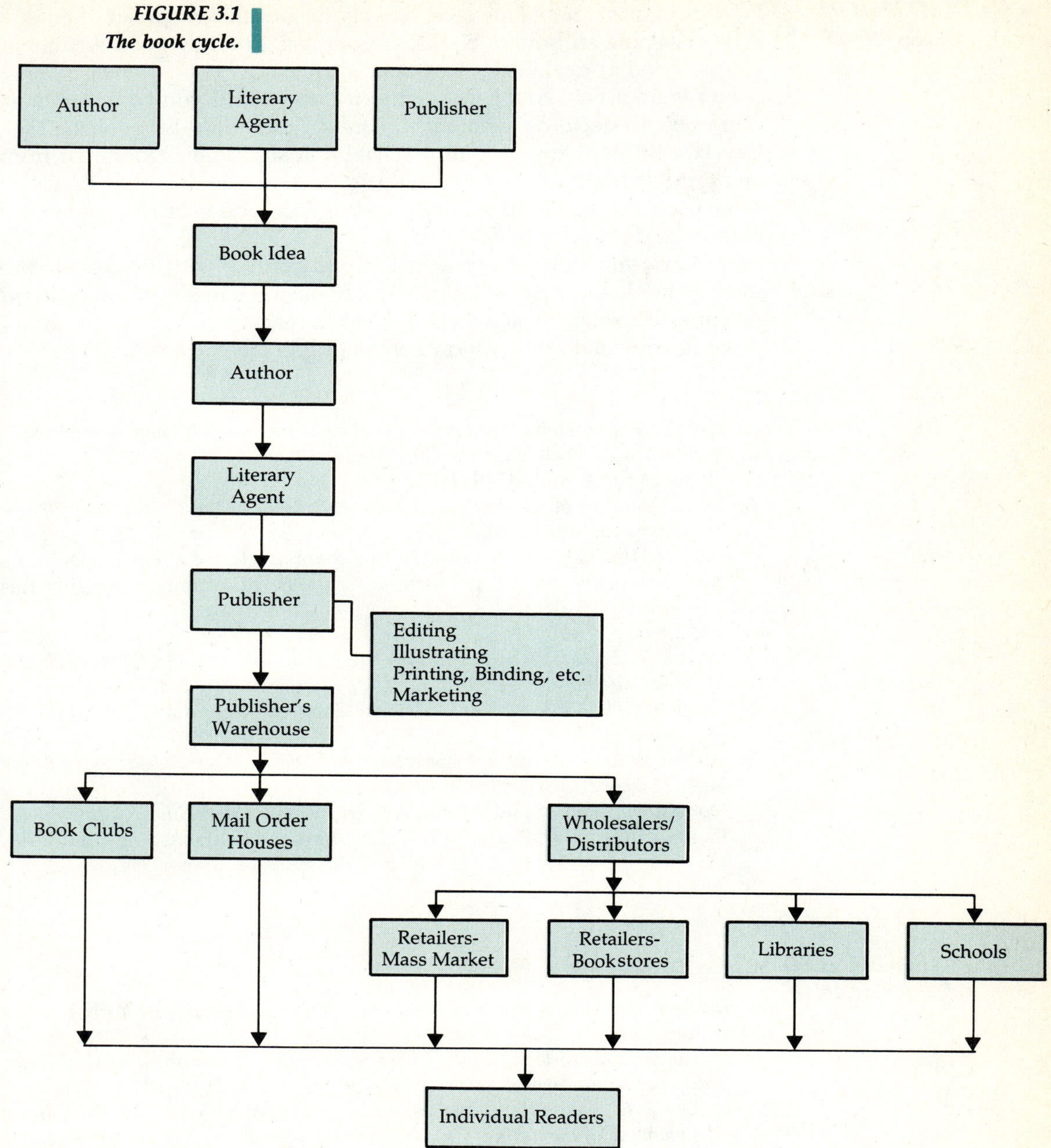

DISCUSSION QUESTIONS

1. Why did governments move so quickly to control the spread of books?
2. Why are some authors of books so popular? Are they good writers or simply good at exploiting the public's taste?
3. If you were a book publisher, what factors would you consider most important in deciding whether a manuscript should be published?
4. Can you think of any kind of material that should be prohibited from being published?
5. What factors are related to book reading? Do you ever read books for pleasure? If so, what kind?
6. Where are you most likely to come into contact with books—at the campus bookstore? At the library? At bookstores in shopping centers? At supermarkets? Or at specialty bookstores?
7. What is your main motivation for reading books?

NOTES

1. Elizabeth Eisenstein, *The Printing Press as an Agent of Change* (Cambridge, England: Cambridge University Press, 1980).
2. Howell's State Trials 1246 (1693).
3. John Tebbel et al., *A History of Book Publishing in the United States* (New York: Bowker, 1972), vol. 1, *The Creation of an Industry,* 1630–1865, p. 1. Much of the historical material in this chapter is based upon Tebbel. For a complete history of the publishing industry, we recommend highly this four-volume work.
4. Ibid., pp. 1-2.
5. Luther H. Evans, "Copyright and the Public Interest," in *Bowker Lectures on Book Publishing* (New York: R. R. Bowker, 1957), p. 258.
6. Public Law 94–553, 90 Stat, 2541, 9th Congress, Sec. 102.
7. Ibid., Sect. 107.
8. Arthur Wallace Peach, ed., *Selections from the Work of Thomas Paine* (New York: Harcourt, Brace, 1928), p. 43.
9. Donald M. Gillmor and Jerome A. Barron, eds., *Mass Communication Law: Cases and Comment,* 3rd ed. (St. Paul, Minn.: West Publishing Co., 1979), p.1.
10. Tebbel, p. 177.

SUGGESTED READINGS

Relevant Contemporary Works

Bowker Annual of Library and Book Trade Information. 35th ed. New York: Bowker Annual, 1990.

This annual work covers the business aspects of the publishing industry, legal aspects, design and technology, and retailing.

Coser, Lewis A., Kadushin, Charles, and Powell, Walter W. *Books: The Culture and Commerce of Publishing.* Chicago: University of Chicago Press, 1982.

Davidson, Cathy N. *Revolution and the World: The Rise of the Novel in America.* New York: Oxford University Press, 1986.

Davis, Kenneth C. *Two-Bit Culture: The Paperbacking of America.* Boston: Houghton-Mifflin, 1984.

Dessauer, John P. *Book Publishing: A Basic Introduction*. New York: Continuum, 1989.

Schramm, Wilbur. *The Story of Human Communication: Cave Painting to Microchip*. New York: Harper & Row, 1988.

Tebbel, John. *Between Covers: The Rise and Transformation of Book Publishing in America*. New York: Oxford University Press, 1987.

Tebbel, John, et al. *A History of Book Publishing in the United States*. New York: Bowker, 1972–1981.

Vol. 1, The Creation of an Industry, 1630–1865.
Vol. 2, The Expansion of an Industry, 1865–1919.
Vol. 3, The Golden Age Between Two Wars, 1920–1940.
Vol. 4, The Great Change, 1940–1980.

CHAPTER 4

NEWSPAPERS: THE FOURTH ESTATE

OBJECTIVES

After studying this chapter, you should be able to

- Trace the history of the newspaper in America from colonial times to the present.
- Describe the organization and operation of a typical newspaper.
- Explain the various constraints on newspapers.
- Describe the trends in circulation and number of newspapers in this country over the past one hundred years.
- Discuss the technological changes that have benefited the newspaper industry.
- Note the trends toward chain ownership and standardization.
- Describe the reading habits of the newspaper audience.
- Discuss briefly the functions and effects of newspapers.

Were it left to me to decide whether we should have a government without newspapers or newspapers without a government, I should not hesitate a moment to prefer the latter.

Thomas Jefferson
Letter to Colonel Edward Carrington
January 16, 1787

The man who never looks into a newspaper is better informed than he who reads them, inasmuch as he who knows nothing is nearer the truth than he whose mind is filled with falsehoods and errors.

Thomas Jefferson
Letter to John Norvell
June 14, 1807

It should come as no surprise that Thomas Jefferson made one of those statements about newspapers before he became president and the other after he assumed the presidency. Most chief executives in this country at one time or another have blamed the press—particularly newspapers—for their political problems. Historian Forrest McDonald claims that the first draft of George Washington's Farewell Address was such a diatribe against the press that Alexander Hamilton had to rewrite it.[1] Ronald Reagan, in one of his last speeches before leaving office, attributed his inability to reduce the huge federal deficit to an "iron triangle" of Congressmen, lobbyists, and journalists.

Reagan's characterization of the press is not unlike that of English historian Thomas Babington Macaulay, who dubbed the press the "Fourth Estate."[2] So important is the press to our form of government that it has been given constitutional protection. The framers of the Constitution believed that the press—which in those days consisted mainly of newspapers, newsletters, and pamphlets—was necessary to ensure an informed electorate and serve as the people's watchdogs on government.

Today, newspapers serve a variety of needs and form an important part of our mosaic environment. We depend more on our local papers than any other medium to stay informed of what is going on in our community, which stores have sales, what movie is playing where, and many other useful bits of knowledge. During the 1989 San Francisco earthquake, one survivor was quoted as saying: "Having a newspaper is like having a piece of gold."[3]

It is probably because they are so important that newspapers receive so much criticism. This criticism serves as a constant reminder of the needs of individuals and society that newspapers are expected to meet. An examination of some of the highlights in the history of newspapers, as well as of the ways newspapers operate, should help you weigh the criticism of present-day newspapers and, most important, to use and interpret more intelligently what you read in newspapers so they better serve your needs.

1600–1799

1665
Early newspapers published in England

1690
America's first paper stopped by King's governor in Boston after one issue

1704
Boston News-Letter begins; soon carries advertising

1735
John Peter Zenger on trial for publishing antigovernment articles

1792
Post Office Act gives newspapers special low mailing rates

1793
Noah Webster begins editorial columns

1800–1899

1828
Freedom's Journal founded—first newspaper in America published by blacks

1831
The Liberator, an antislavery paper, begins in Boston

1833
Penny press initiated in NYC

1844
Samuel Morse perfects telegraph

1848
Associated Press founded in NYC

1851
New York Times established

c1889
Comics appear in New York *World*

1899
Ass'n of American Advertisers hires staff to verify publishers' circulation claims

1900–1949

1904
The Daily Mirror, newspaper for women, started

1906
Gannett newspaper chain begins

1907
E.W. Scripps organizes United Press Associations

1914
Number of U.S. dailies reaches peak of almost 2500

1915
National syndication of comic strips initiated

1917
Newspapers accept voluntary censorship as U.S. enters World War I

1923
American Society of Newspaper Editors adopts Canons of Journalism

1950–1979

1950
Photo offset printing becomes practical

1958
United Press and International News Service become UPI; only 2 major wire services left

1963
Use of computers for newspaper typesetting becomes common

1970
Congress passes Newspaper Preservation Act to save failing newspapers

1973
National News Council established to review national news media

1980–1989

1981
Decline of afternoon daily dramatized by death of Washington *Star*

1982
National general interest newspaper, *USA Today*, is born

1989
Supreme Court permits merger of noneditorial operations of *Detroit News* and archrival *Detroit Free Press*

EARLY NEWSPAPER DEVELOPMENTS

The forerunner of the newspaper in America was the **newsletter,** *a short, periodic report for business and government leaders to keep them informed of shipping and financial transactions and important political events.* Newsletters were written by professionals in the major government and business centers around the world. In addition to the newsletter, during the colonial days periodic pamphlets about important public questions were circulated. The more mundane news—hangings, the capture of a pirate, or local bits of gossip—was often put into poetic form and sung by balladeers to the cadence of some well-known tune.

Regularly issued publications that could be termed newspapers had been published in Great Britain since at least 1665. A few of these found their way to the American colonies. Twenty-five years after the initial newspaper appeared in Britain, a similar publication was started in Boston. From the explicitness of its title, *Publick Occurrences Both Foreign and Domestick,* we can see that newspapers were not familiar objects in the American colonies. The publisher promised to issue the paper once a month, "or if any Glut of Occurrences happen, oftener." Unfortunately, we have no way of knowing whether any "glut of occurrences" happened: the provincial Council and the King's Governor banned the paper after the publication of only one issue because the publisher had no license. The authorities made clear that nothing was to be printed and distributed in the future unless a license was first obtained from the government.

A year earlier, the government of Massachusetts began permitting the publication of an occasional news sheet titled *The Present State of New-English Affairs*. Beneath that heading was the announcement that "This is Published to Prevent False Reports."

A longer-lived American newspaper was started in 1704 by a bookseller and local postmaster named John Campbell. This was the weekly *Boston News-Letter.* It had only one page, about the size of a standard sheet of today's typing paper, and was printed on both sides. It was generally a rather staid publication, except when reporting on pirates. The newspaper's most sensational story was its account of the slaying of the pirate Blackbeard during hand-to-hand combat on the deck of a ship. Then, as now, the line between information and entertainment in the news columns was not always clear.

The Zenger Case

By 1735 there were five newspapers in Boston—a town that then had fewer than 20,000 people. One of the most important events connected with the early history of mass communication occurred that year in New York, then the third largest city in the colonies. A young immigrant named John Peter Zenger had started a newspaper there in 1733 called the *New York Weekly Journal*. He was arrested because his newspaper championed the cause of people who challenged the authority of the Royal Governors. At the trial, which took place in 1735, he was represented by one of the most famous attorneys in the colonies, Andrew Hamilton. Hamilton's final

Benjamin Franklin's older brother, James Franklin, introduced the New England Courant *in 1721. It was noted for its provocative news and comments and high literary style.*

N 27

THE

New-England Courant.

From MONDAY January 29. to MONDAY February 5. 1722.

Aliud eſt maledicere, aliud accuſare. Cic.

A JUDICIOUS Author obſerves, That there is nothing in which Men more deceive themſelves than in what the World call Zeal. There are ſo many Paſſions which hide themſelves under it, and ſo many Miſchiefs ariſing from it, that ſome have gone ſo far as to ſay, it would have been for the Benefit of Mankind, if it had never been reckoned in the Catalogue of Virtues. The fatal Effects of Zeal among our Selves, has almoſt perſwaded me to be of this Opinion. A furious pretended Zeal, which only regards Matters of Opinion, has been improv'd againſt my ſelf with a Deſign to deſtroy my Reputation and Intereſt amongſt thoſe who are Strangers to my Perſon: And that this Deſign might be the better carried on, ſome Perſons have been ſo *undutiful* to the Reverend Dr. *Increaſe Mather*, as to perſwade him to prefix his Name to an Advertiſement in the laſt Weeks *News-Letter* and *Gazette*, wherein the mildeſt Appellation I meet with, is that of a wicked and curſed Libeller. This Charge I now lye under from the oldeſt Miniſter in the Country, and in order to clear my ſelf I ſhall firſt give an Account of the firſt Cauſe of the Difference between us.

The Week before the *Courant* of *Jan.* 1. came out, a Grandſon of Dr. *Increaſe Mather* brought me the following Account of the Succeſs of Inoculation in *London*,

A Paſſage in the London Mercury, Sept. 16.

'Great Numbers of Perſons in the City and the Suburbs 'are under the Inoculation of the Small Pox. Among the 'reſt, the eldeſt Son of a noble Duke in Hanover Square, 'had the Small Pox inoculated upon him.

This he ſaid his Grandfather deſir'd me to inſert in my next, and affirm'd that he had tranſcrib'd it himſelf, and that it was Word for Word with the Account in the *London Mercury*. About Noon on the Day that the *Courant* came out, I ſaw the Four firſt Pages of the *London Mercury* of *Sept.* 16. and found nothing in them, but that *the eldeſt Son of a noble Duke in Hanover Square, had the Small Pox inoculated upon him INCOGNITO*. Here our young Spark was detected in a downright Falſhood, and loſt his Credit with *Couranto*; and I had great Reaſon too to believe that the firſt Part of the above Paragraph was not in the other Half-Sheet of the *Mercury*, becauſe both Paſſages related to Inoculation, and might (no doubt) have been as well inſerted together. The next Week I inſerted a Letter in the *Courant*, which aſſerted, that the former Part of the Paſſage, viz. *Great Numbers of* [illegible] proving it. Whether he remembers it or no, his Grand[illegible] *Biles*, by his Order, deſir'd me to ſet him down as a Cuſtomer ſome Time ago; but upon the Appearance of a Letter in the *Courant*, wherein a certain Clergyman was touch'd upon, he dropt it as a Subſcriber, but ſent his Grandſon almoſt every Week for a conſiderable Time to buy them; by which Method he paid more for the Paper and was more a Supporter of it, than if his Name had been continu'd in the Liſt. At length, being weary with ſending, he became a Subſcriber again, and expreſs'd no Diſlike of the Paper till after Mr. *Muſgrave* had publiſh'd his Grandſon's Letter in the *Gazette* of *Jan.* 15. So that he both had and paid me for one Paper after that which he ſo much diſlikes. The Truth of this I am ready to declare upon Oath, againſt the Teſtimony of all the Men in the Country. And that he has been a Subſcriber, and conſequently a Supporter of the Paper, the following Letter under his own Hand, will ſufficiently prove.

Mr. *Franklin*,

'I Had Thoughts of taking your *Courant* (upon Tryal) for 'a Quarter of a Year; but I ſhall not now. In one of 'your Courants you have ſaid that *if the Miniſters of God 'are for a Thing, it is a Sign it is from the Devil*, and have 'dealt very falſly about the *London Mercury*. For theſe and 'other Reaſons, I ſhall NO MORE be concerned with you.

Your well wiſhing, but grieved Friend,

I. Mather.

In the next Place he ſays, *In one of his vile Courants, he inſinuates, that if the Miniſters of God do approve of a Thing, its a ſign it is of the Devil, which is a horrid Thing to be related.*

The Words in the *Courant* are in a Dialogue (by an unknown Hand) between a Clergyman and Layman, and are exactly as follows,

Cl. But I find, all the Rakes in Town are againſt Inoculation, and that induces me to believe it is a right Way.

Laym. Moſt of the Miniſters are for it, and that induces me to think it is from the D——l; for he often makes uſe of good Men as Inſtruments to obtrude his Deluſions on the World.

The Doctor muſt know, that Satan once ſtood up againſt Iſrael, and provoked *DAVID* to number the People. *Joab*, his wicked General, was not ſo eaſily provok'd to this Evil: The King's Word was abominable to *him*. This is Doctrine which I have often heard from the Pulpit, and if I am condem'd for publiſhing it, I may venture to ſay (in the Words of the Doctor's Grandſon, that I have Company *of which I need not be aſhamed*.

Again, *And altho' in one of the* Courants *it is declared, that the* London Mercury Sept. 16. 1721. *affirms*, That Great Numbers of Perſons in the City and Suburbs are under the Inoculation of the Small Pox; *in his next* Courant *he aſſerts*, That it was ſome buſy Inoculator, that impoſed on the Publick in ſaying ſo.

words in his summation to the jury were eloquent in their defense of freedom of speech and the press:

> *The question before the court and you gentlemen of the jury is not of small or private concern; it is not the cause of the poor printer, nor of New York, alone. No! It may, in its consequences, affect every freeman that lives under a British government on the main of America. It is the best cause. It is the cause of liberty . . . the liberty both of exposing and opposing arbitrary power by speaking and writing truth.*[4]

Although the Zenger trial, which led to an acquittal, set no legal precedent, it strongly influenced Americans' feelings about the importance of freedom of the press.

Because of journalists such as Zenger, newspapers gained great prestige among the colonists during the revolutionary period, and after the war they spread rapidly. This expansion was due in part to the fact that the American press at that time had more freedom than the press anywhere else in the world. American newspapers flourished in the climate that had been created by the John Peter Zengers and the Thomas Paines and by the First Amendment.

The Sedition Act The First Amendment, however, did not resolve all problems of censorship in this new republic. Less than twenty years after the close of the Revolutionary War, when war with France was imminent, Congress attempted to still criticism of the administration by passing the Sedition Act. As explained in Chapter Three, this act specified that anyone who made a "false, scandalous, and malicious" statement against part of the government that was intended to defame it could be sent to prison for up to two years and fined up to $2000.

Cases were brought against a number of publishers under the Sedition Act. One had accused Alexander Hamilton of promoting a scheme to buy and silence an opposition newspaper. Another was prosecuted for criticizing the Massachusetts legislature for not fighting the Alien and Sedition Acts. And yet another was fined and imprisoned for calling President John Adams an incompetent.

One interesting and important aspect of the Sedition Act was the provision that "truth" was an adequate defense against the charge of sedition. A result of that provision was that the journalist who called President Adams incompetent attempted to get the president to appear as a witness at the trial so it could be proven that the charge was true. The court, however, refused to subpoena the president.

This provision of the Sedition Act was important because the relevance of truth as a defense against censorship or prosecution is still an issue. In libel cases, for example, in which a newspaper is accused of harming someone's reputation, proving the truth of what was published is an adequate defense against prosecution in some states but not in others. This raises the more basic issue of whether "truth" or "responsibility" is a necessary condition of the freedom that the First Amendment gives to the press. The question is much debated, at least indirectly, these days. The position of the Supreme Court—so far—is that the First Amendment neither says nor suggests that the press must be truthful or responsible; it says only that it must be free. Thus, presumably, the press can be more courageous, acting without fear of charges that it erred or was irresponsible.

However, this situation may be changing as news media more frequently are finding themselves charged with **libel**—*publishing information that damages someone's reputation*—and many juries and judges are not accepting the First Amendment as an adequate defense. Traditionally, the news media have had more freedom to criticize and report unfavorable

REVIEW

The John Peter Zenger case and the Sedition Act are two examples of early attempts to control the press in America.

information about a political figure or other persons in the news than they did to criticize or report unfavorably on ordinary citizens. This is still the case to some extent, although the distinction appears to be lessening.

BYLINE

Do you agree or disagree with the Supreme Court that freedom of the press should not depend on truthfulness or responsibility? If you disagree, would you rewrite the First Amendment? How? If you agree, does that mean that your local newspaper should be free to publish anything that it wishes about you, whether true or not? How can we balance freedom of the press with the rights of individuals to privacy and their good names? Where should freedom of the press end and the rights of individuals begin?

Partisan Journalism In the history of newspapers, there have been times when publishers were hardly concerned with truth or responsibility. The period from the eighteenth century through the early part of the nineteenth century was such a time. Throughout the eighteenth century, most journalists sprinkled their news stories with personal opinions and arguments, often with little regard for where facts ended and opinions began. The idea of journalistic "objectivity" had not yet become popular. For many journalists, a prime motivation in publishing a paper was the opportunity it gave them to circulate their opinions. One of the worst aspects of this lack of objectivity and the use of a newspaper for the wide circulation of a publisher's opinions was the practice of viciously attacking political opponents. Many of the attacks were quite personal, crude, and dishonest. Consider this "news" story, for example, published during Thomas Jefferson's campaign for the presidency:

> *Should the Infidel Jefferson be elected to the Presidency, the* seal of death *is that moment set on our holy religion, our churches will be prostrated, and some infamous prostitute, under the title of the Goddess of Reason, will preside in the Sanctuaries now devoted to the Most High.*[5]

This type of unobjective, partisan journalism reached its zenith in the early part of the nineteenth century. However, at the same time such newspaper attacks were at their worst, a seed was being planted that was destined to grow and eclipse this highly partisan style of journalism. That seed was the idea of editorial columns or pages, and the sower of the seed was Noah Webster, who later became famous for his dictionary. Webster began an editorial column in the newspaper he started in 1793, *The American Minerva*. The ground was apparently ready for such seed, for by the time of the Civil War, editorial columns and pages were regular parts of a large percentage of American newspapers.

This is not to suggest that any of the news media are, or can be, totally objective. As we have said, news is *about* events, people, or ideas; it is not the same thing as the events, people, or ideas. News is something *constructed* by human beings with words and pictures, using their highly selective and limited knowledge of the world as the basis. The point, then, is not that news is either objective or unobjective but that most journalists today are more concerned about objectivity, fairness, and accuracy than they were a century ago. As a result, readers, listeners, and viewers are better served.

Advertising

Advertising became important early in the history of the newspaper business. By the middle of the eighteenth century it was the chief difference between a newspaper's being profitable and going broke. The *Boston News-Letter* began carrying ads in 1704. By the time the Revolutionary War broke out in 1775, all 37 of the newspapers in the colonies contained them. A leading figure in the American Revolution, Benjamin Franklin, was also responsible for revolutionizing advertising. His newspaper, the *Pennsylvania Gazette,* led the way toward making advertising more attractive through the imaginative use of space and more varied sorts of type. Prior to Franklin's time, all ads looked rather like the classified ads of today, run together in tightly packed columns of type.

Speeding Up the News

You may be surprised to know that newspapers were not always as concerned with up-to-the-minute news as they are today. This value developed in the early part of the nineteenth century. Part of the problem, of course, was that technology for rapid transmission of information did not exist until fairly recent times. News from Europe came by sailing vessel, which meant it usually took about two months to get into print in America. Even American news took time to spread across the country. When George Washington died in 1799, it was two days before the news appeared in the newspaper in his hometown, and that was the first paper in the country to carry the story. Not until a week after his death was the story of our first president's death published in a New York newspaper; 11 days passed before one could read about it in Boston; almost a month went by before it appeared in Cincinnati. Compare this to the speed of diffusion of the assassination of President John Kennedy in 1963. The news appeared within 24 hours in almost every daily newspaper in the world. Because of radio and television, 99.8 percent of Americans knew of his assassination within five and one-half hours of the time the event occurred.

REVIEW

Early newspapers were far from objective. The ads they carried resembled today's classified ads. Also, news traveled much more slowly then.

Newspapers for the Common People

Until the early part of the nineteenth century, newspapers were quite expensive. A year's subscription cost as much as a skilled laborer could earn in a week. As a result, the bulk of the public did not buy or read papers. Because of the importance of newspapers for the development of a society such as ours, the country needed a cheap newspaper that the general public could afford—and we got it. This was the **penny press,** *newspapers that sold for just that—one penny an issue. These were the first newspapers in America published for the general public.* The penny press was crucial to the growth of mass communication in America, for it brought virtually all economic classes into the ranks of newspaper readers. The development of the penny press was closely related to the larger Industrial Revolution, which transformed the entire social structure of much of the western world.

The pioneer among these cheap newspapers was the New York *Morning Post,* which came in with the new year on January 1, 1833. It lasted little longer than two weeks, even though the price per issue was slashed from two cents to one during its final few days. The printer associated with this historic venture was Horace Greeley, later to become one of the most famous newspaper editors in America. The first successful penny newspaper was *The New York Sun,* started later that same year, and edited and published by another printer, Benjamin H. Day. The *Sun's* lively style and emphasis on local stories captured the attention and the pennies of New Yorkers.

Two aspects of the penny press were revolutionary for that day: the price, and the idea of selling newspapers by the individual copy rather than solely by subscription. It was far easier for working people to find a penny or two to pay for each single issue of a paper than to save enough pennies to pay for an entire year's subscription. Thus, for the first time, the working class was brought into the ranks of newspaper readers.

The penny press also contributed to speeding up news coverage. These papers were highly competitive, and their competition was soon reflected in their trying to "scoop" each other. They used speedboats to try to beat each other to incoming ships in order to get the latest foreign news first, and they used horse expresses to get the news from Washington quickly. Even carrier pigeons were used to obtain news stories more quickly. The major advance in speed came with the telegraph, which newspapers began using in 1844. This revolutionary device was quickly adopted by most newspapers. By 1846, for example, all of the papers in New York had a column headed "By Magnetic Telegraph."

The Development of Human Interest Stories

With the development of the penny press came another, extremely important shift. This was the shift from newspapers that were highly partisan politically, often aided financially by the various political factions, to newspapers that were politically independent. In fact, after the Civil War the emphasis on political and governmental news declined. Newspapers broadened the scope of their news coverage. They also broadened their definitions of news to include the human interest story.

One of the more exotic of these human interest stories was the expedition of a former war correspondent, Henry Stanley, into the heart of central Africa to find the lost missionary and explorer, David Livingstone.

This expedition was sponsored by the *New York Herald,* which reported its every detail. (The Stanley and Livingstone story ultimately became a book and movie, as mentioned in Chapter 3.)

The journalist who was perhaps most influential in setting the pattern of modern journalism was Joseph Pulitzer, publisher of the *St. Louis Post-Dispatch* and, later, the *New York World.* He developed many techniques for making his papers more interesting to the mass audience. These techniques proved so successful that they were soon being copied by other papers across the country. Pulitzer began the practice of having reporters continuously searching the city for incidents or situations that could be made interesting to readers, especially if presented in the paper as colorfully and sensationally as possible. He pioneered the newspaper crusade or stunt that could interest and hold the attention of readers, motivating them to buy every issue of the paper. The paper sponsored a drive to collect funds to build a pedestal for the Statue of Liberty, and readers were informed each day of the progress of the drive. Pulitzer also sent a female reporter, Nellie Bly, racing around the world by train, ship, and every other available means and held a contest to see which reader could come closest to guessing how long it would take. He was also the first publisher to use many newspaper illustrations.

In striving to expand their readership, newspapers reported the news in short, snappy stories that were easy to read, and topped them with sensational headlines that caught the attention of potential buyers. As one author wrote, "News was not served raw. It was cooked, overdone, and heavily spiced." Such *excesses in news reporting around the turn of the century* were called **yellow journalism,** a term based on a popular comic strip called "The Yellow Kid." To some critics, the strip symbolized the sensationalism of much of the press during this period.

Nowhere was competition more fierce and yellow journalism more prominent than in the pages of Joseph Pulitzer's *New York World* and William Randolph Hearst's *New York Journal.* Hearst, the son of a wealthy silver miner, had already adopted many of Pulitzer's techniques at the *San Francisco Examiner* before he entered the New York market. With the purchase of the *Journal,* Hearst set out to compete head to head with Pulitzer. He hired away many of the *World's* best journalists, established an evening edition to compete with Pulitzer's *Evening World,* and added a comic supplement with more color than that of the Pulitzer newspaper. The war for talent resulted in both papers producing a version of "The Yellow Kid." At one point during the Spanish-American War—a war fought as much in the newsrooms as on the battlefields—circulations of the rival papers soared to more than a million copies a day.

REVIEW

The penny press, which was intended for the general public, revolutionized the newspaper business. Newspapers were sold by individual copy, news coverage speeded up, and human interest stories and comics were included to appeal to a wider readership of men and women.

As you can see, many of the newspaper practices that we take for granted today, that we assume are simply "natural" parts of the news, developed out of the competition among journalists to catch the interest of potential readers and thus to sell more papers. Although we can and should criticize many of these practices, we must also recognize their benefits. They increase the prominence of newspapers in the communication environments of most of us and therefore increase the probability that we will encounter useful bits of information from newspapers we would not encounter otherwise.

Newspapers for Women Before 1900, newspapers were largely for men only. By the early part of this century, however, women had become an important political force, even though the Nineteenth Amendment to the Constitution, which assured them the right to vote, was not passed and ratified until 1920. In 1904, a newspaper for women was started, *The Daily Mirror,* a forerunner of *Ms.* With its pictorial journalism and illustrated commercial advertising, like the penny press, it captured and held the attention of people not accustomed to reading or, in many cases, not even able to read.

Comic Strips Most newspaper developments in America have been adopted or adapted from Europe, generally from England. A development that has gone the other way, a purely American phenomenon that has spread throughout the world, is the comic strip. Comics began in this country in the 1890s, when publishers started catering to the general public rather than the elite. They were first aimed at children, but it quickly became apparent that adults liked them also. The first national syndication of comic strips began in 1915, the comic book began in 1933, and the "serious" comic strip was inaugurated in 1941 with "Terry and the Pirates." By the 1940s an estimated 27 million people were reading "Dick Tracy" every day. This was six or seven times as many as ever read the most popular novel of the period.

The Wire Services Newspapers, as well as radio and television stations and networks, depend heavily on the **wire services.** These are *organizations that supply international, national, and state or regional news stories and photos to newsapers, radio and television stations, and cable systems.* Two wire services dominate the field in this country, the Associated Press (AP) and United Press International (UPI). Some newspapers supplement the input from one or both of these services with material from Reuters or the *New York Times* news service, the special services for Gannett and Knight-Ridder newspapers, or one of the other small, specialized wire services.

The AP wire is carried by some seventeen hundred newspapers and six thousand radio and television stations in this country and eighty-five hundred foreign subscribers. An audio service, AP Network News, is broadcast on one thousand U.S. radio stations. UPI, which is much smaller than AP, has about three thousand subscribers. Like AP, it also provides an audio news service, the UPI Radio Network.

For a fee, which varies with a paper's circulation, newspapers receive a steady stream of stories over their news wires and regular updates on ongoing stories. Some of the stories come from the state bureau, some from the regional, and some from national and international; as a result, subscribing newspapers have a broad range of stories from which to select. They can also receive photographs and specialized news services, such as all sports, over special lines if they choose.

Newspaper publishers originally developed wire services to save money and, at the same time, improve news coverage. In the 1840s, newspapers in New York became dissatisfied with the reports they were getting from the Mexican War battlefront and with the increasing rates they were being charged for telegraph lines used to transmit stories to the editorial offices. Six of them formed a cooperative to overcome the problem. One of their first ventures was using just one telegraph line, instead of six, to get foreign news from ships coming into Boston Harbor. As these cooperative ventures expanded, the group adopted a name, the New York Associated Press, and began selling news to papers in other cities. The Civil War greatly increased the demand for wire service news, as did the completion of a cable under the Atlantic Ocean in 1866, which brought greater and quicker access to news from Europe.

Despite the attempts by the New York Associated Press to monopolize the wire service field, it was regularly challenged by other groups of newspapers. The original organization was finally driven out of business by the forerunner of what we know today as the Associated Press.

The present-day United Press was formed by E. W. Scripps in 1907 and grew rapidly. In 1958 it merged with the International News Service to become United Press International. Unlike AP, which is a nonprofit cooperative, UPI was supposed to be a profit-making enterprise. However, that has not been the case. After trying for decades to make the service profitable, Scripps sold UPI in 1982. In 1985 the wire service went into bankruptcy. It was purchased the next year by a Mexican publisher and sold again in 1988. Its next owners, Infotechnology Inc., had hoped to capitalize on the success of their other information service, the Financial News Network, which provides news and financial information to cable systems, personal computer users, and news organizations, but went bankrupt before the plans materialized. At present, a consortium of international news media is negotiating to become the newest owners of UPI.

Both the wire services maintain bureaus around the world. AP has 142 bureaus in this country and 84 located in some 70 foreign countries. UPI has a total of 180 bureaus and operates in 90 countries.

Newspaper Chains The major newspaper development between World War I and World War II was the emergence of **newspaper chains,** *groups of newspapers owned by one individual or corporation.* By 1922, William Randolph Hearst owned 20 daily newspapers and 11 Sunday papers in 13 of the largest cities in America. He also owned two wire services, six American magazines, Hearst Metronome News newsreel, a motion picture production company, and King Features Syndicate, which was the largest of the syndicators of comic strips and other feature materials. Scripps-Howard was another major national chain during this period.

Regional syndicates were also developing at this time, generally with groups of small-town newspapers, both dailies and weeklies. Gannett, the chain that today has the largest circulation in the country, was started in 1906 with a group of small-town papers in upper New York State.

The Decline of Newspapers

Newspapers in America began a serious economic decline in the early 1930s—hurt by the Great Depression, the increased strength of labor unions, and the competition from radio. The Depression led to decreased income for newspapers because businesses could not afford to advertise as much; at the same time, labor union demands caused an increase in costs. Radio was a more serious threat, however, than either the Depression or the unions. The growth of radio—especially the growth of radio advertising and the broadcasting of news—was phenomenal. Sales of radio time had reached $19 million a year by the time of the 1929 crash. Even worse, from the point of view of publishers, while newspaper advertising was declining in the early 1930s, radio advertising steadily rose. Thus, newspapers were hit by both the decreased Depression-era budgets of advertisers and the increased share of those budgets taken by radio.

REVIEW

The wire services furnish news and photos to newspapers, radio and television stations, and cable systems. The major ones in this country are AP and UPI. Newspaper chains such as Gannett own groups of newspapers. Newspapers also own radio stations, which compete with them for news.

Newspapers were also much concerned about radio stations broadcasting the news. They were afraid people would stop buying newspapers if they could hear news free on radio. So they tried to prevent radio stations from using news from the wire services and other sources. When that tactic failed, many newspapers accepted the old dictum, "If you can't beat them, join them": They began buying radio stations and starting new ones. As a result, by 1940 one-third of the radio stations in the United States were owned by newspapers.

HOW NEWSPAPERS GET INTO OUR MOSAICS

To understand why you get the news you do in most newspapers today, you need to begin with the fact that our world is an extremely complex place. An infinite number of events and conditions could be reported if adequate time and space were available—but they are not. A major task of all of those involved on the editorial side of a newspaper is to act as gatekeepers, observing the world, interpreting it, and deciding which of their observations or interpretations to let through the gate and in what form.

Organization of the Newspaper Staff

Newspapers vary widely in number of employees and degree of job specialization. In one way or another, however, all have essentially five departments, with some people serving in more than one department—especially on the weekly paper where the owner/publisher and a very small staff do everything.

The *editorial/news department* is responsible for all the printed matter, other than advertising, that appears in the paper. This department is headed by a managing editor or editor-in-chief. On the large paper, there are many subeditors, each responsible for a different type of copy or for a different type of job. The city editor is responsible for local news, assigning reporters to stories and supervising copyreaders. The wire editor is the regional, national, and international counterpart of the city editor. Instead of selecting events to be covered by reporters, however, the wire editor selects stories from the wire services and assigns them to staff members who tailor them to the needs and available space in the paper. The editorial page editor supervises editorial writers and is responsible for all material on the editorial page. Other editors include the sports editor, society or women's page editor, features editor, makeup editor, and photo editor. Some papers have a special editor for the Sunday editon. The larger the paper, the more specialized its editors.

The *advertising department* is responsible for the major revenue-producing activity of the paper, the sale of advertising. Within the advertising department, separate individuals or staffs handle local advertising, national advertising, and classified ads.

The *circulation department* must build as large an audience for the newspaper as possible in order to bring in additional revenues from subscription and newsstand sales and to increase the value of advertising.

The *production department* takes the output of the editorial and advertising staffs and gets it onto the printed page, ready for delivery to readers. The type of personnel in this department depends largely on the method of printing used.

The *business* or *administrative department* is responsible for expenditures and for coordinating all other departments for maximum efficiency, profit, and service.

The *publisher* has overall responsibility for all departments.

This organization is complicated for the newspaper chain because it involves yet another level or two of administration, supervisors of newspapers rather than of a department on one newspaper. In addition, many of the administrative staffs of chains have specialists in editorial management and production, business practices, promotion, mechanical production, and administration; these specialists advise and direct their counterparts on the individual papers. Some chains, such as Gannett, serve their papers even more directly with a news service, columns, central purchasing department, and, in certain cases, an advertising department that sells space for all of their papers to national advertisers.

Mode of Operation The organization of a newspaper staff we have described is designed to perform the following functions: (1) select the events out in the world that are to be covered; (2) create brief and interesting verbal descriptions or interpretations of those events, often with visual illustration; (3) organize them on pages, in the space left over after the advertisements are arranged, in a way that will be attractive to readers and satisfactory to advertisers; and (4) sell the results to as many people as possible.

The major task of selecting ideas and materials to be published in the local newspaper begins with the city editor and the wire editor. The city editor decides to which local events or activities reporters should be assigned and to which reporter each assignment goes. Once the stories are brought in, the city editor decides which stories to use, how much of each to use, and how much prominence each should get. The city editor also affects the kind of story that gets written by the kind of reporter selected to do it. In covering the political campaign of a female candidate for a local office, for example, one is likely to get quite a different story if the city editor sends the regular city hall reporter, a reporter who covers primarily news about the women's movement, or—to take a not-too-extreme case—a sports reporter. The city editor, whether consciously or not, has already made some judgment about how to play a story when the reporter is assigned.

The wire editor has a similar influence. From the thousands of words and hundreds of stories that come over the news wire, only a small percentage can be used, and the wire editor makes the selection.

The city editor and the wire editor must make most of their decisions rapidly. They have little time to think. Information floods in, and there is no time to agonize over decisions. One study shows that an efficient wire editor, dealing with stories of about two hundred twenty-five words each, can read them, decide which to use, and decide on the revisions needed in those retained all within an average of four seconds per story. Even a "slow" wire editor has little more time than that. Given those conditions, habit and the ingrained norms of the profession and of one's own newspaper obviously play a large role in the decisions made.

REVIEW

Newspapers are generally organized into five departments: editorial/news, advertising, circulation, production, and business. The head of the newspaper is the publisher. The city editor and wire editor select most of the current events news that appears in the paper.

Some critics are harsh in their descriptions of the operation of newspapers. Although they acknowledge the operations and problems we describe, they perceive that the primary purpose of American publishers (and American broadcasters) is to sell the largest possible audience to advertisers for the largest possible price. In a sense, that perception is valid. Clearly, the owners and stockholders of the commercial media, including newspapers, are interested in maximizing profits, which means generally that they want large audiences in order to be able to charge high rates for advertising. However, in the vast majority of cases individuals in the operations end of a newspaper (or one of the other media) are also genuinely interested in serving the needs of audience members and of the larger society. Those who think otherwise, who see all decisions on the newspaper as motivated only by the desire to maximize profit, will never understand adequately the American mass media.

Distribution of Space in the Paper

The likelihood that you will encounter some particular bits of information in a newspaper about an event is affected, among other things, by the amount of space your newspaper devotes to that type of news. That, in turn, is partly—but not wholly—dependent on the judgments of the paper's editors. No editors have unlimited freedom in the decisions they make—far from it. First of all, most papers have a formula for determining the proportion of editorial space normally devoted to different sorts of material. (This "formula" is probably not printed anywhere and may not even be talked about, but it is there, clearly understood by all concerned.) One study found that the average newsaper divides its space as shown in Table 4.1.

Keep in mind that these are average percentages. *In a newspaper, the space devoted to nonadvertising material* is called the **news hole.** That term covers not only what we normally think of as news, but comic strips, advice columns, editorials—everything other than advertising. The news hole is as low as 23 percent of the total column space in some papers and as high as 73 percent in others. The average is roughly 38 percent.

You may think that the ratio of news to advertising material in a newspaper also varies with the amount of news there is to report. This is a sensible assumption—but a false one. Except when some extremely unusual occurrence happens, such as the assassination of a president, the advertising-to-nonadvertising ratio on most papers is kept relatively stable. As a result, the amount of news in the paper depends on the amount of advertising that has been sold, not on the number of important occurrences in the world; the more advertising, the larger the news hole. All of that space among the ads must be filled. So when you see a nice fat local newspaper every Wednesday afternoon or Thursday morning, it is not because Wednesdays are especially eventful; it is because Wednesday evening and Thursday morning are the times when all of the supermarkets advertise their weekend specials.

TABLE 4.1 Division of Space in the Average Newspaper

Newspaper content	*Percent of total column space*
Local news	4.5
Foreign and national news	7.5
Leisure time feature	5.0
People, entertainment, and opinion	6.5
Sports	4.5
Data and listings	8.0
Local retail advertising	36.0
National advertising	8.0
Classified advertising	20.0

BYLINE

In Table 4.1, showing the percentage of total column space devoted to various kinds of newspaper content, you may have noticed that more than 50 percent of the average paper is devoted to advertising. Far less than 50 percent of time on any radio or television station is devoted to advertising. Yet broadcasting is criticized far more than newspapers for having too many ads. Why do you suppose that is?

Somewhat less than half of the newspapers in this country have a fixed minimum number of column inches they will devote to nonadvertising content; this minimum is generally a relatively low number, however, so on most days the space for news is still determined by the amount of advertising sold. Some newspapers use a sliding rather than a fixed percentage of their space for nonadvertising material. In those cases, although the amount of editorial matter increases with the amount of advertising sold, it increases at a slower rate so the more advertising sold, the smaller the percentage of nonadvertising matter. The amount of news most of us get in our local papers is thus more a function of the hustle of the advertising sales staff than the hustle of reporters.

This system for determining the size of the news hole, coupled with the way in which the editorial staff must operate in order to get a paper out on time, results in an unwitting bias against late-breaking stories. Because the available space in a newspaper is fairly inflexible once the news hole has been determined by the advertising department, the nearer to press time a story breaks, the less its chance of getting into the paper. Early in the day, the editors are relatively free in their selection of stories to be written or rewritten, and prepared for layout because they must be certain there will be enough. As the day goes on and the editor is assured of having ample material, he or she becomes more selective, and stories are discarded that would have been selected if they had come in earlier. It is expensive to discard the already prepared stories in order to substitute other material. Thus, editors report they are as likely to hold a late-breaking story over to the next day as to replace a story that has already been prepared for the press. Virtually never is a paid ad pulled to make space for the story. In a very small percentage of cases, pages are added to handle the late news.

Because it takes more time to process photographs than print, editors must make final decisions on them earlier in the day and so they have even less flexibility in adding photographic material during the last hour or two before press time.

To compensate for the lag time between the breaking of a story and its appearance in the paper, all large newspapers and most small ones publish several editions. The first edition of the *Miami Herald*—a morning paper—hits the streets between 6:00 and 8:00 P.M. the evening before. A later edition begins rolling off the presses around 1:00 in the morning. Since the printing of the final edition lasts until about 4:15 A.M., there is still an opportunity to stop the presses and make last-minute changes if a story of major importance develops. A more common occurrence is changing the paper "on the fly." In this situation, the presses are stopped for maintenance purposes, allowing time for the inclusion of late bits of news—usually such things as ball scores from the West Coast.

Newspaper Economics

Newspaper income has been rising rapidly in the past two decades, especially income from advertising. In the 18-year period from 1970 to 1988, newspaper advertising revenue rose from $5.7 billion to roughly $31 billion a year, and it has continued to rise since.

REVIEW

The portion of the newspaper devoted to nonadvertising material is called the news hole. It varies with the amount of advertising. News stories that break late in the day have less chance appearing in the next day's paper. Revenues from advertising account for between two-thirds and three-fourths of a newspaper's income.

For the average newspaper, between two-thirds and three-fourths of its income is from advertising, with the bulk of the remainder from subscriptions and single copy sales. About 60 percent of advertising income is from local advertising, with almost 25 percent from classified ads, and just over 10 percent from national advertising. The smaller the paper, the greater the proportion of local and classified advertising.

About one third of the cost of operating the average newspaper is for the supplies, personnel, and equipment needed to carry out the technical production of the paper. Almost 20 percent is for the business departments, including advertising and circulation; about 30 percent is for administration, including the cost of the buildng and plant and employee benefits; and between 15 and 20 percent is for the editorial department.

Controls on the Press

Because newspapers play a vital role in our personal lives and in the life of our society, we must be concerned with ways to maximize the probability of their serving us well. This is not an easy issue.

Government controls. Some countries have addressed this issue by making their newspapers arms of the government, owned and operated as a part of government, so that the control is political. Other countries have avoided government ownership of newspapers but have instituted various degrees of government regulation. In these cases the control is, in a sense, bureaucratic. In the United States, our forefathers opted for an ideal of almost absolute freedom of the printed media with no government controls. That ideal has never been achieved, of course, and there is constant debate about the extent to which it can be or should be achieved. Some critics of the American system claim that government control is preferable to capitalistic control, which they see as the major problem with our mass media. Their argument is that a government agency will be more concerned with the public interest than are profit-seeking organizations.

BYLINE

What is your opinion on the issue of control? Are you more worried about the control of your communication environment by our government or the control of your communication environment by business interests? In what ways is government control likely to influence the news? In what ways is capitalist or business control likely to influence it?

Self-regulation. Beyond regulating libel, pornography, and unfair or misleading advertising, the government leaves control of the content of newspapers largely to the industry: As with other media industry self-regulation, that of the publishing industries is largely ineffectual. The organizations of newspaper people, most notably the American Society of Newspaper Editors and the Society of Professional Journalists, make a great show of self-regulation through the publicizing of their codes. In fact, however, when newspapers ignore the codes, the organizations make no effort to enforce them.

Probably *the oldest of the newspaper industry's self-regulatory codes* is the **canons of journalism,** adopted by the American Society of Newspaper Editors in 1923. Its most recent revision, now called the **Statement of Principles of the American Society of Newspaper Editors,** is simply *a description of journalists' responsibilities to the public.* It briefly points out that journalists should keep the public well informed, protect the freedom of the press, avoid impropriety or conflicts of interest in their own activities, and be truthful, accurate, impartial, and fair. These are important principles. Unfortunately, some journalists ignore them.

Advertisers. Advertisers obviously play an important though generally indirect role in controlling the content of newspapers. Few editors or publishers print material that might displease major advertisers without careful consideration of the potential consequences. Far more important, though, are the constant attempts by editors and publishers to select the type of content for the newspaper that will attract large numbers of the types of readers advertisers want. Those are the types of readers who are most likely to be potential purchasers of the advertisers' products. For example, it is the motivation to attract more potential purchasers of food products, and hence more food advertisers, that leads some newspapers to publish food columns and recipes, materials that are far from anything we are likely to label "news."

Readers. Readers—or, more accurately, those who buy newspapers—also exert substantial influence on reporters and editors. As with advertisers, this influence tends to be indirect; reporters, editors, and publishers produce newspapers for the interests and needs they believe readers have. Most readers, unfortunately, are not very communicative about their needs and interests; at least, they do not communicate about them to newspaper people. As a result, many newspaper personnel seriously misperceive what their readers want and need. Some newspapers are trying to overcome this problem by periodic, systematic studies of their readers and potential readers. Others have appointed **ombudsmen,** *individuals who handle reader complaints and propose to the paper means of satisfying them.*

Press councils. Similar to the ombudsman, but somewhat more representative of the public, is the press council. **Press councils** are *committees, generally comprised of both journalists and private citizens, that investigate complaints about the accuracy and fairness of news stories and attempt to improve press performance through persuasion.* This particular mechanism for criticism and control has been more popular in Europe than in the United States, although councils have been organized in a number of American cities, and a few American publishers have even organized such press councils or "advisory" councils themselves. The major effort of this sort in the United States was the National News Council, established in 1973 with the help and support of a private foundation, the Twentieth Century Fund. The National News Council had two major objectives: to give the public a forum for airing its grievances about unfair and inaccurate reporting by the media and to protect the media's independence. The National News Council lasted barely a decade. It died, in good part, because of opposition from media leaders who resented the implication that they needed a watchdog and who feared that, rather than protecting their independence, the council was inhibiting it.

Audience research. The results of some of the research newspapers conduct or sponsor also serve to control or shape part of the content to which you are exposed. In their research, newspapers are generally concerned with five kinds of information: the number of copies sold per day, the number of people who read the newspaper on the average day, the characteristics of those readers (age, sex, purchasing power, and so on), the particular parts of the paper read by different types of people, and the kinds of material that might attract people who are not buying or reading the paper. Although all newspapers are interested in this information, they vary a great deal in how systematically they seek it.

Because advertising rates and the value of a newspaper's stock depend largely on the number of copies sold per day, and advertisers want to be certain that the figure is reliable, this information is gathered fairly systematically by most papers. In fact, almost all daily newspaper circulation figures in this country are verified and reported in a standard way to ensure reliability and comparability. Such was not always the case.

Prior to the turn of the century, advertisers and others had to take a publisher's word for the number of copies sold, and that word was seldom reliable. This meant advertisers could never be certain which newspapers gave them the most readers for their money. Unhappy with this situation, a group of national advertisers formed the Association of American Advertisers in 1899 and hired a staff to verify the circulation claims of publishers. In 1914, this organization evolved into the **Audit Bureau of Circulations** (ABC).

ABC today is *the organization that checks the circulation claims of newspapers and magazines and distributes these verified circulation data to publishers, advertisers, and advertising agencies*. Because of the ABC, which continues to be an important element in American newspaper and magazine publishing, advertisers can now receive dependable circulation figures. The ABC has three major purposes, outlined in its by-laws: (1) to issue standardized statements of circulation data and other data reported by a member; (2) to verify the figures shown in those statements by auditors' examination of any and all records considered by the bureau to be necessary; and (3) to disseminate data for the benefit of advertisers, advertising agencies, and others interested in facts on the advertising and publishing industries. Advertisers and advertising agencies now routinely check to be certain that a newspaper or magazine's circulation claims have been verified by the ABC.

Other kinds of information—the number and characteristics of the people who generally read each issue of the paper, what they read, and the interests of those who are presently readers—are generally gathered by independent market research firms hired by some newspapers. Although it seems a sound practice to understand one's readers and potential readers as fully as possible, some of this research is highly controversial among journalists. Many fear that newspaper owners and publishers will begin catering too much to the interests of the readers and that public desires as disclosed in this market research will displace the judgment of trained journalists in determining what goes into the newspaper. This is a difficult question. Undoubtedly, the results of market research can be abused. An editor can cater solely to the likes of readers and ignore their needs. On the other hand, it seems the more information about their public that reporters, editors, and publishers have, the more effectively they should be able to serve that public. Whether, in fact, the information from market research is used in this way depends on whether the newspaper personnel are concerned about maximizing their service to the public as well as maximizing profit. The two purposes are not necessarily incompatible.

REVIEW

Newspapers abide by a code of ethics that controls to some extent the practice of news gathering and reporting. Advertisers and readers also exert influence on newspaper content. Press councils, where they exist, provide feedback on media performance, as do audience research and circulation figures.

Recent Developments Many people are concerned today about the seeming decline in the number of newspapers in this country. In fact, however, the number of daily papers has remained fairly constant since World War II, and the number of Sunday papers has actually increased, as has the total circulation of both daily and Sunday papers. The number of daily newspapers reached its peak in 1914, when almost twenty-five hundred of them were in operation in the United States. This number declined to about eighteen hundred in 1945 and is now about sixteen hundred twenty-five. Meanwhile, the number of Sunday papers has reached an all-time peak of 847. Newspaper circulation is also at an all-time high of over 62 million for dailies and Sunday papers. Table 4.2 shows the newspapers with the highest daily circulation. The two leaders, the *Wall Street Journal* and *USA Today,* are considered national newspapers.

One of the factors in the perception that newspapers are decreasing in number has been the well-publicized problems of a few, such as the *Chicago Daily News* and *Washington Star.* However, most of the papers in financial trouble have been bought out, usually by a chain, and continue in operation. Afternoon papers have had the most difficult time in the past two decades, suffering more than a 30 percent drop in circulation; a few of them, in fact, were forced to close. During this same period, however, morning papers more than compensated for the afternoon circulation loss by increasing their circulation some 60 percent.

In this decline of the afternoon paper and the rise of the morning paper, we can see the way in which our media environment is affected by

TABLE 4.2 The Largest Newspapers in the United States: Average Daily Circulation

The Wall Street Journal	1,935,866
USA Today	1,387,233
Los Angeles Times	1,210,077
New York Daily News	1,180,139
The New York Times	1,149,683
The Washington Post	824,282
Chicago Tribune	740,713
Newsday	711,264
Detroit Free Press	639,767
San Francisco Chronicle	569,257
Chicago Sun-Times	532,678
The Detroit News	526,147
The Boston Globe	522,981
The Philadelphia Inquirer	522,020
The New York Post	504,720
The Newark Star-Ledger	470,045
Houston Chronicle	449,755
The Miami Herald	443,216
The Cleveland Plain Dealer	438,066
Minneapolis Star Tribune	410,226

Source: Morton Research; Lynch, Jones & Ryan; and Audit Bureau of Circulations; published in "Facts About Newspapers '90," American Newspaper Publishers Association.

shifts in our social structure. As a larger and larger proportion of Americans turned from industrial employment to white collar and other service employment, more of us started going to work later and getting home later. So we have more time to read a morning paper after breakfast, but less time to read an evening paper before dinner. Television, too, seems to cut into reading time in the evening more than in the morning. Still another factor that contributed to the decline of afternoon papers was the physical change of cities. With gridlock traffic conditions in many urban areas, it became more and more difficult to deliver newspapers to customers.

Changes in the number and ownership of newspapers reflect in large part the economic difficulties faced by the industry in the 1980s. The rising cost of newsprint, increased competition for advertising revenues, higher salary demands, and a host of other financial considerations forced newspaper owners to reevaluate their operations. One avenue available to them was made possible by the **Newspaper Preservation Act** passed by Congress in 1970. The act *enables financially troubled newspapers in the same city to save costs by merging their noneditorial operations.* Until this act was passed, a merger of this nature would have constituted a violation of the antitrust laws. The most highly publicized case involving such a merger took place in 1986 when the Gannett-owned *Detroit News* and Knight-Ridder's *Detroit Free Press* decided to combine operations. After a prolonged court battle in which citizens, employees, and advertisers fought the merger, the U.S. Supreme Court upheld a lower court decision allowing a joint operation agreement between the two papers.

REVIEW

Although the number of afternoon newspapers has declined, overall circulation is at an all-time high. To save failing newspapers, Congress passed the Newspaper Preservation Act.

Minority and Foreign-Language Press

Contributing to the diversity and richness of the newspaper scene in America are the large number of foreign-language newspapers and newspapers published for various minority groups. Like most kinds of papers, foreign-language newspapers were most widespread in this country just before World War I. In 1914 there were about a thousand newspapers (and about three hundred magazines) published here in foreign languages. Most popular were the German language publications, which comprised about 40 percent of the total. These were also the papers hardest hit by the strong anti-German sentiment that swept the country during World War I. In 1914, New York alone had 32 foreign language dailies: 10 German, 5 Yiddish, 3 Italian, 2 Arabic, 2 Bohemian, 2 Greek, and one each of Chinese, Croatian, French, Hungarian, Russian, Serbian, Slovakian, and Slovenian.

At one time or another in the history of this country, about three thousand newspapers have been started which were owned by blacks and directed primarily at a black audience. About two hundred of these exist today, most of them weeklies, but some monthlies and quarterlies. The first black newspaper, *Freedom's Journal*, began publication in 1827. As the name suggests, its major purpose was to fight slavery in America. Other abolitionist papers followed, the most famous of which was Frederick Douglass' *North Star,* introduced in 1847 and noted for its high literary quality. By the turn of the century, almost twelve hundred newspapers had been started by blacks, most of them devoted to civil rights issues ignored by the majority press. Although the average life span of a black newspaper has been nine years, one has lasted for more than a century. *The Philadelphia Tribune,* begun in 1884, is the oldest continuously published black newspaper in America. Others that have lasted almost a century include Baltimore's *Afro-American,* the *Chicago Defender,* Norfolk's *Journal and Guide,* New York's *Amsterdam News,* and the *Pittsburgh Courier.* All were started between 1892 and 1910.

Probably the most rapidly growing group of minority or foreign language publications today are the Spanish-language papers serving largely the growing Hispanic populations of Florida, the New York metropolitan area, and the Southwest—especially Texas and California. Currently there are about fifty major Spanish-language newspapers in this country, but that number is likely to increase. Demographers predict that by 2025, Hispanics will replace blacks as the nation's largest minority group. As this population has grown, English-language newspapers have paid increasing attention to the needs of Hispanic readers. Some have created zoned editions, established bureaus in Hispanic communities, provided editorial

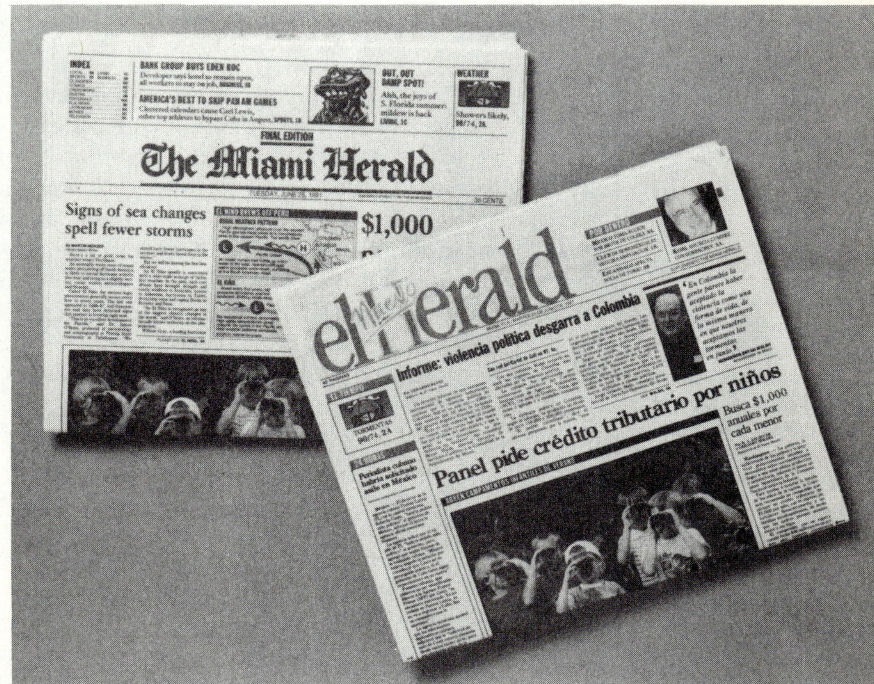

The growing Hispanic population in South Florida—particularly the Cuban-American community in the Miami area—and a large Spanish-speaking market in nearby Latin America have helped increase the circulation and development of the Miami Herald's *Spanish-language newspaper,* El Nuevo Herald.

supplements targeted to Hispanics, and offered bilingual Newspapers-in-Education programs. The *Miami Herald* has attempted to make its English-language paper more attractive to Hispanics—especially to Cuban Americans who make up the largest ethnic group in South Florida—and at the same time upgrade its Spanish-language paper, *El Nuevo Herald*, which has a circulation of about one hundred thousand.

The Suburban Weekly

The development of cheap, offset printing methods for newspapers facilitated the development of the suburban weekly. After World War II, as offset printing was refined and as the suburbs proliferated and grew, the number of weeklies published specifically for the residents of these suburbs increased also. The suburban community is generally an upper middle class audience eager to subscribe to a newspaper and an audience with whom advertisers are eager to communicate because of its high disposable income. In addition, unlike the inner cities, where it is almost impossible to escape unionization, relatively few suburban papers are unionized. These factors, along with the more recent development of low-cost desktop publishing, combine to make the publication of a suburban newspaper a potentially profitable enterprise. About seventy-six hundred weekly newspapers are in operation in this country today. Well over six hundred semiweeklies and triweeklies are also being published. For journalists who want to be their own bosses and who want to create a newspaper in their own image, the small weekly, semiweekly, or triweekly may be their last opportunity.

Rebirth of the Newsletter

Cheaper methods of printing, combined with the reduction in partisanship of newspapers, have led to the rise of a new kind of newsletter. The early newsletters that were the forerunners of our present newspapers were designed to bring relevant news from around the world to business people and government leaders. Today's newsletters are more varied, but in almost every case they are designed to distribute information and ideas to a group of people who have a common interest but who are physically scattered. A large portion of those common interests are political. For example, we have the Common Cause newsletter, the newsletter of the John Birch Society, the United Nations Association newsletter, the National Retired Teachers Association newsletter, the newsletter of the American Civil Liberties Union, the Accuracy in Media newsletter, and hundreds of others. These newsletters serve many of the functions of conventional newspapers for individuals whose special interests cannot be satisfied by those general interest papers.

Probably even more important than their service to people whose special interests are not served by conventional newspapers is the fact that newsletters are providing greater variety in the "marketplace of ideas." Because of the increasing standardization of news, editorials, and features in standard daily newspapers, discussed in greater detail in a following sec-

REVIEW

There are about two hundred newspapers owned by blacks and published primarily for a black audience. Some fifty Spanish-language newspapers exist. Thanks to cheaper methods of printing, there has been a proliferation of suburban weeky newspapers and newsletters associated with various groups and causes.

tion, it is vital to our society that other kinds of news and ideas come from other sources. Newsletters are well suited to providing that service.

Consolidation The development of newspaper chains, previously discussed, continues to the present day. There are about one hundred forty newspaper groups in the country today, ranging in size from two papers to over one hundred. These chains are not only buying individual papers now; they are buying other chains and other kinds of communications media. In 1990 the total number of daily newspapers under group ownership was 1233. This figure represents 76 percent of all the daily newspapers in the United States and 82 percent of the total circulation.

Table 4.3 shows the number of newspapers and circulation of the twenty largest chains in the United States. Gannett, the leader in circulation, accounts for almost 10 percent of the total daily circulation. Like other contemporary newspaper chains, Gannett did not grow by starting new papers; it grew—and continues to grow—by acquiring existing ones. Its most prestigious acquisitions have been the *Des Moines Register* and *Detroit News*, purchased in 1985, and the *Louisville Courier-Journal*, which Gannett

TABLE 4.3 The 20 Largest Newspaper Companies in the United States

	Daily Circulation	*Number of Dailies*
Gannett Co., Inc.	6,022,929	82
Knight-Ridder, Inc.	3,794,809	28
Newhouse Newspapers	2,997,699	26
Times Mirror Co.	2,626,259	8
Tribune Co.	2,608,222	9
Dow Jones & Co., Inc.	2,409,955	23
Thomson Newspapers, Inc.	2,127,123	122
The New York Times Co.	1,919,094	27
Scripps Howard	1,570,957	21
Cox Enterprises, Inc.	1,280,040	18
Hearst Newspapers	1,207,089	13
Media News	1,123,552	19
Freedom Newspapers, Inc.	938,862	27
Capital Cities/ABC, Inc.	898,927	9
The Washington Post Co.	826,871	2
Central Newspapers, Inc.	824,782	7
Donrey Media Group	790,982	57
Copley Newspapers	767,955	12
McClatchy Newspapers	753,558	11
The Chronicle Publishing Co.	742,410	6

Source: Morton Research; Lynch, Jones & Ryan; and Audit Bureau of Circulations; published in "Facts About Newspapers '90," American Newspaper Publishers Association.

Review

Chain ownership accounts for 76 percent of all the newspapers in the United States and 82 percent of the circulation. Some observers fear that chains are more interested in profits than in serving the local community.

bought from the Bingham family in 1986. In 1982 Gannett launched *USA Today*, a national newspaper that revolutionalized the use of color and graphics in contemporary newspapers.

This consolidation of the control of the mass media in America by a relatively small group of companies has concerned many observers. They are worried that such consolidation places too much power in the hands of those who control these communication conglomerates, that it reduces the variety of points of view available in our communication environment, and that it emphasizes cutting costs and maximizing profits more than community responsibility. These are critical questions, and we will return to them in Chapter 11.

Byline

What is your opinion on the issue of newspaper consolidation? Overall, do you see it as a positive or negative development? Are there possible advantages for us as members of the audience? If so, what are they? Should our government encourage or discourage such consolidation?

Printing Methods

The most important technological developments in printing since the time of Gutenberg, five hundred years ago, occurred within the past fifty years. Through the use of computers, coupled with new photo-offset methods of printing, many of the expensive and time-consuming steps in the production of newspapers have been eliminated. Instead of typing their stories on paper, reporters type them directly into the computer and check the result on *the computer screen* (**video display terminal** or VDT in the jargon of the trade). They can correct mistakes, rewrite sections, or rearrange the sections of a story easily by pressing the correct buttons on their keyboards. They can also call up the wire service and other data bases to which the newspaper subscribes and incorporate that information into their story. When a reporter is satisfied with a story, the press of another button causes the story to be stored in the computer's memory bank.

Editors also work with the keyboard and VDT to edit each story, and to set column width, length, typeface, and headline. When they have completed these tasks, the push of yet another button sends the story off to be made into a printing plate or a photocopy.

No longer is it necessary for layout personnel—those who arrange stories and advertisements and other matter on the page—to work with strips of letters formed from molten lead, laboriously laying these out and rearranging them as changes are made in the planned format of each day's paper. They can now do the layout with photocopies. At some newspapers, none of the layout is done manually; the layout editor does the entire job

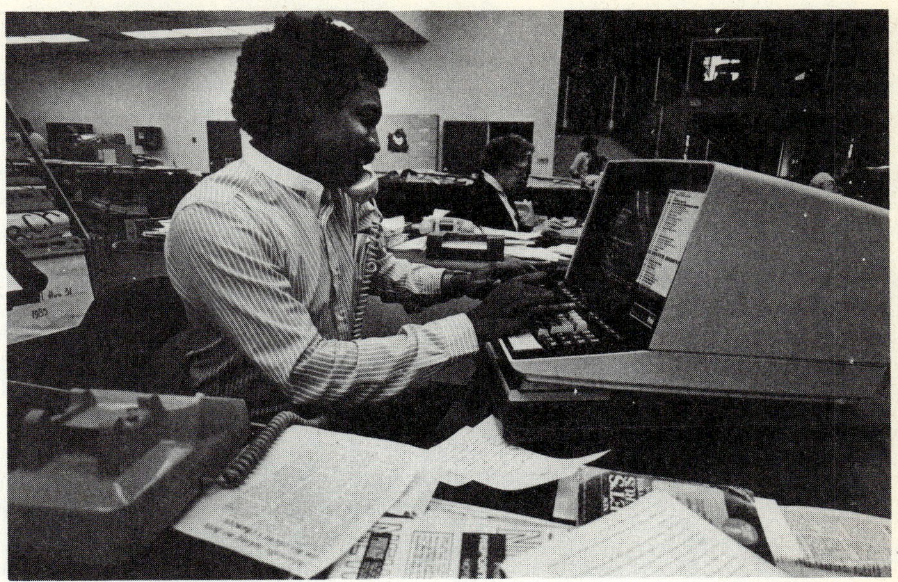

Computer technology has greatly facilitated the means by which news stories are researched, written, and edited, then incorporated into the layout of the newspaper and printed.

with the use of the computer keyboard and the video display terminal. The output goes directly to the press, eliminating the need for a printing plate.

Newspaper personnel are becoming increasingly sophisticated about programming computers to do much of the work previously done by humans. When a portion of a story is deleted, the computer rearranges the remainder of the story on the page. The computer even decides where to hyphenate words that must be carried over to a second line. As experience is gained in these uses of the computer, and as more computer equipment is developed specifically for newspaper, magazine, and book publishers, an even greater number and range of tasks will be done electronically.

Standardization One trend in newspapers that is worrisome to some of us is the steadily increasing degree of standardization. The consolidation of newspapers into chains has contributed to this trend, but it is not the only factor. Many forces have pushed newspapers in this direction. One contributing factor has been the heavy dependence of almost all newspapers on the two major wire services, AP and UPI. An even more important factor has been the increasing use of syndicated materials such as political columns, comic strips, cartoons, crossword puzzles, specialized news, and on and on. Political analysts such as Jack Anderson, William F. Buckley, Jr., and David Broder are carried by hundreds of newspapers. Advice columnists Ann Landers and Judith Martin ("Miss Manners") are likely to be standard fare in "Features" sections of newspapers, and almost anywhere in the country you can follow "Beetle Baily" or "Garfield" or "Doonesbury." So important is syndication that a section of the newspaper industry's trade magazine, *Editor and Publisher,* is devoted to the activities of syndicates. Some of the larger syndicates are Universal Press Syndicate, King Features Syndicate, and United Feature Syndicate.

REVIEW

Today's newspapers feature modern technology that facilitates writing, editing, and layout. They often use the same wire services and syndicated materials, producing a kind of standardization among newspapers. They also tend to imitate successful papers such as *USA Today.*

One other factor that may be responsible for the trend toward standardization is the tendency to "follow a winner." The success of *USA Today* can be measured in part by the many imitations it has spawned. Prior to its introduction, few major newspapers used color or graphics extensively—or imaginatively, we might add. Now, with the exception of several older prestige papers like the *New York Times, Washington Post,* and *Wall Street Journal,* almost all major dailies have color photos on the front page and brightly colored weather maps and other graphics. Many newspapers have also copied *USA Today's* terse writing style, although critics charge that the trend toward shorter and shorter news stories is a disservice to the public. Nevertheless, in the early 1990s, the *USA Today* format is the one most often copied—and most often regarded as the response of the newspaper industry to competition from television.

Our Exposure to Newspapers

Although most Americans say they depend on television for most kinds of news, newspapers still rank extremely high by any measure of importance. Almost two-thirds of American adults read a daily newspaper during the week. Six in ten adults also read a Sunday paper. On any given day, more than 60 million newspapers are produced. Each is read by slightly more than two adults on the average. Not unexpectedly, newspaper reading is positively related to both education and income. There is also a slight relationship with age. Thus we can predict that the probability of your reading newspapers will increase as you get more education, as you get richer, and as you get older.

The results of studies on the relative popularity of different parts of the paper vary widely. Table 4.4 presents a composite of the findings of

TABLE 4.4 Percentage of Adults Regularly Reading Each Section of the Newspaper

Newspaper section	*Percentage of adults reading*
National news	59
Obituaries	50
Ann Landers	48
Display advertisements	42
Comic strips	38
Sports	38
Classified advertisements	35
Business page	29
Editorial page	19

these various studies. It shows the approximate number of adults in this country who regularly read each type of content in the newspaper.

Our data on how much people read and what they read in the paper are less reliable than our information on the number and kind of people who read something. It seems fairly clear, however, that the average amount of time spent with the newspaper each day is declining. About forty years ago the average time was about thirty-seven minutes a day. In 1965 and 1966 it was twenty-eight minutes a day; at last count it was twenty-one minutes a day. Those in the 18- to 24-year age group spend the least amount of time (ten minutes a day on the average), while those between 55 and 65 spend the most (twenty-six minutes a day).

BYLINE

What do the figures in Table 4.4 tell you about why most people read the newspaper? How does your reading compare to those averages? Which sections of the paper do you generally read regularly? What does that tell you about why you read the paper?

Despite the overall decline in newspaper reading, there is at least one group for whom this medium continues to be tremendously important. A survey of America's leaders—the heads of large businesses, presidents of large labor unions, U.S. senators and representatives, national political appointees, and mass media executives and professionals—shows not only that they read newspapers and news magazines a great deal, but also that their reading habits are remarkably similar. Between 50 and 90 percent of every one of these groups except political leaders reads the *New York Times*. Among executives and professionals in mass communication, 88 percent read the *Times*. And although it is read more by business leaders than by others, the *Wall Street Journal* is not far behind. *Time* and *Newsweek* are the most popular magazines with these groups, with well over half of all of these leaders reading one or both. Roughly 80 percent of media executives and professionals read each one.

REVIEW

Roughly two-thirds of American adults read a daily newspaper each week. The amount of reading time varies with age, income, and education. Except for the nation's business, professional, and political leaders, the average time spent reading a newspaper has been declining.

These findings are important for at least two reasons. For one, they indicate that, even though there has been a drop in newspaper and magazine reading among the general population, these media remain important sources of information for people of influence. Therefore, these media undoubtedly have an effect on all of us whether we read them or not.

Second, these publications serve an important function for leaders and, hence, indirectly for our society. They give leaders some common ground, some common knowledge. This common ground facilitates their communication with each other and their working together.

In short, the *New York Times*, the *Wall Street Journal*, *Time*, and *Newsweek* are influential publications, not so much because of the *number* of people who read them but, rather, because of the *type* of people who read them.

FUNCTIONS AND EFFECTS OF NEWSPAPERS

When the word *newspaper* is mentioned to most people, the image that comes immediately to mind is primarily of headlines and news stories about major local, regional, national, and international events. Critics of the press also focus primarily on the quality of coverage of these significant events. However, such "news" makes up only a small part of most newspapers, and for many people in the newspaper business and for many readers it is not the most important part.

Generalizing about newspapers is a hazardous business because there is such a variety of them, from the *New York Times* and *Christian Science Monitor* to the *Village Voice*, *Berkeley Barb*, and Eagle Grove *Eagle*. There are tremendous differences in size and content between the large city daily and the small-town weekly. However, for the vast majority of newspapers in this country, some similarities override those differences, especially in the functions the papers serve.

Functions

Between 55 and 65 percent of the average newspaper is devoted to advertising. This is critical for the owners and staff of a paper because the major part of their income comes from advertising, far more than from sales of the paper to readers. It is also important for readers. They pay less than half as much for each paper as they would need to pay if there were no advertising. Even more important, for a large percentage of readers the advertising matter itself serves an important function. It tells them what movies are available in town, when their favorite television programs are on, which supermarkets have the best bargains on what products, which stores are having sales, what bargains in used automobiles are available, and where one might find a job. They can use the classified ads section themselves to sell their house or boat or to advertise for someone to fix the roof—or, in many papers, to find a lover. And those represent but a small sample of the valuable information and services made available through newspaper advertising.

In addition to presenting news and advertising messages, the newspaper serves a great variety of other functions. It is a community bulletin board, informing readers of club meetings, marriages, births, and deaths, the budget of the school district, when our taxes must be paid, the deadline to register if we wish to vote, and where our polling place will be. It gives us a variety of help and advice, including ways to improve our bridge games, to spice up our dinner menus, and to grow bigger tomatoes.

The newspaper is also a source of entertainment for most of us. Comic strips, for example, are devoted almost solely to our amusement. That these are important parts of most newspapers was emphasized some years ago when the popular "Doonesbury" comic strip was moved from the

Washington Post to the *Washington Star.* During the transition, our nation's capital was without "Doonesbury" for three weeks, which created a crisis rivaled only by the energy crisis, inflation, and unemployment. Within two days of its dropping "Doonesbury," the *Washington Post* was flooded with over a thousand complaints and inquiries. Sales of out-of-town papers that carried the strip boomed in the Washington area. Radio stations read the blacked-out installments on the air and at least one television station showed the comic strip as part of its evening news program. The compilers of the official daily news summary for the president and other occupants of the White House printed the strips throughout the time they were unavailable in a Washington paper. And to still the clamor, the *Star* ran front-page blurbs promising to run all of the missing strips as soon as its rights to carry "Doonesbury" began.

The entertainment function of the newspaper is not served only by its comic strips. Much of the material in the paper entertains in addition to its other functions. Columnists Art Buchwald and Mike Royko use satire to comment on political and social issues. Erma Bombeck uses humor to discuss the complications of family life. And the twists given to many major news stories help make them entertaining as well as informative—in fact, in many cases, the entertainment dominates. Almost any newspaper in the country would give greater play to a president's falling up the steps of his airplane than to the purpose of his trip. (Before condemning journalists for this practice, consider whether, given the choice, you would read a story first about the president's clumsiness or about the trip he is making.)

Effects Newspapers have played an important role in the history of this country and of the world. Together with books, they have made possible a great increase in the accumulation and distribution of knowledge. Printing literally produced the Enlightenment and was a major factor in the revolt against traditional leadership. Pamphlets and periodicals made it possible for revolutionary leaders in many countries to influence people far beyond the range of their voices.

The master printers were an important force in the stabilization and standardization of our language. They became dictators of spelling conventions and guides to acceptable dialects and grammar. The master printer, unfortunately, is being made obsolete by the new methods of printing. Reporters and editors type their stories into computer terminals, and no further human processing is necessary until the paper reaches the reader. Since the spelling and grammar of today's reporters are no better than they were in the past, the loss of the master printer probably means that newspapers of the future will have less and less of a stabilizing and standardizing effect on our language.

Newspapers were also a factor in the spread of literacy, for they motivated the working class in this country to learn to read. Most important, newspapers were the first of our mass media of communication to have a

REVIEW

Newspapers provide a variety of functions for readers. They are a source of entertainment as well as of news and other information. Newspapers have affected our political system, our language, and our reading ability and have brought about a democratization of knowledge.

substantial impact on the democratization of knowledge, making relatively detailed information about our government, foreign countries, the economy, and other important matters equally available to all who could read. As knowledge was distributed, power inevitably followed. Thus newspapers contributed, and continue to contribute, not only to the democratization of knowledge but to our political democracy as well.

NEWSPAPERS IN OUR MOSAICS: A SUMMARY

Although the development of radio and television reduced somewhat the importance of newspapers in our communication mosaics, newspapers are still quite prominent there for most of us. They are especially important as sources of information about local events and local shopping.

The city editor and the wire editor have the greatest responsibility for determining which news stories you are given a chance to read in your local paper. The work of the advertising staff is also important because the more advertising they sell, the larger the news hole; that is, the more space there will be for news and other content.

We normally think of newspapers as publications dedicated primarily to "hard news," but you can go through a good part of most newspapers without encountering such news. World, national, and local news—including sports news—accounts for less than one-fifth of the space in most newspapers. Advertising, on the other hand, accounts for more than three-fifths. Entertainment, features, and editorials account for the remainder.

A variety of external forces influence the content of our newspapers. Press councils, where they exist, are concerned largely with the accuracy and fairness of news stories. Made up largely of respected citizens in a community, they inform both the newspapers and the public when a newspaper has flagrantly ignored one or both of these criteria. Audience research for newspapers consists mostly of gathering accurate data on the number and characteristics of readers. In some cases, information on audience needs and interests is also gathered as a guide to editorial decisions. Other influences, covered in greater detail in Chapters 12, 13, and 14, are the laws regarding freedom of the press, libel, and the right to a fair trial; pressure groups of all sorts; the traditional norms of journalism; and, most important of all, advertising and other economic forces.

You are not as likely to have more than one local daily newspaper to read as your great-grandparents did in the early part of this century. Despite continued growth in population, the number of daily newspapers is less today than it was just before World War I. On the other hand, circulation is at its highest level—but not for all newspapers. While circulation of morning papers continues to rise, there has been a steady drop in afternoon paper circulation, reflecting the changing work habits and lifestyles of Americans, competition from television, and the difficulty of delivering newspapers in congested urban areas during the day. Minority and foreign-language papers continue to dot the newspaper landscape. Spanish-language papers in particular are likely to grow in number as the Hispanic population increases.

The number of suburban newspapers and newsletters has also increased greatly in recent years—in large part because of low-cost offset printing methods and the even less expensive desk-top publishing technology.

In short, although a great deal of concern is expressed these days about the fact that many people seldom read newspapers, the fault does not lie in the availability of the papers. A more justifiable concern, but one we do not hear as often, is the increasing control of newspapers by a handful of giant corporations or chains. This concentration of ownership could result in fewer news sources and points of view and a greater emphasis on profits than performance. Another concern is the trend toward standardization. Newspapers have always relied on the same wire services, AP and UPI, for much of their news. But now they are just as likely to rely on the same syndicates and specialized news services for their political columnists, cartoons, comic strips, and features, and to imitate the format of a single success story—*USA Today.*

DISCUSSION QUESTIONS

1. What was the newspaper like in colonial America? How did it differ from today's newspapers?
2. At what point did the newspaper become truly a mass medium of communication? What changes occurred to make newspapers appealing to large numbers of people?
3. What factors determine or affect the content of a newspaper?
4. What do you think accounts for the decline in the number of afternoon newspapers?
5. How has technology affected the newspaper industry?
6. To what extent do you believe there is a standardization among newspapers—that is, a tendency for them to resemble one another in layout and content? What accounts for this? Can a similar argument be made that radio and television stations are much the same from one community to the next?
7. What functions do newspapers provide? Are they the same functions that other media provide, or do newspapers provide some unique functions?

NOTES

1. McDonald said Washington's remarks were "infused with a bitter, self-pitying defense against Republican calumnies." Forest McDonald, *Alexander Hamilton* (New York: W. W. Norton & Company, 1979), p. 322. In a subsequent lecture, McDonald said Washington's comments were aimed at the Republican press.

2. The term "the fourth estate" derives from the three estates or important classes of feudal times: the nobility, the clergy, and the bourgeoise or commoners of substance. These were the three classes that could influence the monarchy; the peasants, of course, could not. The press, when it developed, could also wield great influence in many countries; hence the label "the fourth estate."
3. "Fear and loyalty in San Francisco: Earthquake inspires awe, sympathy," *Pensacola News Journal*, October 19, 1989, p. 7a.
4. Frank Luther Mott, *American Journalism, a History: 1690–1960*, 3rd ed. (New York: Macmillan, 1962), p. 37. Mott's is the most complete history of American newspapers available. Much of the historical material in this chapter is based on his work.
5. Published in the *New England Palladium* during the campaign of 1800. Cited in Mott, p. 169.

SUGGESTED READINGS

Classic Works in the Field

Berelson, Bernard. "What 'Missing the Newspaper' Means." In *Communications Research 1948–1949*, eds. Paul F. Lazarsfeld and Frank N. Stanton, pp. 111–128. New York: Harper, 1949.

Relevant Contemporary Works

Benjaminson, Peter. *Death in the Afternoon: America's Newspaper Giants Struggle for Survival*. Kansas City: Andrews, McMell & Parker, 1984.

Busterna, John C. "Trends in Daily Newspaper Ownership." *Journalism Quarterly* 65 (Winter 1988): 831–838.

Carter, Nancy M., and Cullen, John B. *The Computerization of Newspaper Organizations: The Impact of Technology on Organizational Structuring*. Washington, DC: University Press of America, 1983.

Ellison, Katherine. "Stars and Stripes and Censorship." *Columbia Journalism Review* 25 (January–February 1987): 8, 10–11.

Emery, Edwin, and Emery, Michael. *The Press in America: An Interpretative History of the Mass Media*. 6th ed. Englewood Cliffs, NJ: Prentice-Hall, 1988.

Gaziano, Cecilie, and McGrath, Kristin. "Newspaper Credibility and Relationships of Newspaper Journalists to Communities." *Journalism Quarterly* 64 (Summer–Autumn 1987): 317–328.

Norton, Seth W., and Norton, Will, Jr. "Economies of Scale and the New Technology of Daily Newspapers: A Survivor Analysis." *Quarterly Review of Economics and Business* 26 (Summer 1986): 66–83.

Oline, Clarice, N., Tichenor, Phillip J., and Donohue, George A. "Relation Between Corporate Ownership and Editor Attitudes About Business." *Journalism Quarterly* 65 (Summer 1988): 259–266.

Peck, Abe. *Uncovering the Sixties: The Life and Times of the Underground Press*. New York: Pantheon, 1985.

Schwarzlose, Richard O. *The Nation's Newsbrokers*. Evanston, IL: Northwestern University Press, 1989.

See also *ASNE Bulletin, Editor and Publisher, Journalism Quarterly*, and *Presstime*.

CHAPTER 5

MAGAZINES: THE SPECIAL INTEREST MEDIUM

OBJECTIVES

After studying this chapter, you should be able to

- Trace the rise of the magazine industry in America from colonial days to the present.
- Explain the demise of the general interest magazine and the trend toward specialization.
- Describe the recent changes in corporate structure in the magazine industry.
- Explain the creative and marketing aspects of the magazine industry.
- List the leading-circulation magazines.
- Discuss the functions and effects of magazines.

There are still groups of people out there who share some special interest or some special way of life and who need a magazine to serve that interest or way of life. And those groups are evolving all the time, faster than the demographers and marketers can keep up with them. And even when the demographers and marketers find them, these groups still may not comprise magazine audiences. Ah, but those who do; those are the ones we look for. In publishing, we dream about those groups with their intense need for magazines to help them, to inform them, to provide them with ideas, information, and inspiration.

James Autry, President
Magazine Group
Meredith Corporation

James Autry's remarks aptly describe the magazine publishing business, which has been called "a colorful, many-headed, every-changing, festive dragon." Indeed it is. Every year some three hundred new magazines representing a veritable patchwork of colors, sizes, and type styles try to find their niche in the American marketplace. In the June, 1989, debut issue of a fashion magazine called *Mirabella*, the publication's director and namesake Grace Mirabella said her first thought was, "Who needs another magazine?" Ultimately she decided that no fashion magazine dealt with "style" in the broadest sense of the word.

Whether her magazine fails or succeeds is not likely to influence other attempts. Publishers already know the odds. Fewer than half will last a year; fewer than 20 percent will last four years. *Manhattan, Inc.*, which won a 1985 National Magazine Award and critical acclaim for its exposés of business practices in New York City, folded in 1990. The magazine *7 Days* received a similar award in April, 1990. Ironically, it had gone out of business the week before. Still, there is that insatiable and tremendously varied appetite for reading material that propels the industry forward—in search of that magic group for whom just the right magazine might be created.

Because of their variability, magazines are probably the most difficult of the media to define. A comparison with newspapers makes clear the reason for the difficulty. The vast bulk of newspapers are fairly similar to each other in types of content, layout, and style of writing. They include roughly the same proportion of national and international news, local news, sports, features, and advertising. Some have more comic strips than others, but most have at least a couple. If you moved from one city to another, you could probably pick up a newspaper that you had never seen before and know where to find the sports section or the latest news about the president.

Such is not the case with magazines. No magazines or type of magazine can be called "typical." In a sense, each one has or creates its own audience—its own "community" of readers. Although these readers are generally scattered across the country and unknown to each other, they have common interests defined, and often created, by the magazine. In many cases, these readers share a specialized vocabulary. The validity of this idea of a community defined by the readership of a magazine is obvious when you consider business or trade magazines. It is less obvious, though no less valid, for many other kinds of magazines, such as *National Geographic*, *Playboy*, *The New Yorker*, or *Better Homes and Gardens*.

EARLY DEVELOPMENTS

The word *magazine* has been traced back to 1583. It comes from an Arabic word meaning storehouse or repository for goods or merchandise. By the middle of the eighteenth century the word came to denote a portable receptacle for items of value. Its first use to refer to anything resembling what we think of as a magazine today was in 1731. And this use

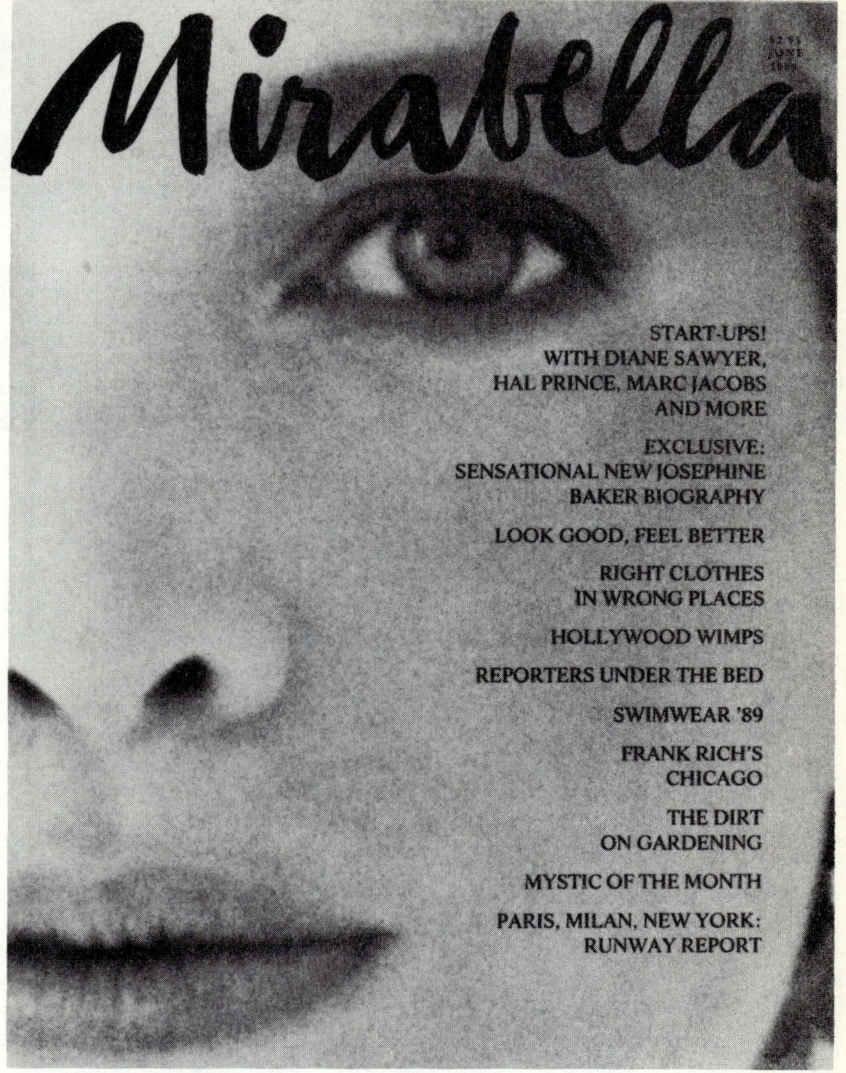

Mirabella *is just one of the thousands of new magazines that make their way onto newsstands each year. In this debut issue editor Grace Mirabella informed readers that* Mirabella *would "attempt to redefine the fashion magazine."*

made good sense, since a magazine publication is a portable storehouse or repository of information and entertainment.

Most of us today use *magazine* to refer to a particular type of portable repository, one in which the articles or stories by a variety of authors are relatively popular. For collections of more serious articles or less popular short fiction and poetry, we use the terms *journal* and *review*. However, the lines between these various types of publications are not clear. In this chapter, all will be referred to as magazines.

1700–1799

1741
America's first magazines appear

1784
Women's magazine, *Gentlemen and Lady's Town and Country*, begins publication

1789
Children's Magazine is first designed for youth market

1794
Congress amends postal regulations to regularize magazine mailings

1800–1849

1806
Yale published *Literary Cabinet*, model for future literary magazines

1820
Antislavery *Emancipator* begins

1821
Saturday Evening Post founded

1845
Magazines copyright contents to reduce chances of plagiarism

1850–1899

1850
Harper's Monthly founded

1865
Weekly opinion magazine, *The Nation*, appears on newsstands

1870
Harper's Weekly begins exposés of Tweed Ring in NYC; corrupt politicians eventually toppled

1892
McClure's is born, pioneer general circulation magazine in U.S.

1900–1949

1903
McClure's exposé of Standard Oil begins trend toward muckraking journalism

1914
Audit Bureau of Circulation evolves

1922–1925
Reader's Digest, *Time*, *The New Yorker* founded

1936
A general interest picture magazine, *Life*, becomes overnight success

1945
Ebony, black counterpart of *Life*, is started

1950–1979

1953
Hugh Hefner sets new trend with *Playboy*

1956
Collier's is first general interest magazine killed by competition with TV

1969
Saturday Evening Post dies

1971
Look dies

1973
Life goes under

1980–1989

1988
Robert Murdoch buys Triangle Publications, which includes *TV Guide* and *Seventeen*, for $3 billion

1989
Time Warner merger creates world's largest media corporation

Starting a new magazine is a risky business today. It was equally so in America's precolonial days. The first two magazines published in this country appeared in January of 1741. The *American Magazine, or A Monthly View of the Political State of the British Colonies,* lasted for three issues. *General Magazine, and Historical Chronicle, for All the British Plantations in America,* started by Benjamin Franklin, lasted for six. (Short, catchy titles obviously were not in vogue in those pre-Revolutionary days.)

The Rise of Specialized Magazines

The publication of magazines in this country had not been going on for long before some entrepreneurs recognized that aiming at the greatest variety of people was not necessarily the most profitable tack for a publisher. They began searching for groups within the population that had identifiable specialized interests yet were large enough to ensure a respectable circulation.

Magazines for women. Women were an obvious choice as one of those groups, and in 1784 a magazine designed specifically for them was published in Boston. It was titled the *Gentlemen and Lady's Town and Country.* Despite the publisher's stated wish "to please rather than to wound, woman the Noblest work of God," it apparently did not please a sufficient number and died within the year. A bit of the flavor of the magazine might be sensed from the title of one of its articles, "Desultory Thoughts Upon the Utility of Encouraging a Degree of Self-Complacency, Especially in Female Bosoms." (This was undoubtedly the forerunner of articles in contemporary women's magazines on assertiveness.) Probably more typical was the sort of advice to women published in Noah Webster's *American Magazine* in March 1788:

> *To be lovely you must be content to be women; to be mild, social, and sentimental—to be acquainted with all that belongs to your department—and leave the masculine virtues, and the profound researchers of study to the province of the other sex.*[1]

Magazines for children. It may be a sign of the attitudes toward women and children in this period of our history that women's and children's magazines first appeared at about the same time. The first women's magazine was published in 1784; the first magazine for children in 1789. The latter was titled just that, *Children's Magazine.* As the early women's magazines strove to educate women for their "proper" role, the children's magazines attempted the same for the young reader with such features as "Moral Tales" and "Easy Introduction to Geography."

Scientific journals. The period during which printing was developing also saw the development of modern science. Each was of inestimable value to the other. A scientific community depends on reasonably rapid and reliable communication among scientists, and science provided the grist for many popular articles.

Magazines targeted toward women first appeared in the 1780s. Harper's Bazaar, *the first magazine devoted to women's fashions and hairstyles, was born in the 1860s.*

At the beginning of the seventeenth century, scientific communication was primarily through word of mouth or through books. However, the normal book was not suitable for reporting simple observations or small experiments. Some of this information was exchanged among a small group of scholars through correspondence, but this was both inefficient and unreliable. In addition, because correspondence was personal, it did not stimulate the sort of criticism and debate essential for scholarly development. The answer was the scientific magazine or journal.

The first scientific magazine was published in France in January 1665. Titled *Le journal des scavans (Journal of Learned Men)*, it contained information about experiments in physics, chemistry, and anatomy and described newly invented machines and meteorological data. Two months later, a

British scientific journal, *Philosophical Transactions,* was published by the Council of the Royal Society. This journal is still being published today, over three hundred years later, a record no other magazine in existence can even approach. It also was the model for almost all scientific journals that followed.

Today, there are probably between thirty-five thousand and fifty thousand different scientific journals being published in the world, between six thousand and seven thousand in the United States alone.

Literary magazines. One of the most important contributions of the early magazines in this country was the encouragement of American writers. The patriotic fervor of the Revolutionary period was shared by the editors and publishers of these magazines. Just as they wanted an American government and American laws as free as possible of European influence, they wanted American writers and an American literature—and they found and nurtured them. In this way, these fledgling magazines played a vital role in the development of a national identity in America.

Probably the magazine most successful at selling short stories to a large and heterogeneous audience was *The Saturday Evening Post*. Started in 1821, it endured as a general interest weekly magazine well past the middle of the twentieth century.

Although Harvard was the first college in the country to have its own printing press, it was Ivy League rival Yale that started the college magazine. The *Literary Cabinet*, published initially in 1806, was the forerunner of a great many literary magazines born and nurtured on college campuses. These magazines were—and remain in the twentieth century—especially important because they are among the few outlets for serious poetry.

REVIEW

The word *magazine* means storehouse or repository for goods or merchandise. Magazines appeared in this country as early as 1741. Specialized magazines were aimed at women, children, scientists, and those who appreciated literature and humor.

Humor magazines. The second quarter of the nineteenth century witnessed the rise of humor in American magazines. Though humor had appeared in magazines on this continent virtually from their beginnings, it became much more prominent in this pre-Civil War period. This example, from a regular section of the *Knickerbocker* magazine, which satirized country newspapers, gives you the flavor of the period's humor:

> *My wife Sally Ann has left my bed and board without provocation whatever. She has been ugly ever since I took her, some fifteen years ago; scratches when she's mad, and gets the histerricks at a moment's warning. She's a dangerous woman. I being entirely taken in by her beauty, which served me right. I never was so sick of any job. I hope nobody will catch her and bring her back. No debts paid of her contracting.*
>
> Dusenberry Snodgrass[2]

The general circulation magazine. During the first half of our present century the magazine became most truly a mass communication medium. This was the era of the mass circulation periodicals—*The Saturday Evening Post, Collier's, Life*—magazines that appealed to a highly varied set of readers. As we shall see later in this chapter, magazines in the past few decades have become increasingly specialized; few attempt to appeal to a broad range of readers.

Until the end of the nineteenth century, magazines were essentially for the elite. Both their content and their price limited their audiences. An important revolution in the magazine industry was the development of popular publications whose content could be enjoyed by a mass audience and whose price made them affordable to that audience.

By the end of the nineteenth century, the improvements in printing technology made practical the publication of very large numbers of copies of a magazine at a low cost. At the same time, the Industrial Revolution increased the need for advertising to market mass-produced goods. With the lure of large profits to be made from advertising, magazine publishers recognized the need to win large circulations in order to demand higher advertising rates. If the magazines had to be sold for less than it cost to produce them, advertising profits could more than make up the difference.

McClure's Magazine, started in 1892, was the pioneer general circulation magazine in America. It sold initially for 15 cents. *McClure's* encountered competition almost immediately, especially from a magazine called *Munsey's*, which cut its price to 10 cents. By 1897 *Munsey's* had a circulation of a half million, probably the largest of any magazine in the world at that time.

Plagiarism in Early Magazines

Plagiarism, or *literary theft*, was a common practice among magazine and newspaper editors in the first half of the nineteenth century. Edgar Allen Poe's "The Raven" was first seen by the public in the *Evening Mirror*, although it had been bought from Poe for $10 by the *Whig Review*. The *Review* had sent out advance sheets, which the *Mirror* simply clipped and published. Newspaper editors were quite upset when literary magazines began copyrighting their contents in 1845, because they lost a good source of free materials. They continued to "borrow" the works of many British authors, however, since those works appeared in magazines that were not protected by copyright.

Rise of the Professional Writer

Most of the early writing in magazines was done by amateurs. Publishers had little choice, for few professional writers were around. As late as 1823 it was estimated that fewer than ten people in the entire country made their living by writing. In fact, even as late as 1842, writing could not have been a very profitable pursuit, if the claim of one editor of that period is to be believed. "The man who depends upon literature for a living," he wrote, "is little better than a fool."

In spite of the economic uncertainties of the profession, by the second quarter of the nineteenth century professional writers were becoming

REVIEW

The magazine became a true mass medium with the introduction of inexpensive mass circulation publications such as *McClure's* and *Munsey's*. In the nineteenth century, literary theft was common, and payment was poor—even for professional writers.

more common. The increasingly popular magazines gave them an outlet and a source of income. That source of income was not generous at first. In the 1820s and 1830s, for example, the going rate was about $1 a page for prose and $2 a page for poetry. Well-known writers got somewhat more; unknown writers often received nothing. Even those meager payments that professional writers were promised did not always materialize because the financial status of most magazines then was precarious.

Editors received comparable payment. Edgar Allen Poe's salary as assistant editor of the *Southern Literary Messenger* was $10 a week. This was raised to $15 a week when he became editor-in-chief. These salaries were not out of line with other salaries of the period: The average male public school teacher was paid about $8 a week then; the average female teacher about $4.

Political Influences In the first hundred years of this country's life, a large number of magazines, like newspapers, were highly political. And a significant political theme was the abolition of slavery. As far back as 1758 magazine articles addressed that subject, both pro and con. In pre-Revolution days, the most frequent emphasis of such articles was on the suffering of slaves, but defenses of slavery were also published. In the post-Revolution period the frequency of articles opposed to slavery increased. A magazine appeared in 1820 that was devoted almost exclusively to that theme; it was called the *Emancipator*. The major publishing figure in the abolition movement was Benjamin Lundy. Through the pages of the *Genius of Universal Emancipation*, begun in 1821, Lundy preached the gospel of gradual abolition and colonization of black people. Most of the antislavery writing of this period grew out of religious commitments, generally Quaker, rather than out of a belief that the American Constitution applied equally to blacks and whites.

This attention to slavery reached its peak in the period just before and during the Civil War. The *Southern Literary Messenger* urged authors to explain to the world that slavery is "a great social, moral, and political blessing." In a western magazine called the *Pioneer*, readers were told that "slavery (is) authorized by God, permitted by Jesus Christ, sanctioned by the apostles, maintained by good men of all ages." By the 1850s an exceedingly large number of antislavery magazines were in print. Many of them, though by no means all, were church-related. Some antislavery magazines were also published by northern blacks. The most important of these was *Douglass' Monthly*.

The magazine publication that probably had the greatest impact on the abolitionist movement was the serialization of Harriet Beecher Stowe's novel, *Uncle Tom's Cabin*, mentioned in Chapter 3. It ran in the *National Era* from June 5, 1851 to April 1, 1852. This story aroused tremendously strong emotions and stirred determination to eliminate slavery as none of the many other appeals to reason, law, or religion had done.

Born into slavery, Frederick Douglass became one of the most eloquent spokespersons of the abolitionist movement in America. A gifted writer and editor, he founded several antislavery newspapers and magazines.

The Muckrakers The early part of the twentieth century was the era of the **muckraker** in American journalism. The term *muckrake* was adopted at this time to refer to *investigative journalists who search out the misconduct of prominent individuals and expose them publicly. Muckrake* originally referred to a special rake for collecting muck or manure. It was an apt term for some of the journalists of that day. President Theodore Roosevelt is said to have been the first person to apply the term to journalists. He thought too many journalists were so busy searching for dirt they failed to see or report more important news.

One of the first magazines to practice muckraking in this country was *McClure's*. From its beginning in 1893 it had rapidly built a strong reputation by publishing fiction from the major writers of the period, such as Robert Louis Stevenson, Thomas Hardy, Stephen Crane, and O. Henry. It also ran many articles about some important personalities of the day.

In 1903, almost by accident, *McClure's* discovered the potential of muckraking for selling magazines. In one issue that year, the magazine published three articles that exposed illegal or questionable practices. One was part of a sensational history of the Standard Oil Company, one was about corruption in Minneapolis, and the third was the first part of a series on racketeering in labor unions. The issue was tremendously successful, and the publishers of the magazine realized they had found their niche in the publishing world. After this, one exposé followed another. There were articles on corruption in various city governments, the copper kings of Montana, the national water power trust, and life insurance companies.

REVIEW

Many early magazines were highly political—especially when it came to issues such as slavery. As the twentieth century dawned, a new type of investigative reporting, called muckraking, made its way into magazines.

The success of *McClure's* lured others into the lucrative muckraking field—*Arena*, *Collier's*, *Hampton's*, and the *American Magazine*, among others. Muckraking flourished for about ten years and then, as quickly as it had developed, it died. Although muckraking articles appear occasionally in magazines and newspapers today, no major magazines are built around the serious investigation and exposure of wrongdoing by major corporations, government officials, or individuals. The closest we have to this sort of thing today are such cheap and questionable newspapers as *The National Enquirer*, which focus almost totally on purported exposés of the sins and misfortunes of the famous.

Advertising in Magazines

Advertising appeared in some magazines almost from the start, although it did not play an important role. In the late 1700s advertisements were occasionally found on the covers of magazines and sometimes on a page inserted between the cover and the text. By the time of the Civil War, however, advertising in magazines was quite common. Only a few publishers still considered it demeaning to have such commercial material in the pages of their magazines. These were primarily publishers of literary magazines.

Manufacturers of patent medicines were among the mainstays of the early advertising business. Because there was little industry or government regulation at that time, all sorts of products were advertised that we are unlikely to see in the pages of publications today. For example, in some magazines in the 1850s there were advertisements for drugs that the manufacturers claimed produced abortions. A great variety of patent medicines were regularly advertised: cancer cures, nerve tonics, and one, Vin's Electric Fluid, that promised to make cripples walk. Although a few of the more reputable magazines tried to screen out the highly questionable advertisements, most did not. Even the *Journal of the American Medical*

Association ran some of the patent medicine ads. Many medical journals were published during this period, and most of them, like most other magazines, depended on advertising to stay alive—a situation still true for a large number of medical journals.

Another questionable practice, one that first appeared somewhat later in the century, was the disguising of advertising to make it appear to be part of the magazine's regular reading material. At that time publishers—even those of some of the religious magazines—did not appear to recognize that this practice was unethical.

Magazines about Advertising

In 1851 the first magazine about advertising appeared, the predecessor of such current trade journals as *Advertising Age* and *Printers' Ink*. And even in general circulation magazines, advertising became a popular subject of analysis and comment. Writers began to warn readers about the dangers of advertising and the tricks of the trade. The following appeared in *Frank Leslie's Illustrated Newspaper* in 1857:

> *The art of advertising is one of the arts most studied by our literary vendors of fancy soaps, philanthropic corn doctors, humanitarian pillmakers, and all the industrious professions which have an intense feeling for one's pockets. Every trick that can be resorted to for the purpose of inducing one to read an advertisement is practised, and, it must be confessed, very often with complete success. How often have we been seduced into the reading of some witty or sentimental verse, that finally led us, by slow degrees, to a knowledge that somebody sold cure-all pills or incomparable trousers.*

REVIEW

Advertisements appeared in magazines almost from the start, although they were not a prominent feature until the time of the Civil War. One of the most common type of advertisements in those days was for patent medicines. The importance of advertising was reflected in the early appearance of trade magazines about advertising.

The sort of seduction condemned by that author in 1857 continues today but receives relatively little publicity. An important part of the art of contemporary advertising is the skillful weaving together of the advertising and nonadvertising matter in a magazine in a way that maximizes the probability that readers will encounter all or most of the ads. When magazines first began to include advertising, this was not done; advertising was carefully segregated from the other content of magazines. In the spirit of the post-Civil War period, this segregation too was struck down. The leader of the movement was the *Ladies' Home Journal* which began interspersing parts of its stories among the advertisements, thus gently leading its readers to those important parts of its contents. Competition among magazines quickly made this a common practice.

BYLINE

Can you find attempts in any of today's magazines to disguise advertisements, to make them appear part of the editorial content or features of the publication? As a reader of magazines, should you be concerned about that practice? Why or why not?

Death of the General Interest Magazines

General interest magazines survived the competition of the motion picture, the automobile, and radio, but television was too much for them. The four major mass-circulation magazines in the country were *Saturday Evening Post*, *Collier's*, *Life*, and *Look*. The first two provided a great variety of fiction and nonfiction, the latter two visual news and feature publications, all for the heterogeneous mass audience. Both *Saturday Evening Post* and *Collier's* had clear antecedents in the early magazines of the nineteenth century. They were simply refinements of the formula, based on shrewd estimates of what the bulk of the public wanted. *Life* and *Look*, on the other hand, were true innovations—the first picture magazines in this country. (The development of *Life* and *Look* is discussed in the next chapter.) These general interest magazines could not compete for the general audience with that new, upstart medium—television. Even the circulation of *Reader's Digest*, one of the largest of any magazine in this country, is small by network television standards—"only" about 18 million. An even more serious problem than audience size was the fact that the general interest magazines could not get high enough rates for their advertising to cover the costs of their large circulations. They could not raise these rates because television was already underselling them. A network television commercial was delivering more potential viewers per advertising dollar than an ad in a major general circulation magazine could deliver. In addition, members of the television audience were more likely to pay attention to that advertising.

To understand the competitive problem of magazines in that situation, you must realize that the print media—newspapers as well as magazines—are at a disadvantage in building circulation when compared to the electronic media. Radio and television can increase audience size with little or no increase in production costs. This is not the case with magazines or newspapers. Although their cost does not double when their circulation doubles, costs for materials, printing, and delivery do increase substantially. Thus, a television network can deliver a very large audience (30 to 40 million people) to an advertiser at a far lower cost per thousand than a magazine or newspaper can.

REVIEW

The general interest magazine did not survive competition from television. *Collier's, Saturday Evening Post, Life,* and *Look* ceased weekly publication in the 1950s, 1960s, and 1970s.

Collier's was the first general interest magazine to succumb, in 1956. The *Saturday Evening Post* lasted for 13 more years, until 1969. Two years later, *Look* went under. In 1973, *Life*, once probably the most effective advertising medium in America, died. Versions of *Life* and of the *Saturday Evening Post* have since been resurrected as monthlies, but the spell is gone. The bulk of the American public ignores them.

SYNDICATES, CROSS OWNERSHIP, AND CONGLOMERATES

The absorption of individual magazines into syndicates, cross ownership, and conglomerates is increasingly common in the magazine industry, as it is in other communication industries. Although these terms are not used consistently in the trade, in general, **syndicate** or **chain** is used to refer to *the ownership of more than one magazine by a single corporation* (or the ownership of more than one newspaper, radio station, and so on). **Cross ownership** is *the consolidation of a variety of media into one corporation,* for example, the ownership of magazines, newspapers, and some broadcasting stations. A **conglomerate** is *the ownership of some communication companies by a corporation that also owns nonmedia companies.*

There are a number of magazine syndicates, each owning many magazines. Some of these also have cross ownership of newspaper and broadcasting properties. The Newhouse newspaper chain, for example, is reported to own about twenty magazines. The New York Times Corporation owns a number. At last count McGraw-Hill, which began as a book publisher under a single imprint, was publishing books under 5 different imprints and 73 magazines and owned 2 educational film companies and 4 television stations. Media ownership changes so rapidly that it is difficult to obtain up-to-date information. The trend, though, is consistently toward larger and more global operations.

One of the fastest growing media corporations is that controlled by Rupert Murdoch, an Australian turned American who has been called "the most voracious media baron of them all" by some and "the Magellan of the Information Age" by others. Murdoch's News Corporation Ltd. claims the largest newspaper circulation in the world—about 14 million in Australia, England, and the United States. In the United States, Murdoch owns daily newspapers, magazines, and television stations, Fox Broadcasting and 20th Century Fox movie studio, and HarperCollins Publishers. He is also this country's largest publisher of evangelical Christian books. In 1988 he purchased Walter Annenberg's Triangle Publications, Inc.; it includes *TV Guide,* which has one of the largest circulations in the country. A recent Murdoch magazine venture is *Soap Opera Weekly,* a publication designed to keep soap opera lovers informed about their favorite programs and stars.

In 1989 the merger of Time, Inc. and Warner Communications, Inc. created the largest information and entertainment corporation in the world, with estimated annual revenues of $10 billion a year. The new media giant includes the largest magazine publisher in the country, one of the top three film studios in Hollywood, the largest worldwide producer of television programming, the largest record company and second largest cable operation in the United States, the country's largest pay TV programmer, and a $900-million-a-year book operation—making it one of the world's largest book dealers and this country's largest direct marketer of books.

The largest privately held media empire is the $11 billion Newhouse Corporation, founded by Samuel Irving Newhouse in the early part of the twentieth century. Newhouse holdings include newspapers, book publishers, magazines, and cable groups. S. I. Newhouse, Jr., oversees the magazine division, which consists of 20 publications in this country and 41 foreign publications. Some of the Newhouse magazines are the *New Yorker*, *Vogue*, *Vanity Fair*, *Self*, and *Mademoiselle*.

Review

Most magazines are owned by larger communications corporations. The merger of Time and Warner in 1989 created the largest information and entertainment corporation in the world. Size enables such media giants to attempt high-risk ventures and absorb the losses when they fail. New technologies allow media corporations to produce and distribute their products more easily and less expensively and to compete worldwide.

Several factors account for the desire of American communications corporations to become larger and more global. First of all, the nature of the business is such that many of its products involve considerable risk on the part of the producer. A new magazine, a new movie, or a new television program may or may not win audience or advertiser approval. So corporations want to be large enough to absorb ventures that fail or require a great deal of risk. Time, Inc., for example, invested $47 million in *TV-Cable Week*, a magazine that lasted less than six months. Rupert Murdoch lost some $260 million in the first year of operation of Sky Television, a four-channel direct-to-homes satellite network.

Another factor that has enabled communications corporations to spread their tentacles is the development of fiber optics and satellite technology, which have made it easier and less expensive to distribute information. The content of a magazine that once had to be mailed from a single distribution point can now be sent by satellite to receiver dishes and printing plants around the world.

Finally, communications industries, as well as other kinds of industries, are cashing in on the ever-growing dominance of English-language markets. Currently, half of the world's economic output comes from English-speaking countries, forcing the rest of the countries of the world to adopt English as a second language—or at least as the language of the marketplace.

Byline

Former *Time* and *Life* editor Thomas Griffith, voicing concern over the possible effects of mergers and takeovers on the editorial independence of news magazines, said: "Among the people who work at *Time* magazine there is a melancholy awareness these days that things have changed forever. No one knows whether the company will wind up in the hands of one aggressive Hollywood titan or another, or on its own as a strong company saddled with an enormous debt." Do you have any concern about the size or composition of media corporations? If a scandal occurred at Warner Bros., do you believe *Time* magazine could report on it objectively and without interference?

HOW MAGAZINES GET INTO OUR COMMUNICATION MOSAICS

The major change in the magazine industry in the past few decades, as noted before, was the decline of general interest periodicals and the parallel rise of special interest ones. *Look*, *Collier's*, *Women's Home Companion*, and *Liberty* were replaced by *Sail*, *Runner's World*, *Entrepreneurial Woman*, *Family Business*, *Model Railroader*, and *Inc.*

The merger of Time and Warner in 1989 created the largest entertainment and information corporation in the world.

What They Bring to the Party

1988 Product, Revenue Breakdowns

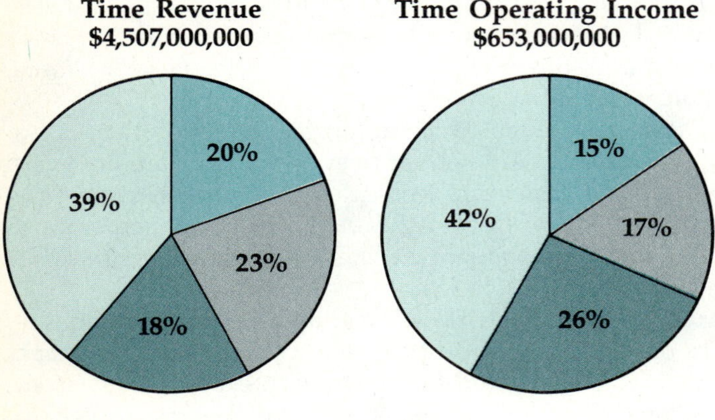

Cable:
American Television and Communications (82% owned), 3,305,000 subscribers, and Paragon Communications (50% owned), 735,000 subscribers*.

Programming:
Home Box Office, 16,500,000 subscribers*, Cinemax, 6,500,000 subscribers*, and HBO Video.

Magazines:
Including Time, Sports Illustrated, People, Fortune, Money, Life, etc. Majority owned magazines: Including McCalls, Parenting, Working Woman, etc. Whittle Communications and other joint ventures (50%).

Books:
Time-Life Books; Scott, Foresman & Co.; Book-of-the-Month Club, and Little Brown and Co., etc.

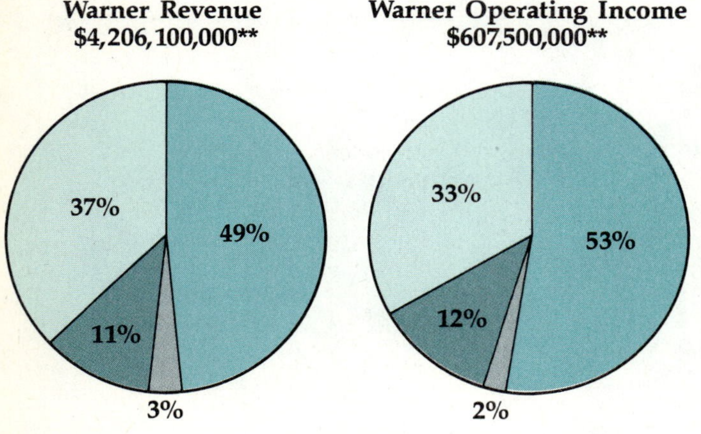

Cable and Broadcasting:
Cable: Warner Cable Communications, 1,500,000 subscribers. Broadcasting***: 42% owner of BHC (which owns 100% of KCOP-TV Los Angeles and KPTV-TV Portland, Ore., and 50% of group owner United Television).

Filmed Entertainment:
Warner Bros. Theatrical Production and Distribution; Warner Bros. Television Production and Distribution; Lorimar Television Production; Licensing Corp. of America, etc.

Recorded Music and Publishing:
Warner Bros. Records, Atlantic Reccords, Elektra Entertainment, Warner Chappel Music, etc.

Publishing and Related Distribution:
Warner Books, DC Comic; Mad Magazine, etc.

* Estimate. **Lorimar results not yet included. ***Broadcasting operations not reflected in revenue and have only minor impact on operating income.

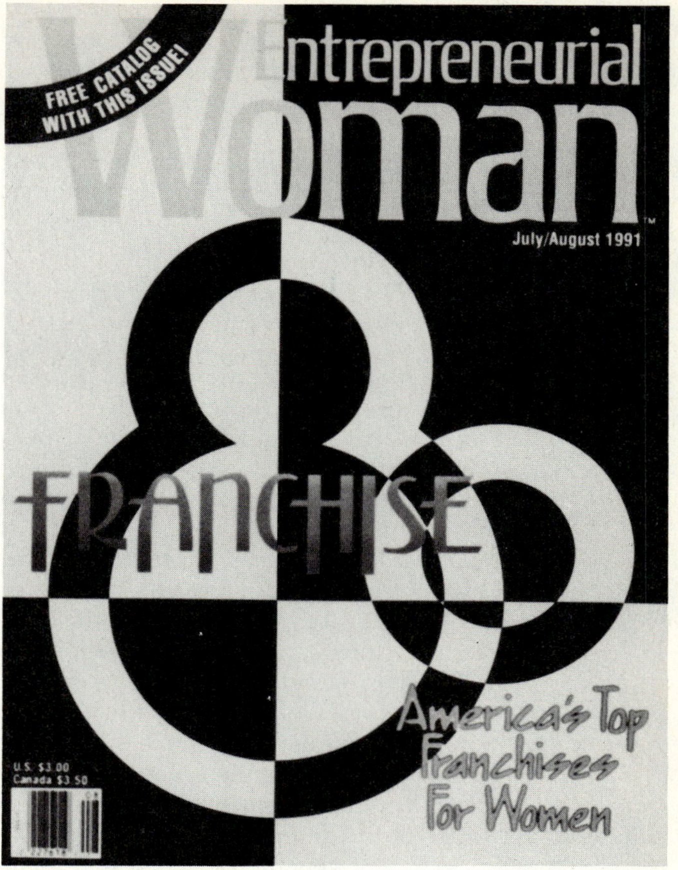

The social changes brought about by the women's movement are reflected in the new kinds of magazines targeted at women. This magazine, Entrepreneurial Woman, *offers ideas and advice to executive businesswomen.*

Something for Everyone: Audience Adaptation

There are magazines for almost every conceivable interest and almost every conceivable type of person. We have magazines for every stage of our lives, from *Jack and Jill* for the very young to *Modern Maturity* for the retired. In between are *YM, Boy's Life, Seventeen, Metropolitan Home, Bride's, Baby Talk, Parents, Working Woman, Family Circle,* and the *Journal of Lifetime Living*.

About twenty-seven hundred business magazines or trade journals are published in this country, at least one suitable for a person in virtually any profession. There is *Modern Packaging, Broadcasting, Sales Management, Editor and Publisher, Medical Economics, The American Brewer,* and many more.

Whatever your hobby—whether taking photographs, building model airplanes, computers, skiing, camping, sewing, or gardening—there is a magazine for you. Nudists have their own magazines, as do most religious denominations and many ethnic groups. There are magazines designed for citizens who are politically conservative and others designed for citizens who are politically liberal or even radical. Many large companies have their own publications for employees. An interest for which a magazine has not been designed would be difficult to find.

Targeting the audience. Publishers have found they must target a particular kind of audience when they design a magazine. Examples of such targeting can be seen in the variety of women's magazines that exist today. Some observers point out that we do not even need to look inside the magazines to determine their target audience; we can often see it from the way they are marketed. Magazines aimed at middle-class homemakers, such as *Woman's Day*, *Redbook*, and *Ladies' Home Journal*, can be found next to the cashier's stand in supermarkets. *Lear's*, which is aimed at sophisticated women over 40, is more likely to be found in a bookstore. *True Story* and *Movie Mirror* are most likely to be displayed on the magazine racks of cut-rate drugstores.

A number of magazines are aimed at people with different kinds of mass communication interests. There is the *Journal of Broadcasting and Electronic Media*, *Journalism Quarterly*, *Printers' Ink*, *Films in Review*, *Journal of Communication*, and many others.

The probability is increasing that you will encounter versions of some popular American magazines in languages other than English. For example, Spanish-language editions of *Good Housekeeping* are now available.

Standard Rate and Data Service, from which advertisers can get information about the media in which they might want to advertise, lists 51 different types of consumer magazines, 12 types of farm magazines, and 159 different types of business magazines—and that is probably an underestimate of the amount of specialization in such publications.

The one general magazine that has bucked the trend toward specialization with tremendous success is *Reader's Digest*. When it was started in 1922, its underlying principle was to make available in short and easily understood form material of interest to the general public from a wide range of other sources. As its name implies, it published digests of articles from other magazines. Most of its material today no longer comes from other magazines, but the type of material remains much the same. Not only is it the third best-selling magazine in America, it is published in 16 different languages and circulated widely in most countries of the world. *Reader's Digest* serves as a good reminder of the fact that, even though we know a great deal about human behavior and economics, both are still sufficiently unpredictable that an idea that runs against the tide still might succeed. For this reason, imaginative people are always needed in mass communication, as well as people who know the research and history of the media. The ideal, of course, is to have people who are both imaginative and knowledgeable.

Impact on magazines of changes in our society. The social movements of the 1950s and 1960s probably affected the content of magazines more than the content of any other medium. Blacks and members of other minorities ceased to be the invisible Americans in general circulation publications. Articles for women, reflecting the rising consciousness of many American women, turned from a focus on gaining and holding a husband to stories on women in business or politics and on the issue of women's rights. Social issues, such as poverty, child abuse, and abortion became popular topics for magazine treatment.

Some magazines had a difficult time adjusting to changes in society. Women's magazines in particular lost readers as a result of changing tastes, work habits, and competition from new magazines targeted to changing needs. The circulation of the so-called Seven Sisters—*Better Homes and Gardens, Family Circle, Woman's Day, Good Housekeeping, McCall's, Ladies Home Journal,* and *Redbook*—dropped from 45 million in 1979 to 37 million in 1989. To attract new readers, the Seven Sisters have undergone considerable change—shortening articles, redesigning covers, changing typefaces, and finding more relevant subject matter.

REVIEW

Among today's magazines, there is one for almost every type of person. Publishers aim these magazines at target audiences—individuals with common interests. An exception is *Reader's Digest*, a general interest magazine. Regardless of type, most magazines reflect the social and political concerns of the day.

The increased interest in radio and television news in the past decade has its counterpart in the magazine business. Although news magazines do not compete in circulation with *TV Guide* or *Reader's Digest*, they are among the large-circulation publications in this country. *Time* has a weekly circulation of about 4.5 million, *Newsweek* has about 3 million, and *U.S. News and World Report* somewhat over 2 million. To estimate their weekly audiences, each of these figures should be tripled or quadrupled, since an average of between three and four persons read each copy. This is 50 percent more than read the average newspaper.

Not only have the three major news magazines been doing well in recent years; an increasing number of other magazines during the 1970s began devoting some of their space to news coverage in order to capitalize on the public's interest in what is going on in the world. *The New Yorker, Esquire, Harper's, Atlantic,* and many other magazines today devote substantial space to detailed treatment of major contemporary news events and issues.

Format and layout. Publishers and editors adapt to their target audiences not only through the content of their magazines and the treatment of the content, but through the format and layout of their magazines as well. The format is the magazine's basic size and shape. A magazine's layout includes a number of ingredients: the order or arrangement of the different types of material, the amount and types of illustration, the amount of color and the way it is used, and the kind of paper stock on which the magazine is printed.

For magazines that depend heavily on newsstand sales, the layout of the cover is especially important. It must attract the attention of the browsers and make them want to pick the magazine up and leaf through the pages. Once someone has picked it up, the chances of a sale are markedly increased. The cover of each issue must be immediately recognizable as the cover of that particular magazine—for example, *Time*—but at the same time be sufficiently different from other issues of that particular magazine to let potential readers know they have not seen it before.

BYLINE

The next time you are in a store with a large display of magazines, examine their covers to see how they attempt to appeal visually to different types of potential readers. How many types of possible readers can you identify just through these visual cues, ignoring what you know about the content of each magazine?

Impact of Advertising on Magazines

One major reason for the greater specialization of magazines these days is advertising. Magazines have become more specialized not only because the general interest publication could not deliver a large audience to advertisers for as low a cost per thousand as television could, but also because many advertisers have come to realize they neither need nor want a general audience. By pinpointing their potential customers, companies can reduce advertising costs because they are not paying for readers who can do them no good. In other words, if you are selling camping equipment, why should you pay for readers who never go camping? That is precisely what you must do, though, if you advertise in a general interest magazine. On the other hand, when you advertise in a camping or hunting magazine, you are getting more relevant readers for each dollar you invest. The same is true whether you are advertising lingerie, pipe tobacco, Rolls Royces, or a laundry detergent. Obviously, there are some products for which almost anyone is a potential purchaser. Most products, though, are bought largely by particular types of persons, and advertisers want to place their messages in the magazines where almost every reader will be one of those types. And that magazine is the specialized one.

Companies obviously find magazine advertising worthwhile, for they are doing a great deal of it. Examine your favorite magazines, and you will probably find that, on the average, almost half the space is devoted to advertising. This percentage has remained surprisingly stable over the past few decades, ranging between about 45 and 50 percent. Though magazines vary a great deal in this respect, some carrying far more advertising than editorial copy, others carrying a far greater percentage of editorial copy, on the average, that 50:50 ratio seems to hold.

Advertising rates. The cost of advertising in magazines today is generally based on a periodical's circulation, the particular kinds of readers that it has, the size of the ad, its use of color or black and white, and the frequency with which the advertiser agrees to buy space. Sometimes renewal discounts are available when an advertiser agrees to continue buying at least as much advertising space for a second, third, or fourth year. Some magazines also charge different rates for advertising in different sections. For example, the inside front cover and the back of a magazine often bring premium prices. Publishers who own a group of magazines may offer a special discount to advertisers who buy space in more than one.

Advertising rates depend in large part on circulation, and when advertising became important, the need arose for reliable circulation figures. Various associations of advertisers and advertising agencies led the drive to establish a systematic and consistent means of obtaining figures. The result was the **Audit Bureau of Circulations (ABC)**, established in 1914, which *verifies the circulation figures of its member magazines and furnishes other information to advertisers about each magazine's subscribers*. The Business Publications Audit of Circulation (BPA) provides similar information. Both services report the number of copies of a magazine that are given away as well as the number sold. ABC refers to the former as *distribution* and the latter as *circulation*.

Impact of advertising on circulation. As with newspapers, advertising made possible the mass circulation magazine because publishers could sell their magazines cheaply, at a price the middle class and working class could afford. The difference in price was more than made up for in advertising revenue. In fact, the total revenue of some magazines today comes from advertising, and copies are distributed without charge. These are usually highly specialized publications, distributed to readers with a high probability of buying the advertised products. For example, a number of medical journals distributed free to doctors contain primarily advertising of medicines and medical equipment. Also, some magazines about closed circuit television are distributed free to users of such equipment. Such magazines are supported by advertisers who want access to these specific potential customers.

REVIEW

A magazine's format and layout are designed with the target audience in mind. The cover is especially important if the magazine is sold at newsstands. By targeting audiences, magazines help advertisers find their customers. The rates magazines charge for advertisements vary according to their circulation. Advertising reduces the purchase price of magazines and at times may influence their content.

Influence of advertising on content. It is difficult to assess the degree to which advertisers have affected the nonadvertising content of magazines. That they have had some effect, both direct and indirect, is clear. But the extent of that effect is unknown. Certainly most magazines select and shape content so as to attract the kinds of readers in whom their advertisers will be interested.

Some magazines also include content that will more directly please their advertisers. One of the most obvious examples of this was the campaign some magazines waged in the 1940s for repeal of the federal government's tax on cosmetics. All of the magazines involved in the campaign were magazines that depend on advertising by cosmetic manufacturers.

This sort of influence is obvious. What is not so obvious is the degree to which magazines have refrained from using material that some of their advertisers might disapprove of: articles on the dangers of some products such as cigarettes, on the tax breaks of some industries, on questionable union-busting tactics, and so on. Not all editors and publishers have succumbed to pressures to include or exclude materials, but such principled behavior has sometimes resulted in lost advertising.

Frequency of appearance in our mosaics. The frequency of publication of magazines varies almost as widely as their content. Roughly 20 percent of those published in the United States today are weeklies, while 6 percent come out twice a month, 42 percent once a month, 11 percent every two months, and 12 percent every three months. Those percentages have not changed substantially in the past fifty years except for a slight drop in the proportion of monthlies and an increase in the proportion of bimonthlies and quarterlies.

It is impossible to determine precisely the total number of different magazines published in the United States today. Some estimates are as high as sixteen thousand, but the figure given by the U.S. Department of Commerce is 11,229. Most of these, however, are trade publications or company publications for employees and customers, and you are not likely to find them in your mosaic. The ones most likely to be seen by the general public are the thirty-one hundred or so consumer magazines such as *Reader's Digest*, *TV Guide*, and *National Geographic*.

Magazine trade organizations. Although you are probably unaware of them, a number of organizations affect the probability of your being exposed to magazines. These are the professional organizations of publishers and others involved in the magazine industry. Such organizations provide guidance to some publishers that can help keep their magazines alive. More important, they lobby for legislation that can benefit publishers financially and thus make it possible for more of them to stay in business. For example, they lobby for lower postal rates for magazines and for corporate tax laws beneficial to publishers. The two most important magazine trade organizations are the Magazine Publishers of America and the American Society of Magazine Editors.

OUR EXPOSURE TO MAGAZINES

Have you ever thought about how you become exposed to different magazines? You or a member of your household may subscribe to some. A friend may pass a few on to you occasionally. Some you may buy on impulse, because you liked the cover or were browsing through a copy on the newsstand and saw something you wanted to read. You almost certainly glance through magazines when you are waiting in your dentist's or doctor's office or while on an airplane. You may even browse through a magazine or two occasionally when you are waiting for someone in the library or at a friend's home. We suspect that if you kept a careful diary for a six-month period you would discover that you do far more magazine reading than you think. The information in the following section will give you a basis for comparing your reading with that of other people.

The Magazine Audience

There are no reliable estimates of the number of people in the United States who read magazines or the average amount of magazine reading they do. We do know, however, that if you consider a single issue of all of the different magazines published in this country, approximately one-and-a-half copies are sold for every adult in the population. We also know, as mentioned in different contexts before, that the average magazine is read by between two and four persons. Thus, quite a bit of magazine reading appears to be going on in the United States. However, this reading is not spread evenly among American adults. Some read many magazines, while others read none at all.

Our data on the kinds of people who are more likely to read magazines are better than our data on the number who do. Surveys show, not surprisingly, that the amount of magazine reading is highly correlated with education. The more educated people are, the more time they are likely to spend reading magazines. We also know that women tend to read magazines more than men do. This is shown by various kinds of data, including the fact that magazines that appeal primarily to women outsell magazines that appeal primarily to men. It may seem strange or out of date to you for anyone in the 1990s to be talking about men's magazines or women's magazines. However, there is little evidence that the sexual revolution is erasing the clear distinctions between men's and women's tastes in magazines. Men are more likely than women to read magazines that cover news on business and finance, mechanics and science, sports, outdoor life, and those that include photographs of women in various states of undress. Men also have a higher probability of reading the general news magazines. Women, on the other hand, are more likely to read magazines with useful household information (recipes, home decor, child care, and gardening) or fashion and beauty information.

Why do people subscribe to magazines in this era when so many other cheaper or even free sources of information and entertainment are available? There is obviously no simple answer to that question, but one important reason is that they want a different kind of material than is readily available elsewhere or they want more of a certain kind of material than they can find in newspapers or the electronic media. Special interests or desires for detailed coverage of a specialized area apparently are not being served adequately by these other media.

Magazine Circulation It should not be surprising that the two magazines with the largest overall circulation, *Modern Maturity* and *NRTA/AARP News Bulletins* ("NRTA" stands for National Retired Teachers Association, and "AARP" for American Association of Retired Persons), are aimed at retired citizens (Table 5.1). The combination of a longer average life expectancy, lower birth rate, and earlier retirement age has made this demographic group one of the fastest growing in America. Although sales of the magazines are based solely on subscription—or, more precisely, on membership in one of the retirement organizations—their circulations of 22 million copies per issue far outdistance most other magazines. For example, 71 of the 100 leading magazines have a circulation of less than 2 million. As Table 5.1 shows, only a handful have circulations of 10 million or more.

REVIEW

There are more than eleven thousand different magazines published in this country. Some of the largest in terms of circulation are *Modern Maturity, NRTA/AARP News Bulletins, Reader's Digest, TV Guide,* and *National Geographic*. Each of these magazines has a circulation of more than 10 million.

What is surprising, perhaps, is the nature of the next two most widely read magazines, *Reader's Digest* and *TV Guide*. The former is a general interest magazine, the kind that so often disappeared after the rise of television. The other, except for its advertising, is devoted exclusively to another medium.

Some magazines do well both in subscription sales and at the newsstand. *TV Guide* sells roughly half of its copies in supermarkets, convenience stores, and other outlets. *National Geographic* and *Better Homes and Gardens*, on the other hand, are sold mostly through subscription, while *Family Circle* depends mainly on newsstand sales.

BYLINE

How do your magazine reading and tastes compare to the dominant trends? Are they similar to or different from those of other adults of your sex? If they are different, how do you explain that difference? Do you expect your magazine reading habits to change when you are out of college? Why or why not?

Distribution of Magazines We take for granted today the easy access to magazines. We can read them in our public or school library, buy them at the drugstore or newsstand, or have them delivered to our homes. It was not always so. Distribution of magazines was a difficult problem in the early days of this country, as you can imagine. People were widely scattered and the roads extremely primitive.

Importance to magazines of favorable postal rates. When the postal service was established, no one thought of it as a means of delivering magazines or newspapers, so these media were not even mentioned in the laws governing that service. As a result, whether magazines could be sent by

TABLE 5.1 The U.S. Leaders in Magazine Circulation: Combined Subscription and Newsstand Sales

1. *Modern Maturity*	22,443,464
2. *NRTA/AARP News Bulletins*	22,105,308
3. *Reader's Digest*	16,396,919
4. *TV Guide*	15,837,064
5. *National Geographic*	10,182,911
6. *Better Homes and Gardens*	8,002,895
7. *Family Circle*	6,159,147
8. *Good Housekeeping*	5,105,094
9. *Ladies' Home Journal*	5,022,414
10. *McCalls*	5,011,473

Source: Magazine Publishers of America, The 100 Leading A.B.C. Magazines, Average Paid Combined Circulation Per Issue, First Six Months of 1990. Reprinted Courtesy of Magazine Publishers Association.

mail was left to the discretion of each local postmaster. Since some of these postmasters also ran small publishing businesses on the side, they were not uninterested participants. Most of them agreed to deliver magazines but, because there was no law to guide them, the arrangements for such delivery were quite varied. Some delivered magazines without charge. Others insisted that whoever wanted to receive a magazine through the mail must pay a fee. In some cases the fee went to the postmaster, in other cases to the horseman who delivered the mail.

In 1794, the United States Congress finally amended the postal regulations to legalize the mailing of magazines. However, that amendment made clear that the delivery of magazines was not the primary function of the postal service; the regulation specified that magazines could be delivered "when the mode of conveyance and the size of the mails will permit it."

From this first amendment, our postal laws have recognized the importance of magazines, as well as newspapers and books, to our country and our people. These publications have always been helped by favorable postal laws that permitted them to be sent through the mails much more cheaply than most other sorts of material. In a sense, this was a subsidy that encouraged and made possible the publication of many magazines. This "subsidy" has been sharply reduced in recent years; postal charges for printed matter have risen considerably.

These rising postal rates have hurt magazines even more than television did. For many publishers, the increase in postal rates consumed their margin of profit. Unable to raise their prices sufficiently while at the same time retaining a large enough circulation to attract advertisers, many of them were forced to cease publication.

BYLINE

The effect of rising postal rates on the magazine industry raises the important policy question of what our society's responsibility should be to the mass media. If you believe that many healthy magazines, as well as newspapers and books, are vital for the sort of society you want, what do you think we should be doing to stimulate and nurture them? Should we ask individuals to pay more for their personal letters and businesses to pay more for their correspondence so that magazines and newspapers can get lower postal rates? Should we insist that individuals and nonmedia businesses pay higher taxes so that the mass media businesses can be permitted to pay less? Taking the position that our government should help magazines and other media survive is easy. It is harder to decide who should pay the price.

Subscriptions. Although most magazines can be distributed either through subscriptions or through the sale of single issues on newsstands, traditionally subscription sales have been preferable. Annual or multiyear subscriptions give the publisher a somewhat more dependable circulation. At least as important, subscribers pay in advance, which helps the company's cash position. Getting subscribers to renew their subscriptions is relatively easy, far easier than finding new subscribers. The bookkeeping is also easier for the renewal than the new subscription. This is the reason publishers are so persistent when your payment for renewal fails to come in on time and they fear you may be planning to drop your subscription.

Many commercial agencies help publishers with their magazine subscriptions. Some are called *catalogue agencies* because they publish catalogues listing most of the magazines published in this country. Libraries, other institutions, or individuals can order subscriptions through the catalogue just as one orders merchandise through the Sears and Roebuck catalogue. *Campus agencies* specialize in selling subscriptions to college students through direct mail and displays on campus. Junior and senior high school students are encouraged to sell subscriptions by the *school plan agencies* in order to raise money for such projects as school trips or band uniforms. There are also *telephone agencies*, which, as their name implies, sell either subscriptions or renewals through telephone solicitation. Increasingly important are the *direct mail agencies*, which solicit subscriptions for a large variety of magazines through the mail, usually by offering special discounts or the chance to win a prize.

Another kind of service agency for magazines is the **fulfillment house**. It *helps publishers with some of their circulation and business tasks.* For example, a fulfillment house might be hired to keep the names and addresses of subscribers and the termination dates of each subscription, mail renewal notices to subscribers at the appropriate times, provide mailing labels for each subscriber, and do all of the billing for the publisher.

Because postal rates are rising so rapidly, magazine publishers are beginning to question whether selling magazines through subscriptions is desirable. Unless some alternative and cost-efficient means of delivery is found, they may drop subscription sales. Some publishers have experimented with "piggybacking" magazine deliveries on newspaper deliveries, that is, having them distributed by the same carriers. Others have considered organizing their own system of carriers.

Competing for newsstand sales. The major alternative to subscriptions as a delivery system is newsstand sales, and an increasing number of publishers are focusing on them as the major means of getting their magazines to readers. You can see signs of this trend in the growing number of magazines with attention-catching covers. Such covers are not a new phenomenon, of course. The warm and attractive human scenes painted by Norman Rockwell for the covers of the old weekly *Saturday Evening Post* have become classics. *Time* magazine's people covers, featuring the man or woman of the week or year, have been attracting attention to each new issue for generations. Most common, of course, is the "cover girl," the photograph of a young, attractive model. The competition among magazines

Which cover do you like? That's the question the Hearst Corporation was interested in when it introduced this new lifestyle magazine in 1991. While most readers saw the cover with the full-bleed picture (left), a test sample received the cover with the border and inset photographs. Newsstand sales will be analyzed to determine reader preference.

for attractive cover girls was so intense at one time that it resulted in fortunes for some New York modeling agencies.

The magazine that depends largely on newsstand sales must compete successfully for attention with the many other magazines on the racks in drugstores, department stores, and corner stands. It must stand out from that mass of color, pictures, and design. For this reason, an attention-gaining cover is crucial. Another important factor in selling magazines through newsstands is getting prime display space on those stands. This is similar to the competition among different producers of canned and packaged foods to get good display space on supermarket shelves. With so much competition, and so little difference among some of the products, distributors want the eyes of the potential customer to fall on their product first. The assumption is that if you find yourself in the mood to read a newsmagazine, whether you buy *Time* or *Newsweek* is in good part a function of which one you happen to see first on the newsstand.

Decline in the Number of Distributors

A relatively new problem facing the magazine industry is the decline in the number of distributors. Fifteen years ago there were 13 major national distributors—companies that convince merchants to stock their racks with the magazines they represent and then arrange for their delivery. Today there are only 5, and 2 of these may be joined as a result of the Time-Warner merger. Where have all the distributors gone? Some were swallowed up in the merger fever that has affected other aspects of the magazine industry; others went bankrupt. Murdoch Magazines, for example, became a major distributor when it purchased Triangle Publications, which had its own distribution division. Until then Murdoch had used Select Magazines as its distributor. Having already lost the *McCall's* account as a result of a joint venture between the owner of *McCall's* and Time, Inc., Select Magazines—the only major independent distributor—was forced into bankruptcy when it lost Murdoch as well.

Although sales from newsstands account for only 24 percent of the total circulation revenues of consumer magazines, publishers rely on such outlets to introduce their products to potential customers. Also, the rising cost of using the postal service makes shoppers with money in hand more attractive than subscribers, who often receive their magazines at considerably less than the cover price.

The main concern among small publishers is that the large distribution companies, which are owned by giant publishing corporations, will provide better representation and placement for the magazines they publish. An attorney for Select Magazines put it this way: "If you have a magazine that competes with one published by Hearst, and if Hearst is distributing yours along with two hundred others, it doesn't take much imagination to figure out where the sales force that works for Hearst will spend its energy."

REVIEW

Since magazines are often distributed through the mail, postal rates greatly affect the cost of distribution. The two ways in which magazines are sold are through subscriptions and newsstands. In recent years the number of magazine distributors has declined. The few that are left are owned by the major publishers, who may give preferential treatment to their own magazines.

BYLINE

Some publishers believe what is happening today in the magazine industry is reminiscent of the movie industry in the 1930s when a few major studios controlled all aspects of the business—production, distribution, and exhibition. That type of vertical integration prevented many independent producers from having their movies shown in theaters owned by the major Hollywood studios. Eventually, government action forced the studios to sell their theaters (Chapter 7). Do you think similar action might be necessary to preserve competition among magazine publishers? Under what circumstances would "bigness" constitute a monopoly—a condition for government intervention?

FUNCTIONS AND EFFECTS OF MAGAZINES

The role of magazines in the United States has probably changed more during this century than the role of any other mass medium of communication.

Functions

Before the days of network radio and television, magazines—and, to a lesser extent, books—provided a common base of information and ideas to the educated elite of our country. Unlike most other countries, until fairly recent times we had no major national newspapers that served this function. Today, with their national editions, as we noted in Chapter 4, *The Wall Street Journal* and *New York Times* have assumed that role, but they continue to be supplemented by *Time* and *Newsweek*. (Although it is a national newspaper, *USA Today* is not influential in this way.)

In the early part of this century, magazines also provided Americans with most of their light fiction, much of it very good. To a large extent, television and the paperback have replaced the magazine as supplier of light fiction. However, neither television nor the paperback provides an adequate source for the imaginative short story, the type of fiction that was developed so superbly in some magazines. As a result, the short story form is in danger.

Another and related function served by magazines prior to the rise of the paperback novel was the nurturance of young writers who were attempting to establish their reputations. Magazines provided the only possible outlet for most of these writers. Authors gained experience and established their names and then were able to move into book publication. In addition, during the late 1800s especially, many books were first serialized in a magazine and then published as a single work in hardcover. The magazine provided a type of test market to see whether a work would be sufficiently popular to justify book publication.

Writers such as John Greenleaf Whittier, Nathaniel Hawthorne, Mark Twain, Oliver Wendell Holmes, and Henry Wadsworth Longfellow

REVIEW

At one time magazines provided a common base of information for the educated elite. They were also an important source of light fiction and an outlet for young fiction writers. These functions have either disappeared or have been replaced by television and paperbacks. New ideas have their best chance for appearance in small-circulation magazines. More popular ideas are likely to find their way into magazines devoted to contemporary political affairs.

depended on magazines for an outlet. Many of their important works first appeared in these publications. A young fiction writer today has no comparable outlet. The paperback is the closest approximation, but it is far more difficult for an unknown writer to get a story accepted for paperback publication than it was to get one accepted by a magazine publisher prior to World War II, when short stories and serials were important features in many magazines.

The small-circulation magazine, the "little magazine," plays an important function in our society, even today. More than any of the other media, it is the nurturer of new ideas. As one former magazine editor put it, "Because new ideas . . . do not always or usually attract large audiences, a diversity of small-circulation media is needed to insure their expression." Being in print, in the types of magazines retained by libraries, new ideas can be passed from mind to mind over an extended period of time. The little magazines serve as seedbeds in which ideas can take root and gain strength before being set out where they must face the harsh elements.

The more popular ideas, those in which there is more immediate interest, can be found in a variety of magazines devoted to commentary on contemporary affairs and, especially, controversial issues. These magazines, such as *The Nation*, *National Review*, *The New Republic*, *Progressive Commentary*, and *Mother Jones*, represent a wide range of political ideologies. If you want to know where the political left or the political right or some other politically identifiable group stands on the major issues of the day, the appropriate magazines are probably your most reliable source.

Effects

The effects of magazines are almost as varied as the publications themselves. The women's magazines have shaped the culinary techniques and the clothing styles of women, just as magazines such as *Playboy* have probably affected the clothing and lifestyles and attitudes of some men. The gardens and home furnishings of many of us have been shaped by what we learned from *Better Homes and Gardens*. The business practices of readers are often adjusted because of ideas gleaned from trade journals: farmers get ideas about new hybrid seeds or types of fertilizer, and medical doctors are persuaded to prescribe a new drug.

Less direct is the effect that some magazines have had on newspaper style and content. New Journalism, in which the reporters are important parts of their own stories and which capitalizes on rather than suppresses the writers' subjective reactions to events, began in the magazines. Writers of fiction, such as Norman Mailer, Truman Capote, and Tom Wolfe, created a new type of writing—a hybrid of journalism and fiction—that helped shatter the once-sacred journalistic ideal of "objectivity." Although newspaper journalists have not carried this style to the extremes that some writers have in magazines, the reporting style of many has moved in that direction.

Magazines appeal to both ends of the poltical spectrum as well as the middle. The liberal Mother Jones *finds its counterpart in the conservative* New American.

For generations, our ideas about the traditional roles and interests of women were shaped and reinforced by the women's magazines. Today, some of the magazines have become a force for change, as *Cosmopolitan*, *Self*, and a host of other publications encourage women to consider new roles, new behaviors, and new outlooks on their lives. If not stimulants for change, these magazines at least give support and comfort to women who are in the process of change.

Needed support has come similarly for many minority groups that found their needs unsatisfied by other media. For example, *Ebony* magazine undoubtedly played an important supportive role for the middle class blacks of America during the period in which they were largely ignored by most other publications. *Essence*, *Jet*, and *Ebony* continue to serve the needs of the black community.

THE FUTURE OF MAGAZINES

The technology for printing and distributing magazines is sufficiently sophisticated now to make it possible to include different kinds of information in an issue of the magazine that goes to different geographical areas. This is already being done with the advertising content of some magazines when advertisers want to target different regions. Such technology also makes it possible not only for magazines to provide specialized information to readers, as they are now doing, but for one magazine to provide specialized sections that go only to particular groups of subscribers. This seems the next logical step in the continuing trend toward greater and greater specialization in all of the mass media.

It is difficult to predict the future impact on magazines of cable television's ability to deliver printed information on demand through the video screen. If cable affects any magazines, it is most likely to be the trade magazines. Information useful to specialists in the various professions will be more profitable to program into the cable system and, equally important, those people with an economic motive for reading magazines are more likely to exert the extra effort required to get their information in this new way. The McGraw-Hill publishing firm has been preparing for some time for this shift in the method of delivering the kinds of information now transmitted by trade journals and specialized newsletters. The entire company has been reorganized to emphasize the electronic marketing of information, which companies, educational institutions, and various professionals will be able to receive—for a fee—through telephone lines to their personal computers. McGraw-Hill president Joseph Dionne predicts that, within the next decade, at least half the company's revenues will be coming from such electronic sale and delivery of information.

REVIEW

Magazines affect our lifestyles, attitudes, and ways of doing business. They even affect other media. They also provide support for those whose lives are in the process of change. In the future magazines are likely to become even more specialized as publishers develop new ways of producing and transmitting information.

Despite cable television, the shortage of wood pulp for making paper, and all the other factors that have led some people to predict the end of magazines as we know them today, magazines will survive. There may be fewer than there are today, but their combination of relative permanence, portability, and types of content they are capable of delivering will keep some of us buying them. If your professional goal is a job on the staff of a magazine, or even to start your own magazine, do not be dissuaded by the prophets of doom.[3]

THE SPECIALIZATION OF MAGAZINES: A SUMMARY

As we have seen in this chapter, the major trend in magazines during this century has been their gradual change from general interest publications, which appealed to a broad segment of the population, to highly specialized publications, each appealing to a relatively narrow or homogeneous group. Magazines will continue to provide something for everyone, but in different magazines rather than in the same one. As printing technology improves even more, the day may soon arrive when you can order almost any kind of print and pictorial material in a unique magazine tailored to your special interest.

A major problem that will remain, however, is distribution. Rising postal rates are making it less practical to distribute magazines by mail. Publishers, therefore, are depending more on over-the-counter sales, although this distribution system does not provide the dependable circulation from week to week or month to month that subscriptions do.

Increased dependence on over-the-counter sales also has some side effects. One is to make the magazine's appearance more critical, since it must compete with the large number of other magazines on the racks in attracting the attention of potential purchasers.

The increased specialization of magazines means you are less likely to find something that interests you when you flip through the pages of a random assortment of magazines. You must search more systematically for the type of magazine you want, just as magazine publishers must work more systematically to design the content, layout, and delivery system of their magazines for their particular target audiences.

Although magazines no longer serve as primary breeding grounds for hopeful young writers of fiction, they still serve many other important functions. To some extent, they provide a common base of knowledge to individuals with similar concerns who are scattered throughout this vast country. More than any other medium of communication, magazines are the testing grounds and nurturers of new ideas. If you want to know what the leading business leaders or political scientists, or the far right or left, are thinking today, you are most likely to find their thoughts in the magazines that are targeted for each of those specific groups.

Magazines thus shape the thinking of many of us, as we learn what our peers and would-be peers around the country are saying. They also shape many of our behaviors as we buy and read those magazines that can provide ideas on nudist colonies and homemaking, farming and jogging, camping and politics. Whatever your needs and interests, there are magazines to serve them.

DISCUSSION QUESTIONS

1. What types of magazines were there in this country prior to the Civil War?
2. When did the magazine truly become a mass medium? What factors increased its popularity?
3. What brought about the demise of the general interest magazine?
4. Why have so many magazines been brought under the umbrella of larger media corporations? Cite some examples.
5. Why are magazines referred to as the special interest medium?
6. In what ways does advertising affect magazines?
7. What are some of the major circulation magazines? What accounts for their popularity?
8. How are magazines distributed and sold? What are some of the concerns expressed by small publishers about the magazine distribution business?
9. What do you see as the major change in the function of magazines in the future? How will new technologies or other media likely affect the magazine business?

NOTES

1. Quoted in Frank Luther Mott, *A History of American Magazines, 1741–1850* (New York: D. Appleton & Co., 1930), p. 64. Mott's four volumes on the history of American magazines from 1741 through 1905 is the best source available for detailed information on this early history. An account of more

recent magazine history, up to 1964, can be found in Theodore Peterson, *Magazines in the Twentieth Century*, 2nd ed. (Urbana: University of Illinois Press, 1964).

2. Mott, p. 424.
3. If starting or managing a magazine is one of your goals, you may want to read the *Handbook of Magazine Publishing*, ed. Marjorie McChanus (New Canaan, Conn.: Folio Magazine Publishing Corp., 1977). This is an excellent source of practical information on all aspects of publishing a magazine.

SUGGESTED READINGS

Relevant Contemporary Works

Bagdikian, Ben H. "The Lords of the Global Village." *The Nation*, 12 June 1989, pp. 805–820.

Benton, Mike. *The Comic Book in America: An Illustrated History*. Dallas, TX: Taylor Publishing, 1989.

Ferguson, Marjorie. *Forever Feminine: Women's Magazines and the Cult of Femininity*. Portsmouth, NY: Heinemann, 1983.

Gordan, Jean, and McArthur, Jan. "Popular Culture, Magazines and American Domestic Interiors, 1898–1940." *Journal of Popular Culture* 22 (Spring 1989): 35–60.

Hubbard, J. T. L. *Magazine Editing for Professionals*. Rev. ed. Syracuse: Syracuse University Press, 1989.

Kanner, Bernice. "Advertisers Talk Frankly About Magazines." *Folio: The Magazine for Magazine Management* 15 (January 1986): 132–137.

Kiely, Thomas. "In Praise of Smallness: Small-Circulation Periodicals Are Vital to Intellectual Life." *The Nation* 13 (April 1985): 417.

Levin, Jack, Mody-Desbareau, Amita, and Arluke, Arnold. "The Gossip Tabloid as Agent of Social Control." *Journalism Quarterly* 65 (Summer 1988): 514–517.

Magazine Publishing Career Directory. New York: Career Publishing Corp., 1985.

Niles, Nicholas. "Personalization Will Reach New Levels Next Decade." *Advertising Age* 60 (May 1989): 76.

Wolseley, Roland E. *The Changing Magazine*. New York: Hastings House, 1983.

See also *Advertising Age*.

CHAPTER 6

Photography: Fixing a Shadow

OBJECTIVES

After studying this chapter, you should be able to

- Describe the major technological developments in the history of photography.
- Discuss the early trends in portrait, landscape, and documentary photography.
- Identify the factors that made amateur photography popular.
- Trace the evolution of photojournalism and its role in development of the tabloid newspaper and picture magazine.
- Discuss the effects of the Depression and World War II on styles of photography.
- Explain the major trends in photography as an art form.
- Speculate on future technological developments in photography.

In his first account of his discovery, written in 1839, Talbot included a subheading titled "On the Art of Fixing a Shadow," where he described what he believed to be the domain of photography. "The most transitory of things," he wrote, "a shadow, the proverbial emblem of all that is fleeting and momentary, may be fettered by the spells of our 'natural magic,' and may be fixed for ever in the position which it seemed only destined for a single instant to occupy."

from *On the Art of Fixing a Shadow: One Hundred and Fifty Years of Photography*, published in 1989 by the National Gallery of Art and The Art Institute of Chicago

Of all the pictorial media, the one with which we have the most experience—as producers as well as consumers—is still photography. Unlike the camcorder, which was introduced just a little over a decade ago, or the super 8 motion picture camera that preceded it, amateur still photography has been around since the turn of the century. Most of our homes are filled with treasured pictures of families, friends, places, and occasions—bits of information embedded in our memories, reminders of who we were, where we came from, and, perhaps, why we are the way we are today. Photography is also an important medium of mass communication, one that is both an integral part of other mass media, such as newspapers and magazines, and a medium unto itself. Published in book form or exhibited in art museums, photographs as works of art range from the avant-garde images of Man Ray and Chuck Close to the stark realism of Dorothea Lange and Walker Evans. Like the motion picture and radio and television, **photography**, which literally means "*writing or drawing with light*" had its origins in scientific invention.

TECHNOLOGICAL DEVELOPMENTS

No one knows for sure when or where the idea originated of obtaining a permanent and objective reproduction of the visible world, but human beings appear to have always had an urge to communicate their views of the environment. Before the development of writing, they did almost all of this communication with pictures. As far back as ten to twenty thousand years ago they were communicating their visual experiences by drawing on the walls of caves in southern France and northern Spain, and some of these early images were remarkably realistic. Continuously since that time, through paintings and sculptures, artists have continued to document their world.

In some instances, as in portrait painting, these early artists achieved great fidelity. But it was not until much later that a different form of painting—painting with light—enabled them to reproduce effortlessly what their eyes perceived. In the early part of the nineteenth century the paths of two scientific discoveries merged to produce a workable system of photography. The first path, which involved an optical system capable of capturing an image, had its roots in pinhole imagery and the discovery of how to make and grind glass into lenses that could project an image. The other path had to do with the chemical reaction that occurs when silver salts are exposed to light.

The Camera The optical principle upon which the camera was developed was known to the ancient Greeks, who observed that sunlight passing through a pin-sized hole in the wall of a darkened room produced the sun's image on the opposite wall. Early astronomers seeking ways to study solar eclipses without damaging their eyes were the first to find a practical application for this phenomenon. It was not until the late Renaissance that the idea of designing a camera for pictorial purposes and incorporating the "pinhole image formation" principle emerged. Inspired by major strides in artistic development that began in the late thirteenth century, Giovanni Battista Della Porta suggested the use of a camera as a sketching device.

The earliest **camera obscura**, or **dark chamber**, was *a darkened room in which a tiny ray of sunlight through a small hole in the wall projected an inverted and laterally reversed image on a white wall opposite the hole* (Figure 6.1). Later, a glass lens was placed over the hole, thereby increasing the brightness of the projected image. By the late seventeenth century, refinements in lensmaking and smaller, more portable cameras made possible a practical means of projecting an image onto a flat surface, placing tracing paper over it, and sketching a reasonably faithful reproduction. A half-century later, cameras were being fashioned to fit specific needs. Depending upon the size of the camera and the focal length of the lens, some were better suited for sketching portraits, while others provided a better perspective for illustrating landscapes and panoramas. The invention of photography—and the development of the camera as we know it—might be thought of as the substitution of a chemical means of recording the camera's images for the laborious task of drawing them by hand.

The Photograph While the chemical action of light—such as sunlight darkening the skin or bleaching a fabric—is a common phenomenon, its application to the photochemical process was not understood until the development of chemistry in the late seventeenth and eighteenth centuries. In 1725, a German chemistry professor, Johann Heinrich Schulze, found that silver salts darkened when exposed to light. Later, a Swedish chemist, Carl Wilhelm Scheele, observed that silver chloride was soluble in ammonia but became insoluble when exposed to light. These discoveries and others that followed provided a basis for chemically producing the imprint of an object on a specially coated surface and then preserving that imprint.

At first, experiments were conducted by pressing objects, such as leaves or insect wings, in contact with a photosensitive material and exposing them to sunlight. The more translucent parts of the objects darkened while the opaque features blocked the light. The result was called a "profile" or "photogram." Unfortunately, at that time there was no way to stop the chemical process, so once the photogram was exposed to further sunlight, it darkened uniformly.

Another forerunner of photography took shape when a French physicist, Joseph Nicephore Niepce, attempted to fix photochemically the image produced by a camera. Having first experimented with **lithography**, *a*

1500–1879

c1558 Camera obscura invented

1727 Johann Heinrich Schulze discovers that light causes silver nitrate to darken

1824 Niepce produces first permanent photograph

1837 L.J.M. Daguerre introduces the daguerreotype

1839 The sale of Daguerre's invention to the French government marks the true beginning of photography

1840 William Henry Fox Talbot invents the calotype process

1840 First commercial photography studio in America opens in New York City

1851 Frederick Archer introduces the collodium wet-plate process

1871 Richard L. Maddox invents the dry-plate process

1880–1900

1880 New York *Daily Graphic* publishes first halftone photograph

1881 George Eastman forms the Eastman Dry Plate Company, later reorganized as Eastman Kodak

1884 Eastman develops flexible film

1887 Discovery of flashlight powder makes night photography possible

1888 Eastman introduces the Kodak box camera and a factory service for processing film

1900 Eastman markets a new camera, the Brownie, for only one dollar

1901–1935

1919 New York *Illustrated Daily News* becomes first newspaper in America illustrated exclusively with halftone photographs

1924 The development of the Leica, a small, lightweight camera with extremely fast lenses, makes candid photography possible

1929 Chemical flash bulbs replace flash powder

1931 Harold E. Edgerton invents an electronic flash

1935 The introduction of Kodachrome and Agfacolor makes high-quality color photography easy to process

1935 AP establishes first wire photo service

1936–1949

1936 Henry R. Luce launches *Life*, America's first picture magazine

1937 The Cowles brothers publish *Look* magazine

1945 National Press Photographers Association formed

1947 Magnum founded to secure copyrights for photographers' works

1947 Polaroid camera develops its own pictures

1950–1989

1971 *Look* magazine folds as a result of competition from television

1972 *Life* suspends publication

1988 Canon introduces the Xapshot, a camera that uses video technology

FIGURE 6.1

The camera obscura or "dark room" was a forerunner of the modern camera. In this drawing, sunlight passing through a small hole in the outer wall projects an inverted image of what the sunlight captures, on the opposite wall. The substitution of a lens for the hole in the outer wall and addition of a means of obtaining a permanent impression of the image formed on the inside wall resulted in the invention of photography.

REVIEW

The principle of pinhole image formation and the making of lenses led to the development of the camera, while the chemical action of light on photosensitive materials provided a basis for permanently recording an image.

printing process that allows chemically treated ink drawings to be transferred from a porous stone or plate to paper, Niepce turned to the camera obscura as a means of producing an image. (One reason Niepce sought the aid of a camera was that his son, on whom he had depended for drawing images, left for the army.) By 1824, he had succeeded in coating a pewter plate with a light-sensitive asphalt varnish and exposing it in a camera to the action of light. The procedure took some eight hours, but gradually the asphalt on the light-exposed parts hardened, while the unexposed parts remained soluble in a mixture of oil of lavender and turpentine and could be removed through a process we now call development. The result was a crude positive image that Niepce called a **heliograph**, from the Greek words meaning sun (*helios*) and to write (*graphein*). *The first complete photographic system* was named **heliography**. Despite its possibilities, heliography was handicapped by the long exposure time required and the delicacy of the operation.

In 1829, Niepce formed a partnership with L. J. M. Daguerre, a successful painter, entrepreneur, and fellow experimenter. Niepce died in 1833, but Daguerre continued the work in heliography and by 1837 had created *a practical photographic process,* which he called **daguerreotypy**, completely *different from the process invented by Niepce*. Daguerre used silvered metal plates that had been fumed with iodine vapor to produce silver iodide (the light-sensitive coating). The plates were placed in the camera for about twenty minutes and afterwards fumed with vapors of heated mercury to develop them. The results were astonishing—exquisitely detailed pictures with a richness and finish that heretofore had been impossible to produce.

Daguerre discovered that he could stabilize the pictures—that is, prevent them from continuing to develop—by bathing them in a strong solution of ordinary table salt. The process was sold to the French government in 1839, the date generally accepted as the beginning of photography. Because of its low cost and relative ease of operation, daguerreotype portraiture became enormously popular in the 1840s and paved the way for the development of commercial photography and a photographic supply industry. Still, daguerreotype photography had one important drawback: there was no way to make multiple copies of a picture. It was a one-of-a-kind process.

The solution to the problem lay in a process that was developed by an English scientist, William Henry Fox Talbot. Working at the same time as Daguerre, Talbot devised a photographic system that produced tonally reversed, or "negative," prints. To re-reverse the tonality, Talbot simply printed the negative onto a new piece of sensitized paper, thereby producing a positive print. The advantage of this new procedure was that more than one print could be made from a negative. The disadvantages were that the finished product had less resolution than the daguerreotype, and exposure time was quite long—as much as two to three hours in bright sunlight. In 1840, Talbot invented an entirely new means of developing negatives. Experiments with a solution of silver nitrate, acetic acid, and gallic acid yielded a much more sensitive negative that reduced exposure time to a minute or two or even, in strong sunlight, to a few seconds. The new **calotype** process, *the first negative-positive system of making photographs*, provided the technical basis for modern photography.

REVIEW

The earliest photographic process was called heliography. In 1839, the date generally recognized as the beginning of photography, L. J. M. Daguerre sold his daguerreotypy process to the French government. The next year the calotype process was introduced, followed by the collodium wet-plate process in 1851 and a dry-plate process twenty years later.

The lack of resolution in finished prints led other scientists to experiment with alternate ways to make negatives. Of particular importance was the work of Talbot's friend, Sir John Herschel, who coined the term *photography*. Herschel had earlier suggested the use of sodium thiosulfate (hypo) as a fixing agent, a practice still in existence today. Later, Herschel experimented with the use of glass plates as an emulsion base.

But the real breakthrough in the development of a glass-plate process was made in 1851 by the amateur English photographer, Frederick Scott Archer. Archer's **collodium wet-plate process** was *a negative-positive system similar to that of Talbot, except that it yielded a much more highly detailed print and was less cumbersome to work with*. Collodium, a highly volatile mixture of ether, alcohol, and nitrated cellulose, bound photosensitive silver salts to a sheet of glass. While still wet, the glass was loaded into the camera, exposed, and then processed before the emulsion dried out. One advantage of the collodium process was that it was far more predictable than the paper negative process and usually more sensitive to light; furthermore, it did away with the poisonous mercury vapors used in the daguerreotype process, and the size of the negatives was limited only by the size of the equipment. By 1856, nearly all photographers had converted to the wet-plate process, although some began substituting *thin metal plates* for glass *to hold the collodium emulsion*. These metal plates became known as **tintypes**. The fact that collodium negatives could be printed quickly and easily by relatively unskilled workers gave rise to the mass production of cheap photographic prints and to a large-scale commercial photography industry and photographic publishing companies.

The next major advancement in photographic technology was a **dry-plate process** introduced in 1871 by an English physician, Richard L. Maddox. *The dry plate substituted a gelatin for collodium*. Until this time, photographers had to carry their equipment with them in order to process the collodium emulsions before they dried. Photographers who ventured outside had to take a wagonload of equipment—camera, glass plates, chemicals, trays, and measuring utensils—and a tent that served as a darkroom. With the dry-plate process, the photographs could be developed later. By the late 1870s, improvements in the gelatin emulsion reduced exposure time to 1/25 of a second and freed photographers from having to use tripods

Using wagons to haul their cumbersome equipment, photographers left the confines of the studio to document the war between the North and South, which lasted from 1861 to 1865.

to take pictures. Subjects who only a few years before had to sit for several minutes while the chemical action of light worked its magic in the camera now merely had to look at the camera momentarily for the photographers to complete their work. This development changed not only the process of photography but also its subject matter.

THE PRACTICE OF PHOTOGRAPHY

Early photographers were fascinated by their ability to record the visible world accurately. For this reason, perhaps, the initial function of photography—one that persists to this day—was to capture the look of things. Faces, architecture, landscapes—these became the major province of the new photographic art.

Portrait Photography

Almost as soon as the daguerreotype process was introduced to the world, portrait studios sprang up in cities across Europe and America, as photographers and would-be photographers pursued commercial exploitation of the new invention. Many of the daguerreotype portraits were modeled after the hand-painted miniatures that preceded them and showed much attention to the pose, placement, and lighting of subjects.

In the United States, the first commercial studio was opened in 1840 by John Johnson and Alexander Wolcott, who constructed their own studio camera and made considerable improvements in daguerreotype photography. An item in the *New York Sun* of Wednesday, March 4, of that year heralded the new enterprise:

> *Mr. A. S. Wolcott, no. 52 First Street, has introduced an improvement on the daguerreotype, by which he is able to execute miniatures, with an accuracy as perfect as nature itself, in the short space of from three to five minutes. We have seen one, taken on Monday, when the state of the atmosphere was far from favorable, the fidelity of which is truly astonishing. The miniatures are taken on silver plate, and enclosed in bronze in cases, for the low price of three dollars for single ones. They really deserve the attention of the scientific, and are valuable acquisition to art, and to society in every respect.*[1]

BYLINE

Early portrait photographs were often framed in a mat, protected by glass, and placed inside an attractively designed miniature case. Some photographs were encased in pieces of jewelry such as lockets or bracelets. Do you or your family have any old photographs displayed in this manner? What do you do with the photographs you take? Do you put them away in a drawer or display them in an album or some other way?

Daguerreotypes soon became familiar household items and an integral part of American culture. Within a decade there were almost a thousand daguerreotype photographers in America and probably five times that many people involved in servicing the new profession. Two of the more famous photographers of that era were Mathew Brady and Jesse H. Whitehurst. Brady, who had studios in New York and Washington, photographed such political luminaries as Andrew Jackson, John Quincy Adams, John C. Calhoun, Henry Clay, Abraham Lincoln, and Jefferson Davis. Whitehurst, a flamboyant organizer-promoter, at one point operated as many as seven studios. Among his many distinguished clients—whose photographs were sold to the public—were General Franklin Pierce, General Winfield Scott, Daniel Webster, Stephen A. Douglas, and numerous theater personalities.

Landscape Photography

Advancements in the process of photography, along with the industrialization of society and the lure of the faraway, offered new possibilities for photographers who wanted to venture outside the studio. Roger Fenton, an English photographer who traveled to Russia in the early 1850s, took pictures of the Crimean War for a London newspaper, which made wood engravings of the photographs in order to print them in the paper.

In America, the gold rush of 1849 and the settling of the West attracted a horde of photographers who doggedly trekked across mountains and plains to document the look of hastily constructed cities, gold diggings, and the exquisite natural beauty they encountered along the way. Among them was an artist-turned-photographer, William Henry Jackson, a Civil War veteran who grew restless in his comfortable New England surroundings and headed west in 1866. Working first as a sign painter and art instructor in Chicago, Jackson saved enough money to travel to St. Louis, where rail lines ended and westbound trails began. He worked on a wagon train hauling food and supplies to Montana goldfields before landing his first job as a photographer's helper. In 1870, he was hired as a photographer for a government geological expedition and within a matter of years was well on his way to becoming the most celebrated landscape photographer in America. Jackson's photographs, mostly albumin prints made from collodium wet plates, included stunning panoramas of some of the West's most beautiful scenery—the Teton and Wind River Ranges, the San Juans, Colorado's central Rockies, and Yellowstone. The photographs of Yellowstone so impressed Congress that in 1872 it created the world's first national wilderness park.

REVIEW

Early photographers were interested in how things looked. Many of them made pictures of people and landscapes.

Another important landscape photographer of that era was Timothy H. O'Sullivan, who, like Jackson, traveled with a government survey team. O'Sullivan introduced the American public to the wonders of the Grand Canyon, the immense waters of Shoshone Falls, and the fissure vents of Steamboat Springs.

Documentary Photography

Rather than emphasizing portraits or landscapes, some early photographers turned their attention to the relationship between people and their environment. Working in the field instead of the studio, these photographers pioneered what is now called documentary photography. One event that helped shape this development was the exploration of the West. In addition to capturing the magnificent natural beauty of the territory west of the Mississippi, photographers documented all aspects of frontier living—wagon trains making their way westward, Indians still largely untouched by the outside world, even themselves loading and unloading their cumbersome gear or standing beside their processing tents.

But more than anything, it was the Civil War that gave photographers the opportunity to show the evocative power of the documentary. Whether it was soldiers enduring the rigors of camp life or bloated bodies strewn across a battlefield, photographers were there to record the moment so the rest of the world could see and experience the many faces and horrors of war. Oliver Wendell Holmes, the American writer whose son—later to become a Supreme Court justice—was wounded several times during the war, said of the battlefield photographs of Antietam:

> *It was so nearly like visiting the battlefield to look over these views, that all of the emotions excited by the actual sight of the stained and sordid scene, strewed with rags and wrecks, came back to us, and we buried them in the recesses of our cabinet as we would have buried the mutilated remains of the dead they too vividly represented.*[2]

Mathew Brady, already a famous portrait photographer, was among the first to conceive of the war—and the prominent figures engaged in the war effort—as subject matter for the camera. Using the improved wet-plate process, he first concentrated on Union troops camped around Washington but soon ventured onto the battlefield, where he and his staff recorded some of the most memorable and shocking scenes of the war. Some of the photographs attributed to Brady were actually made by his talented assistants—Alexander Gardner, George N. Bernard, and Timothy H. O'Sullivan, who would later make his mark as a landscape photographer. Gardner published two volumes of Civil War photographs, which included haunting pictures of the dead at Gettysburg.

Two other photographers who recorded memorable battlefield scenes were John Reekie and Andrew Joseph Russell. Reekie's photographs in particular stirred Northern passions. One showed a burial detail of recently freed slaves going about the grisly business of removing the skeletons of Union soldiers who had been left on the field of battle the year before by victorious Confederate troops. Unlike most of the wartime photographers, Russell was a soldier assigned by the War Department to take pictures for the Corps of Engineers. Many of his photographs were of bridges and pontoons and other types of construction, but he also received permission to record the aftermath of battle. His photograph of dead Confederate soldiers scattered along a low rock wall at Fredericksburg was a grim reminder of what war was all about.

REVIEW

The exploration of the West and the Civil War brought about a new style of photography called documentary. Its emphasis was on the relationship between people and their environment.

Because of the slowness in processing photographs, most Civil War battlefield pictures were of troops waiting to go into battle or of the aftermath of battle.

AMATEUR PHOTOGRAPHY

In the latter part of the nineteenth century, improvements in photographic film and camera design and the rapid growth of the photographic industry resulted in a technology easily available to ordinary people who wanted to record everyday life experiences. Richard L. Maddox's gelatin dry-plate process laid the foundation for popularizing photography on a grand scale. But it was George Eastman who created a mass market for amateur photography when he introduced an inexpensive, easy-to-use, lightweight camera with a roll-film system and a photofinishing industry to take care of the complicated and laborious task of transforming exposed negatives into positive prints.

Eastman Kodak

A little more than a decade after the Civil War, George Eastman, a bank clerk in Rochester, New York, took up a new hobby—photography. At the time, amateurs were generally discouraged by the complexity of picture taking. The collodium wet-plate process was still the predominant means of taking pictures, and while it was an improvement over earlier photographic systems, it was incredibly cumbersome by today's standards. But Eastman, being mechanically inclined, quickly mastered the intricacies of the technology and began experimenting with the recently developed dry-plate process, which he had read about in the *British Journal of Photography*. In 1879, he invented and patented a machine for making the dry plates used in cameras. Two years later, Eastman and a partner, Henry A. Strong, formed the Eastman Dry Plate Company, which was reorganized in 1892 as the Eastman Kodak Company.

The first revolutionary change Eastman brought to photography was the flexible roll of film to replace the bulky glass plate. The roll was made of paper coated with a dry emulsion. Two rollers inside the camera allowed the operator to spool the film continuously through the camera. Shortly after introducing the roll-film system, Eastman switched from paper to celluloid backing, thereby creating a completely transparent, flexible film. (Thomas Edison's assistant, William Dickson, later added sprocket holes to the film and incorporated this advance into the development of the motion picture camera and a device for viewing film. See the next chapter.)

Another revolutionary development in photography occurred in 1888 when Eastman introduced the Kodak box camera. It consisted of nothing more than a lens, film holder, and shutter mechanism. The light, portable camera measured 3¼ by 3¾ by 6½ inches and held a 100-exposure roll of film. The camera—film and all—sold for $25. Over the next several years, the combination of mass demand and modification resulted in a camera that was even cheaper and easier to use—the Brownie, which Eastman introduced in 1900 at the astonishingly low price of $1. According to one report, more than one hundred thousand Brownie cameras were sold that first year.

But the Eastman innovation that really created a mass market for photography was a system for processing film. The greatest obstacle to amateur photography had been the complicated tasks of film developing and printing. But with the Kodak, the photographer simply took the pictures and then sent the camera and its contents to the Eastman Kodak factory. There the camera would be unloaded and the film processed. The developed prints would be returned to the customer along with the camera and a new roll of film. As a Kodak camera advertisement in 1890 said: "You press the button, we do the rest." Public acceptance was instantaneous. By 1895, there were an estimated 1.5 million roll-film cameras in use throughout the world. Photography had become an international hobby.

Personal Photography The development of an inexpensive, easy-to-use camera and a photofinishing industry did more than create a mass market for photography. It gave rise to an entirely new subject matter, new functions, and even a new vocabulary for the medium. While the first fifty years of photography had been dominated by professionals—those who earned their living by taking pictures—the majority of photographers in succeeding generations would be amateurs. Some of them—the so-called true amateurs—took up picture taking as a serious hobby and participated in all aspects of the process.

George Eastman's Kodak and Brownie cameras made amateur photography popular worldwide. This 1909 advertisement shows just how sophisticated cameras had become in the 20 years since the Kodak was introduced.

If it isn't an Eastman, it isn't a Kodak.

Put "KODAK" on that Christmas List.

There's nothing, unless it be the after-delight in the pictures themselves, that more universally appeals to young and old than picture taking. And it's inexpensive now, for Kodak has made it so. There are Kodaks and Brownies for all people and purposes—but none more popular than the simple and compact

FOLDING POCKET SERIES.

No. 1,	2¼ x 3¼	pictures,	$10.00
No. 1A,	2½ x 4¼	"	12.00
No. 1A, Spcl.	2½ x 4¼	"	15.00
No. 3,	3¼ x 4¼	"	17.50
No. 3A,	3¼ x 5½,	"	20.00
No. 4.	4 x 5	"	20.00

Box form Kodaks at $5.00 to $12.00 and Brownie Cameras (they work like Kodaks) at $1.00 to $12.00 and high speed Kodaks with anastigmat lenses at $40.00 to upwards of $100.00 offer an infinite variety, but in none of them have we omitted the principle that has made the Kodak success—simplicity.

Kodak means Photography with the bother left out.

EASTMAN KODAK CO.

Catalogue free at the dealers or by mail.

Rochester, N. Y., *The Kodak City.*

Others merely wanted a visual record of the important people and occasions in their lives. The true amateur experimented with the medium, created special effects, formed or joined photo clubs and photographic societies, and subscribed to photo magazines such as *The American Amateur Photographer*. The other kind of amateur, far more prevalent and less

REVIEW

Amateur photography was made possible largely by the innovations of George Eastman, who founded Eastman Kodak. His contributions included the inexpensive, easy-to-use, lightweight camera and a system for processing film. As photography became more popular, new subject matter, new functions, and even new terms such as *snapshot* were introduced.

intrigued by the technical or artistic aspects of photography, simply settled for pictures that "came out" when they were developed.

Unlike the works of the professional photographers, which were often characterized as "views," "landscapes," or carefully composed "portraits," the works of amateurs were usually distinctly personal recordings of everyday or commonplace occurrences, often hurriedly made with hand-held cameras and with little thought given to any larger meaning. Because of faster emulsions, the camera could freeze in a fraction of a second actions too rapid for the human eye to follow. It could act as a casual observer, capturing the very instant of a smile or frown, gesture or movement.

Sometimes subjects did not even know their pictures were being made. *Photographs produced* in this manner, *instantaneously* and *without deliberation*, were called **snapshots**, after the hunting term to describe a hurried shot of an animal on the run. The ability to make snapshots became increasingly important to professional as well as amateur photographers and facilitated the development of another style of photography—photojournalism.

PHOTOJOURNALISM

The use of the camera by a reporter began long before the technology was available to publish photos on the same page as printed text. **Photojournalism**, *photographs of current events published in newspapers and magazines*, had its roots in the documentary style of photography (discussed earlier) and in the work of sketch artists who furnished illustrations of news events to newspapers and magazines. These illustrations were used to make wood engravings, which could then be printed. Ironically, the artists and engravers whose jobs eventually would be lost to photojournalists often based their drawings and engravings on photographs.

Illustrated News

By the mid-1800s, a number of newspapers and magazines were regularly employing artists to supply them with sketches of important events. Although photography had already appeared on the scene, sketch artists of that day enjoyed several advantages over photographers, including the opportunity to embellish events to suit aesthetic needs and the ability to stop action. Some sketch artists, such as Alfred A. Waud, Thomas Nast, and Winslow Homer, became quite famous. Waud recorded Civil War scenes for *Harper's Weekly* and later traveled throughout the South illustrating the aftermath of the war. Nast also achieved prominence during the Civil War, although he is best remembered as the cartoonist who introduced the donkey and elephant as symbols of the Democratic and Republican parties. Winslow Homer, whose powerful, naturalistic paintings of the sea made him one of America's most famous artists, began his career as a freelance illustrator. *Harper's Weekly* employed him to sketch Civil War battlefield scenes.

newspapers, circulations increased dramatically. By 1910, the hand-drawn engraving had all but disappeared, while the halftone had become a front-page staple.

As competition among newspapers heated up, publishers went to great lengths to bring in more readers, sometimes spicing up stories by customizing facts and photos to suit the occasion. The rush to exploit the Spanish-American War—a war some say was prompted by a circulation battle between rival publishers William Randolph Hearst and Joseph Pulitzer—created the first real photo reporters. Newspapers lavishly used photographs—some of them faked or inaccurately labeled—to trumpet "exclusive coverage" of the war.

One of the most colorful photojournalists of this era was Jimmy Hare, who photographed everything from the wreckage of the U.S. battleship *Maine* in Havana harbor to the charges of Teddy Roosevelt's Rough Riders. Hare's pictures were published in *Collier's*, one of the leading magazines of the day. Before the Spanish-American War, he had been a freelance photographer for the *Illustrated American*, a magazine that had committed itself to the use of halftones. Hare's adventuresome nature took him to the combat lines of the Russo-Japanese War, the Mexican Revolution, the First Balkan War, and World War I. He even managed to take a picture of the secretly guarded experiments of the Wright brothers. The photograph, published in *Collier's* in 1908, was the first of a plane in flight.

Throughout the early part of the twentieth century, newspapers and magazines continued to experiment with ways of combining photographs and text to satisfy the public's seemingly insatiable appetite for news. In 1903, the *National Geographic* magazine published its first halftones of a Philippine woman working in the rice fields. It marked the beginning of a long tradition of pictures of faraway lands and cultures. In 1919, New York's *Illustrated Daily News* became the first newspaper in America illustrated exclusively with halftone photographs. It was also this country's first **tabloid newspaper**, *a newspaper that is half the size of ordinary papers and that contains condensed news and much photographic material*. By 1924, the *Daily News*—as it is now called—had attained the largest circulation of any daily newspaper in America. Chock-full of crime and sex stories and sold for only three cents a copy, it was snapped up from the newsstands by a gullible public indulging itself in titillation. In 1928, the *Daily News* ran a full-page picture of convicted murderer Ruth Snyder's execution, which it had secretly photographed. Ignoring a ban on picture taking in the vicinity of the electric chair, Thomas Howard, a photographer for a sister newspaper, strapped a miniature camera to his ankle and entered Sing Sing prison to witness the electrocution. Using a long cable release that ran from his pants pocket down the leg of his trousers, Howard simply pointed his shoe and lifted his pants leg to capture the moment of execution.

The success of the *Daily News* prompted other publishers—first in New York and then elsewhere—to adopt the tabloid form, and soon the war of "gutter journalism" was on. Hearst's *Daily Mirror* and Bernard Macfadden's *Daily Graphic* entered the competition in 1924, churning out all the juicy crime stories and scandals that happened to come along. The *Daily Graphic* pioneered a technique called the "composograph"—a staged and faked news photograph that often had real faces superimposed on the bodies of actors posed the way the actual scene might have occurred.

REVIEW

Intense competition for readers created a demand for sensational stories and pictures and led to the development of a new style of newspaper called the tabloid.

The tabloid format attracted a number of photographers with a penchant for the seamier—and steamier!—side of life. One of these was freelance photographer Arthur Fellig, known by the nickname of "Weegee"—after the Ouija board—for his uncanny ability to appear at just the right place and time to get a picture. The first photographer to use a police radio for tips, Weegee had a novel way of calculating the price of a photograph of a bullet-riddled corpse—$5 per bullet! Weegee concentrated mainly on urban nightlife—especially crime. With the addition of the flash bulb in 1929, nighttime action became much easier to capture, though cameras were still large and bulky, and bulbs had to be replaced each time a picture was made.

Preparing for a New Era

The demand for photographs in newspapers gave rise to specialized photo services. As early as 1898, George Grantham Bain, a newspaper writer and photographer, began accumulating pictures that he then sold to subscribers. By 1905 he had acquired, catalogued, and cross-indexed a million news photographs. Business was brisk and competition keen as rival picture services battled Bain to provide editors with photographs of "spot" news events. In 1919, the Hearst organization formed International News Photos (INP). Shortly thereafter, two other services appeared—Wide World Photos and Acme Pictures. Associated Press (AP) began its photo service in 1927. Eventually, INP and Acme would become part of United Press International (UPI), while Wide World Photos would be acquired by AP. Although the transmission of photographs by wire began in the 1890s, it was not until 1935 that one of the major news agencies, Associated Press, established a wirephoto service to furnish member newspapers with photographs of current events. With equipment from Bell Laboratories and American Telephone and Telegraph (AT&T) lines, AP set up a 25-station network and ushered in the era of rapid picture transmission. Other news services soon followed suit. Along with AP, they became a main source of photographs for newspapers that did not have their own engraving operations.

The worst excesses of the tabloid newspapers subsided in the 1930s, as journalism and photojournalism reached out in new directions. Technological advancements resulted in new cameras coming on the market that were smaller, lighter, and more flexible. Among the most popular of these cameras was the German-made Leica, which had extremely fast, remov-

REVIEW

The invention of the halftone created a demand for specialized photo services to furnish photographs to newspapers. In 1935, the Associated Press established a wirephoto service. New cameras, such as the German-made Leica and Ermanox, facilitated the work of the photojournalist.

able lenses and used a roll of 35-millimeter motion picture film. Because of its ability to take as many as forty pictures without reloading and under almost any conditions, it was often preferred over the Graflex and the Speed Graphic as the best camera for taking action photos unobtrusively. Another popular camera was the Ermanox, also a product of Germany and small in size, with an extra-fast lens. Its major drawback was that, unlike the Leica, which used spool-wound 35-millimeter film, the Ermanox took individually loaded glass plates. The first news photographer to make extensive use of these miniature cameras was Eric Salomon of Germany. Often referred to as the "father of candid photography" and perhaps the first to use the term *photojournalism* to describe his work, Salomon specialized in taking candid shots of public figures going about their work. His style paved the way for the development of the **photo essay**, *a series of related photographs and text*.

Picture Magazines Until Adolf Hitler took power in 1933, the German magazine industry had been flourishing. Innovative publishers such as Stefan Lorant were shaping the forces for a new photojournalism built around the idea of picture magazines, which had been introduced in the late 1920s. Along with many other editors and photographers, Lorant left his homeland to avoid persecution by the Nazis. After being arrested and then released, Lorant made his way to London and became editor of the magazine *Picture Post*. But his ideas made their way to America, where Henry R. Luce, the publisher of *Time* and *Fortune* magazines, had been studying ways to create a picture magazine. In 1936, with the help of some talented German editors who had fled into exile, Luce launched *Life* magazine, boldly proclaiming his intention:

> *To see life, to see the world; to eyewitness great events; to watch the faces of the poor and the gestures of the proud; to see strange things—machines, armies, multitudes, shadows in the jungle and on the moon; to see man's work—his paintings, towers and discoveries; to see things a thousand miles away, things hidden behind walls and within rooms, things dangerous to come to; the women that men love and many children; to see and to take pleasure in seeing; to see and to be amazed; to see and be instructed.*

The chauvinistic tone of the magazine's manifesto was rather ironic in light of the fact that its most famous photographer—Margaret Bourke-White—was a woman. An extraordinarily talented architectural photographer, Bourke-White also used her camera to document the effects of the Depression and the Dust Bowl, which stretched from the Dakotas to Texas. For the cover of its inaugural issue, Luce selected her photograph of a massive dam under construction at Fort Peck, Montana. One of many New Deal projects begun during Franklin Roosevelt's administration, the dam represented American power and technology—just the right image for a public still searching for a way out of the Depression. The inside of the magazine contained a nine-page photo essay of Bourke-White's depiction of social life in the rough-and-tumble shanty settlements around the construction project. The editors said that they had expected Bourke-White to bring back construction pictures—the kind only she could take—but instead were treated to a "human document of frontier life."

America's first picture magazine was an instant hit at the newsstand. Within a matter of hours, the first issue of *Life* had sold out. Succeeding issues also sold out. By early 1937, a million copies a week were being produced, as *Life* photographers traveled the world over in search of dramatic pictures to serve to a news-hungry public. Besides Margaret Bourke-White, *Life* counted among its pool of talented photographers Alfred Eisenstaedt, Peter Stackpole, and Tom McAvoy. Eisenstaedt, or "Eisie" as he was called, left Germany in 1935, having already established himself as one of the best reporter-style photographers of the day. A master of the 35-millimeter Leica, he had a remarkable eye, lightning-quick reflexes, and an almost instantaneous sense of composition. On September 2, 1945—the day of Japan's surrender in World War II—he took the famous picture of a sailor kissing a nurse in Times Square.

Gardner and John Cowles, brothers and newspaper publishers, were keenly aware of the value of photographs. In the 1920s, they commissioned a young pollster by the name of George Gallup to determine whether readers of their newspapers in Des Moines, Iowa were interested in pictures. They learned that readers liked not only pictures but also, and even better, groups of related pictures. Putting this knowledge to use, the Cowles brothers increased their circulation by 50 percent. When *Life* hit the newsstands, the Cowles were already in the planning stages with their own picture magazine. In early 1937—less than two months after the appearance of *Life*—they launched *Look* magazine. Relying more on feature stories than news events, *Look* was also an immediate success. Along with *Life*, it became one of America's premiere picture magazines until the early 1970s, when television siphoned off its lifeblood—advertising—and forced its demise. *Look* ceased publication in 1971; *Life* succumbed the following year. In 1978, *Life* resumed publication—but this time as a monthly magazine using only freelance photographers.

REVIEW

In the 1930s, two great picture magazines, *Life* and *Look*, made their debuts. They attracted many talented photojournalists such as Margaret Bourke-White and Alfred Eisenstaedt. Television eventually replaced the picture magazine as the most important pictorial medium.

The Depression and War

The documentary tradition of photography established by Jacob Riis and Lewis Hine took on added importance in America of the 1930s and 1940s as photographers joined writers in expressing a new social consciousness aimed at the effects of poverty, hunger, and war. John Steinbeck's *The Grapes of Wrath* and Erskine Caldwell's *Tobacco Road* found their photographic counterparts in the works of Dorothea Lange, Arthur Rothstein, Walker Evans, Carl Mydans, and Margaret Bourke-White. Initially ignored by the press and government, the human misery caused by the Great Depression and the giant Dust Bowl that stretched across America's midsection became grist for the artist's mill. Dramatic stories of south-

Dorothea Lange took this picture of idle farmers in Oklahoma during the great drought of 1936. Lange was one of a handful of photographers who helped the Farm Security Administration document the misery caused by the "Dust Bowl" in the plains states in the 1930s.

ern poverty, the collapse of farming on the Great Plains, and the endless stream of migrant workers pouring into California were magnified by photographic images of destitute people down on their luck. In 1935, the historical unit of the government's Farm Security Administration (FSA), originally the Resettlement Administration, began compiling a photographic record of the impact of the Depression and Dust Bowl and the administration's efforts to alleviate the situation. Under the direction of Roy Stryker, an economist familiar with the work of Riis and Hine, the FSA hired some of the most talented photographers in America. To gain public support for New Deal works, Stryker made FSA photos available to any interested publication, and many of them found their way into newspapers, magazines, and even books. (Stryker also turned to the motion picture for help. See the discussion on Pare Lorentz in Chapter 7.) In 1936, Walker Evans and critic James Agee collaborated on *Let Us Now Praise Famous Men*, a portrayal of the misery of the Depression. It was eventually recognized as one of the classic documents of 1930s America. Margaret

Bourke-White and Erskine Caldwell combined talents to produce *You Have Seen Their Faces*, a stark account of the plight of southern sharecroppers. For the first time, photographs served as more than illustrations for text. They were on equal footing with words—perhaps even superior in power.

Distracted by the crisis at home in the 1930s and disinclined to become involved in matters abroad, Americans were slow to see the significance of troops on the march in Europe and the Far East. But *Life* and other picture magazines and newspapers forced a reluctant public to take notice of a world on the brink of war. As the conflict spread, from China and Spain to Europe and the Pacific, a new generation of photojournalists emerged to chronicle the greatest cataclysm in history, World War II. The most famous war photographers—Henri Cartier-Bresson, Robert Capa, David Seymour (better known as Chim), W. Eugene Smith, George Rodger, Wayne Miller, and David Douglas Duncan—discovered that the best pictures were not of action but of the human costs of war—especially the scars left on children, prisoners, and civilians. Robert Capa risked his life time and again for action shots—and, in fact, he captured the instant a loyalist soldier was killed during the Spanish Civil War—but his most effective photograph was taken in Naples, when he happened to stumble upon a schoolhouse funeral being held for 20 teenagers who, with stolen rifles, had fought the Nazis for 14 days shortly before the city was liberated. Capa lifted his camera and recorded the anguish of grieving mothers about to see their babies carried away in coffins.

REVIEW

The documentary style of photography was refined during the Depression and World War II by photojournalists concerned about poverty and hunger in America and a war in Europe and the Pacific. Walker Evans and Dorothea Lange were among the photojournalists who documented the effects of the Depression and Dust Bowl, while Henri Cartier-Bresson and Robert Capa were two of the many distinguished World War II photographers.

BYLINE

Journalists have often been at odds with the government over how much freedom they should have to report on and take photographs of military operations—particularly invasions. Journalists believe they have an obligation to inform the public of what its government is doing. Military officials argue that censorship is necessary to protect lives. Thus, the press was not informed of the 1983 invasion of Grenada until after it occurred. In the invasion of Panama in 1989, a tightly controlled press pool accompanied U.S. troops. How much freedom do you believe journalists and photojournalists should have? Should they be informed in advance of a pending military strike? Should they be allowed to follow troops into battle? What kinds of restrictions would you impose on reporters and news photographers?

No matter how dangerous or abhorrent an assignment, the photojournalists of World War II rose to the challenge and pointed their cameras at every aspect of the human conflict that engulfed much of the world. And when it was all over, they were there to count the cost. In 1943, Margaret Bourke-White became the first woman to go on an Air Force combat mission. She later accompanied U.S. forces when they liberated the concentration camp at Buchenwald. Her haunting photos of prisoners suddenly set free informed the world of the horrors of the German death camps. Even more grim were the pictures of the dead. George Rodger photographed the mangled pile of bodies found at Bergen-Belsen, while Robert Capa documented what was left of the Warsaw ghetto. When U.S. Marines raised their flag over Iwo Jima near the end of the war, Associated Press photographer Joe Rosenthal was there to record the symbol of victory.

New Challenges and New Directions

By the end of World War II, photojournalists were recognized as artists on a par with writers. Initially, photographers had been regarded as second-class citizens in the newspaper industry—people who chased firetrucks and took snapshots of beauty contests and handshaking ceremonies. But the impressive contributions of photographers throughout the 1930s and during World War II changed that image. Some photographers, aware of their new status and interested in preserving it, formed trade associations and cooperatives. In 1945, a photographer with the *Pittsburgh Sun-Telegraph* began organizing the National Press Photographers Association, the major trade association for photojournalists. Two years later, a cooperative agency, Magnum Photos, was founded by Henri Cartier-Bresson, Robert Capa, Maria Eisner, David (Chim) Seymour, George Rodger, and William and Rita Vandivert to ensure that photographers, rather than the publications in which their photographs appeared, would own the rights to their works. Today, Magnum is considered the most renowned collective of documentary photographers in the world.

For a time, the photojournalist as visual historian reigned supreme. Many of the World War II photographers witnessed the descending of an Iron Curtain in Europe, Gandhi's passive resistance movement in India, the Communist takeover of China, and the Korean War. Their photographs were grabbed up by newspapers and picture magazines eager to show curious readers the world beyond their reach. But about that time, another medium made its appearance and gradually eclipsed the picture magazine as chief chronicler of world events. Television, which entered American homes on a large scale just after World War II, forced all other media to reevaluate their functions and forms. None could compete with television's immediacy and convenience. The Vietnam conflict, in which the United States fought in the 1960s and 1970s, was the first television war—a war brought into the living rooms of Americans on a daily basis.

When television switched to color in the 1960s, photojournalists began using more high-speed color film. By the end of the 1970s, color photos were appearing regularly in news magazines such as *Time* and *Newsweek,* which had begun filling the void left by the collapse of *Life* and *Look*. By the end of the next decade, color photos were common in most newspapers.

BYLINE

There has been a great deal of criticism leveled at reporters and photojournalists for being too intrusive in covering stories involving tragedy. At a memorial service held at Syracuse University for students killed in the crash of a Pan American jet over Lockerbie, Scotland, photographers packed the aisles and balconies of the chapel to take pictures of grieving families and students. Noisy motor drives and frequent flashes of light punctuated the prayer vigil. Should cameras have been allowed in the chapel? If so, what kinds of restrictions should have been placed on their use? What rules of conduct should the photojournalists have observed as a matter of professional ethics?

Despite competition from television, the power of the photograph appears greater than ever. Whether it be of a single man blocking a line of tanks in Beijing or of masses of people dying from famine in Africa, the photograph speaks to us in a way that sometimes words and motion pictures cannot. In an age of information overload and kaleidoscopic visual sensations, still photographs allow us to pause and reflect on the significant—and sometimes insignificant—people, issues, and events of the day. Like paintings, they invite us to consider the personal vision of the photographer against the backdrop of our own experiences. When accompanied by words, as in newspaper or magazine articles, photographs often provide us with the context for constructing the meaning of those articles. (See the discussion of context in Chapter 2.)

As the domain of photojournalism expands and the technology continues to shift—most recently toward digital electronic photography—the challenge to the photojournalist will be to remain faithful to the search for what Cartier-Bresson called "that one moment at which the elements in motion are in balance."[4]

REVIEW

Following World War II, photojournalists formed trade associations and cooperatives. Although the advent of television forced all media to reexamine their functions, the power of the still photograph continues to make the role of the photojournalist important.

PHOTOGRAPHY AS ART

Colin Westerbeck of The Art Institute of Chicago argues that "once a medium is no longer essential as a culture's source of information, it turns into an art form."[5] Thus, the death of the picture magazine, according to Westerbeck, marked the end of the power of photography as a mass medium and of the partnership between journalism and art. It was not mere coincidence, he says, that after this development there was a rise in the number of photography galleries, the number of art school degrees in photography, and auction prices for vintage prints—portents of the historical consciousness with which the medium is now appreciated. But as early as the 1840s, when some photographers were expressing dismay over the lack of resolution in William Henry Fox Talbot's calotype process, others were seeing it as a virtue—an aesthetic creation that only the camera could produce. Throughout the history of photography, there has been the realization that the camera and developing lab were capable of yielding much more than a faithful rendition of the visible world. In the hands of imaginative and sensitive photographers, they offered the possibility for creating a unique art form.

Experimental Art Photography

The first truly self-conscious attempt to create an artistic movement in photography involved *the use of photographs to tell a story*. **Allegorical photographs**, as they were called, were made of subjects who dressed and posed in a symbolic manner, often reflecting the stern morality and sentimentality of the Victorian period. Through a technique known as combination printing, which involved using several negatives to make one picture, the photographer produced a composite photo. One of the most famous of these allegorical photographs, "The Two Ways of Life," created by Swedish photographer Oscar G. Rejlander, was purchased by Queen Victoria, herself an amateur photographer.

The allegorical movement eventually gave way to **pictorialism**, *an attempt to use the camera for subjective expression*. In 1889, an Englishman, Peter Henry Emerson, a leading advocate of the pictorial approach, published *Naturalistic Photography for Students of the Art*, a book that had a profound influence on American as well as English photographers. Emerson rejected the artificiality of the allegorical mode and called for a new aesthetic based on simple equipment and a soft-focus technique. He urged photographers to strive for an impression of nature rather than a literal description of it—in other words, to allow the camera to function as a human eye instead of a mechanical device. In part, Emerson was trying to reconcile the difference between science and art. He believed that if a photograph was nothing more than the product of an optical image striking a light-sensitive surface, it was science. If, on the other hand, it involved the subjective expression of the photographer and presented ideas, it was art.

BYLINE

There has been a long-standing debate about whether photography is an art or a craft. Painters often argue that it cannot be an art because the image is formed optically rather than drawn by hand. What do you think? What distinction would you make between an art and a craft?

Emerson's writings, including his own rejection of what he had said earlier, sparked heated controversy on both sides of the Atlantic. In 1902, an American splinter group of pictorialists formed the Photo-Secession organization. Led by Alfred Stieglitz and Edward Steichen, Photo-Secession was a result of the frustration over a lack of standards in American photographic exhibitions. Stieglitz and Steichen advocated new subject matter and new approaches to photography and sought to emphasize its relationship to other arts. In 1905, they set up a gallery at 291 Fifth Avenue in New York known as "291." Along with photographs, they exhibited sculptures, drawings, and lithographs of other artists—especially artists like Matisse, Picasso, and Cezanne, who were part of the avant-garde of **modernism**, *an artistic movement that attempted a self-conscious break with the past and a search for new forms*. Stieglitz and Steichen also published a magazine, *Camera Work*, in which they introduced subscribers to new styles of photography.

Following World War I, experimental art photography entered one of its most creative periods. Man Ray, an American photographer working in Paris, specialized in darkroom experimentation. Influenced by the ideas of **dadaism**, *a movement in art and literature that rejected traditional art values*, he created abstract works called "Rayograms"—similar in concept to the photograms produced during the earliest days of photographic experimentation. During this period, three of America's most famous photographers—Paul Strand, Edward Weston, and Ansel Adams—began developing a new aesthetic based on the notions of honesty, directness, and objectivity of expression. Strand, a protégé of Stieglitz, became known for his extreme close-ups of machines and large-scale details of natural objects such as cobwebs, driftwood, and plants. His photographs of the people and landscapes of the Southwest had a serene, lyrical quality. Strand wanted photographers to free themselves from the influence of other arts and to recognize the camera's unique aesthetic.

Edward Weston was fascinated by the geometric configuration of natural forms. Unimpressed by the self-conscious manipulation of experimentalists like Man Ray, Weston strived for a precise rendition of his subject: "The camera should be used for rendering the very substance and quintessence of the thing itself, whether it be polished steel or palpitating flesh."[6] Many of his photographs revealed the beauty of natural shapes such as peppers and cabbage.

Like Weston, Ansel Adams found inspiration in nature. Following in the footsteps of early landscape photographers like William Henry Jackson and Timothy H. O'Sullivan, Adams specialized in pictures of mountains and deserts of the West. In 1932, he and a handful of other photographers formed an association called Group f/64 to promote their ideas about straight photography and natural subjects. The name refers to the lens setting that gives a camera its greatest **depth of field**, *the distance between the nearest and farthest points from the camera that are in sharp focus*.

The Great Depression and World War II commanded much of the attention of photographers in the 1930s and 1940s; the result was the strong emphasis on documentary and handheld photography discussed earlier in

Alfred Stieglitz's Camera Works *had a profound influence on the development of Amercian art photography. Published from 1903 to 1917, it attracted a wide audience of painters, writers, critics, and photographers. The final issue of* Camera Works *was devoted to the works of Stieglitz's protégé, Paul Strand.*

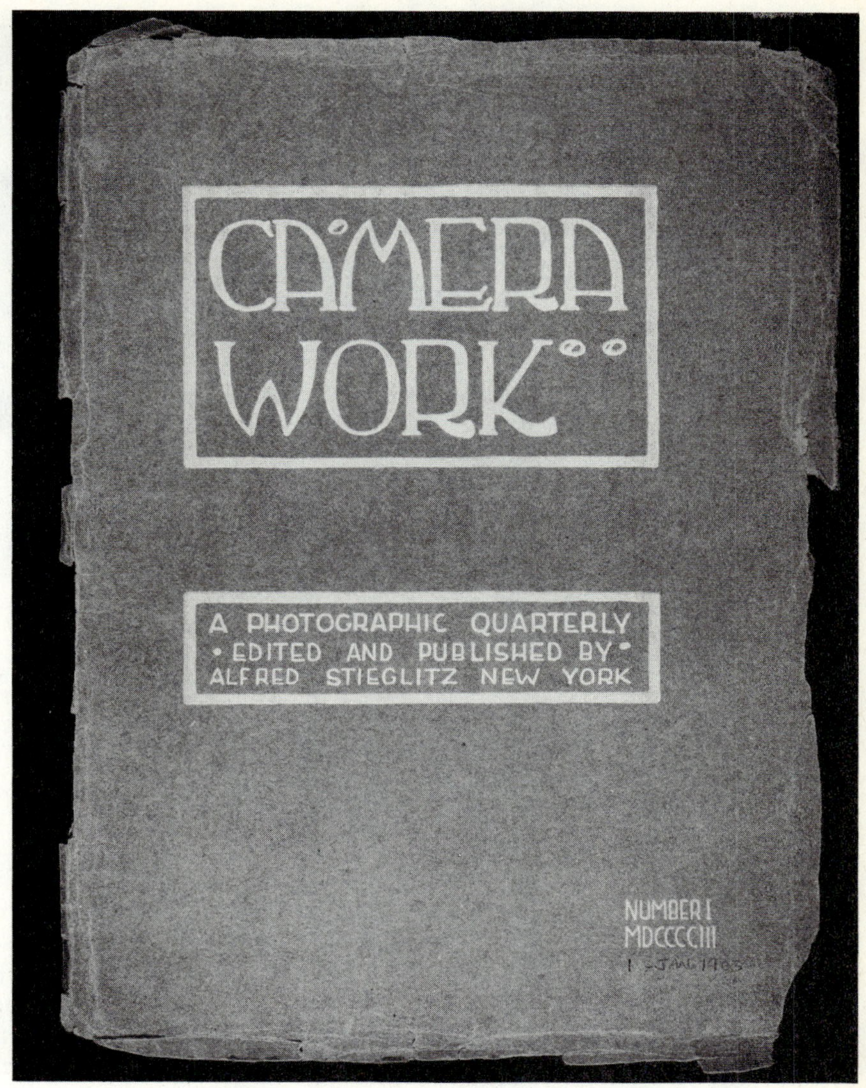

this chapter. But even photographers of that period who were not persuaded to confine themselves solely to social observation or reportage were profoundly influenced by what they had lived through and witnessed. Ansel Adams, for instance, compiled a photographic essay, *Born Free and Equal*, in which he depicted the Manzanar War Relocation Camp, which housed American citizens of Japanese descent. Speaking of President Franklin Roosevelt's order creating the camp, Adams said: "I am sure

In the 1940s Ansel Adams turned his attention away from the panoramic landscape photographs for which he is best remembered to document the conditions of a relocation center where Americans of Japanese descent were confined during World War II. Adams called the internment camp, which was located in Manzanar, California, a tragic problem.

he had no realization of its tragic implications; thousands of loyal Japanese-American citizens were denied their basic civil rights."[7]

The influence of the war—and the cold war that followed—can also be seen in the work of Minor White, who saw active duty in the Philippines. Instead of using photography as a medium of literal description, White saw it as a vehicle for poetic metaphor, a fusion of photography and psychology. White's photographs—seemingly mystical images of oceans, desert nights, or city fog—reflected an inner darkness of anxiety and disorientation as a consequence of the war. Through his photographs, his teaching, and the magazine, *Aperture*, that he cofounded in 1952, White became the most influential landscape photographer of the 1950s and 1960s.

Trends in Photographic Art

As society changes, and new problems replace old ones, artistic movements also change—sometimes just ahead of social trends, sometimes following them. The so-called "street photography" of the 1950s and 1960s—a style characterized by rough, grainy pictures, often of ordinary people on the streets—was a bridge between the lingering effects of World War II and the social upheaval in American cities two decades later. Later trends, such as conceptual art and pop art, challenged assumptions of

REVIEW

Allegorical photographs represented the first attempt to create an artistic movement in photography. Succeeding movements included pictorialism and modernism. Alfred Stieglitz and Edward Steichen were two of the most prominent American photographic artists. Later, Paul Strand, Edward Weston, and Ansel Adams pioneered a style of photography based on honesty, directness, and objectivity of expression. Recent trends include street photography, pop art, and postmodernism.

what art was supposed to be. Andy Warhol, one of the best known of the artists who selected popular culture as their subject matter, referred to his studio as "The Factory"—an acknowledgment of his consumer-goods approach to the production of art. Postmodernist artists, aware of our dependence on media as a source of reality, have recycled and reconstructed existing photographs as a way of expressing their disenchantment with the influence of mass culture—and even with photography itself.

Today, artistic approaches to photography are as varied as photographers themselves. Color, once considered the province of advertising agencies and fashion magazines, has gained greater respectability in artistic photography. Joel Meyerowitz, William Eggleston, and Helen Levitt are just a few of the photographers who helped establish color as a separate genre for landscape and street photography. Composite photographs, like those of Chuck Close, have also received a great deal of attention—partly because of the influence of digitized, computer-generated images of space exploration. At times, the personalities of the artists—like Warhol and Gilbert and George—have overshadowed their works. And, as is the case in every generation, some works—like those of Robert Mapplethorpe and Andres Serrano—have caused public outcries and calls for censorship. All of these developments add up to an art form that is alive and flourishing—stretching our imaginations, shocking our sensibilities, and impressing upon us the deeper meanings of our existence.

THE FUTURE OF PHOTOGRAPHY

While it might be difficult to predict the next artistic trend in photography, it is somewhat easier to see where the technology is headed. The major interest of manufacturers in recent years has been in the development of electronic camera and prepress systems and electronic darkrooms. These technologies offer new ways to record, process, store, assemble, and deliver photographs. Some of the newest still cameras, like the Canon Xapshot, record images on a videodisc much like a video camera and play them back on a television screen. The merging of still and video technologies provides the opportunity to take 35-millimeter pictures, view them immediately, and, if necessary, transmit them instantly by telephone line or satellite to a waiting newsroom. Associated Press recently switched from wirephoto receivers to electronic darkrooms as a means of delivering pictures to newspapers. Instead of sorting through a stack of photographic prints, photo editors who subscribe to AP can now call up digitally delivered pictures on a computer screen.

The push toward electronic publishing has resulted in other new ways of handling photographs once they arrive in the newsroom. The development of electronic prepress systems—digital electronic graphics and pagination, and electronic phototypesetters called imagesetters—may one day replace the halftone process as a way of getting pictures into print. The new equipment scans photographs electronically and then stores them. Before the photos are incorporated electronically into the page makeup and sent to press, they can be retouched and corrected for color—a capability that photojournalists may view with considerable skepticism.

Review

The establishment of electronic newsrooms and continuing explorations in space are likely to result in further developments in photographic technology.

Future missions into outer space will also extend the frontiers of photographic technology, as manufacturers develop ever more powerful lenses to peer into the star-studded darkness of the universe. Once they are focused correctly, the cameras aboard the Hubble spacecraft will beam to us pictures of a world we have never seen—a world that only photographs can reveal.

THE WORLD OF PHOTOGRAPHY: A SUMMARY

The first pictorial mass medium to be developed was photography. Although human beings had tried for thousands of years to communicate through pictures the world they encountered, it was not until the development of photography just over a hundred and fifty years ago that they could do so with such great fidelity. Discoveries in physics and chemistry, which capitalized on earlier observations about the ways in which sunlight could be used, paved the way for the invention of the camera and a means of making a permanent recording of the image formed by the camera's lens.

L. J. M. Daguerre invented the first practical system of producing permanent pictures, which he called daguerreotypes. Daguerre sold his invention to the French government in 1839, the date that marks the beginning of photography. Because they were inexpensive and relatively easy to produce, daguerreotypes led to the development of a commercial photography industry. Other inventors—notably William Henry Fox Talbot, Frederick Scott Archer, and Richard L. Maddox—made various improvements upon Daguerre's system. By the 1870s, it was possible to make multiple copies of pictures—a necessary step for the development of a true mass medium—and to store negatives and develop them at a later time.

In the latter part of the nineteenth century, photographers concentrated their efforts on capturing "the look of things." Portrait photography, landscape photography, and documentary photography became the major provinces for the new medium. Mathew Brady began as a portrait photographer but later turned his attention to documenting the Civil War. After the war, many photographers, like William Henry Jackson, used their cameras to explore the western United States.

Amateur photography became popular when George Eastman invented an easy-to-use camera and provided a service for processing film. The Kodak box camera and film, introduced in 1888, sold for $25. The Brownie, which followed it some twelve years later, sold for only $1. While some amateurs delved into all aspects of photography, joining photo clubs and subscribing to photo magazines, most were content if the snapshots they took simply turned out.

Long before the invention of the halftone photograph, magazines and newspapers tried to illustrate their stories. Sketch artists often supplied drawings of the important activities of the day, and from these drawings, wood engravings were made that could then be printed. The halftone made it possible to print directly from a photograph and gave rise to a new form of photography—photojournalism.

Some photojournalists, like Jacob Riis and Lewis Hine, used their cameras as tools for social reform, while others, like Jimmy Hare and Arthur Fellig, stoked the fires of "yellow journalism" with exciting pictures of combat and crime. The use of halftone photographs led to the development of a new type of newspaper—the tabloid—which made its debut in 1919. About the same time, news organizations formed specialized photo operations to service their newspaper clients. In 1935, Associated Press started a wirephoto service. With the introduction of smaller, lightweight cameras, photojournalists were able to take candid shots of their subjects. Eric Salomon of Germany, the first to describe his work as photojournalism, became a leader in the "candid camera" style of photography.

In 1936, publisher Henry R. Luce launched *Life* magazine, the first picture magazine of its kind in America. With the aid of such talented photographers as Margaret Bourke-White and Alfred Eisenstaedt, *Life* became an instant hit and was soon followed by the publication of another picture magazine, *Look*. Both magazines were highly successful until television chipped away at their advertising revenues and brought about their closure. *Life* returned to the newsstands several years later but with a greatly reduced staff and frequency of publication.

During the 1930s, the effects of the Great Depression and Dust Bowl aroused a new social consciousness among photographers like Dorothea Lange, Walker Evans, and Arthur Rothstein, who carried on the documentary tradition established by Jacob Riis and Lewis Hine. Much of the photographic work of this period was carried out by the historical unit of the Farm Security Administration, a New Deal agency set up to tackle the problems caused by poverty, depleted farm land, and the flood of migrant workers who made their way to California.

War clouds in Europe and the Pacific also attracted the attention of photographers, many of whom later risked their lives to tell the story of a world at war. Henri Cartier-Bresson, Robert Capa, and Margaret Bourke-White were just a few of the distinguished World War II photographers who added stature to the field of photojournalism. While the introduction of television shortly after the war ended the reign of picture magazines like *Life* and *Look*, it did nothing to diminish the need for photographs or their power to inform and persuade.

Photography as an art form had its roots in allegorical photographs, carefully composed pictures used to tell a story. This movement gave way to pictorialism, an aesthetic that likened the camera to a human eye and attempted to draw a distinction between art and science. In America, pictorialists such as Alfred Stieglitz and Edward Steichen helped establish new standards for photography as art. Man Ray, an American photographer working in Paris, created abstract photographs that he called Rayograms. Meanwhile, Paul Strand, Edward Weston, and Ansel Adams were urging a quite different aesthetic, which emphasized natural shapes and large details. The Great Depression and World War II affected notions about photography, causing some photographers to adopt a documentary approach and others, like Minor White, to use photographs as reflections of inner psychological states.

Recent trends in photographic art include street photography, conceptual and pop art, and postmodernist photography. Experiments with color and composite photography are also popular. Sometimes, the works of photographers are overshadowed by their personalities or by the controversies their photographs generate. All of these trends underscore the vitality and uniqueness of this valuable art form.

New technological developments have revolutionized the way photographs can be recorded and processed. Electronic cameras, similar to video cameras, make it possible to record pictures on a videodisc and play them back on a television screen. Wirephotos can be delivered via an electronic darkroom, and electronic prepress systems allow computers to store and select photographs and prepare them for publication. Explorations into outer space hold the promise of further technological developments in photography.

DISCUSSION QUESTIONS

1. What is the principle upon which the development of the camera is based?
2. What were some of the differences among early photographic processes?
3. What styles of photography were popular before the turn of the century?
4. How did George Eastman revolutionize photography?
5. What impact did the halftone photograph have on the newspaper and magazine industries, and on photography itself?
6. Who were some of the important photographers in America in the 1930s and 1940s?
7. What caused the collapse of major picture magazines such as *Life* and *Look*?
8. What were some of the trends in the development of photography as an art form? What are some of the current trends?
9. What are some of the new technological developments in photographic equipment?

NOTES

1. Floyd Rinhart and Marion Rinhart, *The American Daguerreotype* (Athens: University of Georgia Press, 1981), p. 40.
2. Joel Snyder, "Inventing Photography." In *On the Art of Fixing a Shadow: One Hundred and Fifty Years of Photography*, eds. Sarah Greenough, Joel Snyder,

David Travis, and Colin Westerbeck (Washington: National Gallery of Art and The Art Institute of Chicago, 1989), p. 27. Much of the information on the history of photography was taken from this book, which was produced in conjunction with an exhibition commemorating the one hundred fiftieth anniversary of photography.

3. Frank Luther Mott, *American Journalism*. 3rd ed. (New York: Macmillan Company, 1962), p. 529.
4. Henri Cartier-Bresson, quoted by Fred Ritchen, "What is Magnum." In *In Our Time: The World as Seen by Magnum Photographers*, eds. William Manchester, Jean Lacouture, and Fred Ritchin (New York: The American Federation of Arts, 1989), p. 423. This book, which was also produced in conjunction with an exhibition, is an excellent source of information on documentary photography.
5. Colin Westerbeck, "Beyond the Photographic Frame." In Greenough, Snyder, Travis, and Westerbeck, p. 375.
6. Edward Weston, quoted by William Manchester, "Images: A Wide Angle." In Manchester, Lacouture, and Ritchin, p. 25.
7. Ansel Adams and Mary Street Alinder, *Ansel Adams: An Autobiography* (Boston: Little, Brown and Company, 1985), p. 258.

SUGGESTED READINGS

Relevant Contemporary Works

Blaker, Alfred A. *Photography Art and Technique*. 2nd ed. Boston: Focal Press, 1988.

Edom, Clifton C. *Photojournalism: Principles and Practices*. Dubuque, Iowa: William C. Brown, 1976.

Eisenstaedt, Alfred. *Witness to Our Times*. Rev. ed. New York: Viking Press, 1980.

Gernsheim, Helmut, and Gernsheim, Alison. *The History of Photography*. New York: McGraw-Hill, 1969.

Gidal, Tim N. *Modern Photojournalism: Origin and Evolution*. 1910–1933. New York: Macmillan, 1972.

Goldberg, Vicki. *Margaret Bourke-White: A Biography*. New York: Harper & Row, 1986.

Greenough, Sarah, Snyder, Joel, Travis, David, and Westerbeck, Colin, eds. *On the Art of Fixing a Shadow: One Hundred and Fifty Years of Photography*. Washington: National Gallery of Art and the Art Institute of Chicago, 1989.

Kobre, Kenneth. *Photojournalism: The Professionals' Approach*. Somerville, MA: Curtin & London, 1980.

Newhall, Beaumont. *The History of Photography*. New York: The Museum of Modern Art, 1964.

Newhall, Nancy, ed. *The Daybooks of Edward Weston: Volume II, California*. Millerton, New York: Aperture, 1973.

"150 Years of Photojournalism." *Time*, Special Collector's Edition, Fall 1989.

Photojournalism. New York: Time-Life Books, 1971.

CHAPTER 7

MOTION PICTURES: THE START OF MASS ENTERTAINMENT

OBJECTIVES

After studying this chapter, you should be able to

- **Trace the technological developments that led to the creation of "motion" pictures.**
- **Discuss the evolution of the motion picture business.**
- **Cite the reasons for the merging of the film and video industries.**
- **Describe the development of film content and attempts to censor certain types of content.**
- **Discuss current trends in the movie industry—especially the trend toward vertical integration.**
- **Note the changes in audiences for motion pictures, the reasons for those changes, and whether they are likely to continue.**

As a child I was brought up on American movies. My dream life and the part of me that I wanted to see develop had been molded by American cinema.

David Puttnam, British filmmaker and former CEO of Columbia Pictures, in Bill Moyers's *A World of Ideas*.

For better or worse, the wave of the 90's will be huge, well-financed companies that are involved in four or five forms of entertainment and whose competition is not other American companies but Sony in Japan and Bertelsmann in Germany.

Terry Semel, President of Warner Brothers, *New York Times*, October 22, 1989, Section 2, p. 1.

The views expressed by David Puttnam and Terry Semel reflect the dichotomous nature of one of our most cherished institutions—motion pictures. On the one hand, there are the "movies"—those wonderful images on the silver screen that flow from a seemingly mythical world of glamour and glitz to capture our hearts and imaginations. On the other, there is the movie industry—a high-risk, high-cost business struggling to meet the demands of a fickle audience whose choices for entertainment are ever expanding. For most of us, it is the former conception of motion pictures that has meaning. We have our favorite films, our favorite film stars, even our favorite film directors. But for those who control the movie industry, it is the latter perspective that predominates. Movie executives must be constantly on the lookout for new markets, new technology, and new ways of covering rising costs. Although motion pictures have been "big business" almost from the start, they have also been much more than that. They have been our dream factory, our collective psyche, and our most visible barometer of social norms and social change in the twentieth century.

EARLY DEVELOPMENTS IN THE MOTION PICTURE INDUSTRY

The motion picture camera and projector, like the technology of all other mass media, did not arrive on the scene full-blown. They had many precursors, inventions that both stimulated and aided their development. We discussed some of these in the chapter on photography. But a key step in the development of "moving" pictures was a theoretical understanding of how the eye perceives motion. This extremely important contribution was made by an English physician named Peter Mark Roget in a scientific paper, "The Persistence of Vision with Regard to Moving Objects." In this paper, Roget contended that our eyes retain an image for a fraction of a second after the object we are looking at disappears. This idea was put to use in booklets of pictures that you could flip through quickly to make it look as though the people and objects in the pictures were moving. Motion pictures, which are simply series of pictures projected in rapid succession (16 per second for silent films, 24 per second for sound films), carried Roget's idea to its natural conclusion. (Roget, by the way, must have been quite a person. Not only did he develop the fundamental theory for motion pictures, he also developed the famous *Roget's Thesaurus*, which you perhaps use when you are trying to find a synonym for some word.)

Early Motion Picture Cameras and Projectors

The first successful motion picture camera was devised by an Englishman named William Dickson, working in Thomas Edison's laboratory in West Orange, New Jersey. The camera was completed in 1889. Five years later Edison's research team produced the **Kinetoscope,** *a device for viewing films.* On the outside, the Kinetoscope looked simply like a large box with a peephole on the top. One person at a time would look through the

1700–1899

- **1727** Scientists discover light causes silver nitrate to darken
- **1822** Joseph Niepce produces first photograph
- **1889** W.K.L. Dickson develops first successful motion picture camera
- **1896** Motion picture introduced as popular entertainment form in vaudeville

1900–1925

- **1903** Development of Western boosted by release of *The Great Train Robbery*
- **1907** Chicago enacts motion picture censorship law
- **1909** Monopoly comes to film industry: Motion Picture Patents Co. (the Trust) formed
- **1912** *Queen Elizabeth* demonstrates attraction of full-length dramatic films
- **1913** First of the great movie palaces, the Strand Theatre, opens in NYC
- **1914** Charlie Chaplin's character, the Tramp, born in *Kid Auto Races at Venice*
- **1915** The Trust legally disbanded
- **1915** D.W. Griffith's epic motion picture, *Birth of a Nation*, released
- **1919** United Artists formed by director Griffith, actors Fairbanks, Chaplin, Pickford
- **1922** Motion Picture Producers and Distributors of America formed to clean up movies

1926–1939

- **1927** Release of *The Jazz Singer*, starring Al Jolson, heralds age of sound
- **1930** The Motion Picture Production code formalized
- **1934** March of Time newsreel introduced
- **1934** National Legion of Decency formed to fight immorality in movies

1940–1979

- **1948** Courts ban vertical integration of film industry
- **1952** Supreme Court concludes movies somewhat protected by First Amendment
- **1968** Rating System for motion pictures replaces Seal of Approval

1980–1990

- **1987** Rental and purchase of films on videotape exceeds box office sales
- **1989** Sony purchases Columbia Pictures
- **1990** Motion picture association drops "X" rating, adds "NC-17"; Matsushita acquires MCA

peephole while simultaneously turning a crank to make the movie go. Before long, arcades appeared throughout the country, each stocked with a number of Kinetoscopes, in which people could see very short films for one cent each. As you might have guessed, they were called peepshow parlors. These peepshow parlors were quite similar to the later penny arcades.

While the Kinetoscope was being developed in America, two French brothers, Louis and Auguste Lumiére, invented *a new type of motion picture camera that not only took pictures, but also projected them on a screen.* They called it a **Cinematographe.** This is the source of the word *cinematography,* which we use to describe the art of making motion pictures. The advantage of the Cinematographe over the Kinetoscope was that more than one person at a time could view a film. Recognizing the importance of this feature, Edison developed the Vitascope projector.

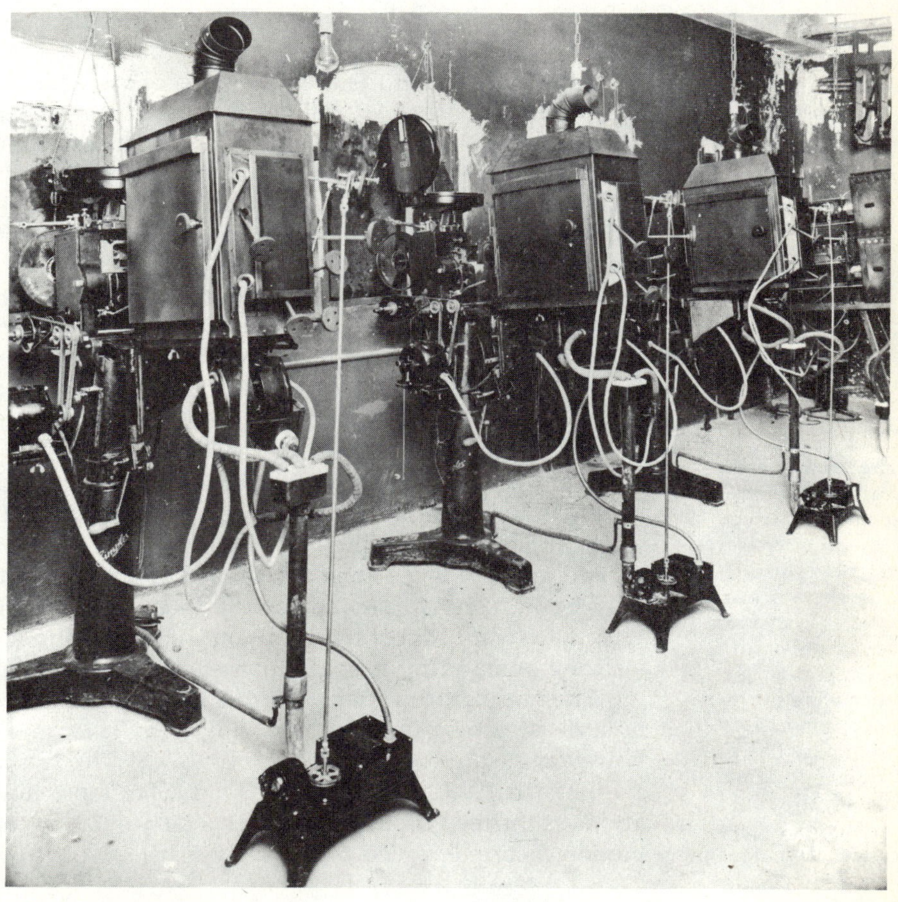

Early motion picture equipment.

Motion Picture Theaters

Early filmmakers in America believed that development of the medium required that they break into the mass entertainment business. However, they found that business to be dominated by the variety shows known as vaudeville. Following that well-known dictum, "When you can't beat 'em, join 'em," the film pioneers began to rent their machines and their films to the vaudeville producers to use as one of the acts on vaudeville bills. This practice was initiated at Koster and Bial's Music Hall in New York City on April 23, 1896. The Vitascope machine Thomas Edison developed was used to project the short film program.

Between 1896 and 1906, vaudeville was the principal outlet for the exhibition of films in this country, bringing this infant medium of communication to national attention. The major vaudeville circuits were quite extensive, with theaters in all major cities and many that were not so major. The novel motion picture "acts" were moved from theater to theater on each circuit, just as the dog and pony acts, the comedians, singers, and magicians were. In a real sense, the movie projector became a star.

After 1906, when the early versions of theaters devoted totally to movies began to develop, *a hybrid film/variety type of theater* that came to be called **small-time vaudeville** also evolved. Small-time vaudeville theaters featured programs balanced equally between film and a variety of live acts. Marcus Loew and William Fox, who later became major figures in the film industry, began the development of their empires with small-time vaudeville houses.

As film projectors became more readily available, the back rooms of the peepshow parlors were curtained off for projected films, or empty stores were converted for the purpose. The *early theaters designed specifically for motion pictures* were called **nickelodeons,** so called because an admission ticket cost a nickel. Most of the nickelodeons ran their films continuously from early morning until late at night.

REVIEW

The earliest device for viewing motion pictures was the Kinetoscope. It was used to project very short films in arcades known as peepshow parlors. Later, motion pictures were incorporated into vaudeville programs. The first theaters designed specifically for motion pictures were called nickelodeons.

Many of the major figures who built the film industry in Hollywood began as film distributors or owners or managers of nickelodeons. They were immigrants from Europe or the children of immigrants, and they exhibited and produced films for their fellow immigrants.

The industry expanded rapidly in the early part of this century. By 1908 there were almost ten thousand nickelodeons across the country and a strong demand for a large and steady supply of films.

The number of motion picture houses that featured silent films peaked in 1929, at nearly twenty-three thousand. This number declined rapidly, however, as the sound houses took over. Twenty sound houses were in business in 1927, eight hundred in 1929, almost nine thousand by 1930, and over thirteen thousand by 1931. The number of theaters playing sound motion pictures peaked in the early forties at over twenty thousand. This number was cut almost in half by competition from television. However, that drop was compensated for somewhat by the rise in drive-in theaters. Until the late 1950s, about four thousand drive-ins operated throughout the country. But as property values increased, land devoted to drive-ins gave way to shopping malls and other commercial developments. A number of other factors, such as the rise in popularity of VCRs and the construction of indoor multiplex theaters, combined to make the drive-in movie practically obsolete by 1990.

A large portion of the motion picture theaters in the United States today are owned by chains. None, though, is as large as the Paramount Picture chain was before the courts ordered a separation of film production companies from film exhibition companies. At the time that separation was ordered, in 1948, Paramount owned 1424 theaters. Each of the largest chains today, General Cinema and United Artists, owns about five hundred theaters. Most of the other chains are considerably smaller.

Monopoly Attempts in the Film Industry

Most industries have a history of constant attempts to control all or as much as possible of the available business. The motion picture industry is no exception.

The Motion Picture Patents Company. The earliest example of such attempts occurred in 1909 when *the nine companies that held the major patents for motion picture cameras, projectors, and film stock* formed the **Motion Picture Patents Company,** often called simply the **Trust.** These companies conspired in a variety of ways to keep competition out. One member of the Trust, Eastman Kodak, agreed to sell film stock only to the other members. The producers in the Trust insisted that if exhibitors wanted any of their films, they could not buy or rent films from a non-Trust producer and could use only projectors made by Trust members. They also insisted that exhibitors pay a two-dollar-a-week license fee in addition to the cost of films. When their agreements with the exhibitors could not be enforced by law, the Trust hired thugs to do the enforcing. In 1910, when they thought some distributors were renting non-Trust films to theaters, they formed their own distribution company and either bought out distributors or simply forced them out of business. Thus, the Trust developed tremendous power.

The independents. Fortunately for the long-range good of the motion picture industry, the independent distributors and producers did not give up easily. Some small distributors began to import films from other countries for their customers. They also distributed films made by "outlaw" producers who, because they were using unlicensed equipment, had to keep moving from one place to another to escape the Trust's private detectives. In fact, this need to elude the Trust's detectives and thugs caused some of the independent producers to move away from the east coast, where the Motion Picture Patents Company members were located, and settle in Hollywood. Southern California provided ample sunshine and a variety of scenery for filmmaking.

By 1913, the monopoly of the Motion Picture Patents Company was broken, and in 1915 the Trust was legally disbanded. There were a number of reasons for its demise, but the main reason was that members failed to understand the way the motion picture medium ought to develop. Their early success made them too conservative; they did not recognize that they could not keep making movies in the same way and stay successful. They assumed audiences would continue to be satisfied with one-reel films, each about twelve minutes long. They also assumed customers would be unwilling to pay more than five or ten cents for an evening's film program. In order to maintain those prices, they refused to pay decent salaries to actors or others involved in their productions.

The independents who were fighting the Trust recognized that their products had to be distinctive, and they were. As we will describe later, they publicized their actors and made them into stars, feeding the public's apparently insatiable appetite for glamor. In 1912 one company imported from England the hour-long Sarah Bernhardt film *Queen Elizabeth* and charged a dollar for admission. It was extremely successful. By 1913 the independents in this country were making their own feature-length films. These factors, and the loss of some important court cases, which stopped the monopolizing of film equipment, broke the back of the Trust.

The three independents most responsible for the demise of the Trust were William Fox, Adolph Zukor, and Carl Laemmle. Zukor and Laemmle continued to influence the motion picture industry greatly during their many years of leadership in Hollywood—Zukor as head of Paramount Studios and Laemmle as head of Universal Studios. Fox, however, was ousted from his own company, Fox Film, in 1931. The company continued to use his name and in 1935 merged with 20th Century Pictures to form 20th Century Fox.

A new monopoly. Less than a decade after the defeat of the Trust, one of the independents who helped bring about that defeat, Adolph Zukor, tried to develop his own monopoly of the motion picture industry. His company, Paramount, already involved in production and distribution, began to buy theaters so that it controlled all aspects of the business—production, distribution, and exhibition. For other theaters that wanted to show some Paramount films, the company insisted on **block booking,** *requiring an exhibitor who wanted to rent a popular film to take an entire block of films, some of which were not very popular.* Other companies soon followed Paramount's lead and began block booking, so that by 1926 much of the production and film distribution in the country was controlled by a small

REVIEW

The Motion Picture Patents Company attempted to monopolize the film industry. Independents eventually brought about its demise. Later, motion picture studios tried to control the industry through block booking and four-walling.

group of companies. This situation remained essentially unchanged until 1948, when the courts ruled that such control restricted competition, and producers were forced to sell their theaters. The courts also made block booking illegal.

The antitrust division of the U.S. Department of Justice continued through the 1970s to monitor film industry business practices that might unduly restrict competition. Their last major action of this sort was the order to Warner Brothers in 1976 to stop **four-walling** motion pictures. Four-walling involves *renting theaters in which to show a film, instead of renting the film to theater owners.* Studios can make more money four-walling than renting if they have a hit movie or have waged a massive advertising campaign.

Motion Pictures and Video

In the 1980s, technological developments and consumer tastes blurred the distinction between the film and video industries. By the end of the decade, box office sales—ticket receipts from the showing of motion pictures in movie theaters—amounted to about $5 billion a year. But the sale and rental of those pictures on videocassette brought in more than twice that amount. In 1980, eight hundred-and-two thousand VCRs were sold. By 1989, VCR sales had risen to more than 12 million. Two-thirds of the households in the United States had at least one VCR; almost a fourth of them had more than one. This development prompted the Japanese electronics giants Sony and Matsushita to stake a claim in the motion picture business. In 1989, Sony purchased Columbia Pictures for $3.4 billion dollars. The trade magazine *Variety* pointed out that it was a "tidy case of hardware meeting software."[1] That is, Sony's intent was to ensure an entertainment product (software) for its electronics production (hardware). In 1988, Sony purchased CBS Records for much the same reason.

Another reason why Sony purchased Columbia Pictures was to position itself for the advent of high-definition technology, in which Sony has invested heavily. It hopes to benefit from that investment in the 1990s. The hardware used in high-definition production and exhibition may eventually replace both motion picture and television technology. According to *Variety,* sales from high-definition computer chips alone will rise from zero to $10 billion a year by 1999.

The Sony purchase, and other acquisitions and mergers that we will discuss later in this chapter, reflect the trend toward total **vertical integration**—*the consolidation under one ownership of corporations engaged in different stages of production of the same or similar products.* This is especially true for the film and television industries. Sony, for example, now has a major motion picture production studio and a library of some three thousand films, as well as eight hundred twenty movie theaters and worldwide theatrical distribution. In addition, it has a television production studio and twenty-three thousand episodes of television programs available for rent. And it is

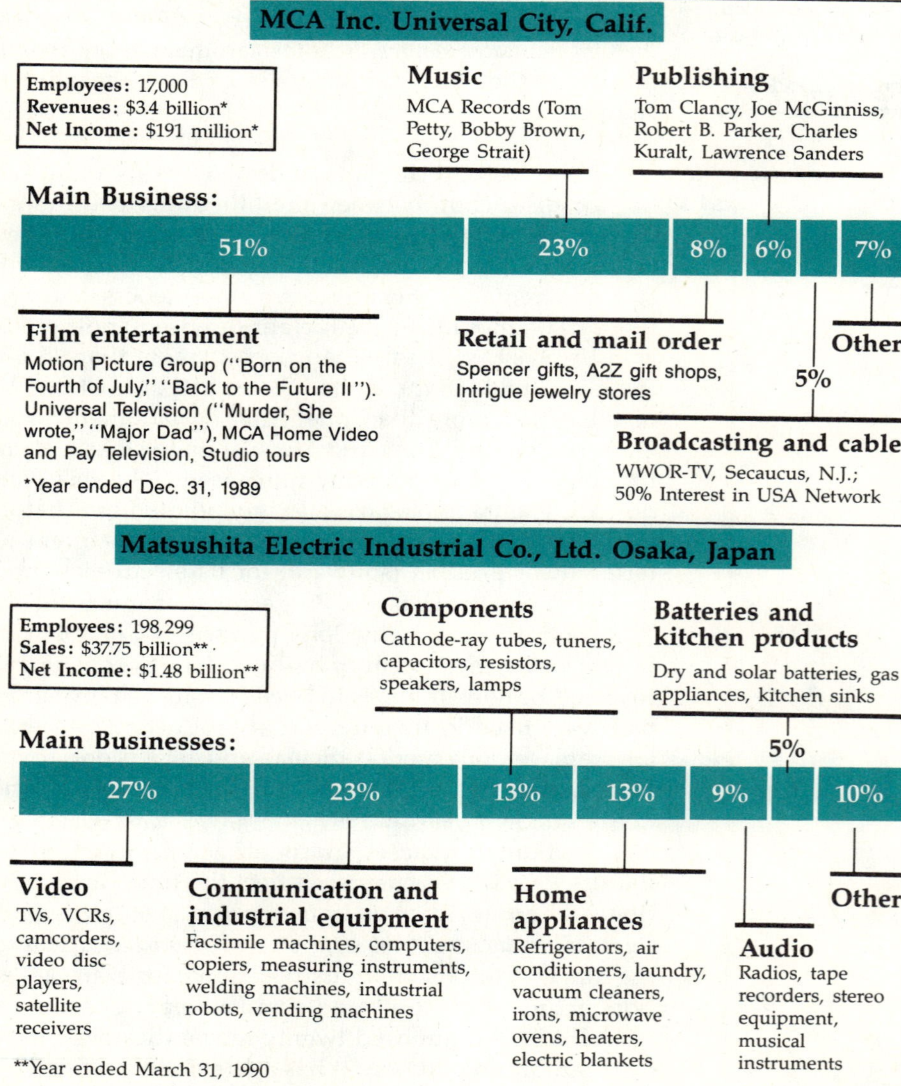
MCA and Matsushita
AT-A-GLANCE
The purchase of MCA Inc. by Matsushita Electric Industrial Co. for $6.6 billion is the largest Japanese purchase of a U.S. company. Here's how the companies compare:
MCA Inc. Universal City, Calif.
Employees: 17,000
Revenues: $3.4 billion*
Net Income: $191 million*
Music
MCA Records (Tom Petty, Bobby Brown, George Strait)
Publishing
Tom Clancy, Joe McGinniss, Robert B. Parker, Charles Kuralt, Lawrence Sanders
Main Business:
51%
23%
8%
6%
7%
Film entertainment
Motion Picture Group ("Born on the Fourth of July," "Back to the Future II"). Universal Television ("Murder, She wrote," "Major Dad"), MCA Home Video and Pay Television, Studio tours
*Year ended Dec. 31, 1989
Retail and mail order
Spencer gifts, A2Z gift shops, Intrigue jewelry stores
5%
Other
Broadcasting and cable
WWOR-TV, Secaucus, N.J.; 50% Interest in USA Network
Matsushita Electric Industrial Co., Ltd. Osaka, Japan
Employees: 198,299
Sales: $37.75 billion**
Net Income: $1.48 billion**
Components
Cathode-ray tubes, tuners, capacitors, resistors, speakers, lamps
Batteries and kitchen products
Dry and solar batteries, gas appliances, kitchen sinks
Main Businesses:
5%
27%
23%
13%
13%
9%
10%
Video
TVs, VCRs, camcorders, video disc players, satellite receivers
Communication and industrial equipment
Facsimile machines, computers, copiers, measuring instruments, welding machines, industrial robots, vending machines
Home appliances
Refrigerators, air conditioners, laundry, vacuum cleaners, irons, microwave ovens, heaters, electric blankets
Audio
Radios, tape recorders, stereo equipment, musical instruments
Other
**Year ended March 31, 1990

REVIEW

Because of advancements in technology and changes in the way audiences experience motion pictures, there is less distinction between film and video. In fact, most films are either sold or rented on videocassette. Large corporations such as Sony and Matsushita have invested in film and video hardware and software.

one of the world's largest manufacturers of video technology. Ironically, this type of integration—with its monopolistic overtones—was labeled illegal in 1948. In today's seemingly laissez-faire atmosphere, it appears both legal and profitable.

Following in the footsteps of the Sony acquisition, Matsushita—better known by such brand names as Panasonic, Technics, JVC, and Quasar—bought MCA Inc., the owner of Universal Pictures, for $6.6 billion. The 1990 purchase was the largest ever of a U.S. industry by the Japanese. Like Sony, Matsushita now has the entertainment software to complement its electronic hardware. In addition to Universal Pictures, MCA—the fourth-largest entertainment company in America—also owns Universal Television, MCA Records, a book publishing company, and broadcasting and cable interests (WWOR-TV and 50 percent of the USA Network). And also like Sony, Matsushita is now poised to push its version of high-definition television (HDTV). In an earlier electronics war involving the VCR, Matsushita's VHS format eventually replaced the Beta format developed by Sony.

BYLINE

Should or shouldn't the Justice Department or some other government agency be concerned about vertical integration, and such other practices believed by many observers to lead to unfair competition? Do you believe the government is right or wrong in reducing or eliminating its role in regulating some of the media? Will deregulation increase or decrease the number and variety of motion pictures you will be able to see in your local theaters?

How the Content of Movies Developed

Not all of the important developments in early film history involved economics or regulation. There were also important developments in film content. Initially, anything that moved was subject matter for the early motion pictures produced for audiences awed simply by the existence of this wondrous technology. Scenes were shown of passengers getting off a train, of London's Trafalgar Square, of a cavalry charge, circus and vaudeville acts, prizefights, and dancers. Even short scenes from popular plays were used. The head-on shot of a train charging toward the camera was always sure to frighten and please an audience. Especially popular for a period were local "actualities," scenes shot in the town where the film program was presented. Filmgoers were thrilled to see their hometowns thus immortalized.

Politics in films. The use of political content in movies apparently was pioneered in a film made for a demonstration of the Biograph projector at Hammerstein's Olympia Vaudeville Theater in New York City on October

12, 1896. A group of prominent local Republicans were invited to the theater where one of the features on the program was a brief film of the Republican presidential candidate, William McKinley. It had been shot in his hometown, Canton, Ohio. Although this film continued to be shown during the remainder of the campaign, there is no record that the Democrats asked for equal time. And apparently no claims were ever made that this use of film accounted for McKinley's election victory over William Jennings Bryan.

Sports. Sports were among the early popular topics for films. A film of the Yale football team practicing was a strong attraction in 1897. The heavyweight championship fight that year between James J. Corbett and Robert Fitzsimmons was less successful, however, because of the film's poor technical quality.

News. Just before the close of the nineteenth century, news footage became a popular film attraction. This development was stimulated by America's foreign involvements, first in Cuba and then in the Philippines, as America fought Spain for control of these islands. Movie patrons were thrilled to see the exotic spots where their heroes Teddy Roosevelt and Admiral George Dewey were protecting "American honor." They saw soldiers boarding troop trains, ships steaming toward Cuba or the Philippines, and the funeral for the victims after the sinking of the American battleship, the *Maine.* They also saw the triumphant parade for Admiral Dewey in New York when he returned after his victory in the Battle of Manila.

Some filmmakers soon discovered that it was easier and safer to shoot the staged war scenes in their studios at home than at the actual sites of the battles. Typical was the producer who restaged the naval battle of Santiago Bay using cutout photographs of warships sailing on a tabletop sea while his wife provided the heavy smoke of the cannons with her cigarettes.

Comedy and trick films. Between 1901 and 1903, comedy and trick films came to the fore. The former were influenced by the comedy routines from the vaudeville and burlesque houses. The latter developed in large part because of the involvement in filmmaking of a French magician, Georges Méliès. Méliès, among other accomplishments, created the science fiction film. His 1902 film, *A Trip to the Moon,* showed a rocket being constructed and shot off, landing in the eye of the man in the moon; the astronauts going down into a lunar crater, being attacked by the moon's inhabitants, fleeing the moon, and splashing down into the ocean back on earth. This fictional film was a fair approximation of the television coverage of America's moon exploration almost three-quarters of a century later, even to its inclusion of the triumphant parade afterward in honor of the astronauts. The only parts of the Méliès fantasy that were not repeated in life, so far as we know, were the attack on the astronauts by the moon people and the man in the moon's shedding of a giant tear when the rocket landed in his eye.

The narrative film. An important early developer of the realistic narrative or fiction film was Edwin S. Porter. He began in the business as a mechanic and cameraman but soon moved into filmmaking. In his first well-known film, *The Life of an American Fireman*, completed in 1902, Porter showed that film could be more realistic than theater. Using both indoor and outdoor scenes, he demonstrated the way in which film could be edited so as to shift attention back and forth to actions occurring at different times or in different places. He also evolved the basic elements of the film chase as he quickly alternated shots of a woman and a child in a burning house and a fire engine racing to save them.

Porter also helped to develop a key film genre, the western, with his second major film, *The Great Train Robbery*, completed in 1903. This was one of the most complex films made up to that date. It had 14 different sequences, including a chase scene as the posse ran down the bandits at the very last possible moment.

The documentary film. From its beginning, film has been used to record or document reality. However, not until 1922 was the full potential of the medium for such a purpose recognized. That year the great American documentary filmmaker and explorer Robert Flaherty completed *Nanook of the North*. The film was Flaherty's record of his study of Eskimo life in northern Canada. For his second full-length documentary film, Flaherty spent almost two years studying native life in Samoa, synthesizing his many observations in the film, *Moana of the South Seas*.

Another influential early documentary filmmaker was a Scot, John Grierson. He organized in Great Britain a production unit devoted solely to the making of documentary films. This unit, supported by the British government, experimented with a variety of documentary forms, including most of those we see in theaters and on television today.

Government support also played an important role in the creation of some of the great documentary films in the United States. During the Franklin Roosevelt administration of the 1930s, Pare Lorentz was hired by the government to document some of the problems of the Depression and their solutions. His 1936 film, *The Plow That Broke the Plains*, was about the poor farming practices that led to the dust bowl. *The River*, released in

REVIEW

From the very start, films concerned themselves with politics, sports, news, and comedy. Editing made the narrative film possible. The first documentary film was *Nanook of the North*. It was followed by other documentaries such as *The Plow That Broke the Plains* and *The River*.

1937, publicized the accomplishments of the Tennessee Valley Authority's soil conservation and flood control programs. These documentary films served a number of purposes for the government: they reached people who couldn't or wouldn't read about these government programs, they served to educate Americans about ways to overcome some serious national problems, and they were effective tools for winning support for the administration.

Besides the uses to which the documentary film can be put, it is interesting and important to us for other reasons. The documentary is similar in many ways to a straight news report. It is also similar in many ways to the dramatic film. The result is that each documentary film raises questions for us as viewers concerning how it ought to be processed. Should we accept it as absolute fact? Should we accept it as fiction? Where does fact stop and fiction begin? The answers to these questions are as varied as the documentary films to which they should be applied.

BYLINE

The next time you see a documentary film, consider these questions: To what extent does the filmmaker present "reality," unvarnished and unshaped by the camera? To what extent does the filmmaker shape that reality in order to affect your attitudes in a particular way? Is that documentary more fact or more fiction?

The impact of the world wars on the film industry. World War I was important to the American film industry for several reasons. One was that it gave an important boost to the development of newsreels. When the war began in Europe, Americans wanted to see what was happening, and the industry obliged. When America entered the war, interest in the newsreels became even greater.

Our entry into the war was also the impetus for President Woodrow Wilson to set up an official American propaganda agency, the Committee on Public Information. This agency encouraged Hollywood to produce films favorable to our cause, controlled which American films were exported to other countries, and insisted that our allies in Europe show American-made propaganda films if they wanted any of our entertainment films.

World War I had its greatest impact on the American film industry, however, because filmmaking in Europe virtually stopped. Chemicals essential for making nitrate film were needed for explosives. As a result, the United States became the dominant supplier of entertainment films to Europe, a position it still retains. This European market for American films is still important for the economic health of the industry. Therefore, a film's potential for doing well in foreign distribution affects the probability that it will be produced.

World War II, as you can imagine, created great opportunities for documentary filmmakers and ample support for their films from every government involved in the war. Among the best-known products in this country are the *Why We Fight* series produced by Frank Capra and the *Battle of Midway* done by John Ford. These were produced to motivate both American troops and those Americans working on the home front. They were so effective that government leaders decided to establish an overseas branch of the Office of War Information for propaganda and information aimed at people in other countries. These materials continue to be produced to the present day by the United States Information Agency (USIA), successor to the Office of War Information.

You may have seen some of those documentaries that were produced during World War II, but you have probably not seen any of the USIA films created since that war ended. The reason is that there is a law against showing these films in the United States. Members of Congress fear that some might be used for internal political purposes if they could be distributed in this country. However, at least one of them won an Oscar, the highest award given in the American film industry. *Seven at Little Rock*, produced by filmmaker and political consultant Charles Guggenheim, documented the problems of school integration in Little Rock, Arkansas. It was selected as the best short subject documentary of 1963.

REVIEW

As a result of World War I, the United States became the film capital of the world. During World War II, a number of Hollywood directors such as Frank Capra and John Ford produced documentary films for the war effort.

The greatest master of the propaganda film was not an American, but a German. Leni Riefenstahl glorified Adolf Hitler and Nazi Germany with such films as *Olympia* and *Triumph of the Will*, both made in Germany in the 1930s. They are classics, both as propaganda and as superb examples of the art of the documentary.

The Rise of the Stars

Initially, the motion picture was a director's medium. Writers were unimportant, for action was often made up as the show went along or borrowed from the classics or the not-so-classy. Employees who sewed costumes, painted scenery, and swept the floors were enlisted as unpaid actors. Even when film acting began to be recognized as a specialized skill, rather than a sideline for technicians and janitors, the major studios, members of the Trust, refused to divulge the names of their leading actors or build on their budding fame because these actors might then use the power of their popularity to demand larger salaries.

Soon, because audiences did not know their names, leading actors became known by the studios for which they worked: "The Vitagraph Girl" or "The Biograph Girl." Others became known by the characters they regularly played, such as "Broncho Billy."

This plot of the major studios to hold down the salaries of the actors finally was foiled when Carl Laemmle, who had started an independent film company, hired the popular Biograph Girl. He not only gave her more

Talking pictures became a hit with audiences in 1927 when Warner Brothers persuaded Al Jolson to star in the screen version of a popular stage play, "The Jazz Singer." Toward the end of the film Jolson turned to his mother (Eugenie Besserer) and said, "Hey, Mom, listen to this." Then he sang two songs. The novelty caught on, and within a few years all the major studios had converted to sound.

money than the Biograph studio had but also promised that her films would be advertised with her own name, Florence Lawrence. When it was discovered that Laemmle more than made up the additional salary paid to Lawrence with the extra ticket sales generated by advertising films with her name, other studios followed suit. This increased visibility proved a financial boon, not only to Florence Lawrence, but also to such leading actors as Mary Pickford, Tom Mix, Gloria Swanson, Carole Lombard, Wallace Beery, W. C. Fields, and many other stars who followed them.

One of the greatest of these stars was Charlie Chaplin. An indication of what the emancipation of motion picture actors meant—or, at least, the emancipation of their names—was the steep spiral of Chaplin's salary. He began as one of the stable of comedians in Mack Sennett's Keystone studio, the home of the Keystone Kops. Because he had some reputation as a vaudeville comic, he was paid what was then considered a large salary, $150 a week. That was in December 1913. A year later he was signed by another film company at $1250 a week. The following year, a third studio increased his salary to $10,000 a week. Four years after joining Keystone, he signed with yet another studio to make eight short films in 18 months for a salary of $1 million. Charlie Chaplin was 27 years old at the time. By 1920, Chaplin and the other Hollywood stars were probably the best-known people in the world.

The "Talkies" Although we talk about the early movies as silent films, audiences seldom experienced them as silent. Some sort of piano music or other accompaniment was almost always played when they were shown in theaters. Each nickelodeon generally employed a pianist who sat with the screen in view so that he or she could synchronize the timing and mood of the improvised music with what was happening on the screen. The music was meant not only to provide mood settings, but also to drown out some of the noise of the early projectors.

By 1912, special musical scores were being written for the major films, and orchestras were often hired to play the music during each showing. The symphonic score for D. W. Griffith's *Birth of a Nation* called for a 70-piece orchestra. Orchestra pits were included in most major movie palaces built after 1914 to accommodate such large ensembles.

Experimentation with synchronizing recorded sound and motion pictures was also conducted virtually from the earliest days. In fact, Thomas Edison was more interested in movies for purposes of visual accompaniment of his recordings than for the movies themselves. He first synchronized his phonograph to the Kinetoscope in 1889. Very short sound films were made in Europe soon after using the same system. The system was not reliable, however. Equally important, as theaters grew in size, the existing phonographs could not produce enough volume to make the sound audible to most of the audience.

A reasonably practical system for synchronizing recorded sound with motion pictures was demonstrated by General Electric and a group of other manufacturers in the early twenties. The major studios showed little interest. Their silent films were highly successful, profits were high, and their block booking practice, described earlier, was holding down competition. They felt no need for change. A company that did feel a need for change however, was one of those being held down by block booking.

In the early 1920s, Warner Brothers was having difficulty finding outlets for its films. In the hope that sound would be a means of overcoming that problem, it bought exclusive rights to *the General Electric sound system* and called it the **Vitaphone.** Warner Brothers made a number of short sound films with this new system, but these did little to change the popular notion that sound films were merely a novelty. The first feature-length film Warner made using the system was a different matter. *The Jazz Singer,*

REVIEW

Audience demand was responsible for the rise of film stars. One of the greatest of the early stars was Charlie Chaplin. In 1927, Warner Brothers introduced the first feature-length sound film, *The Jazz Singer.*

starring Al Jolson, was released in 1927 and became an instant hit. Jolson's songs in that film were, in effect, funeral dirges for the silent film. Within two years, the changeover of the entire industry to sound was virtually complete.

Nothing created as much chaos in the film industry as this changeover. The technical demands of sound required quite different production methods. Different types of writing were required. Many of the major stars were made obsolete overnight because their voices were unsuitable for sound. Perhaps most important, the need for large amounts of capital to finance these changes gave bankers a great deal of control of the film industry.

HOW MOTION PICTURES GET INTO OUR MOSAICS

There were three major stages in the development of the motion picture industry: the *technological stage*, the *artistic stage*, and the *economic stage*. The beginning of the industry, the technological stage, was dominated by the inventors and technicians such as Thomas Edison, William Dickson (who led Edison's research team), and the Lumière brothers. The artistic stage was that period during which directors such as Georges Méliès, Edwin Porter, and D. W. Griffith were exploring the potentials of this new medium for expression and the communication of new forms of content. The third stage, the economic, has continued to the present day. This stage began with the takeover of control by bankers and businessmen (business*men* because few if any of the major entrepreneurs in the early years were women). These were the people who saw motion pictures primarily as a business or an investment. Lines between these three stages are not clear-cut; the stages overlap and many of the individuals identified primarily with one stage were also active in others. Some film inventors also pioneered in the artistic development of the art.

The Business of Motion Pictures

We often forget that motion pictures are the products of large industries that exist primarily because investors want to make a profit. The probability that a film will be produced is dependent on someone coming up with the extremely large sum of money necessary. In a sense, major financial control of the motion picture industry rests with the consumers—those of us who buy tickets to the movies or watch them on our VCRs or commercial television. Long before we get into the act, though, someone must have sufficient faith that we and many other consumers will go for a particular movie to put up the production funds.

In the 1930s and 1940s, the time of the studio-produced film, the bankers were the villains of the film industry. Few films could be made unless a bank backed them, and the "hard-hearted bankers with no aesthetic sensibilities" were blamed when someone's pet idea for a film could find no takers. Today we talk about the independent motion picture producer being dominant in the film industry, and some assume this means that he or she is independent of banker control. Not so. The producer simply has a different banker, usually the old studio—Warner Brothers, 20th Century Fox, or others.

Independent production comes into being in this way: Someone gets an idea or a story that he or she thinks will make a good film and organizes a creative team that can realize that idea or story. This team contains the key personnel. The package is then presented to a financing agency. The agency is generally a motion picture studio because the studio has or can raise the money and has the means to distribute the film after it is made.

If a studio agrees to finance and distribute the film, it is promised a percentage of the film's revenue. Generally this is a percentage of the gross, which means that the studio gets its money first, regardless of whether the film is profitable. Popular stars and directors with a record of successful films also have a great deal of power in this system and can demand a considerable percentage of the film's revenue.

This way of doing business has a conservative influence on the film business. It creates an almost irresistable tendency to go with the kind of film that has made money before, the star whose films have been popular before, the director who has made hits.

For example, of the top-grossing films of the 1980s (Table 7.1), only three—*Batman*, *Beverly Hills Cop*, and *Ghostbusters*—were made without the involvement of either George Lucas or Steven Spielberg, two of Hollywood's most successful directors. And only one of them—*E.T.: The Extra Terrestrial*—was neither a sequel nor a film for which a sequel was planned.

Some observers criticize contemporary trends in the motion picture industry, especially the absorption of the major motion picture companies into large corporations that are involved in many other aspects of the entertainment-information business. The critics say it has become more of a money business than a movie business. There is just one problem with

TABLE 7.1 Top-Grossing Motion Pictures of the 1980s

	Box Office Receipts
1. *E.T.: The Extra Terrestrial*	$399,804,539
2. *Return of the Jedi*	263,000,000
3. *Batman*	251,161,818
4. *Raiders of the Lost Ark*	242,374,454
5. *Beverly Hills Cop*	234,760,478
6. *The Empire Strikes Back*	223,000,000
7. *Ghostbusters*	220,855,498
8. *Back to the Future*	208,242,016
9. *Indiana Jones and the Last Crusade*	195,486,133
10. *Indiana Jones and the Temple of Doom*	179,870,271

Source: Reprinted courtesy of Entertainment Data, Inc.

that observation: it ignores history. Movies have almost always been a money business; the drive to turn a profit has been the dominant force in the industry, at least in this country. You must understand that basic fact if you are to understand this industry, or any of the mass communication industries in America. This economic dominance has its drawbacks, but it also has its positive features. The most important positive value is that the audience's interests and wants are probably more important in this system than in any other conceivable system because the audience ultimately determines what is profitable.

Survival of the Fittest As recently as 1984, there were nine major motion picture studios and more than a dozen independent studios. But as the pressures increased to create bigger and more elaborate films, many of the smaller companies—and even some of the major ones—were eliminated. In 1987, independents released 380 films; that figure dropped to 352 in 1988 and to 287 in 1989. A lack of cash and size needed to produce "blockbuster" films forced a number of companies into bankruptcy, reorganization, or absorption by larger studios. Tri-Star merged with Columbia only to be bought out by Sony. Lorimar was acquired by Warner Brothers, which is now part of the huge Time Warner corporation. By the end of the 1980s, eight major studios accounted for more than 90 percent of the box office sales in this country (Table 7.2). The strongest of them—Paramount Pictures, Universal, Warner Brothers, Walt Disney Studios, and 20th Century Fox—have increased their production, theatrical distribution, television, home video, foreign sales, and cable operations in order to capitalize on a seemingly insatiable appetite for American entertainment product. Time Warner, for example, now owns one of the top three Hollywood motion picture studios, the largest worldwide television production company, the second largest cable system in the United States, and two of the three largest pay cable networks.

TABLE 7.2 The Major Motion Picture Studios

	Number of Films Released in 1989	*Box Office Share in 1989*
1. Warner Brothers	36	17.1%
2. Universal	19	16.3
3. Columbia/Tri-Star	42	16.1
4. Paramount	14	14.1
5. Buena Vista (Disney)	18	13.8
6. MGM/UA	26	6.5
7. 20th Century Fox	17	6.3
8. Orion	17	4.2

Source: Variety, January 3, 1990. Reprinted courtesy of *Variety* Newspaper.

REVIEW

Producing and distributing motion pictures requires huge sums of money, making it difficult for independent filmmakers to find financial support. In the 1930s and 1940s, banks provided much of the backing. Today, eight studios control the industry and account for 90 percent of the box office sales in this country.

Among the major studios, Orion—the smallest of them—is struggling to survive, while two of the others, MGM/United Artists and Universal, have been swallowed up by foreign corporations. Orion had several successes in the late 1980s, including *Amadeus, Platoon,* and *Mississippi Burning*. But *Great Balls of Fire*, released in 1989, was one of a string of box office disasters. Despite the box office success of more recent films—*Dances With Wolves* and *The Silence of the Lambs*—Orion's long-term debt increased from $351 million in 1990 to $509 million in 1991, leaving the studio with huge interest payments. Because of Orion's financial woes, some Hollywood executives speculate that it may be the next major studio sold.

In 1986, television executive Ted Turner purchased MGM/UA and then sold back everything but 3300 films from its film library. A few years later an Australian conglomerate, Qintex, planned to buy MGM/UA, but the deal collapsed. Then, in 1990, the company was bought by Italian financier Giancarlo Parretti's Pathé Communications for $1.3 billion. That same year Universal was acquired by Matsushita.

Censorship and Control of Films

The movies developed a large and loyal body of fans who followed the flickering images from the peepshow parlors to the nickelodeons to the great movie palaces of the 1930s and 1940s. At the same time, the

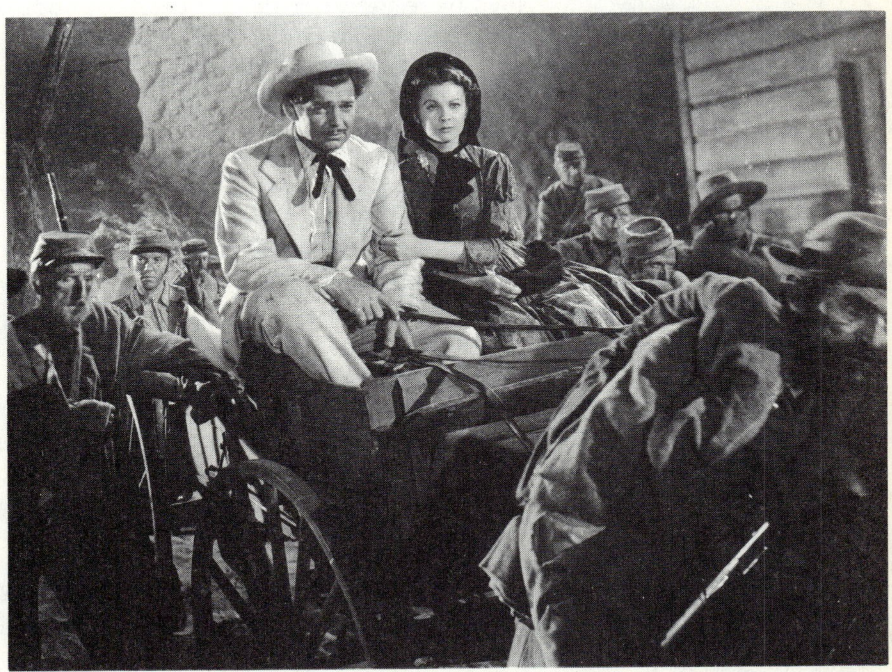

Though it ranks among the all-time film classics, Gone With The Wind *(1939) was a rarity in its time—one of the few true blockbusters of the 1930s and 1940s.*

industry developed its body of critics. Many of the charges leveled against television a half-century later were aimed at movies in these early days. Critics decried their glorification of sex, crime, and violence. They claimed that westerns and gangster movies were inciting young people to crime. In 1905, a publication in Great Britain reported that three youngsters who broke into a store said they had learned how to do it from watching a movie. A short time later, a judge in Belgium cited motion pictures as one of the major causes of crime among children. Does all of this sound familiar?

Such charges, combined with the concerns of other institutions whose business was threatened by the movies—institutions ranging from saloons to churches—brought appeals for censorship. One of the earliest recorded appeals was an unsuccessful attempt in 1896 to have *Dolorita in the Passion Dance* censored.

Chicago was the first of many cities in the United States to enact a censorship law covering motion pictures. That was in 1907. By the early 1920s, the pressures for greater government control of motion pictures became too strong for Hollywood to ignore. Many states were considering censorship bills. Religious groups were organizing against the sinfulness of films. These movements were aided by scandals that were shaking Hollywood at the time and providing lurid headlines across the country. Frequent divorces, frowned on in the 1920s, were common in Hollywood. More serious were the drug-related death of popular actor Wallace Reid, and the trial of comedian Fatty Arbuckle on charges of murdering a young actress during a drunken orgy. This was shortly after the Eighteenth Amendment to the U.S. Constitution had been passed, banning the manufacture or sale of intoxicating liquors. It was a time of righteous zeal.

The Motion Picture Production Code. To stave off government control and to improve its image, the major studios, joined together in the Motion Picture Producers and Distributors Association (MPPDA), in 1922 hired Will Hays to keep the movies clean. The companies agreed to control and censor themselves, under Hays's guidance. An elder in the Presbyterian Church and former Chairman of the Republican National Committee, Hays was a good front man for this purpose. Before release of any motion picture by a member of the MPPDA, the approval of his office was needed. The criteria used by the Hays office in deciding whether to give a film its Seal of Approval were clarified in the **Motion Picture Production Code,** which *listed in detail the do's and don'ts for moviemakers*—primarily the don'ts. The Code banned sexually suggestive acts and language that some people thought offensive. It also insisted that no lawbreaker go unpunished in a movie. By 1940, Hays could boast that 95 percent of America's movie theaters showed only films that carried a seal of approval.

Legion of Decency. In spite of the Code and the efforts of the Hays office, the Catholic Church remained dissatisfied with the amount of immorality it perceived in many films. In 1934, it organized the **Legion of Decency,** *a* *group of Catholics concerned about film morality,* to pressure producers and exhibitors to avoid making or showing questionable films. For at least twenty years, the Legion of Decency was highly effective. Church-goers signed pledges to avoid theaters that showed films disapproved by the Legion. Many Protestant groups also supported the Legion's efforts. And there was close cooperation between the Legion and the MPPDA Code Office, headed during this period by Joseph Breen. Even the satiric sexual humor of Mae West fell victim to the Legion and the Code Office as she was forced to be less suggestive.

Both the Motion Picture Production Code and the Legion of Decency had great influence in Hollywood until television came along. When the video medium swallowed up most of the audience for light entertainment, motion picture producers discovered that one way to combat such competition was to use some of the kinds of sexual scenes, language, and violence that were not permitted on television. This discovery came at the same time that sexual mores in our society were changing and the Catholic Church was becoming more liberal so that the Legion of Decency no longer had either as much power or as much desire to control film content. Since the major studios controlled the MPPDA and, hence, the Motion Picture Production Code, and it was in their financial interest to ease the restrictions of the Code, the Code was liberalized.

The fate of both the Code and the Legion of Decency was sealed in 1953 when a slightly risqué motion picture, *The Moon Is Blue,* was released. Despite condemnation by the Legion and the refusal of the Code office to give it a Seal of Approval, the film reaped large profits. With this example before them, other studios began ignoring the Code and the Legion of Decency and found similar success at the box office.

The Catholic Church became steadily more flexible in its rating of motion pictures and virtually stopped its pressure group tactics on the industry. In recognition of its changed function, in 1966 the Legion of Decency was renamed the National Catholic Office of Motion Pictures.

Film Rating System The Code Office of the Motion Picture Producers and Distributors Association changed radically also, especially after 1968, when it substituted a rating system for its Seal of Approval. This rating system is supervised by a Classification and Rating Administration Board (CARA), which replaced the Motion Picture Production Code Administration. On the CARA board are representatives of the Motion Picture Association of America (MPAA) (successor to the MPPDA), the International Film Importers and Distributors of America, and the National Association of Theatre Owners. Until recently, films were classified as *G*—"for the general audience"; *PG*—"parental guidance suggested"; *PG-13*—"parental guidance suggested for children under 13"; *R*—"restricted, children under 17 admitted only when accompanied by an adult"; and *X*—"persons under 17 not admitted." In 1990, the MPAA made a major change in its movie rating system. It dropped the *X* rating and created a new "no children" category called *NC-17* to prohibit viewers under 17 from seeing films with adult themes or content. The MPAA also modified the *R* classification by furnishing film reviewers and theater owners with brief explanations of why a film was given an *R* rating—usually because it included such themes as sex, violence, profanity, drug use, or suicide.

The reason for the change in the classification system had as much to do with economics as it did with parental concerns about the kinds of films children could see. The *X* rating had become strongly associated with pornography. In fact, producers of pornographic films capitalized on this association by labeling their films *XXX*. But serious films suffered from an *X* rating. Most newspapers and broadcasting stations refused advertising for *X*-rated films, and movie chains refused to book them. As a result, filmmakers often censored their own films to avoid the stigma of the *X*. The new *NC*-17 category has been trademarked by the MPAA to prevent producers of pornographic films from using the new rating as promotional bait. They can, of course, apply for the rating, but it is doubtful that *NC*-17 will carry the same meaning as *X*—at least for a while.

The increased sale and rental of films on videocassette and the fact that many films are released without a rating have prompted demands for a different classification system, one that would be even more explicit. The alternative system, proposed by the Independent Video Programmers Association and the Film Advisory Board, would use six symbols—*C* (children's), *F* (family), *M* (mature), *MM* (very mature), *MMM* (extremely mature), and *X* (pornography and explicit sex). In addition, it would provide the following informational symbols on the back of the cassette boxes—*L* (language), *EL* (extreme language), *V* (violence), *EV* (extreme violence), *E/P/S* (explicit sex), *S* (sex), *N* (nudity), *EN* (extreme nudity), and *SA* (substance abuse). The MPAA opposes the alternative system on the grounds that its rating system accomplishes as much as a voluntary system can and that any additional enforcement should come from parents. Whether the MPAA's recent changes will satisfy criticisms of industry organizations and parent and religious groups that the current rating system is too vague remains to be seen.

BYLINE

Suppose you had an opportunity to devise a motion picture rating system. Would you? Would it resemble the current MPAA system or the alternative one, or would it be different from both of them? Would the classification system be the same for theater exhibition and home video, or would you devise a different system for each? Would ratings be voluntary or mandatory?

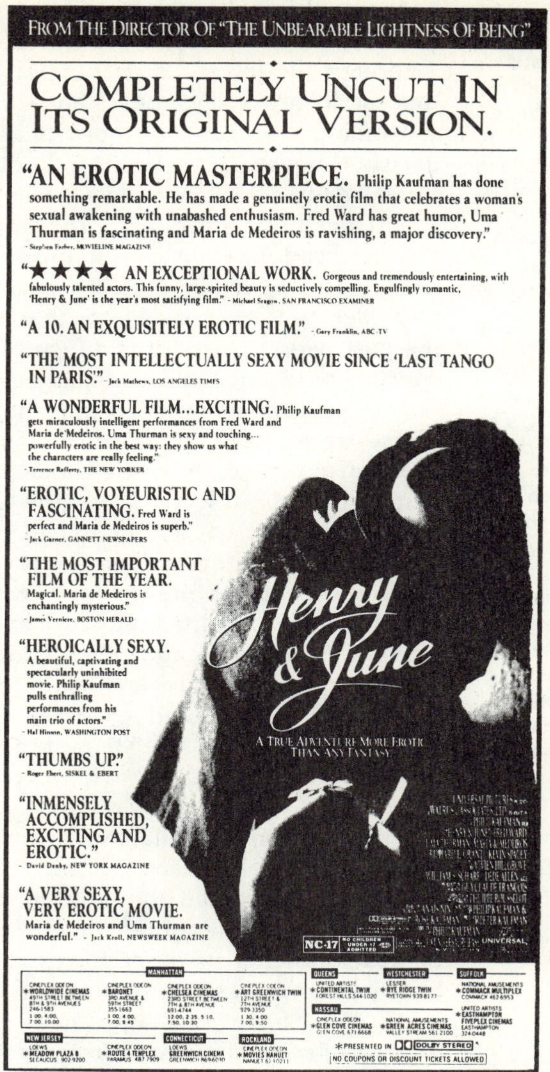

An advertisement for the first motion picture to receive an NC-17 rating.

Decline of film censorship. Decisions by the courts during the past twenty-five years also lessened the threat of government censorship for motion picture producers. The key case was decided in 1952 when the United States Supreme Court first stated that motion pictures were protected from censorship to some extent by the First Amendment. This decision came in a case involving the Italian film, *The Miracle*. In the film, a peasant woman is seduced by a man she believes to be Saint Joseph, and when her child is

REVIEW

Since the earliest days of the motion picture, concerns have been expressed about the amount of sex, crime, and violence in films. To offset possible government control, the film industry created its own self-censorship organization, the Motion Picture Producers and Distributors Association. The Code Office of the MMPDA and the Catholic Church's Legion of Decency exerted a great deal of influence on film content until changing sexual mores, the advent of television, and greater court protection brought about a decline in censorship activities.

born she thinks he is Jesus Christ. The state censorship agency in New York, the Board of Regents, banned the film, charging it was sacrilegious. Although the lower courts upheld the ban, the Supreme Court decided that sacrilege is too vague a standard for censorship and that the New York censorship law unconstitutionally abridged free speech and press. In that decision, however, the Court did not say that all censorship of motion pictures by city and state agencies was unconstitutional.

In decisions since 1952, the Supreme Court has continued to grant greater freedom from censorship to motion pictures. Although the film medium is not totally free of threats of censorship today, it is almost so. Considering the kinds of films that have been exhibited in theaters during the past twenty years, it is difficult to conceive of the sort of film that the courts would say could be legally censored.

At one time many cities and states had censorship boards that licensed films—deciding which ones could be shown in theaters. But a 1965 Supreme Court decision made it much more difficult for such boards to operate. In *Freedman* v. *Maryland*, the Court threw out a prior review statute on the grounds that it constrained protected expression and therefore violated the Constitution. The Court placed the burden of proof on the censor to show that a film was unprotected expression. It also said censorship boards had to expedite their work and either license a film or go to court to prevent its showing, and provide for prompt judicial review. Under these guidelines, one film review board after another collapsed. Ironically, the last state licensing board to close its doors was the one in Maryland. It was put out of business in 1981 by the state's "sunset law" and was not renewed by the legislature.

Influences of Other Media on the Motion Picture

What becomes available to us on movie theater screens is not solely a function of business factors, the pressures of government and other groups concerned about our morality, and the work of talented people in the industry. The content and form of motion pictures are also a product of developments in other forms of communication and entertainment, both past and present.

Sources of many artistic techniques in the film. The history of motion pictures is interesting for many reasons. A primary reason is that it shows us the way in which a totally new mass medium must "borrow" from other arts and media of communication as it searches for an identity and a set of functions it can serve.

Filmmakers borrowed concepts of composition and visual communication from photography and, to a lesser extent, the other visual arts. They borrowed the idea of narrative from the novel and the theater. Ideas about mood lighting came from the theater as well as from photography. Newspapers provided the inspiration for many of the "realities" of the early films as well as the later newsreels and documentaries. And many other sources yielded filmic ideas. Filmmakers experimented with these ideas, and out of their successful—and often unsuccessful—experiments built a unique art of the film. It is an art that has been used primarily to entertain but also to inform and to persuade and even to move to action. The full range of this art has probably not yet been fully explored.

Film in the age of television. The rise of television affected the motion picture industry in a variety of ways, in addition to loosening of standards on sex and violence noted earlier. The first major impact was on attendance: movie attendance peaked between 1930 and 1948, just prior to the television era, then dropped steadily as the competition from television grew. The studios attempted to compete with this new medium in several ways. They went to *very large screens*—**Cinemascope** and **Cinerama**—trying to emphasize their difference from tiny television screens. They attempted to resurrect 3-D movies (the illusion of three dimensions), which had been experimented with some years earlier. Color film began to be used for all films, whereas it had been used only sparingly before. One studio even tried Smellovision—movies that had odors that changed to suit the scene.

For a while, the studios refused to release any of their feature films for showing on television. However, the great profits to be made from such releases were tempting, and finally they agreed to release pre-1948 productions that were no longer of value for theater distribution. These films alone brought the studios millions of dollars in profits. When the pre-1948

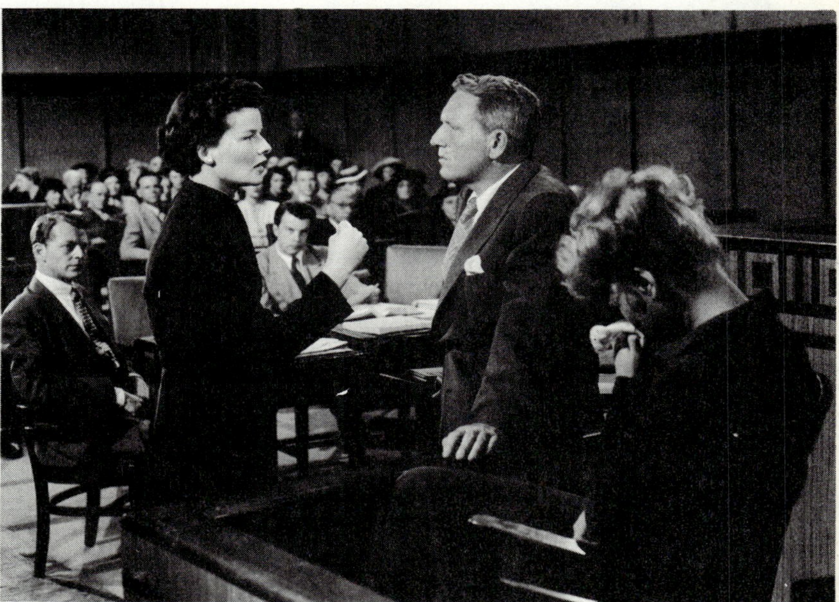

Movie attendance peaked during the pretelevision era, when stars such as Katherine Hepburn and Spencer Tracy (seen here in Adam's Rib*) were popular.*

supply of films was exhausted, they began releasing more and more recent films. Today, television is an important outlet for the industry and a major source of income.

REVIEW

Motion pictures have often been influenced by other media—the novel, theater, newspapers, and particularly television, which has affected the kinds of pictures made and box office attendance. To compete with television, the movie industry introduced Cinemascope, Cinerama, 3-D, and other novelties and refused to release its films for television showing. Today, the motion picture industry is a major producer of television programming.

During the 1961–1962 season, only 45 feature-length pictures were shown on network television. Most of these had their major runs in motion picture theaters some years earlier. After 1962, the number of motion pictures released to television increased steadily; at the same time, the length of time between their original showing in theaters and their showing on television decreased. The potential income from selling the television rights of theatrical motion pictures is an important consideration these days when films are made. However, the greater sexual explicitness and the language in some films can be a problem in television. Producers avoid this problem by shooting two versions of some scenes, the explicit version for theatrical release and a cleaned-up version for television.

Another important trend since the late 1960s has been the supplementing of theatrical films on network television with feature-length films made especially for television. By the mid-1970s, more than half of the motion picture films shown on network television were films made especially for that medium. Such films are generally produced by special divisions of the major studios. These divisions also produce some of the regular television entertainment programs, which account for an important, steady source of income for the studios. During the 1989–1990 season, the television divisions of the major motion picture studios produced 1043 hours of programming for the commercial networks.

OUR EXPOSURE TO MOVIES

Until World War I, movies were largely the medium for the immigrants and the native poor. By 1917, however, as movie houses moved "uptown," a new audience began to be attracted, a better educated and more affluent audience. This greater respectability is also reflected in the fact that newspapers began to review movies about this time.

The attendance at motion picture theaters rose quickly. By 1922, about 40 million movie tickets were sold every week. This figure rose sharply until 1930, when it hit a peak of 90 million. Ticket sales hovered at that level for the next 18 years—from 1930 to 1948—dropping only slightly during the early 1930s when the country was in the depths of the Depression. After 1948, however, as television spread rapidly across the country, many movie patrons abandoned the theaters in favor of the smaller screen that could be viewed at home. Average weekly ticket sales dropped from 90 million a week in 1948 to about 21 million a week today.

The motion picture has always been largely a young people's medium. Since television took over much of the popular entertainment function of the movies for most people, that generalization has been even more true. People between the ages of 16 and 29 comprise about 31 percent of the population of this country, but they comprise about 62 percent of the motion picture theater audience. Interestingly, the relationship between age and movie attendance is almost precisely the opposite of the relationship between age and television viewing. Young children watch a great deal of television. Viewing drops steadily through the school years, with the lowest level in the late high school and early college years. It then climbs steadily as people get older. Movie attendance, on the other hand, is very low for young children, climbs steadily through the school years, and hits a peak through the high school and college years and, to some extent, the immediate postcollege years. From the age of 30, there is a steady drop in movie-going as people get older.

BYLINE

How does your experience jibe with the description of the relationship between age and movie-going? Has your attendance at movie theaters increased during the past ten years? Has that of your friends? How do you explain this?

The one group of older adults for whom movie attendance has not lessened in this half of the twentieth century are the intellectuals. As television took over much of the popular entertainment function for most adults, and as the film industry sought new functions and new audiences, the intellectual and the film seem to have found each other. Initially the intellectual was attracted by the films imported from Italy, Sweden, Japan, and elsewhere. Then Hollywood awoke to this market interested in more complex stories and experimental treatment. This audience is not large, but it is a loyal one. It has given the industry some motivation for developing the artistic as well as the entertainment dimensions of films.

PROCESSING FILMIC INFORMATION

All that was said about information processing in Chapter 2 applies to our processing of the sights and sounds of motion pictures, but that is not the whole story. Most of us approach films in a somewhat different way than we do most of the other mass media; we seem more willing to work at the creation of nonobvious meanings with those sights and sounds from movies. When we read things in the newspaper or see things on television that we can't make immediate sense of, we tend to blame the journalist or the television director. Not so with the motion picture. When we have difficulty immediately creating meaning from a film, we are more likely to blame ourselves and to work harder at constructing some meaning for it.

Some interesting ideas about the way in which we process motion pictures have come from film critics and theorists. Film critics are often thought of as those writers who tell us which movies are good and which are bad. The best critics, however, do far more than that. Along with film theorists they speculate on how films work—that is, why we in the audience perceive films as we do. An intriguing question about our processing and perception of films is raised by a conflict between two of films's major theorists, Sergei Eisenstein and André Bazin.

REVIEW

In 1948, average weekly ticket sales of motion pictures were about 90 million. But the arrival of television resulted in a sharp decline in attendance. Today, about 21 million people—mainly young people—go to the movies each week. Critics and film theorists often speculate on how those movies work.

Eisenstein, one of Russia's early great filmmakers as well as a theorist, believed that we in the audience do not create our meanings from the single shots in a film but rather from the juxtaposition of shots. When shots are edited together, each serves as context for the other and thus affects our perception of the other. As Eisenstein put it, meaning is not created from the individual shots but from the "collision" of shots.

André Bazin, a French film theorist, posited a totally different audience-film relationship. He believed that we create meanings not from the juxtaposition or collision of shots in a film, but rather from the relationships of elements within each shot. Thus spatial arrangement and the movement of the camera and people or things in each individual shot are the elements that affect our processing of meanings from a film. Bazin came to this conclusion in part because he thought the single shot is more natural or realistic for viewers, whereas the montage or series of shots edited together is inconsistent with our everyday experience.

BYLINE

Think about Eisenstein's and Bazin's claims the next time you are watching a movie. Which one seems more consistent with your experience? Is it possible that your decision would be different if you had seen a different kind of film? Could it be that both Eisenstein and Bazin are right?

FUNCTIONS AND EFFECTS OF THE MOVIES

The functions and effects of movies have changed considerably over time. Throughout the first third of this century, the movies, like radio, were a cheap source of entertainment for the many immigrants from other countries. Perhaps even more important, the movies were a major medium of socialization for them. They went to night school to learn the basics of English and civics, but those lessons were driven home as they watched movies and listened to the radio. They learned how Americans were supposed to talk and behave, and their aspirations were heightened by the affluence displayed on the movie screen.

Television has almost totally displaced both radio and the movies in serving these functions for the waves of immigrants since World War II. The functions served by the movies have shifted almost as substantially as their audience. The movies immigrants attend today, especially in the larger cities, are generally from their native country and in their native tongue. Rather than serving as a means of socialization for them, these movies help them keep their ties to their native land and culture. If anything, these foreign language films are retarding socialization. They are part of the means by which an immigrant group can re-create their homeland within these borders of the United States, and the re-creation protects them from the pressures to become Americanized.

Hollywood movies shown in movie theaters serve largely you who are in your teens and twenties. Rather than serving your socialization needs, they are probably serving some of your social needs. They give you a place to go and something to talk about with friends. For many young adults (perhaps for you), they also serve a mating function—a place to go with a date and an aid to becoming acquainted. With an unfamiliar date, the movies save having to think up something to talk about for the entire evening and provide some basis for conversation afterward. The theater provides a good setting in which to become increasingly friendly, when that seems appropriate, and yet a setting in which it is easy to ward off, without embarrassment to anyone, more friendliness than you want. We suspect that few romances today did not evolve to some degree in movie theaters.

THE FUTURE OF THE MOTION PICTURE INDUSTRY

The motion picture industry changed dramtically during the 1980s, as VCRs and pay television altered the way audiences experienced motion pictures. Although the number of people attending movies at movie theaters increased by 63 million from 1980 to 1989, the most

The combination of the VCR and a wide selection of films on videotape has made the video store an integral part of the mass communication scene.

impressive growth occurred in the sale and rental of videocassettes. In 1982, approximately 5 million videocassettes were sold in retail stores; by 1988 sales had reached 135 million, and in 1989 they approached 175 million. While rental sales of movies may be leveling off, they nevertheless account for the bulk of the U.S. revenues for motion pictures—$9 billion a year compared to slightly more than $2 billion a year for the purchase of films on videocassette and $5 billion a year derived from box office sales.

One study of 212 California residents who either owned a VCR or subscribed to a pay-television movie channel showed the change that results when alternatives to traditional movie-going become available. Respondents reported that prior to the purchase of their VCRS or subscription to pay television they attended an average of 2.6 movies a month. After they acquired a VCR or subscribed to a movie channel, their attendance dropped to 1.8 movies a month. VCR owners viewed an average of 7.3 movies a month on their VCRs, while pay-television subscribers watched an average of 10.1 movies a month.[2] This change in viewing behavior, which is likely to continue through the 1990s, will no doubt have a profound effect on the way motion pictures are made and distributed.

REVIEW

Movies function mainly as a source of entertainment. They also perform a social function—especially for young people. But movie-going in the traditional sense may give way to watching films at home on videocassettes or pay television.

As we noted earlier, there has already been a great deal of investment in high-definition television, an electronic technology that makes the quality of a television screen comparable to that produced by 35-millimeter optical film. As this new technology becomes available on a large scale, motion picture production and exhibition as we know it may be replaced by a cheaper and more flexible video system.

MOVIES IN OUR LIVES: A SUMMARY

The movies have been an important part of American life and culture since those first flickering images began moving across the screen near the turn of the century. However, the reasons for their importance have shifted with time. In the first part of this century, the movies were the major source of light entertainment in America, especially for the poor. They were also an important source of education for the numerous immigrants, who learned from them how to be Americans—how to talk and act like Americans. Today they are important for other reasons. Films are increasingly accepted as one of the major contemporary art forms and hence a major source of entertainment for intellectuals. They also serve the young adults who seek entertainment that helps them escape from home—both physically and psychologically.

The motion picture industry has witnessed a number of attempts at monopoly during its lifetime. First the Motion Picture Patents Company, or Trust, attempted to squeeze out all companies except those belonging to the Trust; later, Paramount attempted to control all aspects of the business from production through distribution and exhibition. The Trust was defeated by the conservative business policies of its companies; the independent producers won over audiences by their experimentation with feature-length films, development of the star system, and development of the sound film. Control over all aspects of the business was defeated by the courts, which ruled it inhibited competition. Through vertical integration we see this type of control making a comeback, as major studios seek to extend their media capability.

The development of television has brought substantial change to the film industry, and therefore to the kinds of movies you have the opportunity to see. This competition was largely responsible for the demise of effective self-regulation of the motion picture industry, as the ratings system was substituted for the Code. Television was also largely responsible for the loss of power of such pressure groups as the Legion of Decency to control the sexual explicitness and language found in films. As television largely took over the provision of light, family entertainment, the movie industry sought audiences not adequately served by the video medium. The number of theatrical films produced in this country has dropped sharply since the advent of television. However, motion picture companies are now producing many television series and made-for-television movies, and selling and renting their movies on videocassette.

Film critics and theorists disagree about the way we process information that we get from films, and about the effects films have upon us. A key question is whether our perceptions are shaped more by the interaction among elements within a shot or the integration of elements between shots. This question deserves further study. We believe that both interactions are important to our perceptions, as are the interactions of all of these filmic elements with the bits of information we receive from other parts of our communication mosaics. Whether you agree or not, it should be clear that there is still a great deal we do not know about how we process the movies we see, and about how what we process affects the worlds in our heads.

DISCUSSION QUESTIONS

1. What inventions and innovations led to the development of the motion picture industry? What attempts were made to monopolize that industry?
2. How would you characterize early film content? Of the different kinds or genres of films prior to World War II, which are still found in motion picture theaters? Which are now more likely to be presented as television programming?
3. How did Hollywood filmmakers contribute to the war effort during World War II?
4. What are some of the obstacles to producing and distributing motion pictures? How would you characterize the motion picture industry today?
5. How has the motion picture industry responded to the attempts of government and religious groups to censor films?

6. How did television affect the motion picture industry? How did the motion picture industry initially respond?
7. What evidence suggests that today there is less distinction between the film and television industries?
8. What changes have occurred in the way audiences experience motion pictures? That is, what are some of the alternatives to traditional movie-going?
9. What is vertical integration? To what extent does it characterize the movies industry today?

NOTES

1. Kipps, Charles, "Sony and Columbia: A Tidy Case of Hardware Meeting Software," *Variety,* September 27–October 3, 1989, p. 5.
2. Mazingo, Sherrie, "An Exploratory Analysis of the Impact of VCR Movie Cassette Use and Pay-TV Movie Subscription on Movie Theatre Attendance," *Mass Comm Review* 14 (1987): 30–35.

SUGGESTED READINGS

Relevant Contemporary Works

Allen, Robert C., and Gomery, Douglas. *Film History: Theory and Practice*. New York: Knopf, 1985.

Bordwell, David, and Thompson, Kristin. *Film Art: An Introduction*. New York: Knopf, 1986.

Carroll, Noel. "The Power of Movies: Why Film Is the Dominant Art Form of the 20th Century." *Daedalus* 114 (Fall 1985): 79–103.

Champlin, Charles. "Fifty Years of the Production Code: What Will H. Hays Begat." *American Film* 6 (October 1980): 42–47, 86, 88.

Monaco, James. *How to Read a Film*. New York: Oxford University Press, 1971.

Monaco, James. *Ribbons in Time: Movies and Society Since 1945*. Bloomington, IN: Indiana University Press, 1987.

Wall, James M. "Movies and Censorship: Who Will Protect Freedom?" *The Christian Century* 104 (March 1987): 277–278.

Wasco, Janet. *Movies and Money: Financing the American Film Industry.* Norwood, NJ: Ablex, 1982.

See also *American Film, Variety.*

CHAPTER 8

Recordings: From Bach to Rock and Rap

OBJECTIVES

After studying this chapter, you should be able to

- **Cite the major technological inventions that facilitated the development of the recording industry.**
- **Explain the economics of the recording business.**
- **List the major record companies and describe the means by which records are distributed.**
- **Discuss the functions and effects of music.**

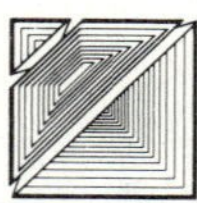

They can beg and they can plead
But they can't see the light, that's right
'Cause the boy with the cold hard cash
Is always Mister Right
'Cause we are living in a material world
And I am a material girl

"Material Girl"
Words by Peter Brown and Robert Rains
Sung by Madonna
1984 Candy Castle Music
Reprinted courtesy Candy Castle Music

What's your definition of dirty baby
What do you consider pornography

Don't you know I love you till it hurts me baby
Don't you think it's time you had sex with me

"I Want Your Sex"
(George Michael)

Got to give us what we want
Got to give us what we need
Our freedom of speech is freedom of death
We got to fight the powers that be

"Fight the Power"
Words by C. Ridenhour, K. Shocklee and E. Sadler
Sung by Public Enemy

No mass medium mirrors the thoughts and feelings of a generation—particularly the younger generation—as much as recorded music. It would be an oversimplification to say that the words from "Material Girl," "I Want Your Sex," and "Fight the Power" reflected the values of the 1980s. But they, like many other songs, touched upon issues that confronted the youth of that era (and this one): material wealth, sexual indulgence, and racial prejudice. While a somewhat older generation was coming to terms with the Vietnam War—and seeing it portrayed realistically in the movies—teenagers and young adults were struggling with other societal problems: the widespread availability of drugs, sexual freedom and its consequences, the pressures to succeed and the tendency to measure success in terms of material gain, the continuing erosion of the nuclear family, and the growing alienation and resentment of many minorities. It should come as no surprise that much of the recorded music of the day echoed these issues. An historian of popular culture explaining what he saw as a decline in "commitment" of the generations of the 1970s and 1980s pointed to a song by Jim Steinman (Meatloaf) as an indication of the change that had occurred. "I want you, I need you, but there ain't no way I'm ever gonna love you," Steinman declares. Then, seeking to console his lover, the singer adds, "Now don't be sad, cause two out of three ain't bad."

Like all of the other mass media, recorded music provides a broad range of entertainment, information, and persuasion. Although we are most familiar with the recordings of popular music, recordings are also a major medium for other types of music, from symphonies to jazz and from operas to hymns. Recordings of poetry and drama, oral history, comedy, sermons, and educational materials are available as well. They provide a way of learning a foreign language on your own or relaxing to great music played by the best musicians.

1800–1899

1877 Thomas Edison files patent application for "talking machine"

1887 Emile Berliner invents flat disc recording

1889 Magnetic recording on wire demonstrated

1896 Motor-driven gramophone developed

1900–1925

1905 Disc with music recorded on both sides, rather than just one, marketed

1925 Electrical system for recording and playing back sound perfected

1926–1949

1942 Musicians' union forbids members from recording, claiming records will reduce jobs

1943–1944 Record companies increase fees to musicians; union lifts recording ban

1945–1949 Industry shifts from discs to magnetic tape for recording masters

1948 Columbia Records introduces long-playing record developed by Peter Goldmark

1950–1969

1950s Record clubs become popular means of merchandising records

1955 "Rock Around the Clock," recorded by Bill Haley and his Comets, starts rock'n'roll boom

1956 Elvis Presley becomes overnight sensation when "Heartbreak Hotel" is released

1959 Payola scandal reveals record companies bribe disc jockeys

1964 The five most popular records in the country are products of the Beatles

1970–1979

1970 Pop music fans mourn disbanding of the Beatles

1979 Recession hits the recording industry

1980–1989

1981 MTV appears on cable, starting music video boom

1983 Compact discs bring higher quality reproduction

1988 Sales of compact discs exceed those of vinyl albums

The record or cassette tape player is most clearly a mass medium in the traditional sense of that term when it is used for popular music. The distribution of a million or more copies of a recording is rare for anything except popular music. Therefore in this chapter we will be discussing primarily popular music recordings, although much of what we consider applies equally to other types. In addition, the term *record* or *recordings* will refer to compact discs (CDs) and to tape or cassette recordings as well as to the older vinyl discs, and, at times, even to music videos. Although music videos do not come anywhere near either discs or cassettes in frequency of use, they are extremely popular.

THE EARLY DEVELOPMENT OF RECORDING TECHNIQUES

Many scientists in the mid-1800s were fascinated with devising a way to reproduce sound. A theoretical paper describing the way it might be done was written early in 1877 by a Frenchman named Charles Cros. But Cros made no attempt to test his theory by building a "talking" machine. The first person to do that successfully was Thomas Alva Edison. The patent application for his machine was filed on Christmas Eve of 1877. Edison called his *talking machine* a **phonograph,** *from the Greek words phone, which means "sound," and graphein, which means "to write."* The records for Edison's phonograph were made of tinfoil wrapped around a cylinder. The recording needle cut a groove in the foil, the depth varying with the sound.

Edison did not perceive his phonograph primarily as a medium for entertainment. In an article he published in the *North American Review* in 1878 he predicted ten ways the device would be used, only two of which involved music or entertainment. He was more interested in the use of the phonographic recording and playback machine for such things as dictation, audible books for the blind, and the preservation of languages or family reminiscences—he even thought a family might want to preserve on the phonograph the last words of a dying relative. Edison saw many educational possibilities for the machine. He also thought it would be a good idea to have a clock that announced in articulate speech when it was time to go home or when it was time to come to the table for a meal. All of these uses that Edison foresaw have come to pass. You can now buy a clock to use when you have guests who do not know when to leave. At whatever hour you preset, the clock can proclaim aloud that it is time for everyone to go home.

Producing Copies of Recordings

One major problem with the Edison record was that making copies was not feasible; one could only play back the original recording. About ten years after Edison's first successful demonstration of the phonograph, Alexander Graham Bell (developer of the telephone) and his associates invented a wax-covered cylinder recording from which copies could be made. Still, only one or two copies were possible, even under the best of circumstances.

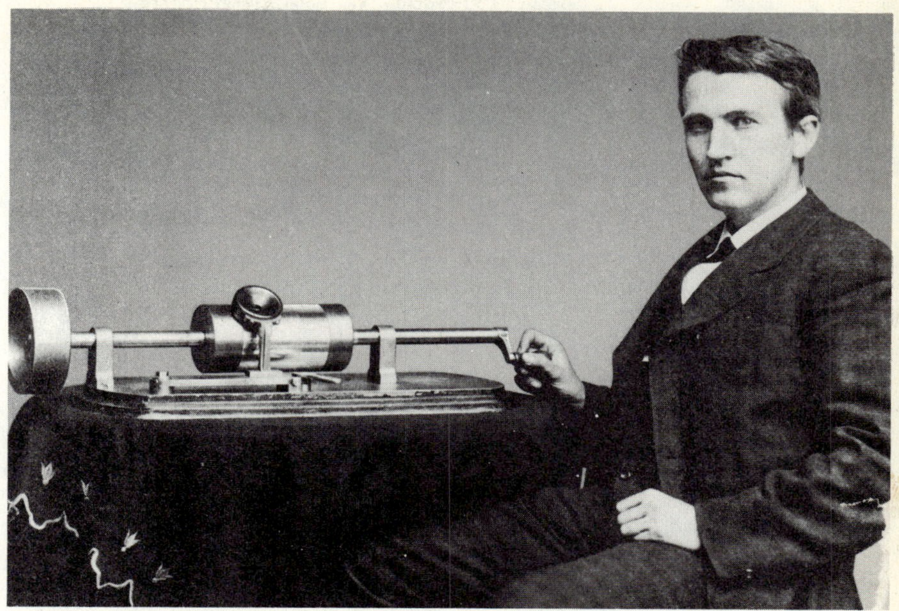

Thomas Edison poses with one of his most famous inventions, the phonograph, introduced in 1877.

An important step toward a commercially successful phonograph and recording industry was the invention of the flat disc recording in 1887 by Emile Berliner. Berliner called his machine for playing the disc recordings a Gramophone, a name still common in Europe. Unlike the cylinder recording, the disc could be duplicated reliably in large numbers. Within a dozen years, the record business was in full swing. Columbia and Victor were the main companies in this country. Opera star Enrico Caruso and bandmaster John Philip Sousa and his marches were among the early stars of this new medium. Little did anyone dream that these musicians would be the forerunners of U2 and Guns N' Roses.

Electrifying the Phonograph

Both the Edison and Berliner machines were completely mechanical. The turntable or cylinder was activated by a wound spring, which had to be cranked regularly. For recording, the sound was picked up by a large horn with a thin diaphragm at the narrow end. The vibrations of the diaphragm caused the recording needle to cut different-sized grooves. For playing sound back, the phonograph simply reversed the process, and the large horn became an amplifier to which one listened. The word *amplifier* might be somewhat of an exaggeration. It was often necessary to put an ear right up against the open end of the horn in order to hear anything.

Following World War I the competition from radio for the interest and cash of the consumer created strong motivation for refining sound recordings. Finally, in 1925, the Bell Telephone research laboratory developed an electrical system for recording and playing back; this greatly improved the fidelity and amplification of sound. The acoustical horn was replaced by a microphone at the recording end and by a speaker at the playback end.

Radio both competed with and promoted the recording industry. Hearing such stars as Bing Crosby, Louis Armstrong, Dinah Shore, and Kate Smith on the radio, along with the great Glenn Miller band, Tommy Dorsey, Benny Goodman, and many others, stimulated people to buy their records. Jukeboxes, which gained popularity in the 1930s, did the same.

Competition among record and phonograph manufacturers also resulted in more aggressive marketing to get their products into the hands of consumers. That competition led the Decca company in the mid-1930s to cut the price of their records from the standard 75 cents to 35 cents. The rest of the major record companies soon followed suit. Some sold records for as low as 25 cents each. This helped gain sales and fans.

Recording Developments Since World War II

Two developments in the years immediately following World War II were important for the recording industry. One was magnetic tape technology, which made possible a long, continuous recording. Until then, long musical numbers needed to be recorded in three- or four-minute segments. Even more important, tape made it easy to correct mistakes and to edit segments from different recording sessions together. Combined with electronic refinements, tape recording permitted improvements—or at least changes—over the actual, live performances.

The other post-World War II development was the *long-playing record* or **LP** *refined by Peter Goldmark, chief scientist for CBS.* Until Goldmark developed the LP record, the standard in the industry was the 78-RPM (revolutions per minute) disc with a maximum of three or four minutes of music or talk per side. The LP disc, recorded and played at 33⅓-RPM and with more grooves per inch, could play for fifteen to thirty minutes on a side. (Goldmark was not the inventor of the 33⅓-RPM recording, although he is usually given credit for it. The Victor Division of RCA introduced a 12-inch, 33⅓-RPM, flexible plastic record in 1931. Because of its poor quality, poor marketing, and poor luck in being introduced during the depths of the Depression, it failed to sell, and Victor withdrew it from the market and returned to its dependence on 78s. Many radio programs during the 1930s and 1940s were also recorded and played back on large discs at 33⅓-RPM. These discs were called electrical transcriptions.) During the postwar period, record companies also experimented with smaller 45-RPM discs, which became the standard means for distribution of pop singles.

REVIEW

The possibility of producing sound fascinated scientists. In 1877, Thomas Edison patented the phonograph, the first talking machine. Later improvements made it possible to copy recordings and to record and play them back electronically. Magnetic tape and long-playing records were introduced shortly after World War II.

Since the introduction of the LP record, the major developments have been high fidelity stereo (hi-fi), the cassette tape, music videos, and continuing improvement in the fidelity of recording and playback equipment—most recently by means of digital recording on compact discs and

Dropping prices are resulting in booming sales for compact discs and disc players, which offer greater durability and purer sound quality than LPs and turntables.

playback machines that pick up the sound by means of a low-powered laser beam rather than a needle. In 1988, sales of CDs exceeded those of vinyl albums for the first time.

HOW RECORDINGS GET INTO OUR ENVIRONMENT

More than two thousand new singles and two thousand new albums, either on LP, CD, or cassette, are released in the United States each year. Although you will not encounter all of them, the chances are high that you will hear a fair number of them. To understand why you are almost certain to hear certain recordings and have little if any chance of hearing others, you need to know about the gatekeepers who influence the creation and distribution of recordings.

"Gatekeepers" are the individuals and groups who control what gets into the media—the individuals and groups who can open the gate and let some material in or close the gate and keep some out. More precisely, a gatekeeper is any individual who can affect the material in our communication mosaics—adding some material, keeping some material from becoming available to us, or changing that material in some way.

Organization and Operation of the Record Company

One important gatekeeper or, more accurately, *set* of gatekeepers, is the record company and those who work within it. There are many facets to such a company; these are four of the major ones:

1. *A&R* (artists and repertoire) staff. These are the talent scouts, the men and women who are constantly visiting the clubs and other spots where young talent can be heard, searching for the next Elvis Presley or Def Leppard.
2. *Production* handles all aspects of the creation of recordings, putting the right talent together and getting them to play the sort of music that best suits their style and that is saleable to the public. The production department is also responsible for recording that combination on tape and mixing tapes to create the final master tape. The key person orchestrating all of these elements is the producer.
3. *Publicity and Marketing* people listen to the tape and devise a strategy for marketing copies. The initial part of that task is determining the kind of audience to whom each single or album is most likely to appeal. The publicity and marketing personnel are then responsible for arranging a total advertising campaign that will get the audience to buy it. Part of the campaign is deciding on the album cover design, for which the publicity and marketing department is responsible, and devising an effective approach to the disc jockeys or MTV producers who control programs to which the target audience listens.
4. *Distribution and Sales* has the responsibility for getting the singles and albums sold. The first task of this division is to convert the master tapes to records (discs, CDs, and cassettes). These recordings are then shipped to distributors who, in turn, distribute them to record and department stores, jukebox operators, supermarkets, and other places where they are sold to the public.

REVIEW

There are four major facets to most record companies: the staff of talent scouts who search for new talent, the production department, a publicity and marketing department, and a distribution and sales division.

In addition to the people in these major departments, accountants and designers, lawyers and engineers, and a great array of other specialists are involved in a record company.

Economics of the Record Business

The economics involved in the business of records is reflected in the figures, shown in Table 8.1, on where the money goes that you pay for a recording. The table shows what percentage of your money goes to each element in the production and marketing process. This distribution, of course, varies somewhat for different companies, different artists, and different albums, but the variance is seldom substantial.

Normally a record company will pay all of the recording costs—the fees to the musicians, vocalists, arranger, studio, editing, and so on—but these costs are treated as an advance and are deducted from the royalties paid to the artist when the record or album is sold. An artist's royalty ranges from 3 to 5 percent of the regular retail price of the recording for an unknown, to 15 percent for a superstar. The amount of royalty is bargained for by the artist's agent before the recording is made.

Major artists not only have agents, as most professional authors do, but also personal managers who handle their business affairs and are often involved in the selection of numbers to be recorded and accompanists to be

David Geffen, who got his start in music entertainment as a business manager for artists' groups, became one of the most powerful executives in the recording industry in the 1980s. His Geffen Records attracted such superstars as Guns N' Roses, Peter Gabriel, Don Henley, Cher, Edie Brickell, and Whitesnake.

TABLE 8.1 Percentage Distribution of Retail Recording Price

Payment to owners of copyrights for music	6%
Musicians' union trust fund fee	2
Manufacturing cost	8
Jacket, inner sleeve	3
Artist royalty and recording fees	14
Freight to distributors	1
Advertising	2
Recording company overhead	8
Recording company's profit	13
Distributor's profit	7
Retailing costs and profit	36

used and in virtually all other aspects of the performers' artistic work. An agent generally receives between 10 to 15 percent of all an artist's fees, including royalties. An additional 10 to 25 percent goes to the manager.

Music Rights Organizations

Authors, composers, and publishers of music have some unique problems ensuring payment for the product of their work. When you buy a record, cassette, or sheet music for your personal entertainment, these interested parties receive a royalty, just as authors of books do when a book is sold. This is no problem. Unlike books, though, recordings and sheet music are also bought by individuals and companies not simply for their personal entertainment but to use for making money.

Imagine that a soloist or musical group uses a song you composed for a concert for which admission is charged, or a radio station uses a recording of that song in order to attract an audience and advertisers. You probably agree that you should receive a larger fee for that use than you receive from the individual who bought the sheet music or record just to play at home. There has been general agreement on this conclusion. The problem, however, is devising a means for collecting that fee. No artist or publisher can keep track of the frequency with which radio stations across the country are playing a particular record. There are some ten thousand six hundred radio stations on the air in this country, together broadcasting over 58 million hours a year—most of which is music from LPs, CDs, and cassettes. No composer or publisher can keep track of which musicians are using their music in concerts around the country; thousands of such concerts are held every day, and a variety of music is played in each. Even if someone could keep track of all of this, the problem of a radio station or concert group making payments to each of the individual artists, publishers, and others involved for each use of their music would be horrendous.

The solution the music industry devised many years ago is the music rights organization, to which a broadcasting station, orchestra, or anyone else making regular commercial use of the music of the organization's members pays an annual fee. For example, broadcasting stations generally pay a percentage of their gross income. Even colleges and universities whose bands or orchestras give regular concerts or which sponsor concerts by professional musicians must pay such fees.

Three major performing rights organizations collect fees from recording companies, broadcasters, film producers, and others who use the music of their members for profit. The organizations then distribute these fees to the composers, authors, and publishers of the music. The oldest of these *performing rights organizations* is the **American Society of Composers, Authors, and Publishers** (ASCAP). Among its members are about thirteen thousand composers and forty-seven hundred music publishers. **Broadcast Music, Inc.** (BMI) has about twenty thousand composers and over nine thousand publishers in its membership. Both ASCAP and BMI are nonprofit organizations. A privately owned, for-profit performing rights organization is **SESAC,** which represents about two hundred publishers.

Broadcasters normally pay somewhat less than 1 percent of their gross income to BMI and about 2 percent to ASCAP. SESAC negotiates a flat fee with each station. For a radio station, this fee can be anywhere from about $200 to $7000 a year. Most stations need to belong to all three of these licensing companies because each controls some of the music they want to broadcast. From this income the performing rights organizations receive, which is quite considerable, they pay each member composer, author, or publisher according to a rather complex formula. The formula is somewhat different for each organization, but the payment is roughly proportional to the use of a composer, author, or publisher's music by stations and others. The music rights organizations estimate that use by sampling the programming of broadcasting stations, concert groups, and so on.

Musicians' Unions Many of the constraints on record makers, factors important in shaping the records that get into your mosaic, are conditions laid down by *the two major musicians' unions.* The union representing instrumentalists, the **American Federation of Musicians** (AF of M), is especially strong. Vocalists belong to the same union as most performers in radio and television, the **American Federation of Television and Radio Artists** (AFTRA). It has never been as powerful as the AF of M. Both unions bargain with recording companies on minimum fees musicians must receive for making a record and on other conditions of employment. They also bargain with film companies concerning when live musicians must be used for a soundtrack, what extra fees for musicians must be paid if the soundtrack is used for advertising or made into records, and so on. If vocalists are involved in multiple tracking—recording more than one vocal to be used with the same musical soundtrack—the AFTRA contract provides that they must be paid for each overtracking as though it were an additional record. Thus, if a duet is created with one singer's voice, that singer must be paid the same amount of money two singers would have received for the same job.

REVIEW

Only 3 to 5 percent of the retail cost of a recording is paid to an unknown artist, while superstars may receive as much as 15 percent. Two music rights organizations, ASCAP and BMI, collect and distribute fees on behalf of composers, authors, and publishers of music. Unions such as AFTRA also represent musicians.

Artist Development An important function of a recording company is the development of young artists. If you think of *artists* broadly, as the creative people—entertainers, writers, journalists—on whom the mass media depend, this is a function every mass communication industry should be serving. However, none serves it as vigorously and consistently as the recording industry, especially the independent record companies. The motion picture industry developed young artists in the old days when the studio system was at its height. But they no longer encourage new talent as systematically as the small record companies do. The major recording firms, like most of the other mass communication industries, tend to depend on hiring well-established artists away from someone else. They apparently feel no serious obligation to do their share of pump-priming with fresh talent.

Small companies are regularly on the lookout for fresh musical groups, vocalists, and songwriters. They groom those they find, shaping all aspects of their professional lives, from musical style to clothing to the kinds of music they perform and where they perform it. The companies are rather like boxing managers who carefully pick the series of opponents who will give their boxers steadily tougher opposition, being certain that they take on no one for whom they are not yet ready. They also pick the sorts of opponents who will give their boxers maximum publicity or visibility. Record companies do the same with their artists.

To demonstrate their talents to record companies, artists sometimes have a demonstration tape, a "demo," made at their own expense. This demo might be made to show and try to sell a musician, a musical group, or perhaps simply a song.

The Independents' Struggle for Survival

The recording industry, like all communication industries, has been strongly affected by the consolidation of giant media corporations. Hardest hit have been the small, independent record companies, the companies whose primary assets are their abilities at finding and popularizing new music styles and previously unknown musicians. These independents were responsible for the discovery of a large percentage of present-day stars.

Independent companies have little overhead because they own neither recording nor distribution facilities. Therefore, they provide a good entry into the business for young people with an ear for talent and the ability to sell. It does not take much capital to start a record company. Owning little but a record label, the independent hires backup musicians and a recording studio to make a master recording, has discs pressed or cassettes and CDs produced at another company, and has distribution handled generally by one of the small companies specializing in the distribution of the output of independents. The rest of the energy of the independent is focused on promotion. This, the independents—at least the successful ones—do superbly.

Because of rapidly escalating costs and increasing control of all phases of the record industry by the six major record companies in this country, many independents have been forced to make exclusive agreements with one of the majors to handle their record pressing, cassette recording, and distribution. A number of the other independents are simply being bought by the majors or by more general communication conglomerates.

The advantage for the independent of having one of the major companies manufacture and distribute its recordings is financial security. The larger company usually gives a cash advance against future royalties. This is important for a small company with little cash flow. On the other hand, the independent will receive less money for each CD, cassette, or LP sold when it is distributed by a major. Thus, security is greater, but potential profit is less.

The Major Record Companies

All of the major record companies are now part of larger communications corporations or conglomerates. The six largest distributors in America—MCA, CBS Records, WEA, BMG, CEMA, and Polygram—

account for more than 95 percent of the record album distribution business and a sizable share of the rest of the entertainment and information industries. For example, MCA—Music Corporation of America—the parent company of Universal Pictures and now a part of the Matsushita empire, is also involved in videocassettes and pay television, motion pictures, television program syndication, studio tours, broadcasting stations, concession and amphitheater operations, and book publishing. In 1988, MCA purchased a 20 percent interest in Motown Records.

WEA—Warner Elektra Atlantic Corporation—is now part of Time Warner, the world's largest media corporation. But even before the merger of Time and Warner, Warner was a media giant. In the recording industry alone, it does some $2 billion in sales each year—making it the world's largest record and music video distributor. Its numerous record companies include Warner Brothers Records and subsidiaries Reprise, Sire, Geffen, Slash, Opal, Qwest, Paisley Park, Tommy Boy, and Cold Chillin'; Elektra and its affiliate Nonesuch; and Atlantic Records and its subsidiaries. WEA also includes WEA International, Warner/Chappell—the world's largest music publisher, Warner Special Products—which markets special compilation recordings, WEA Manufacturing, and Ivy Hill Corporation—a packaging company for the record group.

WEA's major recording artists are Madonna, Prince, Van Halen, Fleetwood Mac, Elvis Costello, REM, and Guns N' Roses (all on the various Warner Brothers labels); Tracy Chapman, Anita Baker, the Cure, 10,000 Maniacs, and Metallica (on Elektra); and Genesis, Debbie Gibson, and INXS (on Atlantic).

CBS Records, which has both the Columbia and Epic labels, is close behind WEA in revenues. However, it seems to have been somewhat slower in recent years in developing new talent. Despite turning out hit after hit by recording artists such as Michael Jackson, Bruce Springsteen, Julio Iglesias, and Barbara Streisand, its market share has dropped. In 1988, CBS Records was purchased by the Sony Corporation of Japan. (Less than two years later Sony bought Columbia Pictures Entertainment, one of this country's largest motion picture and television studios.) The infusion of Sony capital enabled the record company to sign some promising newcomers, including Terence Trent D'Arby, New Kids on the Block, and Living Colour.

Like CBS Records, several of the other major record companies are in foreign hands. Polygram, which bought A&M Records, is owned by the Dutch electronics giant NV Philips. BMG (Broadcast Music Group), the parent company for RCA and Arista Records, is controlled by Bertelsmann AG of West Germany. CEMA, which stands for Capitol EMI Angel, is the distribution arm of Capitol/EMI, which is owned by a British corporation, Thorn EMI.

A major advantage of the large companies is that they are less vulnerable than the small record companies to the fluctuations of the market—the sudden surges and drops in popularity for certain types of records—

A handful of companies control the record distribution business in the United States.

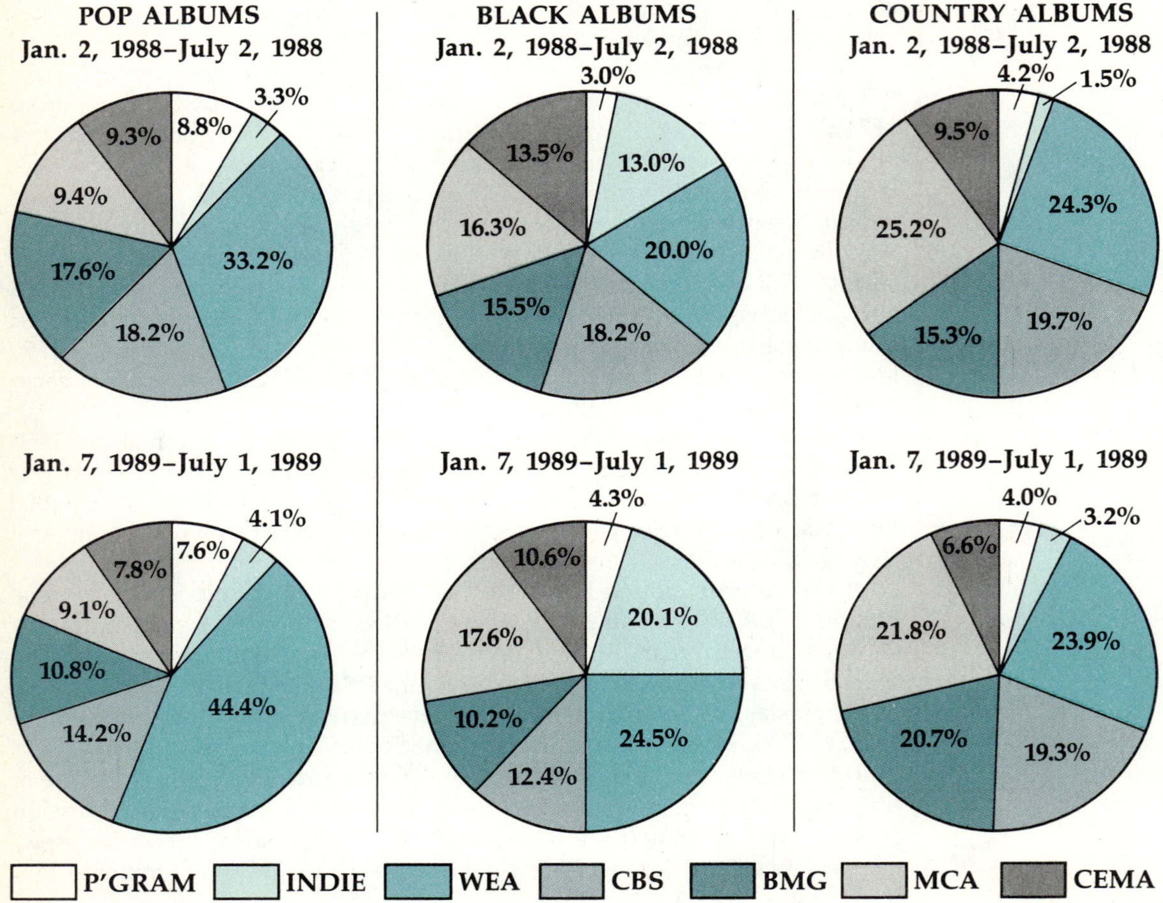

Review

Six major corporations control 95 percent of the record distribution business in America. The largest of these, WEA, is part of Time Warner, the world's largest media corporation.

because they produce a wide variety of recordings. When one type of recording drops in popularity, their sales of other types cushion the shock. Even if the entire record business should have a bad year, the majors, with their many nonrecord interests, can survive. Survival under such conditions is much more difficult for small recording firms like Ruthless Records and First Priority, which have no income from nonmusic interests and, even more serious, usually have all of their stakes on a particular kind of music. Hence when tastes change, they are in trouble.

BYLINE

How important is it that we periodically get new kinds of popular music? What difference does it make? Are there advantages to each generation having its own kind of music? Are there disadvantages?

EXPOSURE TO RECORDINGS

In many ways, the musical recording is like the book. You and other receivers have more control over which record you listen to and when you listen than you have with radio, television, or the motion picture. Like the book also, however, so many records are being made that you have difficulty finding out about all of those you would probably like. You learn about the great hits quite easily; but most recordings that do not become great hits too often remain just outside your communication environment, almost impossible to become aware of.

Available Recordings

The number of recordings manufactured and sold in the United States rose steadily throughout most of this century. At the beginning of the century, close to 3 million recordings a year were being produced. These were the early cylinder recordings. By the end of the World War I, and with the shift to disc recordings, this number had risen to over 100 million. By the end of World War II it had increased to 350 million and by 1978 to 725 million. For about a decade, the number of recordings declined steadily until the introduction of the compact disc and the popularity of cassettes sparked a rebound in manufacturing and sales. Today some 750 million records bring in more than $6 billion in revenues.

One casualty of the new recording technology has been the vinyl disc. Less than a fourth of all the records sold today are vinyl albums (LPs) or vinyl singles (45s). Some major labels have stopped releasing LPs on certain titles, and in 1990 WEA ceased manufacturing 45s except for black music accounts and jukebox operators. WEA's decision was based on the fact that cassette singles were outselling vinyl by as much as 10 to 1. With the advent of CD singles, sales of 45s were expected to drop even more. An editorial in *Billboard* said the passing of the vinyl record—especially the famed LP—marked the end of an era. "Many record buyers . . . will mourn its passing. Even in a period dominated by cassette tapes and headed for the supremacy of CDs, there are still tens of millions of turntables in U.S. homes, and they are likely to keep turning for some time to come."[1]

The Audience for Popular Music

Tastes in popular music vary tremendously from person to person, age group to age group, and, for young people, from year to year. There are even geographical differences in musical tastes. These variations are reflected in the range of radio station formats available to music listeners and in the kinds of recorded music they purchase. A survey commissioned by the Recording Industry Association of America (RIAA) showed that 43 percent of the people who purchased recorded music selected rock music, 17 percent chose pop, 10 percent chose black/dance, another 10 percent purchased country, 5 percent selected classical, 4 percent chose gospel, and 3 percent chose jazz. Other music types accounted for the remaining 8 percent. A study by Mediamark Research found that medium rock—a genre that falls somewhere between hard rock and easy listening—was the favorite of people who purchased records, tapes, and cassettes. These individuals were likely to be between the ages of 18 and 34 and to have household incomes of $40,000 or more. They were also likely to have attended college, to be single or married with children under 12, and to live throughout the country. The second most popular type of music was country. Purchasers of country music were somewhat older—45 to 54—and reported lower household incomes—$25,000 to $35,000. They were likely to be high school graduates, married, with teenagers, living in the West Central and Southwest regions of the country.

REVIEW

Record sales amount to about $6 billion a year, thanks to the popularity of CDs and cassettes, which are replacing the older vinyl discs. Musical tastes differ according to age, family status, income, and education. Today's popular artists are likely to be tomorrow's old favorites.

Because what is popular changes constantly, each generation—or even each subgeneration—has different tastes. A Bing Crosby, Frank Sinatra, or Elvis Presley, with popularity spanning more than one generation, is unusual. It may be difficult to imagine, but years from now when you say your all-time favorite recording artist is Gloria Estefan, Tracy Chapman, or Tom Petty, a younger generation may not be able to appreciate your taste in "oldies."

Distribution of Records

Like books, recordings today are marketed in a wide variety of ways. Traditionally they went from the manufacturer to a specialized distributor who handled just one label or one type of record. From the distributor they went to retail stores or to jukebox operators, and consumers bought them from a retail store or listened to them on jukeboxes or radio.

In the 1950s, when the number of record producers mushroomed, a new type of distributor developed, called the "one-stop." The one-stop distributor handled records from all of the companies, obtaining them through other distributors. Most jukebox operators preferred to work through a one-stop distributor because they could get a wide choice of records without dealing with a large number of distributors. Some retail outlets also depend on the one-stop distributor, although most continue to deal with the traditional, more specialized distributors.

Another marketing innovation in the 1950s was the record club. Record producers sell directly to the record clubs which then market directly to the consumers. Record clubs, like book clubs, have become an important means of distribution. Columbia Record Club's 4 million members purchase records on a regular basis. Other major clubs include the Reader's Digest Record Club and the RCA Club.

The record clubs offer either records at reduced prices or a free record for each one, two, or three records you buy. The clubs are able to make these deals by paying lower royalties to artists for the records they distribute. They also get special prices from the record companies because of the volume involved and, in some cases, because they are record company subsidiaries.

The data we have on the amount of business handled by each type of distributor or retail outlet are inconsistent, but discount stores appear to account for the largest percentage of sales, as much as 45 to 50 percent of the total. Other sorts of department stores account for between 20 and 25 percent and record stores for 15 to 18 percent. Mail-order houses account for most of the rest; a few records and cassettes are sold in drugstores, supermarkets, and other types of stores. Record clubs account for the remaining sales.

As with paperback books, selling from racks in department and variety stores has become an important means of distributing recordings. Because of this development, the **rack jobber** has become a key distribution agent. The rack jobber *furnishes the racks in a store and keeps them filled.* The rack jobber, rather than the store manager, *determines what recordings will be stocked in the store and the way in which they are displayed.* This person also watches the stock to make certain that more recordings are brought in whenever the supply of a particular one is getting low. The rack jobber also keeps track of music trends so that only recordings likely to sell in large numbers are stocked in the racks.

REVIEW

Recordings are distributed through record clubs, "one-stop" distributors, and record stores, department stores, and other types of stores. Distributors who service department and variety stores are called rack jobbers. They often determine what records should be stocked and how they should be displayed.

A change in the returns policy of major recording companies has made it more difficult for you and others to buy recordings that are not very popular. When record and cassette sales dropped sharply in 1979, the companies decided to limit the number of unsold recordings that a store could return. Up until then, some stores were returning to the manufacturer as many as 30 to 50 percent of the recordings they had ordered. In 1980, the major manufacturers limited returns to 20 percent. In 1989, WEA, CEMA, and BMG adopted an even more stringent returns policy for vinyl records, and A&M Records eliminated returns altogether for vinyl singles. As a result, both wholesalers and retailers have had to watch their inventories more closely. They can no longer afford to stock records—particularly vinyl records—or cassettes that may not sell. Therefore, you are less likely to encounter in your mosaic recordings that you might like but that have little probability of high sales.

Advertising and Promotion

Advertising and promotion are tremendously important in selling records and cassettes. In the late 1930s, jukeboxes became both a major market for popular records and a major advertising device. Extremely stiff competition developed among companies to get their records on the jukes.

Two other major ways recordings are advertised today are in print media addressed to teenagers and in television commercials aimed at adults.

Television advertising of albums of famous hits, collections of numbers by a star or group that was once popular, or collections of country and western numbers has been quite successful. Not only has such advertising been successful in selling the advertised albums, but it also increases sales of the artists' other albums. One study showed that sales of these nonadvertised albums could be increased by as much as 30 percent through such television advertisements.

Advertising current hit records to teenagers in the print media is done regularly, but it is not the major factor in record sales to this group. Two other factors are far more important: whether the music is played frequently on radio and whether it appears often on MTV and the other popular music video programs.

Radio and Television: Gatekeepers for Popular Recordings

Until the early 1980s, probably no gatekeeper for any medium of communication had more power than the radio disc jockeys had over which recordings would become hits and which would die. If a recording did not get much play on radio stations across the country, it had little chance for success in the jukeboxes or on sales racks. Disc jockeys exerted strong influence on the musical tastes of young people in this country—especially teenagers, the major purchasers of popular music.

This power of disc jockeys led to a serious scandal in the radio and recording industries in the 1950s. To ensure that their records would be played on radio stations, representatives of artists and recording companies began bribing disc jockeys, producers, and other radio station employees who controlled which records would be played on the air. Sometimes this bribery took the form of giving a disc jockey or a show's producer a direct financial interest in a record or the record company. These various forms of bribery, which became known as "payola," led to a congressional investigation and ultimately to legislation that made them illegal. Promoters of records today must be more subtle and more imaginative in influencing disc jockeys and program producers to play little-known records.

Deciding which records to play is not easy. Most major radio stations with popular disc jockeys are flooded with recordings. One estimate places the number of singles received by the average station at seven thousand a year and the number of albums at four thousand. With about twelve cuts on each album, that makes a total of about fifty-five thousand individual arrangements or numbers sent to the average station each year. It is simply impractical for station personnel to listen to all of these numbers and make informed judgments about which to play.

The average station resolves this problem in two ways. First, it generally gives greater play to records that are high on the national popularity charts published in *Billboard* or one of the other entertainment publications. In addition, it is guided by musical tip sheets to which it subscribes.

Radio disc jockeys serve as important gatekeepers for their unseen audiences. This DJ is broadcasting from an easy listening station in Newport Beach, California.

REVIEW

The most important sources for advertising new records are radio and MTV. On radio, the disc jockey is often the person who determines how much air play a record will receive. Musical tip sheets and popularity charts suggest the kinds of recordings most likely to be popular with a station's listeners.

These tip sheets, generally published by former disc jockeys, suggest which recordings are most likely to become hits and which are most likely to appeal to the station's audience.

Today, although disc jockeys are still important gatekeepers for popular music, they have been surpassed in that role. Since 1982, when Warner-Amex began distributing MTV to cable systems throughout the country, music videos have become the number one influence on the sale of popular music. Recording companies now vie to get their stars on MTV and its imitators. Some are even timing new releases to coincide with a performance of some of the music on one of the major music video telecasts or cablecasts.

Many of the music videos are extremely complex productions, fully utilizing the technical virtuosity of the television medium. In fact, just as rock music stimulated the development of sound recording techniques to an extremely fine and complicated art, it appears to be stimulating the development of television techniques in the same way.

PROCESSING MUSICAL INFORMATION

We do not yet know much about the ways in which people process musical information because we have not studied the subject systematically. From everyday observations, however, we can make some generalizations.

Most of us spend a fair amount of time listening to music from television, radio, or our stereo system. But we seldom give the music our undivided attention. This does not mean, however, that we are not concerned about or interested in the type of music that is playing. Quite the contrary—almost all of us have particular types of music that we like to have on when we are doing different things. We have one kind of music that we believe is good accompaniment for studying and makes studying easier. We have a kind of music that we like when we are driving, and a kind that we like to dance to, or perhaps to have in the background when we are with a date or spouse. For some of us, the same type of music fits all of these situations; for others of us, each situation calls for a different kind of music.

That certain kind of music becomes closely associated in our minds with those activities. The activities are more difficult or less enjoyable without that particular kind of music and the music is made more meaningful by that association. Years later, the music still evokes those associations.

BYLINE

Do your experiences match these of most of us? Are there particular songs that you associate with special events in your life or with special people? Do you find it hard to study without some particular kind of music playing? If so, why do you think that is?

THE FUNCTIONS AND EFFECTS OF MUSIC

You are well aware of the fact that books, newspapers, magazines, motion pictures, radio, and television have been used for persuasive purposes: to sell beer and soap, ideas and political candidates; to bring about social change or to quell a revolution. Few of us think about music or recordings being used for these purposes, but they are and have been for a long time.

Every war has had its songs that whipped up patriotic fervor or, in the case of the Vietnam War, that encouraged protest against it. Some titles of records popular in this country during World War II suggest the extent of the mobilization of the recording industry for the war effort: "Remember Pearl Harbor," "There's a Star Spangled Banner Waving Somewhere," "Any Bonds Today," and "'Round and 'Round Hitler's Grave."

The anti-Vietnam protests of the sixties and early seventies brought forth quite another kind of song. One was "Big Muddy," about a group of soldiers blindly following their commanding officer into a river where many were drowned. Those who sang and heard the song knew that the "Big Muddy" referred to Vietnam and the commander to President Lyndon Johnson, and their antiwar passions were intensified. "Where Have All the Flowers Gone," "The Times, They Are A-Changin'," and "Give Peace a Chance" were other popular songs whose recordings were widely played and used to build resistance to the war.

Music is used not only to add persuasive bits of information to the messages in our heads about war; persuasive music plays an important role in peacetime also. "We Shall Overcome" was a tremendously important force in the civil rights movement, just as the folk songs of Joan Baez, Pete Seeger, and Woody Guthrie have been important to the peace movement. In recent times, music has been used to raise money as well as consciousness for various causes. The Live Aid, Farm Aid, Band Aid, and U.S.A. for Africa concerts and recording sessions raised funds for such causes as famine relief in Africa and destitute American farmers.

Somewhat further back in this country's history, the radical left adopted many old Negro spirituals to communicate its message effectively. "We Shall Not Be Moved," for example, was adopted as the official song of the radical Southern Tenant Farmers Union in the 1930s. In the 1930s also, "Gimme That Old Time Religion" was transformed into "Gimme That New Communist Spirit." That sort of adaptation of songs—giving them new lyrics—has been a favorite tactic of many groups who want to use music for persuasive purposes. The idea is to take a song that people like or that has particular meaning or emotional association for them and use it with new words, hoping that some of the liking, meaning, or emotional associations will transfer to the new ideas being communicated. And it often works.

One of the most recent music forms to carry a persuasive message is rap, also known as "hip-hop." Like other forms of American popular music—blues, jazz, and rock and roll—rap traces its roots to black culture.

Rock groups have helped call attention to some of the world's most pressing social problems. Here saxophone player Clarence Clemons joins John Fogerty and the Grateful Dead's Jerry Garcia during a Fogerty AIDS concert in Oakland, California.

Recording star Marc Morrison of rap group Public Enemy.

Rap music began in urban inner cities in the 1970s when disc jockeys, working as masters of ceremonies at nightclubs and in parks, started experimenting with ways to mix music on their turntables. As disc jockeys cut back and forth between turntables, they often chanted rhymed catch phrases as "Hippity hip hop, don't stop." Eventually, the person chanting the music became known as a rapper or M.C. The first rap-style hit was called "Rapper's Delight." In the 1980s, the message of rap music echoed the attitudes and experiences of many blacks living in inner-city ghettoes. The lyrics, peppered with profane language and a hip lingo, were filled with images of arrogant macho males, savvy in street ways, bragging about sexual prowess and angry about social injustice. The demeaning remarks of rap lyrics were often aimed at whites, women, and gays. The rap group Public Enemy was accused by the Anti-Defamation League of inciting anti-Semitism. Despite such criticism, rap music has become enormously popular—especially among inner-city black youths, for whom rap groups have become important role models. Rap music has also worked its way into the mainstream of pop music, as more mild-mannered rappers like Hammer (formerly known as M. C. Hammer) and Young M. C. have joined a growing number of women and white groups to convey their own message through the rhythms and lyrics of rap.

Threats of Censorship The political uses of music have never caused much controversy in this country. There has been some pressure at times to keep off the air certain antiwar songs or songs associated with the radical left, but this pressure has been neither strong nor consistent. Far more pressure and controversy have been aroused by the lyrics of rock songs that, some critics charge, condone drug use and sexual promiscuity. Recording artists such as the late Jim Morrison of the Doors and the Red Hot Chili Peppers have often been targets of critical and legal attacks. But these attacks pale in comparison to the recent furor over the raunchy language and behavior of the rap group 2 Live Crew. The first shipment of their album, "As Nasty As They Wanna Be," sold a half-million records and sparked a storm of criticism from religious groups, conservative politicians, and prosecutors who objected to the gross language in songs such as "Me So Horny" and "If You Believe in Having Sex." In June 1990, a federal judge in Florida ruled that the album was obscene—the first such ruling on a musical recording—and that police could make arrests at stores selling the album. A few months later, a Ft. Lauderdale storeowner became the first person convicted of selling an obscene recording. A number of retailers in Florida and elsewhere responded by pulling "As Nasty As They Wanna Be" from their shelves.

Several members of 2 Live Crew were also arrested on charges of obscenity when they performed songs from the album at a nightclub in Hollywood, Florida. They were subsequently acquitted when a jury failed to find their performance obscene. The defense had argued that the lyrics were a form of cultural expression commonly used by blacks to make fun of the stereotype that black men are oversexed.

Some community and national groups—especially religious groups—have also applied pressure to broadcasting stations and advertisers to censor objectionable lyrics and performances. A good example is the 1989 flap over Madonna's music video, "Like a Prayer." The video featured Madonna in a low-cut dress singing and dancing among burning crosses, kissing statues of saints, and suffering stigmatalike wounds on her hands. One music critic called the video a confessional feast in which the main course was Madonna's Catholic upbringing. *Rolling Stone* said it was as close to art as pop music could get. But the religious imagery—especially the blending of sexuality and religion—was too much for some Christian groups. The Reverend Donald Wildmon, who heads the American Family Association, denounced the video as blasphemous and called for a nationwide boycott of Pepsi-Cola for its sponsorship of a two-minute commercial featuring Madonna and the "Like a Prayer" tune but in a different setting. Pepsi-Cola, which had reportedly signed a $5 million contract with Madonna, canceled the commercial after it had aired only twice. Ironically, the controversy may have benefited Pepsi. A month after the protest, the trade magazine *Advertising Age* cited a survey showing that Pepsi-Cola was the first product that came to mind when people were asked to name an advertisement they had seen or heard or read during the previous month.

Sometimes the Federal Communications Commission, the regulatory agency charged with overseeing broadcast practices, is called upon to impose more stringent guidelines regarding music programming. The FCC has taken the position, unpopular with many broadcasters, that the station licensee has the same public service responsibility in selecting and rejecting music to be played on the station as it has in selecting and rejecting any other content of the station. The FCC position is that the station should exercise the same supervision of what is sung on the station as of what is said. In a general sense, this is a reasonable position and the only one the FCC could take, given present law. A problem arises with the interpretation of this injunction, however. Does it mean a station should permit no language or ideas in a song that it would not permit on the news or in a sports program? Or does it mean the station should recognize that different forms of communication or entertainment, or programs designed for different kinds of audiences, should have different standards concerning language and ideas? This issue is still far from settled.

Having been largely unsuccessful in keeping sexually suggestive songs or songs that seem to be promoting drug use off the air, some parents' groups in recent years have been attempting to force companies to label their recordings in the same way film companies now label motion pictures. The assumption is that such labels will provide parents with information they need to control the kinds of music to which their young

REVIEW

Sometimes music is used to persuade. War, for example, often gives rise to patriotic songs or songs of protest. But even during times of peace, music takes on social and political causes. Because of its potential effects, from time to time there have been attempts to censor certain kinds of music—especially rock songs that hint of drug use or sexual encounters and rap songs with vulgar lyrics.

The record album, "As Nasty As They Wanna Be," recorded by the rap group 2 Live Crew, became the first ever ruled obscene by a federal court.

children are exposed. One of the major pressure groups involved in this attempt is the Parents Music Resource Center based in Washington, D.C. The leaders in this group include the wives of some powerful congressmen and other government officials, so it is taken seriously by leaders in the music industry. The concern of many people in the music business, though, is that the labeling being advocated could be just a first step toward other forms of control or censorship.

BYLINE

What is your opinion on this issue? Should a station apply the same standards to the language and ideas expressed in the lyrics of songs as it applies to the language and ideas expressed in situation comedies, news programs, or other kinds of programs? Should any songs ever be banned from the air? If so, which ones? Why? If not, why not? Should ratings be used for records as they are for motion pictures?

The Impact of Recordings on Our Perceptions

Whatever the direct effects of musical recordings on our attitudes and behaviors, they are certainly an ever-present and important part of our communication environment, and they contribute to the realities in our heads. No one who listened to popular music during the 1980s could escape the perception that drugs were a major factor in the lives of many people. Popular music of the early 1970s contributed to the belief that most people opposed the war in Vietnam. These messages, sneaking into consciousness from the background music around us, formed an important part of our communication mosaics, just as the messages in the music of the 1990s form an important part of our present communication mosaics.

The Role of Music in Identification and Rebellion

Popular music has two other major functions or effects. It provides each generation of young people a common and cherished experience. Years later, the sound of that music can bring strangers together and stimulate memories of that earlier era. Vivid evidence of the meaningfulness of such experiences can be seen by watching the tourists who are attracted to Graceland, Elvis Presley's former home and now the site of his grave in Memphis. A common sight there is the middle-aged married couple bringing their children—and in some cases grandchildren—to see and, they hope, to feel some of the special magic Presley created for them during their courtship and early married years.

Another major function popular music serves is the provision of a relatively harmless source of rebellion for the young. Each generation of young has its own music, almost invariably unappreciated by parents, just as parents' favorite music was unappreciated by their parents. This music

REVIEW

What sounds immoral to one generation may simply be a means of identification or source of rebellion for another.

is important in part because older people do not like it, and in part because demonstrating one's love of it is part of the ritual of affiliation with peers.

One author has suggested that popular music also serves a "rite of passage" function for young girls. The teenage singing idols may serve as nonthreatening substitutes for actual boys until boys' maturation catches up with that of girls and some semblance of easy boy-girl relationships can be established.

THE FUTURE OF RECORDED MUSIC

Only one major change can be predicted for the recording industry's future: a change in the technology of recording. Digital recording and playback techniques are revolutionizing recorded sound. These techniques involve translation of the sound signal into the type of signal used in computers. Such signals can be manipulated and recorded and rerecorded with virtually no loss in quality. This is not the case with traditional recording techniques in which the sound waves are transformed into electrical impulses which are analogs of the sound, and then recorded. Digital hi-fi techniques result in recordings with far less distortion and noise than the very best recordings made via the traditional analog techniques, and they can be produced more cheaply. Recordings made with this new system are creating a boom in the manufacture and sale of new kinds of high-fidelity playback systems, systems that utilize laser beams rather than metal points, to pick up the sounds from this new type of record.

A development necessary to the survival of the recording industry is some means for controlling the copying of records, tapes, and music videos. Experts estimate that up to 50 percent of the potential income of legitimate recording companies may be lost because so many individuals are taping music from radio or television, or borrowing or renting recordings and making copies for their personal use, or, even worse, rerecording in bulk and selling these illegal copies. The artists, technicians, and business people who are responsible for the creation and distribution of the original recordings, of course, lose much of the payment they have earned for their work because of these practices. Some have already been driven out of business. If some means cannot be found to control pirating, we will soon find few new recordings being produced because no one will be able to make a profit from them.

REVIEW

Record and electronics companies have recently introduced a digital audiotape (DAT) player/recorder system. The recording industry will continue to struggle with the problem of illegal copying.

In 1989, the major international recording and consumer electronics industries reached agreement on a digital audiotape (DAT) player/recorder system to be marketed in the United States. Record companies had feared the loss of sales because of the new home taping technology, but the DAT player/recorder is equipped with a device limiting the number of copies that can be made. The Recording Industry Association of America (RIAA) estimates that $1.5 billion a year is lost to home taping on analog equipment.

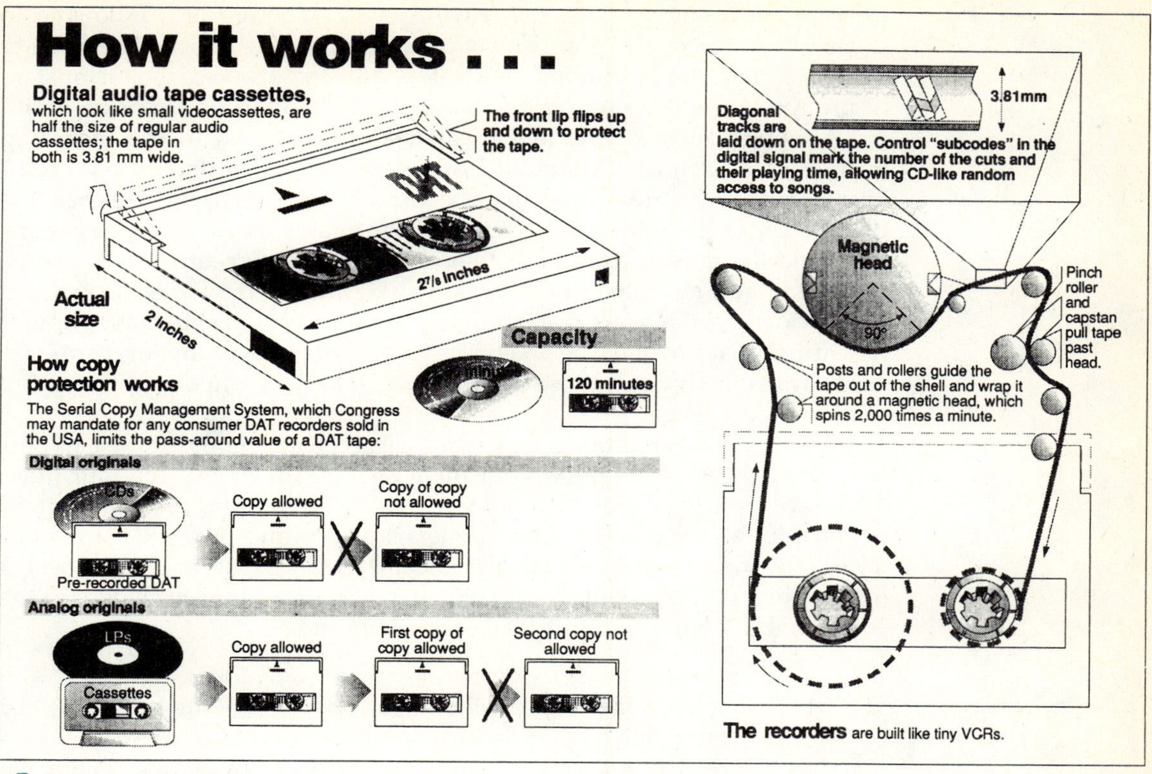
How it works . . .
Digital audio tape cassettes, which look like small videocassettes, are half the size of regular audio cassettes; the tape in both is 3.81 mm wide.
The front lip flips up and down to protect the tape.
Actual size
2 inches
2⁷/₈ inches
Capacity
120 minutes
How copy protection works
The Serial Copy Management System, which Congress may mandate for any consumer DAT recorders sold in the USA, limits the pass-around value of a DAT tape:
Digital originals
CDs
Pre-recorded DAT
Copy allowed
Copy of copy not allowed
Analog originals
LPs
Cassettes
Copy allowed
First copy of copy allowed
Second copy not allowed
3.81mm
Diagonal tracks are laid down on the tape. Control "subcodes" in the digital signal mark the number of the cuts and their playing time, allowing CD-like random access to songs.
Magnetic head
90°
Pinch roller and capstan pull tape past head.
Posts and rollers guide the tape out of the shell and wrap it around a magnetic head, which spins 2,000 times a minute.
The recorders are built like tiny VCRs.

How the DAT works.

RECORDINGS: A SUMMARY

Many people do not consider the musical recording a mass medium of communication, but it meets every criterion. Although it is a subtler medium than most, a medium to which we seldom attend closely, we get a great variety of bits of information from it. In a sense, it provides us with mood settings and emotional associations for many of our other life experiences. It tells us something about our culture and the culture and interests and moods of past generations.

Like the book industry, there is still a place for the small entrepreneur in the recording business. With a small amount of capital, you can find a potentially popular song and a talented singer and have a demonstration tape or record made, just as you can get a book printed by a small printing shop. And like the small, independent publisher, you then face the formidable problem of distribution. For this, your recording must be picked up by one of the major recording companies. This is where radio comes in. If you can get enough disc jockeys to give your record a good play, especially in some of the larger markets, it will develop enough of a following to cause a major recording company or distributor to take notice. Or if you are a sufficiently skilled promoter, you will be able to get one of the major stars or groups to use it for a music video that will truly focus attention on it.

Although most of the major gatekeepers involved in the recording business are somewhat different from those involved in other mass communication industries, they operate on similar principles. Besides the usual economic gatekeepers, there are the major music rights organizations and the musicians' unions that shape the ways recordings can come into being and get into your environment. And the radio disc jockey and music video producer are tremendously important gatekeepers for popular recordings. The owners of jukeboxes, who determine which records are made available through those machines, also have an impact on the future of many recordings.

We may not think much about musical recordings, but they are important in our lives. Whether we use them as a means of showing our independence from former generations, a means of building recognition and support for a political candidate, a means of identification with our country or our God, or a means of protesting a war, racial discrimination, working conditions, or drug laws and sexual mores, our lives would be considerably poorer without those sounds of music.

DISCUSSION QUESTIONS

1. What have been the major technological developments in the history of music recording? What developments are on the horizon?
2. How is a record company organized, and how is its income likely to be distributed?
3. How are musicians' rights—that is, economic rights and working condition rights—protected?
4. What are the major record companies, and how much control do they have over the industry?
5. What factors influence musical tastes?
6. How are recordings distributed?
7. How are recordings advertised? What role do disc jockeys play in advertising recordings?
8. In what sense is music persuasive?
9. Why have there been attempts to censor certain kinds of music?

NOTES

1. "LP Era Saw Many Industry Milestones," *Billboard* 101 (March 11, 1989): 9.

SUGGESTED READINGS

Relevant Contemporary Works

Blau, Judith R. "Music as Social Circumstance." *Social Forces* 66 (June 1988): 883–902.

Chambers, Iain. *Urban Rhythms: Pop Music and Popular Culture.* New York: St. Martin's Press, 1985.

Dannen, Fredric. *Hit Men: Power Brokers and Fast Money Inside the Music Business*. New York: Times Books, 1990.

Denisoff, R. Serge. *Tarnished Gold: The Record Industry Revisited.* New Brunswick, NJ: Transaction Books, 1986.

Dranov, Paula. *Inside the Music Publishing Industry.* White Plains, NY: Knowledge Industry, 1980.

London, Herbert I. *Closing the Circle: A Cultural History of the Rock Revolution.* Chicago: Nelson-Hall, 1984.

Lull, James, ed. *Popular Music and Communication.* Newbury Park, CA: Sage, 1987.

Maultsby, Portia K. "Soul Music: Its Sociological and Political Significance in American Popular Culture." *Journal of Popular Culture* 17 (Fall 1983): 51–58.

Podell, Janet, ed. *Rock Music in America.* New York: H. C. Wilson, 1987. See also *Billboard, Journal of Popular Music,* and *Rolling Stone.*

CHAPTER 9

Radio: Our Sound Companion

OBJECTIVES

After studying this chapter, you should be able to

- Identify the major figures responsible for the development of radio and their key inventions or innovations.
- Explain the reasons for the federal government's involvement in radio regulation and the legislation that resulted from that involvement.
- Trace the development of the networks and the rise of FM radio.
- Discuss the international radio services funded by the U.S. government.
- Contrast pretelevision programming with current programming or programming formats.
- Explain the manner in which commercial and noncommercial radio are supported economically.
- Discuss the reasons for listening to radio—in the past and today.
- Cite the factors that will likely affect the future of radio.

I have in mind a plan of development which would make a radio a "household utility" in the same sense as the piano or phonograph. The idea is to bring music into the house by wireless.

David Sarnoff (later to become chief executive of RCA and NBC), memorandum to Edward J. Nally, Vice-President and General Manager Marconi Wireless Telegraph Company of America, September 30, 1915

Clearly, the most important development in the history of mass communication was the printing press. Just as clearly, the second most important advance was radio. With this development, vast multitudes of people throughout the world for the first time were brought into the mass communication audience. The print medium requires an audience to be able to read; radio is a medium that demands no special skill from its audience, requires little if any payment beyond the small initial investment in a receiver, and reaches listeners over a vast area. For these reasons, the medium of radio continues to be used for educational and propaganda purposes in all underdeveloped parts of the world today and for information and entertainment everywhere in the world.

Radio today does more than simply penetrate our homes; it follows us. Portable radios and car radios have made it the most pervasive of all media. The average household has between five and six radio receivers, and almost all cars (95 percent) are now equipped with radios. The average American over the age of 12 spends more than three hours a day with the radio. During the course of any given week, radio reaches nearly all teenagers in the country. We listen to the radio while lying on the beach or negotiating rush-hour traffic, while eating breakfast or cramming for an exam. Your mail carrier probably carries a radio on delivery rounds. Joggers and roller skaters move to the rhythms of their favorite stations. Some sports enthusiasts even bring their radios to the stadium so they can supplement their first-hand view with an expert account of the game. In few places today can you escape the sounds of radio.

THE BEGINNINGS OF RADIO

To understand the operation of radio and television today, and especially the reasons for some of our present practices, it is important to consider some highlights in the history of radio.[1] The roots of radio, like those of the other mass communications media, are many and varied. One important root is the electric telegraph, conceived by American artist and inventor Samuel Morse in 1832 and successfully demonstrated to Congress in 1844. The electric telegraph was rather simple in theory; it demanded only a wire carrying an electric current between two points and a system for periodically making and breaking an electric circuit in order to send a series of dots and dashes (short and long bursts of current) through the wire.

1800–1915

1832 Electric telegraph conceived by Samuel Morse

1885 American Telephone and Telegraph Company (AT&T) formed

1897 Guglielmo Marconi receives patent for first wireless telegraph

1906 Reginald Fessenden demonstrates first successful radio system

1912 Radio licensing law passed by Congress to control clutter on the air

1916–1929

1916 Lee deForest broadcasts election returns from New York *American* office

1919 Radio Corporation of America (RCA) formed

1920 Westinghouse's KDKA goes on the air in Pittsburgh

1922 First sponsored broadcast: ten-minute commercial on WEAF in New York

1926 National Broadcasting Corporation (NBC) begins programming

1927 Radio Act of 1927 gives Federal Radio Commission firm control of station licensing

1930–1939

1933 Radio's political potential demonstrated by Roosevelt's fireside chats

1933 FM radio patented by Edwin Armstrong

1934 Communications Act establishes Federal Communications Commission (FCC)

1936 CBS carries live H.V. Kaltenborn's eye-witness account of Spanish Civil War battle

1937 American Bar Association adopts Canon 35, limits broadcast coverage of trials

1939 First regular FM radio station goes on the air

1940–1954

1942 Voice of America launched

1946 Networks accept tape recordings, changing radio production and broadcasting

1952 TV replaces radio as major medium for evening entertainment

1953 Voice of America placed in new government agency, the United States Information Agency

1952–54 Rapid development of Top 40 format

1955–1979

1956–59 Most network radio broadcasting ends, except for news, sports, special features

1969 Corporation for Public Broadcasting creates National Public Radio network (NPR)

1978 Audience for FM surpasses AM audience

1980–1990

1981 FCC sharply reduces its regulation of radio content

1982 FCC approves AM stereophonic broadcasting

1988 NAB study shows that nine of ten radio stations use satellite dishes to receive programming

Another important root of radio is the telephone, first demonstrated by Alexander Graham Bell in 1876. Within a year, this device so stirred the imaginations of people that a few foresaw a time when one could speak or play music into one end of the telephone and be heard by audiences long distances away, connected only by the telephone line. And there were demonstrations of concerts in one city heard through telephone connections by audiences in other cities. But the need for a connecting line was a major hurdle to the development of the telephone as a radio system.

During the latter part of the nineteenth century, most people were not interested in using the telephone for mass communication; they did not perceive the potential importance of such use. They were far more concerned with freeing the telegraph from the need for wires because they thought it could then be more useful for business and for the safety of ships at sea. For these purposes, efforts were made to develop a wireless, a telegraph system that did not require connecting lines between the sender and the receiver.

The first workable wireless telegraph system was developed by a young Italian, Guglielmo Marconi, late in the nineteenth century. When Italian authorities showed no interest in his invention, he and his Irish mother took it to Great Britain, where its value was quickly recognized. He patented his wireless system in England in 1897 and found financing to establish Marconi's Wireless Telegraph Company. As Marconi continued his experiments, wireless telegraph systems were installed in lighthouses and aboard naval vessels. More important to the future of mass communication, the "wireless" was first used to speed the transmission of news in 1899. A steamship was fitted with wireless so that it could follow the yachts racing in a regatta and telegraph the details to a shore station, from where they could be phoned to newspapers. The results of the race were published even before the ships returned to land. During that same year, the Marconi Wireless Company of America was incorporated, and the use of the new wireless technology began to spread.

From Wireless to Radio

News of the wireless telegraph stimulated renewed efforts by those who dreamed of music and speech being transmitted over long distances without wires. The first of these to achieve a true realization of the dream was Reginald Fessenden. He did it by radically changing the transmission system developed by Marconi. Marconi's system depended on periodic transmissions of an electromagnetic wave, or short and long interruptions of the wave to signal the dots and dashes of the Morse code. Fessenden instead sent a continuous wave and modulated its amplitude by superimposing on it another wave created by sound, either a voice or music picked up by a type of telephone.

An Iowan named Lee de Forest and an Englishman named John Fleming advanced modern radio a step further. One of the weakest aspects of the wireless telephone at the beginning of the twentieth century was the

In 1899 Italian inventor Guglielmo Marconi traveled to the United States to demonstrate his wireless telegraphy apparatus. The occasion was the America Cup yacht race, and Marconi's reporting of the race for the New York Herald *and* Evening Telegram *established the practical value of radio communication. Here Marconi is shown sending the first wireless marine message in America.*

technology for receiving and amplifying the sound that came over the air. In 1905, building on the idea of a glass bulb detector invented by Fleming, de Forest developed a radio vacuum tube he called the Audion. It was an extremely effective detector and amplifier of radio waves. Useful for both sending and receiving radio signals, the Audion was a key element in the development of radio broadcasting and much of the rest of our modern electronics industry.

In order to gain publicity and support for his ventures, de Forest and his wife spent a night broadcasting music atop the Eiffel Tower in Paris. This broadcast was picked up by listeners within a 500-mile radius of Paris and generated much excitement about the new medium.

An interesting sidelight on these early broadcasting ventures of de Forest's is the fact that he was responsible for the first broadcast on behalf of women's rights. In 1908, he broadcast a speech by his mother-in-law advocating women's suffrage. This occurred 12 years before the ratification of the constitutional amendment that granted women the right to vote.

Like many of the pioneers in mass communication, de Forest was a visionary. He saw radio as a medium that could educate and uplift its audi-

REVIEW

Radio operates on the same principle as the telegraph and telephone but without the wires. The Italian Guglielmo Marconi and Americans Reginald Fessenden and Lee de Forest played key roles in the development of radio transmission and reception components.

ence. As part of his campaign to realize his vision, he broadcast operas from the Metropolitan Opera House in New York City as early as 1916. That same year he also installed a special line from the editorial office of the New York *American* and broadcast the presidential election returns.

Lee de Forest was motivated by more than the desire to uplift and educate when he began regular broadcasts in New York City. He also wanted to advertise his equipment to radio amateurs and give them broadcasts that would make worthwhile the construction of a receiver. A number of the other early broadcasters were similarly motivated, and they were successful. Not only did many amateurs build receivers; they built transmitters as well. In 1913, about a thousand radio transmitters were operating in the United States. By 1917, when the United States entered World War I, close to nine thousand were operating. All were either shut down or taken over by the armed forces when the United States declared war on Germany.

World War I Spurs Radio Developments

The need of the armed forces for dependable communications equipment during World War I hastened many technological developments. This occurred partly through mobilization of the expertise and partly through getting different companies to work together for the period of the war, setting aside the competitive tactics that had sometimes slowed development. Among other things, the needs of the armed forces demanded that the companies cooperate to standardize on key aspects of equipment so that parts could be interchangeable. The American Telephone and Telegraph Company (AT&T), General Electric, Westinghouse, and American Marconi all worked together for an American war victory. Radio was also a winner in the effort.

The ancestor of Voice of America, this country's current international broadcasting arm, was born during the war. The Navy took over a powerful transmitter at New Brunswick, New Jersey, and used it for wireless communication to American forces and foreign receivers throughout the world. In 1918, it transmitted directly to the German people President Wilson's appeal for peace.

Out of the experience of World War I came another development that had an even greater impact on broadcasting in America. The Navy had come to believe that a technology so valuable as radio should remain in government hands. Navy officials, along with some of the leaders in General Electric, were also afraid that the British-dominated Marconi company might win control of world communications. While proponents of a Navy-controlled monopoly of radio failed to persuade Congress to enact legislation that would have placed radio permanently in government hands, Navy officials and General Electric president Owen D. Young managed to engineer the formation of the Radio Corporation of America (RCA) in 1919 and turned over to this new corporation all of American Marconi's wireless stations that were being held by the government. With the support of AT&T and General Electric, RCA soon dominated communications in this country and abroad. Continued American control of the company was made certain by RCA's articles of incorporation, which stated that at least 80 percent of its stock must be held by United States citizens and that all directors and officers must be citizens.

The Early Stations

One important early amateur broadcaster in America was Frank Conrad, a self-educated engineer and inventor at the Westinghouse Electric Company. From a laboratory in his garage, he broadcast recorded music and talked with other radio amateurs around the country. Conrad's call letters were *8XK*. A local music store furnished records for him in exchange for acknowledgments on the air. After World War I, with the help of his sons and friends, Conrad began a regular broadcast schedule. Every Saturday evening, for example, he broadcast a concert of records. In 1920, he broadcast a "remote": It was a piano solo performed in the house by one of his sons and carried to the garage by wire.

The development of broadcasting received a large boost one day in September 1920 when a department store in Pittsburgh advertised wireless receivers for sale with which people could hear Conrad's broadcasts. The receivers sold for $10. A vice-president of the Westinghouse Corporation, realizing the commercial possibilities, instructed Conrad to build a more powerful transmitter to be placed on one of the Westinghouse buildings. It was to be used for regular radio broadcasts that presumably would stimulate the sale of Westinghouse parts for making simple radio receivers.

REVIEW

World War I resulted in many technological developments in radio and the formation of the Radio Corporation of America (RCA), formerly known as American Marconi. In 1920, Frank Conrad, an engineer for Westinghouse, helped establish KDKA, a station still on the air.

The first major broadcast from that transmitter was the election-night coverage of the presidential race between Warren G. Harding and James M. Cox. The call letters of the Pittsburgh station were *KDKA*. This station is still the major hub in the Westinghouse broadcast group.

At first, KDKA was on the air just one hour a night, but gradually the hours of broadcast lengthened. The success of its station in Pittsburgh also encouraged the Westinghouse Company to construct similar stations in Newark, Chicago, and Springfield, Massachusetts, and the sale of Westinghouse receiver parts boomed.

In 1921, stirred by the success of KDKA, RCA moved on two fronts: It began to mass-produce home radio receivers and put its first radio station on the air. Helping to manage these developments was a young man named David Sarnoff.

David Sarnoff

REVIEW

David Sarnoff came to the public's attention when he relayed information about the sinking of the *Titanic*.

David Sarnoff, who had migrated to America from Russia when he was nine years old, came to public attention in this country in April of 1912, while he was a Marconi telegraph operator at a demonstration station in the Wanamaker department store in New York City. He was the telegraph operator who caught the faint SOS signals from the *S.S. Titanic*, which had hit an iceberg far out in the Atlantic and was sinking. Sarnoff stayed at his telegraph key for 72 hours, relaying messages to other ships that might save survivors. He was also the source of information for

GRANDPA HEARS A STRANGE LANGUAGE

—*By Cartoonist Bushnell*

MERRILL SHUDDERS AT THOUGHT OF IT

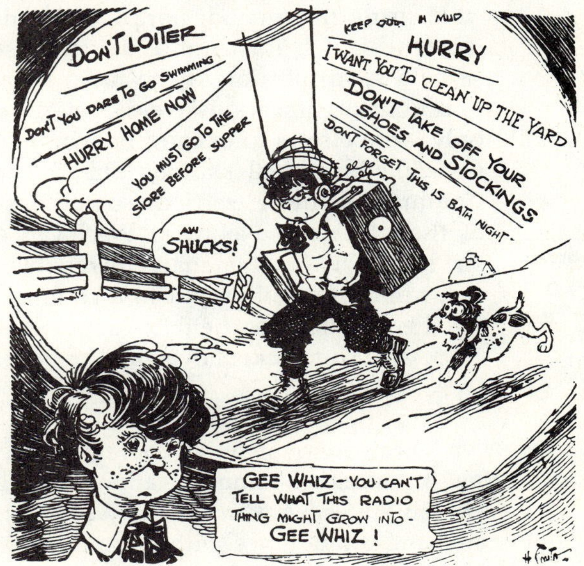

—*Atlantic City Gazette*

The public's fascination with the new medium of radio is captured in these cartoons that appeared in Wireless Age *in 1922.*

American newspapers and for the relatives and friends of survivors. President Taft had ordered all other wireless stations in the country off the air so that there would be no interference. At the age of 21, David Sarnoff was a national hero. At the American Marconi Company, and later at RCA, he became a key figure.

Educational Stations

Experimental stations were developed in the earliest days of radio by a number of universities in the Midwest, primarily by professors of electrical engineering or physics. Initially these were wireless stations; later they became broadcasting stations for voice and music. Even before World War I, educational stations were operating at Nebraska Wesleyan University, the University of North Dakota, and at the University of Wisconsin at Madison. Many of their early broadcasts were designed to serve farmers with weather reports, market reports, and news highlights. The University of Wisconsin station was apparently the first to be officially licensed, in 1914.

By 1927 licenses had been issued to 94 educational institutions. However, the stock market crash of 1929 shook the economic stability of educational as well as business institutions, and by early 1931 that number had dropped to 49; by 1946 there were only 29. Another factor in that drop was the lack of interest in radio on the part of educational administrators. In addition, once radio was beyond the experimental stage, many professors of physics and electrical engineering lost interest, and there was no one else to pick up the reins.

During this period, noncommercial radio had its advocates, but they were no match for commercial interests. All efforts in the 1930s to reserve a small portion of the radio frequencies for educational and other nonprofit organizations were beaten back by the commercial lobby. Not only were efforts to expand noncommercial broadcasting in America defeated; educational stations already on the air were far from secure. Commercial interests tried, sometimes successfully, to take away many of their licenses. Nebraska Wesleyan station WCAJ was forced off the air by WOW in Omaha; University of Arkansas station KUOA was pressured into selling out to a commercial firm. And there were others: Of the 202 licenses held by educational institutions between 1921 and 1936, 164 were taken over by commercial interests or were allowed to lapse.[2]

REVIEW

Educational stations flourished for a while but declined in number after the stock market crash of 1929.

Government Regulation of Broadcasting

The need for some sort of regulation surfaced early in the development of wireless communication. The impetus came initially from the United States Navy in the early 1900s. The Navy was concerned about increasing interference with critical ship-to-ship and ship-to-shore communication by amateur wireless operators. The result was a licensing law passed in 1912. This law, designed to regulate wireless telegraphy, also affected radio broadcasting as the wireless technology began to be used for voice and music transmission.

The Radio Act of 1912 The radio licensing law of 1912 was simple. It required a wireless operator to obtain a permit from the secretary of commerce and each transmitter to be supervised by someone who had passed a special licensing examination. The Radio Act of 1912 gave the secretary of commerce authority to designate the wavelength on which a permit holder could transmit and the hours of such transmission, so that interference could be controlled. The secretary could not refuse a permit. The law also gave the president the power to shut down transmitters in time of war.

The Radio Act of 1927 The 1912 act worked well until the post–World War I period. But as the number of radio stations jumped from 8 to 576 between 1921 and 1923, interference became impossible to control. That fact made many broadcasters eager to have more government regulation because they wanted to reduce the chaos on the air. Another factor that helped bring about regulation was the strong conservationist spirit in America at this time. Many persons were upset by the plundering of this country's oil and other natural resources for private gain. When the Radio Act of 1927 was enacted, it was strongly influenced by one of the leading conservationists in the Congress, Nebraska Senator George W. Norris. At the urging of Norris and others of like mind, the new act made clear that radio frequencies belong to the public, not to the **licensee** (*the individual or group that owns a broadcasting station*). The act specified that anyone granted a broadcasting license had the use of a particular frequency for a limited number of years. In addition, the act stated that each station must operate "**in the public interest, convenience, or necessity**."

That phrase, "the public interest, convenience, or necessity," *appears throughout the act and has been a key factor in the regulation of American broadcasting* ever since it was used in the Radio Act of 1927. Its interpretation has also been a source of some argument. Broadcasters, regulators, attorneys, scholars, consumer advocates, and others have argued whether the "public interest" means that which interests the public or that which someone decides is good for the public. And if it means the latter, who should make that decision? The argument, which began in 1927, is still far from settled.

The other important new element in the Radio Act of 1927 was the principle of the independent regulatory commission. The idea was that the commissioners, although appointed by the president of the United States and approved by the Senate, were to have relatively long terms so that they could be independent of political pressures.

The Communications Act of 1934 The Radio Act of 1927 was superseded during the early years of Franklin Roosevelt's administration by the Communications Act of 1934, but the new act retained all the important features of its predecessor:

1. The interest, convenience, or necessity clause
2. An independent regulatory commission
3. A limited license term, so that licensees could be held accountable
4. A requirement for equal treatment of political candidates

The last feature, usually called the **equal time provision**, stated that *if one candidate for public office is sold or given time on a radio station during a political campaign, all other bona fide candidates for that office must be afforded the same opportunity.*

Since 1934, many attempts have been made to overhaul the Communications Act, but it remains essentially unchanged. One of the few relatively major changes was to extend the period of a broadcast license from three to five years for television and three to seven years for radio.

Although the Communications Act calls for equal opportunities for all candidates for an office, Congress decided in 1959 to exempt certain kinds of news broadcasts from this rule. They exempted bona fide newscasts, bona fide news interviews, news documentaries (if the appearance of a candidate is incidental to the presentation of the subjects covered by the news documentaries), and on-the-spot coverage of bona fide news events. These exemptions make it possible for stations to give news coverage to the major candidates without being forced to give equivalent treatment to all minor party candidates who have little chance for election.

This revision in the equal time provision provided the loophole that has made possible the broadcasting of debates between major party candidates for the presidency without giving the same sort of opportunity to the many minor party candidates in the race. Broadcasters claim that the debates are bona fide news events and that they are simply doing on-the-spot coverage of these events, even though they are often the instructors and stagers of the debates.

Since the exemptions to the equal time provision became law in 1959, a great many debates have been broadcast between major party candidates for state, local, and national offices.

Many arguments have been offered for and against these exemptions. Broadcasters claim they make it possible to give better coverage to the candidates in an election who have a chance of being elected. If stations must provide equal time for the candidates of the many minor parties, such coverage would be impossible. In recent presidential elections, for example, there were candidates not only from the Democratic and Republican parties but also from the Prohibition Party, the Socialist Party, and the States' Rights Party, to name only a few. There was one candidate for the presidency recently whose only goal was to remove "shyster lawyers" from government posts and another whose plan for eliminating crime was to give every citizen a "Saturday Night Special." The argument against loopholes in the equal time provision is that, without decent broadcast coverage of nontraditional candidates, it is more difficult to get fresh ideas into America's political discourse.

The Deregulation Debate

If history is a reliable guide, we can expect to hear more in the years ahead about whether the equal time provision and other regulations should be strengthened or eliminated. In fact, we are almost certain to hear a great deal of debate over **deregulation**—*the elimination of all regulation of radio and television, except for the control of technical standards and interference*. The major argument for such deregulation is that now with more than ten thousand radio and television stations on the air, as well as a variety of cable channels, VCRs, and computerized data banks, competition alone—the marketplace—ensures that the public interest, convenience, and necessity will be adequately served. Opponents of broadcast regulation also argue that the costs of compliance are too high, that regulation is slowing the growth of important and valuable communication industries, and that it is contrary to the First Amendment's freedom of speech and press provision. They claim the media have difficulty fulfilling their traditional function in this country of being watchdogs of government when they are subject to regulation by that government. A recent head of the Federal Communications Commission even argued that "as long as you've got government control, there is the potential that those in authority, with that power of censorship, can use it for evil means."

Proponents of regulation, on the other hand, argue that in today's world the public has less to fear from government than from advertisers and communication industries, whose only serious concern is maximizing profits. They assert that the marketplace will not ensure adequate coverage of the major sides of all important controversial issues or the broadcasting of useful materials to segments of the audience with whom advertisers have little desire to communicate: young children, the poor, the aged, and groups with unpopular views or interests. In addition, they point out that the broadcast spectrum, like our national parks, forests, lakes, and rivers, is a public resource and ought to be protected and regulated in a way that best serves the public interest. Just as the unregulated cutting of timber in national forests can destroy those precious resources, so the unregulated use of the broadcasting spectrum for profit alone can destroy its capacity to serve society.

REVIEW

The first major radio legislation was the Radio Act of 1912, which was followed by a more comprehensive law, the Radio Act of 1927. This law was superseded by the Communications Act of 1934, which covered both wire and wireless communication. Some of the important features of the act included a public interest, convenience, and necessity clause, an independent regulatory commission, a limited license period, and equal treatment of political candidates. In recent years, a number of federal regulations have been eliminated.

The Federal Communications Commission has already eliminated a great deal of broadcasting regulation. Radio, especially, is almost totally free of it. Radio stations no longer need to base their programming on systematic studies of the needs of their communities. They no longer need to keep program logs that are open to the public; to limit advertising; to provide any news, public affairs, or local programming; or to present detailed reports to the FCC to demonstrate that they have served the public interest, convenience, or necessity. The FCC recommendations to both radio and television stations regarding children's programs have been eliminated. The duration of operating licenses has been extended, and the number of stations an individual or corporation can own has been increased. Many other regulations are also slated for softening or elimination.

Perhaps the most hotly debated regulation has been the **Fairness Doctrine**, which *required broadcasters to seek out and present opposing views on controversial issues of importance to their communities*. When it adopted the

Fairness Doctrine in 1949, the FCC was just beginning to navigate its way through the murky waters of "fair" and "reasonable" programming. A few years before, it had declared broadcast editorials inconsistent with the public interest. "The broadcaster cannot be an advocate," the FCC said. But then it reversed its decision. In 1987, after almost four decades of trying to decide what is fair and reasonable, the FCC reversed its stand on the Fairness Doctrine, declaring that in all likelihood the doctrine was unconstitutional. Obviously Congress thought otherwise. It passed a bill requiring the FCC to continue to uphold the Fairness Doctrine. President Reagan, however, vetoed the bill, and President Bush has vowed to do likewise if another such bill is passed.

BYLINE

What do you think about this issue? Should there be less or more regulation of radio and television? For example, should there be a Fairness Doctrine to govern the presentation of issues of public importance, or should the broadcaster be left to decide what to cover and which views to present?

The Birth of Network Broadcasting

As far as we can tell today, the first network was established in 1922 when WGY in Schenectady, New York, and WJZ in Newark, New Jersey, were linked so that both could carry the World Series. Technical quality was poor, but soon AT&T developed ways to improve the fidelity of sound carried over long distances by wire.

As with many of the significant developments in broadcasting, sports and politics were important stimulation for the development of networks. AT&T put together the first coast-to-coast network for an election-eve broadcast by President Calvin Coolidge in November 1924. There were 26 stations in the network and an estimated audience of between 20 and 30 million. No president had ever spoken to so many people.

In 1925, David Sarnoff proposed that stations belonging to the companies involved in RCA be put into a broadcasting company that could become self-supporting, perhaps even profitable, through the sale of advertising. A year later, the RCA Board of Directors approved the idea of the new company to be owned by RCA, General Electric, and Westinghouse; and in August, the National Broadcasting Company (NBC) came into being. The public announcement stressed that NBC would permanently assure listeners a supply of good programs.

A second network, the United Independent Broadcasters, was formed in 1927, when a music promoter and manager, Arthur Judson, found he could not do business with NBC. He lined up 12 stations, arranged financing, and formed his own network. Judson's network became the Columbia

Phonograph Broadcasting System in 1927, when it merged with the recording company, and later the Columbia Broadcasting System (CBS). CBS was beset with problems from its very start, sorely needing large amounts of money and dynamic leadership. It got both in 1928 from a new major stockholder and president, William S. Paley, who was to lead the company for over half a century.

Many other networks were started during the late 1920s and early 1930s, almost all of them restricted to a particular region of the country. Only one other major national radio network developed, although it never achieved the power or prominence of NBC or CBS. The Mutual Broadcasting System was quite a different sort of organization than the other national networks; it was a cooperative. Instead of the network owning stations, the stations owned the network. Most of the programs the Mutual organization carried were produced by one of the affiliated stations rather than by the network. The exceptions were programs produced by sponsors.

Network Functions

Four primary functions of broadcasting networks were set in these early days of their history: (1) to provide programming to affiliates, (2) to arrange relays from the points at which programs originate to the broadcasting stations, and for commercial networks, (3) to sell the time of local stations on the national market and so gain revenue for themselves and for each station, and (4) in the case of NBC and CBS, to earn as much profit as possible for the network stockholders or owners. Each of the networks performed these functions in a somewhat different way. While both networks paid affiliated stations to carry **sponsored programs**—that is, *programs sponsored or financed by advertising revenues*—NBC charged its affiliated stations for **sustaining programs**—*programs that had no sponsors*. CBS, on the other hand, offered sustaining programs to stations without charge but insisted on **option time**—*certain time periods when* it could be assured that the *affiliated stations would carry sponsored programs*.

It soon became apparent that option time was extremely important for networks, and the others picked up the idea. With the same assurance that stations would clear the time for sponsored network programs, it was easier for networks to win advertisers. Option time allowed a network representative to assure a prospective sponsor of a minimum number of stations, including stations in the major cities. Because of its importance, the networks insisted on more and more option time, leaving stations little flexibility to schedule local programs.

Antitrust Action Against Networks

In 1938, the Federal Communications Commission began an investigation of option time and other network practices. The result was the "Report on Chain Broadcasting," which the Supreme Court upheld in 1943. The report had three key provisions:

REVIEW

The NBC network was formed in 1926 and CBS the following year. ABC was formed in 1943 after the FCC forced NBC to sell one of its two networks. All networks have four primary functions: to provide programming to affiliated stations, to relay those programs from their point of origin, to sell time to advertisers, and to make as much profit as possible for stockholders or owners.

1. NBC, which had earlier split its lineup of stations into two—a Red Network and a Blue Network—must sell one of them, because ownership of two gave the company too much power to inhibit competition.
2. Broadcasting stations affiliated with networks could give the network no more than three hours of option time during any of the major parts of the broadcast day (8:00 A.M. to 1:00 P.M., 1:00 P.M. to 6:00 P.M., 6:00 P.M. to 11:00 P.M., 11:00 P.M. to 8:00 A.M.).
3. Networks could not own or control talent agencies, those companies that represent actors, musicians, and so on. The reason for this ruling was that network affiliation gave artists in an agency an unfair advantage in gaining network employment. In addition, control of an agency created a conflict of interest for the network, since it both employed and represented artists.

As a result of this FCC ruling, NBC was forced to sell its Blue Network. Under its new ownership, the Blue Network became the American Broadcasting Company (ABC), and the Red Network reverted to the name of the parent corporation, NBC.

The Development of FM Radio

An important development in radio broadcasting went almost unnoticed by the American public for almost thirty years. This was FM ("frequency modulation") radio, a radically different means of transmission that produced greater fidelity of sound compared to AM ("amplitude modulation") radio and was almost free of static. FM radio was invented by Edwin Armstrong and patented in 1933. Armstrong also built the first experimental FM station a few years later. By the time America entered World War II, about twenty FM stations were on the air.

Following World War II, FM was hurt badly by two developments: the rapid growth of television and a shift in the broadcast frequencies allocated by the FCC for FM broadcasting. The developers of both television and FM fought for the radio frequencies then occupied by FM stations. Proponents of television won that fight, and in 1945 the FCC ruled that the FM allocation would be shifted to a radio band with a much higher frequency. (Actually, the change resulted in the entire FM service being placed between television channels 6 and 7.) Even though the shift created space for far more FM stations, it was a severe setback for the medium because it meant that all of the existing FM transmitters and receivers were worthless; stations had to rebuild their operations and their audiences.

During the first thirty years of FM development, many of the stations were built by AM station owners in the same community, as insurance against an unknown technological future. However, since relatively few

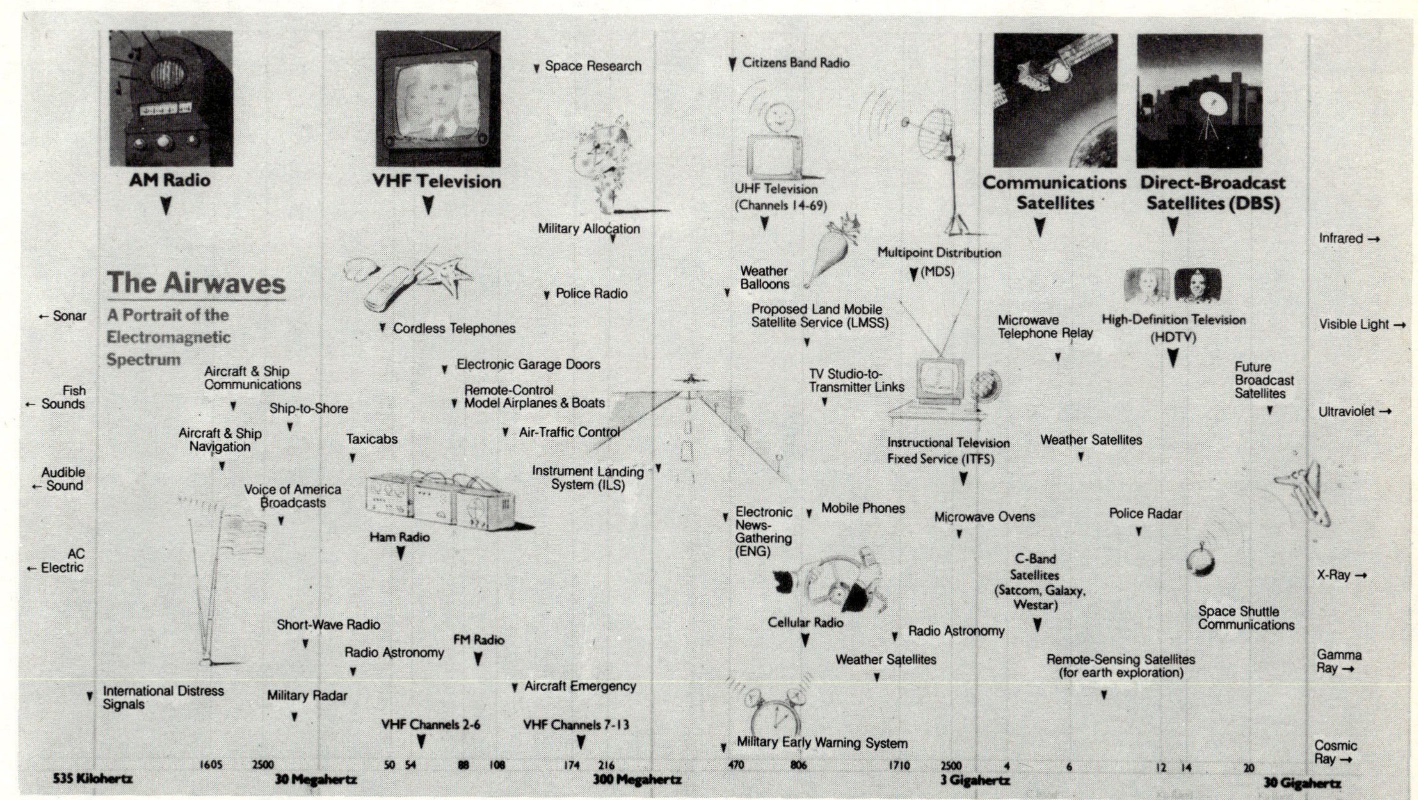

The many services that utilize radio waves are shown in this illustration of the electromagnetic spectrum.

homes were equipped with FM receivers and hence few advertisers were willing to pay for commercials on these outlets, owners saved money on programming by simply carrying the same programs that were on their AM stations. This was known as **simulcasting**—*broadcasting simultaneously on two different frequencies*. Thus, the public had little motivation to buy receivers, and advertisers, without an FM audience, had little motivation to buy time, so stations had little money for special programs. It was, as they say, a vicious circle.

The situation continued well into the 1960s, when FM radio received a tremendous boost from a combination of factors: (1) the virtual saturation of the AM-frequency band at the same time that the financial health of radio was creating a demand for new stations, (2) the widespread distribution of combination AM-FM radios, and (3) the **nonduplication rule** enacted by the FCC. Since its first passage in 1966, the FCC has made the nonduplication rule more stringent. Today, *an owner of both an AM and FM station in a town of more than 25,000 people cannot broadcast programs simultaneously on the two stations more than 25 percent of the time.* This ensures a greater variety of radio material in your communication mosaic.

With the FCC's nonduplication rule, FM stations began striving for programming formats that would distinguish them from their AM competitors and that would attract listeners and, therefore, advertisers. The greater fidelity of FM made music a natural solution. The popularity of stereo broadcasting, perfected in the early 1960s, also contributed to this solution and aided the growth of FM radio.

At the beginning of 1966, when the nonduplication rule went into effect, this country had 4044 AM radio stations and 1525 FM stations. Since then, FM radio has grown far more rapidly than AM radio. By the end of 1984, there were 4823 FM stations on the air compared to 4754 AM stations. Today there are about fifty-six hundred FM stations compared to somewhat less than five thousand AM stations. An even more dramatic change has occurred in the audiences for AM and FM radio. In 1972, FM claimed only 25 percent of the radio audience. In each successive year, its share of the audience has increased—to the point that FM now claims 76 percent of the total radio audience.

Accompanying the audience change was a change in the profit picture. By 1980, the pretax profit of the average FM radio station had surpassed that of the average AM and AM-FM combination station. The result has been a sharp shift in the relative desirability of FM and AM station ownership. In the 1950s and early 1960s, few people were willing to put money into an FM station, whereas there was far greater demand for AM stations than there were frequencies available. Today, in most if not all communities, that situation is reversed.

Review

FM radio was invented by Edwin Armstrong in the 1930s. The development of stereo in the 1960s and the FCC's nonduplication rule spurred its growth. After World War II, magnetic tape replaced wire recordings.

Audio Recording

Another development during World War II, one that went almost unnoticed at the time but that has revolutionized radio and the way many of us receive most of our music, is the tape recorder. Until the war, recording for radio was done with bulky equipment on large, plastic discs. During the war, though, American correspondents used a new, portable device that recorded sound magnetically on a long, thin wire. As our troops overran Germany, they discovered that the Germans had developed an even better medium on which to record—magnetic tape. It had greater fidelity and, unlike wire and disc recordings, could be easily edited. Tape recording was refined rapidly after the war and almost universally adopted for virtually all original recording, radio news gathering, music playback at stations, and home recording and playback.

International Broadcasting

Most Americans are hardly aware of another broadcasting service available to them—shortwave. On any given day, and especially in the evening, shortwave signals bring programming from all over the world. Radio Moscow, Radio Beijing, Radio Deutsche Welle, Radio Havana Cuba, and many other operations sponsored by foreign governments, beam English-language programs to potential audiences in the United States. One of the largest international radio services is the British Broadcasting Corporation (BBC). Unfortunately for these broadcasters and their potential listeners, few Americans own shortwave receivers. Fewer still have receivers with digital scanning to facilitate tuning.

Shortwave broadcasting has been around for a long time. As early as 1923, Frank Conrad, the Westinghouse engineer whose amateur broadcast experiments led to the establishment of KDKA, was exploring the use of shortwave signals. What he and others soon discovered was that they could span incredible distances by *broadcasting at higher frequencies where the radio waves are shorter—hence the name shortwave*. By 1939, NBC, CBS, Westinghouse, and General Electric were all engaged in international shortwave broadcasting.

World War II brought commercial international broadcasting to a halt. The government first took over blocks of time from the international stations and eventually the stations themselves. Shortwave broadcasting became an important propaganda tool during the war and was used effectively by Germany and Japan as well as the United States and its allies. In the summer of 1942, *the government's first official shortwave service*, the **Voice of America** (VOA), began broadcasting in German from tiny studios in New York City. By mid-1944, VOA was producing 119 hours of programming daily in 50 languages.

Had it not been for the cold war in Europe following World War II and the hot war in Korea in the early 1950s, the United States might have abandoned government-sponsored shortwave broadcasting. But the iron curtain descending over Eastern Europe and North Korea's threat to overrun South Korea brought a new purpose to the Voice of America. It would be used to fight communism.

During this period, two other *American-financed shortwave services* were established: **Radio Free Europe** in 1951 and **Radio Liberty** in 1953.[3] Radio Free Europe was aimed at people in Eastern Europe, while Radio Liberty beamed its signal to the Soviet Union. Unlike Voice of America, which depended on Congress for its funding, these services appeared to be financed by American volunteer organizations sympathetic to the plight of millions of people trapped behind the iron curtain. Actually, most of their financing came from the CIA.

It was not until the early 1970s that Congress and the American public learned of the CIA's involvement in Radio Free Europe and Radio Liberty. Critics charged that the two shortwave services were relics of the "cold war" and should be abolished. Supporters saw them as important alternatives to Soviet propaganda and as critical champions of human rights.

With vivid memories of the Berlin Wall and Soviet troops invading Hungary and Czechoslovakia to stamp out attempted democratic reforms, Congress agreed with the supporters and in 1973 passed the **Board for International Broadcasting Act**. This Act *provided a permanent organization to house the two international broadcast services.* Congress could have placed

This Voice of America antenna farm in Greenville, North Carolina, transmits VOA programming to the eastern Caribbean, Latin America, Western Europe, and the northern and western parts of Africa.

Radio Free Europe and Radio Liberty—now called RFE/RL, Inc.—under the **United States Information Agency** (USIA), *an organization created in 1953 to house all of America's media-related public diplomacy operations, including VOA*. It chose not to do so, probably because of differences in the two kinds of services. Radio Free Europe and Radio Liberty were conceived as surrogate home radio stations, that is, radio stations that sound as if they originate in the countries in which they can be heard. The Voice of America, on the other hand, sounds like what it is, an information or propaganda arm of the United States. Its mission is to present America to the world, to explain U.S. foreign policy, and to be a reliable source of news and information in countries without a free press. These ideas were drafted into law in 1976 with the passage of the VOA Charter.

In 1985, our government added **Radio Martí**, an *international radio service aimed at Cuba*. Radio Martí was named after José Martí, the Cuban patriot who led the fight for Cuba's independence from Spain just before the turn of the century. The main support for establishment of the Spanish-language service came from Cuban-Americans in Miami and from the Reagan administration. Both were seeking more aggressive ways to combat communism. Congress, wary of a radio war with Fidel Castro, placed Radio Martí under the management umbrella of VOA and the USIA to ensure high standards of operation. However, the mission and programming of Radio Martí are more like those of Radio Free Europe and Radio Liberty than those of Voice of America.

Programming on the different international radio services varies greatly. The Voice of America, which broadcasts more than a thousand hours each week in 43 languages, is guided by a programming clock or pie chart, representing one hour's worth of programming. That hour is sliced into pieces of news, information, music, Americana, and editorials. In addition to its shortwave broadcasts, VOA broadcasts some programs from stations in foreign countries. It also makes extensive use of satellites to relay programming from its studios in Washington, D.C., to more than a hundred transmitters located in the United States and around the world. The estimated weekly audience for VOA is about 127 million adults.

Communist and other totalitarian countries have frequently tried to jam VOA by broadcasting on the same frequency as the VOA signal. While the Soviet Union ceased such action, China resumed jamming VOA following the 1989 student demonstrations and subsequent government crackdown. Iraq began jamming VOA broadcasts after it invaded Kuwait in 1990.

The programming on Radio Free Europe and Radio Liberty is almost all news and information, with many roundtable discussions and correspondent reports on East-West relations, U.S. foreign policy, human rights, and West European politics. Much of the time is devoted to information about the country in which the broadcast is heard, information audiences would not likely have learned from their domestic media until the recent demise of communism. From their headquarters in Munich, West

Germany, Radio Free Europe and Radio Liberty broadcast over a thousand hours of programming each week in 23 languages to an estimated weekly audience of 55 million listeners. In 1988, the Soviet Union stopped jamming Radio Liberty. Jamming of Radio Free Europe ceased shortly before the overthrow of communist governments in Eastern Europe.

Radio Martí combines news and public affairs programming with entertainment, particularly radio soap operas called novellas, and music, comedy, and variety shows. There are also religious programs and programs about coping with day-to-day life. Interviews with Cuban émigrés suggest that Radio Martí is the most popular station in Cuba. One reason for its popularity is that it can be heard on AM radio as well as shortwave. A series of directional antennae in the Florida Keys enables Radio Martí to reach Cuba on AM radio, while the shortwave signal is broadcast from a VOA relay station in Greenville, North Carolina. In 1990 Congress authorized funds for a television version of Radio Martí that is broadcast from a blimp high above the Florida Keys. As soon as the service was initiated, however, the Cuban government jammed the television signal and superimposed its own radio station on the Radio Martí AM frequency, thereby jamming both Radio Martí and TV Martí.

REVIEW

The shortwave radio services supported by the U.S. government include the Voice of America (founded in 1942), Radio Free Europe and Radio Liberty (begun in 1951 and 1953), and Radio Martí, which began broadcasting to Cuba in 1985. The purpose of the Voice of America is to be a reliable news source and to tell the world about America, whereas the other services provide information about the countries to which they broadcast—information that would otherwise go unreported.

Congress now appropriates almost $500 million a year for some twenty-three hundred hours of weekly programming on the Voice of America, Radio Free Europe, Radio Liberty, and Radio Martí.[4] With the dramatic changes that have taken place in Eastern Europe and the Soviet Union, there may be no need for these radio services in their present form. However, so long as the United States keeps attempting to win friends and influence events in other countries, radio will continue to be a useful tool in that effort. It is a vital part of our public diplomacy, selling America and American ideals to friendly as well as unfriendly countries.

Although commercial shortwave broadcasting all but died following World War II, there are a few such stations in the United States. There are also several religious stations that broadcast on shortwave. If electronics manufacturers ever decide to incorporate shortwave reception in most radios, as they did for FM a number of years ago, new audiences and new functions will likely be found for this valuable long-distance service.

BYLINE

By law, government services such as Voice of America are prohibited from purposefully broadcasting in the United States or from even making transcriptions of broadcasts available to U.S. citizens. This law is known as the Smith-Mundt Act. It was designed to protect U.S. citizens from being propagandized by their own government, but journalists who say their watchdog role is hampered by this prohibition have challenged it in court. What do you think? Should this ban continue, or should it be lifted?

RADIO IN THE AGE OF TELEVISION

World War II was a high point for radio. Never were people more dependent on a mass medium of communication. Radio helped give order to an otherwise chaotic world. Through the efforts of Edward R. Murrow and the many other gifted journalists working in broadcasting, Americans received a meaningful picture of what was happening throughout the world. They were calmed and brought together by the paternal tones of President Franklin Roosevelt and British Prime Minister Winston Churchill. And they felt a sense of continuity when they could still listen each week to Jack Benny and Bob Hope and the many other great entertainers who were almost like family members.

When the battle with Germany and Japan ended, another sort of battle began for radio: the battle with television. Television of some sort had been around for a long time, but not until World War II did it pose a threat to its parent medium, radio. Prior to that, television had been a toy for inventors and a roulette wheel for speculators, as we will see in the next chapter. By the early 1950s, however, technical developments with the medium and an economic boom that provided funds for investment in stations and receivers started television on its path to dominance. Before long, it was the rare home in which the radio set was not removed from its place of honor in the living room and replaced with a television receiver. Popular radio programs featuring stars such as Jack Benny and Arthur Godfrey had made the transition to the new medium. By 1953, radio was no longer the major nighttime family entertainment medium in this country. Those prime-time hours were no longer highly profitable for the sound medium as they had been in the past. In fact, it appeared to many people that no time would be profitable for radio and that the medium was in its death throes. (Table 9.1 shows the impact television had on audience ratings for radio programs.)

The Transformation of Radio

The obituary, as we know now, was premature. Radio of the 1930s and 1940s died, but radio in new forms came back stronger than ever, at least economically. Radio prospered, in spite of the threat from television, because station operators adjusted their programming and manufacturers adjusted the receiving apparatus to serve different functions than those taken over by television. The pretelevision radio receiver was expensive, large, and heavy; it was a major piece of furniture in the living room. The posttelevision radio receiver, helped by the development of transistors, was inexpensive, small, and portable; it followed us wherever we went.

Instead of the traditional radio format of the long drama or situation comedy, which people had to tune in to at a certain time and stay with for at least a half-hour, we now have the sort of programming on most stations that we can turn on or off at any time without feeling we are missing anything special. If we want to listen to some country-and-western music, for example, we do not need to check a schedule to see when such a program is on. Instead, we simply tune to the station that broadcasts such

TABLE 9.1 Top-Rated Radio Programs from the 1930s, 1940s, and 1950s

	January, 1936	
1.	Major Bowes Amateur Hour	45.2*
2.	Rudy Vallee Varieties	28.2
3.	Jack Benny	26.8
4.	Burns and Allen	23.0
5.	Amos 'n' Andy	22.6
6.	Fred Allen: Town Hall Tonight	22.2
	First Nighter	22.2
8.	Maxwell House Showboat	21.1
9.	Al Jolson: Shell Chateau	20.9
10.	Phil Baker	20.4
	January, 1944	
1.	Fibber McGee and Molly	31.9
2.	Bob Hope	31.6
3.	Red Skelton	31.4
4.	Charlie McCarthy-Edgar Bergen	29.2
5.	Jack Benny	27.9
6.	Aldrich Family	26.9
7.	Joan Davis-Jack Haley	24.2
8.	Abbott and Costello	24.0
9.	Mister District Attorney	22.9
10.	Frank Morgan-Fannie Brice	22.5
	January, 1952	
1.	Amos 'n' Andy	17.0
2.	Jack Benny	16.2
3.	Lux Radio Theatre	15.0
4.	Charlie McCarthy-Edgar Bergen	14.7
5.	Walter Winchell	12.8
6.	Our Miss Brooks	11.8
7.	Mr. and Mrs. North	11.5
8.	Suspense	11.3
9.	Dragnet	11.0
10.	Godfrey's Talent Scouts	10.9

*The Cooperative Analysis of Broadcasting, or CAB, was the first program rating service to provide data on program popularity. Figures represent the percentage of homes tuned to a program during a selected week. The last set of ratings shows a marked decline in listening as a result of competition from a new medium—television.

Source: Harrison B. Summers, *A Thirty-Year History of Programs Carried on National Radio Networks in the United States, 1926–1956* (New York: Arno Press, 1971).

music all day long. If we do not know which station that is, we scan the dial and quickly find it. If we want news, we know that most stations carry some "every hour on the hour," or we can just turn to an all-news station.

Much pretelevision radio came from the networks, especially during prime-time hours. It was expensive, with its stars and crews of writers and emphasis on live entertainment. Posttelevision radio discovered that its audience was as willing to listen to recorded music as live music and that the local disc jockey could be as popular with its audience as the network stars of the past had been. Besides, a disc jockey with recorded music provided a flexible format that made it easy to slip in more commercials. If commercial stations rely on a traditional network at all today, it is generally only for news and occasional features.

While the old-style radio network is declining, a new type of network is gaining widespread acceptance. Communication satellites are being used increasingly to distribute syndicated shows and, at times, even commercials to local radio stations for transmission. A great deal of news and sports is also "networked" in this way. At last count, ninety percent of the radio stations in the country had earth stations with which they could pick up program material from satellites for broadcast.

The New Prime Time of Radio

For pretelevision radio, **prime time**, *the time for which the highest advertising rates are asked*, was the evening. With television and cable today attracting the bulk of the audience at night, radio's prime time has shifted to early morning and late afternoon. The largest audience for radio is from about 6:00 A.M. to 9:00 A.M. and 3:00 P.M. to 5:00 P.M. These are the hours that have come to be known as **drive time**, *the time when a large percentage of Americans are driving to or from work.* Stations program those hours specifically for these drivers. In larger cities, for example, road reports are an important service, broadcast every few minutes during drive time to let commuters know about those streets or bridges that are more congested and those on which they can make better time.

Contemporary Radio Rates

The cost for a 30-second radio commercial today can vary from several hundred dollars on a top station in a major market to a few dollars on a small-town station in fringe time. The precise costs for commercials on a particular station are difficult to report because those costs depend on the length of commercial, the time of day it is aired, the number of spots one is buying, how well the buyer bargains, and the size and makeup of the station's audience. Even within the same town, for example, the costs can vary substantially among stations.

The Resurgence of Noncommercial Radio

Noncommercial radio almost died just before World War II but then surged back stronger than ever in the 1960s and 1970s. Three major factors accounted for this resurgence. One was the development of FM radio, which made many more frequencies available for new stations. In fact, the first 20 of those frequencies were set aside specifically for noncommercial use. Another factor in the resurgence of noncommercial radio was the heightened interest in education, stimulated by America's resolve to catch up with the Soviets in space exploration and by the post–World War II baby boom, which flooded schools and colleges with students in the 1960s.

Review

Most of the programming formats of radio were transferred to television in the early 1950s. Radio survived by developing new formats—especially new music formats. Noncommercial radio flourished in the 1960s and 1970s.

The third factor, caused in large part by the second, was the federal legislation that provided for financial help to educational broadcasting.

Today, we have about fourteen hundred noncommercial radio stations operating in this country and a major network, National Public Radio (NPR), to which many of them belong. This network is doing a great deal to make noncommercial radio a national force, even though only about a quarter of the public ever hears any of its broadcasts. NPR's first great coup was probably its live broadcasting of the complete debates in the United States Senate over whether to ratify the treaty that gave the Panama Canal to Panama. This was the first time Congress had ever permitted such broadcasts.

HOW RADIO GETS INTO OUR MOSAICS

To understand why we get the sort of radio content we do in our mosaics, and the conditions that could bring change in that content, some historical background is useful.

The Development of Radio Programming

In the early days of radio, the pioneers of the medium put on the air whatever they could think of that would cost them nothing. However, the development of networks sped the development of quality programming. By the early 1930s, virtually every kind of broadcast programming that we have today on either radio or television had been pioneered. Talks and music dominated the early broadcasting schedules. Vocal, piano, band, and organ recitals filled the air; ballroom dance music became especially popular. And programs were aired on almost any subject someone could be found to talk about. Sports broadcasts came into radio early. Services from a local church were broadcast in Pittsburgh as early as 1921.

Although some comedy programs had been on the air earlier, including a program of "negro dialect stories" broadcast on a station in New York in 1923 (obviously well before the strong civil rights movement), comedy became truly popular during the Depression days of 1930, 1931, and 1932. The first stand-up comedian to have his own show was Eddie Cantor. He was one of the many radio stars in the 1930s who helped variety programs dominate the prime-time hours.

Other broadcasting forms developed to a high level during this period were situation comedies, such as "Fibber McGee and Molly" and "Amos 'n' Andy"; detective and police stories, such as "The Shadow" and "Gangbusters"; and dramas about lawyers and newspaper people, such as "The Front Page" and "Mr. District Attorney." Drama series, such as the "Lux Radio Theatre," also developed in the 1930s, as did soap operas, so called because most of the sponsors were manufacturers of laundry products. These programs included "Ma Perkins," "Our Gal Sunday," and "The Romance of Helen Trent." Children's serials, many of them based on comic strips, were also part of radio's early expansion. "Little Orphan Annie,"

Realistic sound effects kept listeners tuned in to "Gangbusters" and other action-packed radio shows of the 1930s.

"Dick Tracy," "The Lone Ranger," and "Jack Armstrong, the All-American Boy" were favorites.

The Broadcasting of News

News was a key feature on radio from its earliest days, when Lee de Forest, overeager for a scoop, announced on the air that Charles Evans Hughes had been elected president. The year was 1916, and de Forest's announcement was premature; the winner turned out to be Woodrow Wilson.

Newspaper Ownership of Stations

Many newspaper publishers started their own radio stations in these early days, in part because they saw radio as a means of publicizing their papers. Some would read the headlines from the newspaper on the air—teasers—to interest listeners in buying the papers. Some stations not associated with newspapers simply read news stories on the air that they snipped from the local papers. The papers did not object to this practice at first because the stations would usually give them credit: "According to the Quincy Herald Whig . . . " As early as 1921, at least one station,

KDKA in Pittsburgh, was doing newscasts from the newsroom of a local paper. Thus, newspapers served this infant medium of radio, even printing program logs as a service to radio fans, and received free publicity in return.

By the late 1920s, many radio stations were broadcasting regular newscasts. The major wire services even provided special service to them. The networks also were developing regular newscasts and grooming the first of what was to become a long line of news stars: H. V. Kalternborn, Boake Carter, Edwin C. Hill, Walter Winchell, and Lowell Thomas.

Publishers' Attempts to Stifle Radio Competition

As radio became more commercial, competing with newspapers for advertising, their friendly cooperation was undermined. Newspapers began to perceive radio as a threat, especially when they saw their income declining during the Depression while the income of radio steadily rose. The threat became even greater when radio began "scooping" them regularly, getting stories on the air long before any newspaper could even get an "Extra" edition on the streets. Radio was the first to spread the word that the only child of aviation pioneer Charles Lindbergh had been kidnapped and that someone had tried to assassinate President Franklin Roosevelt.

Newspaper publishers fought back. Many stopped printing radio program schedules so that listeners would find it more difficult to find their favorite programs. They put pressure on the wire services not to make news stories available to broadcasters. They were behind the decision by Congress to keep its press galleries closed to broadcast journalists, a ban that was not lifted until 1939.

Finally, in 1933, pressure from newspapers and the wire services forced an agreement from the major radio networks to sharply restrict their news broadcasts. In light of the role of broadcasting in news today, it is hard to imagine that this agreement was made. In exchange for free news service from the wire services (Associated Press, United Press, and International News Service), NBC and CBS agreed that they would do no news gathering on their own and that they would broadcast only ten minutes of news a day—five minutes in the morning and five in the evening—timed to come after morning or evening newspapers had been sold. The networks also agreed that no news story would be longer than 30 words and that special news bulletins would not be issued, except for something of "transcendent importance." Perhaps most surprising of all, they agreed not to permit commercial sponsorship of newscasts. This *pact between the networks, wire, services, and publishers* came to be known as the **Biltmore Agreement** because it took shape during a conference in New York's Biltmore Hotel.

Needless to say, this agreement did not work. Local stations moved in to fill the gap it created. Special news services for local radio stations developed, and before long the networks went fully back into the news business. Attempts to artificially inhibit any mass communication medium in this way have never worked; the demands of the audience, the economic incentives, and the competitive drive of the pioneers in each medium are simply too strong.

Radio Again Goes to War

In the 1930s, another factor was reshaping the role of radio: World tensions were rising, and the story was too important for radio not to cover. From the day in 1936 when H. V. Kaltenborn, squatting in the shelter of a haystack near the Spanish city of Irun, managed to broadcast an eyewitness account of a battle in the Spanish Civil War, it was impossible for anyone to keep a lid on radio news. And the Biltmore Agreement died a quiet death.

The networks began building staffs of correspondents around the world. A national network of news **stringers**—*part-time news reporters*—had been organized by Paul White as part of the CBS News Service, before the Biltmore Agreement killed it. It was now reorganized by CBS, this time on an international scale. NBC did the same. A large reporting staff of this sort was financially feasible because, unlike regular staff reporters, stringers are paid only for the stories they write that are used on the air. By the time German forces began spreading across Europe in 1938, trampling country after country, American radio was there to provide first-hand accounts from a group of superb reporters.

Edward R. Murrow

One of the best of these reporters, one who was to set a standard for broadcast journalism for all who followed, was a young man named Edward R. Murrow. Murrow did not begin his career as a journalist; he became one by a quirk of fate. He joined CBS as director of talks in 1935, when he was still in his twenties. Three years later he was in Europe arranging a program for the American School of the Air when word came that Germany was invading Austria. He flew immediately to Vienna; from there he broadcast to America the story of the city's fall to Adolf Hitler's forces. From that day, Murrow became a legend.

Edward R. Murrow and his colleagues from CBS and the other major networks greatly influenced America's reaction to the war because they brought it into people's living rooms for the first time. Their influence was probably caused by their direct contact with the audience; no editor intervened between Murrow or his other colleagues and that audience. The words were theirs, the voices were theirs, and they largely determined what was emphasized when. Of course, these radio news pioneers were also extraordinarily bright and knowledgeable, and they understood their medium and their audience.

Since World War II, news has been a staple of broadcasting as the public has come to depend more and more on the electronic media as its major source of news.

REVIEW

Almost all programming forms on television today were pioneered by radio in the 1930s. Newspaper publishers, concerned about competition, forced network broadcasters to restrict their news, but the agreement broke down when local stations set up news services and war in Europe created a demand for radio coverage. World War II made news a permanent feature of radio and introduced a new breed of electronic journalists.

The Switch from Programming to Formats

The traditional form of programming in radio was a schedule of programs that would appeal to different segments of the audience and, as often as possible—especially in prime time—that would appeal to as great a variety of people as possible. Since the rise of television and the vast increase in number of competing stations, most radio broadcasters select a segment of the audience they believe they can win and can sell to advertisers, and they broadcast a specialized service for that audience.

In general, this *specialized service* is not made up of 15- or 30-minute programs, in the usual sense of that term; it is made up rather *of continuous entertainment or homogeneous information that the target audience can tune in or out at any point*. Broadcasters recognize that the term programming does not fit this new form of broadcasting; they have adopted the term **format radio** to describe it.

Format Radio

Many kinds of formats exist today, and new formats are constantly evolving. In selecting a format, a station owner or manager studies the market to see what segment of the audience is being inadequately served by other stations and then tries to determine what type of format will attract that audience. For commercial stations, it is critical that the audience attracted be salable to advertisers. That means it must be composed of potential customers for many types of products and must be large enough to warrant broadcast advertising. The larger the city or the **market area**—that is, *the area reached by a station's signal*—the more specialized the audience to which a format can appeal.

For the most part, formats are designed for audiences that fall into certain age, socioeconomic, or ethnic categories. Adult contemporary, rock, and album-oriented rock formats appeal primarily to younger listeners, whereas nostalgia/big band, easy listening, and news formats attract an older audience. Highly educated and more affluent listeners are those more likely to appreciate the classical format, and ethnic groups such as blacks or Hispanics often prefer stations that emphasize their particular culture or language.

Country music, as the name suggests, first became popular in rural areas—especially in the South and West—and in urban areas where listeners felt a special kinship with the folk styles of those regions. Stations with a country format can now be found all over America. Religious stations have also spread throughout the country, aided in part by the ready availability of FM frequencies set aside exclusively for noncommercial use.

When the ratings of a station fall, its management will almost always begin considering a different format. Once such a decision is made, the format can be changed almost overnight so the total sound of the station will be different.

You can find stations throughout the country with the formats shown in Table 9.2 or variations of them. Some formats are relatively faddish; they

TABLE 9.2 The Dominant Radio Formats: Percent of AM, FM Stations in the Top One Hundred Markets Programming Each Format

Format	*AM*	*FM*	*Total AM/FM*
Adult contemporary	18.4%	21.0%	20.7%
Country	19.2	18.8	19.0
Rock/Contemporary hits	2.7	21.0	10.3
Religious	12.9	3.9	9.2
Golden oldies	10.8	3.8	7.9
Nostalgia/Big band	9.0	0.7	5.6
Album-oriented rock (AOR)	0.9	9.4	4.4
Easy listening	2.0	7.8	4.4
News/talk	7.3	0.1	4.3
Urban contemporary	2.4	3.6	2.9
Spanish	3.6	0.7	2.4
Soft contemporary (light)	0.8	2.8	1.6
Black/Rhythm and blues	1.7	0.5	1.2
New Age/Jazz	0.5	1.7	1.0
Classical	0.4	1.6	0.9
Variety	1.0	0.0	0.6
All news	0.6	0.0	0.4

Source: Radio Facts for Advertisers 1989, 1990. Published by the Radio Advertising Bureau, Inc., 1989. Reprinted courtesy of the Radio Advertising Bureau, Inc.

quickly rise in popularity and then die. Disco was one of these. Others are relatively stable, continuing through the years to appeal to a reasonable segment of the potential audience.

Steadily improved radio sound quality has aided the popularity of music formats. FM, stereo and, more recently, compact discs have been the major contributors to better broadcast sound. The past few years have seen a switch from reel-to-reel and carousel tape machines to CDs for the broadcasting of music by stations throughout the country.

The stations that have used the format approach most successfully are those with a highly consistent sound. Once a format is selected, announcers, type of news, and even the styles of commercials are selected or shaped so that their tone and rhythm fit the pattern. The result is a smooth flow back and forth among all of these elements.

BYLINE

Does radio as you know it serve the public interest? Your interest? Can you think of other types of formats that would appeal to you or any of your friends?

Automation and Satellite-Delivered Programming

A number of stations, in order to cut costs, have automated their entire programming or installed satellite dishes so they can broadcast programming that originates elsewhere. At an automated station, the only duties personnel have, other than putting tapes on the machine and starting and stopping them, is either to edit the commercials and station breaks into the tape or to stop the tape periodically for them. Even the latter task is handled by a computer at some stations. A local announcer is necessary only if the station wishes to present local news or other special announcements.

Some of the new automated packages are highly sophisticated. Controlled by a computer, each can run a station for hours without human intervention. The packages switch appropriately from the announcer on the reel-to-reel tape recorder to the next record on a carousel recorder to the commercial on cartridge, starting and stopping each recorder at the right time. They can also switch to the network for news and back to recorded announcements, music, and commercials. Computer packages print a record or log of what has gone out over the air and the time it went out.

Review

Today, radio stations design their programming for particular kinds of audiences. This type of programming is known as format radio. In general, formats are tailored to audiences of certain age, socioeconomic, or ethnic categories who may enjoy a particular kind of music or programming other than music. Many stations have streamlined their operations by employing automated equipment and satellite-delivered programming.

With this sort of automation, switching the format of a station can be exceedingly easy if one buys a format service. One simply inserts the tapes for the new format into the machines and, presto, the station has gone from being a country station to an easy listening station or, more likely, from a classical music station to a contemporary station.

From the point of view of a station's owners, the major advantage of automation is that it cuts down on personnel costs. Very few people are needed to operate a fully automated station.

Satellite-delivered programming also enables a station to save money on personnel. The station manager chooses a programming format available through satellite syndication, installs a dish to receive the programming, and then broadcasts it "live" to the local community. This type of operation has less need for a large investment in recording and playback equipment, since most of the programming is relayed directly from the satellite dish to the broadcast tower. The station manager has only to supply commercials and announcements and whatever supplemental programming might be necessary.

Economic Influences on Radio

In the 1920s, every country in which radio was being developed was exploring ways to fund the operations of this new medium. This had not been a great problem in the early days, because the initial technological developments were funded by large companies that planned to recoup their investments through the lease and sale of equipment. Even the entertainment for broadcasting was readily available without cost because those who sold records were eager for the free advertising, just as musicians and other entertainers were intrigued with the new medium and interested in getting the visibility it offered. Many of the early stations were owned by newspapers and stores, and the owners initially believed that the advertising it gave them justified the costs.

The Effect of Rising Costs

As the costs of broadcasting rose, that justification was questioned. The coverage of on-the-spot news events was becoming increasingly popular, and for these the stations needed to lease expensive telephone lines. Musicians, actors, and other artists, who were happy to perform free in the early days of radio because of the novelty, began to demand payment for their work. The composers and publishers of music began to insist on royalties for works of theirs that were broadcast. They wanted an annual fee paid to the American Society of Composers, Authors, and Publishers (ASCAP). Stores and newspapers that owned some of the early stations found that their businesses did not benefit sufficiently to justify these greater costs. Manufacturers of radio receiving equipment also began to doubt that the cost/benefit ratio of supporting stations was in their favor. Audience members had to have radio receivers, of course, but did not necessarily buy them or the parts to construct them from the companies producing and transmitting the programs they wanted to hear.

This situation created a dilemma unlike those anyone involved with mass communication or entertainment had encountered before. There simply were no precedents that might suggest ways to fund this new medium. When the motion picture came along, its mode of public presentation was so like vaudeville, the legitimate theater, and the circus that it was obvious to everyone that it should be supported in the same way—through the sale of admission tickets. People had to buy books or newspapers, or borrow or rent them from someone who had, before they could read them. In other words, for all previous media, mechanisms were available that permitted control of their consumption and some means of exacting payment from the consumer. Not so with radio. Radio programs were sent out into the atmosphere to be picked up by whoever had the appropriate apparatus. There was no way to control—or even to know—who or where those receivers were.

Possible Methods of Supporting Radio

By the early 1920s, many ideas had been suggested for supporting radio stations, among them:

1. Endowment by public-spirited citizens, much in the manner that many public libraries throughout the country had been endowed by Andrew Carnegie
2. Municipal or state financing, just as municipalities finance schools, museums, and many libraries
3. Ownership and support by the federal government
4. Donations from the general public or a station's listeners. This is the scheme that came closest to the theatrical idea used in financing the motion picture.
5. A tax on radio receivers
6. The sale of advertising

As you know, the last mode of supporting radio ultimately came to be the mode that dominated American broadcasting. This is not surprising, when one considers that capitalism has been a dominant force in American life for much of the history of this country, and the early 1920s was an especially vigorous period for the American economy.

However, do not assume that our present system of financing most broadcasting was a foregone conclusion or that it was the only viable solution to the problem of supporting radio and, later, television. Great Britain, for example, faced with the same problem at the same time, arrived at quite a different solution. That country placed an annual tax on each radio receiver. To this day an annual tax continues to support the radio and television networks of the BBC.[5] No advertising is permitted on these networks, although regulatory changes proposed by former Prime Minister Thatcher's government may force the BBC to seek alternate sources of funding, including advertising. Other countries chose total government support as the proper means to finance radio broadcasting and with that support, of course, government control. You can find almost every conceivable kind of support used at one time or another in some country.

The method by which radio is supported is extremely important because it affects the broadcast content; it affects the bits of information and entertainment that you encounter in your communication mosaic. The differences are not always great, but they are there.

BYLINE

What specific differences in the content of radio would you expect to result from differences in method of supporting the medium? Can you suggest the probable impact of each of the six forms of support?

The Heterogeneous Support System for Radio in the United States

The broadcasting system in the United States is primarily commercial; however, stations here are supported in a variety of ways. Although no station has been totally endowed by a public-spirited citizen like Andrew Carnegie, the Ford Foundation and some smaller foundations have made substantial contributions to many noncommercial broadcasting stations in this country. Some cities own and totally support radio stations. New York City, for example, began radio station WNYC in 1924 and still operates it. Some states also own and operate radio (and television) stations, either directly or indirectly. For example, the state of Iowa, through its three state universities, owns and operates radio stations in Iowa City, Ames, and Cedar Falls. It also owns and operates the Iowa Public [Television] Broadcasting Network. The state of Wisconsin has owned and operated an educational radio network for many years. At least one radio station in this country is owned by a labor union, and a number of noncommercial stations are supported by contributions from their listeners.

In the early days of radio, some members of Congress proposed that the federal government own and operate a powerful radio station that could be received throughout the nation so that the government, and especially the Congress, would have a direct line of communication to citizens. The proposal was promoted by Senator Gerald Nye in 1929. Among other things, the station was to broadcast congressional debates; it was to be a type of audible Congressional Record. This station never became a reality.

One idea for supporting broadcasting that received little publicity in those early days but has since become extremely important is support by churches or religious groups. Radio stations, television stations, and production houses owned and operated by religious groups have become a strong force in American broadcasting, and they continue to spread both in this country and abroad. There are probably between seven hundred and eight hundred radio stations and fifty-five to sixty television stations in this country supported substantially or wholly by religious groups. Most religious stations are also supported by the sale of regular advertising. Only about five hundred of the radio stations carry an all-religious format.

None of this, of course, includes the many syndicated religious television programs. There are between sixty and seventy nationally syndicated devotional programs, many of which are carried by cable systems as well as television stations.

The Commercial Support of Radio

AT&T developed the idea of direct, commercial support of radio. It was analogous to the means that had been used to finance telephone and telegraph service, operations with which AT&T had experience. The idea was that anyone could use a station's studio and transmitter for a fee. Whoever wanted to broadcast something to the world—or to the community—would pay according to the length of the broadcast, just as people paid for long-distance telephone calls in terms of their length. AT&T labeled this practice of *broadcasting for a fee* **toll broadcasting**.

The first organization to take advantage of the toll broadcasting system was the Queensboro Corporation in New York on August 28, 1922. It bought ten minutes of broadcast time for $50 on station WEAF to tell listeners about some apartments it was offering for sale. This ten-minute speech about the virtues of suburban living is considered the first regular commercial in American broadcasting.

Indirect advertising had been used on radio before this time, however. Stores that owned broadcasting stations assumed that the constant mention of their names on the air would bring additional customers in. Theaters furnished talent, and record stores and publishers gave records to radio stations, hoping the credits they received on the air would help sales of tickets or records. Another form of indirect advertising was to give a store or product label to a program or group of radio entertainers.

REVIEW

When radio was first developed, no one was quite sure how it should be supported. Although there were calls for government subsidies and private donations, commercial radio eventually adopted the selling of advertisements as a means of support. The idea came from AT&T, which saw the use of radio as analogous to that of the telephone.

Probably the first of these was the "Wanamaker Organ Concerts," named for the John Wanamaker department store in New York City. Before long, radio listeners could hear the "Eveready Hours," the "Lucky Strike Orchestra," the "Ipana Troubadours," the "A&P Gypsies," and the "Texaco Star Theater."

Advertising then, as now, had its opponents. Herbert Hoover denounced it in the early 1920s when he was secretary of commerce. The Newspaper Publishers Association, obviously distressed about radio competing with them for advertising dollars, argued that "advertising by radio is likely to destroy the entertainment and educational value of broadcasting." One congressman even threatened to introduce legislation to ban advertising from the air. This legislation, like other antiadvertising efforts, obviously failed.

BYLINE

Many people still regularly denounce the support of radio and television by advertising. They charge that these media cannot adequately serve the public interest when they depend on advertising from business and industry. Do you believe their charge is valid? What are the bases for your belief?

Advertising Agencies

Advertising agencies became involved early in commercial broadcasting, just as they had been involved in magazine and newspaper advertising for some time. They were, and remain, the go-betweens for the advertiser and the station or network. They provide the advertiser with the expertise needed to use the media and, best of all for the advertiser, at no apparent cost. The agency fee—normally 15 percent of the cost of air time—comes from the money that would otherwise go to the broadcaster.

REVIEW

Advertising agencies serve as go-between for advertiser and station or network.

For its 15 percent, an agency provides people who are experts at buying broadcasting time, at developing fresh ways of appealing to potential customers, and at producing commercials. Until some years after World War II, advertising agencies also produced many radio programs and, later, television programs for sponsors.

Our Exposure to Radio

Radio reaches more people today than does any other medium. Because advertisers know this, radio's commercial revenues are greater than they have ever been. So for its audiences and its advertisers, modern radio appears highly successful. In fact, almost from the first days that people could hear faint strains of music coming out of thin air or could make out the sound of voices amid the static, radio has been a favorite medium.

Reasons for the Early Popularity of Radio

The reasons for radio's immediate success are easy to discern. Like the motion picture, radio did not demand literacy. The immigrant who had just landed at Ellis Island could enjoy the medium almost as much as the well-educated second- or third-generation American. Not only could radio be enjoyed; it also provided an education about America. Evidence shows that many immigrants and poorly educated people learned how to handle family problems by listening to soap operas. Men and women alike learned to cope with America and American ways from the varieties of radio dramas. Families were entertained and informed by comedy, variety, and musical shows and by the news broadcasts. Through the

Prior to the television age, home life centered around the radio, which occupied a place of honor in the family living room.

worst of the Depression, they were reassured by the fireside chats of President Franklin Roosevelt.

REVIEW

Because radio listening required few educational skills, it was immensely popular as a source of entertainment and news for immigrant families and families strapped by the Depression.

Radio was never more important to the American public than during World War II, as people feared for their sons, husbands, and fathers, their friends and relatives. And all of these benefits of radio were essentially free. Once a family acquired a radio receiver and installed it in its special place of honor in the living room, it delivered its treasures without cost. Children could listen to "Jack Armstrong, the All-American Boy" or "The Lone Ranger" during the late afternoons; women could listen to "Ma Perkins," "My Gal Sal," or "Vic and Sade"; and the entire family could gather about the set to laugh and thrill to "The Shadow," "Death Valley Days," "First Nighter," Jack Benny, Fred Allen, and Charlie McCarthy.

Patterns of Listening Today

Aided by the new radio formats and the fact that radio receivers are available almost everywhere we go, radio listening today is largely unplanned. We tune in at certain times out of habit, at other times because of a special need, and at still other times on a whim—because we want some background sounds.

Our habitual uses of radio center on certain regular activities. For example, some of us always listen to the news while we eat breakfast. Others of us have gotten into the habit of waking up to radio or perhaps are so accustomed to going to sleep with the sounds of radio that we have difficulty nodding off without it.

A good example of radio listening for a special need is the listening commuters do during the morning and evening rush hours in urban areas, which we discussed earlier. Drivers need to know what routes are clogged in order to avoid them, where the traffic is lightest, and so on. They also seek some diversion from the boredom of driving. Popular disc jockeys chatting with one another and bantering with their radio audience seem like familiar friends.

Almost certainly you have had the experience of simply tuning in radio because you wanted some background sounds or diversion—while you are studying or taking a break from studying, while washing dishes, cleaning house, working on your automobile, or perhaps lying on the beach. You don't listen to it very carefully, but you would miss it if it weren't there.

BYLINE

Because of the casual way we listen to radio, most of us are unaware of the amount of time we spend listening to—or at least hearing—the sounds of radio. Estimate your amount of radio exposure and then keep a diary of your radio listening time for a few days. How accurate was your estimate?

Processing Radio Information

Radio, probably more than any other medium of communication, has the potential to stimulate our imaginations. Because of the limitations of time and the audio channel, this medium gives us relatively little information. As a result, we listeners are forced to use our imaginations to the fullest to fill the gaps and to construct visual images in our minds from the sounds we hear. Radio writers and directors have made great use of this characteristic, especially in the creation of dramas and documentaries.

Unfortunately, most people who work in radio, in the United States at least, no longer think of its imaginative or artistic use—the use of the medium to evoke a world of images, a world that can exist nowhere except in the imagination. A psychologist named Rudolf Arnheim is one of the few scholars who dealt extensively with the aesthetic qualities of this medium. In a book titled *Radio*, published in 1936, he stressed the impact of sound on our processing of information. Although most of us do not realize it, in a drama or documentary the sound of a word, because it is more elemental, is often more important than its meaning. Before we recognize the meaning of a word, we sense its sound. And that sound affects us more directly than the meaning of the word. Skillful radio directors and actors can use this phenomenon in creating their art.

A more important factor is involved in our processing of much of the material we hear from radio. From its beginnings, radio has been a source of information and of entertainment, of news and of fantasy. That its reality and its fantasy are confounded is both a strength of radio and one of its problems. This is true in the motion picture also, but in a different way. In a motion picture, there is a confounding of reality and fantasy because we photograph objects that in fact exist but that, through a variety of means, are given symbolic value. The waves seen pounding on a rocky shore in a motion picture are seen as themselves but also as something more: the sign of a storm, a symbol for danger, or the inexorable passage of time.

REVIEW

Today, radio listening is usually the backdrop for some other activity such as eating or washing dishes or driving. Despite its ability to stimulate our imaginations, radio is rarely used as skillfully as it once was. The fact that it blends fantasy and reality is both a strength and a source of problems, especially when news programming and commercials are intertwined.

In radio, the confounding of reality and fantasy occurs at another level; it occurs because the medium is both a source of "real" events and a source of fantasy, and we are switched back and forth between fact and fantasy so quickly and so regularly that fact and fantasy easily become confused.

Unfortunately, some advertisers take advantage of that confusion. The most extreme examples occur during radio newscasts when newscasters go from news stories to commercials without warning, without a change of voice, and with copy written in such a way that the commercials sound like news stories. This practice has been frowned upon by the major networks but is common at many local stations and on some syndicated news programs. Because we associate radio with news and live coverage of actual events, we too often process these commercials in the same way we process news. Hence, we fail to be sufficiently critical of the claims being made; we simply accept them. Paul Harvey's news programs, heard throughout the United States, are among the slickest examples of this practice.

THE FUTURE OF RADIO

The future of radio is difficult to predict; there are too many unknown factors. One unknown is whether Congress will agree to further deregulation of the medium. Although the Federal Communications Commission regulates radio far less than it did a decade or two ago, nearly absolute freedom from regulation might alter the industry quite substantially.

Another unknown factor is the increased use of international communications satellites and cable. Although cable systems and the satellites are thought of largely in terms of television, they are also making available in our homes a greater range of radio materials. As the choices increase and each station must struggle harder for even a small portion of the potential audience, the intense competition may have a substantial impact on the industry. If that impact leads to more imaginative programming and other efforts to woo the segment of the audience with minority tastes that today's offerings fail to satisfy, the result could be positive. On the other hand, if that impact is to reduce the audience for any one station so much that radio becomes unprofitable, there may be no incentive to invest either funds or imagination in the medium, and the result could be negative.

The most serious threat to radio at the moment is to the AM service, which has been experiencing a steady decline in audience, down from 75 percent of the overall radio audience in 1972 to just 26 percent now. In 1988, about half of the AM stations lost money. The biggest handicap has been the inability to compete with FM, which has a more consistent signal, higher fidelity, and stereophonic sound. Many organizations, such as the FCC and Congress, are studying the AM problem and soliciting suggestions on how to improve the service. Some of these suggestions include working with receiver manufacturers to develop high-quality AM radios that feature stereo, higher fidelity, and continuous AM-FM tuning, and requiring by law that all new radios receive the ten new frequencies (from 1605 to 1705 on the AM dial) that just became available, and that all new FM stereos also receive AM stereo.

REVIEW

The future of radio depends in part upon whether there will be more or less government deregulation and whether other media such as cable television will have a positive or negative impact on listening. At the moment, the most serious threat is to AM radio, which has experienced a steady erosion of its audience. Like other communications media, radio stations will increasingly become parts of larger corporate entities.

One thing seems certain about radio's future (and about the future of all communications media): the trend toward consolidation will continue at least for the foreseeable future. A large portion of the radio stations in this country are already parts of groups, a set of broadcasting outlets under single, corporate ownership. For years, many of these groups have included television stations and newspapers. Recently, however, the corporate entities are mushrooming. Although there is a ceiling on the number of radio and television stations that one corporation can own (12 AM stations, 12 FM stations, and 12 television stations), there is no ceiling on the size of the rest of the corporation. Increasingly, radio stations find themselves in corporations that own not only television stations and a growing number of newspapers, but book publishers, billboard companies, and noncommunications industries as well. This development means that ownership is being moved further and further away from the operations end of the broadcasting stations. Many observers fear that with increasing distance will come decreasing concern for the public interest, convenience, or necessity.

THE CHANGEABLE MEDIUM WE CALL RADIO: A SUMMARY

Every medium of mass communication goes through a series of stages in its development to maturity. In none do we see those stages as clearly as we do in the history of radio. First is the stage of technology or invention, in which the medium is dominated by engineers and tinkerers. In the case of radio, these pioneers were concerned with either developing or improving some technical aspects of the medium, such as getting the signal to carry further or to have greater fidelity, or else they were interested in radio as a hobby or toy, something to play with after work or on weekends.

In the second stage, which generally overlaps the first, the medium is perceived, planned for, and used as something other than what it ultimately becomes. In the case of radio, it was initially perceived and used simply as a medium for point-to-point communication—communication from shore stations to ships or from one amateur wireless operator to another.

The third stage is that in which the mature function or functions of the medium are generally recognized and developed. For radio, this stage occurred when the medium began to flourish as an entertainment, information, advertising, and propaganda medium. As with other media, the development of radio's main functions was accompanied by a change in the type of person dominating it; the engineers and tinkerers became less important, replaced by a special breed of entrepreneurs. Not only were they promoters; they were also people fascinated with the medium—in the case of radio, fascinated with the news and entertainment potential of the medium—and they made great contributions to the development of these aspects.

In the fourth stage, as a medium fully matures and becomes a major and complex industry, still another type of person comes to dominate, one concerned primarily with business and management. However, in radio, as with the other major mass media, individuals whose primary concerns were entertainment and information continued to play important roles.

For most of the mass media there has been at least one additional stage. As new media come along and take over some of a medium's traditional functions, it must change, often quite substantially. This happened to radio when television came along. Television took over much of the entertainment and information functions of radio, along with its audience, especially its prime-time audience, and radio had to find new functions and new audiences. In its present stage, although it has not totally abandoned entertainment and information, radio has become primarily a background medium, something unobtrusive and undemanding to listen to while we do other things. In a sense, it is quite a different medium than it was before the advent of television. Whether there will be additional stages in the development of radio, only time will tell.

DISCUSSION QUESTIONS

1. What were the major technological developments in the history of radio?
2. Why was government regulation necessary? How extensive was it by 1934? Is regulation still necessary?
3. What are the functions of networks?
4. What accounts for the dominance of FM over AM radio?
5. Why does the U.S. government broadcast to other nations? What are the differences among the various international radio services funded by the government?
6. How did radio programming change as a result of television?
7. What is format radio?
8. How did commercial support for radio evolve? What other methods were offered for the support of radio? Do any of them survive today?
9. What is the major difference between radio listening in the 1930s and 1940s and radio listening today?
10. What are some of the factors likely to affect radio listening in the future?

NOTES

1. Much of the material on the history of radio is based on the excellent three-volume *History of Broadcasting in the United States* by Erik Barnouw (New York: Oxford University Press 1966–1970). For students of radio, these volumes are fascinating.
2. More details on the early history of educational radio can be found in Werner J. Severin, "Commercial vs. Non-Commercial Radio During Broadcasting's Early Years," *Journal of Broadcasting* 22 (1978): 491–504.
3. From 1952 to 1954, the United States financed the operation of another service, Radio Free Asia. According to Barnouw, few Asians had shortwave receivers, and the service failed to generate the kind of support among intellectuals that Radio Free Europe had. Since 1985, there has been a Radio Free Afghanistan, which was created in response to the Soviet invasion of that country. Administratively, it is part of Radio Liberty.
4. This figure does not include the American Forces Radio and Television Service (AFRTS), which provides programming for U.S. military personnel overseas, nor does it include clandestine broadcasting stations supported by the CIA.
5. The British developed a way to insulate radio from too much government interference by making the British Broadcasting Corporation an autonomous body. The British Parliament does not directly control the tax funds that go to broadcasting. The license fees are paid to the Postal Service, which simply turns them over to the BBC. We should also note that there is a commercial television system in Great Britain today that competes with the BBC for listeners, though not for financial support.

SUGGESTED READINGS

Classic Works in the Field

Barnouw, Erik. *History of Broadcasting in the United States*. 3 vols. New York: Oxford University Press, 1966–1970.

Cantril, Hadley, and Allport, Gordon W. *The Psychology of Radio*. New York: Harper, 1935.

Field, Harry, and Lazarsfeld, Paul F. *The People Look at Radio*. Chapel Hill, NC: University of North Carolina Press, 1946.

Lazarsfeld, Paul F., and Kendall, Patricia L. *Radio Listening in America*. New York: Prentice-Hall, 1948.

Relevant Contemporary Works

Conrad, M. A. "The Demise of the Fairness Doctrine: A Blow for Citizen Access." *Federal Communications Law Journal* 41 (April 1989): 161–194.

Lichty, Lawrence W., and Toppings, Malachi C., comps. *American Broadcasting: A Source Book on the History of Radio and Television*. New York: Hastings House, 1975.

Persico, Joseph E. *Edward R. Murrow: An American Original*. New York: McGraw-Hill, 1988.

Snow, Robert P. "Radio: The Companion Medium." In *Creating Media Culture*, pp. 99–123. Beverly Hills: Sage, 1983.

See also *Broadcasting*, *Radio Television Daily*, and the *Journal of Broadcasting and Electronic Media*.

CHAPTER 10

TELEVISION: THE CENTER OF ATTENTION

OBJECTIVES

After studying this chapter, you should be able to

- **Identify the major technological and programming developments in the evolution of television.**
- **Describe the structure of the television industry and identify the factors that affect its content.**
- **Explain the attraction of television and its use in our everyday life.**
- **Assess the performance of the medium in terms of its various functions.**

Television has transformed the political life of the nation, has changed the daily habits of our people, has molded the style of the generation, made overnight global phenomena out of local happenings, re-directed the flow of information and values from traditional channels into centralized networks reaching into every home. In other words, it has profoundly affected what we call the process of socialization, the process by which members of our species become human.

George Gerbner, former dean,
Annenberg School of Communications,
University of Pennsylvania

Few people would dispute the contention that television is today's dominant medium. Despite concerns about its violent and sexual content, its stereotyped portrayals, its often banal programming, there is hardly a home without a television set. Television is truly the medium that has something for everyone—whether it's pictures of Neptune from the *Voyager II* spacecraft, muppets arguing over the spelling of a word, entertainers like Bill Cosby, Roseanne Barr, and Hulk Hogan, or classical music and classical works of literature.

Television is more than a window on the world; it is the centerpiece of our media world—the most talked-about, trusted, and criticized medium in this country. We blame it for the high level of crime and the low level of reading and spelling, but most of us would not part with it.

In this chapter we examine this wondrous medium: how it came to be, the factors that affect the sights and sounds it transmits, our exposure to those sights and sounds, and the impact that exposure has on us and our society.

THE DEVELOPMENT OF TELEVISION

The dream of seeing at a distance—*tele-vision*—stimulated inventors and speculators for a long time before they were able to convert that dream to reality. Early attempts to realize the dream involved transmitting still pictures by wires, a type of facsimile now used by the news services to send rough reproductions of drawings and photographs to newspapers. Such transmission was demonstrated as early as 1862 by an Italian priest, Abbe Caselli. The development of wireless telegraphy and then radio spurred further efforts to create a practical television system.

Technological Development

The major spurt in the development of television technology occurred between World War I and World War II. During this period, the competition was resolved between the advocates of a mechanical system and those favoring an all-electronic system of television. To understand the issue, it is important to realize that any television image must be made up of small bits or dots, analogous to the newspaper photograph or the giant moving pictures in signs on Times Square in New York. Those moving signs on Broadway are made up of hundreds of electric bulbs of different colors. The newspaper photograph, as you can see if you examine it closely, is made up of hundreds of minute light and dark dots. In both cases, the farther away from the image you are, or the smaller and more numerous the dots or light bulbs, the more distinct the image.

Basic requirements of a television system. A successful television system must accomplish five tasks:

1. Break a picture into minute light and dark bits.
2. Transform those bits into electrical energy or waves.
3. Transmit the energy or waves by a wired or wireless system.
4. Receive and transform the electrical energy or waves back into light and dark bits.
5. Reassemble those light and dark bits into something resembling the original picture.

1890–1939

- **1890s** Paul Nipkow develops system for breaking up and reassembling visual image
- **1919** Vladimir Zworykin experiments with television at Westinghouse
- **1922** Philo Farnsworth diagrams an electronic television system
- **1934** Communications Act of 1934 sets up Federal Communications Commission (FCC)
- **1936** RCA begins extensive field tests of television
- **1939** Commercial television inaugurated

1940–1949

- **1940** Election returns are telecast
- **1941** First commercial television licenses issued
- **1942** Office of War Information formed
- **1948–1952** FCC places freeze on new television licenses
- **1949** FCC reverses itself, decides broadcasting stations can editorialize

1950–1959

- **1951** First network connection between east and west coasts
- **1952** FCC sets up color standards, UHF channels, noncommercial broadcast channels
- **1954** Rise of filmed series on TV
- **1955** Filming of Eisenhower's news conferences permitted
- **1955** Major movie studios start selling or renting old movies to television
- **1956** Videotape recording perfected
- **1959** Revisions in Communications Act weaken equal time provision; include Fairness Doctrine

1960–1969

- **1960** First televised debates—presidential candidates Nixon and Kennedy
- **1965** Extensive network coverage of Vietnam fighting creates first "television war"
- **1965** Early Bird communication satellite launched
- **1966** FCC assumes regulatory authority over cable television
- **1969** Live broadcasts document astronauts' landing on moon

1970–1979

- **1971** Public Broadcasting Services (PBS) formed
- **1975** Home Box Office plans satellite distribution of signals for pay television system

1980–1991

- **1980** Cable News Network (CNN) launched
- **1985** Capital Cities Broadcasting acquires ABC
- **1986** General Electric purchases RCA (NBC) for $6.3 billion and Fox becomes fourth commercial TV network
- **1987** Laurence Tisch, who owns controlling interest in CBS, becomes chief executive officer
- **1990** William Paley, founder of CBS, dies
- **1991** FCC aids networks by changing Financial Interest and Syndication Rules

For a television system with moving images, this process must be rapid so that the movement is smooth and realistic.

A mechanical television system. The mechanical system broke up and reassembled the picture with *a rotating disc invented by Paul Nipkow in the 1890s.* The disc contained 45 holes, arranged in the manner shown in Figure 10.1. Figure 10.2 is a schematic drawing of the entire system, showing how the original image is broken into small dark and light bits, transformed into electrical energy, which activates a light source. A **Nipkow disc,** synchronized with the disc at the sending end, recreates an approximation of the original picture. Early television scanning equipment and an actual transmitted image are shown in the photographs on page 313.

Review

Paul Nipkow's mechanical television system, developed in the 1890s, used a disc to break up an image, transform it into electrical energy, and reassemble it. But it was not until the mid-1920s that a practical television camera and receiver system was available. The mechanical system of that era used a very small screen and produced fuzzy pictures.

It took almost thirty years from the invention of the Nipkow disc for scientists to come up with a more-or-less practical television camera and receiver system. One developed by John Baird was demonstrated in Great Britain in 1926. That demonstration sparked a virtual explosion of television activity, befitting the fast and furious speculative days of the late 1920s. Experimental stations went on the air almost immediately in the United States as well as in Britain. RCA's W2XBS was licensed in the United States by the Federal Radio Commission in 1928. In that same year, the General Electric television station in Schenectady, New York, which had begun a regular schedule of broadcasting, experimented with television drama. Because the early television screens were so small and the pictures so fuzzy, the entire play had to be done in close-ups so that the audience could see the actors.

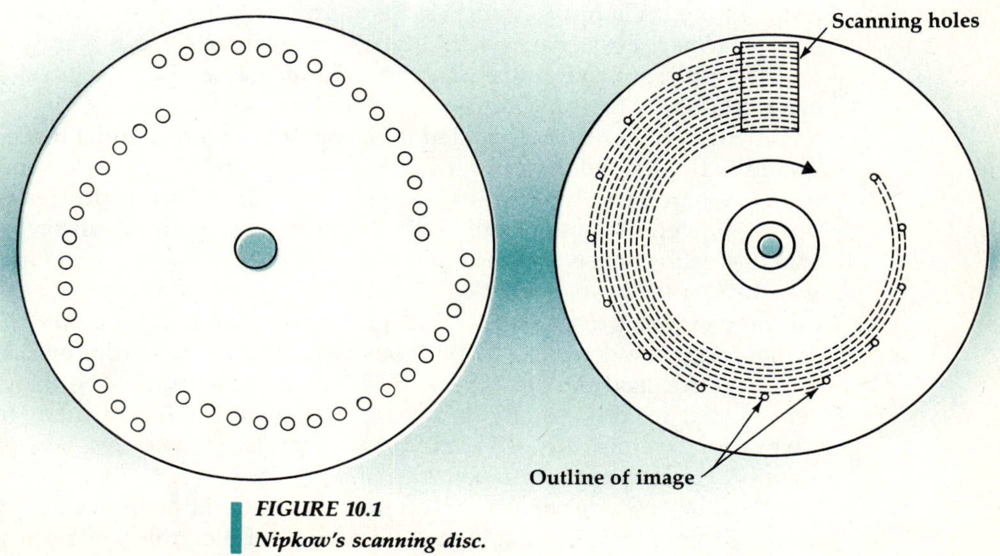

FIGURE 10.1
Nipkow's scanning disc.

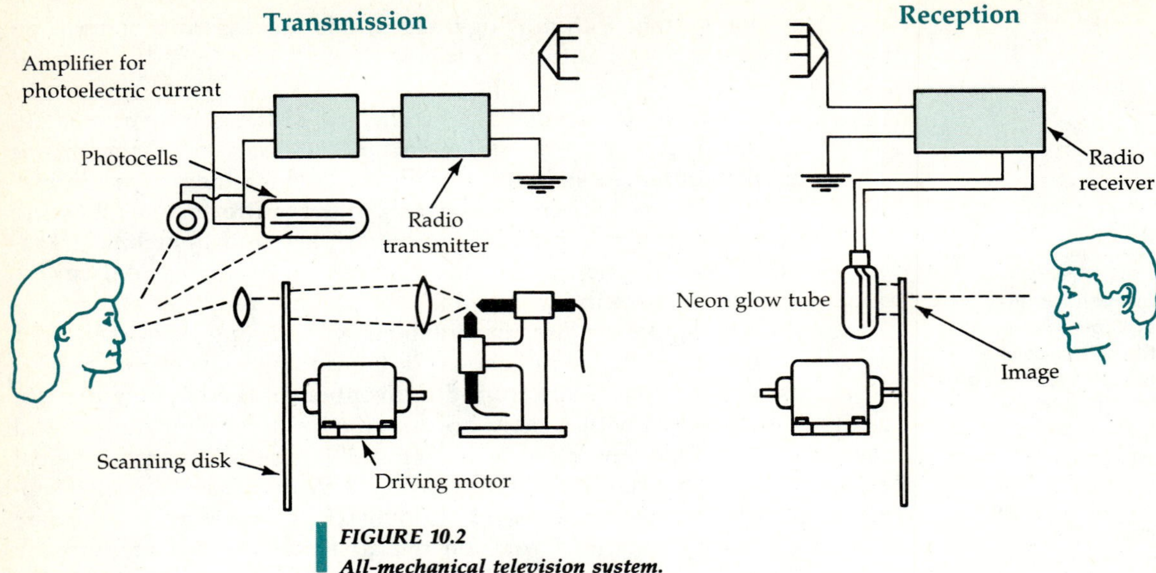

FIGURE 10.2
All-mechanical television system.

An all-electronic television system. The development of television was seriously hampered by its dependence on a mechanical system for breaking up and reassembling images. Not only was the system too vulnerable to breakdowns, but the quality of images that could be achieved was severely limited. A major leap in the development of television came through the independent efforts of two young geniuses, a Russian immigrant named Vladimir Zworykin, and the self-educated son of a Utah sheep farmer, Philo Farnsworth. These men developed the major ideas and technology needed for breaking up and reassembling a visual image electronically.

Zworykin, who had studied electronics in Russia and France, emigrated to the United States immediately after World War I and found a job doing research for the Westinghouse Electric Company. In Russia he had been involved in some of the earliest experiments with television, and he asked Westinghouse for permission to continue those experiments. This was 1919, and the possibilities for television seemed almost nonexistent, but he received permission. In 1923, Zworykin applied for a patent on an iconoscope tube designed to electronically break up a picture by scanning an image focused on the tube with a beam of electrons. The image was reproduced in very rough form by a type of cathode ray tube. In 1929 Zworykin demonstrated *a receiving or picture tube that produced higher-fidelity pictures*. He called it a **kinescope tube.**

Working independently, apparently not even knowing of Zworykin's work, Philo Farnsworth solved the problem of electronic television even

REVIEW

The first all-electronic television system was introduced by Vladimir Zworykin in 1929. His kinescope tube, developed at RCA, became the basis for the present U.S. television system.

sooner. In 1922, he described an all-electronic television system, for which he received two patents in 1930. Zworykin's system was not patented until 1938.

Not surprisingly, the similarity of Farnsworth and Zworykin's television systems resulted in a four-year patent fight, which the court decided in Farnsworth's favor. RCA, for whom Zworykin was then working, agreed to pay Farnsworth $1 million for the use of his patents so that both his inventions and those of Zworykin could be used in the manufacture of modern television cameras and receivers. (See Figure 10.3 for a schematic drawing of the early all-electronic television system.)

The electronic television system simplified the problem of synchronizing the camera and the receiver. It also made possible the breaking down of the image into finer bits, which resulted in better picture quality.

Technical standards. Although solutions were found for the mechanical problems of the early television system, other technical problems plagued the development of the medium. There were disagreements about the standards the industry should adopt: the number of scanning lines per frame, the number of frames per second, whether sound should be AM or FM. More channels were needed for television transmission than the government had allocated. Not enough capital was available for research. Also, businesses and the public were reluctant to invest in either stations

In 1930, NBC-TV broadcast signals into homes of participating experimenters. (left) *Subject of one early transmission was Felix the Cat, here performing in front of the scanning equipment on a phonograph turntable.* (right) *This is how the image broadcast appeared on screen.*

or receivers until they were certain the technical standards would not change and make their investment obsolete. The Federal Communications Commission, aided by the **National Television Standards Committee** (NTSC), *an advisory group for the industry and the FCC*, worked on these problems throughout the 1940s. By 1948, it had become necessary for the FCC to impose a freeze on new license applications. The freeze lasted four years while the FCC wrestled with a host of difficult issues. Finally, in 1952, the commissioners made some critical decisions that have shaped television developments ever since.

1. They added 70 new channels in the UHF (ultra-high-frequency) band to the 12 VHF channels being used up to that time by television stations. This made possible many more television stations in all parts of the country.
2. They added an all-electronic color system as the standard that would be compatible with existing black and white receivers, thus facilitating and speeding the conversion of television to color.
3. They solved the problem of stations interfering with each other by increasing the geographic separation of stations that used the same channel.
4. They reserved channels for 242 stations distributed throughout the country for noncommercial, educational purposes.

It is important to recognize the implications of these decisions made by the FCC, just as it is important to recognize the implications of any decision by a government regulatory agency, even a decision not to regulate something. The decisions concerning color meant that RCA would make more money and CBS would make less, since the standards adopted were those RCA developed. The CBS color system was rejected. Adding UHF channels meant more competition for the VHF commercial channels—competition for viewers and for advertising dollars. The addition of those extra channels also made the reservation of 242 station licenses for educational purposes politically feasible. If the additional 70 UHF channels had not been made available, commercial interests would probably have killed the chances for educational reservations, because the pressure of individuals and corporations wanting to start new commercial stations during this period was quite intense. It took still another FCC ruling in 1962 to make UHF economically viable. That year the FCC began requiring that all new television receivers have UHF as well as VHF capacity.

Another important, although indirect, implication of these decisions by the Federal Communications Commission is that no matter how much one might wish for or advocate a totally free-enterprise system, such a system is impossible in a civilized society. Especially in matters related to broadcasting, the public interest, as well as commercial interests, demands a certain amount of orderly government regulation. Otherwise there is chaos, and everyone loses.

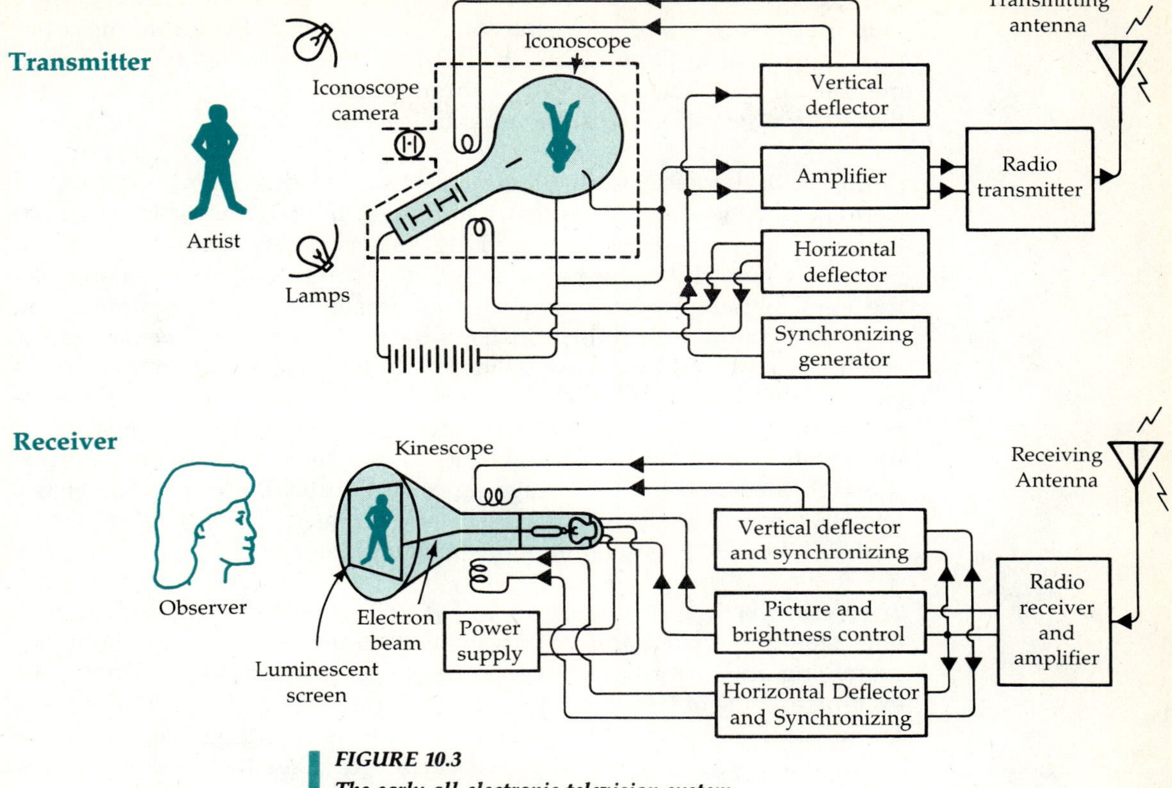

FIGURE 10.3
The early all-electronic television system.

BYLINE

Obviously not everyone agrees on the issue of government regulation. Where do you stand? How do you think technical standards for television, the expansion in the number of channels, and the development of noncommercial television stations could have occurred without government involvement?

By 1952, when the FCC made those decisions on UHF and color and reserved channels for education, 108 commercially licensed television stations were on the air, and national network service had begun. About 15 million homes were equipped with television receivers.

Within two years after the FCC decisions, the number of television stations in the country had more than tripled, and 122 of the new stations were on the UHF band. Three of the new stations were noncommercial.

The growth since then has not been as rapid, but it has been steady. More than fourteen hundred television stations are now on the air in this country, almost half of them UHF. About one-fourth of the total are noncommercial, educational, or "public" stations. This number far exceeds the 242 that were reserved for educational purposes in 1952.

Color. With the decision that the all electronic color system would be the standard for the American television system, the push for color began in earnest. The major pushers were NBC and its parent corporation, RCA, since they held the major patents on the electronic color system and had the most to gain. NBC mounted its first season of color programming in 1954–1955, but not until the mid-1960s did color television become generally accepted by all broadcasters and the public. The cost of television receivers and of converting local stations to color, coupled with the probable reluctance of ABC and CBS to promote color because it would contribute to the profits of NBC and RCA, slowed its development for a decade. Despite the high costs and the heel-dragging of ABC and CBS, by the late sixties television was virtually all color. Black-and-white (monochrome) television in the United States was little more than a memory.

The transition from live television to videotape. The other major change in television in the 1950s and 1960s was the decline of live entertainment programming and the general acceptance of film and videotape. One of the exciting aspects of television during the "Golden Era," from the late 1940s to the mid-1950s, was the fact that most of it was broadcast live. Viewers of variety shows and dramas were not surprised to see the shadow of a microphone boom move across the face of performers or to catch a quick glimpse of a stagehand out of place in a Shakespearean scene. Scripts were written and settings were designed to facilitate the quick movement of actors from one scene to another, often with a change of costume on the way. Some nostalgia buffs believe that much of the excitement of television was lost with the decline of live television.

Until the late 1950s, almost all of the major television programs were produced in New York. As the industry began prerecording the programs—both to reduce the probability of errors and to facilitate reruns, syndication to nonnetwork stations, and sales of programs overseas—the center of entertainment production shifted to Hollywood. No other city in the world had the facilities and the vast number of professionals skilled in the making of motion pictures, whether for theater showing or for showing on this upstart medium, television.

The move to Hollywood was hardly complete before the new videotape technology was sufficiently developed that it began to replace film. Videotape, introduced by the Ampex Corporation in 1956, had a number of advantages over film; for example, it combined most of the speed of live television production (at least if frequent retakes were unnecessary) with the editing and replay possibilities of film.

REVIEW

In order to increase the number of channels available for television, the Federal Communications Commission in 1952 authorized use of the UHF frequency band to complement the 12 channels in the VHF band. The commission reserved channels for 242 noncommercial stations and decided upon a color system compatible with black and white. The introduction of videotape in the 1950s brought an end to most live programming.

The transition from live television to film and videotaped television programming occurred in less than a decade. Between 1955 and 1970, the amount of live network programming declined from 87 to 15 percent. Today, news, sports, and other special events are virtually the only live programming on the networks. Most of the remainder is videotaped or shot on film.

Content Development: In the Mold of Radio

Except for its technological aspects, television's development in this country was totally different from that of any other medium. Every other medium required a long period of search or exploration to discover its role in the society and its mode of operation. When each medium first came along, no one was certain what it was suited for and how it could be operated best. This was not the case with television. Almost from its inception, it was fit into an existing mold, the mold shaped by radio.

Because television was developed and promoted primarily by companies that developed radio, it was conceived simply as radio with

Arthur Godfrey was one of the stars of radio who successfully made the transition to television. By 1952 he was hosting two popular television programs, "Arthur Godfrey's Friends" and "Talent Scouts."

pictures. Thus, the programming, the economic structure, and even the pattern of regulation, that existed for radio were adopted virtually without change for television. Not only did we get the same kinds of soap operas, variety shows, audience participation shows, situation comedies, news programs, police and detective series, westerns, sports and talk shows; we also got television versions of precisely the same programs in some cases. Television commercials were sold in the same way as radio commercials and were distributed between and within programs in the same way. Both the self-regulatory code of the National Association of Broadcasters and the governmental regulations of the Federal Communications Commission that were developed for radio were applied to television.

It probably seems natural to you that television was cast in radio's mold. It certainly seemed so to most of those who were involved in the visual medium during its developmental period because they worked for radio stations and networks. However, this was not the only way in which television could have been shaped. If it had been developed and nurtured by persons other than those involved in radio, it may have been conceived in different ways, thus becoming quite a different medium today.

BYLINE

Think of what television might be if it had been developed by magazine publishers, by some of the major Hollywood studios, or by some large newspaper chains. Or what if the government had decided the educational potential of television was too great to be turned over to the control of profit-seeking entrepreneurs? In each of these cases, how would television differ from what we have today?

You ought to think about the questions in the preceding *Byline* item, not because television is likely to change at this late date, but because it may help you see future communication developments in some new ways. As new media not yet even dreamed of come along, keep in mind this lesson of television. Assuming you are in any way involved in these new developments, as you may well be, remember: Any medium can be conceived of in a great variety of ways. Do not let yourself be stampeded into thinking about a medium in the same way everyone else does. Instead, see how great a variety of other ways you can find to conceive it and explore the implications of each of those conceptions. In this way you may discover far better ways to use each medium.

REVIEW

Most television programming followed the format of radio. Likewise, television commercials were sold in the same manner as radio commercials.

HOW TELEVISION GETS INTO OUR MOSAIC ENVIRONMENT

For an adequate understanding of why you encounter some types of material frequently, and other types rarely, if ever, on television, knowledge about the structure or organization of television in the United States is important. This knowledge is even more important if you want to work effectively at changing the mix or content in your mosaic.

The Structure of the U.S. Television Industry

The television system in this country has three primary components: local stations, networks, and cable systems. There are two major kinds of television stations, and networks: commercial and noncommercial. And we also should include as part of the television industry the rapidly growing field of industrial television, or corporate video communications.

Local stations. Theoretically, the local station is the heart of the American broadcasting system, as defined by the Communications Act of 1934. The part of broadcasting that is regulated is the local channel or frequency. The licensee—the individual or group that receives a license from the FCC—has the legal responsibility for everything coming out of the station's transmitter, whether originated locally or by a network. (The only exception to this legal responsibility is material from a bona fide political candidate. Stations are forbidden from censoring anything that a political candidate says. Hence, they are not legally responsible if a candidate says something libelous over the air.) In a sense, this notion of local licensee responsibility for everything broadcast is an anachronism in this era of network dominance, but it remains the law.

Most local commercial stations are affiliated with one of the national networks. Such network affiliation provides several advantages. The primary advantage is that a network provides the local stations with entertainment programming, news, and public affairs programs, which attract a larger audience than local programs would do, and which no local station could afford on its own. For example, no local stations could afford a news bureau in Washington with two hundred to three hundred fifty staff members like the one each network maintains.

Only about 5 to 10 percent of the programming on the average network-affiliated commercial station is locally produced. About 65 percent of the programs come from the network, and between 25 and 30 percent come from *independent program suppliers* called **syndicators.** Even these syndicated programs are often programs that were formerly on a network, such as "M*A*S*H," "Happy Days," "Miami Vice," and "Dukes of Hazzard." Many of the old movies that you see on television also come to stations through syndication. The local station fully controls the content of only that 5 to 10 percent that it produces. However, as indicated before, the station licensee is also legally responsible for all the rest.

The local station benefits from its network affiliation generally because the network programs attract larger audiences to the station. Therefore, the station can charge more for the programs and commercials that it sells locally and to national spot advertisers who buy time on individual stations. In addition, the local stations get some income from carrying the network-produced programs.

Each station that is part of a national commercial network has an affiliation contract, unless it is an "O & O" station—one owned and operated by the network. This contract assures both the network and the station of certain benefits:

1. The network is assured that the station will carry most network programs at certain times if the network wants it to do so. The network needs this "option time" from its affiliates so it can promise an advertiser that a program and its commercials will be seen on a particular number of stations and in the markets the advertiser wants.
2. Stations are assured that they will get a certain percentage of their standard charge (their rate card) for time devoted to most sponsored network programs or commercials. That amount is generally about 30 percent of what they would get if they sold the time locally for one of their own programs. For programs such as sports, news, and late-night programs like "The Tonight Show," instead of getting payment from the network, a station might be given a certain number of advertising slots within each program that it can sell for commercials. The station thus keeps all income produced during its slots, while the network keeps all income from the advertising it sells for its slots. In addition, the networks do not share the income they derive from the first 24 hours of prime-time programming an affiliate carries each month. Presumably, in this way affiliates pay their share of the networks' overhead costs.

Networks. As you probably know, five national, television networks serve over-the-air broadcasters in this country: ABC (American Broadcasting Company), NBC (National Broadcasting Company), CBS (Columbia Broadcasting System), PBS (the noncommercial Public Broadcasting Service), and Fox Broadcasting Company, the newest network which broadcasts about twenty hours of programming a week to 132 affiliates. In conjunction with production companies, these networks produce or cause to be produced most of the programming transmitted in prime time (7:30 P.M. to 11:00 P.M. on the coasts, 6:30 P.M. to 10:00 P.M. in the Midwest.) This is the time during which television normally has its largest audiences.

The networks spend vast sums of money developing new programs, considering program ideas others bring to them, and financing pilot programs developed by other producers.

Most of the entertainment programs—programs other than news, sports, and public affairs—come from independent production companies. NBC reports that in a normal year it has agreements with about fifty different suppliers of programs.

The selection of the programs that get on the air is a long and expensive process. In one season, for example, NBC reported that it considered more than one hundred fifty actual scripts. It financed the production of 37 pilot or test programs; from that process, it ultimately selected 9 new series to be presented in prime time.

In much the same way that ABC struggled to gain parity with the older networks NBC and CBS, Fox has battled the big three commercial networks with innovative programming and aggressive marketing. Since its debut in 1986, Fox has steadily increased its market share and number of affiliates. A part of the Rupert Murdoch media empire, which includes the 20th Century Fox production company, Fox gave NBC quite a scare at the beginning of the 1990 season when its first original episode of "The Simpsons" finished only one-tenth of a rating point behind the first new episode of its head-on competition, "The Cosby Show." The 18.4 rating—the percent of the audience tuned to "The Simpsons"—was the best ever for the animated cartoon, and the 29 share—the percent of the viewing audience tuned to the program— was the highest ever for a Fox series. These figures are even more remarkable in that Fox has far fewer affiliates than NBC, most of them independent stations on UHF channels. While most of its prime-time programs still finish last in the ratings, two other Fox series that have fared well in ratings competition are "Married . . . With Children" and "In Living Color." To expand its potential audience, Fox recently signed an agreement with Tele-Communications, Inc., to furnish programming to cable systems located in areas that did not have a Fox outlet, thereby making cable systems network affiliates. Fox soon plans to increase its prime-time programming from five to six nights a week and to launch an hour-long national newscast.

Each commercial network today, or any other company, can own 12 television stations, so long as the total coverage area does not include more than 25 percent of the population of the country. (Each can also own 12 AM and 12 FM radio stations.)

The Federal Communications Commission cannot regulate networks directly, even though the networks control most television programming. Networks require no government license as stations do. The FCC can regulate them only indirectly, through regulation of their affiliates and the stations they own themselves (O and O stations). For example, when the FCC wanted to ensure more local programming in prime time, it could not force the networks to stop sending programs to affiliates at every time period during the evening, nor could it force the networks to stop asking their affiliates to provide network clearance for all of the time periods. It could and did, however, insist that each local station, including the O

Though it has consistently rated second in head to head competition with "The Cosby Show," "The Simpsons" has been Fox Broadcasting's highest-rated program.

and O stations of the networks, do some nonnetwork programming each evening during prime time.

BYLINE

Someone has argued that since the networks do a much better job than local stations of producing programs, we ought to license networks and give them control and responsibility, rather than vesting legal responsibility in the local licensees. Do you agree? Why? What are some advantages and disadvantages of the present system?

Network programs sent to over-the-air broadcasting stations are distributed in various ways:

1. *Coaxial cable.* Coaxial cable is similar to a telephone line, except that it can carry far more electronic information at one time. This is necessary for the transmission of video signals.

2. *Microwave relays.* In this system of relaying network programs, the broadcast signals are transmitted from one microwave relay tower to another, hopscotching across the country, at frequencies ordinary television receivers cannot pick up.
3. *Communication satellites.* Each communication satellite circles in a relatively steady position above the earth at such a height that it can pick up signals on special frequencies from a large region and beam them back. For example, one satellite can pick up signals from and send signals to all parts of the United States. In fact, those signals can be picked up and sent from a single satellite to an area far larger than just this country.

Cable systems. The third element in the American television industry is cable. The cable industry began in a few communities that had no local television stations and, because of their geography or distance from towns with stations, could not receive television signals very well. Some entrepreneur would find a high hill near town and install on it a very tall antenna that could receive distant television signals. These signals were amplified and then piped by telephone cable to each home whose inhabitants were willing to pay a monthly fee. These were called Community Antenna Television Systems, or CATV. Unlike over-the-air television, which came into the home by way of an antenna, cable television came by way of wire—much like the telephone. From these rather humble beginnings a multi-billion-dollar cable industry arose.

Cable systems are no longer primarily for communities that do not have their own stations. Because of their ability to provide many different channels through a single wire, the better quality of color most homes get with cable, and the availability of a wide variety of programming to fill those channels, cable systems have emerged as a major television industry, one that rivals over-the-air broadcasting. At present, there are some 50 million subscribers to cable television, and that figure is likely to grow as the number of homes receiving cable increases from the current 56 percent. Cable networks—that is, networks created to provide programming to cable systems—are almost as well known as the older commercial networks. Some of the more popular cable networks are CNN, ESPN, MTV, HBO, and QVC.

Cable has one indisputable advantage over traditional over-the-air broadcasting stations: it is many "stations" rolled into one—including the over-the-air stations. So long as the viewer watches any one cable channel, he or she is part of the cable audience. But the over-the-air broadcaster has only one channel to program—one chance to capture an audience at any particular time. The cable operator, by contrast, can offer at any one moment news, comedy, music video, weather, shopping information, religious programming, programming for children—an array of services restricted only by the number of channels in the system.

The CNN Headline News television control room in Atlanta, Georgia.

Whereas commercial broadcasters are often reluctant to devote time to public affairs programs—programs that fulfill their public interest obligation but generate little in the way of revenue—cable operators can afford to devote entire channels to public affairs. They can even afford to offer public-access channels—channels available to all the people in the community who think they have something worth transmitting.

It is not uncommon for a company to lease a channel from a cable system and then sell the time to local advertisers who use the company's facilities to produce their own programs—a practice reminiscent of the early days of radio. Many of these low-budget programs allow the viewers to phone in questions. A typical evening's fare might consist of advice from a local garden shop, discussion of legal matters by a local attorney, or health tips from a local physician. Despite their lack of sophistication, programs of this nature have proved valuable to their sponsors, who generate "goodwill" for their products or services. And they have enabled the cable operator to serve the local community—even better perhaps than the over-the-air broadcaster whose air time is filled mainly with network programming.

Congress has expressed concern over the increasing concentration of ownership in the cable industry. Unlike television stations, there is no limit on the number of cable systems one company can own. A 1988 study showed that four companies accounted for roughly 27 percent of the cable audience and that the top 25 companies accounted for 68 percent of the audience. (Table 10.1 shows the 20 largest cable networks.)

TABLE 10.1 Top 20 Cable Networks: Ranked by Number of Subscribers

Network	*Number of Subscribers (in millions)*
1. ESPN	57.0
2. CNN (Cable News Network)	56.5
3. TBS SUPERSTATION	55.2
4. USA NETWORK	53.8
5. NICKELODEON/NICK AT NITE	52.9
5. MTV (Music Television)	52.9
7. THE DISCOVERY CHANNEL	52.7
8. THE FAMILY CHANNEL	51.7
9. TNN	51.0
10. C-SPAN	50.6
11. TNT (Turner Network Television)	50.4
12. LIFETIME	50.0
13. A&E CABLE NETWORK	48.0
14. THE WEATHER CHANNEL	46.0
15. HEADLINE NEWS	44.4
16. VH-1 (Video Hits One)	37.5
17. QVC NETWORK	35.2
18. FNN (Financial News Network)	35.0
19. WGN	33.0
20. BET (Black Entertainment Television)	29.1

Source: National Cable Television Association, *Cable Television Developments,* March 1991. Reprinted courtesy of the National Cable Television Association.

The manner and extent of cable regulation has been a matter of controversy since the medium's initial development. Through most of its history it has been regulated both by the FCC and the local governments that granted charters for operation. In a few cases, there was also some state regulation. Just as the federal government has reduced its regulation of broadcasting in recent years, it has reduced its regulation of cable. Perhaps more important, it has also reduced the power of local governments to regulate. The Cable Communications Policy Act of 1984, passed by Congress and signed by the president, freed cable system owners of almost all local regulation, including the regulation of rates. To no one's surprise, cable rates have increased steadily since that time. The General Accounting Office reported that between 1986 and 1988 rates increased more than 25 percent.

In 1985, the Federal Court of Appeals struck down the "must carry rule," an FCC rule that required cable operators to carry the signals of local television stations. Although the principal trade organizations of the cable and broadcasting industries seem to have reached a compromise on the "must carry" policy, there is still concern on the part of over-the-air broadcasters—particularly UHF broadcasters—that their stations will not be

REVIEW

Local stations, networks, and cable systems are the primary means by which television programming is delivered to the home in this country. Most local stations are affiliated with a network, which supplies much of a station's programming. The major networks are ABC, NBC, CBS, PBS, and Fox. Cable systems offer local channels—including the network affiliates in the area—and many additional channels. Currently, there is heated competition between cable and over-the-air broadcasting.

carried on the best (lowest) cable channels. For example, a cable system in Janesville, Wisconsin, announced that it was reassigning four local channels from nearby Rockford, Illinois to Channels 39 to 42. This decision infuriated broadcasters because it relegated local stations to channels that would require a converter to receive. Broadcasters demand not only that cable systems carry the over-the-air stations in their area; they want them carried on Channels 2 to 13, the VHF channels viewers most frequently use.

The fight between cable systems and over-the-air broadcasters is not likely to end soon. Both are in hot competition for viewers. At present, cable seems to be winning the battle. A 1989 Roper poll commissioned by the Television Information Office concluded that the public perceives cable as having better program quality, better children's programs, more educational programs, better entertainment, greater variety, more culture, and more sports. The only bit of good news for over-the-air broadcasters was in news programming. The public thought regular television broadcasters had the edge in this category.

Public broadcasting. As we discussed earlier, in 1952, the Federal Communications Commission produced a revolutionary plan for the development of noncommercial broadcasting in this country. As a result of this plan, 242 television channels were reserved solely for noncommercial licensees—educational institutions, cities and states, and other nonprofit groups that would agree to operate the stations on a noncommercial basis for the best interests of the total community.

Educational and other noncommercial radio stations and a few noncommercial television stations had existed before this, but institutions or organizations wanting to start such stations always had to compete with commercial companies for frequencies and channels. In addition, there were (and continue to be) some educational or nonprofit institutions running commercial television or radio stations, such as Iowa State University and the University of Florida.

After the FCC reserved channels for public broadcasting stations, Congress set aside money that could be awarded to institutions or groups to help them get their stations on the air or improve their facilities. This legislation was the ETV Facilities Act of 1962.

In 1967, Congress passed the Public Broadcasting Act which created the Corporation for Public Broadcasting (CPB) and authorized funds for its operation. The CPB, in turn, created the present network of public broadcasting stations. The CPB also promoted, supported, and helped raise the quality of public broadcasting programs now on the air.

There are now four major types of public television stations:

1. Those owned and operated by colleges or universities, such as the stations at the Universities of Houston, Wisconsin, and Southern Illinois.

2. Noncommercial stations owned and operated by school systems, common throughout the country.
3. Those owned and operated by state or municipal authorities. Generally the licensee is a state agency that has responsibility for a group of stations, as in Georgia, New Jersey, and Iowa. In New York City, the city government owns and operates a television station.
4. Public television stations developed and operated by nonprofit corporations organized specifically for that purpose. Among the best of these stations are the ones in San Francisco, Boston, New York, and Chicago.

Getting adequate operating funds is a constant problem for most noncommercial stations. In addition to funds from the federal government, some stations obtain funds from the general tax revenues of a city or state, from gifts of individuals and foundations, and from selling time and services to public school systems and other agencies. Some school systems, for example, pay a certain amount to a public station for every child in the system in exchange for the station carrying educational programs designed for in-school use. One of the more controversial forms of financing for public television stations is the underwriting of programs by large corporations. Critics charge that the on-the-air credits given to the underwriters are the same as advertising and hence should not be permitted on a noncommercial station. More serious is the fear of some that such underwriting will give these corporations the same power to influence programming on public television that they have over commercial television.

Another hotly debated issue concerning noncommercial television is whether public stations and the public broadcasting network should pursue as large an audience as possible. Those opposed to such a pursuit believe the purpose of public broadcasting should be to serve specialized audiences with material not available on commercial television. They reason that anything that attracts a mass audience will ultimately find its way onto commercial television. Those on the other side argue that they have a responsibility to bring the benefits of public television to as many people as possible.

A third issue, argued primarily within the public broadcasting fraternity, is how control of programming of public stations should be distributed between the national network and the local management. Until recently, stations pooled their programming funds and bid on the programs they wanted PBS to carry. This was known as the Station Program Cooperative. But under a new National Program Plan, the network gained responsibility for the vast majority of programming decisions.

Corporate television. When most of us think about television today we generally think of stations or networks or cable systems. However, there is another, quite different sort of television, one responsible for an increasing portion of the communication mosaics of many people and for an even larger portion of jobs in the television field. According to statistics issued by the U.S. Department of Labor, roughly one hundred ninety-three thousand people in this country make their living in broadcast television; two hundred thirty-five thousand people make their living in nonbroadcast television—in good part, corporate television or video. Another sign of the growing importance of corporate television is the fact that the major growth in sales of professional video equipment in the past decade was in the industrial/business/institutional market, not in the broadcast market.

REVIEW

The ETV Facilities Act of 1962 and the Public Broadcasting Act of 1967 provided funds for noncommercial stations. Funding is a constant problem for noncommercial stations, which provide an alternative to commercial programming and attract a much smaller audience. A wholly different form of television is nonbroadcast in nature. Corporate television provides a variety of programming for industries and organizations.

Major companies throughout the country employ not only video production people but audio, film, and photographic personnel as well. Such professionals are also employed in government agencies, the armed forces, large hospitals, and a variety of other organizations concerned about communicating effectively with their employees, clients, or customers.

These various industries and organizations are producing nonbroadcast television or video to train and motivate employees and to keep their skills and knowledge up to date; to communicate with employees scattered across the country or across the world; to communicate with customers or clients when it is impractical to use broadcast television; and to pass on specialized news to employees. These productions are generally distributed on videotape for playback at a time and place convenient to the recipient, although sometimes a closed-circuit television system within an organization is used. Production facilities in these organizations range from a small consumer-model camera/recorder and editing system to

Satellite communication makes teleconferencing a convenient way to conduct meetings. Many corporations and institutions find that the teleconference saves travel expenses and time.

highly sophisticated television studios complete with the latest color cameras, editing systems, and associated closed circuit systems for distributing live or videotaped materials throughout a plant.

> **BYLINE**
>
> In what ways do you suppose producing materials for corporate television is similar to producing materials for broadcast television? In what ways is it different? Why?

Who Should Determine What Is Put on the Air?

The question of who has the power to determine content is one of the major questions about television in this country—perhaps the major question. And it is far broader than the current debate among broadcasters suggests. Not only is there disagreement over who ought to have the major say—or any say—in deciding what programs to put on the air; there is disagreement about who ought to have a say in deciding the kinds of subjects that are included in or excluded from those programs. In addition, there is disagreement about the criteria that should be used in making those decisions about content.

At least seven possible groups or producers could govern what gets on the air:

1. Open access—Whoever wants to put a program on the air could be given free time.
2. Modified open access—Whoever wants to put a program on the air could be assured the right to buy time for it.
3. The government
4. Some other body appointed by the government or elected by the public at large
5. The station or cable system operators
6. The networks
7. The advertisers

The two open-access systems are impractical given our present technology, although they may become practical in the future as cable operators continue to increase their channel capacity. In the system of broadcasting that currently predominates in this and other countries, some individual or group of individuals must be the final arbiter for any particular channel, deciding what will be transmitted. In this country, a number of these groups share control for our commercial television system, with the general public indirectly holding a great deal of programming power.

The role of programming personnel. In one sense, network and local station programmers have the major say about what will and will not be transmitted. Their dominant criterion is generally what most people will watch, or at least most of the kinds of people who are potential purchasers of advertised products. The reason for this is obvious: station and network programmers want to maximize profits, and the way to maximize profits in broadcasting generally is to get the largest possible audience and to keep it. Advertisers will then want their commercials on that station or network and will be willing to pay large prices for that privilege. Thus, every time you turn the television set on or change channels, you are voting on the kinds of programs you want on the air. If enough people vote the way you do, that behavior will influence the ratings, and your "vote" will be heard. In a sense, it is a highly democratic system; the majority rules. However, it is not perfectly democratic. As indicated elsewhere, if you are between the ages of 20 and 55 and are in a sufficiently high socioeconomic class, your vote carries more weight.

Another important determinant of what gets on the air is the program producer or the person with program ideas. It is impossible for station and network personnel to produce most of the programs they carry, and even if they could, they would not have enough ideas for that many programs. All they can do most of the time is to select from among what other individuals and companies make available. Nothing can get on the air until someone conceives of it as a television program. That seems obvious, but it is a point too often ignored by critics of television. Many people criticize what is on the air; few have ideas for practical alternatives.

Limitations of a free-market system of programming. What we have been describing is a free-enterprise system, a system that makes maximum use of the skill and imagination and hard work of American business people, fighting to give the majority of citizens what they want. At first glance, this seems an ideal system. Why should anyone be unhappy with it?

The principal reason why some people are unhappy with this system is that it does not work as neatly as our description has suggested. First, it is not totally a free-enterprise system; secondly, the system does not serve audiences with minority interests and tastes nearly as well as it serves the majority audience.

It is not entirely a free enterprise system because not everyone who wishes to start a television station, or even a cable system or channel, can do so. Far more individuals or groups want a station than there are channels available in the portion of the spectrum set aside for regular television. Hence, competition is reduced; in many markets only a few stations are vying for audience attention.

The second problem may be more serious. Because the economic situation motivates stations and networks to try for the largest possible audiences almost all of the time, individuals who want information or entertainment of the sort that does not interest a very large number of other people tend to go unsatisfied. For example, you may like a type of music or drama or information that vast numbers of other people do not like. Because the audience for such programs is so small, it is not profitable for a station to broadcast them. The national networks are generally not interested in a program that can attract only 10 or 20 million people. This is an important reason for government regulation—to force stations to provide some service for those whose interests are not shared by the majority. This is also an important reason for an alternative broadcasting system, a public or noncommercial system that is guided by criteria other than popularity so that it provides alternatives to programs aimed at the majority audience.

Distrust of the Dominant Audience Role in Determining Content

The alternative broadcasting system and the limited government regulation that we have in this country do not satisfy all of the critics of American broadcasting. Some are unhappy not only with the important role played by commercial interests in determining programs and program content, but also with the important role played by the majority audience. These critics do not believe the majority of the audience should have so much say about what programs are on the air. They use two primary arguments to support that belief. First, they claim that if the public has free choice, most people will select only programs they are familiar with and can easily appreciate. These critics believe audiences must occasionally be put in a position in which they have little choice but to view other sorts of programs so they will learn to appreciate them. In this view, learning to appreciate more complex forms of entertainment ("high" art) and information (such as documentaries or more detailed news programs) takes time and experience. Taste for such programs does not come naturally; it is acquired. Such critics say that if the audience has a free choice it will continue to avoid "good" programs and so will never acquire that taste.

REVIEW

There is much debate over who should control the content of television programming. Our commercial system is such that, for the most part, audience size dictates the type of programming likely to air, although critics charge that giving the public what it wants reduces the chances for quality programming and limits the audience's choices.

The second argument against giving the public what it wants is the elitist argument that the public simply does not know what is good for it. Interestingly, this argument comes from not only the traditional elitists, those who turn up their noses at the "common folks" and "common tastes," but also from many of those who claim to be fighting for these common folks. Many leaders of the political left believe the media must primarily serve social and political ends. They also believe they know better than the masses what content and style will serve those ends. (Keep in mind, though, that these arguments have been greatly simplified here.)

These issues are presented to you because you will be confronted with them again and again as America debates the future of our system of mass communication. By familiarizing yourself both with the issues and the arguments on various sides, you can determine where you stand and thus be in a position to fight for your point of view.

BYLINE

Consider the popular program "Roseanne." Does it appeal primarily to "common folks" with "common tastes"? What is the reason for your answer? Does the program serve any other purpose than to entertain? If not, should it? What are the values emphasized in "Roseanne"? Are they similar to those of your family and friends?

The Role of the Network in Determining Content

As television developed in the 1950s, 1960s, and 1970s, a major change from the pattern of broadcasting set by radio was the shift in control of prime-time programs from the advertiser and advertising agency to the networks.

The shift in program control from advertiser to network. Initially, television followed the radio pattern of having each program sponsored and largely controlled by a single advertiser. As television became more expensive, however, few advertisers could cover all the costs of a program. In addition, as television became more competitive, networks wanted greater control of both the scheduling and content of programs so they could compete more effectively. They recognized that they needed to be concerned with more than simply the content of each program; they had to plan each entire evening as a package, since each program on a network affects the audience for the program that follows. Further, each network generally wanted the entire schedule for any given evening to attract and hold a particular kind of audience, one that would be lucrative to sell to advertisers. Because of these concerns, networks sometimes refused to carry certain programs, even though a sponsor wanted them, because they did not attract a large enough audience or the right kind of audience. Broadcasters wanted audiences in the 20-to-40 age bracket primarily, audiences of those individuals who are upwardly mobile and, therefore, more frequent purchasers of most products. In the early 1970s, CBS dropped several of its most popular programs—"Beverly Hillbillies," "Green Acres," and "Petticoat Junction"—because they were attracting too many older, rural viewers—those with less purchasing power.

Programming a network became an art, and to practice the art properly required total control. For example, in the mid-1970s, when the ABC television network first began challenging seriously the dominance of NBC and CBS for the prime-time audience, it made major gains for the entire week with just five popular programs. It built its entire schedule around these programs, broadcasting one of them each weeknight at 7:00 P.M. central time. The plan, as the network's president put it, was to "control the center," with those five programs strung across the center of the weekday evenings like a fishing net. Those programs caught a sizable portion of the audience and held them for the rest of the evening. Devising strategies of this sort to attract attention and to counter the strategies of the other networks has become a highly refined art, and programming executives with talent for this art are eagerly sought.

Networks wanted and got not only more control of programming, but also a share of the ownership of most series they broadcast, no matter who had developed and produced them. The reason for this was that the networks wanted to protect their investments and ensure greater profits. Putting a new series on the air entailed certain risks and considerable costs. Ample promotion was needed to increase the probability of success. Each failed series reduced the audience for the programs that followed. The risks were more acceptable if the potential for profit was greater. By sharing ownership, a network got that greater potential for profit. With a share of ownership came a share of the profit from the network rerun rights for successful programs, syndication of a series to other stations after its network run was completed, and sales to stations and networks in other countries.

These practices were so profitable that by 1968 the networks were sharing this way in the control and profits of over 80 percent of the prime-time programs they broadcast, even though those programs ostensibly were made by "independent" producers. An additional 16 percent were produced directly by the network. This left only slightly over 3 percent being produced by totally independent producers.

BYLINE

Where do you stand on the issue of who determines programs and program content? Should broadcasters be forced to program some material for people with minority tastes, even though the audience will be relatively small? Should broadcasters be pressured to program some material that might expand or extend your taste and ours, rather than just programming material that most of us already like?

Reducing the Power of the Networks

The Federal Communications Commission feared that these network practices were reducing competition and hence limiting the diversity of programming. Therefore, in 1970, the FCC passed the **Financial Interest and Syndication Rules**—*rules prohibiting the networks from acquiring partial ownership or syndication rights of programs created by independent producers.*[1] They could buy rights only for network showing. In addition, the antitrust division of the U.S. Justice Department reduced network control further by forcing the major commercial networks to limit the production of their own prime-time entertainment programming to a maximum of two and one-half hours per week. Since that time, the networks have pressed hard for relaxation of the Financial Interest and Syndication Rules—and for a very good reason. When the FCC adopted the rules, the three major commercial networks accounted for 90 percent of the television audience and were practically the sole buyers of programming. Today the networks hold only 60 percent of the audience, and programs are purchased by scores of cable systems and independent stations, and by the networks' newest rival, Fox Broadcasting.

REVIEW

At one time, advertisers exerted a great deal of influence over programming, but gradually the networks gained control. Today, much of a station's programming—especially prime-time programming—is determined by the networks. To reduce the power of networks, the FCC passed the Financial Interest and Syndication Rules prohibiting them from retaining rights to independently produced programs. The Justice Department further restricted network control by limiting the number of prime-time programs they could produce. In 1991, the FCC modified the rerun rules so that networks could acquire financial rights to some syndicated programs. Because of competition among networks, cable stations, and local stations, the rights to certain types of programming—such as sports—have increased substantially.

The major opposition to changing the so-called "fin-syn" rules has been the movie industry, which until recently lobbied successfully to maintain its stake in the syndication market, a market expected to grow to $10.6 billion by 1995. In the early 1990s, the eight largest motion picture studios controlled 63 percent of the domestic syndication market and 80 percent of the overseas market and supplied more than 70 percent of the network programs aired in prime time. Instead of promoting competition, the Financial Interest and Syndication Rules appeared to do nothing more than shift control from the networks to the major Hollywood studios. This change in the marketplace—along with a change in the ownership of the studios, four of which had fallen into foreign hands—prompted the FCC to repeal a portion of the rules. In a 1991 decision that seemed to please no one, the FCC voted 3 to 2 to allow the networks to acquire foreign syndication rights to programs they air and to syndicate domestically programs they produce in-house. But it limited the number of in-house productions to 40 percent of the prime-time schedule and placed restrictions on the manner in which foreign syndication could be carried out. The FCC exempted Fox from any restrictions on syndication until it exceeds 15 hours of prime-time programming a week. The new rulings fall short of the total repeal the networks had hoped for and are likely to be tested in federal court by the networks and the Hollywood studios.

Network competition. Perhaps partly because of this battle over sources of entertainment programming, some of the competition among networks shifted to sports, news, and public affairs programming in the past few years. Consequently, the price of rights to broadcast sports events and the salaries and other expenditures for news and public affairs rose dramatically. In 1989, CBS, ABC, NBC, and ESPN paid some $531 million dollars for the rights to carry National Football League games. What worries traditional networks and over-the-air broadcasters is the increasing number of sporting events that are being sold to cable networks.

Competition among stations and networks in covering the news was once based on the assumption that having outstanding news programs added to one's prestige. This is still an important motivator, but to it has been added a second motivator: the profitability of news and public affairs programs for the network and local station. Not only are news programs drawing large audiences; they are drawing audiences composed largely of mature viewers with above-average expendable incomes.

Self-Regulation of Television

For many years the television industry had a formal system of self-regulation, just as most other major mass communication industries do. The main element in that system was the Television Code of the National Association of Broadcasters. The code stressed in general terms the responsibilities of television broadcasters, set general standards on various types of content, and limited the amount of advertising that should be permitted during any given hour. Each network also has its own code.

Here is a sample of the NAB Code's guidelines:

> *Programs should contribute to the sound, balanced development of children to help them achieve a sense of the world at large and informed adjustments to their society . . . the use of violence for its own sake and the detailed dwelling upon brutality or physical agony, by sight or by sound, are not permissible . . .*
>
> *Special sensitivity is necessary in the use of material relating to sex, race, color, age, creed, religious functionaries or rites, or national or ethnic derivation . . .*
>
> *News reporting should be factual, fair and without bias . . .*
>
> *Commentary and analysis should be clearly identified as such . . .*
>
> *The use of liquor and the depiction of smoking in program content should be de-emphasized. When shown, they should be consistent with plot and character development . . .*
>
> *In prime time on network affiliated stations, non-program material [which means primarily commercials] should not exceed nine minutes 30 seconds in any 60-minute period . . . In all other time, non-program material shall not exceed 16 minutes in any 60-minute period. [Within] Children's Programming Time . . . on Saturday and Sunday, non-program material shall not exceed nine minutes 30 seconds in any 60-minute period . . .*
>
> *In prime time, the number of program interruptions shall not exceed two within any 30-minute program, or four within any 60-minute program . . . In all other times, the number of interruptions shall not exceed four within any 30-minute program period.*

BYLINE

Do the NAB Code's guidelines seem reasonable? Would you change any of these specific regulations? If so, how? From your observations of television, are the networks and stations keeping within these guidelines?

Although you might argue with a few specific points in the code, you probably agree with most of them. The same is true of almost all viewers. Nevertheless, the National Association of Broadcasters has dropped the code, and for a surprising reason: not because broadcasters were unhappy with it, but because the federal government attacked it!

The attack was instigated by a group of advertisers who charged that the agreement among broadcasters to limit commercial advertising illegally restrained trade. As a result, the Justice Department filed suit against the NAB in 1979, charging it to be in violation of antitrust laws. It cited three provisions of the code in the suit: its limit on the number of products or services that could be advertised in a single short commercial, its limit on the amount of time that could be devoted to commercials during any one hour, and its limit on the number of times programs could be interrupted for commercials. The Justice Department said, in effect, that these provisions were analogous to an agreement among the major manufacturers of automobiles or other products to limit production in order to keep prices high, instead of permitting competition to bring about lower prices.

In March 1982, the district court in Washington, D.C., ordered the NAB to stop enforcing the first of those provisions until further notice and said the entire suit would be settled by trial. Instead of fighting that order or going to trial, the broadcasters' organization decided to simply drop the code. As a result, there is no national self-regulatory code for entertainment programs or commercials on television today. The absence of such a code, however, has had little, if any, effect on what you see on television. This is partly because the networks and most of the major stations have their own codes and, more important, because broadcasters do not want to alienate their audiences. That concern has always been a more effective constraint on the industry than any code has been.

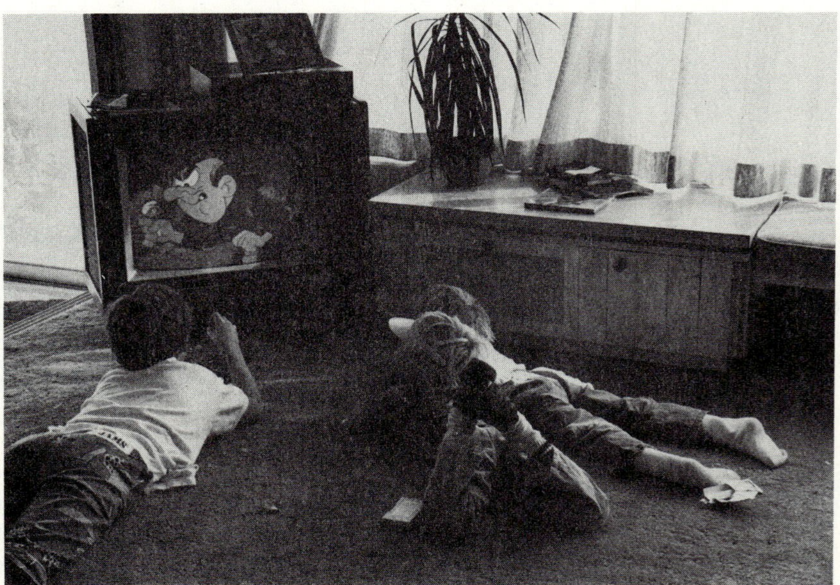

In 1990 Congress passed the Children's Television Act which limits the number of minutes of commercials in programs targeted to children under 12 years old. It also requires licensees to air programs specifically designed to serve the education and information needs of children aged 16 and under.

REVIEW

For many years, the self-regulatory code of the National Association of Broadcasters provided guidelines for television content. But in 1979, the Justice Department charged that the NAB code violated antitrust laws, and the court agreed.

One exception has been in the area of children's programming. For years, citizens' groups such as Action for Children's Television have been pressing commercial broadcasters—with little success—to provide more programming for children and to reduce the number of advertisements in programs aimed at children. These groups claimed that broadcasters largely ignored the guidelines of the NAB Code. In 1990, Congress responded by passing legislation limiting the number of minutes of commercials in each hour of children's programs to 12 hours during the week and 10.5 hours on the weekends. The law also imposed specific programming responsibility on each station and directed the FCC to enact rules regarding toy-based children's shows that might be considered program-length commercials.

Government Regulation of Television

The descriptions of the provisions and activities of the Federal Communications Commission in Chapter 9 are as applicable to television as they are to radio. In fact, they are somewhat more applicable to television. Because of the large number and variety of radio stations that exist in this country today, and because there seems to be less public concern with what they do, the FCC has considerably eased its regulation of radio. To date, however, it has eased its regulation of television only slightly.

REVIEW

The FCC has abolished the Fairness Doctrine and has asked Congress to repeal the Equal Opportunity Provision.

One move to deregulate broadcasting was the decision by the FCC to abolish the Fairness Doctrine. Another was the vote by the FCC to ask Congress to repeal the **Equal Opportunity Provision,** which *requires that a station that gives or sells time to one political candidate must give or sell time under the same conditions to all other bona fide candidates for that office.* Congress has yet to act on the latter proposal, and as we said in the previous chapter, it has threatened to reenact the Fairness Doctrine.

Ratings as Regulators of Television

One effect of television's concern with audience size has been the growing importance of television ratings and other forms of audience research. These, too, have been damned by the critics who believe that excessive concern with attracting and pleasing the audience has hurt the quality of television.

Ratings are estimates of the size of the audience for programs based on information about the viewing of a small sample of that audience. In the industry jargon, a **rating** is *the percentage of all television households (households with television sets) tuned to a program or channel at a particular time.* A **share** is *the percentage of sets in use (households with television sets turned on) tuned to a program or channel during a given time period.*

Ratings are not a new invention. Most of the major methods of obtaining information for ratings were developed for radio, prior to the development of television. These methods have been continuously refined and are generally surprisingly accurate, especially for relatively popular programs.

Nielsen NATIONAL TV AUDIENCE ESTIMATES — EVE. THU. MAY 23, 1991

TIME	7:00	7:15	7:30	7:45	8:00	8:15	8:30	8:45	9:00	9:15	9:30	9:45	10:00	10:15	10:30	10:45		
HUT	43.5	44.3	44.9	46.8	49.1	51.4	52.5	53.9	55.1	56.9	56.7	56.7	54.7	53.7	51.9	49.3		
ABC TV					←FATHER DOWLING MYSTERIES (R)→				MY LIFE AND TIMES		MY LIFE AND TIMES SPCL (PAE)		←PRIMETIME LIVE→					
HHLD AUDIENCE % & (000)					6.9	6,420			5.4	5,030	5.2	4,840	10.5	9,780				
TA%, AVG. AUD. 1/2 HR %					*9.3*	6.7*		7.0*	*6.5*		*6.2*		*16.2*	10.9*		10.2*		
SHARE AUDIENCE %					13	13*		13*	10		9		20	20*		20*		
AVG. AUD BY 1/4 HR %					6.8	6.6	7.0	7.0	5.4	5.3	5.1	5.3	10.6	11.1	10.4	10.1		
CBS TV					←TOP COPS (R)→				←ANTAGONISTS→				←AFI SALUTE: KIRK DOUGLAS→					
HHLD AUDIENCE % & (000)					7.5	6,980			7.6	7,080			7.0	6,520				
TA%, AVG. AUD. 1/2 HR %					*11.4*	6.8*		8.2*	*10.4*	7.3*		7.9*	*10.8*	7.0*		7.1*		
SHARE AUDIENCE %					15	14*		15*	13	13*		14*	13	13*		14*		
AVG. AUD BY 1/4 HR %					6.6	7.0	8.1	8.3	7.3	7.4	7.7	8.2	7.0	6.9	7.1	7.1		
NBC TV					BILL COSBY SHOW (R)		A DIFFERENT WORLD (R)		CHEERS (R)		SEINFELD		←L.A. LAW (R)→					
HHLD AUDIENCE % & (000)					11.5	10,710	13.0	12,100	14.8	13,780	11.7	10,890	10.0	9,310				
TA%, AVG. AUD. 1/2 HR %					*14.0*		*15.2*		*17.9*		*13.9*		*14.8*	9.9*		10.1*		
SHARE AUDIENCE %					23		24		26		21		19	18*		20*		
AVG. AUD BY 1/4 HR %					11.1	11.8	12.5	13.5	14.3	15.2	12.2	11.2	9.9	9.8	10.1	10.2		
FOX TV					SIMPSONS (R)		BABES (R)		←BEVERLY HILLS, 90210 (R)→									
HHLD AUDIENCE % & (000)					9.7	9,030	6.1	5,680	7.6	7,080								
TA%, AVG. AUD. 1/2 HR %					*11.9*		*7.8*		*10.8*	7.1*		8.2*						
SHARE AUDIENCE %					19		11		13	13*		14*						
AVG. AUD BY 1/4 HR %					90	10.5	6.4	5.8	6.8	7.4	8.2	8.1						
INDEPENDENTS (INCLUDING SUPERSTATIONS EXCEPT TBS) AVERAGE AUDIENCE	11.0	(+F)	11.9	(+F)	6.9		7.9		8.8		9.3		13.3	(+F)	11.9	(+F)		
SHARE AUDIENCE %	25		26		14		15		16		16		25		24			
PBS AVERAGE AUDIENCE	1.0		1.2		1.6		1.9		2.3		2.2		1.4		1.1			
SHARE AUDIENCE %	2		3		3		4		4		4		3		2			
CABLE ORIG. (INCLUDING TBS) AVERAGE AUDIENCE	8.2		8.8		8.6		10.0		11.7		12.8		12.2		10.9			
SHARE AUDIENCE %	19		19		17		19		21		23		22		22			
PAY SERVICES AVERAGE AUDIENCE	1.3		1.5		1.7		2.2		3.0		3.3		3.8		3.0			
SHARE AUDIENCE %	3		3		3		4		5		6		7		6			

U.S. TV Households: 93,100,000

This page from the Nielsen ratings book reveals the "winners" in a Thursday night ratings race. The highest-rated program on this particular evening was NBC's "Cheers," which reached almost 14 million homes. This figure is determined by multiplying the rating (14.8) by the number of households each rating point represents (931,000).

Those who make decisions about television programs use ratings to help them decide which programs to leave on the air and which programs to take off or move to another time. Ratings help them decide whether their programming strategy is effective, or whether or not the audience approves of changes in a program. Ratings are also a major determinant of what a station or network can charge for commercials. For example, an average increase of one rating point for the season is worth over $30 million a year in additional advertising revenues to a network. An increase of one rating point means that an additional 1 percent of the country's households or adults tune to the network. For the 1990–1991 season, a Nielsen rating point was equivalent to 931,000 homes.

During the normal year, between one-half and two-thirds of new television series disappear before the season is over, victims of low ratings. Ratings affect not only the longevity of program series, but also the income of networks and stations, the price of a broadcasting stock, and the jobs of broadcast personnel—from executives to actors to news anchors to writers and producers.

An indication of the importance of ratings is that each network spends at least $1.5 to $2 million dollars a year to get them. An even more obvious indication of their importance is the lengths to which networks and stations will go to increase ratings. This is especially noticeable during the so-called "sweeps" months—November, February, May, and July—when the audience for every television station in the country is measured. Those ratings in turn determine the rates each of those stations can charge advertisers during the following quarter, so they have a great effect on

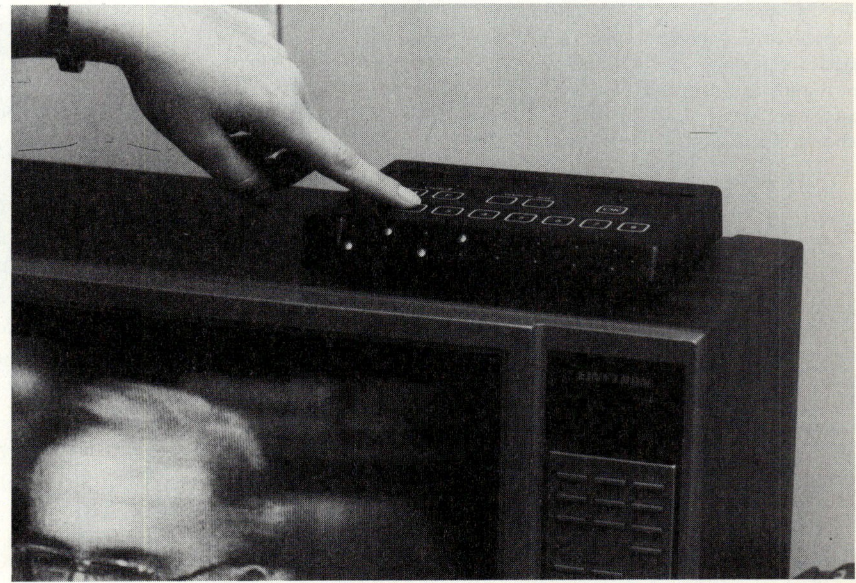

The Nielsen People Meter monitors family television viewing. Unlike previous recording devices, which noted only time and channel, the people meter keeps track of who is watching a program. Each family member is assigned a code number and enters it at the beginning and ending of each viewing session.

income. Sweeps are done by the two major national rating services, Nielsen and Arbitron. The most important sweeps are those in November and February, the heart of the television season. If you ever wondered why an extraordinarily large number of outstanding television attractions are available during those months, that is the reason. Each network attempts to outdo the other in attracting the maximum number of viewers during those critical periods. Local stations also get into the act, many of them running contests during the sweeps months that require people to watch the station in order to have a chance to win.

The advantage of sweeps months for viewers is that we tend to get better programs—the best episodes in series and the best specials and miniseries—or at least programs the broadcasters believe will attract the largest audiences.

Until just a few years ago, Nielsen and Arbitron used two principal means to gather audience data—a diary that respondents in each sample home had to fill out, and a meter attached to the television set that automatically recorded when the set was on and the channel to which it was tuned. In the 1980s, however, a British firm, AGB, introduced another method called the "people meter." Instead of being connected to the television set, the people meter keypad is remotely controlled by the viewer, much like a television or VCR remote control. Each household member can record his or her viewing and indicate demographic information such as age and sex. A device inside the television set or a separate unit outside the set records the data.

REVIEW

Ratings determine not only what programs are likely to survive but also the amount of money that networks and stations can charge for their advertisements. The two major ratings services are Nielsen and Arbitron. They use increasingly sophisticated devices such as people meters to determine audience size and composition.

Although AGB was not able to penetrate the U.S. market successfully, its people meter or a variation of it is rapidly becoming the standard instrument for measuring television audiences. In 1987, Nielsen used the people meter in determining national ratings.

Even more sophisticated devices are currently being contemplated. Both Nielsen and Arbitron are experimenting with electronic scanners that will enable viewers to record product purchases—such as groceries—as well as viewing behavior.

Other Forms of Research Used to Regulate Programming

Another type of audience research is program pretesting. Its purpose is to find out whether a program is likely to be successful with various kinds of people and how it might be made more successful. (Some motion pictures are tested in a similar way.) People are invited into a theater for a preview of a program and are asked to indicate, by pushing buttons or filling out questionnaires, which parts they find interesting or dull. On the basis of such pretesting, some programs are rejected for broadcast, others are rewritten or reedited, or changes are made in the cast before they are scheduled for broadcast. In a sense, such pretesting is like an out-of-town tryout of a play before it opens on Broadway. These tryouts sometimes result in extensive rewriting and other changes, and sometimes in the cancellation of the Broadway opening.

One kind of television research that has become important in the industry in recent years is closely related to program pretesting; this is research designed to discover the sorts of news and newscasters the public prefers. Such research is generally done by news consultants or "news doctors" such as Frank Magid and Associates, the largest firm of this type in the United States. Their aim is to increase the size of the audience for the newscasts produced by the station or network. By testing the reaction of the audience to different newscasters, news formats, and types of stories, the consultant obtains information with which to advise the station. The Magid firm is given credit for developing the idea of "Action News," which swept the country—newcasts filled with short, snappy, filmed or videotaped stories that give the newscasts a rapid pace. Magid is also credited with, or accused of, having developed the "Happy News" format, in which news personnel strive to be informal, friendly, and fun-loving.

REVIEW

Pretesting of programs and the use of consultants also play a role in program decisions.

EXPOSURE TO TELEVISION

A television receiver in the average American household is on for about seven hours a day. Almost every year that figure increases. Just twenty years ago the average time was only five and one-half hours. But along with the increased viewing has come increased competition. During a recent summer "rerun" period—when the networks offer mostly reruns of their entertainment programs—Nielsen "prime time" ratings showed that NBC commanded 23 percent of the audience, ABC and CBS 18 percent, basic cable services 14 percent, Fox Broadcasting 11 percent, and independent television stations 23 percent.

The reason people in the industry label the evening hours "prime time" is evident if you examine data that show the percentage of households using television at each hour of the day. About 10 percent of homes have a television set on between 7:30 and 8:00 in the morning. That percentage rises very slowly during the day until about 4:00 or 4:30 P.M., when somewhat over 30 percent have sets on. At that point, viewing begins to rise sharply and steadily to its peak, which comes between 8:00 and 10:00 P.M. On a winter evening, from 8:00 to 10:00 P.M., a television set is on in more than 60 percent of American households. Somewhat fewer are on during summer evenings.

Relationship of Viewing to Age

Viewing follows an interesting pattern with age. Among children, preschoolers view the most—about 27 hours a week on the average. As children progress through school, the amount of television they view, on the average, drops steadily, with teenagers averaging about 24 hours per week. Then, however, viewing begins to rise, with adults over age 55 doing the greatest amount, an average of about 36 hours per week. In addition, among adults, women view substantially more television than men.

The Role of Television in Our Lives

Some comparisons may help you appreciate the large role that television plays in the lives of most Americans. In this country, more families have a television set than have a refrigerator, vacuum cleaner, telephone, or even indoor plumbing. About 98 percent of households have at least one receiver, and over 55 percent have two or more—and these figures continue to rise. The average child between the ages of 2 and 11 watches over three and one-half hours of television a day and sees an estimated twenty thousand commercials a year. Evidence indicates that Ronald McDonald, the clown who advertises McDonald's hamburgers on television, is second only to Santa Claus in being recognized by children in the United States. When some researchers asked children between the ages of four and six, "Which do you like better, TV or Daddy?" 44 percent of the youngsters said they preferred television.

Some observers claim, and perhaps validly, that more people saw the first television production of *Hamlet* than had seen any of the countless stage productions of this tragedy throughout the world since William Shakespeare wrote it about four hundred years ago. Even a small audience, by television network standards, can be quite impressive in size. For example, a television audience of 30 million is not considered especially large these days. However, a dramatic production staged in an average-sized theater would need to run with capacity houses every night for 137 years to reach that many people.

A news story about an attempted robbery in Cedar Rapids, Iowa, suggests that Americans not only watch a great deal of television; they attend to it closely. According to the news report, a man with a pistol entered a bar in Cedar Rapids one morning when the woman tending bar and her three customers were watching the CBS News. When the gunman warned them not to move, the bartender told him "Nobody is getting robbed while I'm watching the news." Failing to get anyone's attention—even after cocking his pistol twice—the robber complained that he wasn't being taken seriously and left to get some help. When police caught him later and brought him back to the bar, they discovered that one of the customers could not even identify the robber because he had never taken his eyes off the television set during the attempted holdup.

The Greatest Television Attractions

What attracts this sort of attention from so many people? The answer is: almost anything. Vast numbers of people tune to a great variety of types of programs. In fact, almost anything that appears in prime time on one of the commercial networks is likely to gain the attention of millions—perhaps not enough millions to convince the network to keep the program on the air, but a tremendous audience by almost anyone else's standards. Super Bowl games and special miniseries adaptations of best-selling novels have attracted the largest television audiences. During the 1988–1989 television season, the CBS cowboy saga, "Lonesome Dove," had an aver-

REVIEW

In the average household, the television stays on about seven hours a day. Younger children and older adults watch the greatest amounts of television. Some 98 percent of the households in America have at least one television set. In 1980, more than half those sets—amounting to roughly 120 million people—were tuned to an episode of "Dallas."

age audience of 56 million. The ABC miniseries "War and Remembrance" averaged 40 million viewers—less than half the audience for one episode of its predecessor, "Winds of War." One of the largest, if not the largest, television audiences of all time was won by an episode of "Dallas" in 1980. This episode, which aired after a long buildup and torrent of "hype," revealed the identity of the person who shot the series villain, J. R. Ewing. The program had a 53.3 rating (53.3 percent of all television homes in the country) and a 76 share (76 percent of all homes viewing television at that time). It is a reasonable estimate that 120 million people in this country watched that episode. (By comparison, the largest audience ever for public television programming—the 1990 PBS series, "The Civil War"—averaged a 9.0 rating and a 13 share. Approximately 14 million people watched each episode of the 11-hour documentary.)

This amount of exposure and this level of attention to television has made it a major advertising medium. More than $16 billion is spent each year on television advertising, almost half of that for network advertising, and the rest for local advertising.

PROCESSING THE INFORMATION WE GET FROM TELEVISION

Much that we discussed in earlier chapters on processing information from motion pictures and radio is applicable to television. For example, like the motion picture, many images we see on television we perceive both as themselves and as symbols for other things or ideas. Consider, for instance, "The Cosby Show." You probably were familiar with Bill Cosby before he was in that series, so you had some perception of the type of person he is. Thus, when you see him in one of the episodes in the series, you undoubtedly see him as Bill Cosby, but you also see him as Dr. Huxtable, the character he plays in that series; perhaps you also see him as a symbol of the ideal father. Although you probably do not think about those various levels of meaning when you watch the program, or any other program, they almost certainly interact to shape your interpretations of what you see and what you come away with afterward.

The Confusion of Art and Reality

As with both the motion picture and radio, reality and art are confused in television. Because most of us perceive television, like radio, as a news medium as well as an entertainment medium, we may tend to perceive all of what we get from the medium as more "real" than we would otherwise perceive it to be.

The effect of this confusion between art and reality is that the meanings we perceive when we watch television depend in large part on the inferences we make about the television director's intent. For example, when a television reporter overseas is videotaped outdoors giving a report, in the background we might see embassy gates locked with large chains, or soldiers going down the street, or children in a playground, or black clouds in the sky. When you see this report, you might simply assume that

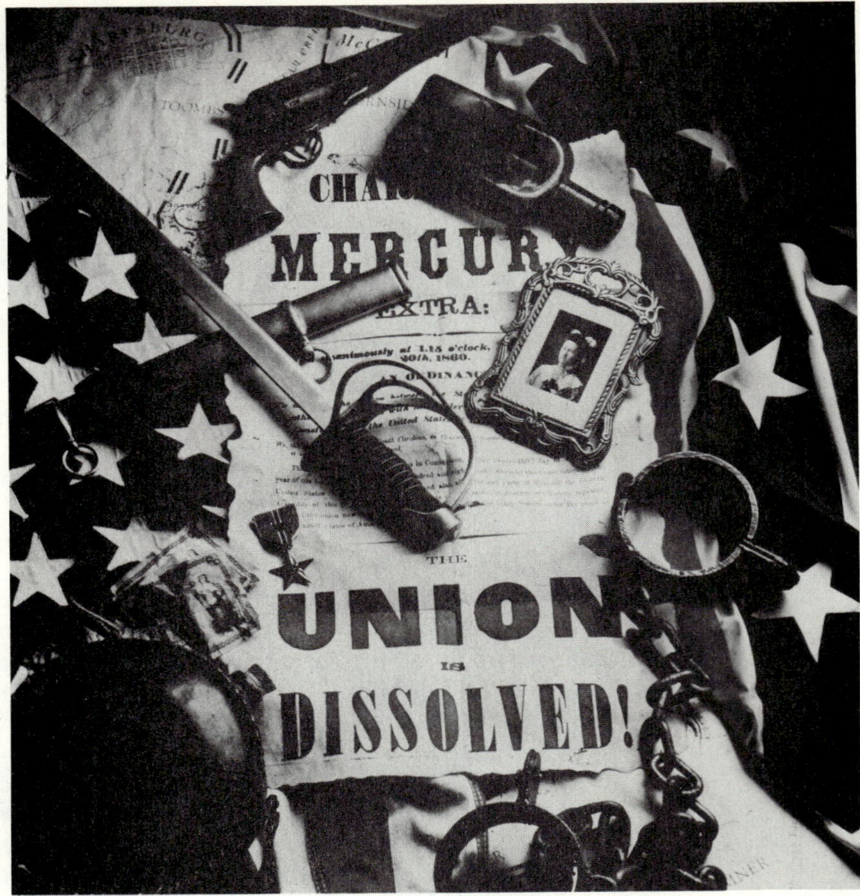

Ken Burns's 11-hour documentary series, "The Civil War," gave PBS its largest audience ever. Burns skillfully combined old photographs, period music, readings from diaries, and interviews with writers and historians to tell the dramatic story of this country's civil war.

the background just happened to be there; the videotape had to be done somewhere. So you ignore the background or simply take it as additional information about the country: "That's just the way it is." On the other hand, if you assume that the background was selected intentionally, you infer that the director is trying to say something more to you, that the background is meant to symbolize something: the detention of political prisoners or hostages, military oppression, the freedom and normality that permit young children to play outdoors very much as they do in America, or danger—the storm clouds heralding possible war or doom. Some of these symbols are so familiar that we perceive them without being aware of it. The clothing a television performer wears, the decor of a room, even the physical characteristics of a performer can be interpreted as symbolic or as nonsymbolic. Because of the nature of television, the appropriate interpretive strategy is seldom clear.

This confusion between art and reality is used not only by directors in television drama or newscasts and news documentaries, but also by producers of commercials. The manufacturers of a brand of decaffeinated coffee used it to get around the NAB code restriction that no physician or actor representing a physician be used in advertising. They cast Robert Young, who had played Dr. Marcus Welby in a long-running television series, in a series of commercials in which he advised other characters who could not drink regular coffee to try decaffeinated coffee. The commercials never stated specifically that he was a physician; they did not need to. Robert Young had played Dr. Marcus Welby on television for so long that, for a large part of the American public, he *is* Marcus Welby, and in the commercials he gives his advice about decaffeinated coffee in the same paternal style that he used in prescribing medications in the Welby series. More recently, Maxwell House Coffee Company ran an ad featuring well-known television journalist Linda Ellerbee. In the ad, Ellerbee claimed that a taste test showed people preferred Maxwell House over Folgers coffee by two to one. Had an actor made such a claim, the public would likely have viewed it as the usual puffery that accompanies advertisements. But

Our processing of television involves more than simply taking in the words and images on the screen. When we laugh at an episode of "The Cosby Show," we are responding both to Bill Cosby, the actor and comedian, and to his character, Dr. Huxstable, the physician and father.

for a bona fide journalist to report the results of a taste test may have confused—or, as the advertiser intended, impressed—viewers who were used to seeing Linda Ellerbee deliver straight, factual information.

Criticizing Television For many Americans, television is a prime target of criticism these days. Some of the criticism is directed at the effects television programs might have on children. Some is directed at the medium's bias in its treatment of political matters, minority groups, women, and our economic system. Much is also directed at the intellectual and aesthetic qualities of television programs. Evidence that indicates whether some of the charges are justified is covered in Chapter 16. Much of the criticism, however, is the sort for which no evidence is relevant. It centers on questions of value, not of fact. For example, whether critics believe television is biased politically depends on whether they disagree with the middle-of-the-road positions the medium generally takes. Whether they charge that it is biased toward the economic system, women, or minority groups depends upon whether they believe the media should be directly and indirectly encouraging social change. And whether they are critical of the intellectual and aesthetic qualities of the medium depends largely on whether they believe that an important responsibility of television is to educate and uplift. Valid arguments can be made on both sides of each of these issues.

BYLINE

Historian Barbara Tuchman said: "Television is moved by the desire to make profits, by appealing not to the audience of quality, but to the largest number—I suppose what used to be called the lowest common denominator. This is not the way to increase the thinking of the public on truth or serious matters, or to help it recognize the values in life that are creative." Does this assessment of television coincide with yours? If not, how would you characterize the medium?

Different perceptions of the nature of television. Another issue that divides critics of television concerns the primary nature of the medium. They disagree about what television is or ought to be. Think about this issue. Is television primarily a medium of entertainment, of information, of expression, or of persuasion? Is it primarily a medium of commerce? Is it an art form? In a sense, it is all of these. Whether it should be all of these is another matter. In any case, we need not worry about the medium's "essential" or "primary" nature. Instead, let us see what interesting insights we can get by looking at it in all of these various ways, and perhaps in some other ways as well.

If we look at television as rhetoric—as information and persuasion—we can consider how good or useful a picture of the world it is presenting and what the relationship of that picture is to the world that we experience directly. What is the picture of marriage that it presents to us? Of education? Minority groups? Israel and Iraq? War? The presidency?

If we look at television as art, we need to consider the originality of programs, their complexity or layers of meaning, their use of symbols, and whether they are expanding our tastes and extending our vision.

Television is often criticized for its lack of originality or variety. When one program becomes successful, a host of imitators are spawned the next season. For example, when a quiz show that awarded a tremendous amount of money to lucky contestants became popular on television, quiz shows soon were popping up all over the dial and the time schedule. From the "$64,000 Question" we expanded to the "$64,000 Challenge," to "High Finance," "Treasure Hunt," "Twenty-One," "Giant Step," and on to the more recent "Wheel of Fortune."

REVIEW

Television shapes our perception of reality, not just in its news programming, but in its entertainment programming and commercials as well. For this reason, critics contend that the manner in which women and minority groups are portrayed on television affects the way they are treated in the real world. Critics are also concerned about the nature of television and the role it should play in society.

This sort of imitation is not unique to television; it has always gone on in every form of entertainment and art. Consider, for example, what happened in motion pictures when the first disaster film was a hit, or to painting when the first Expressionist painting or the first Pop Art painting was recognized. Other filmmakers and other painters began to produce works of the same type, hoping to cash in. You can find imitation in every field that depends for support upon public acceptance or popularity. The problem is that truly original people are a rare breed; not very many of them are around in any generation. The difficulty that the scarcity of originality creates for television is especially acute because of the amount of material the medium consumes and the great expense of each program. We are not suggesting that people should stop insisting on better and more original programs; we are simply pointing out that they are easier to request than to produce.

THE IMPACT OF TELEVISION ON US AND OUR SOCIETY

For most of us, television has become such an integral part of our lives that it is difficult to isolate its impact. Television, more than any other institution, provides a common set of experiences for virtually all Americans—a common base of information, common ways of perceiving issues and ideas, and, to some extent, common values. This set of shared experiences makes it easier for us to communicate with and understand each other. As one observer put it, "Its ceaseless flow of electronic signals pumped into our living and bed chambers affects fundamentally not merely our thoughts but the way we go about the business of thinking collectively." This is not to say that it has solved all of our problems of communication and understanding, but it has made a substantial contribution to their solution.

Most of the major aspects of television's impact will be covered in the later chapters on general media functions and effects. Two related subjects deserve additional emphasis here. One is the fact that television, probably more than any other medium today, shapes as well as reports the news. Just the presence of a camera, for example, alters many people's behavior.

Related to television's shaping of events it reports are the efforts of many individuals and groups to shape the medium's coverage of events. This is most notable in the efforts of political candidates or officeholders to promote and facilitate television coverage of certain events. For example, the president and his staff take great care to ensure that television cameras are present at events that will show the chief executive in a good light. In fact, certain events are staged mostly for the benefit of the cameras and the large audiences they ensure.

Some groups and individuals go to extreme lengths to gain access to the television audience. Terrorists in many parts of the world have hijacked airliners or taken hostages in order to attract the attention of television cameras. Often, terrorists have given as a condition for their release of hostages, the opportunity to have their messages transmitted throughout a country, or sometimes the world.

Hostages were used in a somewhat different way in the confrontation between the United States and Iraq. As a means of deterring the United States and other countries from taking military action in retaliation for its takeover of Kuwait, Iraq decided to detain foreigners who were in Kuwait or Iraq at the time of the invasion. Iraqi authorities referred to the detainees as "guests" rather than "hostages" and regularly provided footage or photo opportunities—what they called "guest news"—for the networks. One interview shown widely on American television featured Iraq's leader, Saddam Hussein, dressed in civilian clothes chatting amicably with nervous but polite detainees about their welfare. Despite Iraq's best efforts to portray him as humane and compassionate—Saddam Hussein coaxed one child to say he had enough milk and cornflakes—the broadcast infuriated many Americans, who saw innocent people being used for propaganda purposes.

During the recent coup attempt by hard-liners in the Soviet Union, television played a crucial role in keeping the world informed of the dramatic events unfolding there and solidifying resistance to the coup. After the apparent overthrow of President Gorbachev, Russian President Boris Yeltsin, who opposed the takeover by reactionary communists, took refuge in the Russian Parliament Building only a short distance from where coup leaders were issuing emergency decrees. Through the use of television, Yeltsin and his supporters were able to undermine the junta's argument that Gorbachev was ill and unable to carry out his duties. Pictures of a defiant Boris Yeltsin standing on a tank and rallying Russians to his side were flashed around the world. The television and the telephone linked Yeltsin to the outside world and to world leaders who offered their encouragement. At one point, when it seemed that Soviet troops were poised to storm the Russian Parliament, ABC's Diane Sawyer entered the Parlia-

Iraq's president Saddam Hussein attempted to project a more compassionate and less militaristic image to the world in this televised interview with foreigners held hostage in Iraq following its invasion of Kuwait. The most memorable part of the telecast, however, was the sight of innocent people—especially children—being used as pawns in a deadly chess game.

ment building and interviewed Yeltsin. A few hours later the world saw the Russian opposition leader calmly preparing for a threatened military attack on his headquarters. However, the attack never came, and shortly thereafter the coup crumbled. A weary but grateful Mikhail Gorbachev was restored to power. *Time* magazine speculated that television not only helped unravel the putsch but forced its own brief attention span upon history.

REVIEW

Television is such an integral part of our lives that it is difficult to isolate its impact. It both shapes and reports the news and is itself shaped by those who wish to influence news coverage. Whether it is the President of the United States or a protest group or even a terrorist group, each plans its activities with television in mind.

What one sees in these examples is a battle of images being waged over the airwaves. Whether it is U.S. preachers and politicians responding to charges of moral corruption, or Palestinian youths hurling rocks at Israeli troops, or Chinese students standing in front of tanks on their way to Tiananmen Square, each group recognizes that the most powerful weapons in the battle for public sympathy and public support are the television cameras that record and shape their actions.

During the 1989 antigovernment demonstrations in China and in the Baltic states of Latvia, Estonia, and Lithuania, many of the signs carried by protestors ("Give Me Liberty or Give Me Death"; "The Baltic States Never Joined the U.S.S.R.") were written in English, clearly for the benefit of camera crews from English-speaking countries. One observer noted that because of television, English has become the universal language of protest.

TODAY'S DOMINANT MEDIUM: A SUMMARY

The signs of television's dominant role among mass media are everywhere. Although it developed in the mold of radio—following the programming structure, the relationship of local licensee and network, and the general economic pattern of its parent medium—it soon outstripped that parent in the affections of the public. Radio and all other mass media have had to change in some way because of television's impact.

Although television in essentially its present form has been with us for some four decades, great debates are still being held about its control—especially its control of content. The amount and kind of government regulation is constantly disputed. The right of the public to access, both paid and free, is also argued regularly. The relationship of local stations, networks, and cable systems is an especially important issue today. The size, functions, and means of support for our public television system in this country are also issues of debate.

Some critics of television believe the networks have too much control. Others think advertisers are too powerful a force in shaping the medium. Still others think the government has too much power. And some think the masses—as represented by program ratings—have too much influence on programming decisions. Television is also criticized strongly for the amount of violence it shows, the sexual attitudes it portrays as normal, its treatment of women and minority groups, and a wide variety of other actions and inactions.

You might believe that a negative relationship would exist between the amount of criticism and the amount of viewing, that since so many people are unhappy about different aspects of television they must not view much. In fact, that relationship is positive. No other medium has ever been so heavily criticized as television, yet no other medium has ever had such a large and loyal following. When a single program such as "Dallas" can attract more than half of the American population, and when audiences of 30 million for programs are common, we must conclude that this medium has a very special place in the hearts and lives of people.

The impact that television has on us and on a great many aspects of our society follows largely from its popularity. When you can reach vast numbers of people simultaneously with a message—whether about a political idea, a candidate, a detergent, or a way of life—that message is going to have an effect. Precisely what that effect is, in many of these cases, we do not yet know. This unanswered question is one of the most interesting aspects of television. This question is also one of the most important opportunities this medium creates for you, if you want to work at answering it for yourself.

DISCUSSION QUESTIONS

1. What are the basic requirements for a television system? Why was the electronic system superior to the mechanical one?
2. What decisions did the FCC make in the early 1950s regarding standards for television? What impact did these decisions have?

3. How is the television industry in the United States structured?
4. Why does cable pose a threat to over-the-air television?
5. How is public or noncommercial television funded?
6. What groups or factors determine the content of television?
7. How would you describe the size and composition of television audiences? What types of programming attract the largest audiences?
8. How does television blend art and reality? What is its purpose in doing so?
9. What are some of the major criticisms of television? Which of those do you agree with?
10. How does television shape the news? How is it used by others to shape or influence news coverage?

NOTE

1. The Federal Communications Commission does not yet have the power to regulate the networks directly. As with a number of other regulations, the FCC got around this limitation by the indirect route of ruling that no television station could affiliate with a network that engaged in those practices.

SUGGESTED READINGS

Relevant Contemporary Works

Allen, Robert C. *Speaking of Soap Operas.* Chapel Hill: University of North Carolina Press, 1985.

Beville, Hugh M., Jr. *Audience Ratings: Radio, Television, Cable.* Hillsdale, NJ: Erlbaum, 1988.

Bower, Robert T. *The Changing Television Audience in America.* New York: Columbia University Press, 1985.

Gitlin, Todd. *Inside Prime Time.* New York: Pantheon, 1983.

Himmelstein, Hal. *Television Myth and the American Mind.* New York: Praeger, 1985.

Oberdorfer, Donald. *Electronic Christianity: Myth or Ministry.* Taylor Fall, MN: John L. Brekke & Sons, 1983.

Williams, Huntington. *Beyond Control: ABC and the Fate of the Networks.* New York: Atheneum, 1989.

See also *Television/Radio Age, Broadcasting,* and *Journal of Communication.*

CHAPTER 11

TOWARD THE TWENTY-FIRST CENTURY

OBJECTIVES

After studying this chapter, you should be able to

- **Explain the major trends in mass communication.**
- **Discuss the various technological developments that are likely to change the manner in which information and entertainment are produced, distributed, and exhibited.**
- **Describe the changes likely to occur in audiences for mass communication.**
- **Explain the notion of demassification.**
- **Discuss the trend toward vertical integration and the emergence of worldwide communications corporations.**
- **Cite some of the legal and regulatory issues that need to be addressed in the last decade of the twentieth century.**

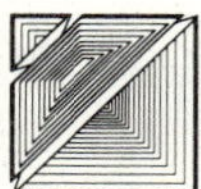

I think the world TV industry and the world cinema industry will disappear over the next decade; they're going to be replaced by a new world in which the two mediums as we know them now can become one.

Vittorio Storaro
Winner of Three Academy
Awards for Cinematography

Ten years from now you'll see more and better laser projection systems. Where present systems still leave plenty to be desired in terms of resolution and brightness, in the future, they'll even be able to use lasers in movie theatres, instead of film and projectors. It could *lead to holographic capability.*

Larry Schotz
Inventor and President
of LS Research

The home will have a compact, erasable laser disk unit that, on signal, can electronically store the day's newspaper. With HDTV it will be as easy as flipping today's pages for a person to read the newspaper. If an individual wants a hard copy of a particular ad, news story or picture, he or she need only touch a button to obtain it from the home's electronic printer.

William D. Rinehart
American Newspaper
Publishers Association

As the twenty-first century approaches, there appears to be general consensus about future developments in communication technology. Whether you talk to the artists who create media products, to the scientists who invent new media technologies, or to the executives who run media industries, the story is the same: there are going to be better and faster ways to create, deliver, and consume media information and entertainment. There will be many a trial and error, as some technologies fail in the marketplace while others succeed, but current trends point toward a world awash in information and entertainment—a world in which you, the consumer, will be increasingly more in control as surviving media industries strive to meet your individual needs and tastes. We have already considered some of the technological changes that lie in store. In this chapter we consider additional changes, both technological and societal, that will shape our use of media in the last decade of the twentieth century.

THE MAJOR TRENDS

We can see seven major trends today that, if they continue, could have great impact on our communication environment:

1. One trend is that information has replaced manufactured goods as the major commodity of business in this and other developed countries.
2. The most visible trend, the one with which most forecasters are concerned—even though it may not be most important in the long run—is the steady increase in the number and kinds of devices or systems for delivering information and entertainment.
3. The computer has become an integral part of all mass media industries.
4. The clear distinctions among most of the major media—such as newspapers, magazines, television, and film—are eroding.
5. The mass media are being "demassified"; audiences are being fragmented as individuals are getting more choices and more control of their particular media mosaics.

6. The audience is changing; it is getting older, and the sexual distinctions in roles and available time for the media are disappearing.
7. The oldest and probably the most important contemporary trend, one that has been building since the early part of this century, is that control of more and more of the sources of communication is being placed in fewer and fewer hands.

THE INFORMATION SOCIETY

This is a period of great technological change in the United States, change that will make mass communication even more important than it has been in the past. Recognizing this fact, some observers have concluded that we have become an **information society,** instead of the industrial society we were through most of the twentieth century.

Evidence for this conclusion is the fact that information occupations have increased during this century from approximately 10 percent to almost 50 percent of the work force, while industrial occupations dropped to 20 percent and agricultural occupations to 4 percent. More than one-fourth of the gross national product of this country comes from the production, processing, and distribution of information goods and services—and this proportion is almost certain to increase. The importance of communication, both for occupations and the generation of wealth, will continue to grow as we become *a society in which communication is a major preoccupation.*

In the earliest days, food was the most important resource, the one essential for existence. As human beings and their civilizations developed, energy increased in importance until the two together, food and energy, were the fundamental resources. As we approach the twenty-first century, we recognize that a third resource is approaching those two in importance, so that three resources are essential: food, energy, and information. The challenge of the twenty-first century will be to manage these resources effectively in order to prevent the destruction of humanity. Much of the responsibility for that management rests on the shoulders of the people involved with the mass media of communication.

If you become one of those people in the media and endeavor to fulfill that responsibility, you must understand some key differences between information and the other basic resources and the different types of challenges they pose.

Food and energy present a challenge because they are in short supply in most areas of the world. We need to find ways to manage those shortages as well as ways to increase supplies as much as possible. Information, on the other hand, is not in short supply. Although there is much we do not know, and great gaps in our knowledge that we must fill through research, the greatest gap exists between the information some people already have and the use of that information. We have far more information than has yet been put to use, perhaps even far more than ever can be put to use.

Information is different from food and energy also because it is not depleted by use, nor does it spoil or diminish when not used. We cannot meaningfully talk about a surplus of information, as we can talk about food or energy surpluses. In fact, unlike food at least, generally, the more information you have, the more you want and the easier it is to get.

REVIEW

The United States has changed from an industrial society to an information society. As a result, information has become an important commodity, one that needs to be equitably distributed throughout the world.

The major problem with information, which must concern us all, is its maldistribution. Some segments of the world's population have an ample supply, while others have painfully little. Those disparities exist not only among countries or regions of the world, but within each country; you can find tremendous gaps in usable information among individuals within a single community. We must find ways to reduce those gaps, not by taking away from those with plenty to give to those without, since that is not necessary with information, but rather by finding ways to give all individuals access to the vast stores of information available and motivating them to grasp that which they need.

DEVELOPING TECHNOLOGIES

As we saw earlier, there is no reliable way to forecast technological developments that exist only in an inventor's mind, or even to predict which of the present technologies will become more or less important in the future. However, we can examine what is happening today and consider their possibilities for tomorrow.

The Telephone

It may seem odd to you that we begin a discussion of developing technologies with the telephone, a gadget invented in 1876 and used with little variation for over a hundred years. However, in 1982 the Justice Department ended the monopoly of "Ma Bell," as AT&T was popularly known, and opened the nation's telephone system to competition, while at the same time freeing AT&T of some of the restrictions under which it operated. The lowly telephone has since taken on a totally new life.

Telephones are no longer simply instruments for calling your mother or closing a business deal. They are complex intercommunication systems in offices. They are connecting links for conferences among individuals who are scattered far and wide. They connect home and office computers to each other and to large computers for data entry and analysis, or for retrieving information. Great masses of data are transmitted by telephone lines regularly across town, across the country, and even across the world.

One recent innovation in telephone technology is the interactive 900 phone exchanges broadcasters are using to solicit viewer responses. Newspapers use a similar service—called a voice information system—to provide timely news, weather, sports, and business information and to promote the newspaper.

In short, the telephone has become the link among many of the other communication technologies and between each of them and the consumer, whether at home or in an office, plant, or laboratory.

Fiber Optics Another development, which may help telephone companies provide an even greater range of services, is **fiber optics.** Fiber optics involve *gossamer strands of glass through which pulses of laser light are transmitted.* This light replaces the electronic signals traditionally used for telephone, radio, video, and computer data transmission.

These glass filaments are much more efficient and take up far less space than copper cables. One pair of filaments can carry about a thousand telephone conversations simultaneously, compared to the two dozen that regular cables can carry. In addition, the glass filaments are easier to install; they are not affected by electronic static and are more secure from industrial and military spies.

With the vastly increased capacity made possible by fiber optics, telephone companies will be in a position to offer an even greater range of services than they do at present. Although Congress now bars telephone companies from providing cable television service, fiber optics will put them into a perfect position to provide most of cable's present services at greater efficiency and lower cost. If the legal barriers to their entry into the field are dropped, telephone companies will be tough competition for present cable operators, unless those operators agree to join forces with them. At present, telephone companies are poised to offer videophone conversations, pay-per-view type programming libraries, health-care monitoring, and a host of other services that fiber optics technology makes possible. Telephone companies might even be tough competition for local television stations if they are permitted to provide a direct link between networks and the home, thereby circumventing local network affiliates.

Computers As discussed in earlier chapters, the computer—especially the personal computer, or PC—is another technological device that has become an integral part of mass communication. Journalists write their stories on computer terminals, and computers control printing of these stories. Computerized editing of television programs and motion pictures is now standard in every major studio. The new computer-based animation equipment permits a level of control and variety of effects that were unobtainable before. The most advanced recording studios for rock and other types of music are largely computer controlled.

Through computers, you can now gain access to vast stores of information. The long-familiar card catalog is being replaced in libraries by computer terminals because they allow indexes to be kept more complete and up to date than do cards. For this reason, there may never be another printed edition of the Library of Congress Catalog.

Computers have also become critical for research on mass communication, whether simple ratings or complex analyses of the roles and influences of mass communication. Research uses will definitely continue and will most likely expand greatly in the years ahead, as both computers and our research methods become more sophisticated.

More and more libraries are replacing card catalogs with computers. This computer has an INFOTRAC periodicals research program.

Computers will soon be able to talk to each other more easily as the industry moves to a universal standard. They will also be able to understand spoken words and print them on a screen. As their vocabularies increase, "talkwriters" will be able to take dictation much as a secretary does. By the end of the decade, you may not be able to tell the difference between a personal computer and a television set. The merging of the two technologies will create what might be called a "smart TV" or a "video computer," which looks like a television set but can perform the software functions of a PC and also store and manipulate images from broadcast and cable signals, VCRs, videodiscs, and video cameras.

Developments in automation. Another portent of our mass communication future with which computers are involved is automation. As suggested in earlier chapters, automation is already significantly affecting the way much of the work is done in most mass communication industries. Automation facilitates the printing of newspapers, magazines, and books. Radio stations are operated almost entirely with prerecorded tapes and computerized controls that automatically turn the tapes on and off and mix them at the proper times of day. Automation is not yet a major factor in television stations, but it probably soon will be. It is already a factor in the operation of major cable systems and in the motion picture exhibition business. It allows an entire motion picture theater to be operated with two people: a combination ticket-seller-usher-manager and someone to run the refreshment stand.

REVIEW

Fiber optics and computers, along with advances in telephone technology, have facilitated the production and transmission of communications products. Computers have also led to the automation of communications equipment.

Ultimately, automation should replace people in doing most tasks that require no human judgment. In each case, the changeover will come at the point at which the cost of automation equipment is less than the cost of labor for the expected life of the equipment. For example, when the cost of automatic money-changing machines (such as those used to sell tickets in some subway systems) falls below the cost of hiring a ticket seller for a year or two, we can expect that movie houses will set a standard admission price for both adults and children and switch over to automatic selling of tickets. They might even use electronically coated tickets so that an automated gate, activated by the tickets, can be substituted for the ticket taker.

Videotex and teletext. Videotex and teletext are technologies for transforming your home television receiver or home computer into a more effective information machine. Commercial videotex and teletext services sometimes go by different names, but the basic technologies are the same. In Miami, Florida, for example, the videotex service that existed until 1986 was called Viewtron.

Videotex is the more powerful of these two technologies. It *links subscribers' television receivers or personal computers to a central computer by either telephone line and modem or two-way cable. Users can communicate with the central computer to get information or, with some systems, to do their banking, pay bills, or shop.*

To date, videotex has been known more for its failures than its successes. The Knight-Ridder Viewtron effort cost $50 million. A similar effort by Times-Mirror cost $30 million. Neither was able to attract more than a few thousand subscribers. Despite its failure in the consumer market, videotex in the professional market is prospering. Nexis, Lexis, Dow Jones News/Retrieval, and other such services offer valuable data bases to professionals. And gradually, businesses are adding consumer-oriented services as they sense a need for home-delivered information. IBM and Sears, for example, recently invested $250 million in a joint venture called Prodigy. J. C. Penney is experimenting with a home-shopping system called Telaction.

A major difference in the current use of videotex is that the delivery of information has shifted from the television set to the personal computer.

Only people with a personal computer and modem will be able to take advantage of the transactional services offered by IBM and Sears or J. C. Penney. In effect, consumers have said they do not want to tie up their television sets with information that has to be read. On the other hand, if that information is useful, they might be willing to call it up on their computer screens and do business from there.

Although used for some of the same purposes as videotex, **teletext** is quite a different technology. It is not interactive; it cannot be used for shopping, banking, and so on. It can be likened to a magazine that *provides specialized types of information. Users of teletext have decoders with which they can call up* whatever pages of that "magazine" they want—the pages that contain *news, weather, sports, stock market reports, and perhaps educational materials. This information reaches your television receiver, if you are a teletext user, through regular broadcast signals, rather than through telephone or cable lines*. The information is brought to your television screen by insertion into some of the otherwise blank spaces in the signals coming into your receiver. You cannot see this information, though, unless you have a decoder.

REVIEW

Videotex and teletext are ways of bringing specialized print information to the home via the television set or personal computer.

At this point, it is impossible to say whether either videotex or teletext will come into widespread use. It is conceivable that their major use will be in businesses rather than in homes. However, if manufacturers begin building decoders for teletext into all television receivers at little or no extra cost, so that people do not need to make a special purchase to get it, it will likely become popular.

Satellites Probably the most important event in recent mass communication history was the launching of the first communications satellite in 1965. That satellite, and the dozens that followed, made possible the instantaneous transmission of sound and pictures, as well as data, over large areas of the earth at low cost. At last count, there were roughly two dozen U.S. satellites serving North America, with the launching of many more planned. By 1984, because of the large number of satellites in orbit and the existing regulations about minimum distance between them, all of the best locations in the sky for satellites transmitting to this country were filled. Since the demand for more communications satellite service was so great, though, the Federal Communications Commission was forced to change the regulations to permit satellites to orbit closer together so that more could be squeezed into those good spots.

The principle of the communications satellite is relatively simple. The satellite is boosted just far enough into space by rocket to get into an orbit that is synchronized with the rotation of the earth. Thus, it always stays in the same position relative to the earth. That so-called "geosynchronous" orbit facilitates the receiving and sending of signals. Once a communications satellite is in orbit, it receives signals from an **uplink,** or *transmitting station on the ground*. It amplifies these signals and transmits them back to earth by means of one of its set of **transponders**—*small transmitters* aboard. These signals are then picked up by **earth stations,** *receiving stations on the ground* which again amplify the signals and send them to cable systems, television stations, networks, and so on, for distribution.

The variety of names that various corporations have given their communication satellites may be confusing. Galaxy, Comstar, Satcom, Westar, Spacenet, Telstar, and SBS are some of the satellites transmitting to various parts of this country. If you go abroad, you will find still different satellite names. As new corporations or conglomerates get into the business, we will get additional names. Despite the variety of labels, all of these communication satellites operate in the same general way, and each serves a variety of mass communication businesses—television and radio networks, stations, cable systems, program or film syndicators, newspapers and news services—as well as many corporations not primarily in the communication business. The latter use satellite service to facilitate the sending and receiving of computer data and other kinds of messages or information, as well as for business meetings involving parties in different locations. These latter are generally called teleconferences or video conferences.

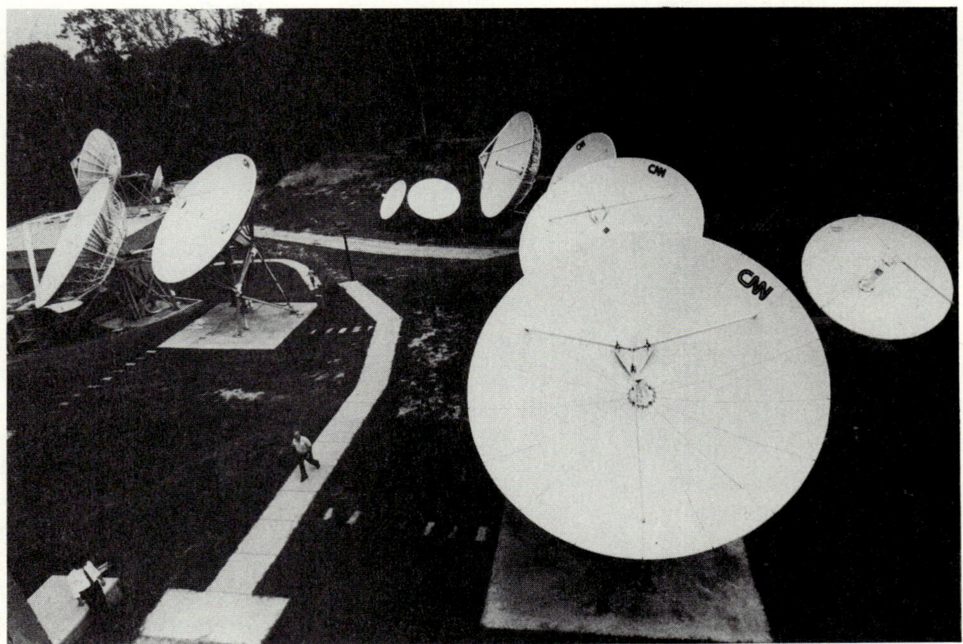

Satellite technology has revolutionized communication. These dishes outside the CNN headquarters in Atlanta pick up satellite feeds from all over the world and relay them to the newsroom. Satellite transmission made it possible for CNN to provide live coverage of the beginning of the U.S. invasion of Iraq and the attempted overthrow of President Mikhail Gorbachev in the Soviet Union.

Communications satellites have freed local broadcasting stations from their dependence on traditional networks; made practical the development of many new, specialized networks; made cable into a major industry by facilitating the distribution of a variety of types of programming; enabled relatively small companies, without a national network of telephone lines, to compete with giant AT&T in supplying long-distance telephone service; and brought into being international video conferencing with conferees who are scattered throughout the world seeing and talking with each other. Most television stations in the United States today have large **dish antennas** or *earth stations* with *which* they *can pick up signals directly from communications satellites.*

Most important, though, the satellite threatens to revolutionize our present system of broadcasting, making the local station, the network, the cable system, and national boundaries irrelevant. This threat comes from the **direct-broadcast satellites (DBS),** which *send signals directly to home television receivers through small home "dishes."*

REVIEW

Satellites are used by all types of communications industries. Soon they may be used to provide a direct-broadcast service (DBS), which would beam a signal from an earth station to a satellite and from there to small home dishes.

The technology for DBS already exists, although it has not yet been widely used. It involves satellites equipped to send out stronger signals so that individual homeowners can use a dish far smaller and cheaper than is required at present. Instead of the large, unsightly dishes we see scattered about the countryside now, we will have dishes that are even smaller and less visible than the regular television antennas that sprout like bushes above most homes and apartment buildings today. With DBS, not only will stations, networks, and cable systems lose their role as gatekeepers; countries will also. When television signals no longer need to be picked up and retransmitted by stations or cable systems, a country has no practical means of controlling the material its people will see. Needless to say, this possibility is causing great anxiety among the leaders in many countries.

Cable As you are well aware, cable has become a major mass communication industry in this country. Almost 60 percent of the households in the United States are hooked in to cable systems. Many specialized programming services are available to cable systems from satellite transmissions. And, as a result of these wider choices available in cable homes, the size of station and network audiences has dropped sharply.

In 1983–1984, television network affiliates commanded a 69 percent share of the audience of all television households, a 58 percent share of the audience of cable households, and a 53 percent share of the audience of pay cable households. By the end of the decade, these figures had dropped to 58 percent for television households, 49 percent for cable households, and 45 percent for pay cable households.

An old idea that has been reborn recently is the so-called "pay-per-view" service. With such service, viewers call the cable company by telephone, or through a two-way communication setup that is integrated into the cable system, and order a particular motion picture. Unlike HBO subscribers, who pay a set fee, pay-per-view subscribers pay only for the programs they order. Rock concerts and sports events have been especially popular as pay-per-view fare. In 1992, cable's coverage of the Olympics will be offered as pay-per-view programming. And NBC, which won over-the-air rights to the 1992 Summer Olympics, will offer six hundred hours of events on three pay-per-view channels.

Two-way cable. A development that has not lived up to its promise is two-way, or interactive, cable. The best known of the experimental interactive systems is QUBE, developed by the Warner Amex Corporation. (Amex—American Express—is no longer a part of the corporation.) The QUBE system was introduced in Columbus, Ohio, in 1977. It was hailed as the television system of the future. Subscribers could respond to or "interact" with a program by pressing buttons on a small, hand-held box wired to the cable. QUBE could be used in many ways. For example, subscribers could respond to questions posed during a program and see those responses immediately tallied and shown on the program. They could vote on issues being discussed by local government bodies and see their representatives taking those votes into account. They could even vote on what the next development in a dramatic program should be and then see the program go in the direction of the majority of respondents. Subscribers could have burglar and fire alarms tied to their cable system to alert the police or fire department in case of an emergency. They could also do some of their shopping through the QUBE system, sending in their orders by pressing the appropriate series of buttons. (This function has been largely replaced by the interactive 900 phone exchanges mentioned earlier.)

Despite widespread publicity about the QUBE experience, and the addition of QUBE to other cable systems, it failed to attract enough viewers to be profitable. In 1984, Warner cut back on the service and sold several systems that featured interactive cable. The one in Columbus still operates, but the interactive part is seldom used. In fact, Warner is in the process of upgrading its Columbus system by replacing copper cable with fiber optic cable. The QUBE box is being replaced by a PIONEER converter, which has greater channel capacity and features an authorization button for pay-per-view programming. For the foreseeable future, pay-per-view may be the only form of interactive television that survives in the marketplace.

Wireless cable. A number of competitors to the usual wired cable systems have developed in the past decade. One such competitor is **SMATV,** or *satellite master-antenna television*. SMATV is used primarily in large apartment buildings or complexes that have a large dish to pick up programs from satellites and then distribute them through a closed-circuit television

REVIEW

Cable television offers a variety of channels along with specialized interactive services. To date, the most successful interactive service has been pay-per-view television. Other forms of two-way cable have failed to capture the public's attention. Some variations of the usual wired cable are the satellite master antenna television system (SMATV) and multichannel, multipoint distribution services (MMDS).

system. This system was highly attractive to persons living in multiple-dwelling units where cable was not available. But as more and more such units were wired, and cable offered a broader range of services, the growth of SMATV declined. SMATV also faced lawsuits from local cable operators who claimed that the satellite master-antenna service violated the cable company's franchise rights.

MMDS, or *multichannel, multipoint distribution system, uses microwave transmitters to distribute programs to subscribers.* This technology is most attractive in large cities where cable wiring is difficult, if not impossible. Because of the relatively small number of channels practical with MMDS, it is used largely for pay channels.

The government has authorized some MMDS systems to be licensed to educational institutions for instructional purposes. These have been labeled **ITFS,** for *Instructional Television Fixed Services.* In some instances, ITFS channels are being used jointly for educational and commercial purposes on a time-sharing basis.

The disadvantage of the microwave transmission used by MMDS and ITFS systems is that the antennas on receiving homes must have line of sight to the transmitters. This sharply limits the number of homes any single system can reach.

The Home Shopping Club, a form of two-way cable, allows cable subscribers to order discounted jewelry, appliances, and other goods from their homes. Program hosts peddle merchandise and chat with viewers on the air, while, off camera, operators process orders taken from around the country.

Low-Power Television Another technology that has yet to fulfill its promise is **low-power television (LPTV).** As its name suggests, LPTV is *a television station that operates at reduced power and covers only a small area.* Introduced by the FCC in 1980, it prompted a flood of applications. By 1983, the FCC had to impose a freeze so it could sort through the forty thousand applications it had received. To facilitate processing, the FCC initiated a lottery system to choose among competing applicants. The FCC predicts that eventually there will be some four thousand LPTV stations in operation, though at present there are only about seven hundred. The greatest challenge to the LPTV stations is to find a specialized function that will attract an audience. Given the considerable start-up cost of a television station, investors have been wary about the profit potential of LPTV. In fact, many LPTV stations have already gone belly up. But John Kompas, president of the Community Broadcasting Association, an LPTV trade association, believes the answer lies in a cooperative arrangement with full-power television stations or cable systems. LPTV stations could serve as subaffiliates to full-power stations, rebroadcasting programs and carrying out some local programming functions. They could also serve as production houses for cable systems and could possibly handle marketing and sales chores. In return, the cable systems would carry the programming of the LPTV stations.

VCRs Beginning about 1980, the spread of VCRs in homes across the United States and in many other countries was almost as rapid as the spread of television receivers in the 1950s. In 1984, only about 10 percent of all households owned a VCR. This figure jumped to 20 percent in 1985 and an additional 10 percent in each succeeding year. Today, 70 percent of the homes in America have at least one VCR. Sales have risen from eight-hundred-two-thousand in 1980 to more than 12 million in 1991.

The same VCR that can be used in conjunction with cable and over-the-air television can also be used to play videocassettes that might have been purchased or rented. Thus, the VCR can both help and hurt cable and over-the-air television. At this point, it is difficult to tell which is more likely. The sale and rental of videocassettes already exceeds $10 billion a year (see Chapter 7), and more and more households are adding a second VCR. By 1990, one in four television households had at least two videocassette recorders. Perhaps the greater threat to cable and over-the-air television—especially the latter—will come from the remote control devices that operate VCRs. Remote units facilitate *playing back programs recorded at an earlier time*—a practice called **time shifting**. But these units also enable viewers to *fast forward* or "**zip**" *through commercials in programs previously recorded on their VCRs* and to *change channels* or "**zap**" *away from ads during regular programs*. Nielsen data indicate that while only 29 percent of viewers had remote control units in 1985, 70 percent of today's viewers have them. The latest viewing trend, which worries many advertisers, is "**grazing**"—*zipping and zapping through commercials and programs* when a lull in the action prompts a search for greener pastures.

Videodiscs In 1981, the electronics giant RCA unveiled what it thought would be the videoplayer of the future—the Selectavision VideoDisc. RCA chairman Edgar Griffiths had every reason to be optimistic. RCA had spent $200 million and 15 years developing a videodisc system that produced a sharper picture than the VCR. It was priced at $499. On the software side, RCA offered an extensive catalog of programming that could be purchased on discs—some for as little as $15. Several other systems based on optical disc technology were also on the market, but their players and discs cost considerably more. Griffiths predicted, by 1990, annual sales of 5 to 6 million players and 200 to 250 million discs. Despite such a rosy forecast and a $20 million advertising campaign, first-year player sales were just over one hundred thousand. By 1984, only five hundred fifty thousand players had been sold—most of them at a considerable discount. That same year, RCA announced it would discontinue production of VideoDisc players. Since its introduction, the VideoDisc operation had cost the company $580 million. RCA had made a colossal error. It had grossly underestimated the popularity of the VCR and videotape rentals.

Despite the spectacular failure of the RCA system, by the early 1990s the videodisc was on the road to recovery. The optical system that Philips had developed proved superior to the RCA system. With only a beam of laser light picking up its signal, the optical disc was practically free of normal wear and tear. And with a picture quality of 430 lines of resolution compared to 240 lines carried by VHS tapes, the laser videodisc system seemed the perfect technology to use in conjunction with the large-screen television sets that were becoming increasingly popular.

Another factor accounting for the resurgence of interest in the videodisc has been the combination player—or "combi" player—which plays CDs and videodiscs, both of which are optical recordings. The digital soundtrack on the videodisc is comparable to that of a CD recording. The newest combi players feature digital frame memory and longer-playing discs. With most feature films and many MTV-style music videos now available on videodisc, sales of players and discs are likely to increase. In 1990, there were roughly a half-million players in the United States. That figure is expected to increase to 2 million over the next three years. Videodisc sales in 1990 reached 6 million. One pressing plant that currently turns out six hundred thousand discs a month expects to produce 3 million a month by 1993. As sales increase, the price of players and discs is likely to drop. In May of 1990, *Billboard* magazine announced that seven different manufacturers were selling laser videodisc players. Six months later, *Billboard* reported 13 manufacturers. One of the new entries was RCA.

REVIEW

Low-power television (LPTV), introduced in 1980, provides programming for specialized audiences. Though it has yet to fulfill its promise, LPTV has generated some forty thousand applications. Currently, there are about seven hundred LPTV stations on the air. VCRs, by contrast, have become so popular that they pose a threat to movie box office sales, cable, and over-the-air television. Videodiscs, after a slow start, have also become increasingly popular—especially among owners of large-screen televisions and combi (CD and videodisc) players.

Improved Production Equipment ***High-definition television (HDTV).*** The television industry has been working for some years to develop equipment that will produce pictures equal in quality to the finest 35-millimeter film, the type used for theatrical motion pictures. That goal may now have been accomplished. The

Billboard® FOR WEEK ENDING JUNE 22, 1991

Top Videodisc Sales™

COMPILED FROM A NATIONAL SAMPLE OF RETAIL STORE SALES REPORTS.

THIS WEEK	LAST WEEK	WKS. ON CHART	TITLE	Copyright Owner, Manufacturer, Catalog Number	Principal Performers	Year of Release	Rating	Suggested List Price
			★ ★ No. 1 ★ ★					
1	1	11	GHOST	Paramount Pictures Pioneer LDCA, Inc. 32004	Patrick Swayze Demi Moore	1990	PG-13	29.95
2	4	3	BONFIRE OF THE VANITIES	Warner Bros. Inc. Warner Home Video 12048	Tom Hanks Bruce Willis	1990	R	29.98
3	15	3	AVALON	Tri-Star Pictures Pioneer LDCA, Inc. SCO55-6107	Armin Mueller-Stahl Joan Plowright	1990	PG	49.98
4	11	3	HAVANA	Universal City Studios MCA/Universal Home Video 81049	Robert Redford Lena Olin	1990	R	39.98
5	2	9	ARACHNOPHOBIA	Amblin Entertainment Image Entertainment 1080AS	Jeff Daniels	1990	PG-13	39.99
6	7	9	PRESUMED INNOCENT	Warner Bros. Inc. Warner Home Video 12034	Harrison Ford	1990	R	29.98
7	9	23	MADONNA: BLONDE AMBITION	Pioneer Artists Pioneer LDCA, Inc. PA-90-325	Madonna	1990	NR	29.95
8	6	31	THE HUNT FOR RED OCTOBER	Paramount Pictures Pioneer LDCA, Inc. LV32030-2	Sean Connery Alec Baldwin	1990	PG	29.95
9	NEW ▶		THE KRAYS	Parkfield Pictures Pioneer LDCA, Inc. 90976	Gary Kemp Martin Kemp	1990	R	39.95
10	3	13	DIE HARD 2: DIE HARDER	FoxVideo Image Entertainment L1850-85	Bruce Willis Bonnie Bedelia	1990	R	49.98
11	12	5	NARROW MARGIN	Live Home Video Image Entertainment ID8236IV	Gene Hackman Anne Archer	1990	R	39.95
12	13	19	PRETTY WOMAN	Touchstone Pictures Image Entertainment 1027AS	Richard Gere Julia Roberts	1990	R	29.99
13	20	3	DUCKTALES THE MOVIE	Walt Disney Home Video Image Entertainment 1082	Animated	1990	G	29.99
14	10	7	CHILD'S PLAY 2	Universal City Studios MCA/Universal Home Video 41024	Alex Vincent Jenny Agutter	1990	R	34.98
15	NEW ▶		JACOB'S LADDER	Live Home Video Image Entertainment ID8239IV	Tim Robbins Elizabeth Pena	1990	R	39.95
16	5	7	MEMPHIS BELLE	Warner Bros. Inc. Warner Home Video 12040	Matthew Modine Eric Stoltz	1990	PG-13	24.98
17	8	9	HENRY AND JUNE	Universal City Studios MCA/Universal Home Video 81050	Fred Ward Uma Thurman	1990	NC-17	39.98
18	24	7	NAVY SEALS	Orion Pictures Image Entertainment ID82060R	Charlie Sheen Michael Biehn	1990	R	29.95
19	17	15	DARKMAN	Universal City Studios MCA/Universal Home Video 80978	Liam Neeson	1990	R	34.98
20	23	15	FLATLINERS	RCA/Columbia Pictures Home Video Pioneer LDCA, Inc. 50386	Kiefer Sutherland Julia Roberts	1990	R	34.95
21	18	17	DAYS OF THUNDER	Paramount Pictures Pioneer LDCA, Inc. 32123	Tom Cruise Robert Duvall	1990	PG-13	34.95
22	NEW ▶		TEXASVILLE	Nelson Home Entertainment Pioneer LDCA, Inc. 7778	Jeff Bridges Cybill Shepherd	1990	R	34.98
23	NEW ▶		GRAFFITI BRIDGE	Warner Bros. Inc. Warner Home Video 12055	Prince Morris Day	1990	PG-13	29.98
24	22	3	ROCKY & BULLWINKLE: VOL. III	Buena Vista Home Video Image Entertainment 1129AS	Animated	1991	NR	39.99
25	14	7	DEATH WARRANT	MGM/UA Home Video Pioneer/Image Ent. ML102170	Jean-Claude Van Damme	1990	R	24.98

◆ ITA gold certification for a minimum of 125,000 units or a dollar volume of $9 million at suggested retail for theatrically released programs, or of at least 25,000 units and $1 million at suggested retail for nontheatrical titles. ◇ ITA platinum certication for a minimum sale of 250,000 units or a dollar volume of $18 million at suggested retail for theatrically released programs, and of at least, 50,000 units and $2 million at suggested retail for nontheatrical titles.

Billboard's *list of top-selling videodiscs.*

new high-definition television, or HDTV, systems increase the number of scanning lines per second from 525 to as many as 1575. The result is a much sharper, or "high-definition," picture. The adoption of HDTV will likely increase the number of network television and cable programs produced on video and speed the conversion of Hollywood theatrical film production from film to video.

At one time, as many as twenty different systems were being considered as the U.S. standard for HDTV. But investment costs and technological edge have reduced the number to five. Once testing on the five remaining systems has been completed, the FCC's Advisory Committee on Advanced Television Service will recommend one as the standard. The FCC is expected to make a final decision on an HDTV system in 1993.

One of the major problems facing broadcasters and the FCC is how to fit HDTV into the space allocated for over-the-air television. Current television stations use 6 megahertz of bandwidth, but HDTV requires 9 to 12 megahertz to carry its brighter and better picture. Compression technology developed jointly by Zenith and AT&T overcomes this problem by squeezing all of the picture information into the conventional 6-megahertz bandwidth. The Zenith-AT&T all-digital system—called the Digital Spectrum Compatible HDTV—offers pictures that are of movie-theater quality and sound comparable to that of a digital compact disc. Two other HDTV systems, one developed by General Instrument and another by the Advanced Television Research Consortium, are also all-digital.

Satellite and cable companies have fewer problems with regard to HDTV. In the super-high-frequency portion of the spectrum where satellites operate, there is plenty of bandwidth for high-definition television. And cable companies can create whatever space they need without seeking government permission. With the advent of fiber optics, converters, smaller satellite dishes, larger flat-screen HDTV sets, and HDTV VCRs, the stage is about to be set for a titanic struggle among direct-broadcast satellite (DBS) services, satellite-linked cable services, and over-the-air television broadcasters, as each tries to capitalize on the latest electronic toy. In hot pursuit will be the movie and print industries, also exploiting the capabilities of HDTV.

Super Slo-Mo. Broadcasters and cable operators who cover sports events have long been interested in better slow-motion video. When standard video signals are slowed down, the resolution of the picture deteriorates. This problem is being overcome in various ways, including Super Slo-Mo, developed by Sony. Super Slo-Mo records at 180 fields per second, rather than the standard 60, so that the playback can be at the normal speed of 60, thus retaining the quality of the rest of the program.

Miniaturization Another continuing development is the miniaturization of almost every technological device used in communication. Not only is equipment being made smaller, it is also being made lighter, better, and, in many cases, cheaper.

Even printed materials are being miniaturized. Microfilm, microfiche, and other photographic reduction techniques already make it possible to store far more printed information in a small space than we can do with conventional books. Further miniaturization of print materials will soon be feasible. These developments are important for many reasons, not the least of which are burgeoning costs of building and maintaining libraries. Miniaturization methods make possible the building and maintenance of a major library without the huge investment of money and space now required. A large part of the cost of any college library is storage space and conventional books. Storage with even our present miniaturized print materials—microfilm and other forms—takes but a fraction of the space needed for books printed on paper, and the difference in cost between a conventional book and the miniaturized forms should become greater, increasingly favoring the latter.

When motion picture cameras were made smaller and lighter so that they could easily be carried about, new kinds of movies were made possible, especially certain kinds of documentaries such as *cinema vérité*, in which cameras literally follow their subjects about wherever they go. The smaller the camera, the more places it could be taken and, hence, the more kinds of subjects we could film.

The same expansion of horizons occurred as television cameras were miniaturized. The portable camera made it easy, for example, for reporters at political conventions to show what was going on in any part of the hall or any other place in the convention city. More spectacular was the placement of television cameras on space rockets so that we could watch astronauts walking on the moon. Still cameras, motion picture cameras, and television cameras can now be made so small that people can be photographed easily without their awareness. That raises again the problem of ensuring privacy.

REVIEW

High-definition television (HDTV) may revolutionize both the film and television industries with its sharply defined, 35-millimeter-like images. The main obstacle to over-the-air broadcasting of HDTV is how to fit the service into the electromagnetic spectrum and make it compatible with existing services. Thanks to the silicon chip, communications equipment is being miniaturized.

Developments in the miniaturization and automation of electronic equipment are being aided by what some scientists believe is the major invention of the twentieth century, the tiny silicon chip. Today, a chip half the size of your fingernail—called a microchip—can be etched with electronic circuitry with enough computation power to operate a radio station or play an expert game of chess. Thousands of integrated circuits can be etched on a quarter-inch square of silicon, giving it the power to do as much as the large computers of thirty-five years ago. Tomorrow, even smaller chips will have even greater power.

The microchips of today are designed for various purposes. Some are electronic memory banks for storing information, some are amplifiers for distributing information, and some are microprocessors for carrying out various computing jobs.

NONTECHNOLOGICAL DEVELOPMENTS

In considering the factors that may affect the future of mass communication, we cannot restrict ourselves to technological developments. Other developments are also important. One is the change in the audience.

The Changing Audience

For the next decade at least, the potential audience for the mass media will continue to grow as the population increases. The rate of increase will not be as steep as it has been in the past, however, and we may reach a "steady state" early in the twenty-first century. At that point, the population will remain relatively stable, neither increasing nor decreasing.

Although the total population in the United States will not change greatly in the next ten or twenty years, its makeup will. The proportion of older people will increase as the birth rate declines and people live longer. The greatest increase now is in the number of Americans in the 25-to-34 age group.

It appears that the number of households will increase far more rapidly than the population, largely because of a great increase in the number of people who choose to live alone—just one person in the household. Population in the southern states and along the Pacific coast will continue to increase more rapidly than in the rest of the country. The suburbs will also continue to gain population at the expense of the large cities. More than half of the adult women in this country now have full-time jobs outside the home, and that proportion continues to increase.

Another important social change that affects the mass communication audience is change in the dominant businesses and industries. These changes are brought about partly by technological developments and partly by changing demands of the public. The result is greater job mobility. The chances are far less that you will work for one company for your entire working life than they were for your parents' or grandparents' generation. You will likely change professions a number of times during your lifetime, or else you will need to keep learning in order to stay in the same profession.

Lifestyles of people in our present society are far more heterogeneous than they were in the past. As you know, new lifestyles are constantly developing, based largely on the changing interests and values of many people, but a substantial portion of the population always retains the more traditional lifestyles. Our improved forms of communication, by their almost immediate and widespread transmission of images of any new lifestyles, increase the number of new styles adopted and shorten the time it takes for adoption to spread throughout the country. The result is proportionately fewer numbers of people with shared interests and values and, hence, smaller audiences for particular kinds of materials in any of the media. The audience is fragmented to a far greater extent.

Implications for the Media of Age Changes

These changes have many implications for the media. The fact that the audience, on the average, is getting older is bound to affect the strong youth orientation that many of the media have today. Appealing to more mature audiences will make good economic sense.

The bulk of the audience for motion pictures, for example, has always been young people in their teens and twenties. As that portion of the population declines, the motion picture industry will need to find ways of attracting more older people into the theaters or of bringing feature films to them. Pay-per-view television and home VCRs may be partial solutions to this problem.

The daytime audience for radio and television is bound to change substantially. In fact, we see it happening already. Better health care is increasing the longevity of people, which means far more quite elderly people in the audience and especially more men who are living many years past retirement. Thus, the proportion of older males in the daytime audience is steadily increasing.

Implications for the Media of Sex Role Shifts

The combination of the sexual revolution and economic need is bringing a far larger percentage of adult American women into the work force and out of the home. This, combined with the increased numbers of males at home, may force broadcasters to rethink totally their daytime programming. By the twenty-first century, female homemakers may no longer dominate the daytime radio, television, and cable audience.

REVIEW

The mass communication audience is changing as the average age of the population increases. There are also lifestyle changes: a larger proportion of women in the work force and less differentiation in the tasks of men and women.

The fact that rapidly increasing numbers of adult women are moving into the work force will probably also affect the readership of books and magazines. Traditionally, women have been the major consumers of light fiction, both in book and magazine form. In good part this has been because they had more leisure time. As they enter the work force, however, and still retain many household duties in most cases, whether married or not, their time for reading fiction will be sharply reduced. Publishers may need to strive harder for older readers to maintain their circulation.

As more women enter the work force, a breakdown is occurring in the sharp division between male and female roles in the home. Men increasingly are sharing in the homemaking tasks, from cooking, caring for chil-

dren, and cleaning to shopping for household necessities. This change in lifestyles will affect mass communication in two ways. It will mean that men have less time to devote undivided attention to the media during prime time and on weekends. Perhaps more important, it will mean that all advertising currently designed to appeal largely to housewives will need to be redesigned to appeal equally to househusbands.

Implications for the Media of Increased Job Mobility

Because people will be changing jobs so often in the future, and because the technology within many jobs is so complex and constantly changing, the demand for continuing education and retraining will increase. Much of the continuing education and retraining will be done by the mass media—or, at the minimum, they will help with that task. The media will need to employ more people who understand the psychology and techniques of teaching and learning and who possess the skills needed to produce newspapers, magazines, books, films, recordings, and radio and television programs.

All of these effects of our changing population are significant. More important than any mentioned so far, however, is the pressure that population changes are creating for "demassification" of mass communication, to be discussed shortly.

THE IMPACT OF TECHNOLOGICAL AND AUDIENCE CHANGES

The developments described in this and earlier chapters have already had considerable impact on mass communication in this country. These past trends are reasonably clear. Far less clear is whether the changes and trends we have seen in the past decade or so will continue and what other changes they might bring about.

Shifting Audience Patterns

As indicated earlier, the movie, sports, and other special types of programming offered by cable systems have already resulted in a decline in the audiences of the three major commercial television networks and, hence, of most local television stations. At this point, we do not know whether the percentage of households subscribing to cable is approaching its maximum, or whether that percentage will continue to climb until it approaches the almost total saturation that regular television has achieved. One estimate shows that by 1993, nearly 86 percent of the households in America will have access to cable, and almost 70 percent of them will be cable subscribers.[1]

The great increase in number of channels of information made possible by VCRs, cable, fiber optics, satellites, computers, and other technologies discussed in this and earlier chapters has made practical the production and distribution of more special interest material for specialized audiences. We need only point to the availability today of all-religious channels on most cable systems, MTV, programs about bowling or female wrestlers, or stock market reports. Editors and programmers in all of the media today are trying to guess the strength of that demand for special interest material. To the extent that there are unsatisfied needs, opportunities exist for special interest publications, videotape productions, interactive computer networks, LPTV, and other forms of mass communication that do not depend on attracting gigantic audiences to some common content. If enough small audiences are attracted to these specialized materials, television as we know it today will pass from the scene. Some futurists have even predicted that our present commercial networks will eventually switch to being simply program suppliers to cable systems and marketers of videotapes for home viewing on VCRs.

Demassification of Mass Communication

To the extent this trend in the popularity of highly specialized content continues and becomes dominant, it will be a revolutionary shift.

The major communication trend up until 1980 was the "massification" of communication—the transmission of the same information or entertainment to a larger and larger percentage of the public. For example, first radio and then television made it possible for a presidential candidate—and even more for a president—to transmit the same message simultaneously to a large portion of American homes. Throughout these years, a large portion of us also were exposed to the same entertainment, the same information, and the same advertising.

The major communication trend of the 1980s and 1990s is **demassification** of communication—making possible *the individualization of messages and of schedules of communication*. This demassification is taking two forms, one controlled by the sender and one by the receiver. Both are made possible by the linking of the computer with various forms of communication, from the printing press to television, cable, and satellites.

Examples of sender-controlled demassification are the "individualized" letters turned out by computer-controlled printers. In these, the name of the letter's intended recipient is inserted periodically, along with information or appeals directed at his or her particular interests. This can also be done—and in fact will be done—with newspapers or magazines, with each reader getting a copy with material that particularly fits his or her wants and needs. A political candidate can send out letters in which combinations of different sentences or paragraphs are inserted that speak directly to the interests of that voter, as indicated by information stored in the computer from regularly updated surveys. It is also possible to update such information banks with data from other sources, such as television-viewing surveys and bank records. Theoretically, a political party or candidate can buy such information in the same way that publishers and advertisers now buy mailing lists of potential customers. The kinds of information that will be legally possible to collect and sell are not yet known. This is a basic issue in the ongoing debate about rights of privacy.

Receiver-controlled demassification will put control of input into the hands of the receiver of communication, rather than the hands of the sender. The number of choices of kinds of information and sources of information for the average citizen is increasing rapidly, and new technologies will increase the choices many times over. The ready availability of cassette videotapes and, even more, the interactive systems that tie each television set or home computer to a vast array of information and entertainment that can be selected and viewed or listened to at any time will offer virtually infinite possibilities for, in effect, editing your own newspaper and building your own television schedule. These developments have been facilitated by the almost limitless computer memory made possible by the new silicon chips.

Potential Advantages of Demassification

There are two major advantages of demassification:

1. As consumers, we will have greater control over what we are exposed to and when we expose ourselves to it. We will be able, in effect, to create newspapers and magazines with exactly the information we want in as much detail as we want it. We will be able to get more of the kinds of entertainment we want. This increased control will be an especially radical change for those of us with specialized tastes who are generally ignored by the mass media today, in particular by the electronic media.
2. Demassification will also provide advertisers and others who want our attention greater opportunities to pinpoint the perfect audience. For example, if some advertisers should want to reach women between the ages of forty and fifty with incomes of over $40,000 per year, they conceivably could pinpoint that audience and get to them with their messages.

Potential Disadvantages of Demassification

In general, demassification is probably a good thing because it gives each of us more control over what we read and hear and see. However, demassification has some potential drawbacks to individuals and to society. Being aware of them, you may be able to help minimize them.

1. Demassification may lead to narrower interests because it will be easier for us to avoid exposure to information or entertainment that is unfamiliar or uninteresting to us. Today, for example, when we read the newspaper or listen to radio or television news, we find it difficult to avoid at least some exposure to foreign news, even if we are not interested in it. In many cases this exposure increases our interest and hence expands our horizons. Even if it does not, at least the exposure gives almost every one of us some knowledge of world affairs, an essential ingredient for public opinion.
2. Because it makes more choices available to all of us, an inevitable result of demassification is a smaller audience for any one choice. This

probably will mean smaller profits for the bulk of producers and publishers. Because a portion of the profits from highly popular programs, books, and films often are used to support important works that are not as popular, such as public affairs programs, specialized or experimental books, and documentary films, a reduction in profits may make it more difficult for such works to get produced.

3. As noted before, the technology that makes demassification possible also makes possible some serious invasions of our privacy.
4. By definition, demassification means we will have fewer experiences in common with most other members of our society. In the past, these common experiences have been a cohesive force, a sort of glue that helped hold us together. That common base made it easier for us to agree on goals and work together toward them. Without such a base, the dangers of disintegration are greater.
5. What is true for our society is equally true for our families. The fewer communication experiences shared by husband and wife, parents and children, the less commonality of values and understanding.

An example of how demassification can lead to less, rather than more, diversification for a single individual can be seen in the homes of many sports fans today who subscribe to cable television. Through cable, the amount of college football available to fans has increased substantially. Within a year after the establishment of ESPN, the amount of college football available more than doubled. An examination of the cable schedule on the West Coast showed that sports junkies on one fairly typical fall weekend could have watched college football almost steadily from Saturday morning until Monday night. They could have watched live broadcasts of the Ohio State-Michigan game on Saturday morning and Alabama versus Miami in the afternoon. That night they could have watched the delayed broadcast of the Harvard-Yale game, Sunday morning Iowa and Nebraska, Sunday night Oklahoma and Missouri, and Monday afternoon UCLA and Stanford. If they missed one of the games or wanted to see any of them a second time, they had another chance: All were repeated later in the week.

Review

The huge increase in the number of channels of communication and the tailoring of messages to specific audiences are likely to result in a demassification of mass communication. While consumers may have more media choices and greater control over the kinds of media they wish to attend, they may also be faced with a reduction in program quality, fewer shared experiences, and less rather than more diversification.

Such saturated exposure on cable and over-the-air television may not be healthy for the viewers but could be very healthy for colleges and universities with major sports programs. The College Football Association (CFA), which represents 64 NCAA Division I-A teams outside the Big Ten and Pacific 10 conferences, negotiated contracts worth more than $300 million for games broadcast by ABC and ESPN from 1991 to 1995. Notre Dame negotiated a separate five-year, $30 million contract with NBC for broadcast of its home games during that period. With the expansion in the number of channels on most cable systems and the need to fill those channels with programming, it is likely that minor sports such as volleyball, lacrosse, track, and soccer will begin receiving greater coverage than in the past and, in return for that coverage, will begin producing income. Women's sports in particular are likely to benefit from cable's constant demand for programming.

THE GIANTS ARE STILL GROWING

Most of the people who write about the future of mass communication focus largely on technological changes in the recent past and those likely to occur in the future. Although such changes are clearly important, they may not be the changes that will have the greatest impact on either the mass communication industries or our society. Developments that could have far greater impact are the trends in the economic structure of the mass media industries. You will not see as much about these changes in your local newspaper or on your favorite television station. They are not trends the media like to publicize. However, because their potential impact is great, you should be aware of them now and as they develop and change in the future.

In a number of the chapters on individual media, we noted the development of a few giant media corporations that control much of the mass media industry. While this concentration of ownership has increased steadily throughout the twentieth century, only in the last decade has it reached worldwide proportions. Some observers predict that by the twenty-first century a handful of mammoth corporations will achieve complete vertical integration and dominate the world's information and entertainment industries. In addition to Time Warner, the world's largest media corporation, the other global media giants include Bertelsmann AG of West Germany, the Sony Corporation and Matsushita Electric Industrial Company of Japan, News Corporation Ltd. of Australia, Hachette S.A. of France, and Pearson PLC and Maxwell Communication of England. Despite their foreign home bases, these corporations own a large chunk of U.S. media. Bertelsmann, for example, owns Bantam Doubleday Dell Publishers, RCA Records, and the Literary Guild. Sony includes among its holdings CBS Records and Columbia Pictures. Rupert Murdoch's company, News Corp., owns newspapers in Boston and San Antonio, and controls Fox Broadcasting, 20th Century Fox movie studios, HarperCollins Publishers, and numerous periodicals and magazines—including *TV Guide, Seventeen,* and *New York.* (Murdoch is now an American citizen.) Hachette is the world's largest publisher of reference books, including the *Encyclopedia Americana.* In 1988, Pearson purchased Addison-Wesley Publishing Company for $283 million, making Pearson one of the world's five largest English-language book publishers. Another giant publisher is Maxwell Communication, which acquired the Macmillan book publishing house in 1988 for $2.62 billion. In 1991, the company's flamboyant owner, Robert Maxwell, wrapped up a deal to take control of the financially troubled *New York Daily News,* one of this country's largest newspapers.

These giant media corporations hope that in the not-too-distant future the acquisition of different kinds of media on a worldwide scale will produce **synergies**—*cooperative* (and presumably profitable) *ventures among subsidiaries of the same corporation.* For example, before the merger of Time and Warner, Time Inc. repackaged the swimsuit edition of *Sports Illustrated* (a Time Inc. publication) into a special for Home Box Office (another Time Inc. property) and an HBO home videocassette. Future such issues might be used to attract subscribers to Time Warner Cable, this country's second-largest cable system. Time Warner can now produce an article that can be transformed into a book, movie, or television program and then sold abroad through an international distributor—all within the corporate framework of Time Warner.

In the 1990s, foreign corporations are likely to continue buying media in this country, as the combination of a weakened U.S. dollar abroad and the potential for making huge sums of money makes American media an attractive investment. While FCC regulations prohibit the purchase of broadcasting stations by foreigners, other media entities are subject to the highest bidders.

To position themselves for media competition in the twenty-first century, U.S. corporations have created their own vertically integrated mega-companies. Time Warner is just one example. Newspaper organizations such as Gannett continue to acquire other media properties as they become available. In 1990, Gannett owned some 82 newspapers, 10 television stations, 16 radio stations, and the second-largest outdoor advertising firm and had begun producing television programming in Hollywood. Another giant media corporation, Gulf + Western, which owns Simon & Schuster books and Paramount Pictures, entered the global race by selling all of its nonmedia holdings and changing its name to Paramount Communications Inc.

Review

Some observers believe that by the twenty-first century, a handful of giant corporations will control much of the world's market of information and entertainment. These corporations will have achieved complete vertical integration. Despite the fierce competition among media businesses, some investments such as direct-broadcast satellite (DBS) will require so much capital that normally rival corporations will join forces and will compete against other corporate coalitions.

The merger and takeover craze of the 1980s led to all three major television networks changing hands. NBC and its parent organization, RCA, were purchased by the electronics giant, General Electric, for $6.26 billion. Laurence Tisch—a billionaire financier who owns Loews Corporation, a conglomerate of movie theaters, hotels, and tobacco and insurance companies—acquired almost a quarter of the stock in CBS and took control of it. Under Tisch's direction, CBS sold its record, publishing, and magazine divisions to concentrate on broadcasting. ABC was taken over by Capital Cities Communications for $3.4 billion. In addition to the ABC network, Cap Cities/ABC has 8 television stations, 21 radio stations, 9 daily newspapers, a magazine and book-publishing division, and an 80 percent interest in the cable sports channel, ESPN. It has interests in two other cable channels as well.

Some ventures of the 1990s are likely to be so expensive that even giant media corporations will be forced into cooperative arrangements with their competitors. For example, the $1 billion financing of a direct-broadcast satellite service (DBS) is bringing together General Motors' Hughes Communications, Rupert Murdoch's News Corp., and General Electric's NBC and Cablevision Systems Co. The four companies—which have a considerable stake in cable systems and programming, broadcast networks, satellite communications, and motion pictures—plan to offer a service called Sky Cable late in 1993. It will provide 108 channels and will have the capacity to transmit high-definition television. The major competitor of Sky Cable is likely to be K Prime Partners, a consortium of nine cable operators—including industry giants Tele-Communications, Time Warner, and Comsat Corp.—and GE Americom, another division of General Electric.

ISSUES RAISED BY DEVELOPMENTS IN MASS COMMUNICATION

The major trends in mass communication discussed in this chapter raise a great many issues. Some must be addressed by our society, both formally, through our government, and informally, through our interactions and development of public opinion and norms. Others each of us must face individually and decide what we ought to do about them to retain or gain maximum control of our lives.

> **BYLINE**
>
> How do you assess the relative dangers and benefits of the trend toward ownership and control of all of the mass media of communication by a relatively few giant corporations? Is this an issue with which the public should be concerned? Is it an issue which the government should do something about? If so, what should the government do?

Legal Issues

Recent developments in mass communication raise a number of legal issues that touch directly on the lives of most, if not all, of us.

Legal conflicts over illegal copying and home recordings. One of the major problems faced by all mass communication industries today—motion pictures, television, book publishing, recording, and others—is that our techniques for making copies of their products have far outpaced our government's ability to provide adequate copyright protection. The technology of the satellite and cable systems permits the importation and sale of television programs produced by stations hundreds or thousands of miles away. Photocopying machines make it easy for anyone to make copies of printed matter without paying a royalty. And audio and video tape recording makes the copying of records or videotapes or television programs as easy as flicking a switch. Our entire copyright system is threatened—which means that our system for adequately rewarding the creators of artistic and intellectual works is threatened. The result could be a decrease in the number of people willing to write and publish books, create records, and produce motion pictures or television programs.

The Recording Industry Association of America (RIAA) estimates that some $300 million a year is lost to record and tape piracy, counterfeiting, and bootlegging. **Piracy** involves *the unauthorized duplication of sounds contained in a recording,* whereas **counterfeiting** is *the unauthorized duplication of the sound and the original artwork, label, trademark, and packaging of original recordings.* **Bootlegging** is *the unauthorized recording of a performance broadcast on radio or television or of a live performance.* The RIAA maintains a full-time antipiracy unit to investigate these activities. In 1986 alone more than 465,000 pirate and counterfeit cassettes were seized. Another problem for the record industry—and a source of lost revenues—is home taping. With advances in recording technology, homemade tapes sound almost as good as original recordings. One of the stumbling blocks to the introduction of digital audiotape (DAT) players/recorders has been the problem of home taping and copyright protection (Chapter 8). All DAT players/recorders sold in this country will be equipped with a Serial Copy Management System (SCMS), which limits the number of digital copies that can be made from a digital source.

The copying of television programs and motion pictures with home VCRs has received a great deal of attention from both producers and the courts, but the situation remains unresolved. At one time, a U.S. Court of Appeals ruled that such recording, even for personal use in one's home, was illegal if permission was not obtained from the copyright owner. However, the Supreme Court struck down that ruling. One of the unresolved problems of trying to collect any sort of royalty payment for such home recordings, even if the law demanded it, is how it could be done practically and fairly. One suggestion is that an extra charge be placed on the blank tapes people buy for home recording, but they are used for many purposes other than recording films or television programs off the air or from rented tapes. Others suggest that a special tax be placed on home recording machines, but many of these machines are never used for such questionable recording. There is also the question of how the income from such special taxes should be distributed, since it is difficult to find out which motion pictures or television programs home users are recording.

BYLINE

Do you believe people who make home video recordings of television programs or motion pictures, that they would otherwise need to rent or buy if they wanted them for self or family viewing in the home, should be forced to pay some sort of fee to the copyright holders? Do you have the same opinion about that as you do about people using electronic devices to get pay cable or long-distance telephone service free? What about getting the services of plumbers or dentists without paying their bills? Is there an essential difference between the obligation to pay dentists for use of their services and the obligation to pay filmmakers?

Information as property. The problem of home recordings is related to another problem we face in the information society—a society in which information is one of our major resources—the problem of social policy. An information society cannot be organized around the concept of private property, as our present society is, because information is totally unlike any of the materials that we consider property today and that make up the wealth of the individual and the country. Unless we make some fundamental changes in our laws and our ways of thinking, information cannot be anyone's private property; no one can "own" it. Although information might be considered part of the wealth of our nation, in no sense (other than metaphoric) can it be considered part of the wealth of an individual. In fact, our society frowns on any person or agency that attempts to hoard information, to keep it from other people.

The question of the property rights to information brings up the question of copyright. As indicated earlier, a major problem with all of the new technologies that facilitate duplication of materials or that make materials available to users in other ways (such as presenting them on call on a video screen) is protecting the rights of copyright holders, whether authors, publishers, filmmakers, record producers, or television stations or networks.

Protecting Our Privacy

The various forms of interactive communications technology—two-way cable, pay-per-view television, computer-delivered videotex, call-tracing telephones—have many potential benefits for people. However, a major drawback, for people concerned about privacy rights, is the capability of identifying with high accuracy who is using, or which households are using, these services. At the source, computers can record which households are using a particular service and how often. This kind of information is of obvious value to advertisers who will be able to pinpoint precisely the audiences they want and tailor their advertising to them. Equally obvious, however, is the potential for the invasion of people's privacy. A related privacy issue has arisen as a result of advances in telephone technology that make it possible for consumer phones to identify the source of phone calls. Despite some of the obvious advantages of this feature, privacy advocates argue that it constitutes an unwarranted intrusion on one's privacy. This dilemma is obviously one that the government must deal with, as it seeks to strike a balance between furthering technological convenience and protecting individuals' rights.

REVIEW

The major trends in mass communication raise a number of important legal and regulatory issues. One such issue is illegal copying and taping. Another is invasion of privacy.

Another technological device that may be producing privacy problems is the fax machine. Actually, facsimile technology has been around for quite some time. In the 1930s and 1940s, a number of newspapers experimented with fax delivery but could not find an appreciative audience. (In the past few years, newspapers have renewed their interest in facsimile and have found a growing audience for timely news summaries targeted to fax users.) Facsimile survived as a means of transmitting photos to newspapers. But it is only in the past few years that businesses and homes have discovered the value of **fax machines**—*machines that deliver copies of letters, documents, and drawings over a telephone line.* Of the roughly 1.6 million fax machines in use, more than half were purchased in the last year. Their use—some would say abuse—has produced a clutter of information from salespersons and publicists who deluge offices with unwanted materials.

Optimizing the Diversity of Views

A major issue with which the various agencies regulating mass communication in this country will need to deal in the future is how to get maximum diversity of viewpoints in the media in the face of pressures toward greater and greater consolidation of ownership. This is not a new issue; the Federal Communications Commission and the antitrust arm of the Department of Justice have been wrestling with it for years. We will probably see the issue arise in the years ahead in the question of cross-ownership. Cross-ownership is the ownership by one corporation of various media in the same market. For example, the Federal Communications Commission struggled with the question of whether the owner of a cable television system could hold a license for a television station in the same community. For years the FCC vacillated on whether a corporation could own both a newspaper and a broadcasting station in a community. Some argue that we can only have maximum diversity in our marketplace of ideas by having no cross-ownership. Others argue that cross-ownership is a problem only where there are no competing media of any sort. Still others argue that cross-ownership is never a problem; public pressure alone, without government intervention, will ensure that the public is adequately served with a wide range of ideas, information, and entertainment. Consider these various points of view and decide what you think about the matter and which side you support.

More Regulation or Less Regulation?

As the twentieth century draws to a close, political pressure is mounting to deregulate some media industries and to strengthen regulation for others. Ever since the breakup of AT&T in 1984, the seven regional Bell operating companies (RBOCs) have been pushing to enter the information business. With annual revenues of $70 billion and the benefit of AT&T's long history of research and development in communications technology, Ameritech, Bell Atlantic, BellSouth, Nynex, Pacific Telesis, Southwestern Bell, and US West would provide formidable competition in any information service field they chose to enter. Although a court order currently prohibits them from producing information transmitted over the lines they own, the relaxation of similar restrictions on AT&T has prompted renewed efforts by the RBOCs to become participants in all aspects of electronic communications. One area that is particularly attractive to the

RBOCs is cable television. Currently, the regional Bells are looking to the courts and to Congress to lift the restriction on offering information services.

Additional pressure to deregulate is coming from the commercial networks, which have experienced a steady erosion in their share of the television audience. The networks fought hard for repeal of the Financial Interest and Syndication Rules (Chapter 10). Now they are likely to challenge the FCC's Prime Time Access Rule (PTAR), which limits the amount of programming a network can furnish during prime time. Although one purpose of the PTAR was to promote localism—that is, to provide an opportunity for network affiliates to offer their own progamming during peak viewing periods—another purpose was to prevent the networks from controlling the airwaves. Some observers believe that now that the Financial Interest and Syndication Rules have been relaxed, the PTAR will be repealed, as both are based on the need for greater diversity in the marketplace. If that diversity has been achieved by other means, through cable, VCRs, and independent television stations, the rationale for such rules may no longer be valid.

While the cry for deregulation is being heard in some quarters, the public's outcry over rising cable rates and poor service is prompting Congress to consider reregulating the cable industry. In 1984, Congress passed a law deregulating the industry. Since that time, average basic cable rates have increased from about $9 a month to $16. One U.S. senator, besieged by complaints from his constituents, declared that the cable industry had no competition and no regulation. That situation is likely to change, as more than a dozen bills have been introduced to deal with such issues as cable rates, local government control of rates, buying and selling of franchises, ownership of cable systems, networks, and programs (an issue much like the one that prompted the FCC to enact financial interest and syndication rules for the over-the-air television networks), the number of cable systems a company can own, siphoning of sports events from over-the-air to cable television, ensuring that cable systems carry local broadcast stations, and providing additional competition. The latter issue might be resolved by allowing the telephone companies to enter the cable business.

The main question for the FCC and Congress to consider in all regulation and deregulation matters is how the public will benefit from any changes in the regulatory structure. At one time, Congress and the FCC thought that more, rather than less, regulation was necessary to protect the public's interest in over-the-air and cable television. But in the late 1970s and throughout the 1980s, the pendulum swung the other way. Some regulations—such as restrictions on the development of cable—seemed to protect broadcasters' interests more than the public's interest; others—like the regulations limiting the number of licenses a company can hold and the terms of those licenses—seemed out of step with market forces. The move to deregulate the communications industry was in keeping with broader goals of decreasing government interference for all types of industries. But in the 1990s, the subject of debate is not likely to be whether regulation or deregulation is better, but what kinds of new laws and regulations will serve the public in an optimum way and what kinds of existing laws and regulations have outlived their usefulness.

BYLINE

What is your opinion? Should we have less government regulation of the media, or should we simply revise our government regulations? Why?

Pressures on Government Created by Rapid Diffusion of News

Many seemingly positive media developments bring with them some potentially negative consequences. The rapid diffusion of news is one such development. When news is diffused as rapidly as it generally is in this country, the public often learns about serious crises as quickly as government officials do. And once the public knows about a crisis, it expects—even demands—immediate government action. But a government can seldom respond so quickly. Government officials need time to think, to consider options, and to plan. In the past, when information was diffused more slowly, the government had ample time for thinking and planning before public pressure for action developed, because the public did not receive the information as rapidly as the government did. Part of the reason for the crisis of leadership we have in this country, some scholars believe, is that government no longer has this lead time over the public and, hence, cannot be ready to act when the public demands action. This is a difficult problem to resolve. The most obvious solution is to slow down or withhold information from the public. But that creates greater problems than the rapid diffusion of information does and is contrary to one of our society's most fundamental beliefs, summarized in the First Amendment of the Constitution.

Regulation of the New Technologies

Another important legal question raised by the new technologies is the extent to which the government can or should regulate various new forms of communication. Part of the answer, although clearly not all of it, depends on how you define those technologies. For example, if a printed story is delivered to homes through some form of transmission over the air waves, is it then television or something else? If it is television, then shouldn't it be regulated in the same way that other television is regulated in this country? If it is not television, is it like the telephone

REVIEW

As the twentieth century draws to a close, there is a demand for both more and less regulation of media. Some new laws and regulations may be needed to best serve the public, while other existing laws and regulations may no longer be necessary.

services? If so, then a different set of regulations applies. Or is it neither television nor telephone but something else? Do we then need a new regulatory agency? Or should the government not regulate this form at all?

All of these are interesting questions that communication practitioners and communication lawyers will be debating for years. We members of the public who use or will use these systems ought to form our own opinions and attempt to shape policy in our interests. Most important, whatever new technologies or uses of the media develop and whatever ways they are regulated, you must determine for yourself how to use them most effectively in order to maintain control of your own life and to live and grow in the way you want. The mass media are a tremendous force in our society. It is up to you whether that force is a constructive or destructive influence on your life.

TOWARD THE TWENTY-FIRST CENTURY: A SUMMARY

In this chapter, we speculated on the future of mass communication. We suggested that during the last decade of the twentieth century there would be better and faster ways to create, deliver, and consume the information and entertainment products created by media industries. We also noted seven major trends that have emerged in mass communication. Probably most important is the rise of the information society. Not only has information become more important to individuals and the society; it has become a commodity of business. It is commonplace today for information to be bought and sold, much like automobiles and loaves of bread. And just as we have always worried about the maldistribution of rice or loaves of bread among the world's population, today we worry about the maldistribution of information.

Unlike the rise of the information society, which has gone largely unnoticed by most people, the large and steady increase in the available means for delivering information and entertainment is clear to everyone. We noted new uses of the telephone that have been developed, cable, the communications satellite—especially its potential for direct transmission to home television receivers (DBS), and the increasing use of fiber optics for carrying information.

At the heart of many of the mass communication developments of the past decade or two is the computer. It is involved in almost every stage and aspect of mass communication today, from the reporting done by journalists to the automated operation of broadcast stations.

Another trend we discussed is the breakdown in the distinctions among the major media. For example, when print news is delivered into your home via telephone line for reading off your television or computer screen instead of paper pages, is it television, magazine, or newspaper news? How we define new delivery services may be important in determining how those services are to be regulated. Also, different services are likely to use the same technology. Satellites, for example, are just as much a part of the newspaper and magazine businesses as they are of broadcasting. And high-definition television (HDTV) will likely be put to use in the production and exhibition of motion pictures and home-delivered newspaper text.

Not only technological trends but also human trends will affect mass communication by the twenty-first century. The proportion of older people in the population is rising, the amount of leisure time available to the average worker is increasing, there are more women in the work force, and the trend toward urbanization continues as small, rural villages die out.

With these technological and human trends have come trends in the economic structure of mass media industries. Newspaper, magazine and book publishers, record companies, motion picture studios, and broadcasting and cable operations have become parts of larger and more complex media corporations, some of them with interests that span countries and continents. By the end of the decade, perhaps as few as a half dozen or so mammoth corporations will control much of the world's information and entertainment market.

Perhaps the most important result of many of these trends has been the increasing demassification of the mass media. This is the decline in common media experiences for the population and rise in the use of specialized materials that match more closely individual interests. Cable, VCRs, and videodiscs, along with the proliferation of low-power television stations, specialized print media, and home computers linked to vast arrays of informational services are among the most prominent causes for this demassification development.

Finally, we discussed some of the major issues raised by the seven trends covered in this chapter. These include the extent to which the free use of copyrighted materials is useful or harmful to a society. The ease with which copyrighted materials can be duplicated without payment of royalty has brought this problem to the fore. The spread of the photocopying machine, VCR, and audio tape recorder are the major causes of this problem. Other communications developments, most notably two-way cable and call-tracing telephone, exacerbate another long-standing problem in mass communication: protection of the privacy of individuals. And the trend toward consolidation of ownership and vertical integration raise fears about a decline in diversity of viewpoints to which the public can be exposed. Given these problems and other changes in the production, delivery, and use of mass communication, the question of the optimum degree and form of media regulation is raised anew.

DISCUSSION QUESTIONS

1. What are the seven major trends in mass communication?
2. What is the difference between videotex and teletext? How is videotex currently being used?

3. What are some of the technologies important to the development and expansion of cable television?
4. In what sense might the VCR and videodisc pose a threat to other media?
5. What is high-definition television? How is it likely to be used?
6. What are some of the changes likely to occur in the last decade of the twentieth century in the audience for mass communication? What life-style changes might we expect?
7. What are some of the causes of demassification? What are some of its advantages and disadvantages?
8. What are some of the world's largest media corporations? What specific media do they own or control?
9. What are some of the legal and regulatory problems that have arisen as a consequence of developments in media technology or the introduction of new media? What are some of the possible solutions to these problems?

NOTE

1. *Communications Industry Forecast: 1989–1993* (New York: Varonis, Suhler & Associates, Inc., 1989), p. 56.

SUGGESTED READINGS

Relevant Contemporary Works

Bagdikian, Ben H. *The Media Monopoly.* 2nd ed. Boston: Beacon Press, 1987.

Bradshaw, Jon. "The Shape of Media Things to Come (A Science-Fiction Story That's All True)." In *Intermedia,* ed. Gary Gumpert and Robert Cathcart. 2nd ed., pp. 636–641. New York: Oxford University Press, 1982.

Communications Industry Forecast: 1989–1993. New York: Varonis, Suhler & Associates, 1989.

Graham, Margaret B. W. *RCA and the Videodisc: The Business of Research.* New York: Cambridge University Press, 1986.

Helsman, Hoyt R. *The New Electronic Media: Innovations in Video Technologies.* Stoneham, MA: Focal Press, 1989.

Schiller, Herbert I. *Culture, Inc.: The Corporate Takeover of Public Expression.* New York: Oxford University Press, 1989.

Williams, Frederick. *The New Communications.* Belmont, CA: Wadsworth, 1984. See also *Technology Review.*

PART THREE

MEDIA CONTROLS

As you are well aware, a great many and varied forces and influences shaped you, led you to become the kind of person you are and to behave the way you do. Similarly, a great many and varied forces shaped, and continue to shape, the mass media. In this section, we will discuss those forces that have the greatest influence on the media.

The chapters that follow generally cover one type of force or control at a time. You should recognize, though, that these forces do not operate in isolation from one another; no one of them deserves all of the praise or all of the blame. For example, even though many critics of our economic system like to place all of the blame on capitalism for whatever they do not like about American media, that approach is naive. Just as naive is the charge of many media executives that the fault lies with the American public's tastes and desires or that the problem is too much government regulation.

Rather than seeking someone to praise or blame, we believe it is more useful to try to understand the *kinds* of influences exerted by each of the agents of control, the *ways* those influences work, and the *relationships* among these influences. For example, rather than worrying simply about whether it is the drive to maximize profit or the drive to please an audience that accounts for a particular television program being on the air, we suggest that it is more valuable to understand how the drive to maximize profit *is related to* the desire to please an audience.

Chapters 12, 13, and 14 are devoted to examining these various kinds of forces and the relationships among them. In Chapter 12, we look at the forces resulting from the fact that the mass media in this country are owned and operated largely by profit-making organizations. Within this general topic, we will look most closely at the advertising and public relations industries. Advertising is important because it is the source of so much media income. Public relations is important because so much of what we get as news and entertainment is the result of public relations efforts.

In Chapter 13, we examine the ways many Americans influence the mass media other than through their reading, listening, viewing, or purchasing. Large numbers of individuals and organizations in this country form pressure groups to shape the content of the media. It is important for you to understand this phenomenon if you want to understand the operation of the media today. It is equally important to understand the way some of our laws and government agencies affect the way our media operate and the kinds of content they make available to you. This, too, is covered in Chapter 13.

The influences discussed in Chapters 12 and 13 come largely from outside the media industries. In Chapter 14, we move inside these industries to consider the ways the traditions and operating methods of media professionals put their own distinctive mark on our communication environment.

As you read these three chapters, keep in mind that all of the forces being discussed are closely related. To some degree or other, most, if not all, of the external and internal factors are influential because they affect profitability. On the other hand, their influence is due to far more than that. You can find many of these same forces operating on the nonprofit media in this country, including your college newspaper and National Public Radio.

CHAPTER 12

Economic Influences on the Media: Advertising, Public Relations, and Ownership

OBJECTIVES

After reading this chapter, you should be able to

- Explain the various kinds of economic controls that affect our communication mosaics.
- Describe the role of the Federal Trade Commission in the regulation of advertising.
- Explain the differences among the direct, indirect, and saliency approaches to advertising and the kinds of products for which each is most appropriate.
- State the media decisions that must be made in planning an advertising campaign.
- Describe the various goals of public relations.
- Explain the major differences between advertising and public relations.
- Point out the major arguments for and against the functions of advertising or its effects on people and on society.

What do the commercial mass media in this country sell? Space and time to advertisers? Laundry detergents and automobiles, beer and breakfast cereals to consumers? Fantasies? Beliefs in our economic and political system? To some extent, they sell all of those things. The major product they sell, though, is you and me and the rest of the millions of consumers in this country; they sell us to advertisers at so many dollars per thousand.

The drive to accumulate as many of us as possible for sale, especially those of us whom advertisers especially want to buy, acts as a major control or influence on the mass media. The media rarely act without considering this goal. Most careful observers blame this drive to build ever more salable audiences on the decline in the amount and quality of serious and important news in the major media. Because most of the media are so inextricably bound to advertising and public relations in this country, directly or indirectly, we must understand those two industries, and the other economic influences, if we want to understand why we get the kinds of media and media content that we do.

VARIETIES OF ECONOMIC CONTROLS

Some media critics take the position that advertising and other economic factors are not merely *part* of the reason we get the kinds of media and media content we do; they claim the economic system is the *dominant* reason. At its most extreme, this argument has been labeled **economic determinism.** This is the *theory that the economic system of a country is the dominant influence on almost everything, including all of the content of the mass media.* Those who believe in economic determinism argue that the individuals and organizations that control most of this country's economic resources, and are always striving to control more, are ultimately the most powerful—and perhaps the only—influences on our communication environment that make any difference.

Review

Although economic determinists probably assume too much influence on the media from the pressures to sell more advertising, tickets, or subscriptions, or from the related drive to maximize profits, those pressures are real. Economic factors clearly play an important role in determining what we can see, read, and hear in the media and in the kinds of media we have.

Economic determinists say, for example, that a new medium of communication develops in our society only when there is a reasonable probability that it will be profitable, and that the particular way it is developed is the way that will be the most profitable. Thus, they say, newspapers are organized as they are because that form has been found to be most profitable. The same is true for radio, television, motion pictures, the record industry, book publishing, and so on. These critics predict that satellite-to-home communication will not become widespread unless and until a way is found to make it more profitable than present cable or network television.

Although most of us would argue that factors other than economics affect our communication environment, we suspect all of us would agree that economics are important. In the United States, as in many countries, the majority of our media institutions are businesses, dependent on the sale of advertising, the sale of the information/entertainment product (the newspaper, magazine, book, recording, or home video), or the sale of admission tickets (to movie houses or for pay television). Almost anyone in the media who ignores the economic factors is soon out of a job, or else the organization is out of business. Even those in the noncommercial media—public broadcasting, university presses, educational film or video production units in schools or colleges—cannot totally ignore economics.

Advertising Controls

The influence of advertising is most obvious in newspapers. There, with few exceptions, the number of pages printed—and, hence, the amount of space available for news—is determined not by the amount of news deemed important, but rather by the amount of advertising sold. (This was discussed more fully in Chapter 4.)

The newspaper is not the only medium affected by advertising, however. Although the length of newscasts on broadcasting stations does not vary daily because of variations in the amount of advertising, the number of newscasts is affected by the availability of sponsorship. More important, other kinds of programming—including documentaries and the discussion of contemporary issues—are strongly affected by economic questions. Not only does availability of sponsorship increase the probability that a program will be aired, but it also increases the probability that it will be aired at a time when there is a large available audience. Even with sponsorship, however, managers of radio and television stations hesitate to place into prime time a program that will not draw a large audience be-

'O.K. Let's say I'm one of those mature spenders. Now: Appeal to me'
wm Hamilton

"Keeping Up" cartoon panel by William Hamilton is reprinted by permission of Chronicle Features, San Francisco.

cause it will not deliver enough viewers or listeners to the commercial programs that follow it. Similarly, live coverage of special events, such as a congressional hearing, will not be presented often because of the great loss of income from regularly scheduled programs and commercials. None of these commercial media can stay alive unless they can attract and hold sufficient advertising to pay all expenses of both the commercial and non-commercial programs and pay a reasonable return on the investment of owners or stockholders. (What constitutes a "reasonable return" and the basis on which it should be calculated are questions no data can answer. An individual or group of individuals must define "reasonable." However, your answers to those questions are critical for your decisions about whether the media could better serve the public interest.)

Advertising affects the content of the media in many ways. One of the most important, as we noted before, is that advertisers want to buy particular kinds of audiences. Consequently, programmers and editors, writers and directors, attempt to create and transmit the sorts of materials that will attract those audiences. NBC increased its profitability tremendously in recent years, for example, with shows such as "Cheers," "The Golden Girls," and "The Cosby Show," which appealed to young, urban audiences—the upwardly mobile, high-consumption audiences that advertisers love. Sports coverage is tremendously important for newspapers, radio, and television because the audience it attracts is not only large but also predominantly male, and therefore easily salable to the advertisers of products whose major purchasers are males.

These kinds of content not only attract the "right" sorts of audiences, but they also provide good contexts for advertising. Companies do not want their commercials or advertisements accompanying a story that will depress the audience and distract them from wanting to buy; they want a context that will put consumers in the right mood—a buying mood. Ideally, the context should help produce a feeling of need. This is the reason special sections of newspapers have developed: travel sections in which ads for airlines and travel agents are buried amidst features on exotic places; fashion sections with features that tell us what we should be wearing this season—and ads that tell us where to buy those fashions; entertainment sections that place glowing reviews of movies and night club acts right next to the ads that tell us where those shows are playing.

BYLINE

How many examples of this kind of newspaper content can you find in your Sunday newspaper? These might be stories or features that create the "right" context for a particular kind of advertising or that attract advertisers in other ways.

The media are not simply distribution systems for advertising, at least not in the minds of advertisers. Advertisers judge each medium in terms of its relative effectiveness as an agent of persuasion. Credibility is one factor in that effectiveness. This is one of the reasons why high-quality news coverage is important for newspapers and television. The credibility gained from carrying news that people want and trust probably generalizes to some extent to the entire paper, station, or network, thus making its advertising more credible.

Review

The drive to attract and hold advertisers affects the amount and kinds of news available in each of the media.

Public Relations

Although few critics blame the public relations industry as much as the advertising industry for the content of the media, it is far more influential than most people realize. Many of the "news" stories we read and see in the mass media originate from press releases written to promote someone or something. Many news stories in the entertainment sections of our newspapers are news releases from motion picture distributors about the stars of a new movie, its plot, writer, director, or anything else that will interest potential theater goers in the film. Many talk show guests are placed there by public relations firms to plug a book, movie, or a major sports event such as the Super Bowl. Much of the "news" we get from Washington and the state capitols originated with the public relations specialists in various government agencies.

Even the plots of some movies and television programs were developed in consultation with public relations agents whose clients want the general audience exposed to those particular ideas.

Review

Public relations is the unseen hand that shapes a large amount of the "news" and entertainment that we encounter in our communication environment.

Ownership Controls

Perhaps the least obvious of all economic controls is ownership. In the days of local ownership, one seldom found negative news in the newspaper or newscasts about the owner's other business interests, family, or friends. This was a fairly trivial problem. But as newspapers, motion picture studios, broadcasting stations and networks, and book publishing firms have been taken over by giant corporations with a great variety of interests, many of them stretching across the globe, ownership controls may be a more critical problem. We must ask whether newspapers or magazines owned by a corporation with heavy financial interest in the power industry are likely to publish exposés of the dangers of nuclear power plants. We must also wonder whether a broadcasting network that belongs to a conglomerate with profitable contracts to supply electronic equipment to Saudi Arabia or Brazil will feel as free to pursue and expose government wrongdoings in those countries as a network without such interests. If all of this sounds farfetched, you must not have heard about the incident at NBC's "Today" show when they were broadcasting a report about the use of shoddy nuts and bolts in airplane engines. One of the major suppliers of those dangerous nuts and bolts was General Electric, the corporation that owns NBC. Viewers of the "Today" show, however, never learned of

REVIEW

When those who own any of the news media also have other business interests, another hurdle is placed in the path of journalistic objectivity.

General Electric's involvement because the network news division edited out all mention of the company before the story was broadcast.

We are not suggesting here that the heads of such corporations as General Electric regularly apply pressure on their communication subsidiaries to cover the news in a particular way. Rather, knowing the interests of the company that pays one's salary can result in a type of self-censorship by individuals in the media.

Ticket sales and sales of the "product." Motion pictures and legitimate drama are also affected by economics. Hollywood and Broadway have often been condemned because of the power of "business people" or "bankers"; however, it seems logical that anyone considering financing a play or motion picture would want to do so only if enough tickets could be sold to recover the original investment plus a reasonable profit. Potential backers for motion pictures, legitimate dramas, and television series also consider the salability of the product in secondary markets—for sale or rental through another medium, for distribution in other countries, and (in the case of television series) for reruns on the network or individual stations. Even the publication of books is affected in this way. A novel with the potential for adaptation to the screen has a better chance of being selected by a publisher than one without this potential. Obviously, all of these factors affect the kinds of products that are financed by or for the media, and hence, the kinds of products that become available in our communication environment.

REVIEW

The content of our media is strongly influenced by the drive to sell more books, papers, and tickets, to export movies and television series overseas, to auction movie and television rights to books, and to merchandise characters popularized in the media—e.g., selling dolls, T-shirts, and other products based on them.

An interesting sort of by-product often important for a company's profitability is one that capitalizes on a character, idea, or person made famous through a motion picture, television series, record, or book. Walt Disney Productions makes more money today from Mickey Mouse toys, shirts, and so on, and from Disney World and Disneyland, which are based on characters and scenes from Walt Disney films, than it does from the films themselves. Even noncommercial television has earned income to support programs through its royalties on toys and clothing featuring characters from "Sesame Street." You may have unwittingly contributed to the support of "noncommercial" television by buying such products.

ADVERTISING

We have discussed advertising at various points throughout this book because of its importance to all media. Advertisements are the major source of income for the media and, hence, are a large part of the content of many of them. In addition, all of the media we considered must advertise themselves in order to attract audiences. It is almost impossible to sell books, magazines, recordings, or newspapers, or to get audiences for a motion picture or a radio or television program, without advertising.

Throughout this book, we have stressed the way bits of information we receive from our communication mosaics affect the worlds we construct in our heads. In thinking about that, do not overlook the fact that advertising—print ads, radio and television commercials, billboards, and advertising's many other forms—contributes many of those bits. Advertisements make up a large part of our communication mosaics.

Origins and Development of Advertising

Some form of advertising has existed ever since the first would-be trader proclaimed the merits of some possession to all within hearing distance. Many town criers were, in effect, professional proclaimers, hired to wander through a village or along the countryside loudly extolling the virtues of particular shops.

The earliest surviving piece of advertising is a clay tablet produced about 3000 B.C. in Babylonia. On it are inscribed notices about an ointment dealer, a scribe, and a shoemaker.[1] Another early form of advertising was the sign placed over a shop or market stall. Such signs led to government regulation of advertising—the first that we know about. A law was passed in England in 1614 restricting signs from extending more than eight feet from a building and requiring them to be sufficiently high off the ground to permit an armored man on horseback to pass underneath.

Like mass communication generally, advertising received a major boost with the development of the printing press. Printing made possible mass production and distribution of advertisements, initially in the form of handbills. As printing presses became more widespread in the fifteenth and sixteenth centuries, the use of handbills and posters for advertising spread with them.

The practice of newspaper advertising began during the seventeenth century in England, and at about the turn of the century in the American colonies. America also followed the mother country in the development of advertising agencies. Agencies were operating in England in 1800, while the first one in this country was organized about 1840. The primary business of this American agency, started by Volney B. Palmer, was to buy space from newspaper and magazine publishers at a special rate and resell it to advertisers at a higher rate. This type of brokerage business was the primary function of advertising agencies for many years.

At the end of the nineteenth century, when substantial growth in selling space was no longer possible and new sources of revenue were being sought, agencies began providing such additional services as writing advertising copy, selecting media for advertisers, and conducting market research.

The early twentieth century saw two important developments in the advertising industry: a struggle to reduce or eliminate unethical advertising practices and the application of social scientific research methods to increase the effectiveness of advertising. In 1911, *Printer's Ink,* a major trade publication for newspaper and magazine publishers, advocated that

REVIEW

Advertising existed at least five thousand years ago, but its modern form started with the printing press. Serious efforts to control misleading advertising, however, did not begin until early in this century.

fraudulent and misleading advertising be made illegal. Such legislation was also pushed by the **Better Business Bureau.** This is *an organization of business people that attempts to eliminate business practices that hurt the image of business—such as practices that are unfair to consumers.* Finally, in 1914, Congress passed the **Federal Trade Commission Act** that *outlawed unfair methods of doing business.* The Act established the **Federal Trade Commission (FTC)** as *the agency charged with developing and enforcing rules to eliminate those unfair business practices.* As we will explain later in this chapter, the FTC today is the primary government agency that controls false and misleading advertising.

How Advertising Gets into Our Mosaics

Advertising gets into our communication environments in a wide variety of ways because of the many different types of advertising and organizations responsible for its appearance. A simple form of advertising is the "For Sale" sign in the window of your automobile, or a call to your local radio station's "trading post" program to announce what you want to buy, sell, or trade. Somewhat more involved is a want ad in your local newspaper. Among the most complex forms of advertising is the large and expensive professional campaign to launch a new product into the national market using a variety of media.

Components of the advertising industry. To understand some of the major ways advertising comes into being and is distributed, you need to be familiar with the large variety of types of organizations and individuals involved. You know something about advertising agencies already, but you may not know that almost every large store, manufacturer, and other kind of business that must attract customers (including book and magazine publishing firms, motion picture companies, and others) has an advertising department. For small businesses that cannot afford an advertising department, planning and supervision of advertising is a large part of the job of one or more executives. In addition, every broadcasting station, newspaper, and magazine has an advertising department that works with individuals, companies, and advertising agencies interested in advertising in that medium.

REVIEW

There are a great variety of types of organizations working to help companies persuade you to buy something. There are advertising departments in businesses and in the media, advertising agencies, production companies, and research firms, to name a few.

Advertising agencies vary tremendously in size and complexity. Some do little more than advise clients regarding the kinds of advertising appeals to use and the media in which to use them, and then how to buy time and space for that advertising. Others have research departments to study systematically the kinds of people most likely to purchase a company's product, the kind of advertising most likely to appeal to such potential customers, and the media that can most likely reach the potential purchasers. They also have creative departments with every sort of media artist who can turn those ideas into advertisements and commercials, media departments that know where and how to get the best media buys, and every other sort of expert needed to inform the public about a product and to persuade as large a portion of that public as possible to spend money for that product.

There are also specialized firms that assist advertising agencies or advertisers in planning, creating, distributing, or evaluating their advertising. There are market research organizations, commercial art firms, motion picture and video organizations specializing in the production of commercials, and firms specializing in selling advertising space and time for local newspapers and broadcasting stations to national advertisers. These are but a sample of the firms involved in some aspect of the advertising business.

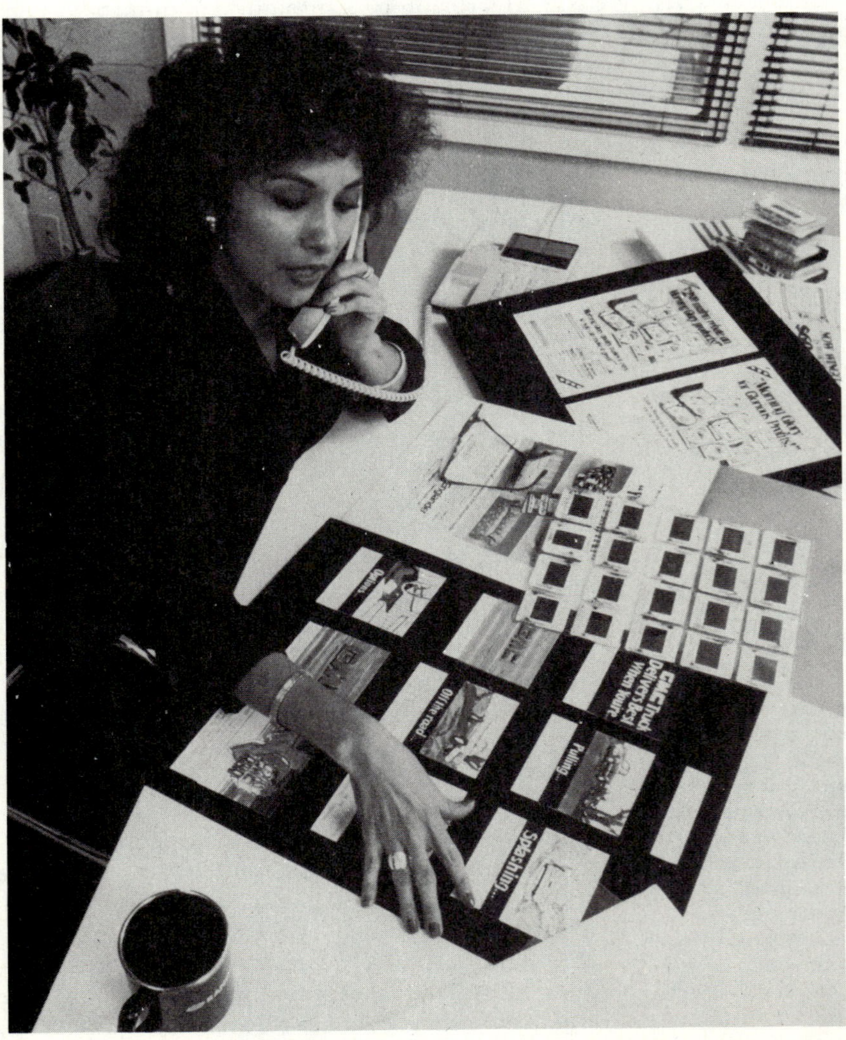

Developing a storyboard for a television commercial is an important function of the advertising agency.

Basic information for an advertising campaign. The planning of every advertising campaign involves answering several basic questions. Among them are these:

1. What sort of product are we trying to sell? Is it the kind that potential customers want a great deal of information about so as to make comparisons before coming to a decision, or is it the sort that people buy on a whim or without much thought? Is it bought largely by adults or children, males or females? What generally motivates people to buy it?
2. In what ways is the product distributed: through department stores, supermarkets, specialty shops?
3. Is this a new product with which potential customers are unfamiliar, or is it one that has been around for a time?
4. Are we striving to gain a larger share of an existing market, to expand the market, or to create a totally new market?
5. Will this be a local, regional, or national campaign?
6. What kind of advertising is the competition doing?
7. What is the current image of our product compared to other similar products?
8. How much money is available to spend for advertising over how long a period of time?

Types of advertising appeals. The answers to these and other questions provide the basis for developing an advertising strategy. A key part of that strategy is determining what persuasive appeal or appeals to build the campaign upon. To be effective, the appeal must be meaningful, believable, and distinctive. Appeals can point out a product's unusual quality, its style, cost, comfort, dependability, safety, convenience, or the status it provides its owner.

Many kinds of appeals and strategies are used in advertising. Essentially, they can be divided into three types: (1) the **direct approach,** which *emphasizes information about the product,* (2) the **indirect approach,** which *attempts to associate the product with something potential purchasers believe to be attractive,* and (3) the **saliency approach,** which simply *tries to make people remember the name or brand.* The direct and the indirect approaches are designed to shape the attitudes of consumers, making them more likely to purchase the product. The saliency approach attempts no attitude change; it simply tries to increase the likelihood that when you consider buying a product you will think of this particular brand or will recognize it in a store.

Much of the criticism of advertising is directed at the indirect approach. The associations developed with the product tell us nothing about the nature or quality of the product. Examples of such advertisements are those that show a lovely model lounging in or on an automobile, an aging actor discussing a particular investment firm, or young couples having a wonderful time on the beach while consuming a particular soft drink. The assumption is that we will associate the product with people we consider beautiful or intelligent or with a situation we find appealing and so will feel more favorable toward the product.

The saliency approach assumes that the purchasing of some products has little to do with beliefs about the quality or other attributes of the product. Consumers either perceive little difference among different brands of these products or perceive that the choice is not important enough to bother considering quality factors. We buy the brand whose name we happen to think of when we need that product or whose label we recognize when we walk down the aisle in the store.

REVIEW

The optimum advertising campaign depends on the kind of product or service, the kind of customer likely to buy it, the form of distribution, the competition, the sales goal, and the advertising budget available. Among the key decisions in the campaign is whether the advertising appeals or strategies will be direct, indirect, or simply aimed at making the brand name salient.

BYLINE

Find a sample of advertisements that take the direct route to persuasion, a sample that take the indirect route, and a sample that take the saliency route. Analyze them to see whether you can explain why the advertisers in each group chose that route over the others.

None of these advertising approaches is right or wrong. Each results from the recognition that different factors are important when we buy different products. In fact, sometimes different factors are important to different people even when they are buying the same product. For example, the cost of an automobile is an extremely important factor for most people. For others, however, the status they associate with certain kinds of cars is even more important.

Gaining the attention of potential customers. The advertising campaign team must next decide how best to ensure that potential customers will confront and pay attention to the selected advertising appeals in their communication environment. The team must consider the characteristics of the advertisement that are likely to gain attention, and the kinds of media and places within those media to which potential customers are most likely to be exposed.

Many factors affect how much attention an advertisement attracts. If it is in a print medium, the layout, use of graphics or photos, color, size of type, and size of ad can affect attention. In television commercials, sound effects, color, composition, editing, and performers are among the many relevant factors. Music, other sound effects, and vocal qualities can make a difference in radio. In all cases, the contrast of the advertisement with adjacent material affects attention. Strong contrast with adjacent advertisements is generally desirable in print media. In radio and television, a minimum of contrast with the regular program is sometimes de-

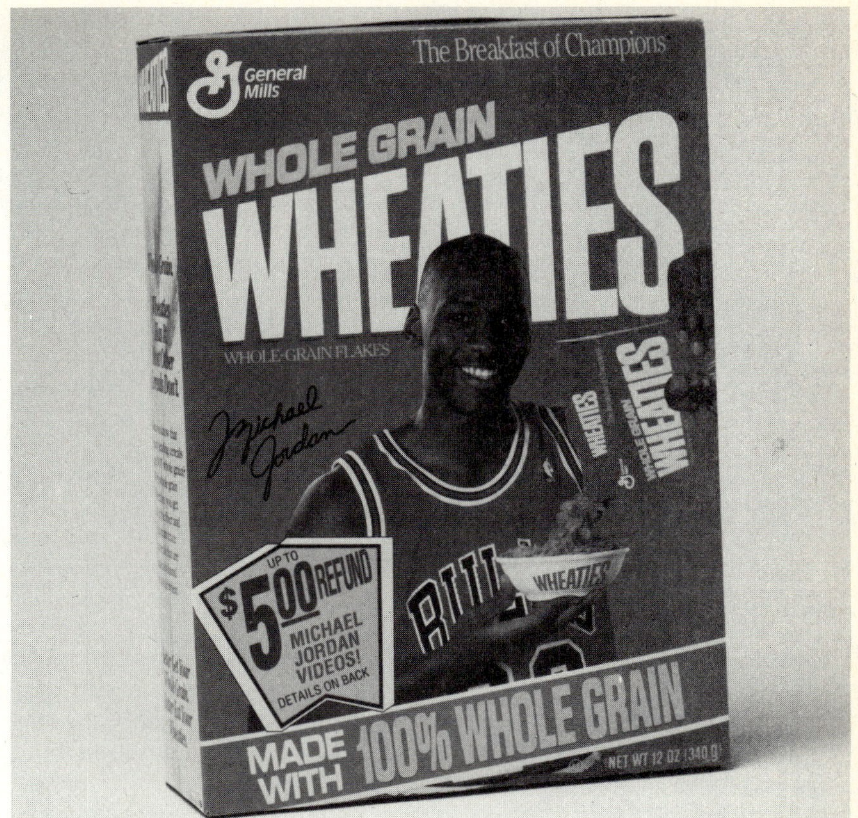

Associating a famous name or face with a product is one of the most common forms of advertising. When that name or face is a great athlete, like Michael Jordan, it can help establish a food product's image as the "Breakfast of Champions."

sirable so the audience does not put its defenses up when program material switches to advertising.

Wise media selection is probably as important as the content of ads in determining how much and whose attention is attracted. The selection of media has many aspects. First is whether to use one medium or some combination of media. Then, for each medium used, decisions must be made about where to place the ads. For example, should they be in the sports section or during a sports broadcast, or are they more likely to be noticed by the right people in the regular news sections of the newspaper or during a break in a newscast? Or are we more likely to catch the attention of the right audience by placing our ads just after a situation comedy or in the middle of a humorous short story in a magazine? Should we place them on billboards along major highways or on the strips leading into small towns?

Another aspect of media selection is deciding on the pattern of exposure. Should we run our ads infrequently over a long period of time, or frequently over a short period of time, or in an irregular pattern? Should our ads consistently be in the same part of the newspaper, magazine, or broadcast, or should they constantly be shifted around? Each of these decisions will affect the kinds of people exposed, the conditions under which they are exposed, and the patterns of repetition with which they are exposed.

Advertising research. Research departments of advertising agencies and independent market research firms can provide information to assist in almost all of these decisions. They conduct different kinds of research at each planning stage of an advertising campaign. They study consumer motivation to determine the potential customers for a product and the needs or wants consumers have that the product might serve. Researchers study the habits of these customers to determine through what media they can be reached and through what outlets the product is best distributed. They pretest advertisements or appeals to see whether they are likely to work with the target audience. Some test **visual efficiency** to discover how an advertisement competes against others for readers' or viewers' attention and how long people must attend to it before they remember it. *The more attention an ad gets and the shorter attention span required for people to remember it, the greater an advertisement's visual efficiency.* A few firms measure the impact of an advertisement on heart rate, dilation of the pupil of the eye, or the degree to which a person's skin conducts electricity. All of these physiological responses are associated with degree of attention and emotional arousal. The presumption is that advertisements that attract a high level of attention or a high level of emotional arousal are more likely to be effective than those that do not.

REVIEW

Advertising research can tell the client the kinds of elements an advertisement ought to have, the kinds of media to use, and when and how often to use them so that the advertising will most likely have the desirable impact on potential customers. Research done to test whether and why an advertising campaign succeeded or failed is as important as research done to guide the development of the campaign.

During or after an advertising campaign, researchers study its success in order to determine what should be changed on this or future campaigns. An obvious method of assessment is examining what happens to sales of the product. Other methods include testing attitudes toward the commercial and the product, assessing recall of the advertisement, and testing association of the product with a slogan or other content of the advertising. Some firms also estimate the number of persons exposed to an advertisement or an advertising campaign. From this information, they can calculate cost per thousand—the cost divided by the number of thousands of people an advertisement reaches. Thus, if an advertisement that costs $150 reaches 20,000 people, the cost per thousand is $150 divided by 20, or $7.50.

Regulation of advertising practices. Although advertising is the subject of much criticism today, pressure groups, self-regulation, and government regulation have eliminated most of its worst abuses. Much of this regulation came as a reaction to the wild and extravagant claims of some patent medicine advertisers during the latter part of the nineteenth century and early in this century. These wild claims seemed even worse than they were because of their number; patent medicines were the most heavily advertised group of products in this country in the 1870s. Finally, some publications banned such advertising.

In 1914, as we indicated earlier, Congress established the Federal Trade Commission and charged it with eliminating questionable business practices. In 1938, the powers of the Commission were expanded to give it control of "unfair or deceptive acts or practices." These increased powers included authority over untruthful or misleading advertising of products sold across state lines.[2]

REVIEW

The government agency charged with controlling unfair and misleading advertising is the Federal Trade Commission. The major self-regulatory groups are the Better Business Bureau and the National Advertising Review Council. The latter two groups work mainly through pressure tactics. The Federal Trade Commission has the power of law to help it.

The *self-regulatory group that probably does the most to eliminate deceptive advertising practices* is the **National Advertising Review Council.** The Council was formed in 1971 by the American Association of Advertising Agencies (AAAA), the Association of National Advertisers (ANA), the American Advertising Federation, and the Council of Better Business Bureaus. The Review Council does its job by putting pressure on advertisers and advertising agencies that engage in deceptive advertising practices. Both the AAAA and the ANA also provide guidelines to their members for various types of advertising.

These groups attack untrue claims for a product, misleading names and labels (for example, a brand name similar to that of a popular brand, or a name of a cigar that implies it is made of Cuban tobacco), exaggeration and misrepresentation, and advertisements that are in poor taste. In recent years, because of public and government pressure, these groups have also become concerned about advertising that misleads or otherwise takes advantage of children.

BYLINE

How effective do you believe these various agencies are in controlling false and misleading advertising? Can you find instances of such advertising today? If so, why do you suppose they have escaped the attention of those control agencies?

Functions and Effects of Advertising

As you know, the effects of advertising and advertisers are greatly criticized in this country. Some of the criticism is part of a general attack on business and capitalism. Other criticism, however, is directed more specifically at advertising. Here, in brief and oversimplified form, are the major criticisms and defenses of advertising:

Anti: Advertising increases the cost of living because advertising costs are added to the prices consumers must pay for goods and services.

Pro: Advertising reduces rather than increases cost because the volume of sales it creates makes possible more efficient production and distribution.

WOLCOTT'S INSTANT PAIN ANNIHILATOR.
Fig 1. Demon of Catarrh. Fig 2. Demon of Neuralgia. Fig 3. Demon of Headache Fig 4. Demon of Weak Nerves Fig 5. 5 Demons of Toothache

This 1863 patent medicine ad promised miraculous relief from virtually every type of pain. Government regulation has since outlawed such outrageous claims.

Anti: The increasingly high cost of advertising gives an advantage to the large and wealthy company, increasing the probability of monopoly.

Pro: The opportunity to advertise gives the new and unknown company or business a chance to win acceptance, thus decreasing the probability of monopoly.

Anti: Advertisers control television, radio, newspapers, and magazines in this country and thus reduce the variety of entertainment, information, or points of view to which we citizens can be exposed.

Pro: Because most media in this country are supported by advertising, we citizens get more radio and television stations, newspapers, and magazines than we would otherwise have, and we get more varied fare than we would if they were supported by any other means.

Anti: Advertising promotes the wrong values in our society—consumer values—leading people to buy goods they do not need and often cannot afford.

Pro: Advertising has helped give the people of our country one of the highest standards of living in the world and has lessened considerably the differences between the rich and poor in what they eat, what they wear, and how their homes are furnished.

Anti: Because newspapers and magazines make so much money on cigarette and chewing tobacco advertising, they will not report the tremendous dangers to people's health from those products as vividly and as frequently as they should.

Pro: Were it not for advertiser-supported newspapers and magazines, the public would know far less today about the dangers of tobacco than they do.

Anti: The media have slanted their news and entertainment toward well-to-do adults under the age of fifty because this is the audience advertisers want to buy. (Among media people and advertisers, these are known as "quality demographics.") As a result, the information and entertainment needs of the poor and the elderly are ignored.

Pro: If the needs of the poor and elderly are being ignored by the mass media, why do these groups spend so much time with the media—especially with television?

BYLINE

What is your position on each of the issues raised on pages 401–403? On the basis of these and other issues, do you believe advertising overall is a positive or negative force in our society?

In much of this chapter, we focused on the effects of advertising on other content of the media. This is important to do if we want to understand mass communication. However, we should not forget that the primary purpose of advertising and public relations is to affect people. Advertising and public relations are designed to influence our beliefs or behaviors—to get us to buy a product, vote for a candidate, watch a

REVIEW

Advertising clearly has both positive and negative aspects. Like public relations, it is designed to influence your attitudes and behaviors. Whether intentional or not, though, advertising is useful for most people in that it saves search time and often makes us more confident about our purchasing decisions.

particular program, contribute money to a particular cause, or simply be more favorably disposed toward an idea, person, or organization.

Nor should we overlook the fact that most people find advertising useful. It saves us search time when we want to know what movies are playing in town, where they are playing, and when. We know precisely where to look in our local newspaper to find the advertisements with this information. Advertising also helps to discover where the sales are and where we can get various kinds of services—someone to repair a leaky faucet or to fix our car.

Advertising also, rightly or wrongly, reduces our worries about some purchasing decisions. Most consumers believe that the more a product is advertised, the better it must be. If they do not see much advertising for a movie, for example, they generally conclude that it must not be anything special. Such inferences are obviously questionable in many cases, but without such cues to help us make decisions about what to buy or what to do, those decisions would be extremely difficult for many of us.

PUBLIC RELATIONS

Throughout this book we discussed the fact that the world in your head is largely your own creation, a product of the many bits of information to which you have been exposed, the order and contexts of that exposure, and your personal needs and attitudes. The job of public relations practitioners is to affect those parts of the world in your head that are relevant to their clients. For example, if their client is IBM, they want that image of IBM in your head to be one of a public-spirited organization that is working to help you. If their client is the Red Cross, they want you to perceive that organization as being on the spot helping people anywhere in the world where trouble strikes; they also want you to know that their continued good work depends on your generosity. If the client is a movie or television performer, the public relations agency wants to increase that performer's popularity with the public and to convince producers and directors to cast him or her in more shows.

Whatever you think of these or any other public relations efforts, you must recognize that communication designed to establish or maintain good relations between a person, organization, or institution and its relevant public(s) is often necessary and desirable. In fact, such communication is often unavoidable. If an individual or organization is involved with the public in any way, it is involved in public relations. The only question is the sophistication and professional help it will choose to bring to the task. In cases where the relevant public or publics are large or widely dispersed, effective public relations requires skillful use of the mass media.

Definitions of Public Relations

Public relations as a field or activity is difficult to define succinctly because it is so varied in both purpose and method. It includes, among other things, all varieties of communication designed to raise funds, to make someone or something better known, to build public support for or against a piece of legislation, or otherwise to affect public opinion about a person, organization, product, or idea. **Public relations** at its best is *the identification, establishment, and maintenance of mutually beneficial relationships between an organization and the various publics on which its success or failure depends.*[3]

REVIEW

No business or organization can avoid involvement in public relations. The only choice is whether to work consciously at creating good impressions on the public or publics with whom one is involved, or whether to leave those impressions to chance. If the decision is to work consciously at building and maintaining good public relationships, one must decide whether to do it on one's own or to hire public relations professionals.

It is not always clear when the activities of someone ought to be viewed as public relations, when they ought to be viewed as advertising, and when they ought to be viewed simply as carrying out one's job with no regard for public opinion. When individuals or institutions have any relationship with the public, everything they do that is visible, or whose effect is visible, affects relations with that public. For example, if you run a business in your home town, you must operate in some sort of building. Whether you intend it or not, the appearance of that building affects the public's opinion of your business, as does the sign outside, the advertising that you do, the quality of the products or services you provide, your statements reported in the media, other news stories about you and your business that appear in the media, and so on. Each of these has a public relations component. In short, you cannot avoid public relations. Your only choice is whether to attempt to shape or control these public relations or simply to leave them to chance.

The Development of Professional Public Relations

Efforts to maintain or improve relations with the public have been made ever since the day that kings and other leaders discovered they needed the support of the people. Early public relations efforts in the American colonies involved such diverse ventures as Sir Walter Raleigh's unsuccessful attempt in 1584 to persuade English citizens to emigrate to Roanoke Island (off the coast of North Carolina) and Harvard College's drive to raise funds in the 1640s. The earliest known press release in this country was one sent to all newspapers in New York City in 1758 announcing the first commencement at King's College (now Columbia University).

The efforts of the Americans to gain their freedom from England brought public relations efforts to a peak, both in number and ingenuity. The Boston Tea Party, for example, was staged to dramatize British tyranny and crystallize American public opinion. The dumping of British tea in Boston's harbor by revolutionaries dressed as Indians was accompanied by systematic efforts to spread the story throughout the colonies and, through letters and leaflets, to appeal for support of the American cause.

Scott Cutlip, Alan Center, and Glen Broom, historians of public relations in America (their book, *Effective Public Relations,* has gone through many editions), identify three antecedents of contemporary public relations: press agentry, advertising, and attacks on business. **Press agentry,** *the flamboyant, show-business type of public relations with little regard for truth,* flourished in America throughout the 1800s, spawning many of our legends of western heroes. Skilled practitioners of the art took ordinary pioneers who had done something notable and built them into myths. The myth of Daniel Boone, for example, was created by a landowner trying to persuade people to settle in Kentucky. The legend of Davy Crockett was constructed in an attempt to win the frontier vote away from presidential candidate Andrew Jackson.

The factor most responsible for making public relations a major industry was the strong antibusiness attitudes aroused by questionable business practices in the late nineteenth and early twentieth centuries. The exploitation of people and resources in this country by the giant industrialists created bitterness and strife. The sort of muckraking journalism discussed in Chapter 4 made the public angry about corruption not only in business but in politics as well. Public demand for government regulation and other reforms swelled. Finally, industry, business, and government leaders realized that public opinion could no longer be ignored, so they turned to public relations experts to improve the public's opinion of them. By the turn of the century, public relations was generally accepted as a major arm of any large business or industry.

Review

The history of public relations in this country stretches from the efforts to encourage British citizens to emigrate to the new world, through the Boston Tea Party, to the "spin doctors" trying to alter the perceptions of journalists about who "won" the latest presidential campaign debates. The major boost to public relations was the antibusiness attitude that prevailed at the turn of the century as a result of shady business practices. American businesses had a clear need to change those attitudes. Since then, public relations has become a sophisticated, research-based profession.

The potential of public relations for government agencies was effectively demonstrated during World War I by the Committee on Public Information, headed by George Creel. Through motion pictures, newspaper stories, posters, and public speeches, Creel and his staff built and sustained strong public support for America's war effort. The Office of War Information in World War II continued and expanded the practices Creel pioneered. The agency won public acceptance of rationing and other sacrifices, promoted the sale of war bonds, and maintained strong public morale. The success of the Committee on Public Information and the Office of War Information spurred the development of public relations departments in virtually every agency of government.

Since the early days of this profession, public relations has become increasingly sophisticated, relying on opinion research and other methods of assessing the beliefs and attitudes of relevant publics. Today, not only do public relations professionals help to improve public opinion of what their clients are doing, but they also advise their clients on all aspects of their operation, suggesting ways to make it more acceptable to the public.

Two of the pioneers in the field of public relations who did much to bring it to its present state were Ivy Lee and Edward Bernays. Among his many contributions, Lee did much to encourage corporations to be more open with the public and the press. He believed strongly that one of the major reasons why American businesses had such a poor reputation was their constant attempt to keep as much as possible of their operation secret.

Edward Bernays successfully promoted the idea that public relations specialists could be of most help to organizations if they were involved in developing policies and practices as well as in publicizing them. Therefore, he argued, the chief public relations professional in an organization should be part of the management team. He coined the term "public relations counsel" to communicate the importance of that role.

Beginning with the 1988 presidential election, a new term was embedded in the political lexicon, "spin doctor." Spin doctors were the members of the political campaign staffs who mingled with journalists before and after the presidential and vice-presidential candidates' debates, trying to shape the way the stories would be reported—attempting to influence journalists' perception of how well a candidate did and what from the debate was important—in short, trying to put a particular "spin" on the story. Whatever their titles on the campaign staffs, these spin doctors were public relations agents.

How Public Relations Information Gets into Our Environment

Between fifteen hundred and two thousand public relations firms operate in the United States. In addition, countless companies, institutions, organizations, and government agencies—even many that employ outside agencies—have public relations departments or personnel. Every government agency in Washington, with the possible exception of the Supreme Court, has a staff of public relations experts whose job is to build goodwill with the public and, even more, with legislators and the administration so that they will continue to support funding for the agency. Our armed forces, for example, have probably the largest battery of public relations personnel in the world. The public relations arm of the Department of Defense became so large and began putting so much pressure on the Congress in the 1970s that it became the subject of a highly controversial television documentary, "The Selling of the Pentagon." The program provided much insight into the public relations operations of government agencies. Probably every senator and representative in Washington also has someone in charge of public relations. And most, if not all, colleges and universities employ public relations personnel.

Methods of shaping our mosaics. In Chapter 14, we discuss in detail how various agencies and organizations use news releases and other handouts to shape the information to which we and other members of the public are exposed. In Chapter 3, which discussed the book publishing industry, we covered the various ways books and authors are promoted through placement on television talk shows and radio interviews, autographing parties in bookstores, and so on. These are only a few of the ways public relations experts shape our communication environment.

Sometimes public relations involves concealing rather than revealing information, although public relations experts disagree on the wisdom of this practice. Consider, for example, the State Department press officer answering questions about some delicate negotiations with another country or about a clandestine operation. Or consider the school board that has ordered the removal of certain books from the school library but does not want to arouse a public outcry. Imagine a college information officer explaining why the college did not expel students who damaged administration offices when protesting cuts in financial aid or increases in tuition. Or think of the public relations representative for a coal mining firm who is asked to explain the deaths of miners in a pit that the company knew was dangerous. Skillful public relations efforts are required in each of these cases, especially since the wisest approach, both for the organization involved and for the public, is not usually obvious.

A difficulty in many of these cases is that any organization has different publics with whom it must communicate: clients/consumers, employees, stockholders, the community, various levels of government, suppliers, distributors, and the media—to name the most obvious groups. Often, those publics have very different values and interests. Think, for example, of the college that does not want to expel student protesters, even though they did extensive damage to college property. The institution's public relations representative must explain the decision in a way acceptable to students, who hold a wide range of individual opinions on the subject, to faculty, to parents, to townspeople, to trustees, to state officials (if it is a public institution), and to other people on whom the college depends for financial stability. No explanation will satisfy all of these publics.

BYLINE

How would you handle the public relations problem outlined in the preceding paragraph? How would you present your solution to each of the publics?

The public relations organization. The structure of public relations departments within large companies or government agencies varies quite extensively. In some cases, separate subdepartments handle community relations, employee relations, and general public relations. Some even have departments specializing in overseas relations or government relations. The structure depends on the public relations tasks the institution's administration wants done and on the particular history of the institution.

To be effective, the director of public relations must work closely with the chief executive of the organization or institution being served. Public relations activities must be consistent with the goals of the organization. Also, the executive and others in the organization must be kept informed of the impact of their present and possible future actions on the organization's relations with its various publics.

Good public relations persons are as much advisers as promoters. If they are doing their jobs well, they bring to an organization and its leaders

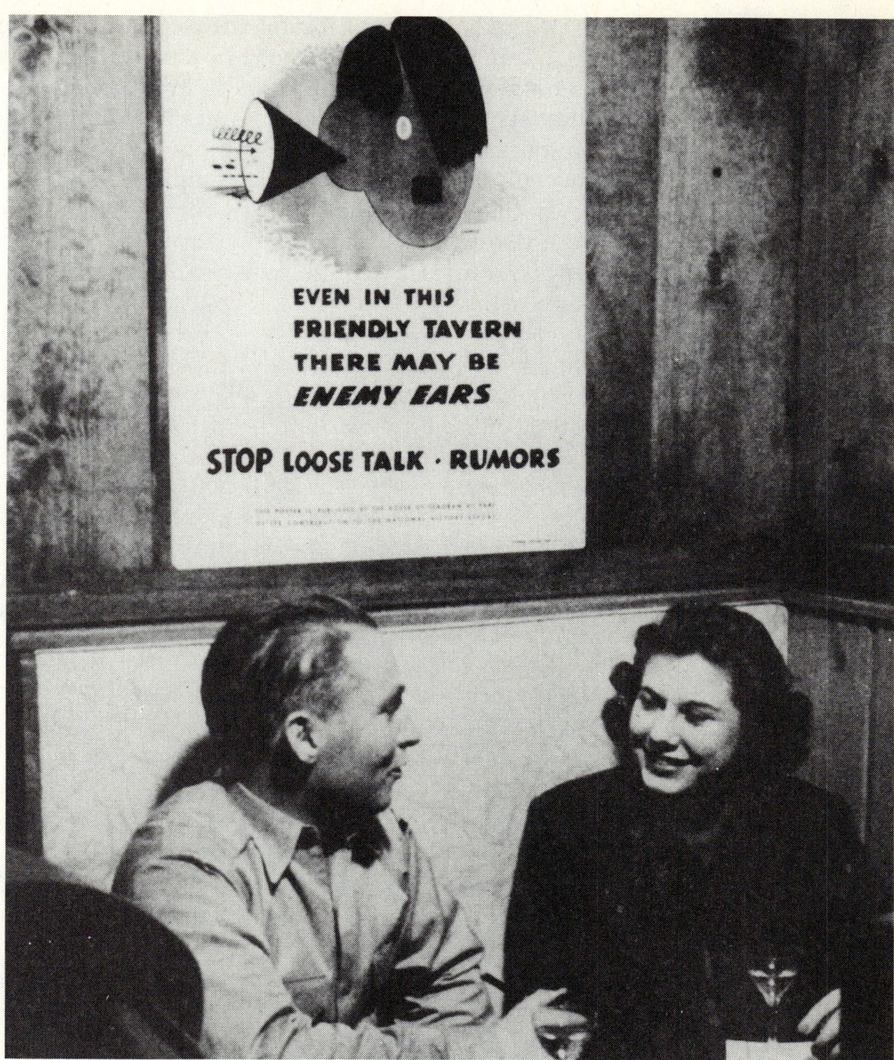

The Seagram distillery improved its image with a lot of publics when it distributed this poster during World War II.

an objective view of the organization's actions. They are expert at giving these leaders an understanding of the concerns of their relevant publics, in a sense helping the leaders place themselves in the public's shoes.

Research plays an important role in public relations, a role somewhat different from that played by advertising. Ascertaining the opinions of the public toward the client, product, or idea being promoted is the key research function for most public relations firms. Before you can do an effective public relations job for the Red Cross or the Pentagon, for example, you must know not only the opinion or image you want to create but also what the present public opinion or image is. You also need to discover whether segments of the public differ in their opinions, what types of information are likely to change the opinions of each segment, and which media can reach these various segments. Research also must be done regularly to determine whether a public relations campaign is working. In short, a good public relations agency or department constantly assesses public opinion to determine whether different types of public relations efforts are needed.

Review

Public relations may involve concealing as well as revealing or shaping bits of information. More often, it involves the attempt to explain actions to a variety of publics, each of which has different concerns. What little regulation exists comes from the organizations of public relations professionals.

Regulation of public relations. Since 1954, the principal self-regulatory code for professionals in public relations has been the Code of Professional Standards of the Public Relations Society of America. Violations of the code have led to censure for some members and expulsion from the organization for others. However, it is unclear whether either censure or expulsion from the society has affected the practices or success of those penalized.

Many public relations personnel have more specialized organizations within the general field. For example, there is the Government Public Relations Association, the Library Public Relations Council, Religious Public Relations Council, and the Bank Marketing Association. Some of these have their own self-regulatory codes.

Exposure to Public Relations

We are exposed to public relations in almost every conceivable way because of the variety of forms it takes. We noted some of these forms earlier in the chapter, but there are many others. The much-heralded annual awards for outstanding motion pictures or television programs, books or recordings, journalistic achievements, and so on, are highly successful public relations for those industries. There is probably no more successful public relations gimmick in the world than the motion picture industry's annual Oscar awards—preceded by weeks of hype, produced as a television extravaganza, and followed with a newspaper, magazine, and television advertising campaign that capitalizes on the awards to sell more tickets for the films that were recognized.

Many newsletters and other publications that companies, institutions, and politicians send to their employees, supporters, and outside groups are intended solely or in part to improve public relations. The letter you receive from a store or manufacturer after you complain about poor merchandise is part of a public relations effort. Television programs in which the station manager and program director answer viewers' questions about the station are part of an effort to improve relations with the public. Even the physical design of stores and industries and the packaging of products are planned in part to shape the public image of that product or institution. In a sense, every time you are exposed to information about individuals or institutions that depend in some way on the public and that had some hand in shaping that information, you are exposed to public relations.

An organization's public relations efforts become most visible when an event occurs that can reflect badly on the organization. Whenever an airliner crashes, a nuclear power company has an accident, a transit system's employees strike, or a college athletic department is accused of violating NCAA rules on recruiting, special public relations efforts are bound to follow. Watch for such events and see how they are handled.

BYLINE

Consider a recent event that might have resulted in bad publicity. How did the organization handle it? As far as you can tell, did the organization try to cover it up, or did it make all possible information available to the media and, hence, to the public? Did it try to demonstrate that this was an isolated incident that is unlikely to recur? Did it publicize actions being taken to prevent recurrence? Did it attempt to isolate blame? Did it communicate different messages to different publics? For each of these and other purposes, how did it use the various media of communication?

Functions and Effects of Public Relations

The intended functions and effects of public relations vary with the initiator and intended audience. At times, the function is to improve image or to generate goodwill. Sometimes the function is to increase sales, expand membership, or, in the case of charities or political candidates, to increase contributions of money or time. Public relations with the members of one's organization or institution are designed to increase morale, build loyalty, and improve job performance. Sometimes the purpose of public relations efforts is to encourage or discourage some government action, either directly, by influencing the views of government officials, or indirectly, by creating pressure from the general public.

Public relations campaigns are begun every day. Broadcasters who want less government regulation of their industry have mounted a public relations campaign to convince both public and relevant government officials of the wisdom of deregulation. The president is constantly building support for his policies through every mode and medium of communication. The American Tobacco Institute is presently faced with one of the most difficult public relations jobs of all: trying to convince the public and members of Congress that the contributions of the tobacco industry to the American economy are greater than the dangers smoking poses to the health of citizens. Industries fighting pollution-control legislation face a similar task. Not much easier is the public relations task of those who are trying to convince motorists not to drive when they drink.

REVIEW

The products of public relations are everywhere in our communication mosaics, although we are seldom aware of them as public relations. The exception is when something bad occurs and an organization must make special efforts to minimize damage to its reputation. Whether we are aware of the fact or not, our perceptions of most organizations and public figures have been shaped by their public relations efforts.

Despite such difficulties as noted previously, our image of many persons, organizations, and regions of the country have been altered successfully because of systematic and sophisticated public relations programs. Consider, for example, how our attitudes toward New York and the South have been affected by the labels "Big Apple" and "Sun Belt." Think about whether you associate the name Rockefeller with *robber baron* or *philanthropist*. When you think of Henry Ford, do you think of an inventor, a strikebreaker, or a master salesman? What image comes to mind when you hear the names AT&T, the Pentagon, NASA, George Bush, the U.S. Postal Service, capitalism, Woody Allen, Chrysler, Xerox, Harvard University, or the Red Cross?

BYLINE

To what extent do you believe your image of each of the people and organizations cited in the paragraph above is the result of their public relations agents? To what extent is it the result of other factors? How confident are you of your answer to that question in each of these cases? Is it likely that your views have been shaped in part by public relations efforts about which you were unaware?

OTHER MEDIA FOR PUBLIC RELATIONS AND ADVERTISING

Covert or indirect forms of public relations and advertising were covered in many of our chapters on the media. They will be discussed further in Chapters 13 and 14, where we consider external and internal media controls. In the remainder of this chapter, we will concentrate on some of the more overt forms of public relations and some media you probably never thought of as part of mass communication. These mass media, which are used for both advertising and public relations, appear to have a substantial and increasing impact on our communication environment.

Direct Mail

The U.S. Postal Service is not often considered a medium of mass communication. And it certainly is not a mass communication medium when it is used for sending personal letters, bills, and other matter directed at a particular recipient. For members of the Direct Mail/Marketing Association, however, it is as much a medium of mass communication as radio, television, or newspapers. These advertisers use the mails to send their materials out "to whom it may concern," just as advertisers in other media send their message to the public at large. This is not to imply that the direct mail/marketing people do not attempt to make the mass mailings appear personal; the use of computer technology has made such "personalizing" quite common. But those using mass mailings are still intent on reaching a large and unknown audience.

A great many businesses today do most of their selling by mail. Roughly $100 billion worth of sales a year are made through direct mail appeals. More obvious evidence of the size of this industry can be found in your mailbox: How much unsolicited, impersonal mail do you receive?

An observation you may have made as the last election approached was the increase in political mail that most of us received. Direct mail is clearly the most sophisticated form of political advertising and public relations today. Virtually all candidates and parties use it extensively. Great amounts of direct mail are used to influence not only attitudes about political candidates, but about almost every conceivable political issue.

Direct mail has been used for political purposes for many years, but it is only since the development of the computer that its use has mushroomed. The major boom in political direct mail began with the congressional elections of 1982. In the final month before that election, an estimated 15 million letters were flooding out to voters every week. That 15 million exceeds, by a considerable margin, the circulation of this country's best-selling daily newspapers, *The Wall Street Journal* and *USA Today*.

The traditional purpose of direct mail in political campaigns is to persuade people to give money to a candidate, a party, or an interest group. An important secondary purpose, especially in recent years, is to serve as an alternative source of information, a type of underground press that makes no pretense of either balance or objectivity.[4]

Pioneers in direct mail marketing. Montgomery Ward and Sears, Roebuck and Company were pioneers of the direct mail/marketing industry. For small-town and rural families, their catalogues were a substitute for the large local department store. Everything from tools to clothing to household goods could be ordered from the catalogue. Although unsophisticated by today's direct mail standards, such catalogues generated a substantial amount of business for Sears, Montgomery Ward, and others.

Buying mailing lists. A sign of the increasing popularity of direct mail for advertising and fund-raising practices is the fact that the sale of mailing lists has become a big business. Many organizations earn extra income through the sale of names and addresses of their members. If you decide to run for office, to raise money for some cause, or to advertise a new product or publication, you can buy a mailing list suited to your purposes. You can buy mailing lists of conservatives or liberals, lists of subscribers to intellectual magazines, sports magazines, farming magazines, or virtually any kind of magazine imaginable. You can also buy the mailing list of registered voters in a county or a state, or a list of the members of a national professional organization such as the American Society of Newspaper Editors or the Future Farmers of America. And you can target people in particular areas of the country or a state, or even particular areas of a large city, simply by the use of zip codes.

The increasing role of the computer in direct mail. Computers make constant updating of mailing lists easy. They also make possible the distribution of different kinds of materials to people with different demographic characteristics. For example, from the basic mailing list, with each individual coded according to such characteristics as age, sex, and socioeconomic status, you can automatically mail advertising for different kinds of products, or gear the advertising appeals to different types of people.

Until recently, advertising appeals that came to us through the mail were quite impersonal. Often they were addressed simply to "Occupant." Now, a computerized printing system can turn out a large number of letters in a relatively short time, each looking as though it were individually typed. Even better (or worse, depending on your biases), it can insert the intended recipient's name at certain places within the letter to make it appear more personal and informal.

REVIEW

Direct mail has become a major form of mass communication in this country, especially for political and sales communication. The combination of easily available mailing lists, computer technology for automated word processing, and the effectiveness of such communication has made direct mail a major mass communication industry.

Most major nationwide fund-raising appeals today depend heavily on these techniques. Major political campaigns are using direct mail more than ever, solely because the computer has made the technique such an effective way to raise funds.

If **electronic mail** becomes common enough, you will be able to place a "personal" message in the homes of almost everyone with a VCR or computer. Electronic mail is *a message delivered electronically via telephone line or communication satellite and received, recorded, and played back by one's home video recorder or a television-computer combination.* Considering the fact that the people with such equipment are likely to be the relatively young, upwardly mobile adults with above average amounts of disposable income, this population will be a prime target for many advertising and public relations appeals.

Buttons and Bumper Stickers

Buttons and bumper stickers have been important forms of mass communication in this country for a long time, especially during political campaigns. It is difficult to assess how effective they are, but most political parties and candidates are unwilling to take a chance and so continue to invest in them. Perhaps that is a good thing, because much of the color and fun and personal involvement in political campaigns would be lost without them.

These media have been used for a wide variety of communicative purposes in addition to formal political campaigns. Slogans such as "Black Power," "Gray Power," and "Fight Pollution" are commonly found on buttons and bumper stickers. Less political suggestions, such as "Support Your Local Debate Team," "Jesus Saves," and "Have You Hugged Your Kid Today?" can be seen on the bumpers of many automobiles. Part of the clean-up-the-environment campaign has been waged through the media of buttons, bumper stickers, and T-shirts.

BYLINE

Have you ever sported a button or T-Shirt with a slogan? Why? What were you trying to communicate? To whom? What feelings did it give you?

REVIEW

Buttons, bumper stickers, and the many related media are interesting forms of mass communication. They are not only persuasive messages but also displays of commitment and membership in some special group.

These forms of communication serve a double function. Not only do they display their messages for anyone who happens to pass by, or whom they pass by, but they also serve as a form of commitment and a bond among those who display them. When you display your Greenpeace T-shirt, your Dan Quayle or Black Power button, or your "America: Love it or Leave It" bumper sticker, you are establishing an identity with others of like mind and like display. You are saying that you are together on this issue and that you are making a public commitment to it. You are also announcing to the world that this is where you stand, and you are adding your prestige or credibility to whatever inherent persuasive power the message itself has as you send that message out "to whom it may concern." And you are adding to the bits of information in other people's mosaics.

Outdoor Advertising: Billboards

Of all the forms of mass communication, probably none has changed our visual landscape more than outdoor advertising. Conversely, no other form of mass communication has been more clearly shaped by other developments in American life. The billboard is like a twin sister of the automobile. Although it has ancestors that existed before the days of the horseless carriage, it was not truly born until the automobile came along. And as the automobile industry grew, the billboard industry grew with it, side by side—the automobile on the road, the billboard on the side of the road.

Although the outdoor advertising industry has never approached the automobile industry in size and profitability, it is still quite substantial. Its revenues run over a half-billion dollars a year. Three main types of outdoor advertising are used: posters pasted on billboards, displays painted on either billboards or the walls of buildings, and neon and electrical signs, as in New York's Times Square.

The history of outdoor advertising. Among the earliest known advertisements were the outdoor ads the Egyptians etched in hieroglyphics on stone tablets about five thousand years ago. On these tablets the Egyptians advertised new laws and decrees and displayed warnings to the people. The Romans used similar inscriptions on buildings and monuments as

Billboards try to attract the attention of motorists with strong graphics and concise messages.

well as on tablets to promote, among other things, their circuses and battles between gladiators.

More recent ancestors of today's billboards and other forms of outdoor advertising displays were the roughly lettered posters announcing the sale of farm animals and equipment, or the annual county fair, or a traveling carnival or medicine show. By the end of the Civil War, about two hundred seventy-five outdoor advertising companies were operating in this country. Most of them were quite small, some employing as few as two people. In those days, such companies were called "billposting" firms; indeed, that is what they did primarily—they posted advertising "bills" on walls and trees and other prominent spaces.

REVIEW

Although outdoor advertising has existed in some form since the days when people first began selling goods and services, the modern outdoor advertising era is largely a product of the automobile age. Developments in lithography also furthered outdoor advertising.

Not until shortly after the Civil War did the owners of walls and fences realize that those spaces were valuable to advertisers and begin to charge for them. Previously, the most owners could expect were free tickets to the circus or a trinket of some kind. At about this same time, billposters were challenged for dominance of the outdoor advertising field by sign painters, those who painted signs directly on walls and fences instead of simply pasting them on.

Another important development in the post–Civil War period was the great improvement in the lithographic process used to print copies of pictures. This improvement boosted the use of posters by making larger, more colorful, and more interesting posters feasible.

With the invention of the horseless carriage, Americans began their love affair with the automobile. And, as growing numbers of people took to the road, billboards along major highways and on the outskirts of cities became effective advertising agents.

Outdoor advertising versus the environmentalists. Billboard development today is under attack. Various government agencies and environmental groups, concerned with retaining as much of the scenic beauty along highways as possible, have tried to control or eliminate billboards that might block views of that beauty. Despite the Highway Beautification Act of 1965, which was designed to limit outdoor advertising displays in areas adjacent to federally funded highways, these groups have had only limited success.

Controversy over the entire issue of controlling outdoor advertising is certain to continue for a long time. This controversy involves the difficult issues of an advertiser's freedom of speech and a society's rights to control what some call "visual pollution." It also involves the question of how far a society should go in limiting the ways in which owners can use their property.

Some of the controversy about outdoor advertising is caused by the strong antiadvertising bias of many people. On the other hand, some of it is caused by the callous disregard for the public shown by some advertisers. Although such disregard is less common today than in years past, in many cases outdoor advertising still contributes substantially to creating an ugly and unpleasant visual environment.

BYLINE

Where do you stand on this issue? Should outdoor advertising be more severely limited? How can such limitation of free "speech" be justified in light of the First Amendment?

Professional associations of outdoor advertising people. We see fewer unsightly and cluttered scenes today, because of government regulations, pressure groups, and the professional organizations in the outdoor advertising field. In response to public pressure and in an attempt to improve their public image and avoid additional government regulation, these professional organizations have developed codes of good practice.

REVIEW

Both government and self-regulation of the outdoor advertising industry have probably reduced the visual pollution caused by outdoor advertising.

The first professional organization for billboard advertisers, formed in 1872, was the International Bill Posters' Association of North America. Billposters organized it in order to combat some of the feuding among competing companies, especially the practice of defacing or pasting over the signs posted by a competitor. Soon after, the Painted Outdoor Advertising Association was formed. These two associations merged in 1925 to become the Outdoor Advertising Association of America, which remains the major professional organization for this field.

Measuring audience size. Outdoor advertising firms find setting and defending their rates more difficult than do newspapers, magazines, radio, and television stations. Rates for ads in these media are based in good part on circulation—the number of copies sold per issue—or on the number of individuals or households that tuned to the station during a particular period. These numbers are collected regularly, in a comparable way for all of a particular medium. No comparable data are available for outdoor advertising. The closest that an outdoor advertising firm can come to a measure of audience size is a traffic count, the number of automobiles or individuals passing a spot during an average day. The more automobiles or individuals going by, the more valuable the billboard space.

REVIEW

The important audience measures for outdoor advertising are traffic count and space position value.

The Traffic Audit Bureau, Inc., sets standards for estimating such potential exposure to outdoor advertising, based on traffic and pedestrian flow, and verifies such estimates. It also prescribes a standard way to assess the **space position value** of a location. Space position value is *a measure of how long and how well someone going by will see a sign in that location*.

Graffiti as Medium

Among newspaper and broadcasting people, a major issue these days is open access or public access—the opportunity for those who wish to say something to the mass audience to have their voices amplified by one of the media. In broadcasting, that call for access is being answered to some extent by the creation of open-access channels in cable television systems. In newspapers, the letters to the editor section serves as that outlet. However, graffiti provide the most open access of all, as many communicators have obviously discovered. A can of spray paint or a felt pen and a fence, the side of a building, a water tower, a subway train, an overpass, or a wall in a public toilet provide a medium of communication "to whom it may concern."

In Pensacola, Florida, near the bridge to the beach is a train overpass beneath which is a rainbow of graffiti. Periodically, the city tries to do something about it. At one time, for example, the overpass was covered with what was supposed to be graffiti-proof paint. It wasn't. The overpass has become a sort of *cause célèbre* for young people who want to preserve the right to express themselves. Similar spots and similar conflicts between young communicators and the establishment can be found throughout the country.

Many graffiti are simply safe forms of exhibitionism. You can feel bold writing dirty words on the walls of a toilet, for example, without risking the criticism you might receive upon saying the words aloud in public. A somewhat different form of exhibitionism is the desire to see your name etched forever on a tree in a public park or on a schoolroom desk.

Although they obviously communicate something, these kinds of graffiti hardly qualify as mass communication in any meaningful sense.

Some graffiti, on the other hand, are as much mass communication as the billboards along the highways and as the local newspaper. The scrawled sign on a wall, "Divest now" or "U.S. out of everywhere!" speaks to the concerns of many people today. There is a great range of such messages, from "Gay Rights" to "Beat Illinois." Graffiti obviously are giving voice to the thoughts of many people and reinforcing them; just as obviously, since many graffiti are antiestablishment, such messages are also designed to discomfort those who disagree.

Some societies have tried to institutionalize graffiti, providing special walls where people can write their messages for all to see. The People's Republic of China has such walls, for example. And some colleges provided similar space for graffiti during the late 1960s and early 1970s when anti-Vietnam feeling was at its height. The colleges hoped that students would use these specially constructed walls instead of painting their antiwar and other messages on the building and sidewalks, where they were costly to remove. Not surprisingly, the ploy did not work. Much of the pleasure from the creation of graffiti clearly comes from putting the messages in forbidden places.

REVIEW

Graffiti are probably the most open and visible of all our "open-access" channels, especially for antiestablishment messages.

Exposure to These Other Media

Throughout this book we have stressed that much of our exposure to the mass media is unplanned and unfocused. We read and hear and see many of the things that we do simply because we happen to encounter them. That unplanned character of exposure is even more true of the media discussed in this chapter than it is of the others. It would be highly unusual for any of us deliberately to set out to see what is on the billboards or bumper stickers today or to search for advertising or public relations letters from direct mail firms (unless we were doing an assignment for class that required such bizarre behavior).

The fact that we do not plan our exposure to these media does not mean it is random, however. Those who design and distribute these various forms of advertising and public relations are quite sophisticated in distributing them in such a way and in such places that make it highly likely that the intended audience will encounter them. So most of us tend to be exposed regularly to a large number of bits of information from these media.

You are probably unaware of the frequency of that exposure because most of it occurs at a low level of attention. This is especially the case for exposure to billboards and bumper stickers. Once in a while we are especially attracted to one and attend to it more closely. On the whole, however, our attention is minimal. In spite of that, for the reason explained in Chapter 2, information from these media may be having a substantial effect on those worlds in our heads.

REVIEW

Virtually all exposure to graffiti, billboards, message buttons, bumper stickers, and direct mail is unplanned *by the receiver.* On the other hand, it is carefully planned by many of the creators of these message forms to ensure maximum exposure by their intended audiences. The low level of attention that results may tend to increase, rather than decrease, the effectiveness of the messages.

ECONOMIC CONTROLS ON THE MEDIA: A SUMMARY

This chapter covered the variety of economic factors that affect the types, forms, and content of the mass media. We discussed primarily two of the forms through which those economic factors exert that influence: advertising and public relations. Also influencing the content the media feed into our communication environment, though, are direct and indirect control by owners and the drive to maximize ticket or product sales.

Advertising dates back to about 3000 B.C. It has become more pervasive and more sophisticated with time and with advances in technology and research methods.

The modern advertising agency plays important and diverse roles: creative work of all sorts, selecting the media to be used for the transmission of ads, liaison with advertisers, and research on the audience and potential advertising appeals, to name a few.

There are three major types of advertising strategies: the direct approach—emphasizing information about the product, the indirect approach—associating the product with something potential consumers find attractive, and the saliency approach—simply making the name or brand of the product impossible to forget. The appropriate strategy depends on the kind of product and the ways most consumers make their decisions for purchasing that product. For these and other reasons, various kinds of research play an important role in the development of a sophisticated advertising campaign.

Public relations, in a sense, is a form of advertising, but it involves a far greater range of an individual's, organization's, or business's activities. Public relations also tends to be less obvious than advertising, even though it may exert as much influence on our communication environment as advertising does. We are often exposed to the products of a public relations campaign without being aware that public relations had anything to do with their existence. That is unlikely to happen with the products of advertising; when we see advertising, we usually recognize it as advertising. As a result, public relations may have a greater influence than advertising on that world in our heads.

Although public relations is relatively new as a profession, it is a major industry today. It is a rare organization, business, or government agency that does not have at least one person handling public relations. Considering the complexity of today's world and the need of most large organizations to communicate skillfully with a variety of publics, it is difficult to operate without professional public relations help.

This chapter considered various types of advertising and public relations, through discussion of some forms of mass communication that are rarely studied: direct mail, buttons and bumper stickers, billboards, and graffiti. We noted the rapid rise in importance of direct mail, especially as it has been facilitated and made more sophisticated through the use of computers. And we noted finally that these forms of mass communication may be "minor" in terms of the conscious attention we pay to them but "major" in terms of the effects they have on the world in our heads—precisely because we are not more conscious of our exposure to them.

DISCUSSION QUESTIONS

1. Thinking of all of the influences on mass media content today, what is the relative importance of economic influences?
2. Which has the most influence on media content today, media ownership, advertisers, or the public relations industry?
3. What is the most effective medium of advertising today? Why?
4. Are some contemporary public relations practices unethical? Which ones, if any? Why or why not?
5. Why is direct mail as effective as it apparently is? For what kinds of goals is it probably most effective? For what kinds is it probably least effective?
6. Should all of these forms of communication—from newspaper advertising to campus graffiti—have full First Amendment protection? Why or why not?

NOTES

1. Otto Kleppner, Thomas Russell, and Glenn Verrill, *Otto Kleppner's Advertising Procedures*, 8th ed. (Englewood Cliffs, NJ: Prentice Hall, 1983), p. 4. Much of the material in this chapter on the history and practices of the advertising industry is based on Kleppner. A wealth of detail on these and other aspects of advertising can be found in this source.
2. Ibid., pp. 677–681. Further details on the authority and procedures of the Federal Trade Commission can be found in these pages.
3. Many of the ideas in this chapter concerning public relations, including this definition, come from Scott M. Cutlip, Allen H. Center, and Glen M. Broom, *Effective Public Relations*, 6th ed. (Englewood Cliffs, NJ: Prentice Hall, 1985). This is an excellent source of information if you are interested in professional public relations work.
4. Ralph Whitehead, Jr., "Direct Mail: The Underground Press of the '80s," *Columbia Journalism Review*, January/February, 1983, pp. 44–46.

SUGGESTED READINGS

Classic Works in the Field

Kirstein, George G. "The Day the Ads Stopped." *The Nation*, 1 June 1964, pp. 555–557.

National Association of Broadcasters. *Advertising Stopped at 10 o'clock This Morning*. Washington, D.C.: NAB, 1962.

Ogilvy, David. *Confessions of an Advertising Man*. New York: Atheneum, 1963.

Relevant Contemporary Works

Bagdikian, Ben H. "Economics and the Morality of Journalism." In *Readings in Mass Communication*, ed. Michael Emery and Ted Curtiss Smythe. 6th ed, pp. 35–44. Dubuque, IA: William C. Brown, 1986.

Boton, Carl H., and Hazelton, Vincent, Jr., eds. *Public Relations Theory.* Hillsdale, NJ: Erlbaum, 1989.

Cutlip, Scott M., Center, Allen H., and Broom, Glen M. *Effective Public Relations.* 6th ed. Englewood Cliffs, NJ: Prentice-Hall, 1985.

Fox, Stephen. *The Mirror Makers: A History of American Advertising and Its Creators.* New York: William Morrow, 1984.

Hendrix, Jerry A. *Public Relations Cases.* Belmont, CA: Wadsworth, 1988.

Jamieson, Kathleen Hall, and Campbell, Karlyn Kohrs. *The Interplay of Influence: Mass Media and Their Publics in News, Advertising, Politics.* Belmont, CA: Wadsworth, 1983.

See especially Chapters 6 and 7: "What is Advertising?" and "Persuasion Through Advertising."

Morton, Linda P. "How Newspapers Choose the Releases They Use." *Public Relations Review* 12 (Fall 1986): 22–37.

Rosden, George, and Rosden, Peter. *The Law of Advertising.* New York: Matthew Bender, 1987.

Schudson, Michael. *Advertising, the Uneasy Persuasion: Its Dubious Impact on American Society.* New York: Basic Books, 1985.

CHAPTER 13

THE INFLUENCE OF GOVERNMENT AND PRESSURE GROUPS

OBJECTIVES

After studying this chapter, you should be able to

- **Define feedback and feed-forward and discuss how they affect media content and the audience exposed to that content.**
- **Describe the various government agencies that affect media operations and the major roles of each.**
- **Explain the First and Sixth amendments and their relationship to mass communication.**
- **Define obscenity and pornography, libel and slander, sunshine laws and copyright laws.**
- **Discuss the role and effectiveness of critics, self-regulation, pressure groups, and consumers as shapers of media content.**

The economic influences on media discussed in Chapter 12 are extremely important. However, it is impossible to adequately explain the content and operations of the communications media in this country on the basis of economic factors alone. In this chapter, we will consider some of the other major external forces that help to shape our mosaic environment, especially those forces that you might be able to affect. You can easily get involved in some of the kinds of pressure groups discussed in this chapter. Although you may not have thought about it before, as a voter you may also be able to influence the kind and degree of government control of the media. The more you understand such controls, the better your chances of affecting them.

CONTROL SYSTEMS

In 1956, three mass communication scholars, Fred Siebert, Theodore Peterson, and Wilbur Schramm, described what they perceived as the four major types of media control systems that could be found in various parts of the world and at various points in history. Because they were primarily interested in the news media, they titled their work *Four Theories of the Press*,[1] but their ideas are equally valid for the entertainment media and the non-news content of all media.

Siebert and his colleagues labeled these control systems Authoritarian, Libertarian, Soviet, and Social Responsibility. The Authoritarian system, they claimed, is that found in totalitarian societies where dictators or rulers maintain total control, trusting neither media professionals nor the public to make their own decisions. Control of the media is usually one of the first steps toward totalitarian control of a country.

Siebert, Peterson, and Schramm defined the Libertarian system essentially as one based on the concept of a "free marketplace of ideas" developed by John Milton in his *Areopagitica* (1644). This is a system in which there are no controls; contrasting ideas, entertainments, and arts compete in the marketplace. The underlying assumption is that truth will win out in the minds of the public when they have free access to all ideas.

The Soviet system that Siebert and his coauthors described was based on the practices of the pre-Gorbachev era in the Soviet Union. It differed little from the totalitarian system, except that the sole function of the media was to teach and perpetuate communist ideals. The media, in that Soviet system, were key tools of the state.

Just as the Soviet system is closely related to the Authoritarian system in Siebert, Peterson, and Schramm's scheme, their fourth system—the Social Responsibility system—is closely related to the Libertarian. The Social Responsibility system, however, recognizes the impossibility of totally free and open media in contemporary societies, so as the price for freedom it assigns ethical responsibilities to the media as the protector of freedom. Government encroachment on freedom of the media, proponents of a Social Responsibility system would probably argue, can be prevented only if the media show social responsibility.

Awareness of those four types of control systems is useful as a starting place in thinking about the regulation of the media, but only if we recognize that they grossly oversimplify what is happening in various countries, including the United States. Media regulation, or control, is far more complicated. In the United States, for example, there is a great variety of types of controls. Some of them are official, written into law; others are unofficial, growing out of traditional practice, out of the profit motive (discussed in Chapter 12), or out of the desires of some individuals to have particular kinds of content in the media—or to keep particular kinds of content *out* of the media. Some of these controls are direct; others are indirect. Some are open and easy to discover; others are more hidden and are generally kept secret from the public. We will describe some of these major types of controls in this chapter. After reading about them, try to think of other types of controls that affect the kinds of information or entertainment you encounter in your mosaic.

The Role of Government

Although the federal and state governments in this country do not control the media to the extent found in some countries, their influence is far from negligible. Television probably experiences the strongest government controls, but no medium is totally free of them. The Congress and state legislatures, the courts, and a variety of government agencies, especially the Federal Communications Commission and the Federal Trade Commission, shape much of the communication flow in our society. In the sections that follow, we will examine some of these government agencies and their impact on our media mosaics.

Congress. Congress has great impact on your communication mosaic through the legislation it passes and the regulatory agencies it creates. The Federal Communications Commission was created by the Communications Act passed by the Congress in 1934, and Congress periodically alters its powers. An example of such alteration is the Cable Communications Policy Act of 1984, in which Congress reduced the power of the states, cities, and the FCC to control the cable industry. The Federal Trade Commission was created by Congress through the Federal Trade Commission Act.

REVIEW

The United States Congress and, to a lesser extent, state legislatures affect our communication environment indirectly by passing laws and establishing commissions and other agencies that regulate the media.

Once in a while, Congress alters our communication environment more directly. Two of the most striking examples of this were its statute banning cigarette advertising on radio or television, passed in 1970, and its statute banning advertising of smokeless tobacco on the electronic media, passed in 1986.

The courts. The courts, together with police departments and the Justice Department, enforce the federal and state laws passed by our legislatures. A few examples can suggest the importance of the courts as controllers of our communication mosaics.

The First Amendment to the United States Constitution, which established the right of the American people to **freedom of the press**, is a keystone of our democratic society. By "freedom of the press," the writers of the Constitution meant *freedom from government control*. The **First Amendment** says:

> *Congress shall make no law respecting an establishment of religion, or prohibiting the free exercise thereof; or abridging the freedom of speech, or of the press, or the right of the people peaceably to assemble, and to petition the Government for redress of grievances.*

This statement is open to many interpretations, especially when applied to media of communication such as radio, television, and cable, which did not exist when the Constitution was written. Hence, for example, it is unclear whether these media are to be considered part of the "press," an institution specifically protected from censorship by the First Amendment. Many major decisions of the Supreme Court have involved rulings on such questions and on others related to the interpretation of this amendment.

The Sixth Amendment to the United States Constitution has come into conflict in recent years with the First Amendment, in the opinion of some observers. The **Sixth Amendment** *promises a fair trial to anyone accused of a crime.* The relevant portion of the Sixth Amendment says that "In all criminal prosecutions, the accused shall enjoy the right to a speedy and public trial, by an impartial jury." However, when the "free" press, prior to a trial, publishes or broadcasts derogatory information about someone accused of a crime, or even merely describes the accusation, many people immediately assume that the person must be guilty. The charges receive added credibility when they appear in the newspaper or on television. As a result, an "impartial jury" can become difficult, if not impossible, to find. The courts have been trying to resolve this problem with minimum limitations on freedom of the press. As yet, though, there is no agreement on a solution.

Cameras in the courtroom may be creating a conflict between the First and Sixth amendments—freedom of the press and right to a fair trial.

The control of obscenity and pornography is another responsibility of the courts that affects the media. Although most of us think we recognize obscenity or pornography when we encounter it, definitions that will stand the test of judicial scrutiny are extremely difficult to develop. The nonlegal definition of **obscenity** is *offensive depiction or description of sexual conduct that appeals to the lustful interest of the average person.* **Pornography** is *any printed, photographed, or recorded form of obscenity.* The courts have generally struck down laws regulating obscenity that are based on these kinds of definitions because of their ambiguity or because they failed to recognize that the context in which the purported obscenity occurs affects its "offensiveness." The most recent definition of obscenity agreed to by the majority of the U.S. Supreme Court (in *Miller* v. *California*, 413 U.S. 24 1973) sets these guidelines as a test for obscenity:

—*The work taken as a whole must appeal to the prurient interest of the average person applying contemporary community standards.*
—*The work must depict or describe, in a patently offensive way, sexual conduct specifically defined by the applicable law.*
—*The work taken as a whole must lack serious literary, scientific, political, or artistic value.*

All of these characteristics must be present for a work to be considered legally obscene. Thus, if a motion picture or a magazine is judged by most of us to be obscene, but it has "serious artistic value," by definition of the court it is not obscene. The courts have come to this position, it seems, because they no longer look upon motion pictures, photography, and so on, simply as businesses but as serious forms of expression—that is, either as forms of speech and, hence, protected by the First Amendment, or as forms of art.

Some problems concerning sexually explicit materials have not yet been resolved, either by the courts or others. For example, the question of whether a book, magazine, or motion picture has "serious literary . . . or artistic value" is as difficult to answer as the earlier questions or tests of whether works were obscene. As a result, it is difficult today to prove that anything is obscene. The other and more serious unresolved problem is how to prevent the thrusting of offensive material on unwilling persons or on children. Even the most extreme civil libertarian, who believes that adults, at least, should be able to read, listen to, or see anything they please, agrees that those who do not want to read, hear, or see something should not be forced to do so. Most also agree that children need some protection in this regard. As a result of these concerns, our legal statutes and the courts today tend to give the greatest freedom to those forms of communication that require the most conscious effort and sophistication on the part of the receiver; they tend to give least freedom to those forms of communication that require the least conscious effort on the part of the receiver to become exposed. Thus, a book that must be bought and read is much freer of controls than a billboard on a public highway. A motion picture shown in a theater where an entrance fee is charged is less restricted than a motion picture on open-channel television where someone can tune it in by accident when switching channels. The degree of restriction that is appropriate for cable has not yet been fully settled, but at the moment it lies roughly midway between the minimal restriction of the theater and the strict restriction of television.

In general, then, the print media have the greatest freedom from censorship; radio and television the least. In addition, broadcasting is most restricted during those times when children are most likely to be in the audience. The Federal Communications Commission has taken the position that an "offensive" broadcast that has literary, artistic, political, or scientific value and is preceded by warnings, so that anyone who might be offended can turn it off, might be permitted in the late evening, but not during the day when children are likely to tune in.

Libel and slander statutes must also be enforced by the courts. These statutes affect what the media can cover and how they can cover it. **Slander** is *spoken defamation, that is, saying something untrue that damages a person's reputation.* **Libel**, technically, is *written defamation,* although some states and courts have held that defamation that is spoken on radio or television is also libel. Libel, of course, is considered more serious than slander because it tends to be more public and to have more impact. Libel laws vary from state to state but, in general, an untrue statement about someone is considered libelous if it harms that person's reputation in the eyes of the community or deters others from associating or dealing with that person.

Anyone who damages someone's reputation in this way, whether through print or electronic media, risks being sued for libel. However, that risk has been reduced somewhat by court decisions that the media have

greater freedom to make negative comments about people who have thrust themselves into the limelight. Public officials, political candidates, and entertainers fall into that category. Journalists can be far freer in what they say about them than what they say about you.

This freedom to comment negatively about public figures was extended considerably by the 1964 Supreme Court decision in the *New York Times Co.* v. *Sullivan*. L. B. Sullivan was the commissioner of public affairs in Montgomery, Alabama, who charged that the *Times* libeled him when it published a political advertisement that contained untrue and defamatory statements. The Supreme Court's decision in this case held that a news medium can publish untrue, defamatory statements about public officials if (1) the statements concern the public, rather than private lives of the officials and (2) the journalists or editors do not know they are untrue and publish them in good faith, not in reckless disregard of the truth. This means the journalists must either have made a reasonable effort to check the facts or must have a persuasive reason for believing them to be true. Prior to the *Sullivan* case, a medium was vulnerable to a lawsuit unless it could prove what it said was true. That is no longer essential.

Some observers charge that libel laws inhibit investigative reporting and freedom of the press. For example, they criticize state laws that prohibit the publication of the names of rape victims because of potential damage or libel to the reputation of such victims. Rather than inhibiting investigative reporting, however, such laws probably increase the chances that the news media will act responsibly. They reduce the probability that innocent people's reputations will be damaged by overzealous journalists under pressure to publish or broadcast material that will attract an audience.

BYLINE

In your opinion, is government regulation of the media an infringement of First Amendment rights to free speech and press? If not, why not? What kinds of laws regulating the media would you permit? If you think the First Amendment injunction that "Congress shall make no law . . . " is an absolute ban on regulation of the media, do you advocate doing away with all such regulation?

Sunshine laws are *statutes that ensure that media and the general public have access to most government documents and the meetings of public bodies.* These statutes are called "sunshine laws" because they force government agencies to expose their activities and documents to the "sunlight" of

REVIEW

The courts have a tremendous influence on our communication environment through their interpretation of government regulations and other laws. They also attempt to balance the First and Sixth amendments by deciding what is and is not "obscene," what is and is not "libelous," and whether copyright or sunshine laws have been breached.

public scrutiny. Most of the sunshine laws include certain exemptions, documents that can be kept secret or meetings that can be closed to the media and public. Many of these exemptions are being clarified through court tests and the resultant court decisions. One exemption that is tending to hold up in the courts, for example, is any discussion or document involving personnel that might harm the reputation of an individual being discussed.

Copyright laws also must be interpreted and enforced by the courts. In general, such laws *give creators and publishers control over who can use their work and the conditions of that use.* Copyright laws, for example, prevent a filmmaker from using, without your permission, a story you created. It also prevents you from copying and selling someone else's film, television program, book, or article. (Copyright was discussed more fully in Chapter 3.)

Often the federal courts are also involved with the work of the other agencies that regulate mass communication because the rulings of any of these agencies—the Federal Communications Commission, the Federal Trade Commission, and others—are subject to challenge in federal court. Most major controversial rulings ultimately go to the Supreme Court for a final decision.

The Department of Justice. The **Department of Justice** is the *legal arm of the federal government*. Headed by the United States Attorney General, its primary function is to represent the government in legal cases. Its major impact on the mass media comes from its antitrust work, trying to prevent corporate mergers that would result in illegal monopolies and undue restraint of trade. For example, in 1967, the Department of Justice challenged the sale of the American Broadcasting Company to the International Telephone and Telegraph Company after the FCC had approved it, finally causing the merger to be cancelled. This prevented what probably would have been the largest communications conglomerate in the world, with holdings in about forty countries. Since 1967, though, as the government reduced its regulation and control of business, similar corporate mergers have gone unchallenged, so we are now getting larger and larger international media conglomerates.

One of the types of limits that the Federal Communications Commission and the Department of Justice have continued to try to enforce, though, is the joint ownership of a newspaper and a radio or television station in the same town, especially if there is little other media competition in the community.

The Department of Justice also becomes involved in mass communication issues when one of the federal agencies that regulates the media, such as the Federal Communications Commission or the Federal Trade Commission, loses a court case. The department has the responsibility for determining whether the case will be appealed.

Federal regulatory agencies. The Federal Communications Commission (FCC) is the government agency charged with regulating radio and television, telephone communication and, to a lesser extent, cable. The major functions of the commission are granting licenses to operate radio and television stations and developing and enforcing regulations that presumably ensure that the stations operate "in the public interest, convenience, or necessity." The activities of the FCC are discussed in more detail in Chapter 9.

The Federal Trade Commission (FTC) was extremely active in the 1970s, when the consumer movement was at its height. Its activity and impact appear to have diminished considerably since then, as deregulation forces have gained control in Washington. The major effect of the FTC on our communication mosaics today results from its efforts to prevent false and misleading advertising and the misbranding or misleading description of products. The critical part of the Federal Trade Commission Act, in terms of our communication mosaic, is Section 5: "Unfair methods of competition in commerce and unfair or deceptive acts or practices in commerce, are hereby declared unlawful." The Act also prohibits the making of false statements about a competitor's products or business.

Among the advertising practices banned by the FTC are visuals in commercials or other advertisements that make a product look substantially better than it is. For example, the agency stopped some food manufacturers from placing marbles in bowls of their soups when they were being filmed or photographed. Marbles force the solids to the top and make a soup look richer than it is. The FTC has forced off the air many commercials for children's toys because the toys were made to appear larger or quite different than they were in actuality. One of the most important cases brought by the FTC was against the Warner-Lambert Company, the manufacturer of Listerine. In this case, decided by the FTC in 1975, the Commission established its power to force a company to do **corrective advertising** if its prior advertising may have seriously misled the public. Corrective advertising is *advertising that attempts to counteract false or misleading information that a company had in earlier advertisements.* Since 1921, Listerine had been advertised as a product that prevented colds and sore throats and lessened their severity. When the FTC found that the product did not do those things, they ruled that the company must

> *cease and desist from disseminating any advertisement for Listerine unless it is clearly and conspicuously disclosed in each such advertisement, in the exact language below, that: "Contrary to prior advertising, Listerine will not help prevent colds or sore throats or lessen their severity." This requirement extends only to the next ten million dollars of Listerine advertising.*[2]

The rationale for the $10 million figure was that this was the average annual Listerine advertising budget between 1962 and 1972; thus, the

Review

The charge of the Department of Justice is to help the FCC, FTC, and other government agencies enforce federal laws. Its antitrust work is especially important for media industries.

corrective advertising, if done at the same rate, would continue for approximately one year. The courts upheld this decision but ruled the company would not need to use the phrase "contrary to prior advertising" in its corrective advertisements.

A major problem with the FTC, according to some critics, is that the agency generally takes an extremely long time to get some kinds of advertising stopped—especially if the advertiser is uncooperative or appeals the FTC ruling to the courts. The average FTC case takes about four years to settle. It took eleven years for the FTC to get the manufacturer of Geritol to stop claiming in its advertisements that Geritol relieved iron-deficiency anemia.

The future of government regulation. An important question raised by the new technologies discussed in Chapter 11 is the extent to which the government can or should regulate the various new forms of communication. Part of the answer, although clearly not all of it, depends on how you define those technologies. For example, if a printed story is delivered to homes through some form of transmission over the air waves, is it then television, or is it something else? If it is television, then shouldn't it be regulated in the same way other television is regulated in this country? If it is not television, is it like the telephone services? If so, then a different set of regulations applies. Or is it neither television nor telephone but something else? Do we then need a new regulatory agency? Or should this form not be regulated at all by the government?

Some scholars argue that with the vast increase in number of sources of information our new technology makes possible, the constitutional basis for regulating any form of mass communication in the United States has disappeared. As indicated in Chapter 9, broadcasting regulation was originally based on the assumption of limited frequencies or channels and the need for a "free marketplace of ideas." If there is no longer a scarcity of channels and frequencies or other sources of information, so that everyone has ample access to the media, can regulation be legally or philosophically justified?

Most advocates of little or no regulation contrast regulation with freedom and argue that the latter must be maximized. But that contrast distorts the issue. The issue is not one of regulation versus freedom. It is, rather, how to *balance* freedoms for the different participants in the communication process: for owners trying to maximize profits, producers trying to create new forms of art or new ways to communicate, advocates of political positions and other points of view who want audiences to hear them, and those audience members—citizens—who have a tremendous variety of interests and needs. Increasing the freedom for one set of players almost invariably decreases the freedom for others. So the critical question is whether some form of regulation is necessary to balance those competing interests.

BYLINE

How would you balance those freedoms? When there is direct conflict among them, should we favor the rights of the readers, listeners, and viewers, the reporters and artists, or the owners of the media? How do you justify your answer?

Another major issue with which the various agencies regulating mass communication in this country will need to deal in the future was touched on in Chapter 11: how to get maximum diversity of viewpoints in the media in the face of pressures toward greater and greater consolidation of ownership. This is not a new issue; the Federal Communications Commission and the antitrust arm of the Department of Justice have been wrestling with it for years. We will probably see the issue arise in the years ahead in the question of cross-ownership. Cross-ownership, as we saw earlier, is the ownership by one corporation of various media in the same market. For example, the Federal Communications Commission struggled with the question of whether the owner of a cable television system could hold a license for a television station in the same community. For years, the FCC vacillated on whether a corporation could own both a newspaper and a broadcasting station in a community. Some argue that we can have maximum diversity in our marketplace of ideas only by having no cross-ownership. Others argue that cross-ownership is a problem only where there are no competing media of any sort. Still others argue that cross-ownership is never a problem; public pressure alone, without government intervention, will ensure that the public is adequately served with a wide range of ideas, information, and entertainment. Consider these various points of view and decide what you think about the matter and which side you support.

Another aspect of the diversity issue is whether particular corporations or types of corporations should have a monopoly on each type of transmission service. For example, should one company have a monopoly on providing telephone service in a region? Should the American Telephone and Telegraph Company have a monopoly on providing land-based coaxial cable and microwave relay service for the television networks? These are now regulated monopolies in the United States, with the Federal Communications Commission setting both rates and minimum technical standards. In the past two decades, in part because the federal government forced the breakup of the AT&T telephone monopoly, competition has increased in long-distance service, telephone rentals and sales, and other aspects of the industry. The question now is whether still more competition would lead to improved services and lower costs, or whether it would lead ultimately to higher costs and a deterioration of services—especially in sparsely populated areas.

REVIEW

Government regulation of the media is highly controversial today. A major question is whether the great proliferation of channels of information has eliminated the need for government regulation or simply changed the kind of regulation needed. The trend toward larger and larger media conglomerates has complicated this issue.

As the twentieth century draws to a close, political pressure for deregulation of the media—doing away with almost all regulation—has become extremely strong. This pressure exists for two major reasons. First, some political leaders are convinced that the great number of sources of information and entertainment we now have, and the even greater number we are likely to have in the future, eliminate the need for regulation. They believe competition among these many sources will force them to serve the public interest in an optimum way. The other reason is that existing regulations have not worked as well as most of us had hoped. About these matters there is no question. The question, rather, is whether market forces will do as well or better, or whether we should be considering some revisions in our system of government regulation rather than its eradication.

BYLINE

What is your opinion? Should we have less government regulation of the media, or should we simply revise our government regulations? Why?

The Media Industries as Self-Regulators

In many ways, the ideal system of media regulation is for the media industries to regulate themselves, guided by pride in their work and a strong sense of responsibility to the public. However, the considerations of pride and responsibility have not always been adequate to bring about sufficient self-control of the mass media industries. Too often, other considerations have outweighed these. One important consideration, of course, is the desire to maximize profit or at least to stay "in the black." But that is not the only motive. There is also the drive to be number one—to have the largest audience of any station in your market, of any newspaper in your area, of any movie distributed that year. Still another factor is the honest disagreement among media professionals about what is and is not in the public interest, or what is and is not in good taste. We see these disagreements clearly, for example, when the media are confronted with whether or under what conditions it is proper to show nudity or sexual behavior.

Whether or not the profit motive is the most important factor limiting the effectiveness of self-regulation, it is highly important and, as indicated in Chapter 12, becoming more so. As mass communication industries have grown and become public corporations, with ownership distributed among stockholders, those who manage each industry are not its owners. Hence, they do not have the pride of ownership. More important, their sense of responsibility must necessarily be to their bosses, the stockholders, rather than to the public.

Before condemning such management and the stockholders who seem interested only in profits, place yourself in their position. For example, if you invested a good portion of your life savings in Paramount Pictures stock, CBS stock, or *New York Times* stock, figuring that this investment would provide your retirement income, would you be more interested in whether that company served the public or whether it turned a profit? Would you vote to retain a board of directors whose primary concern seemed to be serving the public good rather than protecting and building your retirement fund? Although it is possible for a company both to serve the public good and be profitable, we should not be shocked when the latter is given priority over the former.

In light of these considerations, you may be surprised to learn that self-regulation of the media industries has had some limited success. Almost all of the media industries have self-regulatory codes that, at the minimum, provide general guidelines for self-assessment and the assessment of others. The codes for many of the media are described in Part Two in the chapters on individual media.

REVIEW

Self-regulation is an important form of control for most industries in the United States, including the media. At least part of the reason for its success is that self-regulation is in the media's self-interest.

Pure-hearted concern for the public probably has little to do with the success of self-regulation in most cases. It is likely due more to fear of government regulation and to the belief that, in the long run, eliminating practices that are contrary to the public interest is good for business. If the media lose the public's confidence and support, profits are likely to drop. Despite these reasons for self-regulation and the instances of success, fully effective self-regulation of mass communication will always be difficult to achieve because of competing economic pressures.

BYLINE

Given the pressures to maximize profits, why do you believe self-regulation is often effective? Under what conditions, or for whom, might the drive for maximizing profits be consistent with self-regulation?

The Critic as Controller

Critics, especially of popular novels and motion pictures and, to a lesser extent, of television and newspapers, can have a substantial effect on those who work in the media and on the consumer who regulates his or her own exposure to a particular media product. The critic can have a direct influence on who buys a book, attends a movie, or views a particular television program simply by praising or damning it. Most of us think about this sort of effect when we consider the influence of critics. However, in the long run, this immediate influence is not their most important control function. Much more important are their influence on public tastes, their influence on the serious creators in the media, and their influence on industry practices.

Shaping public tastes. Someone once said, "For there to be great art, there must be great audiences." A major function of critics is to help create great audiences. (This also is a function of the educational system.) Good critics can help people learn to see more in a film or book or television series. They can help people learn to read and evaluate newspaper stories. By shaping our ability to understand and see more in these media products, they create in us a demand for better products and decrease our tolerance for shoddy entertainment and trivial news.

Shaping media creators. Although the vast majority of media consumers do not read or listen to the major media critics, almost all of those who create the products being criticized do. In a real sense, critics provide important feedback for people in the media—helping them decide what "worked" and what did not, independent of popularity. In a sense also, the critic is the conscience of some creators, making them strive to do their best.

Serving as industry watchdog. The critic serves as conscience for the industry, as well as for individual creators within the industry. For example, critics who write for the major newspapers are read by broadcasting executives and government leaders concerned with broadcasting policies. Because no network wants to be attacked in the pages of the *Chicago Tribune*, the *Washington Post*, or the *Los Angeles Times*, the critics for these papers can have much influence. CBS was so impressed with former *New York Times* broadcasting critic Jack Gould that they once hired him away from the paper to be a consultant on programming. The marriage did not work, however; Gould was more effective as a gadfly outside the industry—commenting on broadcasting regulations, technical standards, network-affiliate contracts, as well as on programs—than he was as part of the industry "establishment."

REVIEW

Media critics serve at least three major control functions: they shape public tastes, shape media creators, and act as industry watchdogs.

BYLINE

Read some of the criticism of books, movies, and television in recent newspapers and magazines. (You will find such criticism or reviews in any of the news magazines or in the book and entertainment sections of the Sunday *New York Times*, for instance.) Which functions do they seem to be fulfilling? Do the reviews or criticism of different media seem to serve different functions?

Pressure Groups The kinds of controllers described up to this point operate largely in the open, where members of the public can be aware of what they are doing and how they are doing it. Other kinds of controllers generally operate more quietly, so that most of us are unaware of their existence and the impact they exert on our communication mosaics. These are the many pressure groups that consciously and vigorously attempt to shape the bits of information we use to build our messages about the world.

Pressure groups of all sorts are urging that particular kinds of stories or information be distributed or suppressed. Except for isolated instances that have been widely publicized, it is difficult to estimate precisely to what degree these efforts have worked. Clearly, though, their influence has been and is considerable. Pressure groups have increased substantially both in number and sophistication in the past decade or two.

Morality issues. In just one recent year, for example, the number of complaints to the Federal Communications Commission about radio and television content jumped from about six thousand to about twenty thousand a year. Most of these complaints centered on what we can label "morality" issues: obscenity, pornography, and the treatment of religion. In addition, the same groups or individuals that made these complaints also complained about media content they perceived as unpatriotic or un-American.

Probably the most active of these pressure groups have been fundamentalist religious organizations, especially the Moral Majority, founded by television evangelist Jerry Falwell. Among the tactics used by this group, prior to its dissolution in 1989, was wide distribution of its "Moral Majority Clean Up Television Kit."[3] The kit contained a television monitoring form members could use to evaluate programs. Included on the monitoring form were questions such as:

> Would the program help build good character in youth and children?
> Would viewing the program help promote a better family life?
> Did the program contain sexual content, violence, or profanity?
> Was this a program that would help improve the quality of life in our society?

There was also a place on the form for listing the companies advertising on the program. Also included in the kit were the major products advertised on television, the companies manufacturing each one, the address, telephone number, and chief executive officer of the company, and addresses and major officers of the networks. Finally, members were provided with sample letters to companies expressing approval or disapproval of the programs they sponsor.

Children's programming. An organization called **Action for Children's Television (ACT)** is probably the most effective *pressure group for better* *television programming for children and more federal regulation of that programming* in the country. This organization began informally in the living room of a woman in Massachusetts. It now has chapters throughout the country and a tremendously effective lobby in Washington.

The Parent Teachers Association has also been a forceful lobby for better children's programming.

Treatment of women and minority groups. The third major set of pressure groups today were spawned, or at least stimulated, by the civil rights movement of the 1960s and 1970s. Civil rights groups were so successful at influencing the media that they encouraged similar activity from the feminist movement, the gay rights movement, and others. Here again, religious groups have played a major role, although not the dominant role they have played in the fight against obscenity and pornography. The religious groups applying this type of pressure have been the mainline churches such as the Presbyterians, rather than fundamentalist groups. In recent years, though, associations of minority groups, women's groups, gay groups, and so on have been the most insistent, and probably the most effective, pressurers in behalf of their own causes.

You can see some of the clearest examples of their effectiveness if you compare contemporary textbooks with those from the 1950s or earlier. Most obvious will be the influence that women's groups have had in changing the depictions of men and women and the language used to refer to them. Textbook publishers today strongly encourage authors to avoid sexual stereotyping. The result is that such characteristics as financial ineptness, bad driving, or shrewishness are no longer treated in textbooks as typical of women as a group. Girls or women are not shown as more fearful of mice, snakes, or insects than boys or men are. If household duties are discussed, both men and women are usually shown cooking, cleaning, doing household repairs, washing the car, and taking care of children. Such terms as *Neanderthal man, congressman,* and *mailman* are replaced by *Neanderthals, member of congress,* and *letter carrier.*

Groups representing African-Americans, Italian-Americans, Polish-Americans, American Indians or Native Americans, Arab-Americans, and Jews have been equally active and effective in reducing the amount of negative media stereotyping of ethnic and nationality groups. Such efforts have probably had far greater effect on our communication environments than you realize, especially those of schoolchildren.

The reason why all of these groups are so concerned about their portrayals in the media is that unrealistic or negative images of women, minorities, or any of these other groups tend to reinforce stereotypes. The groups also believe that all children, no matter what their sex, race, or background, need to find positive role models in the media. We will discuss this latter rationale further in Chapter 16 in the section on modeling theory.

Review

There are at least five major types of groups pressuring the media for particular types of content or particular approaches to that content. They are distinguished by their concern for morality issues, children's programming, the treatment of women and various minority groups, the treatment of their professional groups, and preventing any sort of control of private ownership of guns in this country.

Professional groups. Groups representing various professions and occupations also strive to promote favorable media treatment of their members. The American Medical Association has probably been the most successful at this task. This group is highly skilled at ensuring that the media present a positive image of physicians. Groups such as the national labor organizations and the National Education Association have come into the field more recently, but they are also working actively to improve the way their professions are depicted.

The gun lobby. Hunting is not a profession for most of its practitioners, but the National Rifle Association—often termed the "gun lobby"—is almost as expert as the American Medical Association in reducing the negative information about guns and hunting. For example, the organization pressured CBS not to broadcast a documentary titled "Guns of Autumn," which they thought showed hunting in a poor light. Although they were unable to force CBS to cancel the broadcast, they succeeded in pressuring some advertisers to withdraw their sponsorship of the program. The NRA's tactics have also been successful in reducing the amount and strength of information in the media that favors gun control legislation.

Reasons for the rise of pressure groups. An intriguing question for us, as we try to understand the forces shaping our communication environment, is why that growth in pressure groups occurred during the 1970s and 1980s. At least part of the answer, we believe, is that the 1970s were a period of rising expectations in America. The passage of key civil rights legislation in the 1960s demonstrated that rapid social change was possible and, perhaps more important, that citizens working together could create irresistible forces for change. The success of Martin Luther King, Jr., and others in the black civil rights movement spurred the many other groups that wanted to bring about change. They saw that the key to change was access to the media—either direct or indirect. With this access, they could tell their stories and get them spread across the land, or at least shape the stories the media were telling.

Another reason for the growth in pressure groups during the seventies was the Vietnam War and the strong antiwar and antigovernment sentiment it generated. People began to question not only the government, but business and industry as well, because they perceived them to be closely tied to government. Many believed that neither business, industry, nor government was working in their interest and concluded that the public must take a more active role in controlling those institutions. For the first time, they got involved in political caucuses and political nominating conventions and insisted on having their say—and their way. We saw the rise of the consumer movement, with Ralph Nader as its hero. And, as part of these developments, we saw the rise of media pressure groups.

Review

Possible reasons for the increase in number of groups pressuring the media were the rising social expectations following passage of civil rights laws in the 1970s, the antigovernment and antibusiness sentiment that grew out of disillusionment with the Vietnam War, the rise of the consumer movement, the reaction against the success of all of these other groups and what was perceived as anticapitalist, antireligious, and anti-American media.

A third factor in the rise of media pressure groups was closely tied to the first two; it was, in fact, a reaction to them. Some people believed the media were becoming *too* favorable to feminist, African-American, and gay causes. They responded to that perceived bias by forming new groups that are pressuring media in the opposite direction.

The last of the major kinds of pressure groups during this period grew largely out of discontent with liberal politics and liberal religion. There was a resurgence of both political conservatism and religious fundamentalism that swept the country, spurred by popular political figures like Ronald Reagan and charismatic televangelists like Oral Roberts, Jerry Falwell, and Pat Robertson. These groups decried what they saw as control of the media by anticapitalist and antireligious forces. They believed people in the media, as well as in education, were undercutting business, industry, morality, and what these groups defined as Americanism. And they dedicated themselves to reversing these biases.

Assessing the impact of pressure groups. Pressure groups have had considerable impact on some aspects of our communication environment. The dominant images of African-Americans on television and in motion pictures will never again be the Amos and Andys and the Stepin Fetchits, shuffling, inane, and foolish. Women will probably never again be relegated solely to the kinds of stereotyped roles accorded them in the past. Homosexuals are unlikely to be the easy butt of humor to the extent they were in the 1940s and 1950s.[4]

This is not to say that all the battles have been won, or that all pressure groups have pushed for the kinds of media fare that you or I want. It is, rather, to say they have clearly made a difference. And because of the success they have had, they will almost certainly continue to be a force affecting the mass media for many years to come. With the decrease in government regulation of the media, these groups appear to be one of the few effective ways relatively small numbers of people can affect their media environment.

Review

Pressure groups have had a great impact on the media, especially in reducing negative and stereotyped images of minority groups and women. The negative aspects of pressure groups are that some may be shaping the media content to which we are exposed without our being aware of it and that they may be making the media less venturesome than some of us might like.

Pressure groups: good or bad? Whether we approve or disapprove of pressure groups depends largely upon which of them we are considering and whether we agree or disagree with their goals. It is difficult to disapprove of groups working to eliminate discrimination against minority groups or women. It is difficult to disapprove of groups trying to eliminate material in the media we believe is harmful or to increase material that we believe is helpful to our children or the society. On the other hand, many of these groups are misguided. They are more concerned with advancing their personal causes than with ensuring that all people have a diverse communication environment that will serve their needs. Many want to reduce the choices available to the consumers of media. Even when their cause is just, pressure groups often go too far or have unfortunate effects. There is a danger that they will make the media more innocuous, more timid, less venturesome than they would otherwise be.

In some ways, it would be well if none of these pressure groups existed. But if we are concerned with maximizing the probability that the mass media serve the public interest—the interest of all segments of the public, rather than simply the interest of the majority—we must have some means for these segments to be heard effectively. No one yet has come up with a better alternative than pressure groups.

The Consumer as Controller

One of the great debates concerning mass communication is over the amount of control regulatory agencies or systems ought to have over our environments and, conversely, the degree to which consumers ought to be the primary means of control—through what they choose to read, listen to, or view and what they choose not to read, listen to, or view.

An extreme position in this debate is taken by advocates of a total free enterprise, laissez-faire, or **free market system**, *a system in which businesses and industries are regulated solely through the competition among them, with no government controls.* At the other extreme are those who advocate total control and supervision of what is available to the public. Neither extreme is desirable or probably even possible, given the complexity of mass communication and of life. Hence, the problem we face is the degree to which consumers must fend for themselves or control for themselves, and the degree to which other agencies—government or nongovernment—will guide the consumers and control part of their communication environments for

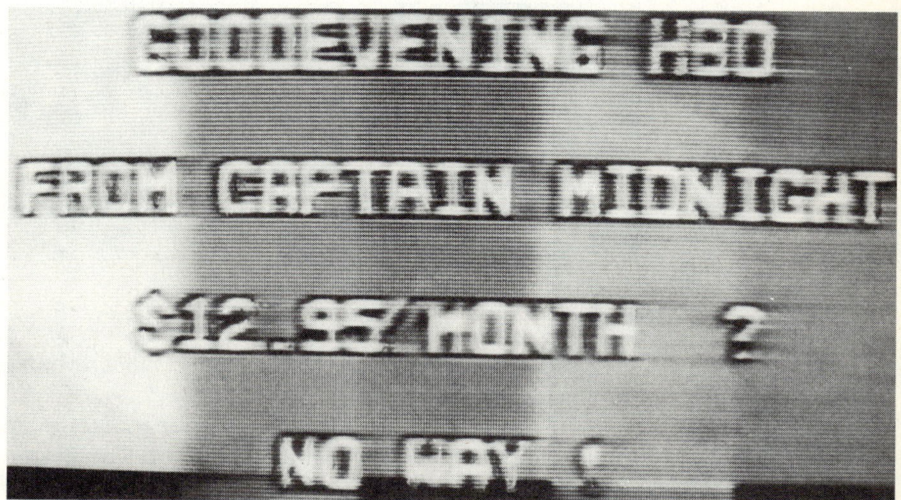

When cable companies began scrambling their signals to prevent nonsubscribers from receiving them, a would-be viewer, using the pseudonym "Captain Midnight," retaliated by breaking into an HBO broadcast with this message.

them. It is not an easy problem to resolve. It is one, though, that deserves a great deal of thought.

BYLINE

How much and what kind of government control of the media do you believe there should be? How much and what kind of control by pressure groups should there be? If consumers are to have the largest degree of responsibility—for control through selection of their own reading, listening, and viewing matter, how can we be sure that there will be an adequate range of information and entertainment from which they can select?

Feedback or feed-forward: who controls whom? Advocates of the free market system of mass communication argue that it is the system that gives greatest control to the audience. They say that if there were no regulation, they would simply give the public what it wants. As evidence, they claim that even today, with our system of minimal regulation, that is what they are doing.

But many critics of the media disagree with that claim. They argue that the public wants what it does because the media have given it little else, and the public learns to accept, even to like, what the media keep giving it.

BYLINE

Consider the claim that the only kinds of films, books, recordings, television or radio programs, magazine or newspaper features that you prefer or would like to have available are the kinds you learned to like because the media gave them to you. Do you agree? Or can you think of some types you would like to have that have never been produced before?

Let's explore these claims of the defenders and critics of the media to see precisely what the arguments are. You can then decide which side has the stronger case.

The first claim is that you and the rest of us members of the public are the major determinants of media content. The more we go to certain types of movies, buy particular types of records, watch specific types of television programs, or read certain types of articles or books, the more those types will be produced and distributed. In other words, the claim is that our mass media content is due to **feedback**, *information about audience be-*

havior or reaction that comes back to a communication source, influencing the future communication of that source. Information about the popularity of different kinds of stories, programs, records, or films feeds back to the producers; on the basis of this feedback, the producers create more of what is popular and less of what is unpopular. For example, when the public reacted positively to color and graphics in *USA Today*, newspapers all over the country began using them also. Similarly, when the first television miniseries based on a popular book was a hit, the other networks began negotiating for television rights to other popular books that they could turn into miniseries, especially series that could be broadcast during sweeps months.

The claim for the dominating role of feedback seems reasonable, but then so does the contrary claim. This second claim is rather like the argument that most of us like the foods we do because we became accustomed to them as children. We were always fed those kinds of foods, so we learned to accept and, ultimately, to like them. In the same way, according to this argument, we audience members simply learn to accept, and often even to like, what we are given in the media. The more entertainment or news of a particular type that is produced and distributed, the more likely we are to encounter it frequently, to become accustomed to it, to feel comfortable with it. This claim is that the relationship between media production and media consumption is not feedback, from audience to producer, but rather **feed-forward**, from producer to audience. That is, feed-forward is *the influence on audience preferences due to frequent exposure to certain types of media content.* In a sense, feed-forward is the influence on audiences to like what they get. According to this thesis, certain types of motion pictures, television programs, newspaper stories, and records become popular because the media industries flood our mosaic environment with them, and we simply choose from what is available and learn to like it. Thus, the major reason so many people have learned to like soap operas and game shows on television is that they want to watch television during the day, and very little else is available then. In this way, some observers argue, the producers, not the public, determine what becomes popular.

In the case of many mass communication products, both claims are valid because feedback and feed-forward are closely related. When most Americans think about the kind of movie they like best, for example, that very thought was shaped in Hollywood. We think only about the kinds of films with which Hollywood has made us familiar. Most of us have difficulty conceiving of any kind of motion picture, television or radio program, record album, novel, or news story other than a kind producers and publishers have given us in the past. On the other hand, there is much copying in the mass communication industries, as there is in other industries. And what producers tend to copy are those things that are most popular with consumers. Thus, whatever the public likes tends to proliferate.

The fact that both feedback and feed-forward operate together in our mass communication system means we are not solely at the mercy of either. If feedback alone were operating, nothing would be available for people whose tastes did not coincide with those of the majority; producers would give us only material that attracted the largest possible audience. If feed-forward alone were operating, we would receive only the material that could be produced and transmitted most cheaply. That would be the way to maximize profits since we and other members of the audience would learn to like it, no matter what it was, if we were bombarded with it long enough. In a sense, feedback and feed-forward serve as safeguards against each other.

Another important safeguard against the dominance of feedback and feed-forward is that at least some television programs, motion pictures, radio programs, newspaper and magazine stories, and so on are created and distributed with little or no clear evidence that they are wanted or needed by the audience or that they are cheaper for the industry to produce. For example, stories about scientific research or scholarship in the humanities do not sell many newspapers and are not cheap or easy to create, but a few journalists and editors believe it is important for our society that they be publicized in the popular press. There was certainly no evidence that the American public was interested in listening to continuous live broadcasts of the U.S. Congress before National Public Radio began carrying them. Nor was there evidence that the motion picture audience wanted or needed a film such as Andy Warhol's *Empire*. (Warhol made this film by simply focusing a stationary motion picture camera on the Empire State Building in New York and letting it run for eight hours.)

These and other atypical media products are created for a variety of reasons: A producer might simply want to make such a product and have the means to indulge that want; he or she might feel a sense of responsibility—might think the public ought to be exposed to a certain kind of information or entertainment whether they want it or not; or the producer might be influenced by some of the control systems or groups that we discussed earlier in this chapter. Whatever the reason such material is pro-

FIGURE 13.1
Who is in control, producers, consumers, or both?

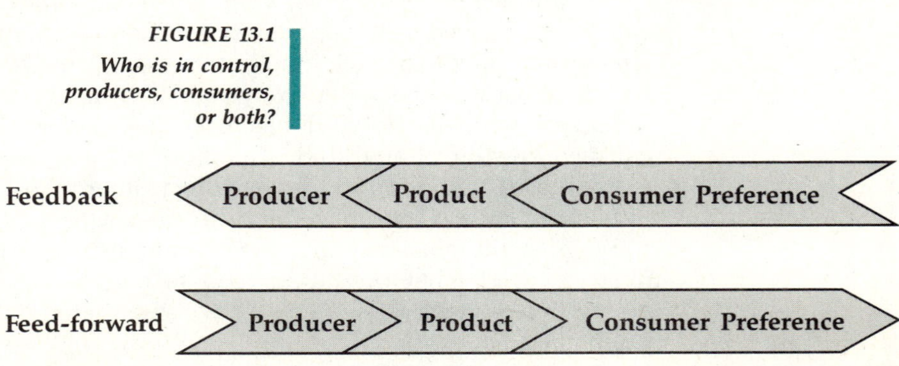

duced, its production has the positive effect of increasing our choices for reading, listening, or viewing.

Another major safeguard against the dominance of both producers and the majority audience is the small group of media consumers in almost any society who do not follow the crowd, whose tastes are consistent and different from those of the majority. Such consumers tend to seek out certain kinds of programs, films, or stories even though these may be scarce and hard to find. Some people will tune to chamber music on radio, even though it is on at an odd hour and on a frequency difficult to receive. Some will seek out the unconventional motion picture or the news stories that few others know or care about. For example, people with minority tastes kept jazz alive even when it was out of fashion.

REVIEW

Feedback is the influence of audience likes on future media products. Feed-forward is the influence of present media products on audience likes. Both feedback and feed-forward, producers who pay little attention to what is popular, and audience members who search out the atypical all affect our communication environment.

This combination of factors—the joint operation of feedback and feed-forward, the producers who pay little attention to what is popular, and the consumers who search out the atypical—results in a mass communication system that serves our society reasonably well.

The idea of feedback and feed-forward, along with the mosaic model developed in Chapter 1, provides a useful framework within which to consider how and why information gets into our communication environment. As you review the material in this chapter and the next, think about feedback and feed-forward forces and the extent to which they account for your particular communication mosaic.

EXTERNAL CONTROLS ON THE MEDIA: A SUMMARY

We began this chapter with a discussion of Siebert, Peterson, and Schramm's four types of media control systems. Having read the entire chapter, you may want to think about how you might refine their four types, perhaps into finer categories that consider more than simply the degree and kind of government control.

We covered many of the external, noneconomic forces that exert some form of control on the mass media. Various agencies of government influence the media in this country: Congress, the courts, the Department of Justice, the Federal Communications Commission, and the Federal Trade Commission. In addition, the First and Sixth amendments to the U.S. Constitution, along with pornography and obscenity statutes, sunshine laws, and copyright laws, impinge directly on media content.

Some self-regulation is done by the media industries, largely through codes of good practice developed by their professional organizations. Although these codes have probably raised the standards of practice somewhat in at least some of the media, their effectiveness has been limited by the economic pressures that seem to be increasing, rather than decreasing, in mass communication.

Critics, too, have played a role in the control of some media in this country, albeit, as with self-regulation, a minor role. They have had some influence on many people's selection of content, especially the selection of books, and they have had an impact on media creators, industry leaders, and government regulators—especially the critics whose work is published in the elite press, such as the *New York Times* and the *Washington Post*.

We also discussed pressure groups that are especially influential in shaping the ways the media treat various moral issues, women and minority groups, professional groups, social issues such as gun control, and materials for children. We suggested some reasons for the rise in the number of pressure groups, attempted to assess their impact, and raised the question of whether, overall, pressure groups are good or bad.

Another difficult issue concerns the extent to which we users of the media ought to rely on ourselves to control what we expose ourselves to, rather than relying on government, pressure groups, and other agencies to control what the media send out. In this regard, we considered the possible influence of audience tastes or preferences on media content and, conversely, the possible influence of media content on audience tastes. We concluded that each has an effect on the other.

During all this discussion of the many forces shaping media content, it may have bothered you that we did not indicate which of these forces are most important, which forces have the greatest impact on our communication environment. We do not believe it possible to do so. No one can say for certain which one of these forces is generally most influential. Some aspects of our communication mosaics are most influenced by legal controls, some by the economic forces discussed in Chapter 12, some by pressure groups, others by traditional norms of the media professions discussed in the next chapter. You may disagree with us on this point and believe, as many observers do, that the economic system is the major factor shaping our communication environment, and that the influence of the rest is merely trivial. Do you? If so, why? Is there evidence that the media are substantially different in countries with different economic systems? If so, in what way are they different? Are all media different, or only some of them? If you are uncertain about the answers to these questions, observe the content of a wide variety of American media for a time to see whether you can discover answers. If you have the opportunity, examine the media of other countries also and compare them to ours. These are important questions for which you ought to be developing answers.

DISCUSSION QUESTIONS

1. What is your answer to the question we raised near the end of this chapter: To what extent should you and all other users of the media rely on yourselves alone to control what you take in, rather than relying on government, pressure groups, and other agencies to control what the media send out?
2. Should the First Amendment be interpreted in absolute terms? That is, should the courts forbid *all* restrictions on free speech or a free press?

3. To the extent that there is government regulation, should its major emphasis be on eliminating certain kinds of materials, such as pornography and misleading advertising, or should it be on increasing the variety of content and points of view available for individual members of the public to choose among?
4. How would you rank the various kinds of controls discussed in this chapter in terms of their probable influence on media content? Include in your ranking pressure groups, government agencies (including the courts), critics, the public, media owners, and advertisers.
5. Do you believe feedback or feed-forward has greater influence?
6. In general, is the existence of media pressure groups good or bad? Why?

NOTES

1. Siebert, Fred S., Theodore Peterson, and Wilbur Schramm. *Four Theories of the Press; The Authoritarian, Libertarian, Social Responsibility, and Soviet Communist Concepts of What the Press Should Be and Do* (Urbana: University of Illinois Press, 1956).
2. *Warner-Lambert Co.* v. *Federal Trade Commission*, No. 76-2239, *Federal Reporter* 562 F.2d 749 (1977).
3. *Moral Majority Clean Up Television Kit* (Washington, D.C.: Moral Majority, Inc., n.d.).
4. We are not suggesting that the NAACP, NOW, and other pressure groups are solely responsible for the more positive images of minority groups and women that exist in the media today. The increasing sophistication of the American public, a growing social awareness sparked in part by the civil rights movement, and fear of social disorder brought about by the racial conflicts of the 1960s all helped to create a climate for change. These groups, however, helped focus that change; they pointed the way.

SUGGESTED READINGS

Classic Works in the Field

A Free and Responsible Press: Report of the Commission on Freedom of the Press. Chicago: University of Chicago Press, 1947.

Chafee, Zechariah. *Government and Mass Communications*. Chicago: University of Chicago Press, 1947.

Federal Communications Commission. *Public Service Responsibility of Broadcast Licensees*. Washington, D.C.: GPO, 1946.

This work, popularly known as "The Blue Book," because of its blue cover, is probably the clearest statement ever made of the original intent of the "public interest, convenience, and necessity" clause in the Communications Act of 1934.

Mill, John Stuart. *On Liberty*, ed. Elizabeth Rapaport. Indianapolis: Hackett, 1978.

Milton, John. *Areopagitica, with a Commentary by Sir Richard C. Jebb*. Cambridge [England]: Cambridge University Press, 1918.

Siebert, Fred S., Peterson, Theodore, and Schramm, Wilbur. *Four Theories of the Press: The Authoritarian, Libertarian, Social Responsibility, and Soviet Communist Concepts of What the Press Should Be and Do*. Urbana: University of Illinois Press, 1956.

This work is especially valuable for its historical treatment of media control systems and the development of the concept of a free press.

Relevant Contemporary Works

Black, Norman. "The Deregulation Revolution." *Channels*, September/October 1984, pp. 52–56.

Champlin, Charles. "Fifty Years of the Production Code: What Will H. Hays Begat." *American Film*, October 1980, pp. 42–46, 48.

Dennis, Everette, Gillmor, Donald, and Glasser, Theodore, eds. *Media Freedom and Accountability*. Westport, CT: Greenwood Press, 1989.

Donahue, Hugh Carter. *The Battle to Control Broadcast News: Who Owns the First Amendment*? Cambridge, MA: MIT Press, 1989.

Hentoff, Nat. *The First Freedom: The Tumultuous History of Free Speech in America*. New York: Delacorte, 1980.

Johnson, Nicholas. "The Myth of the Marketplace." *Technology Review*, January 1984, pp. 55–57.

CHAPTER 14

Influences of Professional Norms and Practices

OBJECTIVES

After studying this chapter, you should be able to

- Explain and justify your definition of "news."
- List and explain the major influences on the news stories we can find in our media.
- Define "gatekeeper" and the major factors that influence gatekeepers' behaviors.
- Describe the dominant norms for journalists in the United States and probable ways in which each norm affects the news stories we find in the media.
- Cite examples, other than those in this book, of how the context of an event can influence or has influenced its news coverage.
- Explain "inferential structure."
- Discuss ways in which the language one uses can bias the report of an event.
- Explain why "accuracy" may not be the best criterion of news quality.

If a dog bites a man, that's not news. If a man bites a dog, that's not news either. If a man keeps a dog on the payroll in exchange for sexual favors, that's news. But it's not the lead story. To be big enough news to open the broadcast [or to warrant a major headline on page one], the dog would have to be under age, and the man would have to be highly placed in government. Or the dog and the man would have to be the same sex—unless both are in the movie business, in which case it isn't news, it's gossip. Unless the dog forges [actor] Cliff Robertson's name on a check—then the story is news again. Unless the dog is a major advertiser, . . . in which case the entire episode may be far less newsworthy than it first seemed.[1]

That satiric view of the news values of journalists reminds us that not all of the forces shaping the content of the mass media are outside the media industries. The traditions, working habits, values, and ambitions of those who work inside those industries are also important.

In this chapter, we will focus largely on news because scholars have studied journalists and their practices more than they have studied those who are responsible for other types of media content. However, this analysis of news practices should give you a model for considering the internal controls on non-news materials in the media as well.

WHAT IS NEWS?

A major reason why such factors as tradition and habit are influential in shaping the news stories we find in the media is that there are no absolutely clear, objective standards for determining what is and is not news. Think about that. What do you believe "news" is? What makes some occurrences more "newsworthy" than others? Why are the social or marital activities of movie or television stars news, whereas the increasing tendency of many hospitals to turn away sick and injured people who cannot demonstrate their ability to pay is not news? Why are ten people running up and down the floor trying to throw a ball through a hoop such important news?

REVIEW

There are no absolute criteria for determining what is and is not news.

Many people seem to think "news" is something that arises naturally out of the world. They assume there is a general, normal flow of life around us and then, somehow sticking out from the flow, there is "the news"—abnormal events that create waves in that normal flow.

News as a Reinforcer of the Status Quo

In fact, what we encounter as news in our newspapers, news magazines, and newscasts, is a highly selected sample of available information about the world. In addition, the kinds of occurrences selected for presentation as news tend most of the time to reinforce and amplify a particular view of life. If you find those generalizations difficult to accept, test them by carefully observing the news media for a week. Check how often something is depicted as normal in your newspaper or television newscast that is inconsistent with the view of the world of most people in this country. For example, in recent months you may have seen stories about:

the government wasting money
Arabs fighting among themselves in the Middle East
welfare cheats
a Latin American drug cartel involved in the drug traffic to the United States
labor unions resisting pressure to increase productivity
an Italian-American with shady business practices, or even ties to the Mafia

REVIEW

News stories tend to reinforce the dominant world view in a society.

Those stories tend to reinforce the pictures of the world that most of us in America already have in our heads; they fit our cultural biases.

The World View of Journalists

Have you ever wondered why you encounter those kinds of stories so often in the news, or in movies and television dramas, but so seldom encounter stories that contradict the view of the world of most of us? For example, stories about:

people who were helped by welfare payments to get on their feet and are now working and contributing to others
members of a labor union who are suffering because of poor management that got a company into trouble
the highly sophisticated culture and intelligence of Arabs in Lebanon
the extraordinary safety record of the airline industry

When journalists seek stories—or create stories from the flow of events around us—it would be just as possible to seek and create the latter set of stories as the former, but they seldom do. The reason is that reporters and editors, and we consumers of news in America, do not have that kind of **world view**. That is, *our beliefs about the way the world is and should be* blind us to some of these possibilities. We simply do not conceive of these kinds of stories and, hence, we do not see them out there in our environment.

WHY IS NEWS?

Why? Why do we so consistently see some kinds of events, and not others, as news? Why do we have that world view? There are many possible explanations. We will suggest just a few that seem to us especially plausible.

Cultural norms. Closely related to our world view, perhaps even the causes of our world view, are the *history and traditions of our society*—our **cultural norms**. Our history and traditions give us a set of mental categories with which to view the world. We construct our worlds in terms of those categories, and we tend to ignore anything that cannot be forced into one of them. Perhaps it would be more valid to say we have difficulty

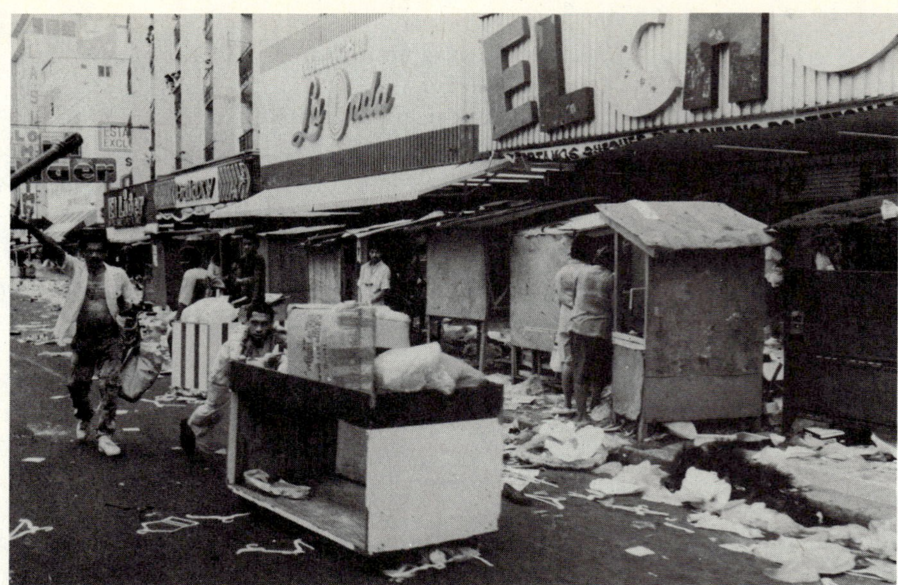

While the press in this country gave a great deal of attention to the United States' military invasion of Panama in 1989 and to U.S. objectives in that campaign, it gave far less attention to the cost of the invasion to Panamanians.

"seeing" anything for which we have no category, or seeing it in a way other than our category system demands. For example, how often do we "see" members of Congress who are more concerned about doing what is best for the country than about what will help them get reelected? How often do we "see" African-American athletes who are not interested in playing professional football or basketball and are competing in college only so they can get a college education? There are many politicians and student-athletes who fit these descriptions. You are probably not aware of them—you probably have no category that helps you "see" them—because the news media seldom describe such individuals in these terms.

Social norms. Journalists and other media personnel, like the rest of us, are guided by a *set of conventions learned from family, friends, and professional colleagues*. These are our **social norms**. We learn from our earliest association with media and other people the kinds of events that are "newsworthy" and the kinds that are not. We learn these lessons so well that we almost always accept those conventions as "natural." It never occurs to us to question why the death of a wealthy person in town is more newsworthy than the death of someone poor.

BYLINE

To see the power of these social and cultural norms and world view, consider the evening newscasts almost any night on ABC, NBC, CNN, and CBS. Notice how similar they are, especially their lead stories. Can you think of any other possible explanation for their similarity than the factors we described?

REVIEW

We find the kinds of news stories we do in the media because of the social and cultural norms of media personnel—their world view. Only the occasional idiosyncratic behavior of a few keeps all of our news from falling into that same rut.

Individual actions. Neither cultural nor social norms can explain all of our media content, but together they account for most of it. The addition of one other factor, though, can make our explanation more complete. This is the occasionally idiosyncratic behavior of a journalist, editor, producer, or media owner. Because of a personal experience, a special interest, personality, or perhaps simply chance, someone in the media will periodically perceive and construct a story we would not predict on the basis of world view, cultural norms, or social norms. These individual actions help to give the media at least a bit of surprise value.

GATEKEEPERS

Reporters, editors, producers, and others who work in the mass media are often called gatekeepers because, presumably, they control what material gets into our environment. Gatekeepers, however, can come from outside, as well as inside, the media. A **gatekeeper** is *anyone with the power to delete, add to, or alter any information or entertainment we get through the media*. Gatekeepers serve a number of control functions:

1. They determine what material is to be gathered or produced for a medium. For example, someone must decide what kinds of films to produce or articles to assign, what news stories to send photographers or reporters to gather, where to maintain news bureaus of correspondents, and whom to interview about an event.
2. They determine the form in which information is to be communicated. A fictional idea might be made into a novel, a motion picture, or a television series. An event might be reported as straight news, a human interest story, or a documentary. It might be reported by the anchor in the television studio or either live or on videotape by a reporter at the scene. Someone must make these choices for each story, and the form of transmission chosen affects the construction of meaning by those of us who receive it.
3. Gatekeepers also determine the means of distribution. A producer can distribute a film through regular motion picture theaters, sell rights to a network for showing it on television, rent it to a cable system, or

Review

Gatekeepers determine what material is gathered or produced for the media, the forms in which it is to be distributed, and the medium of distribution.

syndicate it to local television stations. Someone must decide whether to place a news story on one of the wire services, or whether to serialize a novel in one of the nationally distributed magazines.

At each step of the creation process, as an idea or observation is slowly constructed into a news story, book, program, film, or other media product, it is shaped by different types of gatekeepers. Each gatekeeper has the opportunity to add something, delete something, or reshape what is there before letting that material through the gate.

Gatekeepers: Shapers or Shaped?

Although gatekeepers influence the material transmitted by the mass media into our environment, the amount and kinds of control they have are limited. With few exceptions, if any, gatekeepers are controlled more than they control. However, the control is seldom obvious, even to those responsible. For example, as we indicated earlier, a major influence on gatekeepers is the social pressure from others within their profession—a combination of the norms of the profession at large, those of the gatekeepers' immediate colleagues, and those of their employers or supervisors.

Norms and policies. For a variety of reasons, journalists seem to learn and accept the norms of their profession quite readily. Journalistic practices, developing from a long tradition, are passed on in newsrooms and journalism schools from generation to generation. Journalists also learn professional norms from years of reading newspapers and listening to broadcast news even before entering the profession.

Once one joins the staff of a newspaper or the news department of a station, the norms of the profession and the policies of the organization are reinforced. No one need tell new employees of a newspaper, broadcasting station, or publishing house what the organization's policies are. The employees learn by reading, listening to, or viewing the material produced. When they begin to produce their own materials for the organization—for example, when reporters begin to write stories—they see what the editor changes, what gets into print or on the air and what does not. They also see what they and others are praised for.

Review

Gatekeepers in the media are strongly influenced by professional norms and policies. These norms are learned and reinforced in school, on the job, and in gatekeepers' own reading, listening to, and viewing media.

Most people who work in the media conform to the norms and policies because they like their jobs and want to succeed. In most cases, they hope to win the kind of reputation that will help them get jobs in a larger market. In addition, they generally respect and have a feeling of obligation toward co-workers and bosses. Newsrooms generally are relatively small and intimate, and the staff members are cohesive, similar to a family. A new reporter wants to belong to the group and so is motivated to conform to the norms of the group. Thus, it does not take long for most new employees to identify closely with their co-workers and with the newspaper, station, publisher, or production company for which they work.

A surprisingly large number of journalists and others who work in the media do not agree with the values or policies of their employers and they disapprove of many of the kinds of material being produced. Interestingly, though, evidence shows that the stories and programs and other materials they create are largely indistinguishable from those created by others. The forces to conform are difficult to resist. Unless management strongly encourages the expression of diverse views, most media will tend to reflect a uniform "groupthink." One striking exception to that generalization is the editorial page of many newspapers, where the publication of columnists with diverse political views has become popular.

BYLINE

Study your local newspaper to determine whether its news stories confirm these generalizations. Can you find any news stories that do not conform to the generally accepted norms or values for American news media?

Peer influences. The social pressures of the newsrooms or production organization that affect what gets into our communication environment are much more than simply organization policy or attitudes of "bosses." Ample evidence reveals that those who work in the media are strongly influenced by their perceptions of their fellow workers' attitudes toward their jobs. Journalists, for example, pick up what they believe to be their colleagues' attitudes about management, about news sources, and about the kinds of stories that are important and unimportant. These perceptions of colleagues affect the work of journalists far more than their perceptions either of the audience or of the sources from which stories come. The same can probably be said of many other creative personnel in the media.

Not only is there strong peer influence on news reporters, such influence is also strong on policy makers—editors, publishers, and station managers. The managers and program directors of local radio stations, for example, are greatly influenced by their counterparts in other stations. These decision makers from other stations, with whom they associate regularly or who are fellow members of broadcasting organizations, form a type of "reference group" for the station manager.

REVIEW

Media personnel are strongly influenced by peers. They identify with and learn from each other. The audience has little direct influence.

Audience ratings are obviously important in the decision to retain or cancel a program or programming format, but the radio audience plays only a minimal role as a stimulus for ideas for new programs or formats. The station manager or program director gets programming ideas from discussions at professional meetings of broadcasters, informal visits with other broadcasters, trade magazines, and personnel who have moved from other stations. One of the few instances in which radio station personnel give local citizens a chance to influence programming is when they conduct local surveys to discover which recordings are most popular in the community. From those surveys they develop "play lists" of recordings to be played frequently.

Perceptions of the audience. The perceptions mass communicators have of their audiences obviously affect gatekeeping behaviors. However, these effects are limited mainly to decisions based on ratings or other measures or predictions of popularity. In other words, audience size or potential audience size and, in many cases, audience demographics (proportion of males and females, age distribution, and so on), rather than audience needs and interests specifically, are the primary factors considered.

This neglect of audience interests is not all bad, as the increasing efforts to appeal to those interests demonstrate. **News doctors,** *the consultants some news organizations hire to increase the popularity of their newscasts or papers,* have generally had a negative effect on the quality of news because they give audience *interests,* rather than audience and societal *needs,* primary weight in their recommendations. As a result, hard news gets watered down, while human interest stories and features are increased. For example, many television news departments now insist that stories be kept extremely short and simple because they believe that the audience is easily bored. The kind of news that results has led to speculation such as the following about what would have happened if our ancestors centuries ago had television.

REVIEW

Catering too much to audience interests, as many news doctors apparently recommend, can lead to a substitution of fluff for hard news.

> *If Moses came down from Mount Sinai with the Ten Commandments in an era of television, he would certainly be greeted by camera crews.*
>
> *"What do you have?" they would ask.*
>
> *"I have the Ten Commandments," replies Moses.*
>
> *"Tell us about them but keep it to a minute and a half," they would say. Moses complies and that night on the news, in still more abbreviated form, the story is told. The newscaster begins, "Today at Mount Sinai, Moses came down with the Ten Commandments, the most important three of which are. . . . "*[2]

The power of the audience to punish and reward. Some members of the audience are more visible than others to gatekeepers and are perceived as more able, or at least more ready, to reward and punish certain kinds of performance. Executives of news organizations or broadcasting stations are more likely to look for reactions from business and civic leaders of a community than from a representative cross section of residents. The higher in the organization's hierarchy a mass communicator climbs, the more likely he or she is to participate in civic activities in which he or she will encounter these leaders. In addition, some community groups are

REVIEW

Business and social leaders have far more influence on news media than the bulk of audience members do because they have the power to reward and punish media executives.

more influential than others with media people because of their power to punish and reward. Thus, in general, the Chamber of Commerce has more influence than labor unions on what is printed in a local newspaper because business leaders who control advertising budgets and civic leaders who control some kinds of information are more likely to be members of the Chamber of Commerce than of labor unions. Media executives themselves are also likely to be Chamber of Commerce members.

The norms of the total society: public opinion. As previously mentioned, abundant evidence suggests that the behavior of journalists is seldom directly influenced by the average citizens out there in the audience. However, that audience has some *in*direct influence. Journalists are naturally influenced by the norms of the total society—by public opinion—as are all of us.

We see this influence of societal norms clearly in media use of language and treatment of sexual matters. Shifts in the mores of our society and in the kinds of language generally accepted obviously have been reflected in the media. Much of what is shown on the screen or written about in newspapers would not have been found in these media a few decades ago, when societal norms were more restrictive.

This shift did not occur simply because the media are trying to take advantage of changing mores in order to attract attention; it occurred because the people who work in the media find natural and acceptable today some of the language and behavior they would have found unnatural and unacceptable twenty or thirty years ago. They tend to find natural and acceptable what they see in their everyday lives. Even in television comedies, there is an openness about sexual relations that was rare a generation or two ago. Although certain groups are fighting this openness, as we noted in Chapter 13, most viewers today accept the explicitness of the sexual relationships depicted on programs such as "*Cheers*." Even members of the Moral Majority watched and liked some of the programs the organization condemned.[3]

REVIEW

Society norms, public opinion, and our government's positions all have an influence on media content. This is most evident in the language and treatment of sex found in the media and in the attitude of the press toward other countries.

Although less obvious, public opinion also affects the way the news media treat other countries. As public opinion and our government become more or less favorable toward a country, news coverage of that country becomes more or less favorable. The treatment of the Soviet Union in American news is a fitting example. Before World War II, the media were strongly anti-Soviet. They viewed Russia more favorably during World War II after we became allies, but they adopted negative attitudes again as soon as the war was over and our government resumed its anti-Soviet stance. However, as the 1980s drew to a close and the U.S. government began supporting the reform efforts of Soviet President Mikhail Gorbachev, the U.S. media fell into line again.

BYLINE

As you watch television and read newspapers and news magazines, try to see how the attitudes displayed toward countries such as Nicaragua, El Salvador, Iraq, and China parallel those of our government and of the general public as you perceive them. Can you find any instances in which media attitudes, public attitudes, and government attitudes seem to conflict?

The Effects of Evolving Technologies on Patterns of Gatekeeping

As new technologies develop, we will need to consider, among other things, their effects on patterns of gatekeeping. Each change of technology has brought some change in these patterns. Even a change in living arrangements brings with it a change in the kinds of gatekeeping that are needed and that are possible. For example, as our society moved from a rural to an urban environment in the eighteenth and nineteenth centuries, family and community control of communication flow became more difficult. In contrast, when we moved from an aural to a print society, a wider range of information became available but, at the same time, traditional leaders—heads of the family and the community—were able to exert a greater degree of control. The head of a family or community could control to a great extent the newspapers and books permitted in the house and school and, to some extent, in the library and stores. Limited literacy acted as another type of control. As radio and television brought us back to an aural society, control by traditional leaders again became more difficult because we had the ease of access of the earlier aural era along with the greater range of information that began with the print era. In addition, the key gatekeepers increased in number and moved further and further away from the consumer.

There is much discussion today about how new technologies such as direct-satellite broadcasting, faster and cheaper methods of printing, and electronic newspaper delivery will affect communication flow and the control of that flow. Those new technologies give you much greater choice of what to read, see, and listen to from the vast amounts of information and entertainment available in your communication environment. However, gatekeepers still determine what gets into that environment in the first place. They affect whether you can choose only among bits of information with the same bias or only among commonplace forms of entertainment, or whether you will get alternatives in both substance and quality.

REVIEW

Changes in media technology, like changes in living arrangements, affect the kinds of gatekeeping that are possible and that are necessary.

The implication of this discussion of gatekeepers, and of much of what we have talked about in this book, is that you have two major responsibilities if you want to control the impact of mass communication on your life. First, you must control your own behavior, making conscious choices in your uses of the media. Second, you must actively pressure those who operate the media and those who influence those operators to make available the kinds of services you and others in this heterogeneous society need. You cannot select anything from your mosaic environment that is not there.

JOURNALISTS' NORMS

As noted earlier in this chapter, the kinds of events considered "newsworthy" enough to get into the media are determined in good part by journalists' norms. One norm that has persisted for some time, for example, is to cover the president of the United States every possible moment and, to a lesser extent, his immediate family. This is the reason we see a great deal of rather meaningless videotape of the president hurrying to or from an automobile or airplane. We are more likely to encounter stories and photographs in newspapers, magazines, and on television of the accomplishments of a son or daughter of the president than we are of far more outstanding accomplishments of children of lesser-known parents.

Journalistic Scoops

One of the most familiar norms of the journalism profession, one we encounter in almost every motion picture, novel, and television program about journalists, is the importance of scoops. Journalists encounter strong, constant pressure to beat the competition. For example, the television networks were strongly criticized after some presidential elections for projecting the winner long before the polls were closed in the western part of the country. These projections, critics charged, led western voters to think their votes didn't matter and discouraged them from voting. The networks, though, were more concerned about scooping each other with news of the winner than they were about the possible impact of the news on potential voters.

This drive for scoops did not begin with television, nor will it end there. You can see evidence of it from the pretelevision era if you visit the Harry S. Truman Presidential Library in Independence, Missouri. Prominently featured in the Library is a copy of the *Chicago Tribune* from 1948 with its famous banner headline announcing Mr. Truman's defeat by Thomas E. Dewey. The *Tribune* was so certain Mr. Dewey would win and so eager for a scoop that it went to press with the story before all of the results were in. As a result, it fell flat on its face.

REVIEW

Scooping the opposition is one of the oldest and strongest values or norms of journalism.

We are not suggesting with these illustrations that journalists are unconcerned with accuracy. We are rather suggesting that many factors—economic pressures, professional norms, desires to succeed—affect the importance of accuracy and lead to departures from it.

Standards of Objectivity

Objectivity has been an important value in American journalism for over one hundred fifty years. By **objectivity,** we mean *the reporting of events in a factual way, uninfluenced by attitudes or values of reporters, editors, or publishers*. The media use a number of "strategic rituals" to demonstrate their objectivity and, in a sense, to protect themselves from blame. These

War correspondents gather quickly in any part of the world where war erupts, each trying to get a "scoop."

include such behaviors as verifying "facts," using quotation marks judiciously, and signaling shifts from "objective news" to "analysis." On the whole, devices that enable journalists to claim objectivity probably result in more complete and reliable messages in our communication mosaics. However, sometimes such behaviors can mislead receivers, as when journalists use quotation marks even though they are not quoting precisely, or when they take a quotation out of context, as they frequently do.

An outstanding example of "objectivity" contributing to the misleading of the audience is the coverage given to Senator Joseph McCarthy by most of the media during the 1950s when this country was in the midst of an anticommunist mania. McCarthy was a strong critic of the mass media and most government agencies, charging them with being soft on communism and harboring communists and communist sympathizers in their organizations. When McCarthy charged that there were communists in the U.S. State Department and elsewhere, most of the news media faithfully and "objectively" reported those charges. But they failed to report the numerous inconsistencies and even obvious misstatements of fact in many of McCarthy's charges. They did not report them because they believed that pointing out his inconsistencies and errors would have taken them beyond the "objective" reporting of facts to analysis or even editorializing. As a result, many Americans, relying in large part on media reports, created in their heads invalid visions of a communist conspiracy in the United States; and they responded to those worlds in their heads, thus contributing to the vicious witch-hunts of the period.

The events of the McCarthy era led to a great deal of soul-searching among journalists at the time and a reevaluation of what constitutes "objectivity." For a while, it even resulted in a change in some journalistic practices and norms. Some journalists acknowledged that true objectivity is impossible and that a more useful and reliable communication environment would be created for the public if all journalists or sources made clear what their biases were and then simply communicated about events and conditions as they observed and thought about them.

BYLINE

What is your opinion of this idea? Should journalists discard the attempt to be objective, make their biases clear to the audience, and then report events in whatever way they feel like reporting them?

REVIEW

Although total objectivity is impossible, it continues to be an important and valued norm in journalism. And the "strategic rituals" of journalists for communicating their objectivity continue to be used.

So far, the antiobjectivity voices have not been heeded. The need to build and maintain credibility, the belief that striving for objectivity results in better service to the public, and the practical difficulties of changing long-established journalistic practices combined to quell pressures to discard objectivity as a goal. Although some critics of the news media continue to argue, validly, in our opinion, that journalistic objectivity does not and cannot exist, the goal of objectivity continues to control most practices in newsrooms.

Imposing Sense and Order on Events

In addition to striving for objectivity, the media also try to help the reader, listener, or viewer understand what is occurring in the world by organizing events in a systematic way. This occurs partly by intent and partly because of the way most events must be reported. Only rarely can an event, such as a city council meeting, be reported word-for-word; it must be summarized. In order to cover the key points in a relatively small space or time, media reports must omit the floundering about that city officials sometimes do and the meaningless decisions they make. Because readers and listeners want to be able to understand such an event easily, the report must be structured logically and coherently, even though the meeting itself may have been disorganized and incoherent. No newspaper or broadcasting station could remain long in business if its reports truly reflected the chaotic qualities of most events. If the report of an event is not easily understandable, the reader or listener will blame the reporter, not those involved with the event.

REVIEW

Events are consistently reported as more organized than they were. This practice makes news stories easier to comprehend but, at the same time, misleading.

One result of this journalistic norm of imposing sense and order on events is that news coverage, most of the time, reinforces the credibility of governing bodies, reducing the chances that citizens will question the ways in which they operate.

Audience members, as well as government officials, have become so accustomed to this type of reporting that, when reporters resist the pressures to present these events as orderly and rational—when they describe some of the disorderly or irrational actions—their stories are perceived as biased or malicious.

Good News or Bad News?

In spite of biases that favor the status quo, the media (in the United States at least) are often charged with stressing negative news and underplaying positive news. However, there is no convincing evidence to support that charge. In fact, there is some evidence for the opposite. A study of stories from the Associated Press and United Press International wires in Indiana showed that both wire services were sending more good news than bad news and that only one out of 34 newspapers in Indiana printed a greater proportion of negative stories than came in. Editors also tended to shorten the negative stories more than the positive stories.

The charge of negativism probably results, in part at least, from the tendency of people to be more interested in departures from the usual than in continuation of the usual. When we are in the midst of a peaceful period, the story of a threat of war arouses more interest than a story that tomorrow will be as peaceful as today, just as in time of war a story of possible peace is more interesting than a story indicating that we will be continuing the slaughter.

We see this phenomenon operating in media coverage of race relations in this country. Because the various ethnic groups get along well most of the time, that fact ceases to be interesting to most people and, hence, ceases to be newsworthy. What is deemed newsworthy is the exceptional occurrence: when a fight erupts between black and white teenagers or an Asian shopkeeper is harassed by Caucasians. As a result, the message we in the audience tend to create from these bits of information in the media is that the integration of all of these groups into a unified society is failing. By stimulating us to create that sort of belief in our heads, the media may be making us more suspicious and fearful of each other, thus making the problem worse.

REVIEW

News media do not stress negative news. They do stress the abnormal. This practice may be worsening race relations in the United States.

This is a difficult problem for the media to overcome. Obviously, they cannot constantly repeat the story of smooth racial relations in most parts of the country so that the departures from peace can be perceived in a context more closely reflecting what is actually going on. And so far, the media have not developed other ways to present a balanced picture.

BYLINE

How would you attack this problem? If you were an editor, publisher, or station manager, what would you do to help your audience develop reasonably balanced pictures of racial relations and other problems in their heads and, at the same time, keep your newspaper or station sufficiently interesting that it will attract an audience?

Dramatizing the Event Another factor influencing the way media reports are shaped is the pressure to make the story interesting. As a result, media tend to make of every event a "drama," whatever their prior expectations and whatever the actual interest value of the event. The norms of professionals in the media and, even more important, economic demands of the commercial media make it essential that the interest and attention of the audience be caught and held.

Many events are not inherently interesting. For example, some baseball games are rather dull. But no radio or television station or newspaper can afford to reflect accurately that dullness or it will lose its audience. If a play-by-play announcer of any of these baseball games fails to find an angle that will make the game sound interesting, the audience will turn it off and miss the commercials—and will be less likely to listen to that station in the future. If many broadcasts of that sort were aired, the sportscaster would soon be looking for another job.

Favoring Actions Over Words These criteria of news value have been learned well by many citizens who wish to be heard and need the amplification of the media to make it possible. They have discovered they are more likely to receive this amplification if they *do* something than if they merely *say* something. Thus, when those opposing nuclear power want to communicate their strong concerns to the American public, they know their best chance of being heard is to stage a demonstration at one of the nuclear power plants; the more trouble they create, the more widely their story will be transmitted. If they can force local authorities to call out the National Guard, they will almost certainly get more coverage than if their protest brings out only the local sheriff. If some protesters are arrested and make a dramatic scene of the confrontation between police and protesters, that makes good photographic material and good television. The better the visual display, the more time their story will get on the widely viewed evening news.

This need for dramatic action can even turn advocates of nonviolence into participants in violence. Most of the members of animal rights groups, for example, are extremely peaceful folk. They strongly oppose violence

"Is it sufficiently colorful to send a photographer?"

against any form of living thing, which is the basis for their campaign against the killing of baby seals. They do not believe animals should be killed so that someone can have a fur coat or for any other reason.

In order to get their message across, they have not only photographed the bloody clubbing of baby seals for visual evidence of what they believe is inhumane, but have even provoked those who are harvesting the seals, so that violent confrontations resulted. They know that only actions of these kinds can catch the attention of the media. Speeches and essays, however well done, will not get picked up by the media and so will never reach the public.

This bias toward action or events instead of conditions or trends occurs partly because reporters are like most of us: We do not perceive much of what goes on around us until an event makes some phenomenon stand out from the background. As a result, many important phenomena are insufficiently reported, or the context that can make them meaningful goes unreported. If no startling event attracts our attention to one of these phenomena, most of us remain oblivious to its existence. Most Americans are totally unaware of the poverty in their home towns until some event occurs that focuses on it the attention of a journalist and, through the journalist's report, the attention of the rest of us.

REVIEW

The need to attract and hold attention forces journalists to dramatize events and to favor actions over words.

Ethical Issues Raised by Norms of Drama, Objectivity, and Action

The more dramatic and action-packed a story and its presentation, the more journalists tend to value it. At the same time, the more objective it appears to be, the more it is valued. In pursuit of that "objectivity," journalists believe they must not get too involved with the subject of a story; they must stay aloof. That is a defensible position, but it can lead to ethical problems at times.

An extreme example of such problems is a case that occurred in Anniston, Alabama. Someone phoned the newsroom of station WHMA-TV and asked whether they would like to see someone burn. A photographer and sound technician from the station went to check the call out. They found a drunken, 37-year-old, unemployed laborer. So they set up their camera and lights, started the camera rolling, and then stood and watched as the man doused himself with lighter fluid and then struck a few matches before he was finally able to set himself on fire. By the time one of the reporters realized he might have some human responsibility and tried to stop what was happening, it was too late; the man was a human fireball. In justifying his lack of action, one of the journalists said simply: "My job is to record events as they happen."

This was an unusual case, but far from unique. We have other news footage of people setting themselves on fire that journalists obviously stood by and filmed or videotaped. We have the case in which Phil Donahue and his staff cooperated in keeping secret the whereabouts of a kidnapped child in order to get the child's father to agree to go on Donahue's show. In each of these cases, those involved claimed that their only responsibility was to "get the story."

BYLINE

What is your position on this issue? Under what circumstances should a journalist's responsibility to get a story supersede other responsibilities? Under what circumstances should it not?

WORKING METHODS OF MEDIA PROFESSIONALS

The bits of information we are likely to encounter in our media environments are affected not only by journalists' news values, but also by their working methods. These methods interact with the characteristics of events and media not only to increase and decrease the probability of a story entering our communication mosaics, but also to affect the shape of the stories that are included.

Predicting the Occurrence of an Event

The working routines of journalists are based largely on the predictability of many kinds of events. Predictability will generally determine the way an event is covered, the extensiveness of the coverage, and—in some cases—whether it is covered at all. Reporters cannot be everywhere, so they go or are sent to locations where something worth reporting will most likely occur. It is no accident that we find reporters from all of the major news organizations present when fighting erupts in the Middle East and no one present when an earthquake erupts or fighting breaks out in a country that heretofore had been peaceful.

The Importance of Timing Some scholars suggest that the reason that events, rather than conditions or issues, are more likely to be reported in the media is the frequency of news broadcasts or newspaper publication. They claim that media operating on a daily publication schedule are more likely to cover events that occur within the space of one day than activities or situations that continue over a long period. Thus, a protest demonstration is a likely news event, while the development of a social movement or the condition that gave rise to the protest continues over too long a time to be visible to the daily media. In the same way, the closing of an auto plant is news; the slow but steady loss of sales to overseas competitors that necessitated the closing attracts far less media attention.

REVIEW

The "fit" of an event with publication and broadcast schedules and its predictability affect the likelihood of its coverage. They also affect the style and extensiveness of coverage.

Event Context Obviously, the definitions and norms of journalists are not the only factors affecting news reporting through the media. There is also the **event context**—*the group of events competing for attention and, at the same time, forming a background against which each individual event is perceived*. For example, when Iraq invaded Kuwait in 1990, almost all other events were shoved

The Soviet crackdown on Lithuanian demonstrators in 1991 got little media play because it was crowded out by stories about America's conflict with Iraq.

from front pages and newscasts. At almost any other time, some of those events would have been considered highly newsworthy. On the other hand, some stories that would have escaped the attention of journalists under normal circumstances suddenly became newsworthy because they were related in some way to the crisis in the Middle East.

This consideration of the event context when making editorial judgments is good journalism. When anything causes people to focus attention on some condition, event, or person, they will almost automatically be more interested in and attentive to related events. To take one small example, in the week or two before the annual Super Bowl football game, as the interest and excitement build to a climax, even the most trivial activities and comments of the star players become "news"—activities and comments that would pass unnoticed in any other context. That event context, though, serves as a type of control, making it almost impossible for the news media to ignore some potential stories and making it almost equally impossible to give time or space to some others.

REVIEW

The probability that any particular event will be covered by the media is affected by all of the other events occurring at or about the same time.

Inferential Structure Another important factor affecting our communication environment is the **inferential structure** journalists impose on an event.[4] The inferential structure of an event is *the major interest, news value, or "angle" reporters or news gatherers see in an event when going out to cover it*. It is the *set of expectations through which reporters perceive the event and generally the theme around which they then report it*. When different journalists perceive different news values in an event or have different expectations, they tend to interpret and report the event differently. For example, if three different broadcasting stations decide to do a story on a 22-year-old female socialist who is running for the city council, each might perceive the major news value in the story somewhat differently. One might build the story around the youth and relative inexperience of the candidate, another could focus primarily on the problems of a woman running for office, and the third might concentrate on the implications for the city of the candidate's radical politics. Although there would probably be some overlap in the three stories, quite different messages would be sent into our mosaic environment because each station saw a different news value in the situation; each had a different inferential structure.

The coverage of presidential primaries represents another example of the way in which inferential structuring can distort media coverage of an event. Primary elections are often reported not in terms of winners or losers but in terms of which candidates did better or worse than expected. Thus, candidates have won primaries, but by smaller margins than journalists had been predicting, and the stories treated them as though they had lost. Conversely, when candidates received more votes than expected, even though the total percentage was quite small, news reports sounded as though they had won it all. In this way, these expectations—the inferences journalists had made before the event—supplied the structure within which the story was reported.

REVIEW

Journalists' expectations of an event affect the way they report it, even when their expectations are not fulfilled.

Dependence on Certain Types of Information Sources

Media professionals depend heavily on certain types of sources for much of the information they make available to us. The working relationships they establish with these sources have a far greater impact on our communication mosaics than most people realize.

Community leaders. Obviously, if a mayor, school superintendent, member of Congress, or anyone else does something considered newsworthy, he or she has shaped the news by that action and hence has shaped our information environment. In many cases, though—especially with any government agency or an agency such as the Red Cross, whose function is persuasion—the influence goes beyond this. Because reporters need information from these sources in order to do their job, and because the sources need reporters and their media in order to fulfill their functions, a reciprocal relationship develops. Two communication scholars who studied this phenomenon at the level of local government concluded that reporters tend to become "unwitting adjuncts to city hall. . . . The two groups [reporters and sources] find themselves mutually dependent, and sources and reporters share, in the last analysis, a common interest in the purposes of communication."[5] That relationship is so close, in fact, that the researchers called it a **symbiotic relationship**, to indicate that it is *not only close, but mutually beneficial*.

We find this same sort of mutual dependence, although to a somewhat lesser extent, in the motion picture industry and in the creation of entertainment programs for television. When someone wants to do a drama about the Navy or the FBI, they generally turn to the Pentagon or the FBI for guidance and help—sometimes even for locations at which to shoot. Although a series about the FBI may be fictional, the creators want it to be as realistic and accurate as possible. To achieve this, they need the help of people in that agency. At the same time, people in the agency—as in almost any organization—want positive publicity. Because the creators and the people in the agency being consulted depend on each other, we in the audience generally get a glorified view of the agency and the people in it. There are exceptions to this generalization, of course, such as some of the exposés on the television series "*60 Minutes*," but these are notable largely because they are exceptions to the rule.

REVIEW

The media tend to have a symbiotic relationship with many of the individuals and organizations being covered—they depend on each other. As a result, the independence and objectivity of reporting tends to be lost.

Joseph Turow, in his book *Playing Doctor: Television, Storytelling, and Medical Power*,[6] shows not only how the American Medical Association has influenced the way in which television programs and motion pictures have depicted medical doctors but also how those depictions in turn have influenced Americans' beliefs about the medical profession.

News releases and handouts. At its extreme, the dependence on sources of information leads the media to simply pass on news releases or handouts from these sources, as though they were original products of the reporters and editors. Many audience members who are exposed to such messages misread them. This happens because most of us interpret messages or stories in one way if we think they were produced by an objective reporter, but in another way if we think they were produced by someone with a special interest.

There are many reasons the media use and often even depend on news releases and handouts from these various agencies. The phenomena to be reported may be extremely complex, or the reporter may not have the background to fully understand them, so he or she must rely on experts from the inside or their news releases. This is the case with many issues involving agencies of the federal government or large businesses and industries.

REVIEW

Media often depend on news releases because journalists cannot observe, lack the background to understand the situation, or do not have the time or drive to dig out the relevant information.

The various media must also rely on news releases or news handouts when events to be reported are unobservable. Such is the case with much war coverage. Reporters are unable to observe many of the events in a war or the overall picture of what is going on. Hence, they must rely on military or government spokespersons for their information. Obviously, these are not unbiased sources.

Many events are simply not considered important enough to justify the time and expense of sending a reporter to cover them, but the media will report them if someone else supplies the information or story. Hence, perceived newsworthiness affects whether an event will be reported first-hand or through a press release.

The amount of competition a news medium has and the ease with which a story can be covered also affect the probability that reporters will gather information first-hand and write their own stories. If a reporter must travel far in order to get a story, it is not likely to be covered first-hand. However, when a newspaper or broadcaster has competition from another news medium, the amount of first-hand coverage of local and regional events tends to increase sharply.

REVIEW

Whether a mass medium relies on news releases or handouts depends on the amount of competition a medium has, the importance of the event, and the ease and expense of first-hand coverage.

News sections of the media are not the only sites in which we find handouts. Educational and documentary materials, and sometimes even entertainment, are produced by an industry, organization, or government agency and broadcast or published as though they were part of the regular output of the medium. For example, some television stations broadcast films about the energy crisis that were produced by one of the oil companies, and some newspapers publish recipes for dairy dishes that "just happen" to come from the dairy industry or a government agency promoting the use of milk.

BYLINE

Do you see anything wrong with this practice of relying on handouts? If you have any concerns about this, do they diminish if the broadcaster or publisher announces the source of the material rather than letting the audience believe the publication or station produced the material? How often is such announcing done?

BIAS IN THE NEWS: REASONS

Few journalists set out to intentionally bias the news; they want to do a professional job. Let's consider, then, the reasons why bias occurs in spite of good intentions.

Problems Adapting to Change

One set of reasons is illustrated by media coverage of contemporary social movements, such as the feminist movement, the civil rights movement, the religious right, and the radical left. Such movements, in order to develop and achieve their goals, need the mass media to diffuse their ideas. The problem they encounter, though, is that the constraints of the popular news media lead them to depict new movements in narrow ways, ways not likely to win adherents. For example, when the women's movement was developing rapidly in the 1970s, the story was treated by most of the major media as "soft news"; the media emphasized the novelty of the movement, rather than its concerns and ideas. Instead of reporting the issues, the media trivialized the movement by focussing on such events as bra-burnings. Such media coverage led to jokes and derogatory articles about "women's lib."

In addition, the media wanted to focus on the movement's leaders or spokespersons because that is how journalists traditionally cover organizations. However, the concept of leader or spokesperson was, and is, contrary to the ideology or philosophy of the movement, which is that all women are equal. Journalists could not understand an organization or movement without a leader. As a result, while the women involved tried to define or "frame" the movement in one way, the media kept defining or "framing" it in quite a different way.

Such conflict between the media and a movement or organization is common. And it is serious for any movement, because once the media frame it in a particular way—and media personnel believe the public understands that framing—it is difficult for the movement to change it. For example, once a group is framed as "radical," as a group of "crazy bra-burning women," or as "reactionary," both journalists and the public will continue to view it that way. Everything its participants do will tend to be interpreted within that frame, no matter how misleading it may be.

REVIEW

The media, like many of us, have trouble understanding and adjusting to change. As a result, they often "frame" issues in misleading ways.

The Bias of Language

Not only are stories biased because of the ways journalists frame events, but they are also biased by the choice of what to stress. And we need to recognize that choices of what to emphasize are necessary; no journalist can avoid them.

For example, we sometimes see a great deal in the news media about the percentage of people who are unemployed—6, 7, 8, or 9 percent unemployment—so that the idea of many people being out of work is strongly impressed on the world in our heads. An alternative way of reporting such news was once suggested in a cartoon in the *New Yorker* magazine. The cartoon showed one public relations person in Washington saying to another, "Hey! Why don't we just say we have 91 percent *full* employment."

In one sense, 9 percent unemployment and 91 percent full employment mean the same thing. Have you ever thought about why it is more natural for the media to stress the unemployment rather than the employment figures, or why Washington tries to persuade the media to stress the latter? Neither is right or wrong. However, these two ways of communicating what, on the surface, are the same fact create quite different impressions of the world in the heads of those who read or hear them.

When people assert that the media should just give us the "facts," we need to keep in mind, as this example illustrates, that the problem is not that simple. Not only is there almost always a question of *which* facts out of the infinite possible array they can select from, but there is also the question of what type of language will clothe those facts. And whatever words we choose will bias the message in one way or another.

A different example may clarify this point. Consider the people who periodically create some sort of ruckus around nuclear energy plants or factories believed to be polluting our rivers, lakes, or air. Usually these people passively resist the police who try to get them to move on. When the media report one of these situations, what should they call those who are showing their disapproval of what the plant is doing?

Demonstrators?
Environmentalists?
Law resisters?
Troublemakers?
Concerned citizens?
Law breakers?

They are all of those things, but journalists cannot use all of those terms because they do not have that much time or space to tell the story; if they did, they would confuse readers and listeners.

BYLINE

Put yourself in the place of those journalists. You cannot avoid the problem of labels because you cannot report the story without calling those people something. What are you going to call them? Why?

Were you a reporter, you probably would not give the matter much thought. The label that popped into your mind would likely depend, at least in part, on how our society at the moment and you, as a reporter, look upon what they are doing. If our country is experiencing an energy or economic crisis and we need those plants, you are likely to view those

REVIEW

The language in which facts are clothed has a major effect on the meaning receivers construct. That language, in turn, depends on the historical context of an event, as well as on the sources with whom a reporter talks.

demonstrators as troublemakers. If our energy supply and the economy are in good shape but pollutants in the water supply are reaching dangerous levels, you might instead view them as concerned citizens. The label you use, in turn, will probably help to perpetuate that particular point of view in the society.

Which of those terms you and other reporters use will probably also depend in part on whether you have been talking more with the demonstrators, plant officials, or police. Each of these groups will describe the protest in different ways and thus, consciously or unconsciously, will influence or "manage" the way you cover the story.

MEDIA TREATMENT: BRINGING ABOUT CHANGE

The fact that various biases have existed in the mass media for many years does not mean that those biases are inevitable. The biases are not easy to change, but they can be changed. We have seen a radical shift in the treatment of women in recent years, for example, and an equally radical shift in the treatment of African-Americans and Hispanics. Considering the way these shifts came about may suggest ways you can effect future changes in media coverage toward more balanced treatment of people and issues.

In the case of Hispanics, African-Americans, and women, two major factors accounted for much of the change in their media portrayal. The kinds of pressure groups described in Chapter 13 and innumerable individuals placed both direct and indirect pressure on the media to portray minority groups and women in a greater variety of roles in advertisements, programs, stories, and news. And that pressure had an effect. In addition, more Hispanics, African-Americans, and women entered the media professions, where they could have more influence on what is transmitted. Their entry into the media was helped by those pressure groups, by the affirmative action programs encouraged by government agencies, and by the realization among media leaders that such changes were important for our society.

REVIEW

Social changes, pressure groups, and increased diversity of media personnel have resulted in substantial changes in media treatment of women and minority groups.

Another critical influence on the changing media portrayal of women and minorities is the fact that these groups themselves changed. It is difficult to tell, in fact, how much of the change in media portrayals has been brought about by pressures and concerns about the society and how much has been produced by the change in reality. Women and ethnic minorities are in a greater variety of roles, and many are following more prestigious pursuits, than they were two to three decades ago. So the change may be as much in the society that the media mirror as in the reduction of media bias.

As you consider whether a media portrayal is fair or biased, keep in mind that it is extremely difficult to know precisely what a "true" portrayal is. This is the case when we consider the picture of women and minority groups or when we consider the reports of events or descriptions of individuals. Just as it is impossible for anyone to know what a true portrayal of Barbara Bush or Bill Cosby would be, so it is impossible to know what a "true" portrayal of African-Americans, Hispanics, or women would be. In fact, these groups are more difficult to portray in a valid fashion than any single individuals are. The variety of types of African-Americans in our society, for example, is endless. Almost any portrayal of this group will fit some individuals and not others. Much of the criticism of the media for their treatment of this or any of these groups comes from people who want the media to portray some minority group or women as these critics would like them to become, rather than as they are. A more reasonable and defensible criticism comes from people who simply want the media to reflect the great diversity of Hispanics, African-Americans, women, or almost any other group in our society, rather than treating them in stereotyped ways. For those who work in the media, as well as those who are amateur or professional critics of the media, that sort of diversity of portrayal seems to be a good goal.

BYLINE

Do you agree that the media should merely show the diversity among women or members of minority groups? Or do you think the media have a responsibility to help change society? Should the media work to get injustices righted? If so, who should decide what is just and unjust?

IS ACCURACY THE BEST CRITERION FOR JUDGING MEDIA?

In our discussion of the accuracy or truth of media portrayals, one important question remains: Is accuracy the best criterion for judging the media? The issue of whether women, minority groups, union members, schoolteachers, or any other groups, events, or ideas are accurately portrayed in news stories, motion pictures, or television soap operas or situation comedies is related to a larger issue: What is the primary function of mass communication in our society? Is it to accurately reflect the world, to comment on that world, to entertain, or even—in the case of art—just to be?

One often told story is particularly relevant in this context. It is the story about the famous Hollywood producer who was criticized because his films were merely entertaining; they communicated no moral or important message. "I am not making movies in order to send messages," he responded. "If I wanted to send a message, I would use Western Union."

In short, we ought to keep in mind that the function of much material in the media is to entertain or stimulate; it is not intended to be a slice of life. If our motion pictures, television and radio programs, novels, and so on were accurate depictions of life, they would probably be dull. We would find scant humor or drama to brighten and enlarge our lives.

Even for news and documentary materials, accuracy may not be the most relevant criterion—assuming we can determine what is and is not accurate. When we attempt to picture the amount of violence in society, the financial status of farmers, the quality of education, or the state of religion, there is no way to be "accurate" in any absolute sense.

The sort of picture we paint in our newspaper story or documentary film will and should vary with our purpose. We probably need to depict violence in quite a different way, for example, if we are concerned with the adequacy of our laws than if we are concerned with the factors that cause young people to be more or less aggressive. We might depict it in still a different way if we are trying to explain the antiwar or prowar attitudes of many Americans. In other words, we ought to assess media portrayals most of the time, if not always, not in terms of accuracy but in terms of whether the portrayal is adequate for the purpose of the moment, whether it does the job the creator of the message and its audience desired, and whether it serves our society's needs.

REVIEW

Accuracy is not always the best criterion for judging news or entertainment. The criteria we apply to any media content should depend on the purpose of the content and the degree to which you believe media must reflect reality or try to change that reality.

One further point may help you understand better the position in which media people often find themselves today. In assessing descriptions and evaluations of news and entertainment, and in evaluating that news and entertainment for ourselves, we must separate the beliefs and assertions about what is proper based on the belief that the media should approximate reality from those based on the belief that the media should help to move our society toward some ideal. These are quite different philosophical positions. Media gatekeepers are caught not only between these positions but most of the time also between them and commercial demands, as well as the related demands to entertain or satisfy an audience. The gatekeeper is pressured to be entertaining, to reflect reality accurately, to help change that reality, and to make the audience receptive to commercial messages. In many cases, those four pressures are contradictory.

BYLINE

Can you think of examples you have observed in news coverage and in entertainment content in which such conflicting pressures may have occurred? What about the comedic treatment of women? Of senior citizens? Of minority group members?

PROFESSIONAL NORMS AND PRACTICES IN THE MEDIA: A SUMMARY

In this chapter, we concentrated on some of the major forces within the media that affect the bits of information getting into our communication mosaics—whether news stories, motion pictures, radio and television programs, books, or popular records. We discussed the role of gatekeepers, those individuals or groups through whom media content must flow to get into our environment, those who have the power to delete some of that material, change it, or add to it. Most of the chapter was devoted to explaining the various factors that influence gatekeeping and that therefore, influence the kinds of entertainment and information available to us via the media.

Some influences on the gatekeeper are the same as those that affect all of us, such as the general norms of our society and the people around us whose approval we value or who have the power to reward or punish us. Other influences are more unique to the mass media. The generally accepted values and working practices within the media industries operate as extremely strong controls. The value the news profession places on scoops, objectivity, and well-organized and easy-to-understand stories filled with action and drama sets powerful constraints on those who work in the profession. In the same way, the dependence of journalists on certain types of sources and on their own inferential structures, as well as their susceptibility to the contexts of events, shape the kinds of material we find in our media environment. Even language, the fundamental tool of media professionals, shapes its users and the products of their work.

Given the internal controls on the mass media discussed in this chapter, as well as the external controls covered in earlier chapters, you should consider the degree to which changes in media content and style are possible or even desirable. Think about the criteria by which that content and style, and possible changes in them, are to be judged. In short, whether you are working in the media or are one of their consumers, you need to decide what kinds of media content are desirable and, based on all of the ideas discussed throughout this book, how we might get more of those kinds of content.

DISCUSSION QUESTIONS

1. On the basis of everything you have read so far in this book or elsewhere, as well as on the basis of your own experience and thoughts, how would you define "news"?
2. Which journalistic norms do you believe are essential if our society is to get news that it can rely on? Which norms ought to be adjusted or ignored? Are there other guidelines or norms for journalists that you believe might improve the quality of the news we receive?
3. Would it be good or bad if the general media audience had more influence on the content of the media? If you believe it should have more, how might that change be effected? That is, how might we help the audience have more influence?
4. Overall, do the kinds of gatekeepers now operating in our mass media cause us to receive better or worse news and entertainment?

5. Is the sort of symbiotic relationship between government officials and journalists that we described in this chapter good for our society or not? If you think not, what should be done to change it?
6. Are there any groups in our society that you believe are receiving unfair treatment in the media? What led you to that belief? Why do you think they get the treatment they do?

NOTES

1. Randy Cohen, "What's News." *Channels*, July/August 1983, p. 68.
2. The Glasgow University Media Group. *Bad News* (London: Routledge & Kegan Paul, 1976), p. 84.
3. Churchill L. Roberts, "Attitudes and Media Use of the Moral Majority," *Journal of Broadcasting* 27 (1983): 403–410.
4. Gladys Engle Lang and Kurt Lang. "The Inferential Structure of Mass Communications: A Study of Unwitting Bias," *Public Opinion Quarterly*, 19 (1955–56): 168–183.
5. Walter Gieber and Walter Johnson. "The City Hall 'Beat': A Study of Reporter and Source Roles," *Journalism Quarterly* 38 (1961): 280–297.
6. Turow, Joseph. *Playing Doctor: Television, Storytelling, and Medical Power*. New York: Oxford University Press, 1989.

SUGGESTED READINGS

Classic Works in the Field

Boorstin, Daniel J. *The Image: A Guide to Pseudo-Events in America*. New York: Harper & Row, 1961.

Gieber, Walter, and Johnson, Walter. "The City Hall 'Beat': A Study of Reporter and Source Roles." *Journalism Quarterly* 38 (1961): 280–297.

Schramm, Wilbur. *Responsibility in Mass Communication*. New York: Harper, 1957.

White, Llewellyn. *The American Radio*. Chicago: University of Chicago Press, 1947.

See pp. 68–85 on self-regulation of the media.

Relevant Contemporary Works

Christians, Clifford G., Rotzol, Kim B., and Fackler, Mark. *Media Ethics: Cases and Moral Reasoning*. 3rd ed. New York: Longman, 1991.

Fink, Conrad C. *Media Ethics in the Newsroom and Beyond*. New York: McGraw-Hill, 1988.

Hulteng, John L. *The News Media: What Makes Them Tick?* Englewood Cliffs, NJ: Prentice-Hall, 1979.

Martin, Shannon R. "Proximity of Event as Factor in Selection of News Sources." *Journalism Quarterly* 65 (Winter 1988): 986–989.

Oppel, Richard A. "Readers in the Editor's Chair Squirm Over Ethical Dilemmas," *ASNE Bulletin*, October 1984, pp. 4–8.

Rachlin, Allan. *News as Hegemonic Reality: American Political Culture and the Framing of News Accounts*. New York: Praeger, 1988.

Schudson, Michael. *Discovering the News: A Social History of American Newspapers*. New York: Basic Books, 1978.

Stephens, Mitchell. *A History of News: From the Drum to the Satellite*. New York: Viking, 1988.

Strentz, Herbert. *News Reporters and News Sources: Accomplices in Shaping and Misshaping the News*. Ames, IA: Iowa State University Press, 1989.

Tuchman, Gaye. *Making News: A Study in the Construction of Reality*. New York: Free Press, 1978.

PART FOUR

The Influence of the Media on Your Life

There are many reasons to study mass communication. The mass media are interesting. They have played and continue to play critical roles in the history of our country and world. They are an integral part of our culture. Any one of these would be reason enough to justify your efforts to understand the media. But the most important reason to seek as much knowledge of the media as you can is that, whether you recognize it or not, they greatly influence you and your life. In the final two chapters, you will discover what those influences are and how they work so that, to the extent possible, you can control them.

We will discuss the uses of the media by our society and the effects of those uses, as well as your own and others' uses of the media and the effects of these uses on you. You cannot control the uses and effects on society as easily as you can your personal uses and their effects. However, even the former is not impossible if enough people become knowledgeable and work together to create the kind of society they want.

All of us can influence the effects of the media most directly by changing the ways we use them, since our various uses affect the impact the media have on us. Before attempting to change anything, however, you must become aware of the variety of roles you permit the media to play in your life, the variety of your needs they serve, and the interrelationships among those needs. You must be reasonably certain that when you act to reduce some negative effect, you do not lose even greater positive effects.

Having read and thought about the information and ideas in the first 14 chapters of this book, you probably realize that the impact of the media does not depend solely on what media gatekeepers send through the pipeline. In these last chapters, we want to consider further how the impact of the media depends on a complex interaction of media content and the ways in which you and others process and use that content. Clearly, the media are not neutral. They do both more and less than those who operate them intend. Each medium shapes in particular ways the information and ideas it sends into your environment. But you ignore some of the bits of information they make available to you, and you pick up bits that their creators never thought about. The world that you create in your head is far richer than anything they had in mind and anything they created, for it grows out of a lifetime of experiencing, processing, and shaping messages that fit your needs.

CHAPTER 15

WHAT PEOPLE AND SOCIETIES DO WITH MEDIA

OBJECTIVES

After studying this chapter, you should be able to

- Explain the difference between the "functions" and "effects" of mass communication.
- Differentiate individual and societal functions and provide examples of each.
- Differentiate manifest and latent functions and describe examples of each.
- Explain dissonance theory.
- Discuss ways in which the media enforce social norms.
- Explain how the media facilitate social cohesion.
- Describe at least six of the major functions the media serve for individuals.

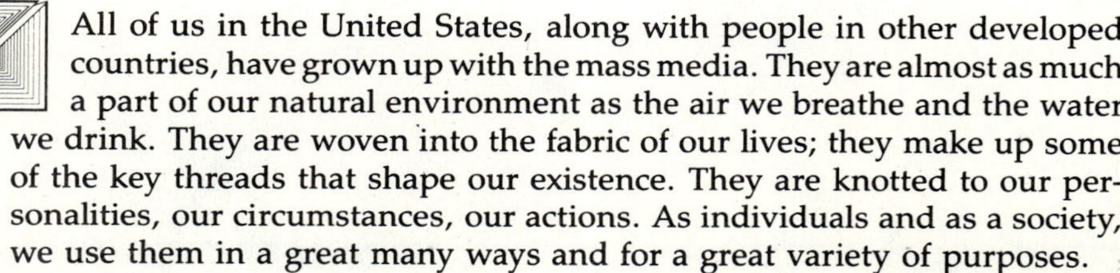

All of us in the United States, along with people in other developed countries, have grown up with the mass media. They are almost as much a part of our natural environment as the air we breathe and the water we drink. They are woven into the fabric of our lives; they make up some of the key threads that shape our existence. They are knotted to our personalities, our circumstances, our actions. As individuals and as a society, we use them in a great many ways and for a great variety of purposes.

Observing these phenomena, some scholars conclude that it is not meaningful to talk about the impact or effects of mass communication (the subject of the next chapter). They maintain that it is more meaningful to talk about and study how and why people use the media as they do. As some critics put it, instead of being concerned about what media do *to* people, we ought to be concerned about what people do *with* media. They suggest further that one of the most important uses of the media is to hold us together as a society and as individuals.

To understand this point, it is helpful to think of each of us, or each of our societies, as a type of system. If we do this, we can then try to understand how the system maintains itself, or how it maintains its equilibrium. In short—using our earlier metaphor—we ought to examine how the media function to help us hold together the many-threaded fabric that is our life and our society.

If the distinction we are making between functions (uses) and effects is not clear to you, think about water. We use water for a great many purposes; it serves many functions for us. Some of the effects of water, such as its effects on health or on irrigated land, depend on how we use it. Other effects, such as the effect of the oceans on our climate or the effect of rain on us and our environment, do not depend on how we use it.

In this chapter, we will discuss some major ideas about the **functions of the media,** the *purposes for which we and our society use them.* As we discuss these functions, however, we should not—in fact, we cannot—discard our concerns about the effects of mass communication if we want to have a reasonably full understanding of its role in our lives. Neither the "functions" approach nor the "effects" approach alone is adequate. Disregarding or rejecting either one is shortsighted. Media are used by people and serve the needs of people and of societies, but the media also *affect* those who use them. We might argue, for example, that it is our use of television, not the medium itself, that affects us. But if television did not exist, we would not have been affected because there would be nothing to use.

Review

Our society and we who live in it are each a type of system. The mass media help to keep these systems running on a relatively even keel.

WAYS TO THINK ABOUT MEDIA FUNCTIONS

Let's begin by establishing some general categories into which media functions fit. Such a category scheme can help you think of additional functions beyond those described in this chapter. It can also give you additional insight into those we describe. We could categorize functions in a variety of ways. Those discussed here are meant to be illustrative, not exhaustive.

Individual Versus Societal Functions

An initial distinction we need to draw is one between the functions the media serve for each of us as individuals and the functions they serve for our society. You might think that societal functions of the media are simply the sum of the functions they serve for all of the individuals in that society. In one sense that is true, but if you view them only in that way, you will overlook some of the most critical roles the media play in contemporary society.

If you consider the questions we might ask about media functions for individuals and for society, the importance of the distinction is clearer. For individuals, we want to know what they do with the media, what gratifications they are seeking, and whether their desires are being fulfilled. For a society, we are more interested in how the media maintain stability or bring about change, how they are used by government or in the political system, and what role they play in the economic structure. So even though, at a very general level, statements and questions about mass media functions for society and for the individual may be similar or even identical, when we frame specific questions we find substantial differences. (You will see the importance of this distinction between the societal and individual level when we consider the effects of mass communication in Chapter 16.)

For example, let's say you are interested in family planning because you believe our planet is getting too crowded. On a societal level, you might ask how the safest and most effective method of birth control is diffused throughout society. You would be searching for ways to speed that diffusion or to make it more complete. Important information for you on this level would be how mass communication helps make people aware of the need to curb population growth, increases the probability that they learn about this particular method of birth control, encourages many of them to adopt it, gives legitimacy to that adoption, and aids the spread of the method's use.

Review

The functions media serve for society are quite different from those they serve for individuals. The societal functions of the media are far more than simply the sum of the functions they serve for individuals.

For a particular couple, however, most of those considerations are irrelevant. At this individual level, you are probably concerned only with whether any of the mass media affected the couple's perception that they ought to limit the size of their family and how mass communication influenced their decision concerning the use of birth control. Even more important, at the individual level, you are concerned with differences among couples and the way those differences affect how they use the media to get information about birth control.

Content Versus Medium Functions

Another useful distinction we can make in considering functions (as well as effects) is the distinction between content and medium. Clearly, some functions are closely tied to the content of the media. Just as clearly, others are relatively independent of content; they are tied solely to the media or the conditions of their use. For example, as you know, the movies serve a mating function in our society. As we indicated in our discussion of motion pictures, they present an excuse to ask for dates, and they provide a good setting for slowly becoming acquainted, especially for those who find it difficult to keep a conversation going for an entire evening. For this sort of mating function, the content of movies is largely irrelevant. The nature of the movie theater is much more important. On the other hand, when we talk about the vote-guiding function of newspaper and television news—the ways in which they provide information about issues and candidates that can help us decide how to vote—content is more relevant than the medium or its form.

BYLINE

Can you think of times when you use one of the media for its content, and its form is largely irrelevant? Can you think of other times when you use one of the media for itself—for the experience it provides—when its content is largely irrelevant?

Manifest Versus Latent Functions

Yet another distinction that is sometimes useful in considering the roles the media play in our lives is the distinction between manifest and latent functions. **Manifest functions** are the *obvious or surface functions of the media,* those we are well aware of when we use them. **Latent functions,** on the other hand, are the *hidden or subconscious functions few of us think about,* especially when the media are serving those functions for us. For example, you may find a couple who listen to radio news each morning while eating breakfast. If you ask them why they do so, they will probably tell you they listen for information—to find out what is going on in the community, what the weather is going to be, and so on. This is the manifest function of their radio news listening. The latent function, on the other hand, may be to have an excuse not to talk to each other. The radio news may save them from having to think of things to talk about; it may even prevent them from arguing.

REVIEW

Manifest functions are those you are aware of. Latent functions are those media serve for you without your realizing it.

A number of years ago, a scholar found that television was often used as a safety valve for tension in families, although the members of the family were probably unaware of this function. He reported that a reasonably reliable measure of the degree of tension in a family was the loudness of the television receiver.

BYLINE

As you think about your uses of the various media or the uses you have observed other people making of the media, can you identify instances in which the media were serving some latent functions? Were you or the others aware of those latent functions at the time? Does it make any difference whether you were aware of them?

Intended Versus Unintended Functions

Closely related to the distinction between the manifest and latent functions of mass communication, but not quite synonymous, is the distinction between intended and unintended functions. Both the source and the receiver of media content usually have particular intentions in mind while developing, creating, or attending to some content, such as a news story. The functions that story actually serves can be quite different from those intended. Think about the incidental learning that goes on when you see a movie; you pick up all sorts of information that neither you nor the producer of the movie thought about.

BYLINE

Have you ever used something in the media for a purpose other than that for which it was intended? Were you aware of it at the time, or is it only in looking back that you realize the medium was serving an unintended function for you?

Another example of the way media can serve functions quite different from those intended has been reported in some of the research literature on **dissonance theory.** (This theory was discussed in Chapter 2.) In essence, *the theory* is *that each of us has some internal pressure to make our attitudes, beliefs, and actions consistent. When they are dissonant, or inconsistent, we try—consciously or, more generally, unconsciously— to make them consistent.*

REVIEW

You almost certainly use media or their contents at times for purposes other than those their creators intended. In fact, you may use them at times for some functions you did not intend.

We sometimes use advertisements for dissonance reduction without realizing it, so that use becomes a latent function of advertising. Advertisements are obviously created to make people want to buy the advertised product. Those who create automobile advertisements intend them for people who are considering the purchase of an automobile. However, dissonance theorists have found that the persons most likely to read an automobile advertisement are those who recently bought that particular kind of car. They read the ad in order to confirm the wisdom of their choice, to help convince them that they made the right decision—in short, to reduce dissonance. This is a function not likely to occur to those who create such advertising.

THE FUNCTIONS OF MASS COMMUNICATION FOR THE SOCIETY

A modern society is impossible without the mass media, and the mass media cannot fully operate except in a modern society. Which is the cause and which the effect is difficult to determine and, at this point, unimportant. What is important is understanding how they serve each other—the functions each performs for the other—so we can try to shape each one to serve those functions better or in a different way when we think that is desirable.

Lasswell's Conception of Societal Functions

One of the first scholars to call attention to the societal functions of communication was political scientist Harold Lasswell.[1] He first considered these functions in terms of categories of specialists that could be found in any society. He identified three types of specialists or functions that must exist in any society.

Surveillance of the environment. According to Lasswell, every society uses both open and secret surveillance to provide intelligence about what is going on in the internal and external environment. Among other things, this surveillance serves as an early-warning system so the society can adjust appropriately when conditions change. This surveillance provides the knowledge necessary to make decisions. Foreign correspondents employed by the media are an important supplement to and check on the reports of diplomats and intelligence experts for surveillance of the external environment. Teachers, reporters, and public opinion pollsters keep the society informed of its internal environment.

Correlation of the response of the society to the environment. The second function mass communication serves for the society, says Lasswell, is correlating the response of the whole society to the environment—that is, developing a reasonably common **public opinion,** that is, *the knowledgeable views of the bulk of the people on important issues in the society.* Through communication, some consensus on these issues can develop. This is important because, in our sort of society, without some reasonable consensus among the public, the government cannot function. There must be some reasonable correlation of the attitudes of society on key issues. Public opinion is brought about, in good part, by creating relatively equivalent degrees of enlightenment among all segments of the society. Lasswell assumed that the correlation specialists were editors, journalists, and public speakers.

Transmission of the social inheritance. The third function identified by Lasswell is transmission of the social inheritance. Parents and teachers have always served this function, but today the media are doing more and more to transmit social values. Broadcasting, newspapers, motion pictures, novels, and other forms of mass communication provide common frames of reference, which are essential for a society. They pass on the knowledge and values of past generations. When people lived almost solely within family units or in small villages where most people interacted face-to-face much of the time, society did not need the mass media for this purpose. With the urbanization, the early abandonment of the family unit, the relative isolation and anonymity, and the frequent uprootings that characterize modern life, the role of the media in socialization and transmission of the social heritage became essential.

Review

Harold Lasswell posited three major societal functions of communication: informing people and society about the external and internal environment, developing consensus, and passing social knowledge on from generation to generation. Lasswell also noted that communication can be dysfunctional as well as functional.

Dysfunctions associated with mass communication. Lasswell recognized that mass communication could be dysfunctional (or harmful), as well as functional, for a society. The development of shared knowledge and consensus in a society can be disrupted or distorted by a ruling class or a government that fears the public and withholds information or, even worse, that uses the media to mislead the populace. In such cases, democratic government is not possible because meaningful public opinion or consensus cannot develop.

Equivalent enlightenment is also impossible to achieve if some people lack the skills needed to use the media effectively. Dysfunction can result from an inability to send information through the media skillfully or an inability to receive and process that information skillfully.

Lazarsfeld and Merton's Conception of Functions

Communication scholars Paul Lazarsfeld and Robert Merton also describe three media functions, which they label status conferral, enforcement of the social norms, and narcotizing dysfunction.[2] In a sense, these functions serve one larger function: to increase the probability of a stable society. Or, if you wish to give this function a somewhat negative value, you might call it "maintenance of the status quo."

Status conferral. In any society there must be a means of *legitimizing or making people believe that certain ideas, issues, people, organizations, and movements are important* (**status conferral**). In contemporary society, the media perform this function. An appearance on the "Tonight" show produces instant fame. An issue discussed by Peter Jennings or Ted Koppel is clearly an issue whose time has come. And making the cover of *Time* is a sure indication that a particular person or idea is truly important.

Treatment by the media does much more than simply bring familiarity or fame to people or ideas—it legitimizes their status. If NBC or the *New York Times* reports on you, you must truly be important, even if what they report is that you embezzled $100 million.

Enforcement of the social norms. Lazarsfeld and Merton suggest that mass media serve to *reaffirm and ensure that social norms are followed* by exposing deviations from those norms (a process known as **enforcement of social norms**). There is often a gap between the public morality and the private behavior of many individuals, between what we say we believe in and what we actually do. These deviations can be tolerated most of the time. They produce no tension, unless they are brought out into the open. Publicity leads to tension, which leads to change. What was privately tolerable

When these four young men from England were featured on the Ed Sullivan Show, *the most popular television program in America at the time, it gave them great status in this country.*

cannot be publicly acknowledgeable. Public norms or values must be maintained. If change does not come about in such cases, the public becomes cynical. Such cynicism developed in many Americans when our government continued to support El Salvador's government, despite the media's publication of the many human rights abuses by the Salvadoran military.

We saw an example in the United States Senate a few years ago of something that was privately tolerable becoming intolerable when it was made public. One of their own, former senator John Tower, was nominated by the president to be secretary of defense. Generally, the nomination of a colleague is strongly supported by senators. However, the news media gave great play to Tower's womanizing and excessive drinking. Senators knew these facts already and under normal conditions would have ignored them. Once the media made Tower's behavior a public issue, however, they could not ignore them. They had little choice but to reject the Tower nomination.

BYLINE

Can you find a recent instance of one of the media enforcing a social norm? How effective does it appear to have been? Since there are ample instances in which public morality and private behavior are at odds, why is it that our media do not serve this function of enforcing social norms more frequently?

Within a society, this pressure for change created by the publicizing of a discrepancy between public morality and private behavior is analogous to what occurs within an individual at times. Your attitude toward a source, such as Chief Justice William Rehnquist, and your attitude toward an issue, such as the public's First Amendment right of access to the media, are relatively independent. Normally, one attitude has no effect on the other. However, if their relationship is made salient for you, they do affect each other. For example, if you have positive attitudes toward both Justice Rehnquist and the right of access, and then you learn that Justice Rehnquist does not believe the First Amendment can be validly interpreted as establishing a right of access to the media—that is, a right to be heard as well as a right to speak, you will experience internal pressure to change your attitude toward Rehnquist, toward the concept of access, or toward both.

Let's consider another example. In some of our home towns, discrimination has existed for years. In some towns, some landlords will not rent homes to African-Americans, Hispanics, people with young children, or some other group. We hear rumors about it, and some of us know it for a fact; few of us do anything about it. Even if we try to do something, we find little support. The town ignores the problem. However, if a local newspaper or radio station begins regularly publicizing these acts of discrimination, we can ignore the problem no longer. Now the town must do something. It can no longer act as though the problem does not exist, and it cannot acknowledge that it does not believe in equality. In this way, the media often serve as enforcers of our social norms.

Review

According to Lazarsfeld and Merton, the two major functions of the media are (1) conferring status on certain ideas, issues, people, organizations, and movements; and (2) enforcing social norms by exposing deviations from them. "Narcotizing dysfunction," according to these scholars, is the media's creation of apathy.

Narcotizing dysfunction. Like Lasswell, Lazarsfeld and Merton also point out that the media can be dysfunctional as well as functional for a society. They stress quite a different sort of dysfunction than Lasswell did, however, one they term **narcotizing dysfunction,** the *creation of apathy by the mass media*. They attribute this apathy to the fact that the media so flood the public with information that we in the audience, rather than being energized—which is the intent—are made numb; we are narcotized. Many of us, according to Lazarsfeld and Merton, spend so much time *learning* about issues that we have little time left to *do* anything about them. We begin to confuse knowing about an issue with acting on that issue.

Servicing the Political Systems

To some extent, much of what Lasswell, Lazarsfeld, and Merton described could be subsumed under the general category of servicing the political system. Mass communication serves that system in a wide variety of ways, some direct, some indirect. In a large and complex society such as ours, leaders can communicate with the public only through the mass media. Think, for example, how much more difficult it would be for statewide or national candidates to campaign if it were not for the media. How would you learn about presidential candidates, the congressional candidates, or the candidates for governor?

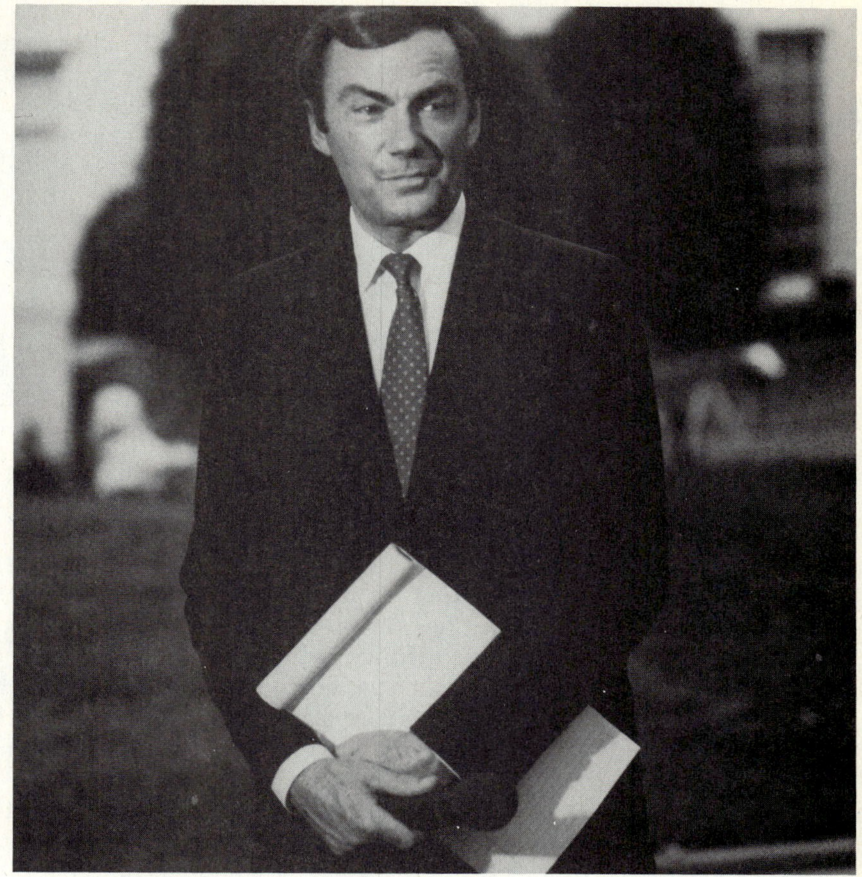

Although White House reporter Sam Donaldson often asked embarrassing questions, he helped the president get his message on the evening news, just as his interactions with the president helped Donaldson's career.

The media are also vital for the diffusion of new information from the government. When our tax laws are revised, for example, we learn from the media about their impact on us and how we should respond.

Our leaders even use the media to communicate with foreign governments. When President Bush wanted to communicate to the world a plan for the reduction of arms or to explain his actions in regard to Central America, he often made the announcement at a meeting widely covered by the world's press. He knew this would result in the immediate, worldwide diffusion of the information, not only to leaders of every country, but also to their people. This method was much more effective than sending the message only to the leaders of those countries because it increased the probability that the citizens of each country would pressure their government to support the plan. Soviet President Mikhail Gorbachev also uses the media this way, and with equal effectiveness, at least with audiences outside the Soviet Union.

The United States Information Agency has made this direct communication between our government and foreign reporters easier by developing Worldnet, an international telecommunications link. Through Worldnet, United States leaders can hold a press conference at almost any time with journalists all over the world to give them our government's version of situations or events and our plans for dealing with them.

BYLINE

Can you find a recent instance in which a government leader or some branch of government used one of the media to help with foreign relations or some other aspect of governance?

Facilitation of Social Cohesion

As we mentioned earlier, the media aid the development of public opinion by providing a base of common knowledge. This shared knowledge increases the sense of community and thus reduces the chances of conflict within a society. In times of crisis, such as during a war, the media do even more to bring about cohesion; the information they transmit unifies people and mobilizes them to support the government. All the mass media need to do is to suggest that there may be a threat to this country, that the enemy is committing atrocities, or that our military and the president are standing up to that evil force. The immediate reaction to such information, as long as it is consistent, is to rally around our country's leader.

It is possible that the media also facilitate social cohesion by challenging dominant values less often then they might. Many social critics today argue that the mass media largely aid the nation's elite in its exercise of power. They claim the media help keep the poor and the powerless quiet and satisfied with their lot. For example, they point out that the popular media seldom point out that the social structure in this country is not equitable. In general, they depict working people as comfortable and satisfied. Even in the coverage of labor disputes, the media do not give us a sense that strikers are representative of working people. In covering other countries, the media almost exclusively show workers who are worse off than those in this country, even though, in fact, workers in some countries have greater benefits or more say in how things are run. Thus, the kinds of entertainment and news we see likely reduce the probability that workers will become dissatisfied.

In this sense, at least, the media support the present economic and social structure in this country. A fundamental question related to this generalization is whether the media *should* be supportive in this way. Should they instead be stirring up dissatisfaction with our economic and social system? Should they encourage Americans to question the fundamental tenets of this society? Would such a challenge be in this country's best interests? Would it lead to a better society or to a more troubled one? We cannot answer these questions definitively. But you ought to think about them as you consider what the role of the mass media should be in this country and, closely related to that issue, the kind of country in which you want to live.

Review

The media facilitate social cohesion by giving people a common base of information and by refraining from criticism of our society's structure and values. To this extent, they support the status quo.

The media have done some such stirring up in the past. Newspaper stories, editorials, and television coverage of the war in Vietnam did much to end American participation in that war. Media coverage of the campaign for civil rights in the 1960s did a great deal to create irresistible pressure for fairer civil rights legislation. One reason there has been less progress—and perhaps even some backsliding—in defending and promoting civil rights in recent years is that the media appear to have forgotten the issue. They give it little attention today.

Interpreting the Society to Itself

The media do more, however, than simply support or challenge the society's power structure, beliefs, and values. They also give expression to them. Many scholars believe the most valid way to discover what a society believes and values is neither to conduct public opinion polls nor to read the essays of philosophers. It is, rather, to examine the kinds of entertainments that are popular. The underlying theory is that the popular situation comedies, soap operas, police shows, novels, songs, and motion pictures have become popular precisely because they are in tune with people's beliefs and values. Thus, one can gain insight into a society by carefully studying these popular materials.

Review

The media reflect and interpret a society's beliefs and values to the people of the society.

Servicing the Economic System

Quite a different type of mass media function is the servicing of a society's economic system. In a capitalist society such as ours, this is one of the media's most important societal functions. Although many people sharply criticize advertising in the media, and some of the criticism is justified, most Americans probably believe we gain more than we lose from advertising, that the servicing of our economic system generally is a positive function rather than a dysfunction of the mass media.

It is not only through advertising that the media service our economic system. They also service it by showing, in dramas, situation comedies, documentaries, news stories, novels, and even in comic strips, the kinds of things an American ought to expect to have. For example, you can read few novels or watch few television programs or motion pictures set in America without assuming, consciously or unconsciously, that every American adult is supposed to have an automobile—even a certain style of automobile.

Review

The mass media service our economic system by creating similar tastes and desires for goods, and then by showing, through advertising, how to satisfy those desires.

A major criticism of advertising and the mass media is that they lead people to want things they don't need, and that they create similar tastes in large segments of our population and, in fact, of the world population. However, it is this creation of similar tastes that makes mass production and mass distribution feasible. Mass production and mass distribution, in turn, make possible a higher standard of living for all.

> **BYLINE**
>
> Overall, is media servicing of our economic system a positive function for our society or a dysfunction?

Integration of New Residents into a Community

Local media advertise not only products and services, but also the community itself. They praise the local sports teams and honor those citizens and former citizens who do something special. They persuade those of us living in the community that this is a good place to live. By so doing, they help integrate new residents into the community. These new residents read the local newspaper, listen to the radio, and watch the local news on television to see what sort of town this is and who and what is important here. By learning about the community, they become part of it. (Some observers criticize local newspapers and broadcasting stations for overdoing such cheerleading. They fear the media lose their objectivity in the process and, with it, their watchdog function.)

REVIEW

Local media help integrate new residents into a community by providing information about the community and by describing features of the community that are a source of pride.

A discussion of the integration of individuals into a community provides a good transition from our consideration of the functions the mass media serve for society to our examination of the functions they serve for individuals, because such a discussion approaches the borderline between the two. Such integration is essential for the smooth functioning of a community; it is also essential for the security and comfort of the individual. Let's turn now to the bulk of the research and theoretical ideas on the functions of mass media for individuals.

THE FUNCTIONS OF MASS COMMUNICATION FOR THE INDIVIDUAL

If asked why we spend so much of our time with the mass media, most of us would probably respond, without hesitation, that we do so to become informed, or to be entertained, or both. Such responses are oversimplifications. For most of us, for most of the time, the media play far more complex and subtle roles in our lives. We use the media for a great variety of purposes, and these purposes change as we and our situations change.

In this section, we shall consider the following functions or uses of media: (1) surveillance or information-seeking; (2) developing a concept of self; (3) helping us professionally; (4) facilitating social interaction; (5) substituting for social interaction; (6) providing relaxation, diversion, emotional release, enjoyment, stimulation, or relief from boredom; (7) aiding escape from tensions and alienation; and (8) ritualizing daily living to give us a sense of order and security.[3]

Seeking Information in the Media

Few of us realize the vast amounts of information we get from the mass media and the variety of ways in which we use that information in the conduct of our lives. In some cases we seek that information consciously, searching for what we need or want. In other cases the search is unconscious, but the uses we make of the information are no less important.

Guiding our behaviors. Media information guides many of our behaviors. For example, it helps us decide whether to go to the basement to avoid a tornado, what horse to bet on in the Kentucky Derby, what movie or television programs to see, and whether to major in anthropology, Chinese history, or business administration.

We also seek information to guide our purchases. We learn who has what for sale, when or whether to buy stock, and what the best tennis racquets or golf clubs are in our price range.

The mass media often shape our voting behaviors; they increase or decrease the probability that we will send contributions to a particular candidate, campaign for a candidate or party, or bother going to the polls to vote.

We also get from the mass media much information that guides our behaviors more generally. For many of us, the media serve as a kind of school of life. We see how people behave in various situations on television, in movies, or in books, and from these observations we build a store of knowledge about how we should behave in similar situations.

Guiding our understanding. Not only do the media provide information that guides our behaviors, but we also get from them information that shapes our understanding of the world around us. We discussed this more fully early in Part One, where we explored the way we construct the worlds in our heads from the bits of information we grasp from our media environment. That world in our heads may or may not be valid, but we would be extremely uncomfortable if it were not there. Believing that we understand our world reasonably well makes it easier for us to go about our business without undue tension.

REVIEW

Information from the media guides our behaviors and understanding of the world.

Developing Our Concepts of Ourselves

In addition to helping us understand our world, the media also help us understand ourselves. Information from the media, coupled with our observation of other people and how they respond to us, are the raw materials with which we develop a concept of ourselves, of who we are. The media function in three ways to help us develop our self-concepts.

Exploring reality. Through the media we explore reality, developing views of ourselves and our lives. As we read, hear, and view a variety of people in various situations—both actual and fictional—we put ourselves into the shoes of many of them. We identify at times with the tough cop in a novel and at other times with the ballet artist on PBS. We empathize with the president or a senator or perhaps with one of the journalists covering Congress and the White House. We feel we are helping to fly that plane in combat or are involved in that operation we hope will save a child's life. Through such identification, and through watching and reading about people like ourselves and how they act and are acted upon, we construct ideas about what our relationships are to other people and what they might be.

Aiding our comparisons and contrasts. In addition to helping us explore and reinforcing our values, the media probably function more directly to help each of us develop a concept of self, or ego. Through comparison and contrast with people we see on the motion picture or television screen or read about in news accounts or fiction, and through observation of the ways others interact with them, we build a sense of who we are, what our values are, and how we ought to play our various roles. Because of the widespread belief that the media serve this comparison-and-contrast function, considerable concern has been expressed in recent years about **sex role stereotyping** in the media, *the constant showing of girls and boys, men and women, in traditional roles*. The media are criticized for not showing them, or members of minority groups in a greater variety of roles. As the child de-

Shots of female soldiers in news coverage of the Persian Gulf War probably led some young women for the first time to think of careers in the military.

velopment experts put it, each child —and, we would add, each adult— needs a variety of role models. For most of us, the media provide many of these role models. We need to see characters we want to be like; we also need to see characters we do not want to be like. And we need to see models that will broaden our vision of what we can do, rather than models that make us think we have few choices.

REVIEW

The media help us develop concepts of ourselves in three ways. Through the media we explore possible roles we might play in life, compare and contrast ourselves with media characters, and get information and ideas for use in our work.

BYLINE

Can you find examples of either sex role stereotyping or minority group stereotyping in the media today? If so, why do you suppose such stereotyping goes on?

Helping us professionally. The mass media often help us professionally as well as personally. Media messages are essential these days in keeping up with many fields (for example, medicine), and they are essential for professional guidance (for example, the farmer's use of market reports, weather reports, and information on new seeds and fertilizers). Most teachers frequently clip articles out of newspapers and magazines or make a note about something seen in a television program or film to use in class.

Facilitating Social Interaction

The media facilitate our social interactions by giving us subjects to talk about and some common background for that conversation. Consider recent conversations you have had about topics other than school matters and determine how many of them could have occurred if none of the participants had obtained information from the media. Information and ideas gained from the media help improve our status by making us better informed. In many of the groups with which some of us interact, for example, we feel inferior if we have not seen the latest French film or read the latest book that "everybody is reading." If we are to be with a group of lawyers for an evening, we know we had better pay attention to news about the latest activities of the Supreme Court.

Our social interactions are aided not only by the specific media products or bits of information we seek out for this purpose, but also by the information and media products we encounter by chance or through our normal media habits. Most of us seem to have an unconscious receptivity to information that will be useful in this way. Research evidence shows, for example, that when people anticipate being involved in political discussions, they seldom search for information. Instead, they simply become more receptive to relevant items during their normal mass media use. All of these media experiences and bits of information then work like oil to lubricate interactions with other people.

Serving as a Substitute for Social Interaction

The media also *function* for us *at times as a substitute for social interaction. They provide vicarious companionship or vicarious interaction.* Communication scholars label this **parasocial interaction.** We have all seen numerous examples of people who develop close, even seemingly personal relationships with individuals or characters they hear on radio or see on television. They send baby gifts to the soap opera characters who are supposedly giving birth to children; they approach television performers on the street as though they are close friends.

One of the most surprising examples of parasocial interaction occurred some years ago when the United Nations Security Council was debating what to do about the Arab-Israeli War. All 51 hours of that debate were covered live on television, and the president of the council, Denmark's Hans Tabor, became a familiar face on the screen. As a result, he received eighty-five thousand letters, most of them from women and many of them extremely personal. A 15-year-old girl began her letter, "My Dear Hans." He was offered advice; people sent him money and other gifts, and asked for his photograph or his autograph. He even received proposals of marriage.

REVIEW

The media help both our social and parasocial interactions. They give us topics to discuss with friends and others and common ground on which to build understanding. They give us characters with whom we can establish parasocial relationships when our real-life relationships are unsatisfactory or nonexistent.

BYLINE

Have you ever fantasized that someone on television or in the movies, or even someone in the news or in a novel, was a friend of yours? How did you show that friendship?

The need for companionship that the media serve is demonstrated in study after study. It is also demonstrated in the conversations you can hear on almost any late-night radio call-in show, and even occasionally in the letters to the editor of your local newspaper. Although our evidence on the matter is not substantial, we assume that this particular function of the media is especially important for many shut-ins and elderly persons who live alone and for people who have difficulty in normal, face-to-face interactions with other people.

Aiding Emotional Release A more obvious function of the mass media for individuals is to offer relaxation, diversion, enjoyment, stimulation, or relief from boredom. These terms are not synonymous. Certainly, being relaxed is not the same as being stimulated, and you could be diverted or stimulated without necessarily enjoying it. However, whether logically or not, most of us turn to the same types of media experiences—at least some of the time—for each of these gratifications. For example, many of us turn on our stereo systems or our radios or television sets when we are bored and need stimulation, and we do precisely the same when we are overstimulated and want to relax. We could also turn to a novel one day for relaxation and to the same novel the next day for stimulation.

BYLINE

What kinds of things do you usually do when bored? Do you turn to one of the media? How about when you want to relax? Like most of us, do you often turn to the same medium for both relaxation and stimulation? If so, how do you explain that apparent contradiction?

There is at least one possible explanation for this seeming contradiction, although as yet there is no evidence to support it. The common element in all of those gratifications we mentioned—relaxation, diversion, enjoyment, stimulation, and relief from boredom—is an emotional experience or release that changes whatever our prior emotional state was. The two important elements we seek, whether we are overstimulated and tense or understimulated and bored, are change and pleasure. We turn to the media and can always find that change. Equally important, it is a change we have learned to enjoy. Very often, the content of what we are reading or watching or listening to makes little or no difference. We enjoy the medium itself. Most of us, when we first began reading novels or short stories, watching movies or television, or listening to music, probably turned to particular kinds of content. The content produced enjoyment, but we almost always got that content from a particular medium. Ultimately, we began to associate the pleasure we got from the content with the medium, so that the use of the medium itself, independent of content, became enjoyable. Psychologists would label this **classical conditioning** because the *control of the response we made to the content was transferred to the medium*. So now many of us can get enjoyment or relaxation or stimulation simply from the act of reading, listening to a record album, watching television, or using some other medium. Think about that explanation and the way you use the various media to see whether it fits your behaviors.

Providing Escape from Tensions and Alienation

Another function that may be indistinguishable from diversion or relaxation is escape. Many people believe that our urbanized, technological, competitive society creates **alienation**—a *feeling of isolation or hostility toward other people*—from which the media offer means of escape. In a sense, they suggest the media serve the same function for some of us that alcohol or drugs serve for others. To put it simply, the media help us forget our problems and worries.

An intriguing question about the use of the media for escape, and to some extent the use of the media for the other functions we discussed, is whether it is the medium, the content, or the situation in which we use the medium that provides the escape or serves the other functions. For example, if you use movies for escape, is it only certain kinds of movies that provide escape for you—such as light comedies and musicals—or does any movie do? If any movie does the trick, is it then the movie that helps you escape and forget your problems, or is it the darkness and isolation of the movie theater? Does watching the movie in your home on your television set provide the same sort of escape? Or, as we discussed earlier, was it originally the movie content that served this function, and you simply learned to associate your content response to the medium itself?

REVIEW

We use the media for relaxation and stimulation, or any time we want a change of mood. The same media experience can either stimulate or relax us.

Ritualizing Our Lives

A great deal of evidence suggests that people vary in their need for organization, for clear structure or order in their lives. To the extent the media function to provide that order for some people, they serve as **ritual.** By "ritual" we mean the *frequent repetition of an act in precisely the same way, like some religious ceremonies*. The ritual of media use provides a sense of security for some of us. When we know that we are going to listen to the radio news at 7:45 A.M. and to television news at 11:00 P.M., that we see "Murphy Brown" Mondays at 8:00 P.M., that on Saturday night we will go to the movies, or that we are going to read a book or magazine when we

Late-Breaking

NEWS

VCR ALERT . . . COMING UP SOON

A handy guide to must-see episodes

• UNTIL WE MEET AGAIN

For **DAYS OF OUR LIVES** fans, it's time to say good-bye to two young favorites — Frankie and Eve will split the Salem scene on **Friday, July 12**.

Stop in the name of love! Mallet (Mark Derwin) does what he can to halt Francesca's (Nadia Capone) wedding.

• WHAT'S UP, SIS?

GUIDING LIGHT went on location in New York City to tape Mallet's trip to the Big Apple on **Tuesday, July 16**. He's there to try and stop Francesca's wedding, but unexpectedly is reunited with his teenage sister, Julie.

• MONTY, MOST FOUL

Tuesday and **Wednesday, July 16** and 17, are definitely not-to-be-missed days on **LOVING**. It's then that, in Agatha Christie style, the mystery of Monty's murder will be explained.

• MAKE ME OVER

Check out **ONE LIFE TO LIVE** on **Wednesday, July 17**, when Tina gets a makeover. Actress Karen Witter (Tina) actually *does* get the beauty treatment on camera, including a haircut. Penn Jillette, of Penn and Teller, makes a guest appearance as a beauty salon owner. Plenty of New York City locations highlight this remote shoot.

Only her hairdresser knows for sure, but Karen Witter (OLTL's Tina) may look very different soon.

36

Late-Breaking

NEWS

• BO'S WOES EXPOSED

DAYS OF OUR LIVES's Carly, who's been growing more and more suspicious about what's going on with Kayla and Bo, finally learns about Bo's illness on **Friday, July 19**. On that same fateful day, Bo locates Emmy.

• MA'AM, I'M SAM

ANOTHER WORLD is the place to be on **Wednesday, July 10**, when Sam returns to town (in the person of newcomer Brian Green). That same day, a mystery blonde signs into a hotel in Bay City.

A broken heart is winging its way to one of the two women in Dr. Bob's life on ATWT: Susan (Marie Masters, left) and Kim (Kathryn Hays).

• EENY-MEENY-MINEY-MO

AS THE WORLD TURNS's Dr. Bob has a tough call to make. Should he give his heart to co-worker/lover Susan, or keep it in the family and stick with estranged wife Kim? Tune in **Tuesday, July 16**, when the tormented doc decides about the two women in his life.

• WHO'S THAT GUY?

Mindy, who accompanied Mallet on his quest to put the kabosh on Francesca's nuptials, spots a mystery man in New York City on the **Friday, July 19**, episode of **GUIDING LIGHT**.

AMC's Dixie (Cady McClain) may not be so happy when she learns that she's being followed.

• PARLOR GAMES

Dixie is stalked, Charlie makes an uncharacteristic overture, and there's an embarrassing scene in the Chandler parlor on the **Friday, July 12**, episode of **ALL MY CHILDREN**. And, a week later, on **Friday, July 19**, the Emily Ann/Joey/Katie triangle takes a bizarre twist.

• GIVE ME THE LETTER

Tracy, put the kettle on — we need to steam open an envelope! Don't miss the show on **Tuesday, July 16**, when those devious Quartermaines try to decide what to do with the mysterious hidden letter addressed to Robert from Edward on **GENERAL HOSPITAL**.

37

Magazines about soap operas, as well as the television programs themselves, serve a great variety of functions for readers and viewers.

go to bed at 11:30, we feel more secure, somehow reassured. Departures from any of these rituals can make us anxious or uncertain. Consider the plight of the unfortunate family whose television receiver is in the repair shop, or the person whose electricity is out and cannot read before going to sleep: "How can I possibly go to sleep if I can't watch the news or read for a while first?"

BYLINE

Make a list of the media uses that order your life. Do you listen to any radio or television newscasts at particular times almost every day? Do you read the newspaper at a particular time and place each day? Do you have a regular night for going to the movies? Are there particular programs you watch or listen to regularly? Do you have some records you listen to periodically that you associate with some particularly happy moments in the past?

These rituals are especially important for some college students who are away from home for an extended period for the first time in their lives.

REVIEW

The media serve a ritual function for many of us; they provide order and regularity. We can almost always depend on them.

Being able to watch the same television programs they watched with their families is somehow reassuring. It ties their present to their past. Such continuity is an important need for many people, and the mass media make it possible. It is also comforting to relive again those days when one had fewer pressures and worries. You can relive those times by watching reruns of the television shows you watched in earlier years at home. One reason for the popularity of VCRs may be that they give us more control of our daily or weekly rituals.

THE FUNCTIONS OF MASS COMMUNICATION: A SUMMARY

In this chapter, we suggested that you think about mass communication in terms of the ways we and our society use them—the functions they serve for us. Instead of just considering *what the media do to you,* consider *what you do with them.* Their effect on you and your society depends in large part on how you and your society use them. It is helpful to distinguish between functions the media serve for you as an individual and those they serve for your society, between functions served by media content and functions served by the media themselves independent of content, between manifest and latent functions, and between functions the media intend and functions they do not intend.

The mass media serve many functions for our society. In a real sense, they are the contemporary manifestations of the tribe and the extended family. They pass on to us our social inheritance; they help socialize us to our environment and hold us together. The media in large part determine who and what is important in the society and create pressure to bring the society's actions into line with its professed values. No political system in a large, urban society could operate well without the mass media. The media are vital both for the election process and in the operation of government. The mass media even facilitate the implementation of our foreign policy. The media help not only our political system but also our closely related economic system. Business and industry are as dependent on the media as government is, not only for advertising but also for stimulating people's desires for various products and a high standard of living. And the media, in large part the entertainment media, interpret and express the beliefs and values of the society. Although some critics of the mass media disagree, it seems clear that most societies are more stable because of what the mass media do. Less clear is whether that is good or bad.

The media serve important functions for individuals as well as for society. As discussed in Chapters 1 and 2, they give us the information we need to shape our understanding of the world, and they help us learn how to behave in various kinds of situations. Even more important, they help us shape self-concepts by giving us models with which to compare and contrast ourselves and situations with which we can identify. They also give us information that can help us professionally and socially, and companionship when it is otherwise unavailable. They bring stimulation, emotional release, and a harmless means of escape when we need it. And, extremely important for many of us, the mass media help us ritualize or organize our lives. Little in the contemporary world is constant and dependable. The mass media, by and large, are an exception; rightly or wrongly, we feel more secure because they exist.

Again, all of these functions of the media exist not primarily because of what the media are or do but rather because of the way we and our society use them.

DISCUSSION QUESTIONS

1. What relationships can you see between the individual functions and the societal functions of the media?
2. Do you believe that manifest or latent functions of the media are generally more important for us to try to understand? What about intended versus unintended functions?
3. How well do you believe the media help to correlate the response of our society to its environment? Should it do better? If so, how?
4. Do you believe the media in our society have a narcotizing dysfunction? Or do they increase involvement in government and politics?
5. In what ways do the entertainment media—movies, novels, comic strips, popular music, and/or prime-time television—reflect the beliefs and values of our society?
6. Do the media in this country generally help women and members of minority groups develop positive self-concepts?
7. In what ways, in addition to those mentioned in this chapter, might the media be serving a ritual function for some people?

NOTES

1. Harold D. Lasswell, "The Structure and Function of Communication in Society," In *The Process and Effects of Mass Communication*, ed. Wilbur Schramm and Donald F. Roberts. Rev. ed. (Urbana: University of Illinois Press, 1971), pp. 84–99.
2. Paul F. Lazarsfeld and Robert K. Merton, "Mass Communication, Popular Taste, and Organized Social Action." In Schramm and Roberts, pp. 554–578.
3. When we develop more sophisticated research in this area, we believe the findings will demonstrate the existence of all of these media functions and more. Such research will also indicate how the various functions relate to each other and to the personal characteristics of those of us who use the media.

   Also, note that we are considering these functions independently of the purposes for which the media materials were intended; that is, independently of the intent of the media creators. The functions media serve for us often bear little relationship to the purposes for which they were intended. A clear sign of this is that the same material often serves quite different purposes for different individuals.

SUGGESTED READINGS

Classic Works in the Field

Berelson, Bernard. "What Missing the Newspaper Means." In *Communication Research 1948–49*, ed. Paul F. Lazarsfeld and Frank N. Stanton, pp. 111–129. New York: Duell, Sloan & Pearce, 1949.

Blumler, Jay, and Katz, Elihu, eds. *The Uses of Mass Communication*. Beverly Hills: Sage, 1974.

Lasswell, Harold D. "The Structure and Function of Communication in Society." In *The Communication of Ideas*, ed. Lyman Bryson, pp. 37–51. New York: Harper, 1948.

Lazarsfeld, Paul F., and Merton, Robert K. "Mass Communication, Popular Taste, and Organized Social Action." In *The Communication of Ideas*, ed. Lyman Bryson, pp. 95–118. New York: Harper, 1948.

Herzog, Herta. "Motivations and Gratifications of Daily Serial Listeners." In *Radio Research, 1942–1943*, ed. Paul F. Lazarsfeld and Frank N. Stanton, pp. 50–55. New York: Duell, Sloan & Pearce, 1944.

Relevant Contemporary Works

Finn, Seth, and Gorr, Mary B. "Social Isolation and Social Support as Correlates of Television Viewing Motivations." *Communication Research* 15 (April 1988):135–158.

Kern, Montague. *30-Second Politics: Political Advertising in the Eighties*. New York: Praeger, 1989.

Payne, Gregg A., Severn, Jessica J. H., and Dozier, David M. "Uses and Gratifications Motives as Indicators of Magazine Readership." *Journalism Quarterly* 65 (Winter 1988):909–913.

Rosengren, Karl Erik, Wenner, Lawrence A., and Palmgreen, Paul, eds. *Media Gratifications Research: Current Perspectives*. Beverly Hills, CA: Sage, 1985.

CHAPTER 16

WHAT MEDIA DO TO PEOPLE AND SOCIETIES

OBJECTIVES

After studying this chapter, you should be able to

- **Explain why particular kinds of studies have dominated mass communication research.**
- **Discuss the reasons why media effects are so complex.**
- **Describe the five different ways in which the media can "cause" effects—the sense in which we can say the media "caused" something to occur.**
- **Explain what the authors mean when they speak of "variable effects."**
- **Describe these major theories used to explain media effects: Modeling theory, Identification, Arousal theory, Schema theory, Cultivation theory, Spiral of Silence theory, Agenda-Setting theory, Consistency theory, Political-Economy theory, and Systems theory.**

The movies are so occupied with crime and sex stuff and are so saturating the minds of children the world over with social sewage that they have become a menace to the mental and moral life of the coming generation.[1]

Movies encourage goodness and kindness, virtue and courage.[2]

Those two generalizations were published in the early part of this century when the motion picture was just becoming one of the dominant media of entertainment. They exemplify the contradictory claims about effects that have been made about every medium of communication from the printing press to the communication satellite. They also exemplify the love-fear relationship that has characterized our society's attitudes toward the mass media since at least the development of radio and the motion picture. Not only has there been continued debate about whether the effects of the mass media are good or evil, but there has also been disagreement about whether those effects are weak or powerful. Some observers believe audience members are little more than puppets, manipulated by the invisible strings of the media. Others believe the media are minor influences compared to other experiences, needs, social relationships, and behaviors.

In this chapter, we will explore the bases for those claims so you can evaluate them and decide, for yourself, which generalizations about media effects are most valid.

THE HISTORY OF RESEARCH ON THE EFFECTS OF MASS MEDIA

Not only have scholars and the general public been concerned since the early days of mass communication about the effects of the media on children, crime, politics, and other aspects of the society, but so have society's leaders. The efforts by kings to control the ownership and use of printing presses, discussed in Chapter 3, stemmed from fear that the spread of information and ideas could lead to unrest and revolution. Some educators were concerned that the widespread use of printed materials in the schools, with the consequent decrease in dependence on memorization, would lead to a loss in children's mental ability. And the media have always been a safe target at which to point the blame for crime and other ills of the society. As a result, dime novels, comic books, movies, radio, and television in turn have been criticized for leading their users astray. On the other hand, as a result of these fears, media also became the foci of research. The most important research on media and children in the early days was the set of Payne Fund studies on the effects of motion pictures on children. (See W. W. Charters's book *Motion Pictures and Youth* in the list of suggested readings at the end of this chapter.)

Not surprisingly, with a capitalist economy such as ours, concerns that arose with the popularity of mass media also centered on advertising. Social critics believed that advertising was distorting the values of Americans, making them too materialistic. Leaders in business and industry, on the other hand, believed advertising benefited society, so they were largely concerned with maximizing its effectiveness. This concern led ultimately to the rise of a major industry devoted to research on marketing and advertising, dedicated to finding ways to make advertising ever more effective. Unfortunately, there has been little research on the possible negative effects of advertising. There is no dearth of literature on the evil effects of

In their early days movies were as popular with children as television is today, so many parents, teachers, and other observers were certain such moving images must be having major effects on these vulnerable youngsters.

advertising, but little of it is supported by research. (See, for example, Michael Schudson's book *Advertising, the Uneasy Persuasion: Its Dubious Impact on American Society* in the list of suggested readings.)

BYLINE

Overall, do you believe that the effects of the media are more positive or more negative?

REVIEW

The mass media have always been accompanied by naysayers and yeasayers—prophets of doom and of boom.

The mass media developed in tandem with modern science. Thus it was inevitable that scholars would become motivated to apply the same logic to the study of human behavior that had been so successful in guiding the development of knowledge about the earth and the heavens. They developed research methods and theories to explain the effects of mass communication on individuals and institutions. They also searched for ways to use media that they or supporters of their research thought would benefit people. Underlying all these developments was a belief that the world is knowable and that, with enough knowledge, we can shape our destinies to some degree.

The Shaping of Research by Social and Economic Concerns

Some examples may help clarify how the kinds of mass communication research done at various times have been shaped by the particular social and economic concerns of those periods. The influence of those concerns seems to be especially strong during periods of change and uncertainty.

The 1960s and early 1970s were just such a period, as both the civil rights and feminist movements spread across the country, heightening people's consciousness and building pressure for legislation against discriminatory practices. The result was a sharp increase in research on media stereotyping of women and minorities, on the forces that cause such stereotypes to get into the media, and on ways media content can stimulate positive or negative self-concepts in females and minority youngsters. (See, for example, the book *Hearth & Home: Images of Women in the Mass Media* by Tuchman, Daniels, and Benet in list of suggested readings at the end of this chapter.)

Periods of political conflict in recent decades almost invariably were accompanied by charges that the media are politically biased. Those charges, in turn, stimulated research on the kinds and degrees of bias and, more important, on the factors that tend to cause such bias. (Some of the results of that research were covered in Chapter 14.)

A related sort of concern marked the decade before World War II, as Americans nervously watched the rise of fascist dictators in Italy, Spain, and Germany. These dictators used the mass media, especially radio, as important persuasive tools to build and retain power. In this country, the fear of such persuasion, or propaganda, led to two kinds of studies: research designed to understand the ways propaganda worked, so citizens could be taught to recognize and counteract it, and research designed to help improve American propaganda efforts abroad. (Descriptions of some of this research can be found in the book *Propaganda, Communication, and Public Opinion: A Comprehensive Reference Guide* by Smith, Lasswell, and Casey, listed at end of this chapter.)

REVIEW

Most media research was stimulated by either social concerns (such as the desire to reduce racial and sexual prejudice, to have fair elections, and resist foreign propaganda) or economic concerns (the desire of advertisers to know the size of the audience for their advertising and to make that advertising as effective as possible).

Ever since advertising became the dominant source of support of the mass media in this country, a constant concern of people working in the industry was to demonstrate the value of the media as carriers of commercial messages. This concern led initially to the development of reliable methods for estimating audience size and later to methods for determining the demographic characteristics (such as age, sex, and economic status) of audiences at different times, for different media, and for different content. It also led to research on the characteristics of advertising that were most persuasive for different types of potential consumers of various products.

A number of research firms now monitor families' grocery purchases, along with their media exposure, to test the effects of different advertising campaigns.

THE COMPLEXITY OF MEDIA EFFECTS

In the early days of media research, scholars underestimated the complexity of mass communication and human behavior. Some people today still do so. You should avoid that sort of oversimplification. As you think about the impact or effects of mass communication, do not assume a simple, direct, stimulus-response relationship between the media and you or other members of the public. Human behavior, as you know, is far more complex than that. The impact of the media on each of us is affected by the functions discussed in the preceding chapter—the way we and our institutions use the media. Our prior knowledge, habits, interests, and attitudes, and the social-cultural milieu in which the communication occurs also affect media impact. The same television program has different effects on different people, and the same medium has a different impact on different types of cultures. Thus, when we speak of media impact or of the media causing something to happen, we do not mean to suggest that the media by themselves are a sufficient cause. Anything as complex as human behavior is not shaped by one factor alone; each behavior usually has been caused by a set of factors.

Different Ways in Which the Media "Cause" Effects

There are at least five different ways in which mass communication might "cause" things to happen:

1. Mass communication could be the sole, direct cause. This is the least likely type of cause, but it is possible that the mere existence of the mass media or just something that the mass media do has some particular kind of effect.
2. Mass communication could be mediated by other factors. Sometimes, the media or their content have an effect on some people or institutions and not on others. In such cases, there are other factors that make individuals more or less likely to be affected. For example, violence on television has a different effect on a child who is frustrated or angry than on one who is not, and political news affects the understanding of people interested and knowledgeable about politics differently than it affects people who are not interested or knowledgeable. These mediating factors may be factors that exist before the mass communication occurs, during the mass communication, or between the time the mass communication occurs and the potential result takes effect.
3. Other factors could be the cause and mass communication the mediating factor. In some cases, rather than the effects of the media being mediated by other factors, the effects of other factors are mediated by mass communication. For example, your reaction to the comments and actions of other people might vary with the particular kinds of background music coming from the stereo. Or your normal reactions to a tragedy, such as the assassination of a national leader, might be strengthened or weakened or otherwise shaped by the kinds of mass media messages you encounter.
4. Mass communication might be a necessary but not a sufficient cause. In such situations, a combination of factors, mass communication among them, is necessary for an effect to occur. In these cases, exposure to mass communication must occur, but that alone is not enough to bring about the effect.
5. Mass communication might be a sufficient but not a necessary cause. In such situations, alternative causes are possible. Mass communication may have been the cause for some people; something else may have been the cause for other people. As a trivial example, you may have read in the newspaper that a bridge is closed for repair. Reading that newspaper story is the cause of your knowledge. On the other hand, someone else may know that same thing who did not read the paper; he or she could have encountered a detour on the way to school.

REVIEW

The processes by which mass communication can "cause" effects are complex. Mass communication might be the sole, direct cause. Its effect might be increased or decreased by other factors, or it might increase or decrease the effects of other factors. It might be a necessary but not sufficient cause, or it might be a sufficient but not a necessary cause.

The point is that mass communication affects us and our society in a variety of ways. The fact that most of those ways are indirect, that they almost always involve other factors, and that the effects are not the same at all times or for all individuals does not mean the media are not really the cause. All of these complications, along with the multiple sources of information and influence from the communication mosaic that we discussed in the first chapter, make it difficult for scholars to pin down the precise influences of the media and especially of any one medium. Nonetheless, many of these effects have been established with reasonable certainty, and mass communication scholars continue to seek understanding of others.

A single chapter, or even a single book, cannot cover all of the effects of the mass media. However, it is possible to examine a cross section of them to provide some notion of the importance of the media in our lives and of ways we can control their impact on us.

Sources of Media Impact

When we speak of the impact of the media, precisely what do we mean by "the media"? The answer is: "It depends." At times we mean the content of the media; at other times we mean the media themselves, as operated in a particular culture, independent of content. For example, when we speak of the effects of the media on whether young women aspire to be engineers or medical doctors—vocations traditionally limited largely to males in this country—we are considering the effects of media content. On the other hand, when we speak of the effects of the media on family structure or interactions among family members, we are probably considering the media themselves, not their content. For example, the fact that first radio and then television motivated family members to gather to listen and watch together and then discuss was relatively independent of content. The effect of movie theaters on the mating behaviors of young Americans is probably also relatively independent of content.

When we speak of the impact of the media, we may be thinking of media in general, of some particular group of media, or of one particular medium. For example, when we speak of the impact of the media on a culture, we generally mean all media. When we speak of the effects of media on sports, we are considering largely the news media (newspapers, radio, and television). And when we speak of the effects of new media on old, obviously we are thinking of individual media.

REVIEW

Effects of the media might be due to the media themselves, their content, or the milieu in which we experience them. They might be due to the particular medium, the media in general, or some subset such as the news media.

Despite the impression you may have gotten from much of the criticism of mass communication, few of the major effects with which we are concerned are attributable to one medium alone. Although television gets most of the credit and blame today for effects the mass media have or that someone believes they have, the credit and blame must be shared with all of the media that contribute to our communication mosaics.

Variable Effects

Too often, when people who do not understand mass communication processes or mass communication research think about the effects of the mass media, they think in all-or-none terms. That is, they think that if mass communication has a particular effect on one person, it must have the same effect on everyone who uses the mass media or who was exposed to that content. If they do not see an effect on everyone, they believe its absence must be due to something other than mass communication.

These people do not understand that mass communication scholars are not trying to discover simply, or even primarily, a total or average effect of the media. Instead, they are trying to understand why the same sort of mass communication experience has different effects on different people. They know that there is great variability in the behaviors of people who use the media, and they are trying to explain that variability. For most mass communication scholars, the question of whether watching a lot of television reduces children's creative imaginations is not as important as the question of why watching a lot of television seems to affect the creative imaginations of various children in quite different ways. Research on this latter question is more likely to lead to useful understandings and to the development of better theories about the effects of mass communication on human behavior.

REVIEW

Mass communication has different effects on different people and institutions. Scholars are trying to find the reasons for this variability.

In the sections that follow, for the sake of brevity we will sometimes talk about the effects of the media on institutions or people rather than talking about the variable effects of media or effects of media on variability. In every case, though, keep in mind that what we are discussing and explaining is variability.

Levels of Media Impact

We can think about these variable effects of the mass media in many ways. As with the functions of mass communication discussed in Chapter 15, there are individual effects and societal or collective effects. To cite but a few examples, media may have an effect on the aggressiveness of individuals, their attitudes or knowledge, the kinds of products they buy, the way they vote, their aspirations and beliefs in themselves, or the way they use their time. On the other hand, at a collective or societal level, mass communication can reshape a political system, sports, religion, the court system, the economy, or the general culture.

In considering the impact of mass communication, we also need to distinguish between short- and long-term effects. The short-term effects are usually more noticeable. Consider, for example, the rapid way in which, in 1986, the vivid television pictures of the explosion of the space shuttle *Challenger* and the memorial services for the crew that followed evoked our collective shock and sorrow. Another relatively short-term effect is the emotion that tends to arise quickly among Americans when the media publicize children starving in Africa or a terrorist attack on American citizens.

REVIEW

Mass communication might affect individuals, institutions, or societies. Effects might be short- or long-term.

The long-term effects, although usually less noticeable and harder to determine with certainty, are probably far more important in most cases. Among the countless examples are effects the usual mass communication content has had on the values of our society, on our trust in government, on the shape and health of our economy, and on the way politics and government are carried on.

News photos of Isaac Stern continuing his concert in Israel during a SCUD missile alert, which prompted some members of the audience to don gas masks, but none to seek shelter, heightened viewers' beliefs in Israeli courage.

EXPLANATIONS OF EFFECTS

To understand the effects of mass communication, it is not enough to know whether violent media content increases the aggressive behavior of some children, or whether political advertising affects the way many people vote. You need to understand the *reasons* why effects do or do not occur. Knowing the reasons, in fact, is far more important than knowing the specific effects because knowledge of the reasons gives you a better basis for predicting other kinds of effects and, equally important, it gives you a better basis for controlling or changing the effects mass communication has on you and on others.

Review

Theories are important because they help us understand reasons for an effect and therefore help us predict and control it. Most effects can be explained by more than one theory. The best theory, in such cases, is the one that explains the most variability.

Therefore, this section is organized in terms of major explanations or theories about effects that scholars have advanced, rather than in terms of specific effects. Within the discussion of each theory, we will consider some of the effects for which it may account. Keep in mind, however, that any effect can usually be explained by more than one theory. For this reason, scholars are not merely concerned with whether a particular theory can help to explain an effect; they are trying to discover which one, from among some group of theories, explains an effect better or, in the terms we discussed earlier, which theory explains more of the variability in human behavior. We touched on some of these theories briefly in earlier chapters as we talked about exposure to and processing of information, but it is useful to consider them together and in relation to each other.

One further note about this section: It is impossible to fully explain each theory here; such explanation would take a number of volumes. We can present only a brief and oversimplified summary. Each of these theories is far more complex than its summary suggests. You can gain a fuller understanding by reading further about the theories that particularly interest you, or by taking advanced courses in mass communication or other social sciences.

Modeling Theory

Modeling theory is a sophisticated refinement of the old-fashioned idea that much of what we know and do we learned by example. It suggests that we learn to behave the way we do, in large part, by watching and imitating models. Children watch their parents, friends, and others and then try out some of the things they see them do. If their trial behavior is reinforced in some way, they are more likely to continue it. Children, and even adults, find models to imitate not only from among the people they live with and meet, but also from the true and fictional characters they see, hear, and read about in the mass media.

Through exposure to these various kinds of models, little boys learn how boys are supposed to behave, and little girls learn how girls are supposed to behave. Somewhat older boys and girls learn from models how to dress, what to do in different kinds of situations, and what roles they are going to have to play and how to play them: student, lover, parent, working man or woman, and consumer.

A theory of Modeling explains the ways in which the media help to socialize children—help to integrate them into their society. Many children see the same models on television, but because the models they have at home and elsewhere differ and because their imitation of models is reinforced in different ways, those media models affect them differently.

REVIEW

Modeling theory explains the way we learn many of our roles and behaviors by imitating people we see on or off the media and then having that imitation reinforced.

Modeling theory can be used to explain the influence of the media on the learning of and variability in a great number of behaviors. It is used to explain how the media, along with other factors, contribute to the differences among children in their use of cigarettes or chewing tobacco, in their aggressiveness, and in the degree to which an increasing number of females are interested in what our society once viewed as male occupations—such as law and engineering.

Identification

The idea of identification is closely related to the theory of Modeling. This is the idea that we vary in the degree to which we admire and want to be like some of the people we know or see, hear, and read about in the media. The more we identify with a model, the more we are likely to imitate and learn to behave as that person does. For example, television characters with whom children identify, either positively or negatively, influence their self-concepts and behaviors more than television characters or other models whom they neither like nor dislike. The same is probably true of you, whether you are aware of it or not. To take a trivial example, you are probably more likely to buy clothes that are similar to those of people, on or off television, with whom you identify.

BYLINE

Have you ever been conscious of the fact that you adopted some behavior or style of clothing from someone in the media? If so, was the person similar to you or merely someone you admired?

REVIEW

Identification explains why some models affect us more than others. We tend to identify most with characters we perceive as most similar to ourselves or whom we most admire and want to be like.

The importance of identification for the development of self-concept and other kinds of learning from the media is well established. It is for this reason that people concerned about improving the self-concepts and aspirations of young women and both male and female members of minority groups pressure the mass media to show more women and members of minority groups in nontraditional and positive roles, whether in programs, commercials, or news stories or as news anchors. Cast in such roles, women and minority group members can become important models with whom many youngsters will probably identify.

Arousal Theory Arousal theory, along with Modeling, is used to explain the variability in aggressiveness shown by children who are exposed to violent media content. A variety of communication and psychological studies have found that people undergo certain physiological changes when they are emotionally aroused, perhaps by mass communication content that is especially

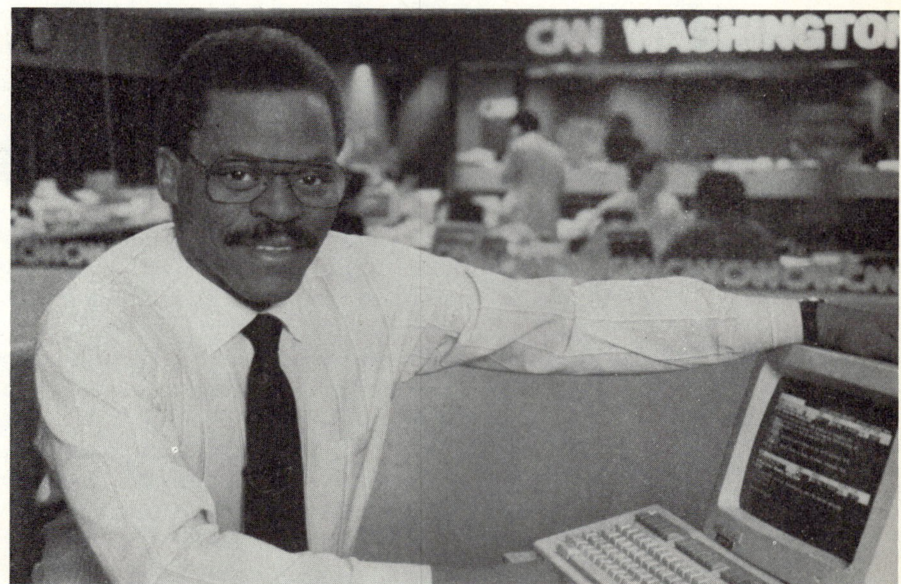

CNN news anchor Bernard Shaw serves as a positive role model for many minority youngsters, who are more likely to identify with media figures who are similar to them in some way.

absorbing or exciting. Their heart rate goes up, the pupils of their eyes dilate, and their skin becomes a better conductor of electricity. More important, these changes seem to be accompanied by a release of extra adrenaline in their systems. An increasing number of behavioral scientists believe that when people become emotionally aroused by something they see, hear, or read in the mass media, that arousal will affect more than their response to media content. If called on to do something unrelated to that content or medium, they will do it more quickly and with greater intensity. So it is not only the arousal from violent television or movie content that might cause a child to behave more aggressively; arousal from a comedy or even a romantic drama could have the same effect.

But the effects of arousal are not necessarily negative. Arousal can speed up and intensify pro- as well as antisocial behavior.

REVIEW

Emotional arousal from media or other experiences can affect the speed and intensity with which you do something, as well as how well you learn. Moderate arousal affects learning positively; high arousal affects it negatively.

A certain amount of arousal is also important for learning. If your instructor uses some instructional films, audiotapes, or television programs to cover part of this course, they should be those that arouse your emotions to some extent. You are more likely to remember the content of the program better if you are somewhat aroused than if you are simply coolly taking notes. On the other hand, if the material is too arousing, it will be distracting. The trick with such materials is finding some that arouse a moderate amount of emotional response from most members of the class. (A fuller discussion of arousal and the media can be found in Percy Tannenbaum's book *The Entertainment Functions of Television*.)

Script or Schema Theory

In Chapter 2 we discussed the ways in which individuals fill gaps in the bits of information to which they are exposed. As we noted there, through prior experiences people develop expectations about the usual components of an object or message, or about the usual steps in a sequence of events. These expectations help us process and make sense of all of those bits of information with which we are constantly bombarded.

Some scholars label these images of objects or sequences of events that people learn "schemas" or "scripts." All of us have well-developed schemas or scripts about our normal, daily experiences, such as washing up in the morning or going to school. It takes little thought; we do those things automatically. And when we hear or read of someone else washing up in the morning or going to school, we easily conjure an image of that event because we use the well-learned script we have in memory.

We also have scripts for almost every experience with which we are familiar, even if we have not experienced it ourselves. We have a script for the police movies or television programs we have seen. This is the kind of script literary scholars label a "genre." The first time we saw such a show, we had to concentrate and think about it in order to follow the plot. The more of them we saw, though, the more we learned the "script." Consequently, it became easier to follow the plot of each new police drama we encountered; we could do so almost unconsciously, even when we failed to see all of it.

We also have scripts for news stories about murders, accidents, and political campaigns. These scripts are our expectations concerning content and form for such stories, based on all of the similar stories we encountered in the past. With these scripts, it takes little concentration to process new stories about murders, accidents, or politics that we come across. Doris Graber, for example, in her book *Processing the News: How People Tame the Information Tide*, examines the role of script theory in comprehending the news.

REVIEW

All of us have many scripts or schemas in our heads—standard sequences of events or images of objects that we learned from prior exposures to similar events or images. These scripts or schemas guide our behaviors and help us predict and make sense of new objects or events by serving as analogies.

Because people vary greatly in their past experiences with particular objects, actions, or ideas, they necessarily vary in their schemas or scripts for that category of objects, actions, or ideas. For the same reason, they vary in the ease or naturalness with which they use a script to process exposure to such phenomena.

These variations in scripts help explain why different people construct different meanings from the same media content and respond differently to that content. This is important, since a major effect of the mass media is their influence on the worlds all of us construct in our heads, which represent, in various degrees, the reality outside our heads.

Cultivation Theory

One group of researchers in this country explains those worlds in our heads—our beliefs about the external world—in a somewhat different way. They claim the mass media have a strong, direct, and homogeneous effect on people's perceptions of the external world, at least those people who are exposed to a great deal of mass communication. Cultivation theorists attribute this common image of the world to the repeated exposure of people to similar kinds of messages or images.

These scholars place special emphasis on the power of television to cultivate these images because it is such an important part of most people's lives, especially in developed countries such as the United States. Television is also a potent cultivator, they say, because the messages it transmits are so consistent. For example, it gives us the same picture of crime, of police, and of teachers over and over again. Frequent viewers of television, according to the theory, develop images of the world that are more consistent with what is presented on television than with what exists in the real world outside their doors.

For evidence of the cultivation effect, scholars have analyzed the content of television programs to demonstrate the ways the medium consistently distorts various aspects of American life. They have also surveyed television viewers to see whether there is a relationship between frequency of television viewing and the belief that American life is indeed like it is portrayed on these programs. The results of such analyses provide some support for the theory, but not absolute proof. As a result, cultivation theory has both supporters and detractors.

Some of the strongest evidence for Cultivation theory comes not from the research of those theorists but from independent research on the effects of repetition on attitudes and beliefs. A number of studies demonstrate that simple repetition of a stimulus—even an apparently meaningless stimulus—will tend to make people feel more accepting and positive toward that stimulus. This evidence on the effect of repetition is one of the reasons some scholars are worried about the number of sadomasochistic films that have become popular with many young adults, films that show women being tortured and raped. Evidence suggests that frequent exposure to such films will tend to make people more accepting of the behaviors shown and more lenient toward those who abuse women in those ways. The major proponent of Cultivation theory has been a scholar named George Gerbner. (See the article by Gerbner et al. included in the list of suggested readings.)

REVIEW

Cultivation theory argues that people who watch a great deal of television will tend to develop a distorted view of the world, one that more closely approximates that of television than of the "real" world.

Cultural Imperialism

A theory similar to the Cultivation theory, in focus as well as name, is the theory of Cultural Imperialism. This theory holds that mass media content from developed western countries—primarily the United States, Great Britain, and France—is changing the beliefs and values of the populations of the developing countries because it dominates their television channels, movie screens, and radio frequencies in the same way that the United States and developed countries of Europe dominated the political and economic systems of many countries prior to World War II.

Cultural Imperialism theory is far broader than Cultivation theory, however, in that it focuses also on the economic factors involved in importation of media products from America and other developed nations into these developing countries and the way these imports inhibit the continued development or maintenance of native cultures. Because mass media materials can be imported more cheaply than they can be produced within most countries, and because a large proportion of the population of these countries prefers these western products, local writers, musicians, filmmakers, and television producers have great difficulty competing. In addition, because of the popularity of these materials from the West, local artists and media personnel feel pressure to imitate them instead of creating works more consistent with their countries' traditional culture. The pressures toward imitation appear strongest in those countries in which the media are primarily commercial, and so there is less incentive to protect the native culture or to nurture native talent. In *The Media Are American*, British scholar Jeremy Tunstall lays out the argument for the Cultural Imperialism theory.

REVIEW

Cultural Imperialism is the domination of a country's media by materials from other countries—usually the domination of poor or low-technology countries by rich, high-technology countries. Because it is cheaper to import such materials as television programs and films, these foreign products tend to dominate and shape beliefs, values, and customs. They inhibit the maintenance of an indigenous culture.

Spiral of Silence Theory

The Spiral of Silence theory also considers the consistency of the messages we get from the mass media, but it focuses on and explains a different type of effect. This theory was developed by German scholar Elizabeth Noelle-Neumann to explain the impact of the media on public opinion. (One of her key articles is listed among the suggested readings.)

Review

Most people, wanting social acceptance, will remain silent when they believe their opinions are inconsistent with majority views inferred from the media. They will tend to speak up more when they perceive their views to be consistent with the majority. This creates an even stronger sense that the media represent the majority and so even stronger pressures to be silent or speak up. In this way, there is an ever-increasing "spiral" of silence.

Some research has shown that, when the media have taken a consistent position on an issue over some period of time, the opinions of the general public will tend to move toward that position. According to the Spiral of Silence theory, this media effect occurs because most people want others to accept them; they fear isolation. If they believe their personal opinions are different from those of others, they will be less likely to speak up. On the other hand, if they believe their personal opinions are consistent with those of the majority, they will be more likely to voice them. But in most cases they have no way of knowing how most other people feel about an issue, so they infer that public opinion from what they read, hear, and see in the mass media. As those who disagree with the media position stay quiet and those who agree with the media speak up, the perception that the media position is the majority position gets stronger, creating even greater pressure to remain silent or speak up. In this way, we get a spiraling effect, with public opinion moving more and more strongly toward the original media position, no matter what the majority of people thought initially.

Agenda-Setting Theory

The Spiral of Silence theory predicts and explains the effect of the media on *what people think about some issues*. Agenda-Setting theory predicts and explains the effects of the media on *what issues people think about*. Research supporting this theory suggests that the beliefs of most people about the relative importance of, say, campaign issues, are shaped in good part by the relative amount of space the media—especially newspapers—devote to each one. The more space the media give to an issue, the more important most people believe it to be. Since, in most elections, some candidates are stronger on some issues while their opponents are stronger on others, to the extent the news media shape people's perceptions of which issues in the election are most important, they probably influence votes. (The major developers of Agenda-Setting theory are Maxwell McCombs and Donald Shaw.)

Review

The more attention the media give an issue, the more important most people will believe it to be. Similarly, the media lead us to believe we have certain needs and often even provide models to follow to fulfill those needs. This is how beliefs and practices get diffused in our society.

Agenda-Setting theory, together with Modeling theory, may also partly explain the kinds of innovations that get diffused in a society. The history of many kinds of diffusion, such as the spread of hybrid seed corn or the gradual acceptance of certain health practices, supports that claim. Evidence indicates that publicity through the mass media frequently makes people aware of options they did not know they had—for example, that they do not need to accept their current crop yields or the current amount of sickness. The shaping of such beliefs or the evoking of such needs by the mass media is a type of agenda setting.

Once a need is established by this sort of agenda setting, the media almost always provide models to imitate. These models might be presented in news stories or features about people who have adopted the new product or practice. If other potential adopters can identify with these people, the probability increases that they also will accept the change, and in this way, the innovation will be diffused.

Consistency Theory

Consistency theory, also discussed in Chapter 2, is based on the generalization that we human beings tend to feel uncomfortable if any of our beliefs, attitudes, and behaviors are inconsistent with each other. This discomfort, in turn, creates pressure within us to make our beliefs, attitudes, and behaviors consistent—that is, to change some of them so all are in line. This theory predicts and explains why the media sometimes influence us. The new information they give us can change our beliefs about something so that they become inconsistent with our attitudes or behaviors. We then must either convince ourselves that the information is wrong, change our attitudes and behaviors, or learn to live with more discomfort than most of us like.

Review

We human beings tend to feel uncomfortable if we become aware of an inconsistency among our beliefs, attitudes, and behaviors. This discomfort pressures us to change attitude, belief, or behavior so all three will be consistent. The media can sometimes affect us by making such inconsistencies salient.

Few, if any, of us do not have some inconsistency among the things we believe to be true, our attitudes, and the ways we behave. For example, some of us know that smoking cigarettes or chewing tobacco is dangerous to people's health, and yet we chew or smoke. Somehow we manage to avoid facing up to the link between our smoking or chewing behavior and our knowledge of its dangers. The mass media can affect or change many of our behaviors by frequently stressing that link between our tobacco use and our health so the fact of their relationship is unavoidable. At that point, the pressure to change the behavior will become too strong to resist for many smokers, especially if the message concerning the effect of tobacco on health is strong and persuasive enough to prevent denial tactics.

The most interesting description and argument for Consistency theory is Leon Festinger's book, *A Theory of Cognitive Dissonance.*

Political-Economy Theory

The idea underlying Political-Economy theory is a relatively simple one, that the forces created by the economic interests of the media have an impact on what the media do and, therefore, on the population and institutions of the society in which the media are embedded. Also important in this theory is that the economic and political system are closely linked; government passes laws that facilitate business, while business supports government and political candidates through taxes, contributions, and other help. Because the media in the United States are primarily commercial, with profit as a dominant motive, certain effects can be expected, as we have suggested throughout this book. (The case for Political-Economy theory is persuasively argued by Graham Murdock and Peter Golding.)

Antismoking advertising is intended to create inconsistency in teenagers' minds between the behavior of smoking and knowledge of its unattractive aspects. Pressure toward consistency should lead more youngsters to stop smoking or not to start.

Economic demands in a commercial system of mass communication lead to pressures to get the particular kinds of audiences that will be attractive to advertisers. Some political economists even speak of the media's "creating" audiences. This description makes sense when you think about the fact that there was little audience for activities such as tennis or parlor games before television picked them up, promoted them, and created audiences for them—audiences that many advertisers are eager to talk to through their commercials.

The political economy of sports. The effects explained by Political-Economy theory are probably most easily seen in the relationship of television to sports. Not only has television created a large audience for sports such as tennis, professional basketball, and professional football, but it has also made them highly profitable for the players as well as for television stations, networks, and cable systems. It has also changed those sports, to make them more attractive to viewers and more compatible with the video medium and its economic demands.

Sports are desirable sources of programming for the mass media because they attract a large, adult, male audience—an audience with money to spend for products such as automobiles, beer, and shaving cream. Because of the interest in sports created largely by television, and the almost insatiable appetite of the video medium for more sports programming, the number of teams has been expanded and the length of the season extended. Many sports that were once confined to relatively short and distinct seasons are becoming almost year-round activities. Football is probably the most obvious example.

To meet the demands of television, many sports have also been altered. Additional timeouts have been added to football and basketball games to make space for more commercials—the "television timeouts"—thus lengthening the games. At the same time, to better predict and control length, the tie-breaker has been added to tennis. Before the invention of the tie-breaker, tennis sets continued until one player had won at least six games and at least two more than the opposition. Sets could go on for so long that either the television schedule was thrown off or the network had to cut away to other programming, leaving frustrated viewers wondering how the match ended. The quick tie-breaker when a set reaches six games all solved that problem. Basketball has been speeded up for the television audience by the shot clock, which prevents interminable stalling, and by elimination of the jump ball except at the beginning of a game.

Even the timing of sports events is affected by the broadcasting schedules of radio and television. This is true not only of professional sports but also of college sports. For example, many college basketball games have been shifted to weekend afternoons to accommodate the schedules of television stations and networks. Some are even played on Sunday afternoons, which would have been taboo in a pretelevision era.

Review

Political-Economy theory explains most of what happens in the media in terms of economic and government forces and the symbiotic relationship between the two. Sports coverage, for example, is shaped to attract the kinds of audiences advertisers want to address.

Newspapers have taken advantage of the increased interest in athletics television created by expanding their sports coverage. In this way, they attract additional advertising aimed largely at men.

All of this media attention has made stars out of major sports figures and has driven the salaries of professional athletes into the stratosphere. It has also affected the salaries of college coaches. Among the fringe benefits now used to attract head coaches for major college football and basketball teams is the extra money they can earn from television and radio interviews and appearances on rebroadcasts of their teams' games.

The political economy of religion. Religion has always played a major role in the mass media, especially radio and television. In radio, the public service broadcasting of regular religious services from established Christian churches was long a Sunday morning staple. There were no commercials or requests for funds on these broadcasts, and there was no charge to the churches for the air time. These broadcasts made some of the Christian religious experiences available to a wider range of people. Economic forces have altered the nature and availability of those experiences.

Television in its early days followed the model of radio in broadcasting religion. But as the medium became more popular with audiences and advertisers, as production costs increased, and as FCC pressure to broadcast a certain percentage of unsponsored, public service programs eased, television stations looked for ways in which those time slots being given away to churches could generate income. The result was the sale of time to religious groups that in turn used that time to raise money. Many radio stations, searching for new sources of income to replace what they had lost to television also turned to religion for pay.

Review

Increased pressures from stockholders to maximize profits and decreased pressure from government to carry unsponsored programs led to a shift from public service broadcasting by mainline churches to fund-raising broadcasting by nontraditional evangelists and more fundamentalist churches. In the process, religious broadcasting became a major industry.

This development had many effects. One was its contribution to a shift in the relative popularity of established churches and nontraditional evangelists. The established churches dominated religious broadcasting when radio and television time was free. The nontraditional groups have dominated the paid broadcast market, and it has proved highly profitable for them. In fact, religious broadcasting is a major industry in the United States today. A number of evangelists, building on their radio and television popularity, have developed multimillion dollar empires. Many of them today not only buy time on commercial television stations for their broadcasts, but they also own strings of radio and television stations and syndicate programs to cable systems across the country. Not surprisingly, a new label has been attached to these *religious leaders for whom television is a pulpit*—**televangelists.**

The visibility and popularity gained through television, radio, and cable have also given some televangelists a strong base from which to exert political influence. The attempt by the Reverend Pat Robertson, master of ceremonies of television's "700 Club," to win the Republican presidential nomination in 1988 probably attracted the most attention, but he is not alone. Many televangelists have used their television-generated popularity to influence politics.

BYLINE

What other effects do you believe Political-Economy theory might explain?

Systems Theory Systems theory is probably the broadest or most all-encompassing of the theoretical ideas that have been used to explain effects of the mass media. It was developed by a biologist named Bertalanffy who based it on the general assumption that all parts of a social system are interrelated and that there is constant pressure toward balance or equilibrium among those parts. When there is change in one part of the system, it tends to throw the system out of balance, creating pressure for change in other parts of the system that will bring them to a new equilibrium. Systems theorists label this *state of balance, stability, or equilibrium* **homeostasis.**

In thinking about ways the idea of systems might help us understand the effects of mass communication, keep in mind that the theory or analogy can be applied to different kinds and levels of systems. You can think of American society as a type of system, or you can think of a newspaper office or broadcasting operation as a system. Whatever level of social system you are concerned about, Systems theory should lead you to think about how change in one part of a system affects other parts.

A variety of effects of the mass media can be explained to some degree by Systems theory, by the tendency of a system to seek homeostasis. It can explain phenomena as different as the effect of the mass media on political processes and the effect of one mass medium on another.

An examination of the history of mass communication will show that the development of each new major medium of communication has affected our political processes in some way. When radio came along, because it was more useful for political campaigning than the print media had been, candidates began to use this sound medium and decreased their dependence on the campaign train and the newspaper. Newspapers were then forced to find other functions to serve during a campaign. More important, radio and television decreased the dependence of candidates on the political parties. They no longer needed party workers to carry their message door to door or to organize campaign rallies at which they could speak. Candidates could enter homes through the radio or television receiver and speak directly to voters in their living rooms. But speaking to people in their homes was very different from speaking to people en masse at rallies or gathered around the rear platform of a train. There was no need to shout to be heard. In fact, voters resented being shouted at as they sat in their living rooms or around the kitchen table, even when the shouting was being done through the radio receiver. Candidates were forced to adopt a totally new speaking style for the radio medium, one more akin to conversation with friends than to the great oratorical style of the previous century. And this speaking style carried over to all political speaking, not just to that done over the radio.

Systems theory might also help to explain why the introduction of a microphone or camera at the scene of an event, or even the pad and pencil of a journalist, can change the event being covered. The presence of one of these media seems to throw things out of balance, and the event is often changed to accommodate and balance that medium, to reduce the possible harm it might bring, or to maximize the possible benefits of its presence.

The substantial change that took place in the presidential nominating conventions when radio coverage and then television coverage were introduced are but one set of examples. The microphones and cameras changed the dynamics of those events. Those planning the conventions became more concerned with communication to the listening and viewing public than with communication to the delegates in the convention hall. Today the conventions tend to be long political commercials instead of occasions for debate on party positions and the selection of presidential and vice-presidential candidates. Most of the essential business is done off-screen, where it will not bore the audience or reveal too much of political manipulation.

REVIEW

Systems theory argues that there is constant pressure in any system to keep its parts in balance, whether the system is a person, a family, a newsroom, a network, or a society. The theory explains why each new medium of communication changed our political system, why the news media change the events they cover, and how even the desire for media coverage leads people to change events.

The timing of many events, political and nonpolitical, is now planned to increase the likelihood of maximum media coverage. Some are timed to make the late editions of newspapers; others are timed to get prime-time television coverage. Groups that want to communicate to the general public shape their actions in a way that maximizes media coverage.

Almost any group that wants to mount an effective protest today—whether for or against abortions in the United States or apartheid in South Africa—must not only time that protest to maximize media coverage but must also adapt it to the visual demands of television. Plain talk, no matter how eloquent, will seldom make the late evening news. The protest must be visual, action-filled, and dramatic. This is a lesson that almost every type of protest group has learned well. It was certainly learned well by the group that telephoned a television reporter one day to announce they were planning to protest and wanted her to cover it. When the reporter asked how many pickets would be there, the caller asked how many she would need. Similarly, when asked what time they would be picketing, the reply was that they would picket whenever it would be convenient for the station. This is the way events are tailored to the demands of the media—to the recognition that they must be adapted to the state of the social system at that time, a social system of which the mass media are an integral part.

Systems theory helps us predict and explain these actions. It also helps us explain the changes in existing mass media that occurred when new media came along. It may also help us predict the changes in current media that will occur when new media develop in the future.

One of the most dramatic examples of the effect of one medium on another is the change in American radio broadcasting that occurred when television came along. When it became obvious that television was going to replace most of the entertainment and news functions radio served in the pretelevision days, many observers predicted that radio would die. But displaced from that part of our system, radio re-established itself by serving needs that television could not meet. It did this by adapting its receivers so they could follow people literally wherever they went—to the kitchen, the beach, the barn, or the automobile. The content of radio was shifted from an emphasis on distinct, regularly scheduled, 15-, 30-, or 60-minute programs to an emphasis on programming formats one could tune in or out at any time without losing the sense of what is going on. (This shift was described in greater detail in Chapter 9.)

REVIEW

The changes in some of the mass media as other media developed can also be explained by Systems theory. The major weakness of the theory is that it cannot explain alteration of the overall social system; it only explains change within that system.

A major weakness of Systems theory is that it fails to account for change in an overall social system. It is far better suited to explaining the difficulty and slowness of such change. Some observers accuse the media of resisting change because those who own and control them want to maintain the status quo. Systems theory reveals that as a gross oversimplification. The mass media are embedded firmly in a much larger system of organizations and relationships, and, to survive, they must maintain reasonable consistency with that system. This would be the case whether the media were commercial or noncommercial. Alone, the media have little chance of being effective agents for change.

THE IMPACT OF THE MEDIA ON OUR LIVES: A SUMMARY

That the media of communication have had a major impact on our lives is beyond question. Less clear is precisely which parts of our lives have been affected and the relative influence of the media compared to other factors. Also unclear in some cases is which theories are most useful for explaining those effects and for guiding our attempts to control them: maximizing their positive effects and minimizing their negative ones.

Here we encounter what may be the most difficult question of all for us and our society: Which effects of the media are positive and which are negative? The answer to this question depends not only on facts, the evidence of change, and the role of media in that change, but also on your values, the goals you have for your life, and the kind of society in which you want to live. In assessing the impact of the media then, consider the theories that might explain an effect, consider the evidence for that effect and the role of the media in bringing it about, and then consider the values that determine for you whether such change is good or bad and what you ought to do about it.

Consider theory, evidence, and values in thinking about the ways the media have affected your life and the lives of others whom you care about:

the ways they affected your self-concept and behaviors, the information and attitudes that you have, the issues you think are important, and your beliefs about the world. Consider also their effect on the important institutions in our society: politics and government, religion, education, business and industry, and perhaps even sports. Most important, consider not only the impact the media have had, but also the impact they can have in the future, and what you and others can do to increase the probability that impact will be positive.

DISCUSSION QUESTIONS

1. What are all of the probable effects the media of communication have had on education?
   a. Overall, have these effects been good or bad?
   b. Which of the theories best account for what you believe to be the major effects of the media on education?
2. Do you believe it is valid to blame the mass media for much of the crime and violence in our society?
3. Of the five ways in which we can speak of the media "causing" things to happen, which one do you believe best describes the process by which *most* media effects occur?
4. Which one of the theories described in this chapter do you believe is most useful for explaining the kinds of media effects that are most important?
5. Which of the theories described in this chapter best explain(s) the effects the media have on you?
6. Which of the theories described best explain(s) why our contemporary media operate as they do, create the content that they do, and so forth?

NOTES

1. *World's Work*, March, 1913, p. 40.
2. *Christian Century*, January, 1930, p. 110.

SUGGESTED READINGS

Classic Works in the Field

Bertalanffy, L. von. *General Systems Theory*. New York: Braziller, 1968.

Charters, W. W. *Motion Pictures and Youth*. New York: Macmillan, 1933.

Festinger, Leon A. *A Theory of Cognitive Dissonance*. New York: Row Peterson, 1957.

Smith, Bruce Lannes, Lasswell, Harold D., and Casey, Ralph D. *Propaganda, Communication, and Public Opinion: A Comprehensive Reference Guide*. Princeton: Princeton University Press, 1946.

Relevant Contemporary Works

Criscuolo, Nicholas P. "The Public's Attitude toward Education: What Effect Do the Media Have on Formulation of Opinions?" *Editor and Publisher* 118 (March 1985):16–17.

Entman, Robert M. *Democracy Without Citizens: Media and the Decay of American Politics.* New York: Oxford University Press, 1989.

Gerbner, George, et al. "Living With Television: The Dynamics of the Cultivation Process." In *Perspectives on Media Effects,* ed. Jennings Bryant and Dolf Zillman, pp. 17–40. Hillsdale, NJ: Lawrence Erlbaum, 1986.

Graber, Doris. *Processing the News: How People Tame the Information Tide.* 2nd ed. New York: Longman, 1988.

Infante, Dominic A., Rancer, Andrew S., and Womack, Deanna F. *Building Communication Theory.* Prospect Heights, IL: Waveland, 1990.

See especially the appendix, pp. 401–430, for a clear discussion of the general methods by which most social scientific research on the processes and effects of mass communication is done.

Lichter, S. R., and Lichter, L. S. "Does Television Shape Ethnic Images?" *Media and Values* 43 (Spring 1988):5–8.

Lowery, Shearon A., and DeFleur, Melvin L. *Milestones in Mass Communication Research.* 2nd ed. New York: Longman, 1988.

Lowery and DeFleur summarize and discuss many of the major, classic studies of mass communication, including some of those referred to in this chapter.

McCombs, Maxwell E., and Shaw, Donald L. "The Agenda-Setting Function of the Press." *Public Opinion Quarterly* 36 (1972):176–187.

McQuail, Denis. *Mass Communication Theory: An Introduction.* 2nd ed. Newbury Park, CA: Sage, 1987.

See especially Chapter 7, "Processes of Media Effects."

Meyrowitz, Joshua. *No Sense of Place: The Impact of Electronic Media on Social Behavior.* New York: Oxford University Press, 1985.

Murdock, Graham, and Golding, Peter, "Capitalism, Communication and Class Relations." In *Mass Communication and Society,* ed. James Curran, Michael Gurevitch, and Janet Woollacott, pp. 12–43. London: Edward Arnold, 1977.

Noelle-Neumann, Elizabeth. "Return to the Concept of Powerful Mass Media." *Studies of Broadcasting* 9 (March 1973):67–112.

Rader, Benjamin G. *In Its Own Image: How Television Has Transformed Sports.* New York: Free Press, 1984.

Schudson, Michael. *Advertising, the Uneasy Persuasion: Its Dubious Impact on American Society.* New York: Basic Books, 1984.

Tannenbaum, Percy H. "Entertainment as Vicarious Emotional Experience." In *The Entertainment Functions of Television,* ed. Percy H. Tannenbaum, pp. 107–131. Hillsdale, NJ: Lawrence Erlbaum, 1980.

Tuchman, Gaye, Daniels, Arlene Kaplan, and Benet, James, eds. *Hearth & Home: Images of Women in the Mass Media.* New York: Oxford University Press, 1978.

Tunstall, Jeremy. *The Media Are American.* London: Constable, 1977.

See also *Communication Research* and *Journal of Communication.*

Credits

Page 59: "1(a" is reprinted from *Complete Poems*, 1913–1962, by E. E. Cummings, by permission of Liveright Publishing Corporation. Copyright © 1923, 1925, 1931, 1935, 1938, 1939, 1940, 1944, 1945, 1946, 1947, 1948, 1949, 1950, 1951, 1952, 1953, 1954, 1955, 1956, 1957, 1958, 1959, 1960, 1961, 1962 by the Trustees for the E. E. Cummings Trust. Copyright © 1961, 1963, 1968 by Marion Morehouse Cummings.

Photo and Illustration Credits

Unless otherwise acknowledged, all photographs are the property of ScottForesman. Page abbreviations are as follows: (T) top, (C) center, (B) bottom, (L) left, (R) right, (INS) inset.

Page 3: Ron Blakeley/Uniphoto. **Page 7:** Gilles Bassignac/Gamma-Liaison. **Page 9:** MacNelly/Reprinted by permission: Tribune Media Services. **Page 28:** Focus on Sports. **Page 34:** R. Maiman/Sygma. **Page 36:** Reprinted with permission, Copley News Service. **Page 49:** UPI/Bettmann. **Page 51:** Spencer Grant/Stock Boston. **Page 55:** Lisa Quinoes/Black Star. **Page 72:** David Muench. **Page 76:** New York Public Library, Astor, Lenox and Tilden Foundations. **Page 91:** Courtesy of People for the American Way. **Page 97:** Rare Book Division/New York Public Library, Astor, Lenox and Tilden Foundations. **Page 106:** Courtesy of American Antiquarian Society. **Page 129:** Alan Carey/The Image Works. **Page 142:** From *Harper's Bazaar,* Nov. 1868. **Page 146:** Library of Congress. **Page 152:** Reprinted courtesy of *Broadcasting* magazine. **Page 177:** The Bettmann Archive. **Page 181:** The National Archives. **Page 183:** Culver Pictures. **Page 191:** Dorothea Lange Collection/Library of Congress. **Page 197:** International Museum of Photography at George Eastman House. **Page 198:** AP/Wide World. **Page 207:** The Bettmann Archive. **Page 212:** AP/Wide World Photos. **Page 218:** Culver Pictures. **Page 223:** Culver Pictures. **Page 227:** Copyright © by Universal Pictures, a Division of Universal City Studios, Inc. Courtesy of MCA Publishing Rights, a Division of MCA, Inc. **Page 229:** Culver Pictures. **Page 233:** Alan Carey/The Image Works. **Page 241:** Library of Congress. **Page 243:** Bob Sacha. **Page 245:** Michael Childers/Sygma. **Page 250:** © 1989 BPI Communications, Inc. Used with permission of *Billboard*. **Page 255:** Spencer Grant/Stock Boston. **Page 257:** AP/Wide World. **Page 258:** Marc Morrison/Shooting Star. **Page 260:** Art by Julie Stacey, reprinted with permission of *USA Today.* **Page 261:** Laura Luongo/Gamma-Liaison. **Page 270:** Library of Congress. **Page 273 ALL:** From the *Wireless Age*/Science & Technology Research Center, The New York Public Library, Astor, Lenox and Tilden Foundations. **Page 281:** Illustrations by Andrea Baruffi. © 1983 Channels of Communications. **Page 284:** Tom Forrest for U.S. Information Agency. **Page 291:** Culver Pictures. **Page 301:** Library of Congress. **Page 313:** Courtesy of NBC. **Page 317:** The Bettmann Archive. **Page 322:** TM & © 1991 20th Century Fox Film Corp. **Page 324:** Michael S. Vamashita/Woodfin Camp & Associates. **Page 328:** Sepp Seitz/Woodfin Camp & Associates. **Page 338:** Courtesy of Nielsen Media Research. **Page 336:** Peter Menzel/Stock Boston. **Page 341:** Nielsen Media Research. **Page 344:** A General Motors Mark of Excellence Presentation. **Page 345:** Viacom/Shooting Star. **Page 349:** Katz Pictures/Woodfin Camp & Associates. **Page 357:** Dion Ogust/The Image Works. **Page 360:** Jean-Louis Atlan/Sygma. **Page 363:** Courtesy of the Home Shopping Network. **Page 366:** © 1991 BPI Communications, Inc. Used with permission from *Billboard*. **Page 370:** © 1990/Reprinted by permission: Tribune Media Services. **Page 390:** Chronicle Features, San Francisco. **Page 396:** Bob Daemmrich/Tony Stone Worldwide. **Page 402:** Library of Congress. **Page 409:** Pat Coffey. **Page 416:** Courtesy of Brookfield Zoo, Chicago/

Photo by Mike Green, Chicago Zoological Society. **Page 426:** Ellis Herwig/Stock Boston. **Page 428:** Washington Post Writers Group. Reprinted with permission. **Page 441:** HBO/*Time* magazine. **Page 452:** UPI/Bettmann. **Page 460:** Lionel DeLevingne/Stock Boston. **Page 464:** © *Punch*/Rothco. **Page 466:** Reuters/UPI/Bettmann. **Page 487:** UPI/Bettmann. **Page 489:** Mark Reinstein/Uniphoto. **Page 492:** Mike Luckovich/*New Orleans Times-Picayune*/Reprinted by permission: Tribune Media Services. **Page 495:** Tom Stoddart/Woodfin Camp & Associates. **Page 505:** Culver Pictures. **Page 507:** Hans Kluetmeier. **Page 511:** Esaias Baitel/Gamma-Liaison. **Page 513:** Douglas Kirkland/Sygma. **Page 519:** Courtesy of American Cancer Society.

INDEX